(Continued on back endsheets)

Dictionary of Literary Biography • Volume Seventy

British Mystery Writers, 1860-1919

Dictionary of Literary Biography • Volume Seventy

British Mystery Writers, 1860-1919

Edited by
Bernard Benstock
University of Miami
and
Thomas F. Staley
University of Tulsa

A Bruccoli Clark Layman Book
Gale Research Inc.
Detroit, London

Printed in the United States of America

Published simultaneously in the United Kingdom
by Gale Research International Limited
(An affiliated company of Gale Research Inc.)

The photographs on pp. 305, 307, and 314 are reproduced courtesy of A. P. Watt Ltd. on behalf of the Literary Executors of the Estate of H. G. Wells and courtesy of the University of Illinois Library, Urbana-Champaign.

The paper used in this publication meets the minimum requirements
of American National Standard for Information Sciences—Permanence
Paper for Printed Library Materials, ANSI Z39.48-1984. ∞™

Contents

Plan of the Series

. . . Almost the most prodigious asset of a country, and perhaps its most precious possession, is its native literary product—when that product is fine and noble and enduring.

Mark Twain*

The advisory board, the editors, and the publisher of the *Dictionary of Literary Biography* are joined in endorsing Mark Twain's declaration. The literature of a nation provides an inexhaustible resource of permanent worth. We intend to make literature and its creators better understood and more accessible to students and the reading public, while satisfying the standards of teachers and scholars.

To meet these requirements, *literary biography* has been construed in terms of the author's achievement. The most important thing about a writer is his writing. Accordingly, the entries in *DLB* are career biographies, tracing the development of the author's canon and the evolution of his reputation.

The purpose of *DLB* is not only to provide reliable information in a convenient format but also to place the figures in the larger perspective of literary history and to offer appraisals of their accomplishments by qualified scholars.

The publication plan for *DLB* resulted from two years of preparation. The project was proposed to Bruccoli Clark by Frederick G. Ruffner, president of the Gale Research Company, in November 1975. After specimen entries were prepared and typeset, an advisory board was formed to refine the entry format and develop the series rationale. In meetings held during 1976, the publisher, series editors, and advisory board approved the scheme for a comprehensive biographical dictionary of persons who contributed to North American literature. Editorial work on the first volume began in January 1977, and it was published in 1978. In order to make *DLB* more than a reference tool and to compile volumes that individually have claim to status as lit-

erary history, it was decided to organize volumes by topic, period, or genre. Each of these freestanding volumes provides a biographical-bibliographical guide and overview for a particular area of literature. We are convinced that this organization—as opposed to a single alphabet method—constitutes a valuable innovation in the presentation of reference material. The volume plan necessarily requires many decisions for the placement and treatment of authors who might properly be included in two or three volumes. In some instances a major figure will be included in separate volumes, but with different entries emphasizing the aspect of his career appropriate to each volume. Ernest Hemingway, for example, is represented in *American Writers in Paris, 1920-1939* by an entry focusing on his expatriate apprenticeship; he is also in *American Novelists, 1910-1945* with an entry surveying his entire career. Each volume includes a cumulative index of subject authors and articles. Comprehensive indexes to the entire series are planned.

With volume ten in 1982 it was decided to enlarge the scope of *DLB*. By the end of 1986 twenty-one volumes treating British literature had been published, and volumes for Commonwealth and Modern European literature were in progress. The series had been further augmented by the *DLB Yearbooks* (since 1981) which update published entries and add new entries to keep the *DLB* current with contemporary activity. There have also been *DLB Documentary Series* volumes which provide biographical and critical source materials for figures whose work is judged to have particular interest for students. One of these companion volumes is entirely devoted to Tennessee Williams.

We define literature as the *intellectual commerce of a nation:* not merely as belles lettres but as that ample and complex process by which ideas are generated, shaped, and transmitted. *DLB* entries are not limited to "creative writers" but extend to other figures who in their time and in their way influenced the mind of a people. Thus the series encompasses historians, journalists, publishers, and screenwriters. By this means readers of *DLB* may be aided to perceive litera-

*From an unpublished section of Mark Twain's autobiography, copyright © by the Mark Twain Company.

ture not as cult scripture in the keeping of intellectual high priests but firmly positioned at the center of a nation's life.

DLB includes the major writers appropriate to each volume and those standing in the ranks immediately behind them. Scholarly and critical counsel has been sought in deciding which minor figures to include and how full their entries should be. Wherever possible, useful references are made to figures who do not warrant separate entries.

Each DLB volume has a volume editor responsible for planning the volume, selecting the figures for inclusion, and assigning the entries. Volume editors are also responsible for preparing, where appropriate, appendices surveying the major periodicals and literary and intellectual movements for their volumes, as well as lists of further readings. Work on the series as a whole is coordinated at the Bruccoli Clark Layman editorial center in Columbia, South Carolina, where the editorial staff is responsible for accuracy of the published volumes.

One feature that distinguishes DLB is the illustration policy–its concern with the iconography of literature. Just as an author is influenced by his surroundings, so is the reader's understanding of the author enhanced by a knowledge of his environment. Therefore DLB volumes include not only drawings, paintings, and photographs of authors, often depicting them at various stages in their careers, but also illustrations of their families and places where they lived. Title pages are regularly reproduced in facsimile along with dust jackets for modern authors. The dust jackets are a special feature of DLB because they often document better than anything else the way in which an author's work was perceived in its own time. Specimens of the writers' manuscripts are included when feasible.

Samuel Johnson rightly decreed that "The chief glory of every people arises from its authors." The purpose of the Dictionary of Literary Biography is to compile literary history in the surest way available to us–by accurate and comprehensive treatment of the lives and work of those who contributed to it.

The DLB Advisory Board

Foreword

The writing of mysteries, generally in the form of novels and short stories but also at times as dramatic presentations, has provided an increasingly significant contribution to literature in Britain (as well as in America and on the European continent) since the advent of the Gothic novel at the end of the eighteenth century. Scholars have enjoyed tracing the roots of the mystery form back to much earlier cultures, particularly to Greek tragedy, inadvertently acknowledging that, as long as criminal acts and behavior are an aspect of human activity, crime will provide subject matter for works of literature. Yet nineteenth-century writers laid the foundation for modern mystery fiction, which in its various forms and manifestations has held sway in the twentieth century as a highly popular component of both mass culture and serious literary expression.

Despite the attempts of writers to define the mystery form during the so-called Golden Age of the mystery in England (the period from about 1913 to 1930 when the puzzle mystery reached a degree of heightened preciosity) the genre is remarkable for its varying guises and classifications. The relationship between the Gothic novel, which flourished in Victorian England, and the mystery is clear, for example, in the works that Sheridan Le Fanu began writing in the early 1860s and in precursors of the mystery such as Angus Reach's romance *Clement Lorimer* (1848-1849). Although the fiction of the supernatural has continued to influence the mystery, Edgar Allan Poe's four detective stories published in the 1840s established an emphasis on ratiocination over atmosphere that has been far more influential in determining the overall direction of detective fiction. The success of Wilkie Collins's *The Woman in White* (1860) and *The Moonstone* (1868), along with Sir Arthur Conan Doyle's Sherlock Holmes (created in 1887), popularized the basic detective narrative, focusing on the investigative detective, frequently a "serial" figure like Holmes himself, appearing throughout a succession of novels and stories.

Detective fiction has its analogue in the crime story and in its unusual variant, the inverse crime narrative, where the emphasis shifts from the reader's assembling the pieces of the puzzle into a revelatory pattern along with the detective to the observation of the investigator arriving at (or in some cases failing to arrive at) the completed puzzle already known to the reader. In both types of crime narrative the crime and the criminal are featured at the expense of the detective, and detection is limited to an ancillary function. Many of these crime narratives are essentially psychological thrillers, with focuses ranging from the elements of aberrant human behavior to the workings of the thoroughly pathological criminal mind, and a fine line, if any at all, separates mainstream psychological fiction from the psychological crime thriller.

Crime/detection fiction also shares roots with the pure adventure story, and elements of the adventure tale have often been retained in the less genteel variants of the crime/detective story, often resurfacing in fictions that feature or culminate in "the chase" or "the hunt," depicted either from the perspective of the hunter or the hunted—or both. In turn, the adventure/chase phenomenon of exciting crime narratives evolves naturally into the espionage novel. This variant of the mystery has increased in popularity since World War II, but the espionage novel came to prominence at the time of World War I in the works of Edgar Wallace, John Buchan, William Le Queux, and E. Phillips Oppenheim. Spy fiction more often than not retains its affinities with crime and detection in methods of operation, while frequently containing strong political implications and propagandistic intentions.

What is frequently termed the thriller or the suspense novel covers a wide area, subsuming the detective story, which in itself has often been divided between the genteel puzzle narrative that looks to be almost exclusively English (with American imitators) and that reached its zenith (or nadir) in the Golden Age of the 1920s and 1930s, and the fiction of hard-boiled "realism" that was its contemporary American cousin and alternative (but has been adopted by occasional British practitioners as well). Scholars have viewed that violent American phenomenon as either a reaction against the effete English variety of detective novel or a native by-product of nineteenth-century Western fiction urbanized and brought up to date. Yet bloody crime fiction already existed during the formative period of detective fiction in Victorian Britain, and violence, with its own didactic purposes, was characteristic of serious fiction of the age as well.

The nineteenth-century phenomenon of "middle-culture" literary art blurred the distinction between serious literature and popular fiction, a balanced attitude that only a handful of authors in the twentieth century have sought to establish for themselves. Most mystery fiction since the cultic prominence of Conan Doyle's detective has been written by authors who specialize almost exclusively in it, although an author of prestige has on occasion been known to indulge in the writing of thrillers, usually under an assumed name. From the nineteenth century on, writers best known for their work in other genres have tried their hand at the popular form, at times creating literature that satisfies both worlds. With prose fiction, and particularly the novel, fixed as the primary literary vehicle of the bourgeois era of the nineteenth and twentieth centuries, the mystery novel in its various guises has claimed a prominent position, with a pedigree of its own, in mainstream literary art. Thus it is appropriate for the *Dictionary of Literary Biography* to include these writers, who have not only played a significant role in the tradition of popular fiction but who have also affected the development of so-called mainstream literature.

This is the first *DLB* volume of British mystery writers; subsequent volumes will cover the period from World War I to the present. Because there has been little scholarship devoted to individual mystery writers except for the most prominent, this volume is particularly useful as a stimulus to further study. Writers are best defined by what they wrote, and so the primary bibliography for each entry contains as many published books as could be verified in reliable sources. Since mystery writing of the period covered here is often formulaic, it has frequently been adequate to discuss works representative of an author's career or to describe in general terms the fiction a writer produced.

The history of mystery fiction, in Great Britain as in America, recounts the evolution of a literary form from a means of popular entertainment to a mode of expression through which the exigencies of everyday life are examined. There is no more compelling subject than crime, particularly murder; the century-and-a-half-long tradition of mystery fiction, which is the systematic literary attempt to come to terms with violent crime, deserves our closest attention. The writers in this volume were the pioneers of that tradition.

—Bernard Benstock

Acknowledgments

This book was produced by Bruccoli Clark Layman, Inc. Karen L. Rood is senior editor for the *Dictionary of Literary Biography* series. Charles Lee Egleston was the in-house editor.

Production coordinator is Kimberly Casey. Art supervisor is Cheryl Crombie. Copyediting supervisor is Joan M. Prince. Typesetting supervisor is Kathleen M. Flanagan. Laura Ingram and Michael D. Senecal are editorial associates. The production staff includes Rowena Betts, Charles D. Brower, Patricia Coate, Mary Colborn, Mary S. Dye, Sarah A. Estes, Cynthia Hallman, Judith K. Ingle, Maria Ling, Warren McInnis, Kathy S. Merlette, Sheri Neal, Joycelyn R. Smith, and Virginia Smith. Jean W. Ross is permissions editor. Joseph Caldwell, photography editor, and Joseph Matthew Bruccoli did photographic copy work for the volume.

The editors also wish to acknowledge the admirable research and organizational support of Joan Seay.

Walter W. Ross and Rhonda Marshall did the library research with the assistance of the staff at the Thomas Cooper Library of the University of South Carolina: Daniel Boice, Cathy Eckman, Gary Geer, Cathie Gottlieb, David L. Haggard, Jens Holley, Dennis Isbell, Jackie Kinder, Marcia Martin, Jean Rhyne, Beverly Steele, Ellen Tillett, Carol Tobin, and Virginia Weathers.

Dictionary of Literary Biography • Volume Seventy

British Mystery Writers, 1860-1919

Dictionary of Literary Biography

Grant Allen
(24 February 1848-28 October 1899)

Phyllis Rozendal
York University

BOOKS: *Physiological Aesthetics* (London: King, 1877; New York: Appleton, 1877);

The Colour-Sense: Its Origin and Development (Boston: Houghton, Osgood, 1879; London: Trübner, 1879);

Anglo-Saxon Britain (London: Society for Promoting Christian Knowledge, 1881; New York: Young, 1881);

The Evolutionist at Large (London: Chatto & Windus, 1881; New York: Fitzgerald, 1881; revised, London: Chatto & Windus, 1884);

Vignettes from Nature (London: Chatto & Windus, 1881; New York: Fitzgerald, 1882);

The Colours of Flowers as Illustrated in the British Flora (London: Macmillan, 1882; London & New York: Macmillan, 1891);

Colin Clout's Calendar: The Record of a Summer, April-October (London: Chatto & Windus, 1883; New York: Funk & Wagnalls, 1883);

Flowers and Their Pedigrees (London: Longmans, 1883; New York: Appleton, 1884);

Biographies of Working Men (London: Society for Promoting Christian Knowledge, 1884; New York: Young, 1885);

Philistia, as Cecil Power (London: Chatto & Windus, 1884; New York: Munro, 1884);

Strange Stories (London: Chatto & Windus, 1884);

Babylon, as Cecil Power (3 volumes, London: Chatto & Windus, 1885; 1 volume, New York: Appleton, 1885);

Charles Darwin (London: Longmans, Green, 1885; New York: Appleton, 1885);

In All Shades (3 volumes, London: Chatto & Windus, 1886; 1 volume, Chicago: Rand, McNally, 18??);

Common Sense Science (Boston: Lothrop, 1886);
Kalee's Shrine, by Allen and May Cotes (Bristol:

3

Arrowsmith/London: Simpkin, Marshall, 1886; New York: New Amsterdam Book Company, 1897?); republished as *The Indian Mystery; or, Kalee's Shrine* (New York: New Amsterdam Book Company, 1902);

For Maimie's Sake: A Tale of Love and Dynamite (London: Chatto & Windus, 1886; New York: Appleton, 1886);

The Beckoning Hand and Other Stories (London: Chatto & Windus, 1887);

A Terrible Inheritance (London: S.P.C.K., 1887; New York: Crowell, 18??);

The Devil's Die (3 volumes, London: Chatto & Windus, 1888; 1 volume, New York: Lovell, 1888);

Force and Energy: A Theory of Dynamics (London & New York: Longmans, Green, 1888);

A Half-Century of Science, by Allen and T. H. Huxley (New York: Humboldt, 1888);

This Mortal Coil (3 volumes, London: Chatto & Windus, 1888; 1 volume, New York: Appleton, 1889);

The White Man's Foot (London: Hatchard's, 1888);

Falling in Love, with Other Essays on More Exact Branches of Science (London: Smith, Elder, 1889; New York: Appleton, 1890);

Individualism and Socialism. Reprinted from "Contemporary Review" of May 1889 (Glasgow: Scottish Land Restoration League, 1889);

Dr Pallser's Patient (London: Mullen, 1889);

The Jaws of Death (London: Simpkin, Marshall, 1889; New York: New Amsterdam Book Company, 1897);

The Tents of Shem (3 volumes, London: Chatto & Windus, 1889; 1 volume, Chicago: Rand, McNally, 1889);

A Living Apparition (London: S.P.C.K., 1889);

The Great Taboo (London: Chatto & Windus, 1890; New York: Harper, 1891);

The Sole Trustee (London: S.P.C.K., 1890);

Wednesday the Tenth; a Tale of the South Pacific (Boston: Lothrop, 1890); republished as *The Cruise of the Albatross, or When Was Wednesday the Tenth? A Story of the South Pacific* (Boston: Lothrop, 1898);

The Duchess of Powysland (1 volume, New York: United States Book Company, 1891; 3 volumes, London: Chatto & Windus, 1892);

Dumaresq's Daughter (3 volumes, London: Chatto & Windus, 1891; 1 volume, New York: Harper, 1891);

Recalled to Life (Bristol: Arrowsmith, 1891; New York: Holt, 1891);

What's Bred in the Bone (London: Tit-bits Offices, 1891; Boston: Tucker, 1891);

Blood Royal (New York: Cassell, 1892; London: Chatto & Windus, 1893);

Science in Arcady (London: Lawrence & Bullen, 1892);

An Army Doctor's Romance (New York: Tuck, 1893; London & New York: Tuck, 1894);

Ivan Greet's Masterpiece (London: Chatto & Windus, 1893);

Michael's Crag (Chicago & New York: Rand, McNally, 1893; London: Leadenhall, 1893);

The Scallywag (3 volumes, London: Chatto & Windus, 1893; 1 volume, New York: Cassell, 1893);

The Lower Slopes (London: Elkin Mathews & John Lane, 1894; Chicago: Stone & Kimball, 1894);

At Market Value (2 volumes, London: Chatto & Windus, 1894; 1 volume, Chicago & New York: Neely, 1894);

Post-Prandial Philosophy (London: Chatto & Windus, 1894);

Under Sealed Orders (1 volume, New York: Collier, 1894; 3 volumes, London: Chatto & Windus, 1895);

The British Barbarians: A Hill-top Novel (London: John Lane, 1895; New York: Putnam's, 1895);

The Desire of the Eyes and Other Stories (New York: Fenno, 1895);

In Memoriam: George Paul Macdonell (London: Lund, 1895);

The Story of the Plants (London: Newnes, 1895; New York: Appleton, 1895);

The Woman Who Did (Boston: Roberts/London: John Lane, 1895);

A Bride from the Desert (New York: Fenno, 1896);

Moorland Idylls (London: Chatto & Windus, 1896);

A Splendid Sin (London: White, 1896; New York: Buckles, 1899);

An African Millionaire: Episodes in the Life of the Illustrious Colonel Clay (London: Richards, 1897; New York: Arnold, 1897);

Tom, Unlimited: A Story for Children, as Martin Leach Warborough (London: Richards, 1897);

The Evolution of the Idea of God: An Inquiry into the Origins of Religion (London: Richards, 1897; New York: Holt, 1897);

The Type-writer Girl, as Olive Pratt Rayner (London: Pearson, 1897; New York: Street & Smith, 1900);

Front cover for the first British book publication of Allen's twelve stories about a self-described "parasite upon capitalists" who takes repeated advantage of a wealthy colonialist (courtesy of Otto Penzler)

Grant Allen's Historical Guides, 12 volumes (London: Richards, 1897-1912);

The Incidental Bishop (London: Pearson, 1898; New York: Appleton, 1898);

Flashlights on Nature (New York: Doubleday & McClure, 1898; London: Newnes, 1899);

Linnet: A Romance (London: Richards, 1898; New York: New Amsterdam Book Company, 1900);

The European Tour: A Handbook for Americans and Colonists (London: Richards, 1899; New York: Dodd, Mead, 1899);

Miss Cayley's Adventures (London: Richards, 1899; New York: Putnam's, 1899);

Rosalba: The Story of Her Development, as Olive Pratt Rayner (New York & London: Putnam's, 1899);

Twelve Tales (London: Richards, 1899);

Hilda Wade: A Woman with Tenacity of Purpose, by Allen and Arthur Conan Doyle (London: Richards, 1900; New York & London: Putnam's, 1900);

Plain Words on the Woman Question (Chicago: Harman, 1900);

The Backslider (New York & London: Lewis, Scribner, 1901);

County and Town in England (London: Richards, 1901; New York: Dutton, 1901);

In Nature's Workshop (London: Newnes, 1901);

Sir Theodore's Guest and Other Stories (Bristol: Arrowsmith, 1902);

Evolution in Italian Art (London: Richards, 1903; New York: Wessels, 1908);

The Hand of God and Other Posthumous Essays, edited by Edward Clodd (London: Watts, 1909);

The Reluctant Hangman and Other Stories of Crime, edited by Tom and Enid Schantz (Boulder, Colo.: Aspen, 1973).

OTHER: Richard A. Proctor, ed., *Nature Studies*, comprises studies by Allen, Thomas Foster, Andrew Wilson, Edward Clodd, and Proctor (New York: Funk & Wagnalls, 1883);

The Attis of Caius Valerius Catullus translated into English verse, with dissertations on the myth of Attis, on the origin of tree-worship, and on the Galliambic metre by Grant Allen (London: Nutt, 1892);

Gilbert White, *The Natural History of Selborne*, edited, with notes, by Allen (London: John Lane, 1902).

Most of Grant Allen's fiction is now forgotten and nearly all of it is out of print. His detective stories, however, many of which first appeared in the *Strand Magazine*, have earned critical praise, and volumes of his detective fiction are now sought by book collectors. Allen's chief contribution to the genre, *An African Millionaire: Episodes in the Life of the Illustrious Colonel Clay* (1897), was listed by Ellery Queen as one of the "cornerstones" of detective fiction and cited by Hugh Greene as "one of the most amusing collections of crime stories ever written." Besides creating the first great rogue of mystery fiction–the illustrious Colonel Clay–Allen produced two lively series of stories featuring female amateur sleuths, collected in *Miss Cayley's Adventures* (1899) and *Hilda Wade: A Woman with Tenacity of Purpose* (1900), as well as two novels in which detectives play parts, *The Scallywag* (1893) and *A Splendid Sin* (1896), and several other novels and stories that may be linked, albeit loosely at times, to the mystery genre. Most of Allen's crime fiction does not fit the mold of the classical whodunit. Howard Haycraft has called him one of the "borderliners," an author whose work "falls somewhere between the undoubted detective story and such related forms as mystery, criminal adventure or intrigue." Allen's fiction reflects the eclecticism of his tastes and experience and is often as difficult to categorize as the man himself.

In his lifetime Allen was best known as a popularizer of science, though he was praised by Charles Darwin, A. R. Wallace, and Herbert Spencer for his original contributions to science. From 1877 until his death at age fifty-one in 1899 Allen published books and articles on an astonishing range of subjects, from biology and botany to physics, philosophy, geography, history, and art. Allen started writing fiction only after discovering that he could not make a living from his scientific writing. In the last fifteen years of his life he turned out more than forty novels and collections of stories, while continuing to produce volumes with titles such as *Force and Energy: A Theory of Dynamics* (1888) and *The Evolution of the Idea of God* (1897), as well as a series of historical guides to the major cities of Europe. For one of his novels, *What's Bred in the Bone* (1891), he received a £1000 prize from *Tit-bits* magazine, but the book that won him widest recognition and instant notoriety was his best-seller *The Woman Who Did* (1895), a serious novel of purpose that shocked England with its portrayal of a high-minded young woman, Herminia Barton, who chooses to have a child out of wedlock, rejecting marriage on principle and making herself a martyr to the cause of female emancipation. Allen's mystery fiction was thus a small part of a large and enormously varied literary output.

Charles Grant Blairfindie Allen was born near Kingston, Canada, on 24 February 1848. His father, J. Antisell Allen, was an Irish clergyman who had immigrated to Canada in 1840. His mother, Charlotte Catherine Ann Grant, of Scottish and French ancestry and the only daughter of the fifth baron de Longeueil, belonged to one of the oldest and most prominent Canadian families. Allen's lifelong love of nature was rooted in his early childhood years, spent happily, by his own account, wandering the woods and fields near his home and observing the plants, flowers, insects, and animals that later became the subjects of his scientific studies. Taught by his father until the age of thirteen, Allen then moved with his family to New Haven, Connecticut, where the boy was given a Yale tutor. In 1862 Allen was sent to the College Impériale in Dieppe, France, and he also attended King Edward's School in Birmingham, England, before matriculating at Merton College, Oxford, in 1867. His colonial birth, mixed parentage, and peripatetic upbringing were all significant influences on a man whose work was to stretch and cross so many boundaries and who retained a fine and critical eye for the provincialism of manners and morals exhibited by many of his contemporaries. He married while at Oxford, but shortly after their wedding his wife became ill. She died two years later.

Because Allen's university education was in the classics (having received a scholarship at Merton, he went on to earn a first-class degree in Mods. in 1869, a second class in Greats in 1870, taking his B.A. in 1871), he remained an amateur in the field that interested him most–

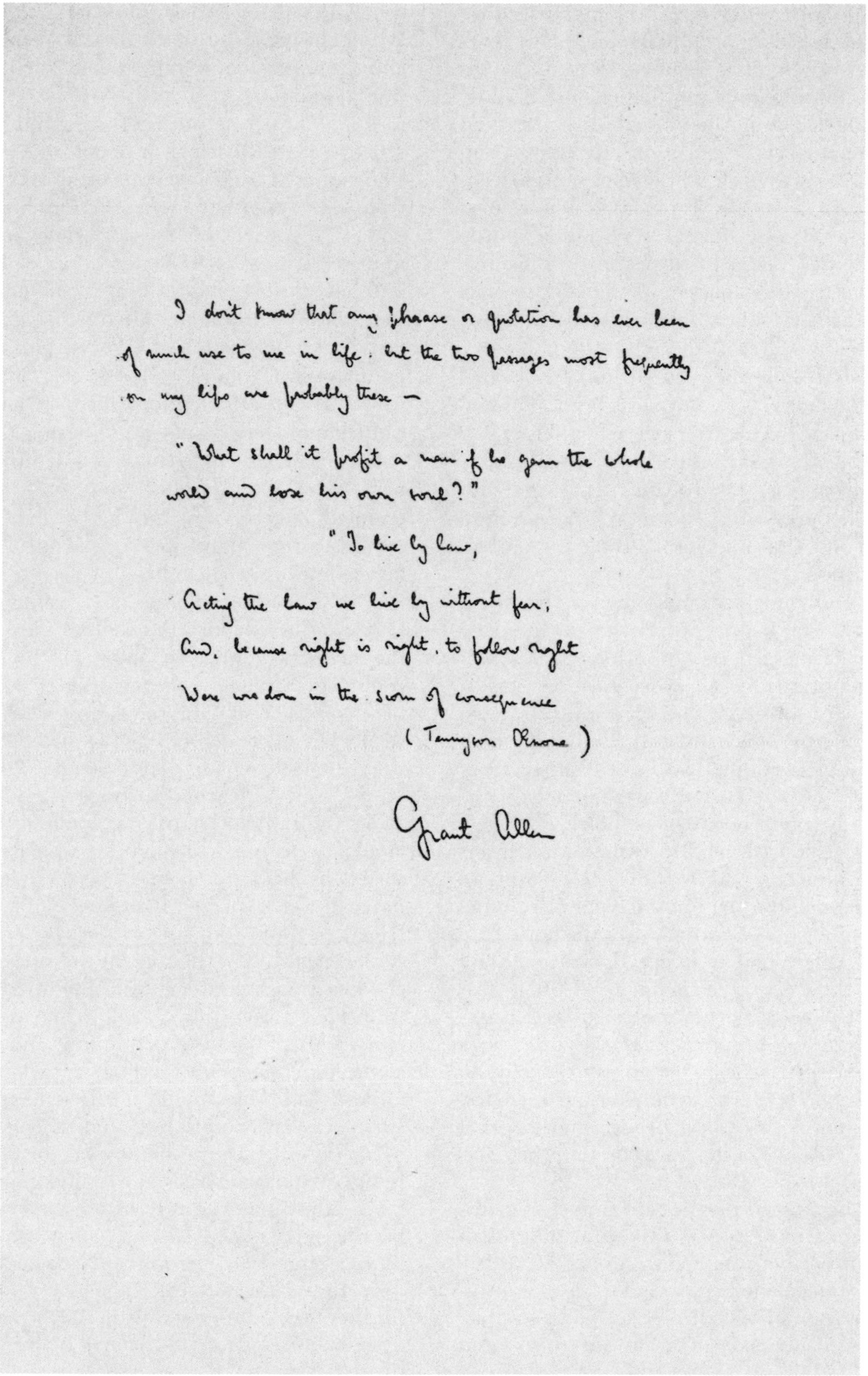

I don't know that any phrase or quotation has ever been of much use to me in life. But the two passages most frequently on my lips are probably these —

"What shall it profit a man if he gain the whole world and lose his own soul?"

"To live by law,

Acting the law we live by without fear;

And, because right is right, to follow right

Were wisdom in the scorn of consequence

(Tennyson Œnone)

Grant Allen

Manuscript reproduced as the epigraph for Edward Clodd's memoir, Grant Allen *(1900)*

science. At Oxford Allen first developed his enthusiasm for the evolutionary philosophy of Herbert Spencer, whose ideas remained central to his own work and thinking for the rest of his life. After leaving Oxford Allen spent three years at the "uncongenial task" of teaching Latin and Greek in various English schools before proceeding, in June 1873, to the more exotic post of professor of moral and mental philosophy at the recently founded Government College in Spanish Town, Jamaica. He was accompanied by his second wife, formerly Ellen Jerrard, whom he had married that spring. Although Allen became head of the school when the original principal died of yellow fever, his tenure was brief. The college closed in 1876 due to a lack of qualified students. The experience did, however, provide material for some of Allen's later fiction and also gave him the opportunity to study Jamaican flora and fauna and continue his reading in philosophy and science.

Upon returning to England in 1876 Allen, with characteristic energy, produced "a hundred or more magazine articles on various philosophical and scientific subjects, every one of which," he said, "I sent to the editors of leading reviews, and every one of which was punctually 'declined with thanks' or committed without even that polite formality to the editorial wastepaper baskets." Undaunted, he published his first book, *Physiological Aesthetics* (1877), at his own expense, an enterprise which left him £50 poorer but with an enhanced reputation, the book having sold somewhat under 300 copies. Shortly after the book's appearance, Leslie Stephen accepted two of Allen's articles for the *Cornhill* magazine, and other articles soon followed. Over the next few years (1877-1883) Allen supplemented the precarious income from such articles by working briefly on the staff of the *Daily News*, contributing regularly to the short-lived periodical *London* and assisting Sir William Wilson Hunter in compiling the *Imperial Gazetteer of India* (1881).

Allen began writing fiction almost inadvertently in about 1880 and as a natural outgrowth of his scientific interests. While doing an article for *Belgravia* magazine he decided to cast his argument, about the impossibility of a man's recognizing a ghost if he saw one, in the form of a narrative: "I did not regard this narrative as a story: I looked upon it merely as a convenient way of displaying a scientific truth." The editor of *Belgravia* thought differently, however, and asked Allen to contribute more "stories." He did,

using the "prudent pseudonym" of J. Arbuthnot Wilson, fearing, he said, that "these my tentative tales . . . might stand in the way of such little scientific reputation as I possessed. . . . " Allen was led, in his own phrase, "further on the downward path which leads to fiction" by James Payn, who, upon taking over editorship of the *Cornhill* from Leslie Stephen, sent Allen a letter rejecting one of his scientific articles while at the same time sending another letter addressed to J. Arbuthnot Wilson inviting him to submit more stories. Thus encouraged, Allen wrote a number of tales for the *Cornhill* and other magazines, collecting them in a volume called *Strange Stories* (1884), which he published under his own name with a rather apologetic preface explaining that he was "by trade a psychologist and scientific journeyman," not a storyteller and that he had attempted to give most of his "short sensational tales . . . some slight tinge of scientific or psychological import or meaning."

The volume *Strange Stories* cannot be classified as crime fiction, but it does have links with the mystery genre. In some of the stories accounts of strange and apparently supernatural happenings create an atmosphere of eeriness and suspense that is dispelled only at the conclusions when logical explanations emerge. The "simulacrum" that a learned professor encounters in "The Mysterious Occurrence in Picadilly," for example, turns out to have been an elaborate hoax staged by his future son-in-law. While the technique is the same as that used later by Allen's friend Arthur Conan Doyle in *The Hound of the Baskervilles* (1902), the tone of the stories is generally less intense and less skillfully managed.

The stories that Allen wrote in the 1880s and 1890s illustrate a continuing and significant connection between his scientific background and interests and his mystery fiction. As a scientist Allen was an evolutionist, and as a novelist one of his most persistent themes was the effect of heredity. A character's racial past and genetic inheritance often play the role of a ghost, evoking the horror, terror, and suspense that other mystery writers achieve by introducing elements of the supernatural. The title of "The Beckoning Hand," for instance, refers not only to the "strange and indescribable fascination" which is exercised over the narrator by Césarine Vivian, an extraordinary beauty with "something uncanny and weird about her," but it refers also to Césarine's own irresistible attraction toward the cannibalistic "Voudoux" rites of her African ancestors. The narrator is led through a series of increasingly horrifying revelations as he secretly follows the dark-eyed beauty he has married, first to a village in Haiti, where he discovers she has a black, voodoo-worshipping grandmother, and then into the jungle, where he watches her take part in the ritual sacrifice of a human child. Filled with revulsion at being married to a murderer, yet unwilling to turn his wife over to the police, the narrator finds his dilemma resolved when Césarine conveniently dies of yellow fever. The story could easily have had a supernatural cast, but Allen presents the fateful power as biological, a disposition passed down irrevocably from generation to generation.

The same note is struck in "The Third Time," collected like the previous story in *The Beckoning Hand and Other Stories* (1887). A woman is troubled by the mysterious disappearances of her otherwise loving and considerate husband. The third time he goes away without warning or explanation she accidentally stumbles upon him lying in the road in a drunken stupor, and, while she is still reeling from the horror and shock of this discovery, the husband shoots himself, leaving a note to explain that both his parents were drunkards and that he has decided to dispose of himself rather than repeat a pattern he cannot break. The theme is further elaborated, with some variations, in Allen's later work *A Splendid Sin*, in which Hubert Egremont discovers that a shabby drunken stranger, well on the way to alcoholic insanity, is in fact his mother's husband and thus apparently the father he has always wished to know and has never been allowed to meet. The stranger, Colonel Egremont, tells Hubert that it "runs in the blood with all my family to be hoary old reprobates. . . . We've been hoary old reprobates now for five generations." Since the young man is a physiologist who believes that "heredity is everything," he is convinced that he himself will go mad before the age of thirty. The "splendid sin" of the title is his mother's secret affair with a noble American poet, who turns out to be Hubert's true father. This revelation frees the young man from his horror and despair and enables him to go on living in spite of the colonel's underhanded efforts to disinherit him because of Mrs. Egremont's youthful infidelity. While the theme is appropriate to a naturalistic novel, the tone, again, is closer to that of a ghost story or tale of terror.

One explanation often given for the burgeoning popularity of detective fiction in the 1890s is the dramatic increase in scientific discoveries at the end of the nineteenth century, a phenomenon which, according to A. E. Murch, aroused admiration for men who were clever at finding things out. The archetypal detective hero, who possessed both brilliant analytical powers and a vast store of specialized technical knowledge, is, of course, Sherlock Holmes, who made his first appearance in print about the time Allen was venturing into fiction. Although Allen did not produce any detectives in the Sherlock Holmes mold, his stories frequently contain characters who are doctors, geologists, botanists, or experimental scientists. Interestingly, however, when such characters are featured in his crime fiction they are more often villains than heroes, using their professional expertise to commit rather than to solve crimes. In *The Devil's Die* (1888), for example, Harry Chichele is a medical doctor and bacteriologist who deliberately shortens the life of a patient in order to prove his new germ theory. When he escapes detection and wins acclaim for his theory, Harry decides that medical science offers the means for the perfect murder, one indistinguishable from death by natural causes. He later injects his wife with cholera germs, hoping to free himself for life with another woman, and it is not the police but a medical colleague who suspects the truth. This doctor is spared the task of trying to prove his suspicions because Harry's wife recovers, while Harry himself is stricken with cholera and confesses everything just before he dies. In *Hilda Wade* the motive for murder is the "sacred thirst for knowledge" of Professor Sebastian, a renowned doctor who has killed a colleague, Hilda's father, because the man objected to his using helpless patients as the subjects of his medical experiments. In the course of the story Sebastian also attempts to do away with Hilda (by, among other methods, injecting her with a blood-poisoning bacillus) because her investigation threatens to cut short his research. As Hilda notes: "He is a man of high ideals but without principle. He would stab a man without remorse, if he thought that by stabbing him he could advance knowledge."

If Allen presents professional scientists in a less-than-favorable light, his professional policemen and detectives do not fare much better. In "The Great Ruby Robbery," collected with "The Conscientious Burglar" in *Ivan Greet's Masterpiece* (1893), the police detective himself turns out to be the thief. This tale is also noteworthy in that it contains, in a form unusually pure for Allen, sev-

Illustrations by Gordon Browne from the June 1896 issue of Strand Magazine, *which published the first of Allen's twelve stories about the South African millionaire Sir Charles Van Drift and his nemesis, Colonel Cuthbert Clay, whom Frederic Dannay called "the first great thief of short mystery fiction"*

eral elements of the classical detective story: the puzzle to be rationally solved, the mystery unraveled in a final confrontation of all the suspects, and the "least likely suspect" motif (as Officer Gregory announces when he first comes to investigate the disappearance of the rubies: "Our experience teaches us that if there's a person in the case whom nobody ever dreams of suspecting, that person's the one who has committed the robbery.").

The private investigator who appears in *A Splendid Sin* is similarly shrewd and unscrupulous. Fletcher is hired by the drunken reprobate, Colonel Egremont, to break into his wife's escritoire and find the evidence (love letters) that will enable him to disinherit Hubert. Although he appears in the climactic scene and takes part in some rather exciting action, disarming and handcuffing the colonel when he succumbs to the final stages of megalomania, Fletcher's job is not glamorized ("Divorce is my bread and butter," he remarks at one point), and he is definitely less than a disinterested pursuer of justice. While preferring to operate within the law ("Legal methods are safest," he says), he also believes that the "first duty of every intelligent private inquiry agent is to look after Number One" and is therefore prepared to play on whichever side will pad his pocket. Apart from playing a minor role in the plot, the character of Fletcher serves mainly to reinforce the novel's contention about the corruptness of conventional morality, the same morality that keeps Hubert's mother tied to a man she despises. The alliance of Fletcher and the colonel, two men with the laws of society on their side, helps to make Allen's point that Mrs. Egremont's "sin" against those laws was indeed splendid. As Hubert says: "Such sins are purer far than half this world's purity. It is love—and natural fitness—not the word of a priest or a law, that sanctifies."

When Allen's professional detectives are not distinctly shady characters, they generally play minor roles in stories mainly concerned with other matters. In *The Scallywag*, for instance, Detective Sherard from Scotland Yard does succeed in tracking down the man who stole Mr. Solomon's money, and some detail is expended on how he has followed clues to make this discovery, but the detective appears only briefly in volume three, and the theft itself is not a major element in the plot, which concerns the efforts of the impoverished Paul Gasgoyne to pay his and his father's debts and to prove that he is deserving of the inherited title of baronet.

Given all these examples of untrustworthy or ineffectual guardians of the law, it is perhaps not surprising that Allen's most engaging creation is a self-confessed rogue who openly thumbs his nose at the establishment, outwitting all the police forces of Europe and proving himself a far more attractive character than the pillars of respectability he consistently outsmarts. *An African Millionaire*, which ran in the *Strand Magazine* in 1896 and 1897, consists of twelve episodes in a continuing battle between Sir Charles Van Drift, South African millionaire and famous financier, and his nemesis Colonel Cuthbert Clay, who declares himself a modern-day Robin Hood, "a microbe of millionaires, a parasite upon capitalists." The appropriately named Clay is a master of disguise, appearing variously as a Mexican seer, a fresh-faced curate, a Tyrolean count, a German professor who has invented a scheme to mass-produce diamonds, and, in the most devastatingly effective of his incarnations, as "the best and cleverest detective in England." In each role Clay plays upon Sir Charles's greed and capitalistic instincts—as well as on his weakness for Clay's sidekick Madame Picardet—to relieve him of increasingly large sums of money. Keeping the reader as well as the authorities off guard, those episodes in which Sir Charles is hoodwinked by a disguised Colonel Clay are interspersed with those in which the millionaire wrongly suspects and falsely accuses an innocent and usually highly distinguished gentleman. Ellery Queen captures the spirit of the book when he refers to Clay as the rogue "who playfully pilfered, purloined, and pluck-pigeoned his way to pecuniary profits, and who was clever enough to go scot-free." Actually the colonel does not go scot-free. In the end he is caught, tried, and sent off to fourteen years imprisonment with hard labor. The operations of justice, however, are thrown into question even as they are technically served. Clay turns his trial into an indictment of Sir Charles, forcing him to confess publicly to his own greed and fraudulent dealings. As the convicted criminal says to Sir Charles: "We are a pair of rogues. The law protects *you*. It persecutes *me*. That's all the difference."

After *An African Millionaire*, and while also writing a great deal of nonmystery fiction, Allen produced two more detective series for the *Strand Magazine*, both featuring female sleuths. Allen's choice of women (amateurs perforce) as

Illustration by Gordon Browne from Miss Cayley's Adventures *(1899), the first of two series of stories by Allen about female detectives*

the only detectives to play central and positive roles in any of his fiction was conditioned, apparently, both by his long-standing interest in the "woman question" and by that distrust of the establishment evident in so much of his other writing. *Miss Cayley's Adventures* and *Hilda Wade* were intended as light entertainments, unlike *The Woman Who Did,* which was written, Allen said, "For the first time in my life wholly and solely to satisfy my own taste and my own conscience." Although the two later heroines do not challenge Victorian sexual morality and end their adventures with traditional, happy marriages, they are in other ways distinctly unconventional, and in their brisk independence and wide-ranging capabilities they present a more appealing picture of the possibilities of liberated womanhood than does their dour and single-minded predecessor Herminia Barton in *The Woman Who Did.*

In *Miss Cayley's Adventures* a penniless young Girton College graduate, Lois Cayley, rejects the respectable but boring job of teaching and chooses instead to go round the world in search of adventures, a project she finances with the same enterprising pluck that makes her a successful (though rather casual) sleuth. While serving as a lady's companion in Germany, a bicycle sales agent in Switzerland, and a journalist in Egypt, Lois rescues her employer's diamonds from a thief, unmasks a quack healer, and in the final epi-

sode, "The Adventure of the Unprofessional Detective," proves a disputed will and clears her fiancé's name. Like Hilda Wade after her, Lois Cayley operates mainly through "flashes of intuition" rather than by any process of deductive reasoning, but this feminine quality is supplemented by a high degree of resourcefulness and intrepidity. Among her other exploits, for instance, she rescues a male friend who has fallen over a precipice, and she kills a rampaging tiger in India. Although it shares many of the same features, *Hilda Wade* is a more tightly plotted book than *Miss Cayley's Adventures;* the heroine is a more substantial character, and the detective element is more dominant. Hilda's intellectual abilities are so formidable that the narrator feels obliged to assert at one point that "she laid no claim to supernatural powers ... she was simply a girl of strong personal charm, endowed with an astounding memory and a rare measure of feminine intuition." Hilda's immediate goal in life is to unmask Professor Sebastian as the murderer of her father. This overriding purpose unifies the plot, but individual episodes show Hilda solving other mysteries along the way, using her expertise in the analysis of handwriting as well as her great store of esoteric knowledge (an understanding of Buddhist prayer wheels, for example). Her major strength as a sleuth, however, is her extraordinary insight into character, a trait that distinguishes her from her more plodding counterparts on the police force. She is a psychologist, and, as she says, "the police are not; they are at best but bungling materialists. They require a clue. What need of a clue if you can interpret character?" A particularly memorable flight scene–one that suggests both the pace and the tone of the book–occurs in South Africa, where Hilda has been pursued by Professor Sebastian. After the professor has stirred up a rebellion in one of his many attempts to kill her, Hilda escapes by pedaling madly across the veldt on her bicycle, steering with one arm and in the other holding a baby she has rescued from a massacre. Accompanied by her friend Hubert on a pony, she is pursued by spear-throwing natives.

Like Lois Cayley and many other of Allen's characters, Hilda Wade is an inveterate globetrotter. Making use of his own cosmopolitan experiences, Allen frequently exploited exotic settings to create variety and heighten the interest of his tales. Setting has further significance in *Under Sealed Orders* (1894), a tale that combines romance and international intrigue as Owen

Cazelet, reared on English soil but nephew of a Russian general, is drawn into a nihilist plot to assassinate the czar. The foreign episodes provide an additional narrative bonus in that they allow for shipwrecks on the way home, a plot device used in *Hilda Wade*, *The Scallywag*, and *The Devil's Die*, among other novels. ("I am learning," Allen had written as early as 1885, "to do the sensational things that please the editors.")

Hilda Wade is noteworthy also because the final episode was written by Arthur Conan Doyle, Allen's friend and neighbor in Hindhead, where he had moved in 1893. Stricken with his final illness while *Hilda Wade* was still running in the *Strand*, Allen on his deathbed told Conan Doyle his plans for the serial's ending, and Conan Doyle completed it for him after Allen's death on 28 October 1899. Doyle was only one of many leading literary men who respected Allen and valued his friendship. Another was George Meredith, Allen's neighbor in Dorking, where he had moved in 1881.

Although Allen regarded his fiction as merely the work of "a good sound hack," something that allowed him to make a comfortable living for his wife and son (Jerrard Grant Allen, born in July 1878), and as a departure from the serious work of his life, the stories are nevertheless of a piece with his total output. They reflect the multifarious interests and abilities of a man who, according to his friend and biographer Edward Clodd, "was from early manhood till death a soul in revolt against conventions that dwarf and corrupt, and against political and economic conditions that enslave." Even his lightest and most popular productions evidence not only his scientific outlook but also his persistent questioning of established convention and of the institutions and officials that uphold it. With its tales of crime and terror and intrigue, its sinister scientists, appealing rogues, and amateur detectives, Allen's fiction also offers a particularly good exam-ple of the many and diverse strands contributing to the development of the mystery genre at the end of the nineteenth century. The most witty and original of his own contributions, *An African Millionaire* and *Hilda Wade*, still make delightful reading today.

Biographies:
Edward Clodd, *Grant Allen: A Memoir* (London: Grant Richards, 1900);
Marcus Woodward, "Life of Grant Allen," in *The Story of the Plants*, revised and annotated by Woodward (London: Hodder & Stoughton, 1926), pp. 11-17.

References:
Edward Clodd, "Grant Allen," in *Memories* (London: Watts, 1926), pp. 21-36;
Patricia Craig and Mary Cadogan, *The Lady Investigates: Women Detectives and Spies in Fiction* (New York: St. Martin's Press, 1981), pp. 25-28;
Arthur Conan Doyle, *Memories and Adventures* (London: Hodder & Stoughton, 1924), pp. 261-263;
Hugh Greene, Introduction to *More Rivals of Sherlock Holmes: Cosmopolitan Crimes*, edited by Greene (London: Bodley Head, 1971), pp. 9-18;
Howard Haycraft, *Murder for Pleasure: The Life and Times of the Detective Story* (New York: Biblo, Tanner, 1968), pp. 80-81;
A. E. Murch, *The Development of the Detective Novel* (London: Owen, 1958; New York: Philosophical Library, 1958);
H. G. Wells, *Experiment in Autobiography* (New York: Macmillan, 1934), pp. 461-466.

Papers:
The manuscript for *The Tents of Shem* is at the University of Toronto library. The manuscript of *Under Sealed Orders* is located in the Berg Collection of the New York Public Library.

Robert Barr

(16 September 1850-22 October 1912)

Alison Janice McNabb Cox

BOOKS: *Strange Happenings,* as Luke Sharp (London: Dunkerley, 1883);

One Day's Courtship, as Luke Sharp, in *The Record of Badalia Herodsfoot, by Rudyard Kipling. One Day's Courtship, by Luke Sharp* (London: Detroit Free Press, 1890);

In a Steamer Chair and Other Shipboard Stories (New York: Stokes, 1892; London: Chatto & Windus, 1892);

From Whose Bourne (London: Chatto & Windus, 1893; New York: Stokes, 1896);

In the Midst of Alarms (Philadelphia: Lippincott, 1893; London: Methuen, 1894);

The Face and The Mask (London: Hutchinson, 1894; New York: Stokes, 1895);

One Day's Courtship and The Heralds of Fame (New York & London: Stokes, 1896);

The Mutable Many (New York & London: Stokes, 1896; London: Methuen, 1897);

Revenge! (New York: Stokes, 1896; London: Chatto & Windus, 1896);

A Woman Intervenes. Or, The Mistress of the Mine (New York & London: Stokes, 1896; London: Chatto & Windus, 1896);

Tekla. A Romance of Love and War (New York: Stokes, 1898); republished as *The Countess Tekla* (London: Methuen, 1899);

Jennie Baxter, Journalist (New York: Stokes, 1899; London: Methuen, 1899);

The Strong Arm (New York: Stokes, 1899; London: Methuen, 1900); revised and abridged as *Gentlemen: The King!* (New York: Stokes, 1899);

The Unchanging East (2 volumes, Boston: Page, 1900; 1 volume, London: Chatto & Windus, 1900);

The King Dines (London: McClure, 1901); republished as *A Prince of Good Fellows* (New York: McClure, Phillips, 1902; London: Chatto & Windus, 1902);

The Victors. A Romance of Yesterday Morning and This Afternoon (New York: Stokes, 1901; London: Methuen, 1902);

The O'Ruddy. A Romance, by Barr and Stephen Crane (New York: Stokes, 1903; London: Methuen, 1904);

Over the Border. A Romance (New York: Stokes, 1903; London: Isbister, 1903);

A Chicago Princess (New York: Stokes, 1904); republished as *The Tempestuous Petticoat* (London: Methuen, 1905);

The Woman Wins (New York: Stokes, 1904); republished as *The Lady Electra* (London: Methuen, 1904);

The Speculations of John Steele (New York: Stokes, 1905; London: Chatto & Windus, 1905);

A Rock in the Baltic (New York & London: Authors & Newspapers Association, 1906);

The Triumphs of Eugène Valmont (New York: Appleton, 1906; London: Hurst & Blackett, 1906);

The Watermead Affair (Philadelphia: Altemus, 1906);

The Measure of the Rule (London: Constable, 1907; New York: Appleton, 1908);

Young Lord Stranleigh. A Novel (New York: Appleton, 1908; London: Ward, Lock, 1908);

Cardillac (New York: Stokes, 1909; London: Mills & Boon, 1909);

Stranleigh's Millions (London: Eveleigh Nash, 1909);

The Girl in the Case. Being the Manoeuvres of the Inadvertent Mr. Pepperton (London: Nash, 1910);

The Sword Maker (New York: Stokes, 1910; London: Mills & Boon, 1910);

Lady Eleanor, Lawbreaker (Chicago & New York: Rand, McNally, 1911);

Lord Stranleigh, Philanthropist (London: Ward, Lock, 1911);

The Palace of Logs (London: Mills & Boon, 1912);

Lord Stranleigh Abroad (London: Ward, Lock, 1913);

My Enemy Jones. An Extravaganza (London: Eveleigh Nash, 1913); republished as *Unsentimental Journey* (London: Hodder & Stoughton, 1915);

A Woman in a Thousand (London: Hodder & Stoughton, 1913);

The Helping Hand and Other Stories (London: Mills & Boon, 1920);

Tales of Two Continents (London: Mills & Boon, 1920).

PLAY PRODUCTIONS: *An Emperor's Romance*, adapted by Barr and Cosmo Hamilton from *Tekla*, Hartlepool, Grand Theatre, 1 January 1901;

The Conspiracy, by Barr and S. Lewis Ransom, Dublin, 8 November 1907; London, Adelphi Theatre, 9 September 1908;

The Hanging Outlook, by Barr and John Savile Judd, London, Court Theatre, 11 July 1912;

Lady Eleanor, Lawbreaker, Liverpool, Repertory, 14 December 1912.

OTHER: "A. Conan Doyle and Robert Barr; Real Conversation Between Them," in *Human Documents: Portraits and Biographies of Great Men of To-Day* (New York: McClure, 1896), pp. 188-199;

The Conspiracy, by Barr and S. Lewis Ransom, in *Short Modern Plays, second series*, edited by S. R. Littlewood (London: Macmillan, 1939).

Although often considered a North American writer, Robert Barr is perhaps more accurately placed in context as a British author. He has been identified as one of the "displaced" writers of the nineteenth century by R. G. Moyles in his *English-Canadian Literature To 1900* (1976). From the age of four to the age of twenty-six he lived in Canada, developing his individual perspective, though an early review by Arthur Kimball in an 1896 issue of *Book Buyer* notes and explains Barr's successfully cosmopolitan outlook as that of "a Scotsman by birth, a Canadian by emigration, an Englishman by long residence, and a man of the world by travel."

Robert Barr was born in Glasgow, 16 September 1850, to Jane Watson Barr and Robert Barr. He was the eldest in a family of eight children. They immigrated to Canada in 1854 on a ship called the *Mayflower* when Robert was four. The family settled in Wallacetown, Ontario, in the township of Dunwich, where Barr worked with his father during the summer months, learning the trade of carpentry in the burgeoning settlement areas and attending school as he could during the winter months.

An article in *Canadian Magazine* (April 1895) devotes considerable attention to Barr's family, finding in them all the virtues of the middle-class Scottish immigrants who enriched the young dominion with their qualities of sobriety, intelligence, and worthy industry. In addition to Barr's own considerable writing success, his sister Jeannie marketed her stories to newspapers; brother James of the *Pall Mall Gazette* wrote under the pen name Angus Evan Abbott; and another brother, John, was the commercial editor of the *Detroit Free Press*.

Barr's reputation as a raconteur began early; in "Former Days" his brother John recalled that young Robert "had an active brain and brilliant imagination. We would see an accident. Ten minutes later in telling of it, he would add several features to intensify the happening. Fifteen minutes later he would give a much more elaborate description with more trimmings and half an hour afterward the original incident had been so changed and improved as scarcely to be recognized." His story-telling inclination was first supported by what he read in the popular journals

Barr at his desk in the Idler *office circa 1894, the year before he lost control of the magazine to his partner, Jerome K. Jerome (photograph by Fradelle & Young)*

available to a minimally educated rural youth, and when he came to mail the countless letters, sketches, and short "fillers" to these journals, he modeled his work on the form of these periodicals—a robust, broadly drawn rural satire. What resulted was a distinctive style, which, in spite of the valid criticism it provoked, he was never to change substantially, though he varied its uses.

Although he had not yet completed high school, Barr was employed in his early twenties at small country schools, where he taught under a temporary certificate while simultaneously studying for his senior grades, eventually taking a first-class grade in the finals of grade twelve in 1873, an achievement with which he was unself-consciously delighted.

His experience of the Toronto Normal School—which he entered in January of 1873 and attended for four months, earning a third-class certificate—resulted some years later in one of his strongest novels, *The Measure of the Rule* (1907), a caustic commentary on the contemporary educa-

tion system which also includes, almost as an afterthought, a romantic plot line.

In the spring of 1875 he was offered the principalship for that year of the central school in Windsor, Ontario, and it seemed as though his future was secure. He was responsible for supervising two assistants and was to earn a salary of $600 per year. He tried to find a teaching position nearby for Alexander McNeil, his friend from normal-school days, and he began to plan a summer holiday with McNeil to follow their studies for their grade thirteen exams in 1875. Barr's humorous fictional account of their boating trip along the shores of Lake Erie began with hypothetical absurdities related in letters written to McNeil long before their actual departure, letters that became the nucleus for what was to be his first published work. Although rejected by every Canadian newspaper and publisher to which it had been sent, it was accepted immediately by the editor of the *Detroit Free Press,* William E. Quimby, and ran from October until December of 1875 in the Sunday supplement under the title

"A Dangerous Journey." Barr's literary career dates from the acceptance of this manuscript, as did his lifelong friendship with Quimby and his frequent public acknowledgments of Quimby's gifts as an editor. It was essentially on the strength of this manuscript that Quimby offered him a permanent position on the staff of the *Detroit Free Press* in 1876. In 1876 Barr also married Eva Bennett, the daughter of a trustee at the first school which had employed him. They were to have two children.

Once in Detroit, Barr quickly passed from general reporting to the authorship of several popular columns of humor and commentary and finally to the position of exchange editor. His brother John joined the staff in 1880, to eventually become the commercial editor. A third brother, James, was on the general staff in Detroit until he followed Robert to England, where he continued to contribute to the *Detroit Free Press* frequent articles under the name Angus Evan Abbott.

Much of Barr's journalistic writing was anonymous, according to the protocol of the time, though from his earliest professional days he frequently wrote his more humorous material under the pseudonym Luke Sharp, a name he discovered on an undertaker's sign near the boarding-house where he lived while he was at the Toronto Normal School; he also published his first short-story collection, *Strange Happenings* (1883), under this name. He continued to use this pseudonym when he contributed material to British as well as American journals during these years, and it was given new life when he came to write for his own magazine a decade later. It was in this persona that Barr and his cheerfully iconoclastic humor became known to a wide readership.

In 1881, after only five years in Detroit, Barr was offered the editorship of the first overseas edition of an American newspaper, the London edition of the *Detroit Free Press*, a weekly which was published regularly for the next twenty years, quickly becoming a dependable North American perspective on world events. With his outgoing personality and authoritative opinions, Barr easily took his place in the British newspaper establishment, while his youth and gregarious nature assured him of acceptance and friendship of the young working journalists and writers he met and employed. Barr became a member of several London clubs and actively encour-

aged literary and social activities, delighting in his frequent discoveries of new talent.

A decade of successfully managing the London *Detroit Free Press* brought Barr considerable financial success, but by 1891 no professional writer in London was unaware that he was bored and in the market for a new venture and for a creative partner to share in the development of a different type of popular magazine tailored for the young suburban market.

Barr narrowed the choice of partner down to two popular young writers, Rudyard Kipling and Jerome K. Jerome. He chose Jerome because, he explained, Jerome lacked Kipling's sturdy jawline and would, he believed, be an easier partner to "manage." (Another factor in Barr's decision was probably Jerome's record of four successful humorous publications in the past two years.) Jerome proved not to be as tractable as Barr had hoped. In fact, at one point he took over control of the magazine, but the two remained close friends notwithstanding.

Barr planned his venture, the *Idler Magazine*, as direct competition to the *Strand Magazine*. In 1891 the *Strand* was just beginning publication, as a modestly respectable younger brother to the vulgar and unpretentious *Tit-Bits*, John Newnes's earlier magazine. Where the *Strand* was aimed for a middle-class family market, Barr hoped to capture the imagination of the young, single, businesspeople of London with a glossy, irreverent, humorous journal, an adult version of extremely successful English juvenile publications such as *Boy's Own Paper*, the *Magnet*, and the *Gem*. The first issue of the *Idler* was offered to an enthusiastic public in February 1892, following the *Strand* into the new field of literary entertainment with spectacular success. With each succeeding issue the *Idler* managed to make the *Strand* look more and more like a journal for provincials while the *Idler* presented a liberal, casually sophisticated, racy image. Breezy, irreverent, and sentimental, the *Idler* began in strength and continued to gain in popularity.

Barr undoubtedly contributed the organizational skills learned in his fifteen-year apprenticeship as a newspaper editor and was personally responsible for cultivating the long list of contributors to the immediately successful magazine; but he kept a deliberately low profile when it came to his many written contributions to the magazine, often using pseudonyms or leaving work unsigned. The public tended to identify the *Idler* with Jerome and the New Humorists, not least be-

Barr and Arthur Conan Doyle at the Doyle house in South Norwood, just outside London, circa 1894 (photograph by Fradelle & Young)

cause of the magazine name, a direct play on the title of Jerome's most recent success, *The Idle Thoughts of an Idle Fellow* (1886).

Given the pool of acquaintances from which Barr drew his staff, it comes as no surprise to find that most contributors had served their apprenticeships as penny-a-line journalists for the newspapers and other magazines.

Among the contributors in the early years of the magazine were Arthur Conan Doyle, James Barrie, A. E. W. Mason, Max Pemberton, Gilbert Parker, G. K. Chesterton, Israel Zangwill, Eden Philpotts, Barry Pain, Marie Corelli, Anthony Hope, Grant Allen, Robert Louis Stevenson, and W. W. Jacobs—most if not all recruited by Barr. Over the years they not only wrote articles and stories in the magazine but also contributed to the "Idler's Club" feature. Initially 'this section of the magazine was just a facetious imitation of the short-lived "Strand Club" which appeared in the *Strand*. It began as a column of unorganized table talk, but it quickly developed into articulate symposia which addressed a wide variety of topical and often controversial subjects. Contributors were identified by name, and their

views provided a cross section of contemporary opinion. Women wrote a significant share of feature material as well as publicizing their views in this column.

Conan Doyle supported the magazine from the beginning, and his close ties with Barr are obvious in Barr's informal and intimate interview of Doyle, part of which was published in the November 1893 issue of *McClure's*. Longer versions subsequently appeared in the October 1894 *Idler*, the November 1894 *McClure's*, and in *Human Documents: Portraits and Biographies of Great Men of To-Day* (1896). Doyle's *Stark Munro Letters* (1895) was published serially in the *Idler* in 1894-1895.

The influence of newspaper editing was obvious in all the work of Barr and Jerome; Barr, of course, was entirely a product of the American newspaper environment; his editing has been described by Louis K. McKendrick as being "saturated by the technologies of newsprint and its attendant formalities," and this influence is apparent when the *Idler* is compared to other popular magazines of the time. The frequent contemporary criticism of Americanized vocabulary and irreverence leveled at the New Humorists and

Illustration by George Hutchinson for Barr's "Detective Stories Gone Wrong: The Adventures of Sherlaw Kombs," published under the pseudonym Luke Sharp in the May 1892 issue of Idler *Magazine. This story is one of the earliest Sherlock Holmes parodies.*

their magazine become more understandable in this context.

Established authors and traditions of writing were passing from public taste as the newly educated classes turned to journalism rather than literature for entertainment. London was crowded with young men writing for the new magazines. With a quarter century's hindsight Conan Doyle remarked in his autobiography, *Memories and Adventures* (1924), on the "most amazing crop, all coming up simultaneously." Other critics were not so encouraging. A more typical response was that of T. W. H. Crosland, who in his *The Suburbans* (1905) compared these writers to the traditionalists and found them "despicable"; he went on to particularize his dislike by noting that "their ideal comic author was Mr. Jerome K. Jerome, and when they wanted pathos, they turned to the 'weepier productions' of J. M. Barrie."

By the summer of 1895 Jerome was announcing in the pages of the *Idler* that Barr's editorship

had come to an end. For the next several years Barr devoted himself to full-time writing, but he resumed his editorship of the magazine in 1902, continuing until the final issue, in March 1911. He died a year and a half later from what his biographer, Louis K. McKendrick, describes as "cumulative effects of dropsy."

During his retirement from journalism Barr met Stephen Crane, who settled in England in 1897. The two writers became friends, and in 1900 the dying Crane requested that Barr complete Crane's adventure-romance novel, *The O'Ruddy* (1903). Having been told Crane's plans for the unfinished portion of the book, Barr feared that "The contrast in the work would be too horrible . . . ," but he agreed because Crane "was too ill for me to refuse." Despite his reservations, Barr was able to adapt his style to fit Crane's. The reviewer for *Book News* (December 1903) praised Barr's ability to enter "into the spirit of his deceased friend" and said that he had "finished the story with fitness."

Dust jacket for the first British edition (1906) of Barr's stories about a French detective. This collection includes "The Absent-Minded Coterie," Barr's most widely anthologized story.

Two of Barr's magazine publications in 1896 and 1897 were "How to Get Out a Book" and "How to Write a Short Story," and during his hiatus from work at the *Idler* he proved that he knew exactly what he was writing about. In addition to a steady output of novels published almost annually during the remainder of his life, his magazine contributions and short-story production barely slackened. Even among his successful contemporaries, his income from writing was enviably secure, reportedly bringing him more than £50,000 annually.

Given his background in newspapers and magazine writing, it is not surprising that he remained the essential journalist, the columnist, in his novels and short stories. He admitted that the plot, to him, was the story. On the whole his characters remain merely devices required by the contingencies of the story line, seldom taking on any

life of their own. He was a master at creating good plots, whether in undemanding adventure tales or improbably complex romantic suspense novels, all narrated with his characteristic ironic, deadpan humor. The public clamored for more.

The modern reader, however, finds less to recommend in his work, depending as it does on nineteenth-century literary conventions and melodramatic resolutions. His solidly middle-class morality and outlook prevented him from delving more deeply into his characters' environments, and his employment of purely conventional rather than psychological motivation weakened many of his more promising ideas.

It is against his background and style that Barr's contributions to the field of mystery writing must be evaluated. In spite of his relative unimportance as an author, he can be credited with two developments that have had a long-lasting effect on the genre: the humorous pastiche or parody and the character of the foreign detective. Both these contributions were recognized and appreciated by his contemporaries. The two best examples of these are "Detective Stories Gone Wrong: The Adventures of Sherlaw Kombs" (first published in the May 1892 issue of the *Idler* under the byline Luke Sharp; collected in *The Face and The Mask*, 1894, as "The Great Pegram Mystery") and "The Absent-Minded Coterie" (in his later book of short stories about his French detective, *The Triumphs of Eugène Valmont*, 1906).

While "The Great Pegram Mystery" was not the earliest parody of Conan Doyle's Sherlock Holmes, it was one of the most successful and the earliest to be published for a wide popular audience. The first story of Conan Doyle's *The Adventures of Sherlock Holmes*, "A Scandal in Bohemia," had appeared in the July 1891 issue of the *Strand*, and succeeding stories continued for a year. Appearing nine months into the *Strand* series, Barr's parody in the rival *Idler*, predates the first volume of Sherlock Holmes stories, *The Adventures of Sherlock Holmes*, published later in 1892. "The Great Pegram Mystery" remains a marker of the deep friendship between Barr and Conan Doyle, which was to end only with Barr's death twenty years later. Barr's parody benefits significantly from the reader's enjoyment of Sherlock Holmes, but even on its own merit the parody still succeeds today.

In *The Misadventures of Sherlock Holmes* (1944) Ellery Queen comments on Barr's shrewd grasp of the character of Sherlock Holmes and his equally penetrating comprehension of Conan

Doyle's style. The story begins with descriptions of Kombs's execrable violin playing, his idiosyncratic attitude to knowledge, and his bizarre excursions into deductive reasoning; and the climax is a delightful exaggeration of Holmesian deductive reasoning, while the denouement rivals any of Watson's finest epilogues.

Once Conan Doyle had established the detective as a series character, a half-dozen imitations followed, including the stories in Barr's *The Triumphs of Eugène Valmont*. However, Valmont is different from the others in two significant ways. He is not only the first foreign detective to delight the British middle class but also a deliberately humorous character. Critical recognition of Barr's contribution to mystery fiction has centered on this short-story collection, in which "The Absent-Minded Coterie" is undoubtedly the best-known and most frequently discussed story. Barr's treatment of Valmont gives full play to his highly developed sense of the ridiculous, with frequent excursions into heavy irony and caricature. Here there is no master sleuth but an incompetent bungler, no high romance or adventure but a series of mundane events which are badly misinterpreted and minor mysteries imperfectly resolved.

In *Queen's Quorum* (1951) Ellery Queen reminds modern readers that the adventures of Valmont, the comic literary forefather of Agatha Christie's Hercule Poirot, were in fact a "trenchant" commentary on the deteriorating relationship between England and France in the days preceding World War I, and that they presented a thoughtful comparison of two different legal philosophies, the Napoleonic Code and English Common Law. A. E. Murch notes in *The Development of the Detective Novel* (1958) that the fact of Valmont's nationality and his inherently ridiculous presentation are "not unconnected."

In general Barr's contemporaries were less impressed with his achievements. A reviewer for the *Critic* (June 1906) found the stories in *The Triumphs of Eugène Valmont* "readable but not absorbing," while the *Spectator* reviewer (7 July 1906) acknowledged the "ingenuity" of the stories, while concluding that "it is extremely hard for anyone at the present day to make detective stories original." The review in the *Athenaeum* (21 April 1906), however, called Valmont's personality "distinctive" and drew a comparison with Sherlock Holmes. The review concludes, "The creation of Eugène Valmont may, indeed, be counted one of Mr. Barr's best achievements."

Although Barr published several other collections of tales that could also be called mystery stories, the majority of them fall as easily into the general "romance of fortune" category, though they include moments of high suspense and clever use of dramatic irony which recall the best of contemporary mystery-suspense fiction.

One such borderline story collection is *Jennie Baxter, Journalist* (1899), in which Barr enlarges on an earlier character from his episodic novel *A Woman Intervenes* (1896) to develop the character of Jennie Baxter, whose romanticized career recalls his own early investigative journalistic days. (The narrator notes, "her sketches . . . are considered the finest things in the little volume. They have been much copied as typical examples of American humor.") In comparison to Valmont, Baxter falls short, though she is typical of his use of the literary vogue of the "new woman," whose virtues include independence, competence, achievement, and, of course, beauty.

Never a great novelist, Barr nonetheless remained a popular and accessible spokesman for a large number of the newly democratic and prosperous middle class. What his light adventure tales or humorous social commentaries lacked in depth and subtlety they more than made up in their whimsical presentation of social awkwardness. His short stories ran almost continuously in magazines and newspapers, during his lifetime while his novels appeared in quick succession. The application of his gifts to the field of mystery fiction has enriched the genre. His influence on the literary taste of the period and his encouragement of an entire school of vital young writers through the *Idler* magazine remain his most significant contributions to literature.

References:

C. Stan Allen, "A Glimpse of Robert Barr," *Canadian Magazine*, 4 (April 1895): 545-550;

John Barr, "Former Days," review of G. B. Burgin's *Memoirs of a Clubman, Detroit Free Press*, 22 October 1922;

Walter James Brown, "Robert Barr and Literature in Canada," *Canadian Magazine*, 15 (June 1900): 170-176;

G. B. Burgin, *Memoirs of a Clubman* (London: Hutchinson, 1921);

Burgin, *More Memoirs. (And Some Travels)* (London: Hutchinson, 1922);

John Dickson Carr, *The Life of Sir Arthur Conan Doyle* (New York: Harper, 1949), pp. 67-68, 78, 93, 194;

John A. Cooper, "Canadian Celebrities. IX.– Robert Barr," *Canadian Magazine*, 14 (December 1899): 181-182;

Arthur Conan Doyle, *Memories and Adventures* (Boston: Little, Brown, 1924);

Frederick A. Stokes Company, "The Robert Barr Canard Denied," *Critic*, 28 (30 May 1896): 394;

Hamlin Garland, *Companions on the Trail: A Literary Chronicle* (New York: Macmillan, 1931);

Garland, *Roadside Meetings* (New York: Macmillan, 1930);

Donald B. Gibson, *The Fiction of Stephen Crane* (Carbondale & Edwardsville: Southern Illinois University Press, 1968), p. 145;

Lillian Gilkes and Joan H. Baum, "Stephen Crane's Last Novel: *The O'Ruddy*," *Columbia Library Columns*, 6 (February 1957);

Sir Hugh Greene, Introduction to *More Rivals of Sherlock Holmes: Cosmopolitan Crimes* (London: Bodley Head, 1971); republished as *Cosmopolitan Crimes: Foreign Rivals of Sherlock Holmes* (New York: Pantheon, 1971);

Francis W. Halsey, ed., *Authors of Our Day in Their Homes: Personal Descriptions and Interviews* (New York: Pott, 1902);

Howard Haycraft, *Murder for Pleasure; The Life and Times of the Detective Story* (New York: D. Appleton-Century, 1941), pp. 66, 303;

Jerome K. Jerome, *My Life and Times* (New York: Harper, 1926);

Samuel S. McClure, *My Autobiography* (New York: Stokes, 1898);

Louis K. McKendrick, Introduction to Barr's *The Measure of the Rule* (Toronto: University of Toronto Press, 1973);

McKendrick, "The Life and Work of Robert Barr," M.A. thesis, University of Toronto, 1966;

A. E. Murch, *The Development of the Detective Novel* (London: Peter Owen, 1958), p. 199;

Desmond Pacey, *Creative Writing in Canada* (Toronto: Ryerson Press, 1964);

John Parr, Introduction to *Selected Short Stories of Robert Barr* edited by Parr (Ottawa: University of Ottawa Press, 1977);

Parr, "The Measure of Robert Barr," *Journal of Canadian Fiction*, 3, no. 2 (1974): 94-97;

J. B. Pond, *Eccentricities of Genius: Memories of Famous Men and Women of the Platform and Stage* (New York: Dillingham, 1900);

"Portrait," *Outlook*, 69 (16 November 1901): 697;

Ellery Queen, "The Detective Short Story: The First Hundred Years," in *The Art of the Mystery Story*, edited by Haycraft (New York: Simon & Schuster, 1946), pp. 476-491;

Quentin Reynolds, *The Fiction Factory* (New York: Random House, 1955), p. 136;

"Robert Barr at Home," *Critic*, 43 (November 1903): 435;

"The Six Prigs to Robert Barr," *Canadian Magazine*, 14 (January 1900): 248-252;

R. W. Stallman, *Stephen Crane. A Biography* (New York: Braziller, 1968).

Papers:

Barr's papers are in the Crane collection at the Butler Library, Columbia University, and at the Regional History Department of the University of Western Ontario. Other papers are privately held.

E. C. Bentley

(10 July 1875-30 March 1956)

Thomas M. Leitch
University of Delaware

BOOKS: *Biography for Beginners*, as E. Clerihew, editor (London: Laurie, 1905);

The Woman in Black (New York: Century, 1913); republished as *Trent's Last Case* (London: Nelson, 1913; New York: Grosset & Dunlap, 1913; revised edition, London & New York: Knopf, 1929);

Peace Year in the City, 1918-1919: An Account of the Outstanding Events in the City of London During the Peace Year (London: Privately printed, 1920);

More Biography (London: Methuen, 1929);

Trent's Own Case, by Bentley and H. Warner Allen (London: Constable, 1936; New York: Knopf, 1936);

Trent Intervenes (London: Nelson, 1938; New York: Knopf, 1938);

Baseless Biography (London: Constable, 1939);

Those Days (London: Constable, 1940);

Elephant's Work: An Enigma (London: Hodder & Stoughton, 1950; New York: Knopf, 1950);

Far Horizon; A Biography of Hester Dowden, Medium and Psychic Investigator (London & New York: Rider, 1951);

The First Clerihews, by Bentley and others (Oxford & New York: Oxford University Press, 1982).

OTHER: "Greedy Night," in *Parody Party*, edited by Leonard Russell (London: Hutchinson, 1936), pp. 77-96;

Damon Runyon, *More Than Somewhat*, edited by Bentley (London: Constable, 1937);

Runyon, *The Best of Runyon*, edited by Bentley (New York: Stokes, 1938);

Runyon, *Damon Runyon Presents Furthermore*, edited by Bentley (London: Constable, 1938);

The Second Century of Detective Stories, edited by Bentley (London: Hutchinson, 1938);

"The Ministering Angel," in *To the Queen's Taste*, edited by Ellery Queen (Boston: Little, Brown, 1946), pp. 291-305;

"The Feeble Folk," in *Ellery Queen's Mystery Magazine* (March 1953).

Portrait of E. C. Bentley drawn in 1915 by H. G. Riviere (National Portrait Gallery, London)

E. C. Bentley wrote *Trent's Last Case* (1913), a landmark in the golden age of the English detective novel, that time around World War I when the traditional mystery story flourished. Edmund Clerihew Bentley was born the eldest son of John Edmund Bentley and Margaret Richardson Clerihew in Shepherd's Bush, London, on 10 July 1875. Bentley's autobiographical memoir, *Those Days* (1940), describes his education at St. Paul's School. There he first met G. K. Chesterton, who was to become the great friend of his life and the formative influence on his detective stories. At Merton College, Oxford (1894-1898), he achieved greater distinction in debate, on the crew, and as president of the Oxford Union than in his formal studies, which he concluded with a second in Greats. His son Nicolas, who grew up to become an artist and writer and to illustrate his father's collections of verse and anthologies of Damon Runyon, has called his father's academic failure "a fundamental clue to his character, to the hesitancy, the aloofness, as it seemed to some, the withdrawal from any approach to intimacy, which kept him on the sidelines throughout his life instead of his having a place on the field, to which his intelligence would seem to have entitled him."

This judgment may well account for the curious mixture of extroversion and aloofness in *Those Days*, which gives a great deal more information about Bentley's milieu, the world of England from 1880 to 1914, than about the particulars of his life. But if Bentley's sense of his own failure accounted for his diffidence, his achievements were minor only compared to those of such Oxford friends as Hilaire Belloc and John Buchan, for Bentley's writing career was long, varied, and extremely productive. When he was called to the bar in the Inner Temple in 1902, he had been writing light verse, burlesques, and parodies since his days at St. Paul's, where, in 1890, he invented the clerihew, a four-line verse form (named after himself) whose initial example has never been excelled:

> Sir Humphry Davy
> Abominated gravy.
> He lived in the odium
> Of having discovered sodium.

Although the element of fancy obvious in this clerihew prevailed in the verse Bentley contributed to *Punch* throughout his twenties and in the ballades he claimed to have brought back into fashion, it was as a journalist and editorial writer that he was to make his living. He began to write for the *Speaker* in 1899 and joined the staff of the *Daily News* in 1902, with the responsibilities of compiling a daily column, "Notes and News," writing short nonpolitical editorials, reading and reporting on manuscripts submitted, and performing sundry administrative work. Perhaps Bentley's most characteristic contribution to the *Daily News* was a column called "Table Talk," which Bentley later described as "consisting of comment upon anything that could be made amusing without the paper being thereby landed in difficulties." The ability to make ordinary events amusing may not be evident throughout the 5,000 editorials Bentley wrote at the *Daily News* and later during 1912-1934 at the *Daily Telegraph*, but it is a primary impulse in his fiction.

In *Those Days* Bentley has described in detail the inception of *Trent's Last Case* in an idea he had in 1910 that "it would be a good idea to write a detective story of a new sort." Enthusiastic in his admiration for Sherlock Holmes, Bentley nonetheless bridled at Holmes's stylized unreality and self-seriousness and so determined "to write a detective story in which the detective was recognizable as a human being, and was not quite so much the 'heavy' sleuth." Bentley made his detective human by allowing him to fall in love with the widow of the murdered millionaire (a woman who was the chief suspect in the case). He has him reveal a wrong–but clever–solution to the mystery, and (more fundamentally) he gives him a personality and a voice so like his own–witty, urbane, self-deprecating, yet cultured and knowledgeable about a wide range of subjects–that readers could not help seeing themselves in Trent. If Conan Doyle had created in Holmes the detective as superman, approachable only through the audience surrogate Dr. Watson, Bentley re-created the detective as Everyman, himself a surrogate for a cultivated and literate audience.

Toward the end of 1911 Bentley submitted "Philip Gasket's Last Case" to Duckworth in the hope of winning a prize of fifty pounds for the best first novel. On learning from Edward Garnett that the novel was not in serious contention for the prize and hearing that a detective story would probably make much more than fifty pounds, Bentley withdrew the novel from the competition and sent it to Century in New York. They first published it in 1913 under the title *The Woman in Black*, its hero now called Philip Trent. A British edition, published by Nelson, followed the same year under the title *Trent's Last Case*. Under this title the book, Bentley's first extended narrative of any kind, has sold steadily in a dozen editions and several translations and remains today unusually fresh and undated, ingeniously plotted and alive with wit and intelligence–the most influential British detective fiction since Doyle's.

Indeed, Bentley's influence on golden-age detective fiction has been so pervasive that it is difficult to assess *Trent's Last Case* properly. Most of Bentley's leading figures (the murdered millionaire, his mysterious widow, the secretaries and servants of his household) and plot motifs (the

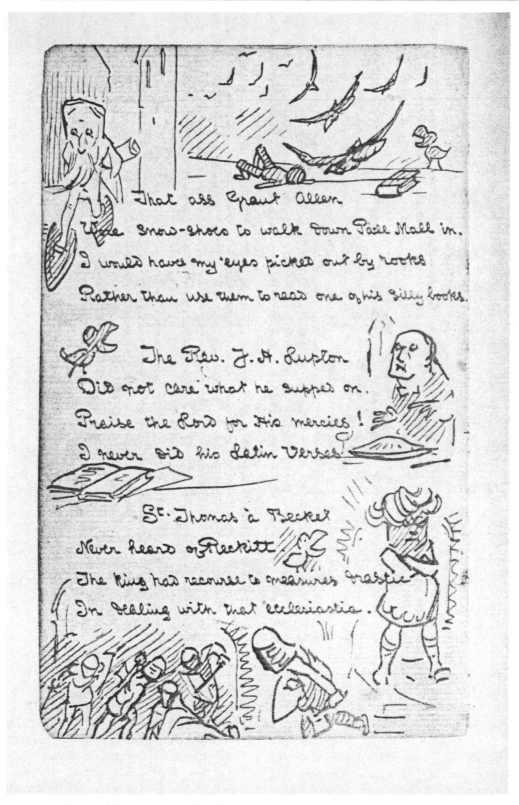

Page from Dictionary of Biography, *a notebook from the early 1890s in which Bentley and his friends recorded their "Cleri-hews," a biographical verse form Bentley devised and named after his mother's family. Most of the verses in this notebook are by Bent-ley, and all are in his handwriting. The author is signified by a coding system; a drawing of a dodo bird designates Bentley. The illustrations are by G. K. Chesterton (courtesy of the library, St. Paul's School, London).*

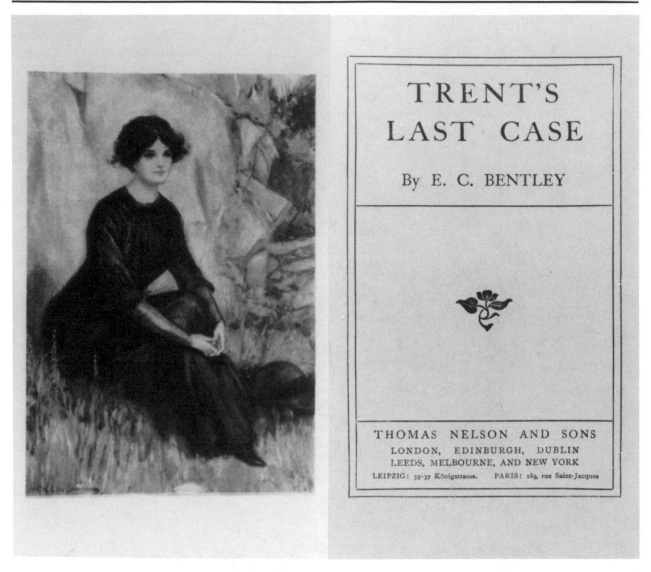

Frontispiece and title page for the first British edition of the novel that is said to have inaugurated the golden age of the English detective novel

suspicious quarrel, the perfect alibi, the frantic trip by car) were already clichés when he wrote; it is his handling of them that makes them seem fresh. In the chapter of Chestertonian fantasy which opens *Trent's Last Case*, in which Sigsbee Manderson's death turns Wall Street into "a clamorous inferno of pale despair," the tone is elaborately satiric without ever becoming farcical. Raymond Chandler surely misses the point of Manderson's personality when he concludes that "I have known relatively few international financiers, but the author of this novel has (if possible) known fewer." H. Douglas Thomson is more judicious: "Sigsbee *is* such a good name for the murdered man. It is also an additional motive to murder." Bentley remarked that "it does not

seem to have been generally noticed that *Trent's Last Case* is not so much a detective story as an exposure of detective stories." Bentley's burlesque of detective conventions has seldom been appreciated (so that Chandler, for example, could take *Trent's Last Case* perfectly straight). The tone of light comedy which he created for his dilettante hero (which allows Trent to take the mystery seriously as an intellectual challenge and even to fall in love with Mrs. Manderson without ever taking himself too seriously or acknowledging any elements which might threaten his civilized world) remains constant throughout British detective novels of the golden age. Bentley's handling of murder as light comedy has had an obvious influence on writers (Dorothy Sayers, Henry Wade,

Margery Allingham, Cyril Hare) who use the detective plot as a means of introducing episodes that are amusing individually. The Englishness of his milieu, which his first American publisher complained about and which is characteristic of all Bentley's work (as a boy he had been asked, "If you were not an Englishman, what would you like to be?" and he replied, "I should like to be an Englishman"), is sometimes accompanied by the class-conscious snobbery characteristic of the formal English detective story. Villains in the short stories which followed *Trent's Last Case*, and which were later collected in *Trent Intervenes* (1938), are identified as such because they do not know which wine to order with fish, or why no one ever rowed for All Souls College. In general, however, Bentley's snobbery is relatively unconscious and urbane: he seems simply to regard himself as a gentleman writing about gentlemen for an audience of gentlefolk. His careful attention to the planting of clues, in which he excels even Chesterton, is, of course, a hallmark of golden-age detective fiction. Although Bentley's clueing is deceptively casual–almost all the clues leading to Trent's solution of Manderson's murder are slipped into chapters four and five of *Trent's Last Case*–he is, with Chesterton and A. E. W. Mason (whose *At the Villa Rose* had appeared in 1910), the first writer of English detective fiction to play scrupulously fair with his readers, allowing them the same chance the detective has to solve the crime. Not only the characteristic tone of the golden-age detective story but the convention which defines its intellectual appeal can therefore be ascribed largely to the influence of *Trent's Last Case*.

Bentley's colleagues and later critics alike have especially praised the construction of *Trent's Last Case*, in which not only Trent's solution to the mystery–revealed little more than halfway through the novel–but also the solution which replaces it turn out to be wrong. But Bentley's plot construction is a tour de force in another way as well. Apparently without any awareness of the problems involved in extending a detective puzzle to novel length–a problem which plagues most of Doyle's novels–he manages to make *Trent's Last Case* continually absorbing without resort to the fundamental cliché of golden-age novels, the red herring. Even though Bentley presents two false solutions to the mystery, he does not spend any time multiplying suspicions of peripheral suspects or developing irrelevant subplots. The story involves a small number of

important characters, and its focus on the personality of the late Sigsbee Manderson allows Trent to solve (apparently) the riddle of Manderson's death without expressing portentous or irrelevant opinions of any of the suspects. The short stories which follow *Trent's Last Case* continue this pattern: Trent simply examines the evidence, interviews the principal witnesses, and presents his solution, often in a long dispatch to his newspaper. Hence stories such as "The Genuine Tabard," "The Sweet Shot," and "The Clever Cockatoo" achieve their effect without generating suspense about which suspect committed the crime; for Trent, ever the gentleman, never seems to regard his informants as suspects. Indeed Bentley is virtually incapable of creating vicious characters, and the problem of creating someone evil enough to be a convincing criminal but plausible enough to masquerade as innocent–a problem so brilliantly solved in *Trent's Last Case*–tends to undermine his later novels.

The first of these later novels, *Trent's Own Case* (1936), written in collaboration with, and evidently at the urging of, Bentley's friend, the minor detective-novelist H. Warner Allen, did not appear for more than twenty years after *Trent's Last Case*. Critics have often speculated about why Bentley did not pursue the success of his first novel, and they dismiss his later work as a postscript to a career consisting properly of only one book. But Bentley seems to have taken his first title literally. Convinced that he was writing a parody of detective fiction, and unaware that his parody was in fact establishing the conventions for a new generation of detective-story writers (a generation whose next impetus did not come until Agatha Christie's *The Mysterious Affair at Styles*, written in 1916 but published in 1920), he seems to have regarded the book as an unrepeatable experiment in the manner of Chesterton's *The Man Who Was Thursday* (1908), to which he refers in the book's dedication to Chesterton. Instead of allowing his creation to reshape his career, as Doyle had done, he returned to his journalistic work and his family. He had married Violet Boileau in 1902; the couple had a daughter, Betty (who died in childhood), and two sons, Neil and Nicolas. Bentley continued to write short stories about Trent, stories notable less as intellectual puzzles than as anecdotes about Trent and illustrations of criminal ingenuity. The crimes are nearly always more ingenious than the solutions, and nearly half the culprits escape unpunished. The stories do not fully pre-

E. C. Bentley

pare for his return to detective fiction in 1936, with the publication of "Greedy Night," a burlesque of Dorothy Sayers which is perhaps the most effective parody of detective fiction ever written. There followed *Trent's Own Case*, the collection *Trent Intervenes* and the anthology *The Second Century of Detective Stories* (1938). This second chapter in Bentley's detective-story career was concluded by the publication of *Those Days* and his return to the *Daily Telegraph* in 1940 as chief literary critic.

Bentley's later work in detective and mystery fiction is on the whole disappointing. *Trent's Own Case* is a story of great anecdotal charm, more appealing in its parts than as a whole. Ben Ray Redman has observed that it is "the work of a writer who believed that in detective fiction the solution is not all, that it is the author's duty to provide entertainment along the way—as great a variety of entertainment, verbal and otherwise, as

possible." But in *Trent's Own Case* the diffuse episodes of the Tiara of Megabyzus, the Comte d'Astalys, the cork labeled Felix Poubelle 1884, and the unacknowledged relatives of the late James Randolph neither lead to the solution of the mystery nor generate the suspense of false leads; they simply broaden and extend what is fundamentally a simple, unoriginal, and obvious story, one which has in fact dated more obviously than its predecessor.

Bentley's last novel, *Elephant's Work: An Enigma* (1950), which he called a shocker, is a story about an amnesia victim, an English nobleman, mistaken for an American gunman. Despite Bentley's extravagant premise and his cast of colorful characters, the story lacks the conviction of the adventure stories of John Buchan, to whom it is dedicated, not only because Bentley seems so completely outside his element but because his plotting is so niggardly; so little happens in *Ele-*

phant's Work that it must be the most sedate shocker ever written. Bentley is incapable of writing a truly shocking story because his characters, however irregular their activities, so often turn out to have the souls of English gentlemen; the villain of *Elephant's Work*, like that of *Trent's Own Case*, is kept offstage for virtually the entire book (he is killed offstage in a motor accident). At times the gentility of Bentley's characters can be surprisingly affecting, as in the denouement of *Elephant's Work* in Glasminster Cathedral when General Justo de la Costa, lately of the Latin American country of Peligragua but originally brought up in England, makes a gesture which leads Lord Severn to realize who he really is. In general, however, *Elephant's Work* is interesting chiefly because of the way it illuminates Bentley's characteristic concerns, not because of his skill in developing them.

Elephant's Work belongs to the last period of Bentley's career, a dark period beginning, according to Nicolas Bentley, when his house was bombed during the war. Bentley retired again from newspaper work in 1947, living with his wife thereafter in a series of hotels; after her death in 1949 he became bedridden until his own death on 30 March 1956.

References:

Nicolas Bentley, *A Version of the Truth* (London: Deutsch, 1960), pp. 14-42;

Raymond Chandler, "The Simple Art of Murder," *Atlantic Monthly,* 174 (December 1944): 53-59;

Howard Haycraft, *Murder for Pleasure: The Life and Times of the Detective Story* (New York: Appleton, 1941), pp. 112-119;

Ben Ray Redman, Introduction to Bentley's *Trent's Case Book* (New York: Knopf, 1953), pp. v-xii;

Julian Symons, *Mortal Consequences: A History from Detective Story to Crime Novel* (New York: Harper, 1972), pp. 93-95;

H. Douglas Thomson, *Masters of Mystery: A Study of the Detective Story* (London: Collins, 1931), pp. 147-155.

M. McDonnell Bodkin

(8 October 1850-7 June 1933)

Gerald H. Strauss

Bloomsburg University

BOOKS: *Poteen Punch, Strong, Hot and Sweet, Made and Mixed by "Crom a Boo"* (Dublin: Gill, 1890);

Pat o' Nine Tales, and One Over (Dublin: Gill, 1894);

Lord Edward Fitzgerald: An Historical Romance (London: Chapman & Hall, 1896);

White Magic (London: Chapman & Hall, 1897);

Paul Beck, the Rule of Thumb Detective (London: Pearson, 1898);

A Stolen Life (London: Ward, Lock, 1898);

The Rebels (London: Ward, Lock, 1899);

Dora Myrl, the Lady Detective (London: Chatto & Windus, 1900);

A Bear Squeeze; or, Her Second Self (London: Ward, Lock, 1901);

A Modern Miracle (London: Ward, Lock, 1902);

Shillelagh and Shamrock (London: Chatto & Windus, 1902);

In the Days of Goldsmith (London: Long, 1903);

A Modern Robyn Hood (London: Ward, Lock, 1903);

Patsey the Omadaun (London: Chatto & Windus, 1904);

A Madcap Marriage (London: Long, 1905);

A Trip through the States and a Talk with the President (Dublin: Duffy, 1907);

The Quests of Paul Beck (London: Unwin, 1908; Boston: Little, Brown, 1910);

The Capture of Paul Beck (London: Unwin, 1909; Boston: Little, Brown, 1911);

True Man and Traitor, or the Rising of Emmet (London: Unwin, 1910);

Young Beck, a Chip of the Old Block (London: Unwin, 1911; Boston: Little, Brown, 1912);

Grattan's Parliament, Before and After (London: Unwin, 1912);

His Brother's Keeper (London: Hurst & Blackett, 1913);

Behind the Picture (London: Ward, Lock, 1914);

Recollections of an Irish Judge: Press, Bar, and Parliament (London: Hurst & Blackett, 1914; New York: Dodd, Mead, 1914);

The Test (London: Everett, 1914);

Pigeon Blood Rubies (London: Eveleigh Nash, 1915);

Old Rowley (London: Holden & Harrington, 1916);

Famous Irish Trials (Dublin & London: Maunsel, 1918; revised and expanded edition, Dublin: Duffy, 1928);

When Youth Meets Youth (Dublin: Talbot, 1920; London: Unwin, 1920);

A Considered Judgment: Report of Judge Bodkin (Dublin: Talbot, 1921);

Another Considered Judgment: Second Report of Judge Bodkin (Dublin: Talbot, 1921);

Hunt the Hare (Dublin: Duffy, 1926);

Kitty the Madcap (Dublin: Talbot, 1927);

The Lottery; A Comedy in One Act, as Crom a Boo (Dublin: Duffy, 1927);

Guilty or Not Guilty? (Dublin: Talbot, 1929);

Paul Beck, Detective (Dublin: Talbot, 1929).

In the wake of Arthur Conan Doyle's success, many writers created superhuman sleuths in the manner of Sherlock Holmes. At the same time, sometimes in conscious reaction, others created detectives who were just ordinary men, two of whom are Arthur Morrison's Martin Hewitt and M. McDonnell Bodkin's Paul Beck. (According to Bodkin's son, Father Mathew Bodkin, S. J., Beck "was deliberately conceived as the opposite of Sherlock Holmes, unromantic.") When his detective debuted in 1897 (in *Pearson's Magazine*) Bodkin called him Alfred Juggins, but he soon dropped that name, and in 1898 he published his first collection of Paul Beck stories, *Paul Beck, the Rule of Thumb Detective*, which was favorably received. These and subsequent Beck adventures–as well as Bodkin's stories featuring Dora Myrl, whom Beck eventually marries, and their son, Paul Beck, Jr.–are still good reading.

Matthias McDonnell Bodkin was born in Ireland on 8 October 1850 to Dr. Thomas Bodkin and Maria McDonnell Bodkin. Educated at Tullabeg Jesuit College and Catholic University, he became a barrister, a Queen's Counsel, and a

PRICE SIXPENCE

Paul Beck
The
Rule of Thumb Detective

BY
M. McDonnell Bodkin, K.C.
Author of "Dora Myrl," etc.

"Of Absorbing Interest"
SCOTSMAN

"Set forth with
unflagging animation"
DAILY NEWS

C. ARTHUR PEARSON Limited

Front cover of a post-1900 printing of Bodkin's first collection of stories about the stout detective conceived as Sherlock Holmes's opposite (courtesy of Otto Penzler)

member of the Irish Bar. He married Arabella Norman of Dublin in 1885, and they had two sons and four daughters. One son, Thomas, became director of the Irish National Gallery. Bodkin served in the British Parliament as a Nationalist M. P. from North Roscommon from 1892 to 1895 but did not stand for reelection. In 1907 he was made County Court Judge of Clare and held that position until 1924. Before he began writing detective stories in his late thirties Bodkin had written other short fiction, mainly in a comic vein, as well as historical romances. After a little more than a decade of detective-fiction writing he gave up the form, but he continued to write, primarily nonfiction, including a historical study of Henry Grattan, *Grattan's Parliament, Before and After* (1912); a book about notable Irish trials, *Famous Irish Trials* (1918); and a volume of memoirs, *Recollections of an Irish Judge: Press, Bar, and Parliament* (1914), in which he says nothing

about his work as a writer of detective fiction, though he touches upon most other aspects of his career. He died in Dublin on 7 June 1933.

In *Paul Beck, the Rule of Thumb Detective*, Bodkin's first sleuth is said to be a "stout, thick-set man" who looks "more like a respectable retired milkman than a detective." (Arthur Morrison's Hewitt, who made his first appearance several years before Beck, is described as a "stoutish, clean-shaven man, of middle height.") Beck does not appear especially bright and says of his detection method: "I just go by the rule of thumb, and muddle and puzzle out my cases as best I can." (Hewitt similarly claims that "he has no system beyond a judicious use of ordinary faculties.")

Despite his self-deprecating manner, Beck succeeds in solving some difficult mysteries, relying upon his ingenuity and sound common sense. Bodkin's son Mathew recalls hearing his father say that he deplored the detective story's having become a murder story because he believed, "Murderers . . . were the most stupid criminals and con-men the best material." Nevertheless, "Murder by Proxy"—an early "locked room" whodunit—is one of the best stories in *Paul Beck, the Rule of Thumb Detective*.

The action takes place at the country home of Squire Neville, who is shot to death while sleeping on a sofa in his study. Aside from the servants, the only others home at the time are his nephews Eric and John. Eric had left the house and was talking to a gardener when the shot rang out; John, the squire's heir, claimed that he was in his room when he heard the shot and ran to the study, where Eric found him at the squire's body. Apparently the irascible squire, who previously had fought with John and a neighbor, Colonel Peyton, was alone in the closed room when he was killed. John calls in Wardle, the local constable, and Paul Beck. Pending the inquest, Wardle places John under house arrest for the murder of his uncle. Beck, however, examines the squire's study with deliberate care and at the inquest accuses Eric (who is next in line as heir after John) of murdering his uncle. Beck explains that by aiming a half-cocked pistol at the sleeping squire and placing a filled water bottle between it and the window to generate heat, Eric had "made the sun [his] accomplice!" Years later American writer Melville Davison Post used a variation of this means of murder in "The Doomdorf Mystery," a "locked room" whodunit in which the sun also is the long-range assassin.

Bodkin introduced Dora Myrl, his second sleuth, in *Dora Myrl, the Lady Detective* (1900). Just as Beck is historically important as a "plain man" detective type, Myrl is significant as an early female sleuth. In 1929 Dorothy L. Sayers wrote, "There have . . . been a few women detectives, but on the whole they have not been very successful"; twenty-nine years earlier there were even fewer. Indeed, Myrl is one of the first female series detectives and is an important predecessor of Baroness Orczy's Lady Molly of Scotland Yard. Nevertheless, critics over the years have ignored Myrl, and Julian Symons, one of the few even to mention her, disparagingly remarks that the 1900 collection in which she is featured is "no less absurd than other stories of the time about women detectives, who retained an impossible gentility of speech and personality while dealing with crime."

In a typical Myrl story, "How He Cut His Stick," a bank clerk is robbed of a bag containing £5,000 while he is in a locked train compartment. Inexplicably, the thief has managed to escape from the moving train. The clerk's boss hires Myrl to solve the case, and–after learning that the telegraph line along the route was broken down at a place where "the line was embanked and the wires ran quite close to the railway carriage"–she goes with Jim Pollock, the clerk, to the town closest to the place where the robbery occurred. There they "look out for a stranger with a crooked stick instead of a black bag." After locating such a man, they apprehend him when he goes to retrieve the loot. At the end of the story Myrl explains that a spry man leaning out of a moving train could easily slip a crooked stick over telegraph wires "and so swing himself into the air clear of the train." Further, "the friction of the wire . . . with a man's weight on it, would bite deep into the wood of the stick," and in fact a deep notch on the thief's stick cuts through the varnish into the wood.

In all of the Dora Myrl stories Dora is a quick-witted and resourceful person, both cerebral and action-oriented. Femininity never gets in her way, and she holds her own physically and emotionally with adversaries of both sexes. Frequently she solves a puzzle soon after hearing the facts of a case, but then she typically withholds her explanation until she has everything confirmed. Though Bodkin sometimes leaves loose ends, the Myrl stories offer intriguing puzzles with clever resolutions.

Front cover for the first American edition of a collection of stories about the detective Paul Beck, Jr., son of Paul Beck and Dora Myrl, the fictional sleuths for whom Bodkin is best known (courtesy of Otto Penzler)

In *The Capture of Paul Beck* (1909) Bodkin unites Beck and Myrl. Phil Armitage is victimized by unscrupulous financier Abe Lamann, a false friend who had been Armitage's unsuccessful rival for Norma Lee. Armitage is able to turn the tables on Lamann but in so doing commits a technically illegal act. Lamann hires Beck to prove Armitage's culpability and thus make him liable to criminal prosecution, but Dora Myrl, Norma Lee's friend, takes the case on behalf of Armitage. The result is a fast-paced battle of wits between Beck and Myrl, with both detectives using everything from their bags of tricks, including masterful disguises that strain credibility. Beck prevails in the sleuthing contest, though by that time he has fallen in love with his opponent. After learning the truth about his deceitful and amoral client, however, he switches sides, and he and Myrl together bring Lamann to bay. The novel closes with Armitage and Lee planning their marriage and Myrl revealing that she and Beck already have wed.

Because the novel presents a pair of love stories as well as a competition between two detectives, it is more complex than most of its contemporaries in the genre. It is unconventional, too, in that the primary purpose of the multiple action is to prevent anything ill from befalling the young hero, Phil Armitage (the possibility that Lamann will prevail, due to Beck's efforts, providing the only suspense in the book). At the close the villain is denied the satisfaction of revenge but is not punished in any other way. Bodkin devotes little time to substantive characterization: likable as they are, Armitage and Lee are just two-dimensional stereotypes; and Beck and Myrl are no different from what they were like in earlier books.

The Capture of Paul Beck remains entertaining because of Bodkin's novel device of pitting two shrewd detectives against each other on the same case and then having them join forces. The book is dated, however, because the central element upon which everything depends is the improbably similar appearance of Armitage and an American named Thornton. They are veritable identical twins: "One of them wore a beard at that time and the other was clean shaven, but apart from this they were as alike as two peas. When the shaven man grew a beard there were all kinds of mistakes. Figure, features, complexion, colour, they were as two eggs from the same hen. An old doctor at the hospital told me that he had never seen twin brothers so like." The whodunit credos of Willard Huntington Wright (1928) and Ronald A. Knox (1929) effectively foreclosed the use of twins in detective fiction.

Two years after he married off Beck and Myrl, Bodkin produced *Young Beck, a Chip of the Old Block* (1911), a collection of stories featuring Paul, Jr., mainly while he is a university student and soon after. The cases are varied and original (a card-cheating story is superb), demonstrating that Bodkin was still at the top of his form; but he published just one other Beck volume, *Paul Beck, Detective* (1929), a collection of ten stories from Beck's bachelor days.

Reference:
Hugh Greene, ed., *The Crooked Counties* (London: Bodley Head, 1973).

Papers:
Many Bodkin family papers are on deposit in the Record Office, the Law Courts, Dublin.

Mary Elizabeth Braddon

(4 October 1835-4 February 1915)

Virginia B. Morris
John Jay College of Criminal Justice

See also the Braddon entry in *DLB 18, Victorian Novelists After 1885.*

BOOKS: *Three Times Dead* (London: W. M. Clark/ Beverley: Empson, 1860); republished as *The Trail of the Serpent* (London: Ward, Lock & Tyler, 1861); republished as *Three Times Dead* (New York: Dick & Fitzgerald, 1864?);

Garibaldi and Other Poems (London: Bosworth & Harrison, 1861);

The Lady Lisle (London: Ward, Lock & Tyler, 1862; New York: Dick & Fitzgerald, 1863?);

Lady Audley's Secret (3 volumes, London: Tinsley, 1862; 1 volume, New York: Dick & Fitzgerald, 1863?);

Ralph the Bailiff and Other Tales (London: Ward, Lock & Tyler, 1862; enlarged, 1867);

The Captain of the Vulture (London: Ward, Lock & Tyler, 1863); republished as *Darrell Markham; Or, The Captain of the Vulture* (New York: Dick & Fitzgerald, 1863);

Aurora Floyd (3 volumes, London: Tinsley, 1863; 1 volume, New York: Harper, 1863);

Eleanor's Victory (3 volumes, London: Tinsley, 1863; 1 volume, New York: Harper, 1863);

John Marchmont's Legacy (3 volumes, London: Tinsley, 1863; 1 volume, New York: Harper, 1864);

Dudley Carleton; Or, The Brother's Secret and Other Tales (New York: Dick & Fitzgerald, 1864);

Henry Dunbar (3 volumes, London: John Maxwell, 1864; 1 volume, New York: Dick & Fitzgerald, 186?);

The Doctor's Wife (3 volumes, London: John Maxwell, 1864; 1 volume, New York: Dick & Fitzgerald, 1864);

Only a Clod (3 volumes, London: John Maxwell, 1865; 1 volume, New York: Dick & Fitzgerald, 1865?);

Sir Jasper's Tenant (3 volumes, London: John Maxwell, 1865; 1 volume, New York: Dick & Fitzgerald, 1865?);

Mary Elizabeth Braddon, circa 1877

The Lady's Mile (3 volumes, London: Ward, Lock & Tyler, 1866; 1 volume, New York: Dick & Fitzgerald, 1878?);

What Is This Mystery? (New York: Hilton, 1866); republished as *The Black Band* (London: Vickers, 1877);

Circe, as Babington White, 2 volumes (London: Ward, Lock & Tyler, 1867);

Rupert Godwin (3 volumes, London: Ward, Lock & Tyler, 1867; 1 volume, New York: Dick & Fitzgerald, 1867);

Birds of Prey (3 volumes, London: Ward, Lock & Tyler, 1867; 1 volume, New York: Harper, 1867);

Diavola (New York: Dick & Fitzgerald, 1867); republished as *Run to Earth*, 3 volumes (London: Ward, Lock & Tyler, 1868);

Charlotte's Inheritance (3 volumes, London: Ward, Lock & Tyler, 1868; 1 volume, New York: Harper, 1868);

The White Phantom (New York: Williams, 1868);

Dead-Sea Fruit (3 volumes, London: Ward, Lock & Tyler, 1868; 1 volume, New York: Harper, 1868);

The Octoroon; Or, The Lily of Louisiana (New York: DeWitt, 1869);

The Factory Girl (New York: DeWitt, 1869?);

Oscar Bertrand (New York: DeWitt, 1869?);

Fenton's Quest (3 volumes, London: Ward, Lock & Tyler, 1871; 1 volume, New York: Harper, 1871);

The Lovels of Arden (3 volumes, London: John Maxwell, 1871; 1 volume, New York: Harper, 1872);

Robert Ainsleigh (3 volumes, London: John Maxwell, 1872; 1 volume, Berlin: Asher/Philadelphia: Lippincott, 1872); republished as *Bound to John Company; Or, Robert Ainsleigh* (New York: Munro, 1879);

To the Bitter End (3 volumes, London: John Maxwell, 1872; 1 volume, New York: Harper, 1875);

Milly Darrell and Other Tales (3 volumes, London: John Maxwell, 1873; 1 volume, New York: Carleton, 1877); republished as *Meeting Her Fate* (New York: Carleton, 1881);

Strangers and Pilgrims (3 volumes, London: John Maxwell, 1873; 1 volume, New York: Harper, 1873);

Lucius Davoren; Or, Publicans and Sinners, 3 volumes (London: John Maxwell, 1873); republished as *Publicans and Sinners; Or, Lucius Davoren*, 1 volume (New York: Harper, 1874);

Taken at the Flood (3 volumes, London: John Maxwell, 1874; 1 volume, New York: Harper, 1874);

Lost for Love (3 volumes, London: Chatto & Windus, 1874; 1 volume, New York: Harper, 1875);

A Strange World (3 volumes, London: John Maxwell, 1875; 1 volume, New York: Harper, 1875);

Hostages to Fortune (3 volumes, London: John Maxwell, 1875; 1 volume, New York: Harper, 1875);

Dead Men's Shoes (3 volumes, London: John Maxwell, 1876; 1 volume, New York: Harper, 1876);

Joshua Haggard's Daughter (3 volumes, London: John Maxwell, 1876; 1 volume, New York: Harper, 1877);

Weavers and Weft, and Other Tales (3 volumes, London: John Maxwell, 1877; 1 volume, New York: Harper, 1877);

An Open Verdict (3 volumes, London: Robert Maxwell, 1878; 1 volume, New York: Harper, 1878);

Vixen (3 volumes, London: John & Robert Maxwell, 1879; 1 volume, New York: Harper, 1879);

The Cloven Foot (3 volumes, London: John & Robert Maxwell, 1879; 1 volume, New York: Harper, 1879);

The Missing Witness: An Original Drama in Four Acts (London: John & Robert Maxwell, 1880);

The Story of Barbara, 3 volumes (London: John & Robert Maxwell, 1880); republished as *Barbara*, 1 volume (New York: Harper, 1880);

Just as I Am (3 volumes, London: John & Robert Maxwell, 1880; 1 volume, New York: Harper, 1880);

Asphodel (3 volumes, London: John & Robert Maxwell, 1881; 1 volume, New York: Harper, 1881);

Dross, or The Root of Evil: A Comedy in Four Acts (London: John & Robert Maxwell, 1882; New York: DeWitt, 188?);

Married Beneath Him: A Comedy in Four Acts (London: John & Robert Maxwell, 1882);

Marjorie Daw: A Household Idyl in Two Acts (London: John & Robert Maxwell, 1882); prepared for the American stage by Henry Llewellyn Williams (New York: DeWitt, 1885);

Mount Royal (3 volumes, London: John & Robert Maxwell, 1882; 1 volume, New York: Harper, 1882);

Flower and Weed. A Novel (London: John & Robert Maxwell, 1882 [as a volume of *The Mistletoe Bough*]; New York: Harper, 1882); enlarged as *Flower and Weed and Other Tales* (London: John & Robert Maxwell, 1883);

The Golden Calf (3 volumes, London: John & Robert Maxwell, 1883; 1 volume, New York: Lovell, 1883);

Phantom Fortune (3 volumes, London: John & Robert Maxwell, 1883; 1 volume, New York: Harper, 1883);

Under the Red Flag (London: John & Robert Maxwell, 1883 [as a volume of *The Mistletoe Bough*]; New York: Harper, 1883); enlarged

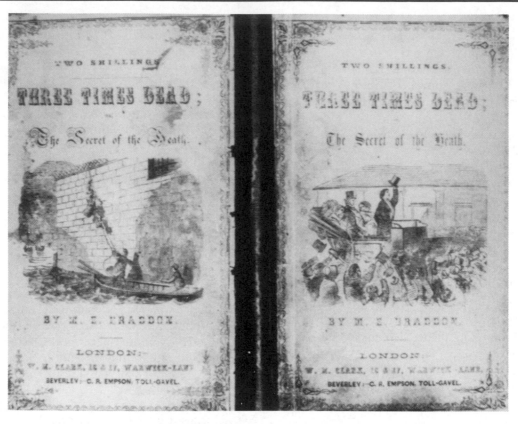

Front and back covers for the 1860 first edition of Braddon's unsuccessful first novel. "Death stalked in ghastliest form across my pages. . . . I wrote with all the freedom of one who feared not the face of a critic," she recalled thirty-two years later.

as *Under the Red Flag and Other Tales* (London: John & Robert Maxwell, 1886);

Ishmael (3 volumes, London: John & Robert Maxwell, 1884; 1 volume, New York: Harper, 1885);

Wyllard's Weird (3 volumes, London: John & Robert Maxwell, 1885; 1 volume, New York: Harper, 1885);

The Good Hermione, as Aunt Belinda (London: John & Robert Maxwell, 1886);

One Thing Needful (3 volumes, London: John & Robert Maxwell, 1886; 1 volume, New York: Harper, 1886); republished in part as *Cut by the County* (London: John & Robert Maxwell, 1886);

Mohawks (3 volumes, London: John & Robert Maxwell, 1886; 1 volume, New York: Harper, 1886);

Like and Unlike (3 volumes, London: Spencer Blackett, 1887; 1 volume, New York: Munro, 1887);

The Fatal Three (3 volumes, London: Simpkin, Marshall, 1888; 1 volume, New York: Harper, 1888);

The Day Will Come (3 volumes, London: Simpkin, Marshall, 1889; 1 volume, New York: Harper, 1889);

One Life, One Love (3 volumes, London: Simpkin, Marshall, Hamilton, Kent, 1890);

Gerard; Or, The World, The Flesh, and The Devil, 3 volumes (London: Simpkin, Marshall, Hamilton, Kent, 1891); republished as *The World, The Flesh, and The Devil*, 1 volume (New York: Lovell, 1891);

The Venetians (3 volumes, London: Simpkin, Marshall, Hamilton, Kent, 1892; 1 volume, New York: Harper, 1892);

All Along the River (3 volumes, London: Simpkin, Marshall, Hamilton, Kent, 1893; 1 volume, New York: Cassell, 1893);

The Christmas Hirelings (London: Simpkin, Marshall, Hamilton, Kent, 1894; New York: Harper, 1894);

Thou Art the Man, 3 volumes (London: Simpkin, Marshall, Hamilton, Kent, 1894);

Sons of Fire, 3 volumes (London: Simpkin, Marshall, Hamilton, Kent, 1895);

London Pride; Or, When the World Was Younger (London: Simpkin, Marshall, Hamilton, Kent,

1896); republished as *When the World Was Younger* (New York: Fenno, 1897);

Under Love's Rule (London: Simpkin, Marshall, Hamilton, Kent, 1897);

In High Places (London: Hutchinson, 1898);

Rough Justice (London: Simpkin, Marshall, Hamilton, Kent, 1898);

His Darling Sin (London: Simpkin, Marshall, Hamilton, Kent, 1899; New York: Harper, 1899);

The Infidel (London: Simpkin, Marshall, Hamilton, Kent, 1900; New York & London: Harper, 1900);

The Conflict (London: Simpkin, Marshall, Hamilton, Kent, 1903);

A Lost Eden (London: Hutchinson, 1904);

The Rose of Life (London: Hutchinson, 1905; New York: Brentano's, 1905);

The White House (London: Hurst & Blackett, 1906);

Dead Love Has Chains (London: Hurst & Blackett, 1907);

Her Convict (London: Hurst & Blackett, 1907);

During Her Majesty's Pleasure (London: Hurst & Blackett, 1908);

Our Adversary (London: Hutchinson, 1909);

Beyond These Voices (London: Hutchinson, 1910);

The Green Curtain (London: Hutchinson, 1911);

Miranda (London: Hutchinson, 1913);

Mary (London: Hutchinson, 1916).

PLAY PRODUCTIONS: *The Loves of Arcadia*, London, Strand Theatre, 12 March 1860;

Griselda; or, The Patient Wife, London, Princess's Theatre, 13 November 1873.

Mary Elizabeth Braddon, a popular and successful Victorian novelist, mounted an audacious challenge to the codes of literary propriety. A major force in the development of the modern crime novel, she turned conventional morality on its head by describing respectable murderers–aristocrats, philanthropists, professional people–who often got away with their crimes and rarely felt remorse. Perhaps more daring, many of her boldest criminals were outwardly perfect Victorian ladies who were capable of fraud, bigamy, cruelty, even murder, if it served their purposes. The lasting impact of her work, with that of her contemporaries Wilkie Collins and Charles Reade, was to domesticate crime, moving it from the slums to the country house, where most English mystery writers and their readers still find it. In Henry James's words, these sensation novel-

ists wrote of "those most mysterious of mysteries, the mysteries which are at our own doors."

One sure sign of Braddon's popularity was the financial success that marked her career. In part it was the result of her exceptional productivity and the speed with which she wrote, but it also grew from her astute sense of what the middle-class reading public wanted. She produced at least eighty novels under her own name, many of them serialized in newspapers or monthly journals and then published in three-volume editions shortly before their concluding episodes appeared. In addition she turned out a stream of short stories and novellas for *Belgravia*, the journal she founded in 1866 and edited until 1876, as well as occasional plays and pseudonymous potboilers aimed at the lower end of the literary scale.

There is little doubt that the straitened circumstances of her childhood and young adulthood contributed to her drive for economic security and her willingness to work hard to achieve it. She was born in 1835 into an old and affluent middle-class Cornish family, but Braddon's parents, Henry and Fanny White Braddon, separated in 1839, and her ne'er-do-well father provided little support. Without a formal education but determined to provide for her mother, Braddon became a modestly successful actress in the late 1850s. Flouting the unwritten rule that no lady should earn a living on the stage was her first act of social defiance.

But by early 1860, when her short comedy *The Loves of Arcadia* was produced in London to complimentary reviews, she abandoned acting for the more respectable career of writing and editing. Fiction offered the greatest potential for success, and Braddon combined her vivid imagination with her skill at plotting to help create a new genre, the sensation novel. Grafting an obsession with crime onto an unlikely hybrid of social realism and Gothic romance, it became the dominant form of popular fiction in the 1860s.

Often her themes hinge on a moral paradox: either good people are guilty of crimes they must expiate or, more radical, those who seem good because they follow all the external rules of conduct are evil. Although her writing is often formulaic, in her best novels there are serious ideas and telling observations about Victorian manners and morals. As Braddon's biographer Robert Lee Wolff has observed, she used her fiction to direct cleverly discreet social criticism against the hollow morality of affluent Victorian life and in par-

Notebook sketch by Braddon for the scene from Lady Audley's Secret *in which Lady Audley causes her first husband's fall into an abandoned well shaft (courtesy of Houghton Library, Harvard University)*

ticular against the fatal combination of "beauty, luxury, and wickedness" which characterized her worst villains.

When *Lady Audley's Secret*, a novel which capitalizes on the wickedness of a beautiful woman, was published in October 1862 and went into eight printings before Christmas, Braddon became a literary force almost overnight. The titillation of a tale that hinged on bigamy, murder, and arson certainly accounted for some of that success, but *Lady Audley's Secret* continued to be popular long after the bizarre convolutions of the story were common knowledge. By some reckonings, it was the best-selling novel of the nineteenth century, and it is the only one of her books still in print.

The eponymous heroine is no heroine at all, but a ruthless and clever woman hiding behind a beautiful face and a charming public personality. Believing she has been abandoned by her husband, who has gone away and has not written to her in several years, Helen Talboys assumes a new identity and finds a job as a governess, that most appropriate of all ladylike occupations. When a wealthy, widowed baronet proposes, Helen, now known as Lucy Graham, does not hesitate long before she accepts, eager to move into the world of privilege and security. But, just as she becomes Lady Audley, George Talboys returns from a profitable venture in Australia, expecting to find his wife waiting for him.

Rather than admit her bigamy, Lady Audley embarks on an elaborate campaign to get rid of Talboys and cover the evidence of her past. Then the plot twists once more: her newly acquired nephew, Robert Audley, is Talboys's best friend. Together the young men visit Audley Court, and Robert, once entranced by his uncle's beautiful bride, is now, quite accurately, convinced she is responsible for his friend's mysterious disappearance. In fact, she has caused his fall into an abandoned well shaft and left him for dead. At this point the convoluted romance becomes a detective story, as the once-indolent Robert Audley doggedly pursues the secrets of Helen's past, driven at least as much by his dread of her self-assurance and determination as he is by the desire to protect his uncle and avenge his friend.

For most of the novel Lady Audley is a formidable foe, but finally, driven to desperation, she sets fire to the inn where Audley is staying, believing she has doomed him by locking him in his room. Though he escapes, the innkeeper–a nasty drunk who has been blackmailing her–dies. Robert Audley seizes the chance to unmask her crimes to his uncle and have her privately committed to an insane asylum without even the pretense of a judicial hearing. For many readers Lady Audley gets what she deserves, even though Talboys has not been murdered after all, having escaped from the well to live a long, self-pitying life. But for others she is the archetypal feminine victim of hypocrisy and chauvinism, condemned for her independence and intelligence.

For the Victorian critics who raged against the immorality of the novel, Lady Audley's worst crime was bigamy. They condemned it as a deliberate assault on social integrity: if a woman could not be trusted to be honest when she married, the institution of the family was threatened. And though Lady Audley's motives for bigamy are obviously financial rather than sexual, her action raises a specter of passion inappropriate to the Victorian conception of womanhood.

Braddon credited Wilkie Collins's *The Woman in White* (1860) as one of the major influences on the development of *Lady Audley's Secret*. Both have convoluted plots unraveled by amateur detectives, irregular marriages, bizarre disappearances, and the corrupt use of insane asylums to control threatening women; both are designed to shock and astound the reader. But Braddon takes the greater risk in making her criminal a woman who seems to epitomize the Victorian ideal in looks and manners while cleverly hiding her deceptions behind the appearance of innocence. Because Lady Audley comes so close to carrying off her schemes, Elaine Showalter suggests that the novel is subversive. Although Braddon's contemporaries missed her criticism of a society that rewarded conventionality and perpetuated the idea that a woman's value was measured by the marriage she made, there is little question that in its treatment of women, of marriage, and of crime and punishment it signaled a new direction in English fiction.

Unlike the horrified Victorian arbiters of literary taste or the modern reader who may be put off by the novel's undeniably overblown rhetoric, Robert Audley's self-righteousness, or the shifts in perspective that transform Lady Audley from victim to victimizer, Braddon's readers were eager for more. Her publishers, the Tinsleys, had paid £250 for the copyright and agreed to pay a £50 bonus if it was reviewed (as it was, enthusiastically) in the *Times*. The bonus was increased to £500 when she agreed to accept £1000 for a two-year copyright on her next novel, *Aurora Floyd* (1863), and £2000 apiece with the same provision for two novels in 1863. No wonder she could write to her mentor Sir Edward Bulwer-Lytton that she felt the four novels would provide enough money to keep her mother comfortable for the rest of her life.

But she was not telling Bulwer-Lytton the whole truth about how she was spending the money she was making. Her private life was almost as complicated and shocking as the plot of a sensation thriller. Between 1862 and 1866, as she established herself as an author and editor, she produced nine three-volume novels, a copious collection of hackwork, and four children from her liaison with the Irish-born publisher John Maxwell, whose mentally unstable first wife was living in a Dublin asylum. She had been his companion since at least the spring of 1861, and—until they married on 2 October 1874 after his wife's death the previous month—their irregular union, though kept secret to some extent, left her open to social ostracism and vituperation. It may explain the personal attacks that frequently were part of the reviews of her novels as well as the pointed criticism of Victorian hypocrisy so evident in her own fiction.

Despite earlier assumptions that Braddon's incredibly prolific writing habits were driven solely by the need to rescue her lover from bankruptcy, Wolff argues convincingly that Braddon's quest for her family's financial security was the real motivation. In 1866 a firm holding a mortgage on one of Maxwell's business ventures withheld money due Braddon as partial payment for Maxwell's debt to them, but she fought their decision and the matter was settled to her satisfaction in arbitration. There is no question the money she earned was welcome. After all, the family, about to move into a large house in Richmond, included Braddon, Maxwell, her mother, their four children (one of whom died that summer), five children from Maxwell's first marriage, and a staff of servants. (Braddon and Maxwell had five surviving children, three sons and two daughters.) Braddon's generosity to family and friends is also well documented, and as she became more affluent she used her money for others' benefit as well as her own.

Her letters to Bulwer-Lytton, one of the few sources for Braddon's thoughts on her own work, support the idea that her desire for money drove her to work quickly although she knew her writing would benefit from a more moderate pace, as well as revision and polishing. Ironically, too, the public seemed to prefer her genre fiction to the more powerful novels with different themes and settings which she sometimes produced. It is probably fair to say that she saw writing as a business rather than an art, and it was a business at which she had few equals.

The Braddon-Maxwell family in 1872. Standing: John, Jr., and Polly, two of Maxwell's children by his first wife, who resided in an Irish insane asylum; seated on bench: Braddon and John Maxwell; seated on the ground: Will, Gerald, Fanny, and, on Maxwell's knee, Rosie, Braddon and Maxwell's children. (Another child, Teddy, an infant at the time, is absent.) Braddon and Maxwell married in 1874 after his first wife died.

Some of Braddon's ambivalence toward her work is evident in the opinions of Sigismund Smith, the sensation novelist who is a character in *The Doctor's Wife* (1864) and *The Lady's Mile* (1866), two early novels which break out of her usual mode. "What the penny public want," he says, "is plot, and plenty of it; surprises and plenty of 'em; mystery as thick as a November fog." The great majority of Braddon's novels provide just that. With their contemporary settings and seemingly ordinary middle- and upper-class English characters, they are full of shocking incidents. From bigamy and murder in *Lady Audley's Secret* and *Aurora Floyd*, she moved on to depict fraud, kidnapping, blackmail, and every other conceivable crime except explicit adultery, incest, and homosexuality. Overt treatment of sexual crimes was not acceptable in English fiction, espe-

cially fiction intended for circulation by the lending libraries, as Braddon's work certainly was. But sexual tensions lurk close to the surface of her work and are often the motives for the nearly inevitable murder that has to be solved before the novel can end. A powerful study of sexual repression, *John Marchmont's Legacy* (1863), explicitly describes one woman's obsession with duty and good works as sublimation and self-deception.

While her convoluted plots can hardly be described as realistic, Braddon's novels nevertheless provide an accurate view of the domestic details of Victorian life–the way people dressed and ate, decorated their homes, and lived their daily lives. This careful use of setting demonstrates a clear connection between the crime novels she was writing and twentieth-century detective fiction. And while social criticism is characteristically subsidiary to incident in her work, just as it is in modern detective fiction, the personal failings of the superficially perfect Victorian (as opposed to the failings of society at large) are held up to scathing criticism.

Although she relaxed her pace somewhat after 1866 and stopped producing anonymous hackwork for readers of halfpenny fiction, Braddon continued, for most of her life, to turn out two novels a year under her own name and to read constantly as a source for new ideas and approaches to her work.

In 1867 and 1868 she published two intricate crime novels, *Birds of Prey* and its sequel *Charlotte's Inheritance*, which describe murder committed for profit rather than passion and social success established through sleazy financial deals. The primary plot centers on the heroine, Charlotte Halliday, who is cheated of her inheritance and gradually poisoned by her corrupt stepfather before she is rescued by her lover. While Wilkie Collins's influence shows in the first-person narration, the detailed regional descriptions, and the convoluted search for the heir to an enormous fortune, Braddon's reading of Honoré de Balzac is surely apparent in the characters of the three grasping villains. The ringleader, Philip Sheldon, a dentist who has killed Charlotte's father and married her mother, praises Balzac's candor in describing an evil man who is much more successful than his virtuous brother: "That is *real* life," Sheldon remarks. "Your English novelist would have made his villain hang himself with the string of his waistcoat in a condemned cell, while his amiable hero was declared heir to a dukedom and forty thousand a year. But this fellow Balzac knows better than that." As Wolff points out, there is no way to prove that Braddon was putting her own ideas in the mouth of an unscrupulous killer, but since he, too, manages to escape punishment, it is tempting to credit his creator with a realism atypical in most popular English fiction of the time.

After a brief hiatus from writing in 1869-1870 Braddon tried new genres as well while regularly recycling sensation formulas. Her popularity remained high, despite the uneven quality of her fiction. After a final burst of critical vitriol directed at her in 1868, including a scathing attack by Margaret Oliphant, her books were generally well reviewed in the press as the work of a highly accomplished popular writer. Many of her more literary contemporaries, among them William Makepeace Thackeray and Robert Louis Stevenson, were unabashed in their enthusiasm for her work.

In *Taken at the Flood* (1874) she varied the Lady Audley story, keeping the bigamy and insanity and once again making an ambitious and calculating young wife the villain. This time, however, the wife, Sylvia Carew Perriam, wants to rid herself of her husband. She stages his funeral with the body of his brother, who has conveniently died, and has her husband committed to an asylum with the connivance of a corrupt doctor so that she can marry Edmund Standen, the man she adores. Shadrach Bains, Sir Aubrey Perriam's loyal retainer, uncovers the truth just in time to halt the wedding, and Sylvia promptly dies, abandoned and disgraced. Though the story moves along easily and Sylvia's cool-headed treachery is clearly developed, it lacks the ingenuity and dramatic tension of *Lady Audley's Secret*. In *Taken at the Flood* the critics saw no depraved disregard for morality in the elaborate twistings and turnings of the plot or in uncontrollable passion that inspired Sylvia's machinations. Perhaps a decade of sensation fiction had had its effect on conventional Victorian morality.

A far better book of the 1870s, *Joshua Haggard's Daughter* (1876) demonstrates, in contrast, that Braddon's talent was still fresh and that her writing was powerful when she took the time to refine her work. Despite some overly simplistic development of the characters of the doomed young lovers, there are strong themes at work in the family tragedy of Joshua Haggard, a Methodist preacher and shopkeeper; his young wife, Cynthia; his maiden sister, Judith; his devoted daughter, Naomi; and the effete, aristocratic prospective son-in-law, Oswald Pentreath. In this novel murder is the consequence of inflamed passion: Haggard's jealousy is deliberately fed by Naomi's thinly veiled incestuous adoration for her father and her consequent resentment of his child-bride, Cynthia. Unlike novels in which a murder's investigation provides the tension, the emphasis here is on the crime's consequence for the culprit: the repentance and death of a good man pushed by his daughter into murdering Oswald in the mistaken belief that Oswald has seduced Cynthia.

The interactions of the Haggard and Pentreath families reveal another of Braddon's recurrent themes. Much of her best work is concerned with destructive consequences of strong emotions and the potential for violence in the

Braddon in the 1880s

most powerful bondings. The evil that well-bred people do is not the simplistic consequence of poor home environment but more often the result of too-intense devotion coupled with the perverse need to control the life of another person. Several critics have seen Emile Zola's influence in this novel about the forces that control human destiny; others have called it Euripidean or Hardyesque. Clearly it is a book that deserves to be better known.

Braddon's powerful naturalistic novel *Ishmael* (1884), set in Paris during the 1850s and 1860s, is in many ways the least typical of her books. Though there is ample violence and even an unscrupulous private detective, it is not primarily crime fiction. The hero, Sébastien Caradec, calls himself Ishmael—the outcast—as he struggles to succeed against repeated personal and political setbacks. Unloved by his aristocratic father, he becomes a bricklayer in Paris, where he achieves financial security on his own but is abandoned by his wife, who elopes with his friend. Torn between his own success as a capitalist and his sympathy with the workers' cause, Ishmael at long last accepts his inheritance and finds a devoted, if somewhat insipid, wife. But overshadowing his

hard-won peace is the agony and ultimate failure of many other characters in the novel.

Ishmael includes classic Braddon touches. She describes the Parisian setting in meticulous detail and develops complex characters whose motives are comprehensible even when they are repellent. It is hardly surprising that her readers and some of the critics preferred the recognizably English characters and typically sensational incidents of her next novel, *Wyllard's Weird* (1885), which, for today's reader, is most interesting for its idiosyncratic French detective. Wolff describes him as a kind of "Braddonian Maigret" but he might also be compared to the better-known Sherlock Holmes, who made his debut about the same time.

Thirteen years later another, more fully realized, detective was a featured player in two of Braddon's novels, *Rough Justice* (1898) and *His Darling Sin* (1899). John Faunce is English, an admiring student of the great literary detectives from both England and France. He relates in the first person some of his adventures in solving murder cases and disproving libel, a technique Braddon borrowed from Wilkie Collins. In *Rough Justice* Faunce is the voice of normalcy as he carefully uncovers the clues that point to the guilt of a wealthy, radical-socialist philanthropist, who has murdered his "fallen" cousin who lived in the London slums so he can spend her unanticipated inheritance doing good for other unfortunates. Oliver Greswold, a cold and passionless man obsessed by solving the problems of the poor, is best described in Wolff's phrase as a "totalitarian liberal," someone who is convinced he is right and believes he can make his own rules.

Typically Braddon surrounds the seemingly improbable crime with so much realistic social and physical detail that the reader is drawn into Faunce's world and given a persuasive education in the excesses of the Victorian social "crusaders" as well as in the techniques of Victorian detection. Characteristically, too, the conclusion is ambiguous; since there is not enough evidence to bring the case to trial, the perpetrator goes on being publicly revered while his guilty conscience makes him physically ill. Braddon is too honest an observer of human nature to force a confession, and the result is a complex and suspenseful tour de force.

The public scandal over Braddon's private life faded as her fame grew, and for most of her career Braddon enjoyed the friendship and admiration of a wide circle of literary and creative

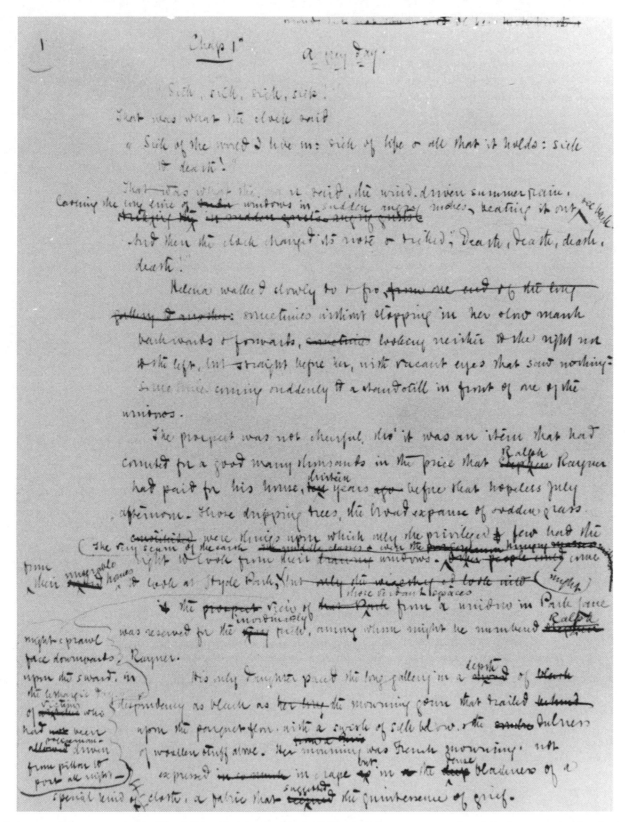

First page of the manuscript for The White House, *Braddon's 1906 novel about a woman whose inheritance carries the stipulation that she must never marry (Robert Lee Wolff,* Sensational Victorian, *1979)*

people, entertaining and being entertained almost as energetically as she wrote. But several major changes during the last decade of the century affected her life and work. Her beloved husband died in 1895 after a long illness, ending a personal and professional alliance that had lasted more than thirty years. Since he had managed the financial details of her career, as well as publishing many of her novels himself, his death meant many new challenges for her. Additionally the circulating libraries–losing business because of the availability of inexpensive one-volume editions–were forcing an end to the three-volume novel, which had been the standard format since mid century, by decreasing the rates by which they paid publishers for these books. Though she resisted briefly, Braddon, as always, was attuned to the demands of the market and switched, without apparent effort, to writing one-volume works. She continued to experiment with subject and genre, always including enough crime in her stories to generate excitement, yet making serious social and moral issues a central focus.

She wrote, somewhat less prolifically, until her death in 1915, and her novels remained best-sellers long after their publication. After the death of her mentor Bulwer-Lytton, she revealed little about her attitudes toward her work or her aspirations as a writer, but in the last years of her life she did write a childhood memoir, "Before the Knowledge of Evil," that provides some details about her formative years. Robert Lee Wolff has used it to identify autobiographical elements in several of her novels.

While her work is little known to the modern reader, she made a lasting impact on the substance and style of English fiction. Her recurrent theme, the hidden nature of crime and the suspect respectability which masks the evil that men and women do, is still timely, and her meticulous attention to detail sets the standard for the successful modern mystery novel.

Letters:
"Devoted Disciple: The Letters of Mary Elizabeth

Braddon to Sir Edward Bulwer-Lytton, 1862-1873," edited by Robert Lee Wolff, *Harvard Library Bulletin,* 22 (January 1974): 1-35; (April 1974): 129-161.

Interviews:
Joseph Hatton, "Miss Braddon at Home," *London Society,* 53 (January 1888): 22-29;
Clive Holland, "Fifty Years of Novel Writing. Miss Braddon at Home. A Chat with the *Doyenne* of English Novelists," *Pall Mall Magazine,* 48 (November 1911): 697-709.

Biography:
Robert Lee Wolff, *Sensational Victorian: The Life & Fiction of Mary Elizabeth Braddon* (New York & London: Garland, 1979).

References:
Norman Donaldson, Introduction to Braddon's *Lady Audley's Secret* (New York: Dover, 1974), pp. v-xiv;
Winifred Hughes, *The Maniac in the Cellar* (Princeton: Princeton University Press, 1980);
Henry James, "Miss Braddon," review of *Aurora Floyd,* in his *Notes and Reviews* (Cambridge, Mass.: Dunster House, 1921);
Benjamin M. Nyberg, *The Novels of Mary Elizabeth Braddon* (Ann Arbor, Mich.: University Microfilms, 1965);
Michael Sadleir, "Mary Elizabeth Braddon," in his *Things Past* (London: Constable, 1944);
Elaine Showalter, *A Literature of Their Own: British Women Novelists from Bronte to Lessing* (Princeton: Princeton University Press, 1977).

Papers:
Some of Braddon's notebooks are held at the Houghton Library, Harvard University. The collection of Robert Lee Wolff, which includes the manuscript of her unpublished memoir, manuscript diaries for 1890-1914, notebooks, essays, and letters, is held at the University of Texas at Austin.

Ernest Bramah

(20 March 1868-27 June 1942)

Joan Seay
University of Tulsa

BOOKS: *English Farming and Why I Turned It Up* (London: Simkin, Marshall, Hamilton, Kent/ New York: Scribners, 1894);

The Wallet of Kai Lung (London: Richards, 1900; Boston: Page, 1900);

The Mirror of Kong Ho (London: Chapman & Hall, 1905; Garden City: Doubleday, Doran, 1930);

What Might Have Been: The Story of a Social War (London: Murray, 1907); republished as *The Secret of the League* (London: Nelson, 1909);

Max Carrados (London: Methuen, 1914);

Kai Lung's Golden Hours (London: Richards, 1922; New York: Doran, 1923);

The Eyes of Max Carrados (London: Richards, 1923; New York: Doran, 1924);

The Specimen Case (London: Hodder & Stoughton, 1924; New York: Doran, 1925);

Max Carrados Mysteries (London: Hodder & Stoughton, 1927);

The Story of Wan and the Remarkable Shrub and The Story of Ching-Kwei and the Destinies (Garden City: Doubleday, Doran, 1927);

Kai Lung Unrolls His Mat (London: Richards, 1928; Garden City: Doubleday, Doran, 1928);

A Guide to the Varieties and Rarity of English Regal Copper Coins: Charles II-Victoria, 1671-1860 (London: Methuen, 1929);

Short Stories of To-day and Yesterday (London: Harrap, 1929);

A Little Flutter (London: Cassell, 1930);

The Moon of Much Gladness, Related by Kai Lung (London: Cassell, 1932); republished as *The Return of Kai Lung* (New York: Sheridan House, 1938);

The Bravo of London (London: Cassell, 1934);

The Kai Lung Omnibus (London: Philip Alan, 1936);

Kai Lung Beneath the Mulberry Tree (London: Richards, 1940).

Ernest Bramah occupies a small but secure place in the history of British detective fiction as the creator of Max Carrados, the remarkable blind sleuth. The Carrados tales belong to the golden age of short detective stories that flourished before World War I. During this era many unusual variants of the fictional detective were invented in an effort to give originality to the detective story. Max Carrados is one of these unique probers of mysteries. A cultivated, erudite gentleman who pursues detection as a hobby, Carrados is a thoroughly classic British detective hero. Unlike sighted private investigators, he must rely to a far greater degree on other senses and follow a somewhat different course in his investigations, thus providing new twists and novel approaches to solving mysteries.

Ernest Bramah, pen name of Ernest Bramah Smith, was born near Manchester in 1868. He was the younger son oɪ Susannah Brammah Smith (he dropped the other "m") and Charles Clement Smith, a businessman. After leaving the Manchester Grammar School at seventeen, he tried his hand at farming. This experience was the subject of his first published book, *English Farming and Why I Turned It Up* (1894), an amusing treatise on the disadvantages of farming. His venture lost money, but a weekly column he wrote between 1890 and 1892 from his Warwickshire farm for the *Birmingham News* earned him ten shillings a week and seemed to offer a more promising career. In 1892, aided by a generous allowance from his father, he went to London to find newspaper work and pursue his writing. A shorthand and typing course helped him obtain a secretarial job with Jerome K. Jerome, who edited the magazine *To-day*. Bramah became an editorial assistant, handling fiction and literary articles by such writers as Thomas Hardy, Rudyard Kipling, George Moore, and Bret Harte, whose work he particularly liked. After several years at *To-day* Bramah found his job was becoming routine. He joined a new firm and edited a magazine, the *Minster*, for two years until late 1897 when he left to become what he called an "outside writer." Bramah married Lucie Maisie Barker on 31 December 1897 in London. He died on 27 June 1942 at Weston-super-Mare, Somersetshire.

If the basic facts about the life of Ernest Bramah are scanty, even less is known about his personal life. So carefully did he guard his privacy that there was speculation that Ernest Bramah did not exist at all but was instead a pseudonym of another British author or a syndicate of authors perpetrating a literary hoax. An American publisher wrote to Bramah, "I have always had a feeling that you were a mythical person." The only recorded account of Bramah by someone who actually had met him was from publisher Grant Richards, who found him to be "one of the kindest and the most amiable of men." To an inquiry from Howard Haycraft, Bramah replied, "I am not fond of writing about myself and only in less degree about my work. My published books are about all that I care to pass on to the reader."

Bramah was also the author of a wide range of works that include a book on numismatics, a science-fiction novel (*What Might Have Been: The Story of a Social War*, 1907), short stories published in magazines, and short plays once popu-

Front cover for volume one of the 1923 two-volume "gift edition" of Bramah's first collection of fiction. Doran published this special edition twenty-three years after the book first appeared, to coincide with the publication of the second collection of tales, Kai Lung's Golden Hours, *narrated by Bramah's Chinese storyteller (courtesy of Otto Penzler).*

lar with radio and amateur theater audiences. He is remembered today only for the Carrados stories and his Kai Lung tales featuring an itinerant Chinese storyteller. The Kai Lung stories spanned his writing career—the first written before 1900 and the last shortly before his death in 1942. Praised for their literary craftsmanship and subtle humor, these stories have had many distinguished admirers such as Hilaire Belloc, Sir Arthur Quiller-Couch, Sir John Collings Squire, Dorothy Sayers, and J. B. Priestley.

In a rare interview with the BBC in 1935 Bramah recounted how he was inspired to invent a blind detective. The idea occurred to him at a theater while watching a "crook" play in which the plot and action were so contrived that the characters would have to have been blind not to see that a theft was taking place. His initial idea focused on the "humorous and ironic—the incongruity of a man so handicapped taking part in what was generally supposed to be a particularly open-eyed occupation." Bramah knew he must keep him serious and "tread warily" with his satire or he would risk offending readers.

Max Carrados, like Sherlock Holmes and R. Austin Freeman's Dr. John Evelyn Thorndyke, is endowed with a striking personality that dominates the stories. Abundant details of his life are supplied, making him a convincing and engaging human figure. He is a wealthy bachelor who has inherited a fortune from an American cousin on the condition that he change his name from Wynn to Carrados. If he were not blind, his activities would be considered quite ordinary. In addition to detective work, his special hobby, which figures in several of his investigations, is collecting antique Greek coins. He enjoys chamber music and opera; he boxes and fishes; he plays golf, bowl, croquet, and cards; and he goes punting on the river near his comfortable house, The Turrets, just west of London in Richmond. As Bramah wrote, "If there was one thing more than another about Max Carrados that came as a continued surprise, even a mild shock to his acquaintances, it was the wide and unrestricted scope of his amusements."

Some twelve years before his detective work began, Carrados lost his sight when a branch hit his eyes while he was horseback riding. His particular form of blindness is amaurosis, which leaves the external appearance of the eyes unchanged. He has courageously overcome many of the limitations of his condition, and, Bramah noted, "so far from that crippling his interests in life or his energies, it has merely impelled him to develop those senses which in most of us lie half dormant and practically unused." Carrados himself says there are unexpected compensations: "A new world to explore, new experiences, new powers awakening; strange new perceptions; life in the fourth dimension." His supertrained surviving senses allow him to do many things. For example, he can read newspaper headlines with his fingers. His sense of smell enables him to deduce that a man is wearing a false mustache because the odor of glue is emphasized by perspiring skin. He can detect sound inaudible to others

and remember voices perfectly. Should the blind sleuth's feats seem incredible, Bramah, in the preface to *The Eyes of Max Carrados*, describes some of the recorded achievements of blind people in history.

Although Carrados is singularly independent, he relies on the services of his secretary, Annesley Greatorex, and, especially, his valet, Parkinson, who possesses a highly trained faculty of observation and retention. Carrados also has his Watson—Louis Carlyle, a capable, but somewhat naive, private-inquiry agent whom he had known during his days at St. Michael's school.

Besides his supertrained senses, Carrados is equipped with a keen intelligence and what Bramah calls an "elusive sixth sense," which is often no more than an intuitive perception of human psychology. Finally Carrados is endowed with an agreeable personality. Sometimes cynical and satirical, he is always good-natured and unfailingly kind. Bramah's blind sleuth is generally regarded as a memorable and successful fictional detective. Willard Huntington Wright (who wrote the Philo Vance detective novels under the pseudonym S. S. Van Dine) said of Max Carrados: "To be sure, he was endowed with gifts which recalled the strange powers of the citizens of H. G. Wells's *The Country of the Blind*, but so accurately and carefully has Mr. Bramah projected him that he must be given a place in the forefront of famous fictional sleuths."

Bramah's gifts for invention, characterization, description, and humor give the Carrados stories special appeal. The blind sleuth, who is interested in unusual crimes, pursues his diverse investigations in realistic settings that include London back streets, modest rooms, and remote rural locations, as well as the genteel environments favored by many detective writers of the era. Adding authenticity, Bramah occasionally ties episodes to events in the news such as suffragette protests, Sinn Fein plots, and British rule in India. The Carrados tales are also distinguished by Bramah's winning personal style. The tone is witty, ironic, and gently satirical. His gift for expression is reflected in clever dialogue and lively third-person narration.

Not all of the Carrados fiction stands up well. It is uneven in quality, and the weaker stories (mostly later ones) tend to be ponderous and unconvincing. But even when logic fails and the solution to a mystery is absurd, Bramah's style is engaging.

Illustration by Warwick Reynolds for Bramah's "The Missing Witness Sensation," a Max Carrados story in the July 1926 issue of Pearson's

Max Carrados, the first book of Carrados stories, appeared in 1914. Most of the eight stories are first-rate, and Ellery Queen has described it as excellent. The opening episode, "The Coin of Dionysius," depicts the initial meeting between Carrados and Louis Carlyle, a private investigator. Carlyle is referred to the amateur numismatics expert for an opinion about the genuineness of a Greek tetradrachm and discovers that Carrados is an old friend with a new name and changed circumstances. Carrados soon amazes Carlyle by quickly solving the Greek coin mystery without leaving his study. This bit of armchair detective work is rare for Carrados, for he usually performs on-the-spot investigations.

Against the backdrop of Edwardian London, "The Knights Cross Signal Problem" features a tragic train crash, stock-exchange speculation, a Bengal Indian, and a surprising ending. As in many Carrados tales, newspaper information plays a role and indicates Bramah's familiarity with the newspaper trade.

The *Max Carrados* collection contains what some critics regard as Bramah's best Carrados story. "The Tragedy at Brookbend Cottage" concerns a husband's attempt to kill his wife by the simulation of lightning. Although there is the usual breezy conversation and good-natured banter between Carrados and Carlyle, this story has what Jacques Barzun and Wendell Hertig Taylor refer to as a classic quality: "where the mood is still felt as tragic and the pebbles rattling on the window pane as a master touch." The essentially lighthearted mood of Bramah's stories often has undertones of a darker side.

Less serious situations are treated in "The Clever Mrs. Straithwaite," a domestic farce with a make-believe jewel theft and a fraudulent insurance claim, and the amusing "The Comedy at Fountain Cottage." Both of these have skillfully portrayed and individualized female characters.

"The Last Exploit of Harry the Actor" deftly sets up an interesting puzzle: someone is breaking into and stealing from safe-deposit boxes in an impregnable safe in a steel-encased basement, even though reliable guards are always posted, and they follow a fail-safe procedure for obtaining keys to the boxes. Carrados adroitly figures it all out, and a comical denouement provides a happy ending.

The least successful stories in this volume are "The Tilling Shaw Mystery" and "The Game Played in the Dark," neither of which includes Louis Carlyle. The first contains too much description of past events and too little action. The second lacks substance, but it does show the advantages a blind man has when surrounded by villains in a dark room.

It was nine years before the second collection of Max Carrados stories appeared. Generally well received, *The Eyes of Max Carrados* (1923) offers an interesting variety of clever tales. Reviewing the collection for the *Literary International Book Review* (May 1924), Louise M. Field wrote: "It is not only that these tales are perplexing, entertaining, ingenious and very well written; they have an attention to detail, and air of verisimilitude, which makes the reader believe in the reality of the events they record. The book is full of flesh-and-blood characters and dextrously turned phrases, phrases which will give abundant delight to the lover of fine craftsmanship in the art of writing."

Among the best of the nine stories in this volume is the frequently anthologized "The Ghost at Massingham Mansions." This is an intriguing mystery with puzzling circumstances, interesting investigative work, clever characterization, and some sparkling dialogue. "The Disappearance of Marie Severe" presents another fine puzzle. Carrados, ingeniously, if not quite believably, uses his highly developed senses to track clues in the case of a young girl who has vanished leaving no apparent trace. Another missing-person case, "The Missing Actress Sensation," has charm, but its complicated situation and far-fetched resolution make it an inferior Carrados tale. Also weak is "The Eastern Mystery" involving a holy Hindu talisman with mystic powers. Better is the exploration and explanation of what appear to be supernatural occurrences in "The Secret of Dunstan's Tower," an old-fashioned tale with ancient legends, an inbred old family, Druid stones, and a secret passage.

The solution to "The Mystery of the Poisoned Dish of Mushrooms" requires digging deeper and deeper, pursuing and discarding possible explanations, until the truth is found. A rare book disappears at an auction and reappears in different forms in "The Virginiola Fraud." "The Kingsmouth Spy Case" has an elaborate plot in which Carrados uncovers a German spy. In "The Ingenious Mr. Spinola," he solves the mystery of a large card-playing machine to find there is still another revelation.

Eight more Carrados tales appear in *Max Carrados Mysteries* (1927). This volume is uneven in quality and is considered the weakest of the

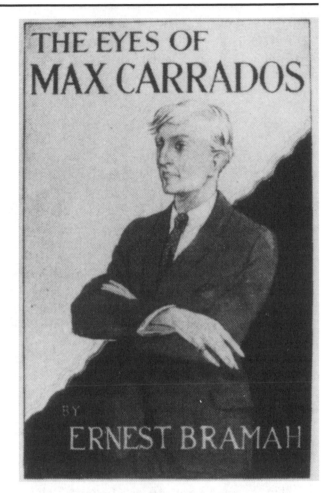

Dust jacket for the first British edition of the second collection of stories about Bramah's blind detective. In his introduction Bramah discusses the ability of the blind to compensate for their handicap and explains the genesis of Max Carrados (courtesy of the Lilly Library, Indiana University).

three collections of Carrados short stories. "The Holloway Flat Tragedy" and "The Mystery of the Vanished Petition Crown" are the best in the book. The first is one of the rare Carrados and Carlyle cases involving murder, and it displays Carrados's combination of logic and understanding of human psychology. In "The Mystery of the Vanished Petition Crown" Bramah puts some of his own experience with coin dealers and journalism to good use with a plot in which Carrados helps to exonerate a female reporter accused in the disappearance of a valuable coin. After expertly finding the missing coin Carrados explains one secret of his success when he says that "there is no form of villainy that I haven't gone through in all its phases. Theoretically, of course, but so far as working out the details is concerned and preparing for emergencies, efficiently and with craftsmanlike pride. Whenever I fail to get to

sleep at night–rather frequently, I'm sorry to say–I commit a murder, forgery, a robbery or what not with all its ramifications . . . the criminal mind is rarely original, and I find that in nine cases out of ten that sort of crime is committed exactly as I have already done it."

Social commentary figures in several of the stories. "The Ingenious Mind of Mr. Rigby Lacksome" offers an amusing parody of the wealthy, American self-made industrialist in Hiram Nogg, who is seeking a major acquisition for his Shakespeare collection. In this story suffragettes make an appearance, along with an American woman who is "de-voted" to the cause of the emancipation of her British sisters. Sinn Feiners create problems in "The Missing Witness Sensation." Carrados is locked up in a cellar by a band of extremists in order to keep him from identifying a key witness at a trial. His brilliant but improbable escape is memorable. A German spy working in a natural-history museum is discovered sending secret coded signals as war is declared in "The Secret of Headlam Height." In the farcical "The Curious Circumstances of the Two Left Shoes," a so-called Monkey Burglar is at the height of his fame and is suspected in the disappearance of a silver chest.

The least successful stories in this collection are "The Strange Case of Cyril Bycourt," where Bramah indulges in pseudoscience, and "The Crime at the House in Culver Street," a complicated, implausible case. Yet even these stories are marked by Bramah's exemplary style.

The Specimen Case (1924), a sampling of short stories spanning the first thirty years of Bramah's published stories, contains one Max Carrados piece, "The Bunch of Violets," in which Carrados again has a momentary advantage over adversaries in a darkened room.

The Bravo of London (1934), the only Carrados novel, demonstrates that Bramah was much better as a writer of short detective fiction.

It features a completely detestable villain, Mr. Joolby, operator of a shady antiques business. He masterminds an elaborate counterfeiting scheme that hinges on an unbelievable impersonation. While characterizations are excellent and there are some delightful episodes, the pace is tedious, the telling is at times ponderous, and key elements of the plot are unconvincing. Max Carrados's phenomenal escape from a locked room in a cellar repeats the method used in "The Missing Witness Sensation."

One indicator of the success of the Max Carrados stories is their continued availability in print. At least sixteen have appeared in thirty anthologies. New editions of *Max Carrados* appeared in 1975 (in Hyperion's Milestones of Mystery Series) and in 1976 (in Garland's Crime Fiction Series), and selected stories were published in *Best Max Carrados Detective Stories* (1972). Characterized by individuality and stylistic merit, the Carrados tales have stood the test of time.

Bibliography:
William White, "Some Uncollected Authors XXXVII," *Book Collector*, 13 (Spring 1964): 54-63.

References:
Grant Richards, *Author Hunting By an Old Literary Sports Man* (New York: Coward-McCann, 1934), pp. 272-275;

William White, Introduction to "Ernest Bramah on Max Carrados: An Unpublished BBC Talk," *Armchair Detective*, 15, no. 1 (1982): 80-83;

White, "Is There an Ernest Bramah?," *American Book Collector*, 6 (Summer 1966): 12-19.

Papers:
The Humanities Research Center, University of Texas, Austin, includes manuscript material and letters. The University of Illinois library holds correspondence from Bramah to his literary agent.

John Buchan

(26 August 1875-11 February 1940)

J. Randolph Cox
St. Olaf College

See also the Buchan entry in *DLB 34, British Novelists, 1890-1929: Traditionalists.*

BOOKS: *Sir Quixote of the Moors* (London: Unwin, 1895; New York: Holt, 1895);

Scholar Gipsies (London: John Lane/New York: Macmillan, 1896);

Sir Walter Ralegh; the Stanhope Essay (Oxford: Blackwell/London: Simpkin, Marshall, Hamilton, Kent, 1897);

John Burnet of Barns (London: John Lane, 1898; New York: Dodd, Mead, 1898);

The Pilgrim Fathers: the Newdigate Prize Poem, 1898 (Oxford: Blackwell/London: Simpkin, Marshall, Hamilton, Kent, 1898);

Brasenose College (London: Robinson, 1898);

Grey Weather: Moorland Tales of My Own People (London: John Lane, 1899);

A Lost Lady of Old Years (London: John Lane, 1899);

The Half-Hearted (London: Isbister, 1900; Boston & New York: Houghton Mifflin, 1900);

The Watcher by the Threshold and Other Tales (Edinburgh & London: Blackwood, 1902; enlarged edition, New York: Doran, 1918);

The African Colony (Edinburgh: Blackwood, 1903);

The Law Relating to the Taxation of Foreign Income (London: Stevens, 1905);

A Lodge in the Wilderness, anonymous (Edinburgh & London: Blackwood, 1906);

Some Eighteenth Century Byways and Other Essays (Edinburgh & London: Blackwood, 1908);

Prester John (London: Nelson, 1910); republished as *The Great Diamond Pipe* (New York: Dodd, Mead, 1910);

Sir Walter Raleigh (London: Nelson, 1911; New York: Holt, 1911);

The Moon Endureth: Tales and Fancies (Edinburgh & London: Blackwood, 1912; New York: Sturgis & Walton, 1912);

The Marquis of Montrose (London: Nelson, 1913; New York: Scribners, 1913);

John Buchan in his library at Elsfield Manor, which he acquired in 1919 (courtesy of Lady Fairfax-Lucy, Lord Tweedsmuir, and the Hon. William Buchan)

Andrew Jameson, Lord Ardwall (Edinburgh & London: Blackwood, 1913);

Britain's War by Land (London & New York: Oxford University Press, H. Mitford, 1915);

Nelson's History of the War, 24 volumes (London: Nelson, 1915-1919); revised as *A History of the Great War,* 4 volumes (London: Nelson, 1921-1922; Boston & New York: Houghton Mifflin, 1922);

Salute to Adventurers (London: Nelson, 1915; Boston & New York: Houghton Mifflin, 1915);

The Buchan family, circa 1903. Standing, from left: John, Anna, Willie, and Walter; sitting: Rev. and Mrs. John Buchan and Alastair (courtesy of Lady Fairfax-Lucy, Lord Tweedsmuir, and the Hon. William Buchan).

The Thirty-Nine Steps (Edinburgh & London: Blackwood, 1915; New York: Doran, 1916);

The Power-House (Edinburgh & London: Blackwood, 1916; New York: Doran, 1916);

Greenmantle (London: Hodder & Stoughton, 1916; New York: Doran, 1916);

The Battle of the Somme, First Phase (London & New York: Nelson, 1916);

Poems, Scots and English (London & Edinburgh: T. C. & E. C. Jack, 1917; revised and enlarged edition, London: Nelson, 1936);

The Battle of the Somme, Second Phase (Edinburgh, New York & London: Nelson, 1917);

Mr. Standfast (London: Hodder & Stoughton, 1918; New York: Doran, 1919);

These for Remembrance (London: Privately printed, 1919);

The Island of Sheep, by Buchan and Susan Buchan as Cadmus and Harmonia (London: Hodder & Stoughton, 1919; Boston & New York: Houghton Mifflin, 1920);

The History of the South African Forces in France (London: Nelson, 1920);

Francis and Riversdale Grenfell: A Memoir (London: Nelson, 1920);

The Path of the King (London: Hodder & Stoughton, 1921; New York: Doran, 1921);

Huntingtower (London: Hodder & Stoughton, 1922; New York: Doran, 1922);

A Book of Escapes and Hurried Journeys (London: Nelson, 1922; Boston & New York: Houghton Mifflin, 1923);

The Last Secrets (London: Nelson, 1923; Boston & New York: Houghton Mifflin, 1924);

Midwinter (London: Hodder & Stoughton, 1923; New York: Doran, 1923);

Days to Remember: The British Empire in the Great War, by Buchan and Henry Newbolt (London: Nelson, 1923);

The Three Hostages (London: Hodder & Stoughton, 1924; Boston & New York: Houghton Mifflin, 1924);

Lord Minto: A Memoir (London & New York: Nelson, 1924);

The History of the Royal Scots Fusiliers (1678-1918) (London & New York: Nelson, 1925);

John Macnab (London: Hodder & Stoughton, 1925; Boston & New York: Houghton Mifflin, 1925);

The Man and the Book: Sir Walter Scott (London & Edinburgh: Nelson, 1925);

The Dancing Floor (London: Hodder & Stoughton, 1926; Boston & New York: Houghton Mifflin, 1926);

The Fifteenth-Scottish-Division 1914-1919, by Buchan and John Stewart (Edinburgh: Blackwood, 1926);

Homilies and Recreations (London: Nelson, 1926; London & New York: Nelson, 1926; Boston: Houghton Mifflin, 1926);

Witch Wood (London: Hodder & Stoughton, 1927; Boston & New York: Houghton Mifflin, 1927);

The Runagates Club (London: Hodder & Stoughton, 1928; Boston & New York: Houghton Mifflin, 1928);

Montrose (London & Edinburgh: Nelson, 1928; Boston & New York: Houghton Mifflin, 1928);

The Courts of the Morning (London: Hodder & Stoughton, 1929; Boston & New York: Houghton Mifflin, 1929);

The Causal and the Casual in History (Cambridge: The University Press, 1929; New York: Macmillan, 1929);

The Kirk in Scotland, 1560-1929, by Buchan and George Adam Smith (London: Hodder & Stoughton, 1930);

Castle Gay (London: Hodder & Stoughton, 1930; Boston & New York: Houghton Mifflin, 1930);

The Blanket of the Dark (London: Hodder & Stoughton, 1931; Boston & New York: Houghton Mifflin, 1931);

Sir Walter Scott (London & Toronto: Cassell, 1932; New York: Coward-McCann, 1932);

The Gap in the Curtain (London: Hodder & Stoughton, 1932; Boston & New York: Houghton Mifflin, 1932);

Julius Caesar (London: P. Davies, 1932; New York: Appleton, 1932);

The Magic Walking Stick (London: Hodder & Stoughton, 1932; Boston & New York: Houghton Mifflin, 1932);

The Massacre of Glencoe (London: P. Davies, 1933; New York: Putnam's, 1933);

A Prince of the Captivity (London: Hodder & Stoughton, 1933; Boston & New York: Houghton Mifflin, 1933);

The Free Fishers (London: Hodder & Stoughton, 1934; Boston & New York: Houghton Mifflin, 1934);

Gordon at Khartoum (London: P. Davies, 1934);

Oliver Cromwell (London: Hodder & Stoughton, 1934; Boston: Houghton Mifflin, 1934);

The King's Grace (London: Hodder & Stoughton, 1935); republished as *The People's King: George V* (Boston: Houghton Mifflin, 1935);

The House of the Four Winds (London: Hodder & Stoughton, 1935; Boston & New York: Houghton Mifflin, 1935);

The Island of Sheep (London: Hodder & Stoughton, 1936); republished as *The Man from the Norlands* (Boston: Houghton Mifflin, 1936);

Augustus (London: Hodder & Stoughton, 1937; Boston: Houghton Mifflin, 1937);

Memory Hold-the-Door (London: Hodder & Stoughton, 1940); republished as *Pilgrim's Way* (Boston: Houghton Mifflin, 1940);

Comments and Characters, edited by W. Forbes Gray (London & New York: Nelson, 1940);

Madeleine Carroll and Robert Donat in a scene from Alfred Hitchcock's 1935 film version of Buchan's The Thirty-Nine Steps

Susan Grosvenor, whom Buchan married in July 1907 (courtesy of Lady Fairfax-Lucy, Lord Tweedsmuir, and the Hon. William Buchan)

Canadian Occasions (London: Hodder & Stoughton, 1940);

Sick Heart River (London: Hodder & Stoughton, 1941); republished as *Mountain Meadow* (Boston: Houghton Mifflin, 1941);

The Long Traverse (London: Hodder & Stoughton, 1941); republished as *The Lake of Gold* (Boston: Houghton Mifflin, 1941).

OTHER: *Essays and Apothegms of Francis Lord Bacon*, edited, with an introduction, by Buchan (London: W. Scott, 1894);

Izaak Walton, *The Compleat Angler, or the Contemplative Man's Recreation*, edited, with an introduction and notes, by Buchan (London: Methuen, 1901);

The Long Road to Victory, edited by Buchan (London: Nelson, 1920);

Archibald Philip Primrose, *Miscellanies, Literary and Historical*, edited, with a prefatory note, by Buchan (London: Hodder & Stoughton, 1921);

Great Hours in Sport, edited by Buchan (London: Nelson, 1921);

A History of English Literature, edited by Buchan (London: Nelson, 1923; New York: Ronald, 1938);

The Nations of Today, edited by Buchan (London: Hodder & Stoughton, 1923-1924; Boston & New York: Houghton Mifflin, 1923-1924);

The Northern Muse: An Anthology of Scots Vernacular Poetry, compiled by Buchan (London: Nelson, 1924).

Despite his achievements as historian, biographer, historical novelist, and statesman, it is for his thrillers that John Buchan has found an enduring reputation in popular letters. The "Buchan touch" is a name applied to fiction which shares his appeal: his characters are romantic but not preposterous, his sense of setting and climate is superb, and his plots move swiftly. Written with unassuming ease, his thrillers and tales of high adventure have been read by many. He introduced to spy fiction its basic theme: that evil and worldwide conspiracies can lie just beneath the surface veneer of so-called civilization–"Away behind all Governments and Armies there was a big subterranean movement going on, engineered by very dangerous people" (*The Thirty-Nine Steps*, 1915). According to Andrew Lumley in *The Power-House* (1916), it is civilization that is the conspiracy that holds chaos and anarchy at bay.

Born in Perth on 26 August 1875, John Buchan was the son of John Buchan, a minister in the Free Church of Scotland, and Helen Masterson Buchan. His family moved to Fife where he grew up along the coast. The woods in which he played with his sister Anna and his brothers Walter and William became the setting for imaginary adventures based partly on family stories and partly on the Bible and *Pilgrim's Progress*. In the border country near Peebles and Broughton (where his mother's family lived) Buchan found new vistas for his imagination in reenacting stories from Scottish history. As he grew older and explored the countryside, first on foot and then by bicycle, he added to a store of places where his fictional characters would live, fight, and even die.

Climbing the Tweedside hills led to greater efforts, the Swiss Alps and the Dolomites in particular. At Oxford (Brasenose College), where he took his First in Literae Humaniores (Greats), he did not go out for team sports, but he participated in some strenuous activities. In his autobiography, *Pilgrim's Way* (1940; originally published as *Memory Hold-the-Door*, 1940), he speaks of canoeing, walking to the limit of his strength, or riding a course marked out on a map. His fictional characters would follow his example in this as in other things.

In London Buchan studied law at the Middle Temple and continued the writing he had begun while at Oxford. He added foreign travel to his experience, spending two years (1901-1903) on the staff of Lord Alfred Milner, high commissioner for South Africa. After his return to London and a period of time as a barrister, Buchan accepted a position as literary adviser for the publishers Thomas Nelson and Sons in their Edinburgh headquarters. He moved back to London and worked in Nelson's office there soon after his marriage to Susan Grosvenor. The couple had four children.

Much of Buchan's writing before 1910 had been nonfiction: articles and books on Africa and on the tax law. His fiction had been written in emulation of Sir Walter Scott and Robert Louis Stevenson, drawing on the rich romantic traditions of Scotland. His first contemporary novel, *The Half-Hearted* (1900), introduced the characteristic Buchan theme that self-sacrifice could overcome cowardice. In 1910 he published *Prester John*, a boys' adventure novel which opened new fictional fields for him. In the decade since he wrote *The Half-Hearted*, Buchan learned how to

Front wrapper for the English-language edition of Greenmantle *published in Paris by Thomas Nelson and Sons*

blend the exaggerated world of romance and adventure with a style of his own. With the opening sentences of David Crawfurd's story, which foreshadow terrors and excitements to come, he has the reader's attention. This story of a black uprising includes a skillful depiction of Africa based on Buchan's recent experiences there. Africa had been a subject for British writers since Rider Haggard, but Buchan created new interest by giving John Laputa, the black leader, a majesty that is memorable.

The Power-House was published in hardcover in 1916, the year after *The Thirty-Nine Steps* appeared, but its periodical appearance preceded the more famous novel by two years. The Buchan theme of the precarious nature of civilization was given its simplest and most direct form in *The Power-House*. Edward Leithen, first seen in the short story "Space," is called on to find Charles Pitt-Heron. While Tommy Deloraine goes halfway around the world to bring him back, Leithen encounters, in London, the man behind Pitt-Heron's disappearance—Andrew Lum-

Lt. Col. John Buchan during World War I. When the Ministry of Information was formed in 1918, Buchan was appointed Director of Intelligence (courtesy of Lady Fairfax-Lucy, Lord Tweedsmuir, and the Hon. William Buchan).

ley, in charge of the "Power-House," an organization to provide leadership to international anarchists. The details of the plot are sketched in lightly. By not overdrawing the picture, Buchan is able to leave the reader with the impression that he has been privy to marvelous secrets and profound ideas, and that there is more to the spy story than is readily apparent.

The Thirty-Nine Steps was written while Buchan was in the hospital, recovering from an operation for a duodenal ulcer. Richard Hannay, a young Scotsman visiting England after thirty years in South Africa, finds himself bored by London. He meets Scudder, an American adventurer, who hints to him of some secrets important to England before he is murdered in Hannay's flat. Hannay realizes he is the object of interest to two sets of people: Scudder's enemies and the police, who suspect him of the murder. With Scudder's notebook in his possession, Hannay must remain free to deliver its message himself. Here the dangers to the hero are more

concrete than in *The Power-House* and the use of a hurried journey enhances the suspense. The story takes on the characteristics of a folktale or even a parable for modern times. It is a series of cliff-hanging scenes leading to the final revelation of the meaning of the book's title and the thwarting of the plot of the spy organization, the "Black Stone." Like Andrew Lumley in *The Power-House*, the master spy masks his true nature under a cloak of respectability.

The basis of a Buchan thriller is always the story and the setting. With Scott and Stevenson as his models he could hardly write otherwise. The chase across Scotland in *The Thirty-Nine Steps* might have been inspired by the flight in the heather of David Balfour and Alan Breck in *Kidnapped*. Buchan pays tribute to the economy of detail which Stevenson uses when he describes this effect in his essay "Literature and Topography." Stevenson gives the reader a view of the terrain so that he has a map in his mind. He selects the place names artfully. The effect is not speed but distance and accompanying fatigue. Buchan strives for the same effect in his own work. The reader is given enough detail to get his bearings and learn how vital it is that the hero reach his goal.

The popularity of *The Thirty-Nine Steps* called for a sequel, *Greenmantle* (1916). Eventually Buchan had characters and plots for a cycle of eleven novels and several short stories–including most of the contents of *The Runagates Club* (1928)– about Hannay, Leithen, John S. Blenkiron, Peter Pienaar, Archie Roylance, Sandy Arbuthnot, and their companions in adventure. To these works should be added the trilogy of adventures of the retired Glasgow grocer, Dickson McCunn, and another novel, *A Prince of the Captivity* (1933), in which several of the same characters are mentioned and some of the themes of the other thrillers are continued.

Greenmantle is both longer and more complex than *The Thirty-Nine Steps*. Hannay is no longer the lone man on the run. Buchan has filled in the background since the previous adventure with swift strokes which convince because the reader is not told more than he needs to know. Convalescing after a wartime leg wound at Loos, Hannay is entrusted with a secret mission by Sir Walter Bullivant of the Foreign Office. In the company of Sandy Arbuthnot and an American, John S. Blenkiron, he seeks to discover the meaning of the words "Kasredin," "cancer," and "v.I." found on a scrap of paper. The three

Buchan and his daughter Alice outside Bank House in Peebles, Scotland (courtesy of Lady Fairfax-Lucy, Lord Tweedsmuir, and the Hon. William Buchan)

make the journey to the Middle East by different paths. Hannay's route takes him through wartime Germany in the company of an old Boer, Peter Pienaar. The title character is the long-awaited leader to unify Islam against its (and Germany's) enemies—Britain in India and Africa and Russia in Turkey. The three men are able to prevent the holy war. As with other Buchan thrillers, a plot summary conveys few of the reasons this novel has remained so popular. The explanation is in the manner in which it is told, and the sense that the reader is privy to secrets not given out to just anyone. There is also the sense that the enemy is a worthy sort, both as adversary and human being.

World War I is still on in *Mr. Standfast* (1918), and there is the same quiet recapitulation of events in Hannay's career since the Greenmantle affair. Bullivant pulls strings to get

Hannay assigned to home-front duty under the guise of a pacifist. At Fosse Manor he meets Mary Lamington, a member of the Voluntary Aid Detachment, who is the one to give him his orders. They are hunting the most dangerous man in the world, and the outcome of the war will be determined by their success. The enemy, Moxon Ivery, is another of those whose guise of respectability is so convincing it nearly fools Hannay.

Mr. Standfast has underlying themes and ideas that raise it above the mere well-plotted thriller. Buchan's treatment of the conscientious objector, Lancelot Wake, is both objective and humane. Even more moving is the scene in which Peter Pienaar gives his life while performing one final noble deed. Although Pienaar attempts to emulate the character of Mr. Standfast from *Pilgrim's Progress*, Hannay suggests that in his death he more closely resembles Mr. Valiant-for-Truth,

Buchan wearing the headdress given him along with the title "Teller of Tales" by a tribe of Canadian Indians during his tenure as Governor-General of Canada, from 1936 until his death in 1940 (courtesy of Lady Fairfax-Lucy, Lord Tweedsmuir, and the Hon. William Buchan)

whose scars were witness that he had fought the good fight, and that the trumpets would sound for him as he passed over to the other side.

Richard Hannay returns in two later novels and one short story (in *The Runagates Club*), but not before the first volume of a new series was published. *Huntingtower* (1922) is a tale of royal Russian exiles and evil Bolsheviks. It was the first thriller written at Elsfield, the home near Oxford that Buchan moved into in 1920. It introduces a new protagonist, Dickson McCunn, who had read Scott not so much for the story as the setting. The books provided him with material to construct journeys of the imagination, and with this sort of preparation he enters the world of high adventure aided by a sort of Boy Scout group from the Glasgow slums known as the "Gorbals Die-Hards."

McCunn, filled with spring fever, sets out on foot through the Scottish countryside. At an inn he meets John Heritage, a poet who becomes his companion in adventure, and the two men become intrigued by an old house known as Huntingtower. Heritage has heard the voice of a woman he had seen in Rome coming from the house. Young Dougal, chieftain of the Die-Hards, informs them the house is inhabited by two women. Instantly McCunn's dreams of gentle bookish romance are replaced by a kind of crude melodrama. They decide to burgle Huntingtower and find a veritable princess who requires rescuing. To balance the romantic trappings in the novel, McCunn's common sense serves as a kind of framing device through which the reader willingly suspends disbelief.

Buchan alternated his thrillers with historical novels, works of history, biographies, and books on various subjects about which he was enthusiastic. Richard Hannay returned in 1924 in *The Three Hostages*, in which Buchan proposed a justly celebrated "formula" for writing thrillers: take any three disparate objects or situations and proceed to demonstrate their relationship to one another. Retired to his country estate, Fosse Manor, Hannay has everything he could want, including a wife and son, Peter John, but he is frustrated by the lack of excitement in his peaceful life. Dr. Tom Greenslade, a neighbor, presents Hannay with the opportunity for adventure. Julius Victor, the richest man on earth, whose mission in life is to secure peace in the world, has learned his only daughter is being held hostage by his enemies—an underground group of anarchists. Two more people vanish: the heir to the greatest dukedom and the only child of a national hero. Six lines of verse sent to each of the families proves the abductions to be connected. Hannay takes up the challenge even though the search leads him to Norway, to the inner world of psychology, and finally to the highlands of Scotland. Ultimately the riddle is solved, and the tale climaxes in an old-fashioned chase scene.

The Buchan thriller for 1925 was *John Macnab*, a lighthearted, improbable, yet compelling account of a poaching expedition in the Highlands and its aftermath. The protagonists include Edward Leithen, last seen in the more serious venture, *The Power-House*. Accompanying him are John Palliser-Yeates and Charles Merkland, Lord Lamancha. All three are bored with their lives so their doctor, the great Acton Croke, suggests they add excitement to their existence. Their thrill seeking takes the form of poaching from three Scottish estates with letters announcing the intention of one "John Macnab" to take a stag or a salmon on the property specified within a specified time period, adding an extra element of risk to the venture. None of the three can afford to be caught at such a scheme, and the chase and evasive maneuvers on the part of each provide enough excitement to stave off boredom.

The next entry in Leithen's career was more in keeping with the serious-minded high adventure of *The Power-House. The Dancing Floor* (1926) is a haunting and complex novel in which old magic and a reenactment of Greek myth are made credible. Vernon Milburne, student at Oxford with Sir Edward Leithen's nephew, solicits the help of Leithen in determining the meaning of his annually recurring dream in which he finds himself in a suite of rooms, and each door he opens leads to yet another room. Each year a new door opens, and behind the final door is a fear which "transcend[s] word and thought" and symbolizes a tremendous experience he is to have. The knowledge that his destiny will not be revealed until the opening of the final door gives him extraordinary courage through World War I. The Vernon Milburne plot soon develops into another plot featuring Koré Arabin, mistress of the troubled Greek island of Plakos, who comes to England to forget that a tragedy awaits at home.

In the end there is no discovery of hidden treasure, no winning of great moral victories, but a granting of insight to Leithen. As critic David Daniell says, he "becomes an interpreter working out the significance of the central factors of the fear of evil in Vernon's dream and Koré's inheritance." The ancient world of the Greeks is replaced by a modern one in which the two young people find courage. The pagan rituals on the island are cleansed through a Christian epiphany of fire. Buchan was to mine a similar vein the following year with a historical novel, *Witch Wood* (1927). *Witch Wood* is a leisurely paced story of the survival of the witch's sabbath in the seventeenth century and what happens to the Reverend David Sempil when he discovers the true nature of his parishioners. The novel was the fictional result of Buchan's research for his biographies (1913, 1928) of the Scottish supporter of Charles I, James Graham, first Marquis of Montrose (1612-1650). In *Pilgrim's Way* Buchan writes of a time "when the rigours of the New Calvinism were contending with the ancient secret rites of Diana." The pagan rites in *Witch Wood* are described obliquely instead of in detail.

Dust jacket for Buchan's best-known novel (1915), inspired in part by Robert Louis Stevenson's Kidnapped *(1886)*

In 1927 Buchan was elected to Parliament representing the Scottish universities. He served in this capacity until 1935 when he was raised to the peerage as the first Baron Tweedsmuir and appointed Governor-General of Canada, a post he held until his death in 1940.

The Runagates Club, a collection of short fiction, is presented as if told by members of a London dining club, many of them protagonists of Buchan's thrillers: Hannay, Palliser-Yeates, Lord Lamancha, and Leithen. The tales are varied in theme–African witchcraft, the power of old magic, a wager between friends with comic results. "Sing a Song of Sixpence," a story of the attempted assassination of a South American president on the streets of London, appears in anthologies of modern spy stories.

In *The Courts of the Morning* (1929) Sandy Arbuthnot has a more dominant role than the one he played in *Greenmantle*. Hannay narrates the prologue in which Arbuthnot vanishes, then is seen disguised as a waiter in a South American café in Paris, and John S. Blenkiron, whose own obituary had been widely disseminated in the public press, sends Hannay a note to put his mind at ease. Such is the entry into the account of the doings of the companions in the Republic of Olifa, a country whose economic future is determined by its mineral resources and by Castor, its dictator. Archie Roylance and his bride, Janet, are honeymooning in Olifa when they meet Arbuthnot. Castor, he tells them, is no benevolent despot, but a megalomaniac whose new "power house" is plotting a great dictatorship. With the help of Blenkiron, Arbuthnot is determined to restore Olifa to its former free condition. Arbuthnot (El Lobo Gris) leads a band of commandos, this time into Olifa. Having discovered his better self, Castor dies with honor while saving Janet's life.

Castle Gay (1930) is the second of the Dickson McCunn trilogy, a humorous excursion into Ruritanian romance set in the imaginary central-European state of Evallonia, where republicans rival royalists. A kidnapped newspaper magnate, a prince, and suspicious foreigners all contribute to the novel's high adventure and romance. McCunn has the soul of a romantic but, being a plain Scotsman and a plain businessman, keeps his head throughout the critical moments.

In *The Gap in the Curtain* (1932) several people (including Leithen) are presented with the opportunity to glimpse a moment of time one year into the future. The fantastic part of the tale is told with such scientific plausibility that the results of the experiment in time seem equally plausible. The novel relates the effect this knowledge has on five lives. Leithen is distracted and does not see into his own future, but two of the others see their own obituaries. Businessman Arnold Tavenger's glimpse of an international merger actually costs him money, for he doesn't have the broad view; David Mayot sees the name of the new prime minister but loses his own seat in Parliament; Reginald Daker sees himself as a member of an expedition to Yucatan but not the reason for his trip; Sir Robert Goodeve and Captain Charles Ottery face knowledge of their own deaths with varying degrees of bravery. The worlds of finance and politics are particularly well depicted in this fine satire.

The House of the Four Winds (1935) rounds out the Dickson McCunn stories. McCunn, banished to Germany for his health by an Edinburgh specialist, encounters not only Dougal Crombie (formerly of the Gorbals Die-Hards, now a force

in journalism) but Prince John of Evallonia. His adventures include preventing a plot to overthrow the Evallonian monarchy as well as an encounter with Juventus, a nationalist youth movement, and serve to make him content to return to his fireside and travel only in the pages of his beloved books.

The last Richard Hannay adventure is *The Island of Sheep* (1936), published in the United States as *The Man from the Norlands*. Marius Eliaser Haraldsen, mining engineer and treasure-hunter–the "Man from the Norlands"–and his son call on Hannay for aid in combating an old enemy. A gang from London is after the Haraldsen fortune. Richard Hannay, Peter John Hannay, Archie Roylance, and Sandy Arbuthnot come to the rescue of Haraldsen, his son, and his daughter. Although Hannay is the narrator, his son shares much of the adventure and the danger. The climax of the novel, on the rocky cliffs of the Faroe Islands, is like something out of the Norse sagas and is as well written and vividly realized as anything Buchan had done before. It is dedicated to Buchan's oldest son, who shared young Peter John Hannay's interest in nature.

There is a special place in the Buchan canon for *Sick Heart River* (1941). As in *Mr. Standfast* there is the theme of the dying man performing one more noble deed. This last adventure of Leithen was completed just before its author's death, and there is an ironic parallel between the two. Leithen, going on a mission into the Canadian northwest, finds the man he seeks but, being himself ill, sacrifices his chance of recovery in working to save an Indian tribe from destruction. Buchan, too, sacrificed health and life to his iron sense of duty.

Critics continue to disagree about what makes Buchan so notable and what keeps him in print. Howard Swiggett claims the adventures to be prosaic but the characters to be memorable. Richard Usborne claims his plots are exciting while his characters (heroes and villains) are dull. There is tacit agreement that, unlike many writers of thrillers who depend largely on action for their effects, there is more beneath the surface with Buchan.

The Buchan hero is generally modest, almost too modest to be heroic, and part of his success is due to luck or coincidence. Success is also due to patience in waiting for the right moment to act. He is essentially an amateur and a more plausible figure than many heroes who are equipped with special abilities or talents. The talent of a Buchan hero is his common sense. This, plus the matter-of-fact, no-nonsense tone of Buchan's style, explains the high degree of plausibility surrounding even the most improbable events. The reader is drawn into the vortex of the situation along with the hero, neither one aware of what will happen next.

Bibliographies:
Archibald Hanna, Jr., *John Buchan, 1875-1940: A Bibliography* (Hamden, Conn.: Shoe String Press, 1953);

B. C. Wilmot, *A Checklist of Works By and About John Buchan in the John Buchan Collection, Douglas Library, Queen's University* (Boston: Hall, 1961);

J. Randolph Cox, "John Buchan, Lord Tweedsmuir: An Annotated Bibliography of Writings about Him," *English Literature in Transition*, 9, nos. 5-6 (1966): 241-325; 10, no. 4 (1967): 209-211; 15, no. 4 (1972): 67-69;

Robert G. Blanchard, *The First Editions of John Buchan* (Hamden, Conn.: Archon Books, 1981).

Biographies:
Anna Buchan, *Unforgettable Unforgotten* (London: Hodder & Stoughton, 1945);

Susan Tweedsmuir, *John Buchan by His Wife and Friends* (London: Hodder & Stoughton, 1947);

Arthur C. Turner, *Mr. Buchan, Writer* (London: SCM Press, 1949);

Janet Adam Smith, *John Buchan: A Biography* (London: Rupert Hart-Davis, 1965);

Smith, *John Buchan and his World* (London: Thames & Hudson, 1979; New York: Scribners, 1979);

William Buchan, *John Buchan: A Memoir* (London: Buchan & Enright, 1982).

References:
Barbara B. Brown, "John Buchan and Twentieth-Century Biography," *Biography*, 2 (Fall 1979): 328-341;

John Cawelti, "The Joys of Buchaneering," in *Essays in Honor of Russel B. Nye*, edited by Joseph Waldmeir (East Lansing: Michigan State University Press, 1978), pp. 7-30; reprinted in Cawelti and Bruce A. Rosenberg's *The Spy Story* (Chicago & London: University of Chicago Press, 1987), pp. 79-100;

J. Randolph Cox, "John Buchan: A Philosophy of High Adventure," *The Armchair Detective*, 2 (July 1969): 207-214;

David Daniell, Introduction to *The Best Short Stories of John Buchan*, 2 volumes, edited by Daniell (London: Joseph, 1980, 1982);

Daniell, *The Interpreter's House, A Critical Assessment of John Buchan* (London: Nelson, 1975);

Francis R. Hart, *The Scottish Novel from Smollett to Spark* (Cambridge: Harvard University Press, 1979), pp. 169-181;

Gertrude Himmelfarb, "John Buchan, an Untimely Appreciation," *Encounter*, 15 (September 1960): 46-53;

Gavin Lambert, *The Dangerous Edge* (London: Barrie & Jenkins, 1975), pp. 79-104;

M. R. Ridley, "A Misrated Author?," in his *Second Thoughts* (London: Dent, 1965), pp. 1-44;

Alan Sandison, *The Wheel of Empire: A Study of the Imperial Idea in Some Late Nineteenth and Early Twentieth-Century Fiction* (London: Macmillan, 1967; New York: St. Martin's Press, 1967), pp. 149-194;

Leland Schubert, "Almost Real Reality: John Buchan's Visible World," *Serif*, 2 (September 1965): 5-14;

Richard Usborne, *Clubland Heroes* (London: Constable, 1953), pp. 83-139.

Papers:
Buchan's manuscripts, correspondence, notebooks, and much of his private library (with the exception of popular fiction) are in the John Buchan Collection, Douglas Library, Queen's University, Kingston, Ontario; additional material is in the National Library of Scotland, Edinburgh; and in the Edinburgh University Library.

G. K. Chesterton

(29 May 1874-14 June 1936)

Thomas M. Leitch
University of Delaware

See also the Chesterton entries in *DLB 10, Modern British Dramatists, 1900-1945, DLB 19, British Poets, 1880-1914,* and *DLB 34, British Novelists, 1890-1929: Traditionalists.*

BOOKS: *Greybeards at Play: Literature and Art for Old Gentlemen, Rhymes and Sketches* (London: Johnson, 1900);

The Wild Knight and Other Poems (London: Richards, 1900; revised edition, London: Dent/ New York: Dutton, 1914);

The Defendant (London: Johnson, 1901; New York: Dodd, Mead, 1902);

Twelve Types (London: Humphreys, 1902); enlarged as *Varied Types* (New York: Dodd, Mead, 1903); abridged as *Five Types* (London: Humphreys, 1910; New York: Holt, 1911); also abridged as *Simplicity and Tolstoy* (London: Humphreys, 1912);

Robert Browning (New York & London: Macmillan, 1903);

G. F. Watts (London: Duckworth/New York: Dutton, 1904);

The Napoleon of Notting Hill (London & New York: John Lane/Bodley Head, 1904);

The Club of Queer Trades (London & New York: Harper, 1905);

Heretics (London & New York: John Lane/Bodley Head, 1905);

Charles Dickens (London: Methuen, 1906; New York: Dodd, Mead, 1906);

The Man Who Was Thursday (Bristol: Arrowsmith/ London: Simkin, Marshall, Hamilton, Kent, 1908; New York: Dodd, Mead, 1908);

All Things Considered (London: Methuen, 1908; New York: John Lane, 1908);

The Ball and the Cross (New York: John Lane, 1909; London: Gardner, Darton, 1910);

Orthodoxy (London: John Lane, Bodley Head/ New York: John Lane, 1909);

Tremendous Trifles (London: Methuen, 1909; New York: Dodd, Mead, 1909);

George Bernard Shaw (London: John Lane, Bodley Head/New York: John Lane, 1910);

G. K. Chesterton in 1935 (photograph by Howard Coster)

What's Wrong With the World (London, New York, Toronto & Melbourne: Cassell, 1910; New York: Dodd, Mead, 1910);

Alarms and Discussions (London: Methuen, 1910; enlarged edition, New York: Dodd, Mead, 1911);

William Blake (London: Duckworth/New York: Dutton, 1910);

Appreciations and Criticisms of the Works of Charles Dickens (London: Dent/New York: Dutton, 1911);

The Innocence of Father Brown (London, New York, Toronto & Melbourne: Cassell, 1911; New York: John Lane, 1911);

The Ballad of the White Horse (London: Methuen, 1911; New York: John Lane, 1911);

Manalive (London, Edinburgh, Dublin, Leeds, New York, Leipzig & Paris: Nelson, 1912; New York: John Lane, 1912);

A Miscellany of Men (London: Methuen, 1912; enlarged edition, New York: Dodd, Mead, 1912);

The Victorian Age in Literature (London: Williams & Norgate, 1913; New York: Holt, 1913);

Magic (London: Secker, 1913; New York & London: Putnam's, 1913);

The Flying Inn (London: Methuen, 1914; New York: John Lane, 1914); enlarged as *Wine, Water and Song* (London: Methuen, 1915);

The Wisdom of Father Brown (London, New York, Toronto & Melbourne: Cassell, 1914; New York: John Lane, 1915);

The Barbarism of Berlin (London, New York, Toronto & Melbourne: Cassell, 1914); republished as *The Appetite of Tyranny, Including Letters to an Old Garibaldian* (New York: Dodd, Mead, 1915);

Letters to an Old Garibaldian (London: Methuen, 1915); republished in *The Appetite of Tyranny, Including Letters to an Old Garibaldian* (New York: Dodd, Mead, 1915);

Poems (London: Burns & Oates, 1915; New York: John Lane, 1915);

The Crimes of England (London: Palmer & Hayward, 1915; New York: John Lane, 1916);

A Short History of England (London: Chatto & Windus, 1917; New York: John Lane, 1917);

Utopia of Usurers (New York: Boni & Liveright, 1917);

Irish Impressions (London, Glasgow, Melbourne & Auckland: Collins, 1919; New York: John Lane, 1920);

The Superstition of Divorce (London: Chatto & Windus, 1920; New York: Doran, 1920);

The Uses of Diversity (London: Methuen, 1920; New York: Dodd, Mead, 1921);

The New Jerusalem (London: Hodder & Stoughton, 1920; New York: Doran, 1921);

Eugenics and Other Evils (London, New York, Toronto & Melbourne: Cassell, 1922; New York: Dodd, Mead, 1927);

What I Saw in America (London: Hodder & Stoughton, 1922; New York: Dodd, Mead, 1922);

The Ballad of St. Barbara and Other Verses (London: Palmer, 1922; New York & London: Putnam's, 1923);

The Man Who Knew Too Much and Other Stories (London, New York, Toronto & Melbourne: Cassell, 1922; abridged edition, New York: Harper, 1922);

Fancies Versus Fads (London: Methuen, 1923; New York: Dodd, Mead, 1923);

St. Francis of Assisi (London: Hodder & Stoughton, 1923; New York: Doran, 1924);

Tales of the Long Bow (London, New York, Toronto & Melbourne: Cassell, 1925; New York: Dodd, Mead, 1925);

The Everlasting Man (London: Hodder & Stoughton, 1925; New York: Dodd, Mead, 1925);

William Cobbett (London: Hodder & Stoughton, 1925; New York: Dodd, Mead, 1926);

The Incredulity of Father Brown (London, New York, Toronto & Melbourne: Cassell, 1926; New York: Dodd, Mead, 1926);

The Outline of Sanity (London: Methuen, 1926; New York: Dodd, Mead, 1927);

The Queen of Seven Swords (London: Sheed & Ward, 1926);

The Catholic Church and Conversion (New York: Macmillan, 1926; London: Burns, Oates & Washbourne, 1927);

The Return of Don Quixote (London: Chatto & Windus, 1927; New York: Dodd, Mead, 1927);

The Collected Poems of G. K. Chesterton (London: Palmer, 1927; New York: Dodd, Mead, 1932; revised edition, London: Methuen, 1933; New York: Dodd, Mead, 1966);

The Secret of Father Brown (London, Toronto, Melbourne & Sydney: Cassell, 1927; New York & London: Harper, 1927);

The Judgement of Dr. Johnson; A Comedy in Three Acts (London: Sheed & Ward, 1927; New York & London: Putnam's, 1928);

Robert Louis Stevenson (London: Hodder & Stoughton, 1927; New York: Dodd, Mead, 1928);

Generally Speaking: A Book of Essays (London: Methuen, 1928; New York: Dodd, Mead, 1929);

The Poet and the Lunatics: Episodes in the Life of Gabriel Gale (London, Toronto, Melbourne & Sydney: Cassell, 1929; New York: Dodd, Mead, 1929);

The Thing (London: Sheed & Ward, 1929); republished as *The Thing; Why I Am a Catholic* (New York: Dodd, Mead, 1930);

G. K. C. as M. C., selected and edited by J. P. de Foneska (London: Methuen, 1929);

Four Faultless Felons (London, Toronto, Melbourne & Sydney: Cassell, 1930; New York: Dodd, Mead, 1930);

The Resurrection of Rome (London: Hodder & Stoughton, 1930; New York: Dodd, Mead, 1930);

Come to Think of It . . . (London: Methuen, 1930; New York: Dodd, Mead, 1931);

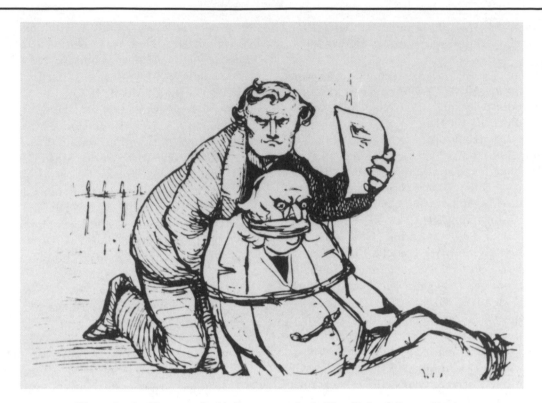

Illustration by Chesterton for his first mystery book, The Club of Queer Trades

All Is Grist: A Book of Essays (London: Methuen, 1931; New York: Dodd, Mead, 1932);

Chaucer (London: Faber & Faber, 1932; New York: Farrar & Rinehart, 1932);

Sidelights on New London and Newer York and Other Essays (London: Sheed & Ward, 1932);

All I Survey: A Book of Essays (London: Methuen, 1933; New York: Dodd, Mead, 1933);

St. Thomas Aquinas (London: Hodder & Stoughton, 1933; New York: Sheed & Ward, 1933);

Avowals and Denials: A Book of Essays (London: Methuen, 1934; New York: Dodd, Mead, 1935);

The Scandal of Father Brown (London, Toronto, Melbourne & Sydney: Cassell, 1935; New York: Dodd, Mead, 1935);

The Well and the Shallows (London: Sheed & Ward, 1935; New York: Sheed & Ward, 1935);

As I Was Saying (London: Methuen, 1936; New York: Dodd, Mead, 1936);

Autobiography (London: Hutchinson, 1936; New York: Sheed & Ward, 1936);

The Paradoxes of Mr. Pond (London, Toronto, Melbourne & Sydney: Cassell, 1937; New York: Dodd, Mead, 1937);

The Coloured Lands (London: Sheed & Ward, 1938; New York: Sheed & Ward, 1938);

The End of the Armistice (London: Sheed & Ward, 1940; New York: Sheed & Ward, 1940);

The Common Man, compiled by F. J. Sheed (London: Sheed & Ward, 1950; New York: Sheed & Ward, 1950);

The Surprise (London & New York: Sheed & Ward, 1952);

A Handful of Authors, edited by Dorothy Collins (London & New York: Sheed & Ward, 1953);

The Glass Walking-Stick and Other Essays from the Illustrated London News, 1905-1936, edited by Collins (London: Methuen, 1955);

Lunacy and Letters, edited by Collins (London & New York: Sheed & Ward, 1958);

Where All Roads Lead (London: Catholic Truth Society, 1961);

The Man Who Was Orthodox: A Selection from the Uncollected Writings of G. K. Chesterton, edited by A. L. Maycock (London: Dobson, 1963);

The Spice of Life and Other Essays, edited by Collins (Beaconsfield, U.K.: Finlayson, 1964; Philadelphia: Dufour, 1966);

Chesterton on Shakespeare, edited by Collins (Henley on Thames, Oxfordshire & Chester Springs, Pa.: Dufour, 1971);

The Apostle and the Wild Ducks, and Other Essays, edited by Collins (London: Elek, 1975);

GK's Weekly: A Sampler, edited by Lyle W. Dorsett (Chicago: Loyola University Press, 1986).

OTHER: *The Floating Admiral*, includes contributions by Chesterton, Victor Whitechurch, Dorothy Sayers, and others (London: Hodder & Stoughton, 1931; New York: Doubleday, Doran, 1932);

"Dr. Hyde, Detective, and the White Pillars Murder," in *To the Queen's Taste*, edited by Ellery Queen (Boston: Little, Brown, 1946), pp. 306-321.

Gilbert Keith Chesterton, journalist, essayist, master ideologue of religion and politics, and a seminal figure in the development of the modern detective story, was born on 29 May 1874 in Campden Hill, in the Kensington neighborhood of London. Chesterton's father, Edward Chesterton, was a Unitarian bourgeois whom his son memorialized in his posthumously published *Autobiography* (1936) for his devotion to his many hobbies; his mother, Marie Louise Grosjean Chesterton, had roots in French Switzerland but came from an Aberdeen family of Keiths. Chesterton was educated at Colet Court, St. Paul's School, and the Slade School of Art (1892-1895). Chesterton's clearest legacy from his parents, as his younger friend and biographer Maisie Ward has pointed out, is a sense of the romantic possibilities of the middle class. Chesterton himself observed in his study of Robert Browning that "it is in the middle classes that we find the poetry and genealogy; it is the suburban grocer standing at his shop door whom some wild dash of Eastern or Celtic blood may drive suddenly to a whole holiday or a crime." The whole range of Chesterton's work, including his detective fiction, may be described as an attempt to discover and dramatize the poetry, and indeed the melodrama, implicit in everyday middle-class life.

Chesterton developed slowly throughout his childhood and adolescence; he was an undistinguished student, whose master described him at fifteen as "a great blunderer with much intelligence." Though he attended lectures in English literature at University College during his tenure at Slade, Chesterton received no formal training in the writing which was to become his life's work. From his earliest school days, however, he had shown great interest and considerable aptitude in debating. The formation of the Junior Debating

Club at St. Paul's, a forum which constituted Chesterton's ideal model of friendship, confirmed his intimacy with several lifelong friends, including Lucian Oldershaw, who would later marry Chesterton's sister-in-law, and E. C. Bentley, who would join him in changing the face of the English detective story. Indeed all the most important relationships in Chesterton's life, including his childless marriage and his close attachments to children, seem to have been based on ideals of friendship.

In a chapter of the *Autobiography* entitled "How to Be a Lunatic," Chesterton recounts the spiritual crisis of his late adolescence in terms which recall the breakdown of J. S. Mill. The leading symptom of this crisis was an extreme skepticism which made him feel "an overpowering impulse to record or draw horrible ideas and images." Long after Chesterton's two-year period of skepticism and depression ended, he concluded of his dabblings in spiritualism that although in his experiments with a ouija board something had happened "which is not in the ordinary sense natural, or produced by the normal and conscious human will," and although he could not tell whether the effects produced could be attributed to subconscious or to external forces, he could say "with complete confidence, about that mystic and invisible power, . . . that it tells lies."

The acknowledgment of the possibility that otherworldly powers are either deceptive or ultimately nonexistent and the affirmation of rationality (the power to distinguish lies from truth as the hallmark of the healthy intellect) remain throughout in Chesterton's most characteristic fiction, which is shaped by an alternating rhythm in which reason is first challenged and then reaffirmed. As early as 1890 he had written that "the world is a story and every part of it," and all his writing (especially his detective stories) constantly proclaims that the world, despite frequent appearances to the contrary, makes sense. Chesterton therefore saw his task as the discovery and manifestation of the order implicit in the worlds of art, literature, philosophy, economics, and religion, rather than as the attempt to impose his personal sense of order on a world in flux. This position, which would have been unexceptionable for centuries, set Chesterton at odds with nearly all the leading intellectual figures of his day, and together with his personal habits–his theatrical dress and bearing; his notorious absent-mindedness (on one occasion he was forced to buy a copy of his own weekly newspaper in order

G. K. Chesterton, circa 1900

to remind himself of the location of his new office; on another he sent to his wife the immortal telegram: "Am in Market Harborough. Where ought I to be?"); his pride in his amateur status as philosopher, historian, and economist; his willingness to debate the most unlikely opponents on the most trivial subjects—gave him a reputation as a heroic crank.

Even before completing his studies at the Slade School, Chesterton (who had never persuaded himself or anyone else that he was preparing for a career as an artist) began to work as a book reviewer for the *Academy* and the *Bookman*, a monthly issued by the publishing firm of Hodder and Stoughton. Upon leaving the Slade School Chesterton went to work first at Redway's and later at Fisher Unwin. In the meantime, he had met and fallen in love with Frances Alice Blogg. After a long engagement they were married, despite the opposition of Chesterton's mother, on 28 June 1901.

Chesterton first came to prominence through his journalism as a result of his outspoken opposition to the Boer War in 1899. His first volumes of verse, *Greybeards at Play* and *The Wild Knight*, were published the following year, and the second collection was respectfully reviewed. Even so Chesterton continued in the popular imagination a journalist despite the hundred books he eventually published—largely perhaps because so many of his books were journalistic in subject and tone. As early as *The Defendant* (1901) Chesterton presented himself as a universal polemicist; in such later volumes as *What's Wrong with the World* (1910), *The Crimes of England* (1915), and *The Superstition of Divorce* (1920) he ventured repeatedly into politics and sociology. All of Chesterton's writing is fundamentally moralistic in impulse. The economic theory of distributism, for example, which plays so large a role in his story cycle *Tales of the Long Bow* (1925), is based on the theory that the English citizens' right to private property is being endangered by the increasing concentration of property in the hands of a small number of landowners. It is therefore fair to say that a polemical impulse underlies not only Chesterton's journalism but also the fiction for which he is best remembered today.

Chesterton himself drew a sharp distinction in his *Autobiography* between himself and "a real novelist" who would not have spoiled so many of Chesterton's promising ideas for novels: "I could not be a novelist; because I really like to see ideas or notions wrestling naked, as it were, and not dressed up as masquerade men and women. But I could be a journalist because I could not help being a controversialist." Speaking of his eschatological fantasy *The Napoleon of Notting Hill* (1904) Chesterton was even more succinct: "I have never taken my books seriously; but I take my opinions quite seriously."

The *Autobiography* itself offers striking evidence in support of this judgment. As a record of the principal events of Chesterton's life it is almost useless because Chesterton devotes so little attention to the people and events (for example, his wife and his books) presumably most important to the readers of a book about him. Chesterton's mind is resolutely unhistorical: he rarely dates particular events, organizes his material thematically rather than chronologically, and devotes far more space to his opinions than to their causes or effects. Throughout the *Autobiography*, Chesterton's fondness for moralizing the events of his life transforms the data of personal history into rhetorical exempla; each chapter is organized like an expository essay for which Chesterton's life is merely providing the premises. This tendency is equally clear in his studies of Robert Browning, Charles Dickens, Geoffrey Chaucer, and Thomas Aquinas; all are written with a serene conviction that accuracy of historical detail is less important than gnomic, often intuitive insight. Whether he is giving particulars of his life, debating the vices of colonialism, or, in his later years, defending the Catholic Church, Chesterton is always ready to leave behind particular circumstances in order to debate the moral and metaphysical (and so, for him, timeless) issues they raise.

Chesterton's fondness for debate and his tendency to moralize the events of history and indeed of his own life indicate the essentially antithetical nature of his imagination, its dependence on a universe governed by intelligible rules within which the mind would be free to play—a universe which, his adolescent crisis once

Frontispiece by Sidney Seymour Lucas for the first British edition of the second collection of Father Brown stories, The Wisdom of Father Brown

behind him, Chesterton never felt in danger of losing or misconstruing. His philosophy is therefore optimistic and positivistic, in accord with his sanguine temperament. Throughout his adult life, Chesterton was an extraordinarily friendly and cheerful man, whose "great ambition," as he wrote in 1896, was "to give a party at which everybody should meet everybody else and like them very much." He remained on cordial terms with a great number of his most cherished ideological enemies, a list which soon grew to include H. G. Wells, G. B. Shaw, and hundreds of lesser figures.

The antithetical cast of Chesterton's mind apparently found complete fulfillment in intellectual debate; his theatricality, which led him to treat the events of his life as grist for a series of characteristically brilliant apothegms and which affected a florid and fantastic style first in drawing and later in writing, demanded a stage whose conventions took the form of stable and immutable laws. Writing of the fear the English have of the unwritten law of libel, Chesterton observed: "This is the English way of maintaining a Terror.

The Latins, when they do it, do it by rigidity; but we actually do it by laxity. In plain words, we increase the terror of law, by adding to it all the terror of lawlessness. The machine is felt to be dangerous, not so much because it strikes by rule, as because it strikes at random."

It was perhaps inevitable that such a law-abiding controversialist and metaphysician of the press as Chesterton would eventually be attracted by Catholicism, and Chesterton ends the *Autobiography* with an explicit reference to the Church's account of divine law as the perfect expression of the law he had always sought as the source of life and freedom: "It was my instinct to defend liberty in small nations and poor families; that is, to defend the rights of man as including the rights of property; especially the property of the poor. I did not really understand what I meant by Liberty, until I heard it called by the new name of Human Dignity. It was a new name to me; though it was part of a creed nearly two thousand years old." In short, Chesterton, who had seemed from his early years to combine the disposition of a determined amateur, the imagination of a fantasist, and the temperament of a gadfly, was confirmed by the publication of *Heretics* (1905) and *Orthodoxy* (1909) as the most unexpectedly and aggressively orthodox of writers.

Chesterton's inveterate amateurism—there was no important current debate in morals, politics, religion, or political philosophy to which he did not turn his attention—has made his work a problem for literary historians. Despite the great quantity of his writing, Chesterton's pretensions as a mainstream writer are dismissed without mention by theorists of religion, sociology, economics, and literature. Instead he has remained a cult figure, an outsized personality whose interests were too diffuse to guarantee him mastery of any single area. Chesterton is less than a serious writer, critics agree; at the same time, he is more than a apologist for orthodoxy, more even than a journalist of genius. The one genre in which Chesterton's mastery remains unquestioned is that of the detective story, a genre whose aesthetic pretensions, appropriately enough, are even more modest than Chesterton's own. Chesterton made no secret of the fact that most of his detective stories were written in order to subsidize a series of weekly newspapers: the *Eye Witness*, later the *New Witness*, which he founded with his brother Cecil and Hilaire Belloc in 1911; and its successor *GK's Weekly*, which Chesterton edited from 1925 until his death on 14 June 1936. Never-

theless, as with Arthur Conan Doyle's stories about Sherlock Holmes, the ephemeral fiction has outlived the more ambitious project it was meant to support.

Virtually all of Chesterton's fiction, apart from millennial novels like *The Napoleon of Notting Hill* and satiric romances like *The Ball and the Cross* (1909), comprises detective stories of different sorts. Chesterton's marked originality in conceiving the structure and material of his detective stories makes it difficult to distinguish sharply between his formal detective stories and his other work; virtually all of his fiction contains such typical detective elements as the posing of a riddle and its logical solution; many of his stories have the structure of formal detective stories without the presence of a detective; and in his novel *The Man Who Was Thursday* (1908) detectives appear in wild profusion. Because detective and nondetective elements are combined so frequently, and in so many different ways, in Chesterton's fiction, a fair assessment of his contribution to the detective story depends on an appreciation of the relation between his detective fiction and his other fiction. All of Chesterton's novels and stories are essentially fantasies, allegories and anatomies of good and evil, humility and pride, concealment and revelation. All of them are extensions or dramatizations of Chesterton's favorite trope of paradox, in which a logical premise is used to demonstrate an apparently contradictory conclusion. Auberon Quin, the randomly chosen King of England in *The Napoleon of Notting Hill*, for example, rarely speaks except in paradoxes: "All ceremony consists in the reversal of the obvious," he says as he begins his rule by removing his coat and putting it on backwards; and each of Chesterton's other heroes talks or behaves in a way that seems nonsensical until the underlying paradox is elucidated.

Chesterton's dependence throughout his writing on paradox and antithesis as tools for educating his readers irritated readers like T. S. Eliot, who complained that Chesterton "seems always to assume that whatever his reader has previously believed is exactly the opposite of what Mr. Chesterton knows to be true." In his detective stories, however, Chesterton's paradoxical rhetoric operates not only in the service of a religious view of the world but, more immediately and more unexceptionably, as the rationale for his climactic reversals of plot. Throughout Chesterton's fiction the world is treated as a Book of Life whose mysteries, which take the form of appar-

Frances and G. K. Chesterton in 1922 (photograph by Alice Boughton)

ent logical contradictions, can be read with the aid of paradox, which reveals their solutions as the timeless apothegms of which Chesterton was so fond. The difference between the detective stories and the nondetective fantasies is primarily the presence of an expert paradox-reader, who is more often than not a paradox-monger, and who serves as mentor, guide, and scandal to the more active, less perceptive characters who are surrogates for the audience's own bewilderment.

Taken as a group, however, Chesterton's readers of paradoxical riddles are the most unlikely detectives imaginable. Except for Gabriel Syme, the police agent in *The Man Who Was Thursday*, none of them are professional detectives; and even Syme finds himself involved in an investigation outside his professional competence. Basil Grant, in *The Club of Queer Trades* (1905), a former judge who "suddenly went mad on the bench," is presented as "a star-gazer, a mystic, and a man who scarcely stirred out of his attic"—and, typically, the brother of a private detective. Horne Fisher, in *The Man Who Knew Too Much* (1922), the cousin and secretary of an important politician and friend of a rising journalist, is him-

self retiring and unworldly. Mr. Pond, in *The Paradoxes of Mr. Pond* (1937), is a faceless civil servant. Innocent Smith, in *Manalive* (1912), is a lunatic, and Gabriel Gale, in *The Poet and the Lunatics* (1929), is the keeper and companion of a lunatic. Chesterton did create one professional detective, Dr. Adrian Hyde, in the story "Dr. Hyde, Detective, and the White Pillars Murder" (1925), but here the real detection is performed by Hyde's young assistant Walter Weir, who has just joined Hyde's agency without any previous experience. Thus all Chesterton's detectives have a strong family resemblance to the most successful of them all, the moon-faced little Essex priest, Father Brown.

If Chesterton had not created Father Brown, his detective fiction would rarely be read today, but his place in the historical development of the genre would still be secure. Chesterton's impact on the structure of the detective story and his originality in ordering and recording its elements can scarcely be overestimated. More important he was the first habitual writer of detective stories (as against occasional practitioners like Dickens and Wilkie Collins) to insist on the conceptual unity of the form, a criterion he expounded at length in several essays on the subject. "The whole point of a sensational story," he writes in "On Detective Novels," in *Generally Speaking* (1928), "is that the secret should be simple. The whole story exists for the moment of surprise; and it should be a moment." A plot whose solution, however ingenious, cannot be summarized in a few words explaining the leading mystery (for example, "The Archdeacon is Bloody Bill") will depend on a purely mechanical interest, for it has no epigrammatic, conceptual strength, no rhetorical or dramatic authority of its own. Since "it is the business of a shocker to produce a shock," as Chesterton writes in "About Shockers," in *As I Was Saying* (1936), the best detective stories will lead to a revelation which does not simply confirm the audience's suspicions of one character or another but allows them to see the world of the story in a completely new way.

The secret of deceiving the audience therefore lies to a great extent in encouraging them to misinterpret the nature of the fictional world they are exploring, the relationships among the characters, and indeed the function of each individual character. In "How to Write a Detective Story," in *The Spice of Life* (1964), Chesterton contends that "a great part of the craft or trick of writing mystery stories consists in finding a con-

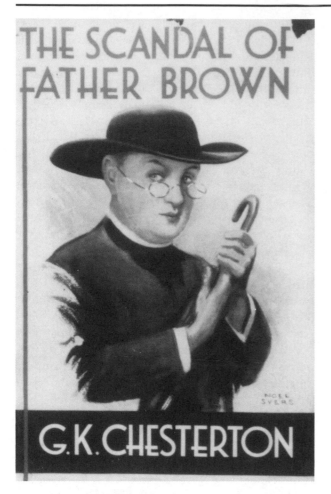

Dust jacket for the first British edition of the fifth, and last, collection of Father Brown stories. The drawing is by Noel Syers (courtesy of Otto Penzler).

vincing but misleading reason for the prominence of the criminal. . . . The art of narrative consists in convincing the reader for a time, not only that the character might have come on the premises with no intention to commit a felony, but that the author has put him there with some intention that is not felonious. For the detective story is only a game; and in that game the reader is not really wrestling with the criminal but with the author."

The audience's enjoyment of detective stories is based on the expectation that the author will observe the rules of the game because the point of a detective story is not so much mystification as revelation. In an essay, "On Political Secrecy," in *All Things Considered* (1908), Chesterton observes that "mystery stories are very popular . . . but that is because the author of a mystery story reveals. He is enjoyed not because he creates mystery, but because he destroys mystery. Nobody would have the courage to publish a

detective-story which left the problem exactly where it found it." The point of mystifying the audience is ultimately to enlighten them, just as "being an agnostic [is] the best and purest preparation for receiving the happy revelations of St. John," and the best detective stories are those which give their audience the climactic shock of seeing the world of the story in a completely new way, a way they have never suspected before. Chesterton argues in "About Shockers" that an author who multiplies suspicions by setting his story in the world of professional criminals or who attempts to distract attention from his criminal by apparently clearing him at the beginning of the story and then bringing in new evidence at the end has foregone the single most powerful effect of the detective story: the thrill of "finding out that men are worse or better than they seem, and that by their own choice. . . . There can never be quite so much excitement over the mere mechanical truth of how a man managed to do something difficult as over the mere fact that he wanted to do it." In sum, it is a mistake to suppose that "our interest in the plot is mechanical, when it is really moral."

In "A Defence of Detective Stories" (*The Defendant*, 1901), his earliest essay on the genre, Chesterton set forth two moral functions of the detective story. In the first place, "it is the earliest and only form of popular literature in which is expressed some sense of the poetry of modern life," especially of modern London. By "poetry" Chesterton means the capacity of the minutiae of reality to imply hidden meanings: "A city is, properly speaking, more poetic even than a countryside, for while Nature is a chaos of unconscious forces, a city is a chaos of conscious ones. The crest of the flower or the pattern of the lichen may or may not be significant symbols. But there is no stone in the street and no brick in the wall that is not actually a deliberate symbol—a message from some man, as much as if it were a telegram or a post-card." The capacity of the modern city simultaneously to assert and conceal symbolic meanings, Chesterton argues, has been exploited only by the detective story, which alone of all popular genres "declines to regard the present as prosaic or the common as commonplace" and so nourishes the audience's sense of wonder at their own world. The second function of the detective story is closely related: by focusing on the frontiers of the social order, "it tends to remind us that we live in an armed camp, making war with a chaotic world, and that the criminals, the children of chaos, are nothing but the traitors within our gates." The detective story suggests that "civilization itself is the most sensational of departures and the most romantic of rebellions" and that "morality is the most dark and daring of conspiracies. It reminds us that the whole noiseless and unnoticeable police management by which we are ruled is only a successful knight-errantry." Chesterton therefore concludes that "the romance of the police force is the whole romance of man."

Given this emphasis on the symbolic importance of the audience's progression from ignorance to enlightenment and on the figure of the detective, it is not surprising to find Chesterton insisting, in "The Domesticity of Detectives," in *The Uses of Diversity* (1920), that "the great detective story deals with small things; while the small or silly detective story deals with great things." A detective story whose setting is domestic and whose range of suspects and motives is limited will invoke the audience's own world, with all its unsuspected promise of mystery; a story dealing with international conspiracies and criminal masterminds will simply be understood as a romance of the otherworldly. The apparently ambitious scope of the international conspiracy genre actually serves to limit its symbolic efficacy, for the world it presents is too lawless and unbounded to serve as a figure for either the audience's domestic world or the world of God's creation. And it is clear throughout Chesterton's essays on detective fiction that for him the structure of the detective story, and the audience's experience in reading it as a progress from darkness to blinding light, is itself symbolic. He observes pointedly in "How to Write a Detective Story" that "the secret may appear complex, but it must be simple; and in this also it is a symbol of higher mysteries." The world's mystery, when the audience has finally understood it, will turn out to be based on a secret so simple that no one could have appreciated it.

Because the world of the detective story reflects in its initial concealment and ultimate revelation of a universal order the larger world as Chesterton conceives it, his decision to provide all the clues necessary for the audience to solve the mystery has more than procedural importance. In the detective stories of Edgar Allan Poe, Emile Gaboriau, and Conan Doyle the emphasis is on the detective's personality or his methods, not his competition with the reader to solve a mystery to which the author has presented all the clues. Sherlock Holmes is particularly given to picking up bright objects which Dr. Watson

and the reader only glimpse, or making inquiries about which the reader has no direct knowledge. The revelation of Jefferson Hope as the murderer in *A Study in Scarlet* (1888) is thus logically as well as dramatically unexpected. Fair play—the presentation of all evidence to the reader, who therefore has as good a chance as the detective to solve the mystery—does not become firmly established as a criterion of the detective story until *Trent's Last Case* (1913), by Chesterton's great friend E. C. Bentley, and Chesterton's Father Brown stories, the first of which appeared three years earlier. For Chesterton, writing to demonstrate not only the romance of the ordinary but also the accessibility of its secrets to every reader, fair and detailed clueing has philosophical implications: a reader who is given the opportunity to discover the secret of a detective story is thereby offered a model for perceiving the world of God's reason.

Chesterton's determination to provide his audience with all the clues available to his detectives has been so widely imitated as to become the defining characteristic of the formal or golden age period (roughly 1920-1940) in detective fiction. His other principal innovation in the form of the detective story, however, has been far less influential: the variation, from volume to volume and sometimes from story to story, of what secret is hidden from the audience. Modern readers, for whom the term *whodunit* has become synonymous with *detective story*, forget that the concealment of the criminal's identity as the central mystery of the story is a relatively modern convention: in Poe's story "The Purloined Letter" (1845) and in Conan Doyle's "A Scandal in Bohemia" (1892), the culprit is known from the beginning, and the interest lies in the battle of wits between the detective and his quarry. Chesterton's Father Brown stories, many of which present murder puzzles in which the murderer's identity constitutes the climactic revelation, are the most orthodox of his stories in the context of the succeeding golden age, whose conventions they so largely established. In his other stories, however, Chesterton's mysteries are much more original in construction—so much so, in fact, that several volumes constitute nonrepeated experiments. Chesterton's stories characteristically present a nonsensical series of events which may or may not involve crime but which are understood in the light of a single conceptual revelation. *The Club of Queer Trades*, as its title suggests, presents a series of stories each of which involves someone who has in-

Chesterton, Prof. William Lyon Phelps, and George Russell at Phelps's home in New Haven, 1931, during Chesterton's second visit to the United States

vented a completely new method of making money, a method whose effects create the story's mystery and whose identification its conclusion. In "The Awful Reason of the Vicar's Visit," for example, the narrator Swinburne, as he is dressing for a dinner party given by a female friend of his acquaintance for a Captain Fraser, is interrupted by a Rev. Ellis Shorter, who tells him an incredible tale of impersonation and kidnapping. Hours later, when the vicar has finished his story and Swinburne has missed his party, he takes the old man to Basil Grant, who produces a duplicate vicar who has been telling him a similar story and explains that both of them work as Professional Detainers, "paid by [their] clients to detain in conversation, on some harmless pretext, people whom they want out of the way for a few hours." In this case Captain Fraser had hired two such Detainers, in their most expensive impersonations as clergymen, to prevent his fellow guests at dinner from interrupting his last dinner with the lady who had invited them all.

Chesterton's other collections are less whimsically original than *The Club of Queer Trades* but more pointedly symbolic in their mysteries. The

four parts of *Four Faultless Felons* (1930) present a Moderate Murderer, an Honest Quack, an Ecstatic Thief, and a Loyal Traitor; it is the task of each part to explain the paradoxes of these titles, and to demonstrate how apparently criminal actions can be inspired by the most ardent love for others. *Manalive*, seldom considered a detective story, expands the structure of *Four Faultless Felons* to novel length. Its first part presents the evidence for considering Innocent Smith a criminal lunatic; its second part reveals the circumstances behind his apparent crimes of assault, burglary, and polygamy and demonstrates that he is far more sane than his accusers and that all his alleged crimes have been the means of making himself and other people more keenly alive. The stories in *Tales of the Long Bow* take the form of riddles, each of which is resolved as the attempt to literalize a cliché (for example, Colonel Crane wears a cabbage on his head in preparation for fulfilling his promise to eat his hat); the stories in *The Paradoxes of Mr. Pond* are extended glosses on the paradoxes which introduce them (for example, "I did know two men who came to agree so completely that one of them naturally murdered

Chesterton at a BBC microphone delivering one of his radio talks, the first of which was broadcast in 1932 (courtesy of the British Broadcasting Corporation)

the other"). What the stories conceal in each case, whether or not there are any allegations of lawbreaking, is the logical principle which will explain the paradoxes of an agent or a world which has apparently lost its reason, and the effect of each story is based on the audience's faith that, however absurd the world may appear, it is not only reasonable, but its reason may be grasped in the revelation of an instant.

Chesterton's pronounced fondness for organizing his stories each around a single paradox naturally inclined him toward the short detective story rather than the novel. In "On Detective Novels" he went so far as to rule that "the *roman policier* should be on the model of the short story rather than the novel," because, since "the detective story is, after all, a drama of masks and not of faces," it follows that "the author cannot tell us until the last chapter any of the most interesting things about the most interesting people. . . . We cannot really get at the psychology and philosophy, the morals and the religion, of the thing until we have read the last chapter." Chesterton's

few novels, whether or not they are dominated by detective elements, are episodic, structured most often by repetitions of the same events (the battles in *The Napoleon of Notting Hill*, the aborted duels in *The Return of Don Quixote*, 1927, the unmaskings of the police agents in *The Man Who Was Thursday*). Nonetheless, if Chesterton is a short-story writer rather than a novelist, his volumes of stories themselves incorporate lines of progression which give the final story a climactic force. *The Club of Queer Trades* ends with a story showing Basil Grant's own unique profession as a private judge of morals and establishing his status as president of the club. *The Poet and the Lunatics* ends with the revelation that a putative madhouse is actually an asylum for a gang of criminals masquerading as madmen. *The Man Who Knew Too Much* ends with two stories which present first Horne Fisher's brother and then Fisher himself as criminals. In fact, so many of Chesterton's detectives turn out to be criminals that the relation between the two is an intimacy amounting virtually to identity.

73

The intimacy between detective and criminal is the paradox at the heart of Chesterton's best-loved detective, Father Brown. In the last chapter of his autobiography, Chesterton describes the inception of Father Brown as the moment in which he realized that his friend Father John O'Connor, who would receive him into the Catholic Church in 1922, knew far more about the "perverted practices" of evil and crime than the worldly young men who condescendingly dismissed his cloistered way of life. The Father Brown stories, Chesterton decided, would be "a comedy in which a priest should appear to know nothing and in fact know more about crime than the criminals." Accordingly, Father Brown was made the most inconsequential detective in fiction, stumpy, clumsy–he is continually misplacing his umbrella–with "a face as round and dull as a Norfolk dumpling" and a habit of falling asleep during police interrogations. Unlike Sherlock Holmes, Father Brown is much less interesting and even less definitely established than the riddles he investigates. He has no first name or fixed abode; he has no personal habits apart from an absentmindedness presumably based on Chesterton's own and a cryptically paradoxical way of talking; and he is introduced as a minor character in almost every story in which he appears. ("The Hammer of God" contains a typical introduction: "In the yard of the smithy were standing five or six men, mostly in black, one in an inspector's uniform. They included the doctor, the Presbyterian minister, and the priest from the Roman Catholic chapel to which the blacksmith's wife belonged.") The stories are never told from the priest's point of view, nor do they present his thoughts except through his speech.

Nevertheless Father Brown dominates his stories, though in a peculiar way. Chesterton's villains, who, taken as a group, are much more personable than Father Brown, are seldom unsympathetic, and it might seem that Chesterton had failed in his attempt to present the priest's grasp of evil when the evildoers he confronts seem so often attractive. In the Father Brown stories, however, the imaginative failure of evil lies precisely in its unoriginality, its lack of an independent motivating principle. Chesterton's criminals are lovers, avengers, impostors, and thieves who nearly always have plausible explanations for their crimes; they are less often monsters of evil than sinners ripe for conversion, and Father Brown is less interested in proving their guilt than in hearing their confession. Father Brown often sur-

prises the other characters with revelations of the *victim*'s hidden sins (as in "The Sign of the Broken Sword," "The Three Tools of Death," and "The Arrow of Heaven"–a technique which Bentley also adopts in *Trent's Last Case*). He often reveals innocent secrets, as in "The Absence of Mr. Glass," or in "The Duel of Dr. Hirsch" (a story evidently inspired by the whimsical suggestion, in a 1909 letter to the *Bystander*, that Bernard Shaw and Chesterton were so completely antithetical to each other that they must be the same person). Father Brown also discovers unexpected goodness– the servant's mysterious code of honor in "The Honour of Israel Gow," and the dreadful love inspiring the manifestations of "The Insoluble Problem." The true mystery in the Father Brown stories is the mystery of goodness, so much more profound than that of evil, which appears in these stories as its mere counterfeit–a mystery represented most pointedly by the figure of Father Brown himself.

The intimate relation between good and evil is nowhere more economically illustrated than in the relationships between Chesterton's detectives and the criminals they pursue. Horne Fisher, the man who knew too much, begins by identifying particular criminals and ends by indicting the class and property structure of English society. Innocent Smith is universally considered a lunatic. Gabriel Gale, who first appears mad, is the companion of madmen, and who ends by exposing an asylum as a nest of sane criminals. Father Brown is a successful detective primarily because his own personality is not too strong to allow him to assume, for the purposes of his calling, the personality of the criminals he seeks. As he tells Grandison Chace in "The Secret of Father Brown" (1927), "It was I who killed all those people. . . . I had thought out exactly how a thing like that could be done, and in what style or state of mind a man could really do it. And when I was quite sure that I felt exactly like the murderer myself, of course I knew who it was. . . . I thought and thought about how a man might come to be like that, until I realized that I really *was* like that, in everything except final consent to the action." In the first of the Father Brown stories, "The Blue Cross," Chesterton's moral categories seem unequivocal: the detective is Valentin, the criminal is Flambeau, and the victim of the theft is Father Brown. By the end of the story, however, Father Brown turns out to be Flambeau's nemesis rather than his victim. Valentin returns in the following story, "The Se-

Alec Guiness (left) as Father Brown in the 1954 Columbia Pictures film The Detective, *based in part on Chesterton's story "The Blue Cross"*

cret Garden," only to be identified as the criminal; and by the fifth story, "The Invisible Man," Flambeau has reformed and become, like so many of Chesterton's Watson figures, a private detective. As in the other stories, the line between detective and criminal is not only thin but frequently crossed.

Despite its deceptiveness in presenting Valentin and Flambeau, "The Blue Cross" does establish many of the themes and conventions for the fifty Father Brown stories which follow. The most important of these is the power of human reason to explain the mysteries of the world. The story begins with Valentin, head of the Paris police, arriving in London in order to arrest Flambeau, a criminal of gargantuan height and imagination. Because Valentin has no clues to Flambeau's exact plans or whereabouts, he proceeds to follow a trail of curious circumstances which have no rationale—and no clear connection with Flambeau. When he stops in a restaurant and finds salt in the sugar bowl and sugar in the salt shaker, he follows the trail of the two clergymen who had last eaten there. This trail leads him to a greengrocer's, where placards have

been exchanged and a cart of apples overturned; to another restaurant, where one of the two priests paid three times too much for their bill and then broke a window; and finally to a confectioner's, where the same priest left a parcel to be posted. Since "Valentin could not follow the train of the reasonable, he coldly and carefully followed the train of the unreasonable," trusting that "we must either follow one wild possibility or else go home to bed." When he overtakes the two clerics, they are sitting on a secluded hill in Hampstead Heath discussing whether reason is a supreme principle of the divine order. The taller of them suggests that "other worlds may perhaps rise higher than our reason," but the short priest asserts that "reason is always reasonable" because "God Himself is bound by reason." When the tall priest reveals himself as Flambeau, in search of a jeweled cross the other is carrying, the short priest, Father Brown, replies that he has already left the cross behind to be posted and that he has spent all day behaving unreasonably in order to attract the attention of Valentin, whose mind, like his own, he knows will insist on rational explanations for his behavior. In effect, Father Brown has substituted for Flambeau's intended theft a detective story, complete with striking and baffling clues, for the benefit of the policeman who earlier observed: "The criminal is the creative artist; the detective only the critic." The climactic paradox of the story, that Father Brown, like Chesterton's friend Father O'Connor, has a much more profound grasp of evil than the criminal who thinks himself evil, is prepared by the paradox of its structure, which, by posing a series of unreasonable tableaux whose logical explanation is their very unreasonableness, suggests that reason itself is more profound and wonderful than the most bewildering mystery.

The reasonableness of apparently unreasonable things is the revelation at the heart of "The Blue Cross." As in a number of the Father Brown stories, the identity of the criminal is known from the outset: Valentin, following the two clerics to Hampstead Heath, feels that "he had grasped the criminal, but still he could not grasp the clue." In the stories which follow, such circumstantial mysteries are often heightened by Father Brown's teasingly paradoxical hints at the solution. When Dr. Simon asks how the unknown victim in "The Secret Garden" entered the locked garden, Father Brown denies that there ever was a strange man in the garden. "He hadn't got into the garden, I suppose?" asks a servant. "Not entirely," the priest observes. To Dr. Simon's impatient remark that "A man gets into a garden, or he doesn't," Father Brown replies, "Not necessarily." Exchanges like this one–there is one such conversation in nearly every story–crystallize the mystery by presenting it in its most paradoxical form while making Father Brown thoroughly exasperating to his fellow characters; indeed he is the only fictional detective whose explanations invariably begin by making the mystery sound even stranger, for nearly every Father Brown story turns on a moment when what the priest himself calls "perhaps the worst thing that can fall on [men]" happens: "We have found the truth; and the truth makes no sense." The drama of the Father Brown stories lies in the detective's attempt, and the reader's, both guided by their faith in reason, to make sense of the truth.

The Innocence of Father Brown (1911), Chesterton's first collection of Father Brown stories, presents twelve stories divided about equally between what would soon become known as whodunits (of which "The Secret Garden," "The Hammer of God," and "The Eye of Apollo" are exemplary) and stories like "The Blue Cross" in

which the leading question posed does not concern the identity of a criminal. Stories like "The Queer Feet," "The Honour of Israel Gow," and "The Sign of the Broken Sword" pose mysteries which are not fundamentally mysteries of the perpetrator's identity. The greater number of such stories are in *The Innocence of Father Brown* and its immediate successor, *The Wisdom of Father Brown* (1914). Beginning with *The Incredulity of Father Brown* (1926) and continuing through *The Secret of Father Brown* (1927) and *The Scandal of Father Brown* (1935), stories of the whodunit variety predominate as Chesterton's structures become more conventional. Many of these later stories–"The Man in the Passage," "The Arrow of Heaven," "The Miracle of Moon Crescent," "The Ghost of Gideon Wise," "The Mirror of the Magistrate"– are models of golden age construction. The nonwhodunits, however, are more original and characteristic.

A quintessential example of Chesterton's skill in setting forth a mystery at once bewildering, misleading, and thematically portentous is his early story "The Sins of Prince Saradine," in which Flambeau and Father Brown, traveling on holiday, visit Prince Saradine, an Italian exile living on a secluded island in the Norfolk Broads in hiding from the son of a man he had killed long ago. Reed Island, which Flambeau compares to fairyland, seems insubstantial, alluring, and deceptive, and the prince's home, a crystal palace full of mirrors and old photographs, seems to turn the characters into images of themselves and each other. Father Brown, observing that "we have taken a wrong turning and come to a wrong place," explains: "We here are on the wrong side of the tapestry. . . . The things that happen here do not seem to mean anything; they mean something somewhere else." The avenger the prince had been fleeing vindicates Father Brown's intimations of Doomsday by arriving with the announcement, "This is the end of the world–and of you," and killing the prince in a duel, but the priest still feels as if "he had not seen the real story, but only some game or masque" and tells Flambeau: "I, for one, don't know whether I'm in this world or the next." The climactic revelation about the import of the duel and the true nature of Prince Saradine is given an eschatological resonance: Reed Island is presented as a geographical figure for the end of the world, and the final explanation places Father Brown and his audience for the first time on the right side of the tapestry. More explicitly than Chesterton's other

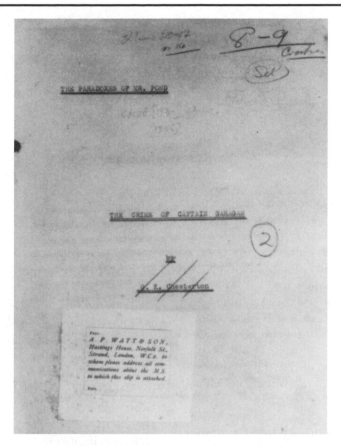

Cover sheet for the agent's typescript of the second story in Chesterton's posthumously published collection The Paradoxes of Mr. Pond *(Biblioasis Two [Idyllwild, Cal.: A. Hime, 1981])*

stories, "The Sins of Prince Saradine" takes the process of detection, whereby mysteries are resolved and sins revealed in the light of right reason, as a metaphor for the second coming. Each of the Father Brown stories implicitly presents a movement from worldly confusion to the dazzling clarity of apocalypse, a movement which is thematically central to all Chesterton's work.

Such a movement could of course be imputed to any detective story, but Chesterton alone among notable writers of detective fiction makes his apocalyptic scheme explicit, not only in "The Sins of Prince Saradine" and other Father Brown stories but in his masterpiece, *The Man Who Was Thursday*, the world's only eschatological detective novel. *The Man Who Was Thursday* concerns a group of anarchists ruled by a council of seven men named after days of the week. Gabriel Syme, a police detective who has penetrated the council, offers himself for election to the vacant post of Thursday and speaks so much more violently than his opponent, the real anarchist, that he is elected. Thereafter Syme goes in fear of his fellow council members, but as he plots against

them, they reveal themselves, one by one, all to be members of the police–all, that is, except the fearsome and enigmatic Sunday, the council's president. As in Chesterton's other novels, the plot develops by means of a series of formulaic repetitions; and as in his other detective stories, the mystery of evil, which takes the form of lawlessness and chaos, is only a mask for the mystery of goodness. Every one of the chief anarchists is a spy for the powers of the moral order: even Sunday, after staging a climactic pageant clearly based on the allegorical pageant which concludes Dante's *Purgatorio*, speaks to Syme in the voice of Christ. When Syme realizes that the elegiac farce of the anarchists' council has been staged solely in order to make romance and adventure available to the most law-abiding citizens, "so that each man fighting for order may be as brave and good a man as the dynamiter," he concludes that because of the detectives' fears of each other, "We have been broken upon the wheel.... We have descended into hell," and asks Sunday, who has deceived them all, "Have you ever suffered?" Sunday's answer, which seems to end Syme's vision and return him to the everyday world of London, is, "Can ye drink of the cup that I drink of ?" Detectives who follow the path from the muddle of the commonplace to the dazzling clarity of moral revelation are here, as in Chesterton's other fiction, the true modern imitators of Christ.

Long before he published his last Father Brown stories, Chesterton was widely regarded as the father of the modern English detective story. When Anthony Berkeley founded the Detection Club in 1928, it was Chesterton, not Conan Doyle, who became its first president and served in this capacity until his death. When Chesterton wrote a prologue for *The Floating Admiral* (1931), a detective novel to which each member of the club contributed a new chapter and a solution to the mystery so far, he was privileged, unlike all the other contributors except for Berkeley himself, to read the complete manuscript before writing his own chapter.

Chesterton's influence on later detective fiction has manifested itself in several ways. With E. C. Bentley, he decisively turned the emphasis of the detective story away from heroic glorification of the detective's personality toward the engagement of the audience in a fairly clued puzzle. More specifically his fondness for allegory and Christian apologetics influenced the satiric detective stories of Ronald Knox; Margery Allingham's novel about the mystery of evil and the deeper mystery of good, *The Tiger in the Smoke*; and the revelatory structure of *The Nine Tailors* and other novels by Dorothy L. Sayers, who acknowledged Chesterton's formative influence on her own work in her preface to his play *The Surprise* (1952). Chesterton's proclivity for invoking supernatural forces for mysteries which would ultimately be solved by natural and logical means clearly inspired a similar tendency in the work of John Dickson Carr, who modeled his detective Dr. Gideon Fell on Chesterton himself because he wished to create a detective whom everyone would like. Perhaps Chesterton's most interesting influence was on the Argentine short-story writer Jorge Luis Borges, who repeatedly cited Chesterton as one of his masters. Like Chesterton, Borges has concentrated on the shorter fictional forms; like Chesterton, he has written several formal detective stories and many more stories containing detective elements. Borges's riddles and labyrinths have different metaphysical overtones from Chesterton's but carry an equally explicit suggestion that detective work is a metaphor for the modern experience of the world. His Babylonian lottery and library of Babel are very much like agnostic versions of Chesterton's council of anarchists and Book of Life. If Borges's world assigns to language and fiction a far more ambitious role than Chesterton's, the difference between the two accurately reflects the difference between the constitutive power of words–which comprise the ultimate reality of Borges's fictions– and the redemptive power of the Word–which manifests in all Chesterton's work a reality beyond all telling.

Chesterton's influence on later detective fiction has been considerable, but his true legacy is his body of work apart from its direct influence on later writers. Unlike writers like Agatha Christie and Ellery Queen, whose mastery of the conventions of the detective story create a form to be valued in and of itself, Chesterton always, and unabashedly, used the structure and figures of detective fiction as a vehicle for dramatizing a moral and eschatological view of the world. Critics who denigrate Chesterton's achievement because of his impure motives in writing fail to realize that the concepts–reason, mystery, innocence, evil, inversion, paradox, recognition–for which his stories create metaphors are the essential concepts of detective fiction, and that his figures–the foolish or criminal or lunatic detective, the assistant handicapped by worldliness, the mysterious secret which can be summarized in a single breathless paradox–not only dramatize the conflict of reason and the unreasonable but illuminate the salient conventions of literary detection. Chesterton's work provided the detective story with a structural and thematic integrity approached before only in Wilkie Collins's *The Moonstone* (1868) and never since surpassed.

Bibliographies:

John Sullivan, *G. K. Chesterton: A Bibliography* (London: University of London Press, 1958);

Sullivan, *Chesterton Continued: A Bibliographical Supplement* (London: University of London Press, 1968).

Biographies:

W. R. Titterton, *G. K. Chesterton: A Portrait* (London: Organ, 1936);

Maisie Ward, *Gilbert Keith Chesterton* (New York: Sheed & Ward, 1943);

Dudley Barker, *G. K. Chesterton: A Biography* (New York: Stein & Day, 1973);

Alzina Stone Dale, *The Outline of Sanity: A Life of G. K. Chesterton* (Grand Rapids: Eerdmans, 1982).

References:

Hilaire Belloc, *The Place of Gilbert Chesterton in English Letters* (London & New York: Sheed & Ward, 1940);

Anthony Mattheus Adrianus Bogaerts, *Chesterton and the Victorian Age* (Hilversum: Rozenbeek en Venemans, 1940);

Ian Boyd, *The Novels of G. K. Chesterton: A Study in Art and Propaganda* (New York: Barnes & Noble, 1975);

Margaret Canovan, *G. K. Chesterton: Radical Populist* (New York & London: Harcourt Brace Jovanovich, 1977);

Sister M. Carol, *G. K. Chesterton: The Dynamic Classicist* (Delhi: Motilal Banarsidass, 1971);

Cecil Chesterton, *Gilbert K. Chesterton: A Criticism* (London & New York: John Lane, 1909);

Chesterton Review (Thomas More College, Saskatoon) (Fall/Winter 1974-   );

Cyril Clemens, *Chesterton as Seen by His Contemporaries* (Webster Groves, Mo.: Mark Twain Society, 1939);

Lawrence J. Clipper, *G. K. Chesterton* (New York: Twayne, 1974);

John Coates, *Chesterton and the Edwardian Cultural Crisis* (Hull: Hull University Press, 1984);

D. J. Conlon, ed., *G. K. Chesterton: A Half Century of Views* (Oxford & New York: Oxford University Press, 1987);

Conlon, ed., *G. K. Chesterton: The Critical Judgments, Part I: 1900-1937* (Antwerp: Antwerp Studies in English Literature, 1976);

Christopher Hollis, *The Mind of Chesterton* (London: Hollis & Carter, 1970);

Lynette Hunter, *G. K. Chesterton: Explorations in Allegory* (New York: St. Martin's, 1979);

Hugh Kenner, *Paradox in Chesterton* (New York: Sheed & Ward, 1947);

John O'Connor, *Father Brown on Chesterton* (London: Muller/Burns, Oates, 1937);

Rufus William Rauch, *A Chesterton Celebration* (Notre Dame: Notre Dame University Press, 1983);

Joseph W. Sprug, ed., *An Index to G. K. Chesterton* (Washington: Catholic University of America Press, 1966).

Papers:

The largest collection of Chesterton's papers is held in the Robert John Bayer Memorial Chesterton Collection at the John Carroll University Library, Cleveland, Ohio. Other materials are held at Columbia University, Marquette University, and the British Library.

Erskine Childers

(25 June 1870-24 November 1922)

Gareth W. Dunleavy

University of Wisconsin-Milwaukee

BOOKS: *In the Ranks of the C.I.V.* (London: Smith, Elder, 1900);

The H.A.C. in South Africa, by Childers and Basil Williams (London: Smith, Elder, 1903);

The Riddle of the Sands, A Record of Secret Service Recently Achieved. Edited by Erskine Childers (London: Smith, Elder, 1903; New York: Dodd, Mead, 1915);

War and the Arme Blanche (London: Arnold, 1910);

The Framework of Home Rule (London: Arnold, 1911);

German Influence on British Calvary (London: Arnold, 1911).

OTHER: *The Times History of the War in South Africa*, volume 5, edited by Childers (London: Low, Marston, 1907).

Erskine Childers intended *The Riddle of the Sands* (1903) to be a warning, in the guise of a light adventure story, about England's vulnerability to invasion by sea. Today it is viewed by many as the first important British spy novel, a genre that runs from Childers to John Le Carré. Its steady popularity is reflected in numerous reprintings, including translation into French, American republication (1976), and a British film version (1979).

Robert Erskine Childers was born in London on 25 June 1870, the son of Anna Mary Henrietta Barton Childers and Robert Caesar Childers, the famous Orientalist. On the death of his father from consumption in 1876, Childers was sent from England to live with relatives at Glendalough House, County Wicklow, Ireland. He seemed destined to enjoy the privileged life of an Anglo-Irish gentleman. Educated at Haileybury and Trinity College, Cambridge, he became a clerk in the House of Commons and spent weekends indulging his craving for adventure and love of the sea with solitary sails in the Thames estuary. In the summer of 1897 he made the first of six cruises along the Dutch, German, and Danish coasts and in the North Sea that provided intimate knowledge of the Frisian Islands, the setting for *The Riddle of the Sands*.

He was among the first to join the City Imperial Volunteers for the Boer War. *In the Ranks of the C.I.V.* (1900), his first published book, was the personal record of his experiences. He coauthored, with Basil Williams, the official history of his company, *The H.A.C. in South Africa* (1903), and edited volume five of *The Times History of the War in South Africa* (1907). He also wrote *War and the Arme Blanche* (1910) and *German Influence on British Calvary* (1911), two books arguing for modern weapons and training.

He began writing *The Riddle of the Sands* in the winter of 1901. In September 1903 on a visit

Erskine Childers, circa 1903

Childers in 1899. He was among the first to join the City Imperial Volunteers for service in the Boer War (courtesy of BBC Hulton).

to Massachusetts he met Mary Alden (Molly) Osgood. They were married in Boston on 5 January 1904 and returned to England. The couple had two sons, Robert and Erskine (elected president of Ireland in 1973).

Although of a unionist family, Childers came back from the Boer War with inclinations toward home rule for Ireland. His argument for this position, *The Framework of Home Rule*, was published in 1911. In July 1914 after passage of Herbert Asquith's home rule bill and the subsequent arming of the Ulster Volunteers, Childers and his wife ran their yacht, the *Asgard*, laden with Mauser rifles and ammunition, from Hamburg into Howth Harbor north of Dublin and delivered to waiting Irish Volunteers arms that were used in the 1916 Rising of Easter. After distinguished service in the British Army in World War I, Childers returned to Ireland to become immersed in the cause of Irish independence. A member of the Irish Treaty delegation to London in 1921, he renounced the treaty establishing the separation of Ireland into north and south and sided with Eamon de Valera in the civil war. He was captured by Free State soldiers and condemned to death. Robert Erskine Childers died on 24 Novem-

ber 1922 before a Free State firing squad in Dublin after he had shaken hands with his executioners and asked them to step closer.

In *The Riddle of the Sands* Childers places at nautical play in the Baltic, North Sea, and Frisian Sands two Oxonians, Carruthers and Davies. A deadly game ensues in which they uncover a sinister scheme that threatens the security of England. Carruthers, a snobbish, self-absorbed Foreign Office dandy, affects ennui with duties that leave him alone in an empty London in September to move in a dignified rut between club and chambers. With lofty condescension, for he regards Davies as an indifferent dresser and eccentric, boring nonentity, he accepts an invitation to join him on his *Dulcibella*, ostensibly to sail and shoot ducks in the Baltic.

Carruthers's kit contains "two faultless pairs of white flannels" when he boards the seven-ton, thirty-foot, flat-bottomed craft that offers, instead of the "creamy purity of Cowes," the reek of "paraffin, past cookery, tobacco and tar" and impossibly cramped and grimy quarters. Despite discomfort Carruthers comes to respect Davies, "a sun-burnt, brine-burnt zealot who draws inspiration from the wind and spray" and who "com-

Molly and Erskine Childers in 1910 aboard their forty-nine-foot ketch, the Asgard *(courtesy of BBC Hulton)*

muned with his tiller." Such nautical talk combined with the technical details of inshore sailing packed into Childers's story attracted and held the interest and admiration of sailor readers. Davies's literary hobby is naval warfare, represented in part by a worn copy of Alfred T. Mahan's *The Influence of Sea Power on History, 1660-1783* (1890) on his shelf, a clue to those readers who were Whitehall and Admiralty strategists that this book was more than an adventure yarn.

Various clues suggest that Davies has invited Carruthers for more than duck hunting. Carruthers is taken aback when his host declares there are no ducks in the Baltic and proposes that they sail into the North Sea and explore the sandbanks and shallow channels of the Dutch and North German coasts. Carruthers gives skeptical consent to this dangerous passage in the course of which Davies confesses that he had sailed the same waters earlier in the year and had encountered a luxurious German yacht, the *Medusa*, whose master is a mysterious figure named Dollmann. On pretense of guiding Davies on a shortcut through the sands, Dollmann had raced ahead in the *Medusa* to disappear in the fog, leaving Davies and the *Dulcibella* stranded

and in imminent danger of breaking up. Convinced that Dollmann had tried to murder him, Davies has resolved to return and confront the man whom he believes to be an Englishman in German service. Why did Dollmann try to lead him to his death? Davies suspects the motive was to prevent discovery of vital information about this flat and dreary coast that seemingly has no strategic importance.

This, then, is the riddle of the sands, and Davies realized that to solve it he needed Carruthers, who knew the German language and the rudiments of sailing. For Davies the trip is "a little secret service on the high seas"; for Carruthers it becomes medieval romance, "the gay pursuit of a perilous quest" that has injected welcome excitement into his dull life as a haunter of clubs, a diner-out and dancer, a smug Foreign Service junior careerist who had nothing but contempt for meddlesome alarmist journalists.

But Carruthers finds that "to reduce a romantic ideal to a working plan is a very difficult thing." The sudden revelation of Dollmann's true identity, Davies's infatuation with Dollmann's daughter (inserted grudgingly in revision by Childers in response to his publisher's insistence

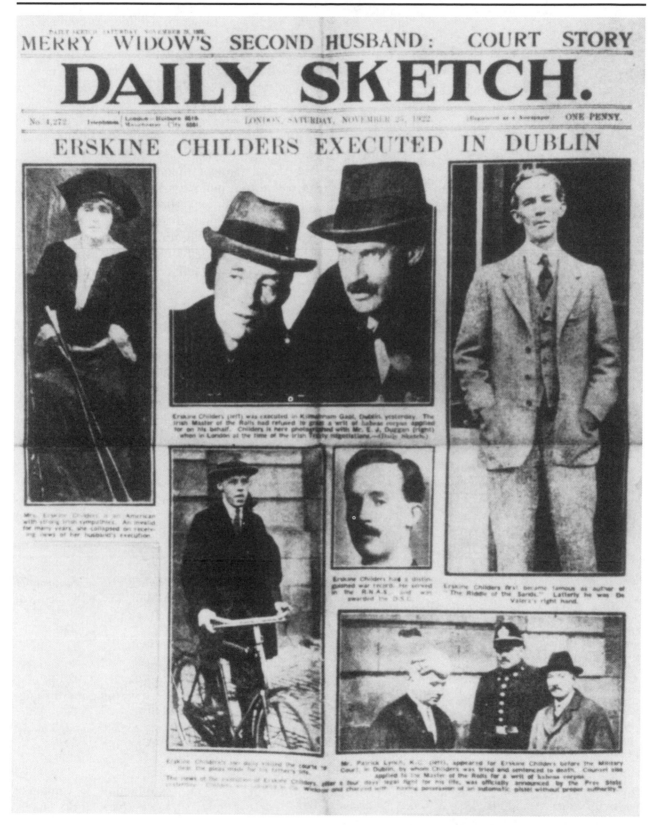

Front page of the London Daily Sketch *reporting Childers's execution by an Irish Provisional Government firing squad after a secret trial for possession of an automatic pistol*

Molly Childers (left) and Mary Spring Rice aboard the As-gard, circa 1914, running guns from Hamburg to the National Volunteers around Dublin. The Childerses and Rice were members of a committee composed of Anglo-Irish Protestant liberals in London who supported home rule in Ireland.

In a long "Epilogue" Childers presents skeptical readers, who may fear that "a baseless romance has been foisted on them," with a half-burned "memorandum" in cipher recovered from Dollmann's stove. It contains the details of the German invasion plan. "Perfect organization and perfect secrecy" underlie the riddle of the sands, writes Childers, and no one should doubt the German capacity for executing the plan at the critical moment when Germany might have little to lose and much to gain.

To its author's surprise *The Riddle of the Sands* met with immediate public and critical approval. Convinced of England's vulnerability to an invasion launched by Germany from the desolate Frisian sands, Childers had registered his concern in an adventure story based on firsthand observations set down in logbooks in the years he had cruised those shoals. Many of the book's minor characters are based on real-life encounters during those excursions, and the main figures of Carruthers and Davies, two English innocents abroad, appealed to readers as first they cope with the dangers of the sea and then find themselves involved in solving a riddle that is fraught with explosive geopolitical implications. For a decade *The Riddle of the Sands* helped fuel a national debate on England's supposed state of military unreadiness. For yachtsmen it remained an excellent tale of men against the sea, and in its many republications the book has continued to attract readers who admire a good spy story.

that the story contain "love interest"), and the ominous presence of a commander in the Imperial German Navy force Carruthers to the foreground to become the tactician of the pair. Davies, the remarkably self-possessed sailor, begins to lose control when the action shifts from sea to land. It is Carruthers who figures out connections, makes associations, and fits clues into meaningful theories. Disguised as a common seaman, Carruthers penetrates the veil of secrecy with which the Germans have surrounded their scheme to invade England by landing on the flat Lincolnshire coast, north of The Wash. Singlemindedly he pursues his objective: "to get Dollmann, secrets and all, daughter and all, away from Germany altogether." On the hairbreadth perilous homeward journey Dollmann (revealed to be Lt. "X," a disgraced British naval officer) jumps into the sea rather than face humiliation.

Bibliography:

Patrick S. O'Hegarty, *A Bibliography of the Books of Erskine Childers* (Dublin: Privately printed, 1948).

Biographies:

Basil Williams, *Erskine Childers, 1870-1922* (London: Women's Printing Society, 1926);

Burke Wilkinson, *The Zeal of the Convert* (Washington, D.C.: Luce, 1976);

Andrew Boyle, *The Riddle of Erskine Childers* (London: Hutchinson, 1977).

References:

Norman Donaldson, Introduction to Childers's *The Riddle of the Sands* (New York: Dover, 1976), pp. 1-11;

John N. Young, *Erskine H. Childers, President of Ireland* (Gerrards Cross: Colin Smythe, 1985), pp. 3-32.

Wilkie Collins

(8 January 1824-23 September 1889)

Jeanne F. Bedell
Virginia Commonwealth University

See also the Collins entry in *DLB 18, Victorian Novelists After 1885*.

BOOKS: *Memoirs of the Life of William Collins, Esq., R. A.*, 2 volumes (London: Longman, Brown, Green & Longmans, 1848);

Antonina; or, The Fall of Rome (3 volumes, London: Bentley, 1850; 1 volume, New York: Harper, 1850);

Rambles Beyond Railways; or, Notes in Cornwall Taken A-foot (London: Bentley, 1851);

Mr. Wray's Cash-Box; or, the Mask and the Mystery: A Christmas Sketch (London: Bentley, 1852); republished as *The Stolen Mask; or, the Mysterious Cash-Box* (Columbia, S.C.: De Fontaine, 1864);

Basil: A Story of Modern Life (3 volumes, London: Bentley, 1852; 1 volume, New York: Appleton, 1853; revised edition, London: Sampson Low, 1862);

Hide and Seek, 3 volumes (London: Bentley, 1854); revised as *Hide and Seek; or, the Mystery of Mary Grice*, 1 volume (London: Sampson Low, 1861; Philadelphia: Peterson, 1862);

The Holly-Tree Inn, by Collins and Charles Dickens, *Household Words* (Christmas 1855); (New York: Dix & Edwards, 1855);

After Dark, includes material by Dickens, 2 volumes (London: Smith, Elder, 1856; New York: Dick & Fitzgerald, 1856);

The Wreck of the Golden Mary, by Collins and Dickens (London: Bradbury & Evans, 1856);

The Dead Secret, 2 volumes (London: Bradbury & Evans, 1857; New York: Miller & Curtis, 1857);

The Two Apprentices. With a History of Their Lazy Tour, by Collins and Dickens (Philadelphia: Peterson, 1857); republished in *The Lazy Tour of Two Idle Apprentices. No Thoroughfare. The Perils of Certain English Prisoners* (London: Chapman & Hall, 1890);

The Queen of Hearts (3 volumes, London: Hurst &

Wilkie Collins, 1873 (photograph by Napoleon Sarony, New York; courtesy of the Houghton Library, Harvard University)

Blackett, 1859; 1 volume, New York: Harper, 1859);

The Woman in White (3 volumes, London: Sampson Low, 1860; 1 volume, New York: Harper, 1860);

No Name (3 volumes, London: Sampson Low, 1862; 2 volumes, Boston: Fuller, 1863);

My Miscellanies (2 volumes, London: Sampson Low, 1863; 1 volume, New York: Harper, 1874);

Armadale (2 volumes, London: Smith, Elder, 1866; 1 volume, New York: Harper, 1866);

No Thoroughfare. A Drama in Five Acts, by Collins, Charles Fechter, and Dickens (New York: DeWitt, n.d.); republished in *The Lazy Tour of Two Idle Apprentices. No Thoroughfare. The Perils of Certain English Prisoners* (London: Chapman & Hall, 1890);

The Moonstone (3 volumes, London: Tinsley, 1868; 1 volume, New York: Harper, 1868);

Black and White, by Collins and Fechter (London: Whiting, 1869);

Man and Wife (3 volumes, London: Ellis, 1870; 1 volume, New York: Harper, 1870);

Poor Miss Finch: A Novel (3 volumes, London: Bentley, 1872; 1 volume, New York: Harper, 1872);

Miss or Mrs?: And Other Stories in Outline (London: Bentley, 1873; revised edition, London: Chatto & Windus, 1877);

The New Magdalen (2 volumes, London: Bentley, 1873; 1 volume, New York: Harper, 1873);

The Dead Alive (Boston: Shepard & Gill, 1874); republished as *The Frozen Deep and Other Stories*, 2 volumes (London: Bentley, 1874);

The Law and the Lady (3 volumes, London: Chatto & Windus, 1875; 1 volume, New York: Harper, 1875);

The Two Destinies (2 volumes, London: Chatto & Windus, 1876; 1 volume, New York: Harper, 1876);

My Lady's Money and Percy the Prophet (Leipzig: Tauchnitz, 1877); *Percy the Prophet* republished (New York: Harper, 1877); *My Lady's Money* republished as *My Lady's Money: An Episode in the Life of a Young Girl*, 2 volumes (New York: Harper, 1878);

The Haunted Hotel, A Mystery of Modern Venice (Toronto: Rose-Belford, 1878); republished as *The Haunted Hotel, A Mystery of Modern Venice, to Which is Added: My Lady's Money*, 2 volumes (London: Chatto & Windus, 1879);

The Fallen Leaves (3 volumes, London: Chatto & Windus, 1879; 1 volume, Chicago: Rose-Belford, 1879);

A Rogue's Life: From His Birth to His Marriage (London: Bentley, 1879; New York: Appleton, 1879);

Jezebel's Daughter (3 volumes, London: Chatto & Windus, 1880; 1 volume, New York: Munro, 1880);

The Black Robe (3 volumes, London: Chatto & Windus, 1881; 1 volume, New York: Munro, 1881);

Heart and Science (1 volume, New York: Munro, 1883; 3 volumes, London: Chatto & Windus, 1883);

"I Say No"; or, the Love-Letter Answered (New York: Harper, 1884); republished as *"I Say No,"* 3 volumes (London: Chatto & Windus, 1884);

The Evil Genius: A Domestic Story (3 volumes, London: Chatto & Windus, 1886; 1 volume, New York: Harper, 1886);

The Guilty River (Bristol: Arrowsmith, 1886; New York: Harper, 1886);

Little Novels, 3 volumes (London: Chatto & Windus, 1887);

The Legacy of Cain (1 volume, New York: Harper, 1888; 3 volumes, London: Chatto & Windus, 1889);

Blind Love, by Collins and Walter Besant (3 volumes, London: Chatto & Windus, 1890; 1 volume, New York: Appleton, 1890);

Under the Management of Mr. Charles Dickens: His Production of "The Frozen Deep," by Collins and Dickens, edited by Robert Louis Brannan (Ithaca: Cornell University Press, 1966).

PLAY PRODUCTIONS: *The Lighthouse*, by Collins and Charles Dickens, London, Tavistock House, 15 June 1855; London, Olympic Theatre, 10 August 1857;

The Frozen Deep, by Collins and Dickens, Tavistock House, 6 January 1857; London, Olympic Theatre, 27 October 1866;

The Red Vial, London, Olympic Theatre, 11 October 1858;

A Message from the Sea, London, Britannia Theatre, 7 January 1861;

No Thoroughfare, by Collins, Charles Fechter, and Dickens, London, Adelphi Theatre, 26 December 1867;

Black and White, by Collins and Fechter, London, Adelphi Theatre, 29 March 1869;

The Woman in White, London, Olympic Theatre, 9 October 1871;

Man and Wife, London, Prince of Wales's Theatre, 22 February 1873;

The New Magdalen, London, Olympic Theatre, 9 May 1873;

Miss Gwilt, London, Globe Theatre, 15 April 1876;

The Moonstone, London, Olympic Theatre, 17 September 1877;

Ranks and Riches, London, Adelphi Theatre, 9 June 1883.

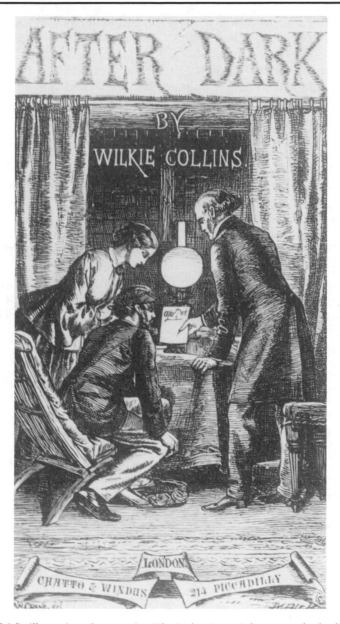

Cover, with E. G. Dalziel's illustration of a scene in "The Stolen Letter," for a paperback edition of Collins's 1856 collection of short stories

Although best known to modern readers as the author of *The Woman in White* (1860) and *The Moonstone* (1868)–which T. S. Eliot and Dorothy Sayers have called the best English detective story–Wilkie Collins made contributions more substantial than his current reputation indicates to the development of mystery and suspense fiction. As early as 1865 Henry James noted that Collins had "introduced into fiction those most mysterious of mysteries, the mysteries which are at our own doors." Writing before the detective story had become established as a genre and before it had hardened into formula, Collins (like other mid-Victorian authors who emphasized secrecy, mystery, and crime in their fiction) was considered by contemporary reviewers a sensation novelist, and James's comment singles out an innovation crucial to the creation of modern suspense fiction. Sensation fiction, generally viewed as domestication of the Gothic romance, established an atmosphere of mystery and terror in realistic settings and relied upon factually accurate detail and believable characterization to give verisimilitude to often lurid plots. Collins shared the Victorian belief that fiction should be true to nature;

and in the "Letter of Dedication" to *Basil* (1852) he wrote that he founded the novel "on a fact within my own knowledge" and stressed his adherence to the "actual" and to "everyday realities." In simultaneously emphasizing his reliance upon experience and retaining his prerogative to exercise his imagination and to include "those extraordinary accidents and events which happen to few men" as "legitimate materials for fiction," Collins fused the romantic and the realistic and provided a model for subsequent suspense and mystery fiction. His plotting, called by a contemporary "almost as ingenious as the knot of Gordius," was intricate and closely meshed. Praised for his skill in "the gradual unravelling of some carefully prepared enigma" and his ability to make "every circumstance subordinate to his leading idea," Collins established plot techniques of such obvious importance to detective fiction that without his contributions, as Sayers maintains, "the English novel of intrigue would either never have developed at all or would have developed much later and upon much narrower and more Gothic lines," and "the modern English detective story could never have risen to its present position of international supremacy."

Collins's own background, which combined the artistic with the practical, proved ideal for his future career as an author. Born 8 January 1824, the first son of William Collins, R.A., and Harriet Geddes Collins, William Wilkie Collins spent his childhood in London in the parish of Marleybone. William Collins, who had been elected to the Royal Academy in 1820, was a successful painter but definitely not a bohemian. To his sons Wilkie and Charles, born 25 January 1828, he emphasized the importance of religious piety, filial obedience, and aristocratic connections. Wilkie was apparently an obedient son–his first book (1848) was a laudatory biography of his father–but the scathing attacks in his novels upon religious hypocrisy and social pretentiousness reveal divergence from his father's principles. His powerful portrayal in *Hide and Seek* (1854) of the rigors of an English Sunday and the effects of narrow religiosity upon a sensitive child may be partly autobiographical, but there is no real evidence that Collins's childhood was unhappy or that it differed markedly from that of other middle-class Victorian children. In fact, his notable eye for landscape and his skill in descriptive writing can be attributed to his familiarity with painting and to the occasional sketching expeditions on which he accompanied his father. His

appreciation of art was enlarged and deepened during the years 1836-1838, which the family spent in travels through Italy. While William Collins studied Italian masterpieces, the adolescent Wilkie savored not only the beauties of art but also the contrasts between Italy and England. His enchantment with Rome is evident in the Roman setting of his first novel, *Antonina* (1850). His exposure to Italian culture gave him, at an impressionable age, a vivid and fascinating alternative to the narrow rigidity of Victorian society and perhaps provided a basis for the critical attitude toward that society he was later to display.

The journey to Italy interrupted Collins's formal education, begun at Maida Hill Academy in 1833; on his return to England it was continued at a private school in Highbury. In 1841 he was apprenticed to Antrobus and Company, a large firm of tea merchants. Aside from giving him a distaste for a business career, described in *Hide and Seek* as "nine hours of the most ungrateful labour," Collins's five years with Antrobus seem to have had little influence upon his development. An expedition to Scotland and the Shetland Islands with his father in the summer of 1842 and a trip to Paris with Charles Ward in the early autumn of 1844 broke the monotony of his business career, as did the writing to which he devoted his leisure time. His first verifiable publication, "The Last Stagecoachman," a short lament for the disappearance of stagecoaches as a consequence of railway expansion, appeared in the *Illuminated Magazine* of August 1843. Collins was fortunate to attract the attention of the magazine's editor, the popular author and playwright Douglas Jerrold, who became a lifelong friend. Jerrold introduced him to the theater and to theatrical melodrama, a style of importance in the development of his literary technique.

In 1846 Collins was released from his apprenticeship with Antrobus and entered as a law student on the rolls of Lincoln's Inn. Although he qualified for admission to the bar in November 1851, Collins did not pursue his law studies seriously after the death of his father in February 1847. Their effect upon his writing is, however, significant. The number of characters associated with the legal profession, plots which turn on detailed knowledge of law, and the narrative structures of *The Woman in White* and *The Moonstone*–both of which are designed to resemble the methods by which evidence is presented in court–reveal the impact of Collins's tenure as a law student.

The death of his father actually marks the beginning of Collins's literary career. Freed by inheritance of the necessity to earn a living, he first carried out William Collins's request that he write a memorial of his life. *Memoirs of the Life of William Collins, Esq., R.A.* was published by subscription in 1848 and attracted favorable attention for its young author. The reception of this book undoubtedly owed more to the reputation and popularity of its subject than the skill of the biographer, but Collins wrote in a pleasant, unpretentious style and made ample use of diaries and letters to reveal his father's personality. Detailed discussions of his father's paintings offered good practice in descriptive writing, an ability for which he became justly known.

Once his filial obligations had been completed, Collins returned to the historical romance on which he had been working for years. *Antonina*, written under the influence of Sir Walter Scott and Edward Bulwer-Lytton, did not display his talents to advantage. Turgid, inflated prose and a plot which moves with soporific slowness combine to produce a novel Sayers appropriately calls "impossibly melodramatic and impossibly dull." In depicting the adventures of a pure-minded and beautiful adolescent girl during the Gothic invasion of Rome, the religious fanaticism of her father, the opposing fanaticism of a pagan high priest, and the consuming desire for vengeance of a Gothic woman whose husband and children were massacred during the sack of Aquileia, Collins produced a blood-drenched but implausible narrative. Surprisingly, the novel was favorably reviewed by critics who found its portrayal of Roman life accurate and moving. A warning note, however, was sounded by H. F. Chorley in the *Athenaeum*. Chorley, later one of Collins's most virulent critics, warned him "against the vices of the French school—against the needless accumulation of revolting details—against catering for a prurient taste by dwelling on such incidental portions of the subject as, being morbid, ought to be treated incidentally." The commentary is significant as a harbinger of the attacks on the morality of Collins's fiction which became commonplace with the publication of his next novel, *Basil*, and continued throughout his career.

Both professionally and personally, mid century proved an exciting and influential period for Collins. Through his brother Charles's association with the Pre-Raphaelite brotherhood, he met such artists as William and Dante Gabriel Ros-

setti, William Frith, J. E. Millais, Augustus Egg, and Holman Hunt. In 1849 he submitted a landscape to the Royal Academy; it was accepted, probably out of respect to his father's memory, but hung near the ceiling where it was practically invisible to viewers of the exhibition. According to Holman Hunt, Collins later kept the painting in his study and narrated its history to guests with ironic self-mockery.

The reception of his painting convinced Collins that his future lay in literature, and a walking tour of Cornwall with his new friend artist Henry C. Brandling in the summer of 1850 led to the writing of *Rambles Beyond Railways*, published in 1851. An anecdotal travelogue of the sort popular with mid-Victorian audiences, *Rambles* is slight but charming and shows that Collins possessed a sense of humor and a talent for humorous characterization not indicated by *Antonina*.

Early in 1851 Collins's passionate interest in amateur theatricals led to his first meeting with Charles Dickens. Learning of Collins's ability as an amateur actor from their mutual friend Egg, Dickens wrote to ask him to take a small part in Bulwer-Lytton's *Not So Bad As We Seem*. The first performance of the play was given 14 May 1851 at Devonshire House in the presence of Queen Victoria and Prince Albert. This auspicious beginning led to a close personal and professional relationship which lasted until the death of Dickens in 1870. A bachelor and bon vivant twelve years Dickens's junior, Collins became a favored companion for dinner, theater parties, and extended rambles about London. Dickens's biographer, John Forster, says that Collins was "one of his dearest and most valued friends," and although the friendship apparently cooled in the late 1860s, it proved profitable, in both financial and literary terms, to both men. Collins became a paid contributor to Dickens's *Household Words* in 1853 (the same year in which he toured Switzerland and Italy with Dickens and Egg) and an editor in 1856. The encouragement of Dickens, who considered Collins the most promising young writer of his time, and the association with *Household Words* were influential in shaping both his approach to fiction and his career as a popular author.

The first evidence of Dickens's influence appears in *Mr. Wray's Cash-Box* (1852), a Christmas tale published in *Household Words* in December 1851. The story features Reuben Wray, a retired actor, and the theft of his most prized possession, a bust of Shakespeare; it concludes with a Christ-

The amateur cast for the 1857 production of The Frozen Deep *included the play's authors, Charles Dickens (reclining at center) and Collins (kneeling with head on hand), and various friends and family members (courtesy of BBC Hulton)*

mas feast and is notable only for its use of Collins's experience in amateur theatricals (material presented to better effect in *No Name*, 1862) and in its contemporary setting. Collins's forte, as he himself realized, was not the historical novel, and in his next book, *Basil*, his most significant novel of the 1850s, he turned to the present.

The reality in *Basil* was too strong for many contemporary critics who found in it the "aesthetics of the Old Bailey" and condemned it because it did not "elevate and purify." Collins referred to these criticisms in prefatory remarks to the revised 1862 edition of the novel:

> On its appearance, it was condemned offhand, by a certain class of readers, as an outrage on their sense of propriety. Conscious of having designed and written my story with the strictest regard to true delicacy . . . I allowed the prurient misinterpretation to assert itself as offensibly as it pleased, without troubling myself to protest against an expression of opinion which aroused in me no other feeling than a feeling of contempt.

Collins's contempt for middle-class morality and the limitations it imposed on the artist, only thinly disguised here, was to culminate in later ref-

erences to the "clap-trap morality of the present day." He refused to accept "young people as the ultimate court of appeal in English literature" or to succumb to "this wretched English claptrap" which forbade a writer to "touch on the sexual relations which literally swarm around him."

Collins's appreciation of human sexuality is evident in *Basil* where his depiction of sensuality is remarkably candid for the early 1850s. Its hero is a young man of aristocratic background, the second son of a father whose pride in his lineage is fanatical. In pursuit of realistic detail about human nature for a historical romance he is writing, he boards a London omnibus and becomes immediately infatuated with one of the passengers: "I had helped to hand her in, as she passed me; merely touching her arm for a moment. But how the sense of that touch was prolonged! I felt it thrilling through me—thrilling in every nerve, in every pulsation of my fast-throbbing heart." The young woman under whose sexual spell he falls is Margaret Sherwin, the daughter of a linen draper. Basil knows that she is an unsuitable wife (that he cannot introduce her to his father or sister), but his desire for her is so great that he consents to a secret marriage and even accepts the stipulation of Margaret's father that the marriage not be consummated for a year. He feels "guilty"

Wilkie Collins, circa 1865

and "humiliated" and comes to see "certain peculiarities in Margaret's character and conduct, which . . . gave me a little uneasiness and even a little displeasure." Margaret, as the reader understands at once, is vain, shallow, and materialistic; she feels no affection for Basil and is interested only in his wealth and social position. The uneasy and unnatural situation of Basil, who calls on his wife in the evening and is chaperoned during the visits, is further complicated by the appearance of Mr. Sherwin's clerk, the mysterious Robert Mannion, a reticent and sinister figure whose relationship with Margaret creates a sense of foreboding. Basil's humiliation becomes complete when, shortly before the year is up, he follows Margaret and Mannion to a seedy hotel and learns that they are lovers. Infuriated, he attacks Mannion and permanently disfigures him.

Despite a melodramatic conclusion in which Mannion tries to murder Basil and is himself killed, the novel is successful. The anonymous critic of *Bentley's Miscellany* who found "a startling antagonism between the intensity of the passion, the violent spasmodic action of the piece, and its smooth, commonplace environment" identifies

Collins's achievement: he uses crime, passion, and domesticity in "the secret theatre of home," employing the technique he was to put to such masterful use in *The Moonstone* and *The Woman in White*. Secrecy and crime in a mundane suburban villa bring suspense and terror close to the reader's own experiences and prove more frightening and more significant than similar crimes committed in the ruined castles so commonplace in the Gothic romance. Like Dickens, Collins was able to see "the romantic side of familiar things." *Basil* also anticipates Collins's future work in its use of letters and journals (to vary the narrative) and dreams (to express unconscious feelings and give a sense of inevitability to plot action).

Morally, *Basil* is ambiguous: the hero's older brother, a man of the world with a mistress whom he jokingly refers to as "the morganatic Mrs. Ralph," presents an implicit contrast to Basil whose humiliating experiences are, as William Marshall rightly observes, caused by "the honorable quality of his intentions. . . . Had he not wished to marry Margaret but to seduce her—in effect, to follow that aristocratic ethic that Ralph himself has consistently personified—had he not sought to enter with Margaret the state which for the Victorian bourgeois was at the center of all social order—then he would have avoided all his difficulties." In simultaneously criticizing the aristocratic ethic in his portrayal of the arrant snobbery of Basil's father, and affirming its value in his depiction of the competent and practical manner in which Ralph straightens out the mess Basil had made of his life, Collins neglects to provide the consistent moral focus so important to Victorian critics, but he has presented a realistic portrait of a young man caught between two value systems, both of which have obvious flaws.

Although much less powerful than *Basil*, Collins's next novel, *Hide and Seek* (1854), was more favorably received by critics who found its morality unobjectionable and who praised its humor. In creating Valentine Blyth, a second-rate painter devoted to an invalid wife and an adopted daughter who is a deaf-mute, Collins put to good use his knowledge of the art world. The basic plot, which turns on the parentage of the deaf-mute Madonna, relies too heavily on a series of improbable coincidences, but the novel is noteworthy for containing Collins's first piece of sustained detection and for the characterization of Matthew Grice, also known as Mat Marksman. An eccentric wanderer who has spent most of his life in the wilds of North America and had been scalped by Indians, Grice is derived from James Fenimore Cooper's Leatherstocking. Dickens considered him "admirably done," as well he might since Collins had clearly profited from studying Dickens's own touch with eccentricity. Grice's detection is admirable for its pertinacity rather than its skill. His search for his lost and ruined sister and his discovery of her death and subsequent identification of her seducer and her child, especially the detailed reconstruction of past events, indicates the approach Collins was to follow in later novels. *Hide and Seek* also displays his antipathy toward narrow religiosity and the association of morality with respectability, attitudes at variance with his own moral vision which consistently emphasized charitableness and forgiveness.

Because of the outbreak of the Crimean War at the time of its publication, *Hide and Seek* failed to attract a large audience. Although Collins was discouraged by readers' temporary preference for newspapers over fiction, he persevered in his work and was rewarded by the serialization of his next novel, *The Dead Secret* (1857), in *Household Words*. As the title indicates, Collins was moving closer to sensation fiction, a genre Kathleen Tillotson has aptly christened the "novel-with-a-secret." Once again the discovery of a young girl's parentage is the focal point of the plot, but the secret itself, evident in the early chapters of the novel, is less important than the characterization of the custodian of the secret, Sarah Leeson, and its effect upon her mental and physical health. Her weak heart and mental instability establish her as a precursor of Anne Catherick, the title character in *The Woman in White*. Collins's sympathetic treatment of her and her illegitimate daughter, Rosamund Frankland, as well as Leonard Frankland's dismissal of class distinctions when he learns that his wife is the daughter of a lady's maid and a miner, embody Collins's divergence from usually strict Victorian attitudes toward sexual morality and social stratification.

Two volumes of short fiction (largely pieces previously published in *Household Words*), *After Dark* (1856) and *The Queen of Hearts* (1859), display an increasing preoccupation with suspense and an innovative approach to detection. Collins provided a frame narrative for both collections, but the main interest in each lies in the short stories and novelettes collected. "A Terribly Strange Bed," usually considered Collins's best short story, appears in *After Dark*, as do "Sister Rose," a short novel set during the French Revolution and a possible influence on Dickens's *A Tale of Two Cit-*

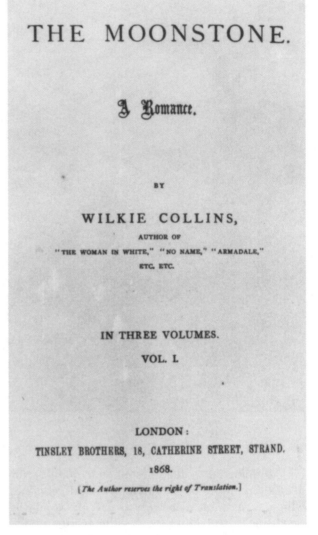

THE MOONSTONE.

A Romance.

BY

WILKIE COLLINS,

AUTHOR OF

"THE WOMAN IN WHITE," "NO NAME," "ARMADALE,"
ETC. ETC.

IN THREE VOLUMES.

VOL. I.

LONDON:
TINSLEY BROTHERS, 18, CATHERINE STREET, STRAND.
1868.

[*The Author reserves the right of Translation.*]

Title page for the novel in which Collins introduced Sergeant Cuff, whom T. S. Eliot called "the ancestor of the healthy generation of amiable, efficient, professional but fallible inspectors of fiction among whom we live today"

ies (1859), and "The Yellow Mask," which features a Machiavellian priest—a character type developed at greater length in *The Black Robe* (1881). "A Terribly Strange Bed" is a horror story of considerable merit with debt to Poe's "The Pit and the Pendulum" and the tradition of Gothic haunted-chamber fiction. Two young Englishmen in Paris visit a shady gambling house where the narrator breaks the bank at *rouge-et-noir* and overindulges in champagne in celebration. Persuaded to spend the night at the house instead of risking robbery during the return to his hotel, he is unable to sleep and lies in his canopied four-poster bed watching "a dark old picture" on the opposite wall. Gradually he realizes that his view of the picture has changed and that the canopy of the bed is descending. Paralyzed with fear, he rolls off the bed, "just as the murderous canopy touched me on the shoulder," he says. Macabre though it is, the story builds suspense through careful revelation of detail and the somewhat befuddled mental condition of the narrator which makes the slow realization of his plight more terrifying and more believable.

Generally, the stories in *The Queen of Hearts* are better than those in *After Dark*. The frame narrative–in which three elderly men tell stories to amuse a young woman who, by her father's will, must spend six weeks each year with her guardian at an isolated Welsh estate–is more convincing. "Mad Monkton," which Dickens had declined for *Household Words* because he thought its theme of hereditary insanity might offend readers, is an interesting study of an abnormal mental condition and the impact of family legend upon an unstable personality. "The Dream-Woman," in which a man's dream precisely predicts future action, maintains a feeling of inescapable doom. "The Biter Bit," an epistolary tale usually considered the first humorous detective story, features an inexperienced policeman who is consistently misled by the thief he has set out to catch. The reader is (or, ought to be) aware of the criminal's identity, a circumstance which adds to the story's ironic humor. "Anne Rodway," though sentimental, has an unusual heroine-detective, a poor seamstress who succeeds in finding the murderer of her friend after the incompetent police have failed to find a single clue. Collins's always ambivalent and frequently critical attitude toward the official police figures prominently here. The chief investigator is a "big, thick-voiced, pompous man, with a horrible unfeeling pleasure in hearing himself talk before an assembly of frightened, silent people."

Collins's attempts throughout his life to make a career in the theater were not successful. Many of his attempts to dramatize his own novels failed either to find a producer or to hold an audience, but the theatrical experiments were beneficial to his work as a novelist and contributed to the effectiveness of such superb set scenes as the opening of *The Woman in White* and the dramatic intensity with which he maintains suspense in the major novels.

No doubt the most important personal event of the late 1850s was Collins's liaison with Caroline Graves, a widow with a child. As related by John G. Millais in his biography of his father (1899), their meeting was dramatic: in the late summer of 1855 as Collins, his brother, and John Everett Millais were walking to Millais's studio in Gower Street in north London, they were startled by a woman's scream from the garden of a nearby house:

> It was evidently the cry of a woman in distress; and while pausing to consider what they should do, the iron gate leading to the garden was dashed open, and from it came the figure of a young and very beautiful woman dressed in flowing white robes that shone in the moonlight. She seemed to float rather than to run in their direction, and, on coming up to the three young men, she paused for a moment in an attitude of supplication and terror. Then, suddenly seeming to recollect herself, she suddenly moved on and vanished in the shadows cast upon the road.

Collins ran after the woman and did not reappear until the next day when he told his friends that she had been kept prisoner for several months by a man who used "threats and mesmeric influence" to prevent her escape. Whatever truth there may be in this story, and it resembles the opening chapter of *The Woman in White* far too closely to be accepted without reservations, Collins meeting with Caroline, however it may have occurred, effected significant change in his life. Cautiously, he remained living at home with his mother and brother until 1859 when he set up housekeeping with Caroline and her daughter, Lizzie. The move restricted Collins's extensive social life–his mother was a noted hostess–because his friends, although sympathetic, did not introduce Caroline to their wives. Millais concluded his account of her with typical Victorian reticence: "Her subsequent history, interesting as it is, is not for these pages." The conspiracy of silence with which Collins's friends and acquaintances treated his affair and the absence of letters to Caroline or his later mistress, Martha Rudd, account for the paucity of information about his private life. In 1868 Caroline married Joseph Clow, a plumber, and Collins formed a liaison with Martha Rudd, who became the mother of his three children (born in 1869, 1871 and 1874). Caroline's marriage was apparently unsuccessful, and by the early 1870s she was again living with Collins. At his death he left the income from his estate divided between Caroline and Martha and their three children, who were acknowledged in his will. It seems fairly certain that

Publicity poster by Frederick Walker for the 1871 production of Collins's dramatic version of the novel that a decade earlier had inspired "Woman in White" cloaks, bonnets, perfumes, waltzes, and quadrilles

Collins's sympathetic fictional treatment of illegitimacy and the problems of fallen women, as well as his frequently caustic comments about those who confused morality with respectability, reflect his personal situation and his sensitivity to the difficulties faced by the two women in his life. The reasons for his personal antipathy to marriage are not known, but both his long and lively bachelorhood and the rheumatic gout from which he began to suffer in the mid 1850s, and which led to an eventual addiction to laudanum, may have produced an aversion to the responsibilities of marriage and sustained domesticity.

The contributions of his relationship to Caroline to his career are purely conjectural, but the decade of the 1860s did mark the end of his apprenticeship and inaugurated the period of his greatest success. *The Woman in White*, serialized in *All the Year Round* (successor to *Household Words*)

from 26 November 1859 to 25 August 1860, and published in book form by Sampson Low in August 1860, was his most popular book and one of the most popular novels of the century. The first impression sold out on the day of publication and was followed by six impressions in the next six months. Public acclaim was shared by such notable figures as Prince Albert (who sent a copy to Baron Stockmar), William Gladstone, William Thackeray (who read it straight through), and Dickens who told Collins that he found it "a very great advance on all your former writing." "Woman in White" cloaks, bonnets, perfumes, waltzes, and quadrilles became the rage. This gratifying response was, however, diminished by negative critical responses to the novel. While most critics agreed that *The Woman in White* was "in point of intricacy a masterpiece" and praised its maintenance of suspense, many agreed with the

Saturday Review that Collins was "an admirable story-teller . . . not a great novelist." The Victorian distinction between the novel of incident and the novel of character worked to Collins's disadvantage, and although he himself professed contempt for such criticism, it is significant that in the preface to *The Moonstone* he wrote that he was attempting "to trace the influence of character on circumstances" rather than "the influence of circumstances upon character" as he had previously done. Modern criticism, following Henry James, sees plot and character as inseparably interrelated and is perhaps better able to understand Collins's achievement than either he or his contemporaries. This is especially true of the narrative technique used in both *The Woman in White* and his second masterpiece, *The Moonstone*. Contemporaries recognized that multiple narrators contributed to the dramatic development of the story and to its "lifelike" quality without, apparently, seeing that Collins, in making subjectivity and the peculiarities of perception central to his method, had made not only a major advance in the possibilities of narrative but had also devised a method for the revelation of personality that is inextricable from plot.

The Woman in White contains two secrets: the first, of secondary importance, is the identity of Anne Catherick (the title character); the second, and chief motivation for the novel's main action, is the illegitimacy of Sir Percival Glyde. Sir Percival marries Laura Fairlie to gain access to her income and then, when that proves insufficient to meet his debts and because he thinks she knows his secret, imprisons her in a private asylum under Anne Catherick's name and buries the dead Anne under Laura's name. In these nefarious activities he is aided or, one might better say, masterminded, by the most engaging villain in Victorian fiction, the Italian Count Fosco, and opposed by one of its most fascinating heroines, Marian Halcombe, who "has the foresight and the resolution of a man," and Walter Hartright, the drawing master whose love for Laura and desire to restore her identity make him an amateur detective of outstanding ability. Collins's use of a witness as narrator not only enriches the novel but emphasizes the legal predicament of Laura and the desperate position of married women who were, as John Stuart Mill said, "legal slaves." It is the fat and charming Fosco, surrounded by his pet white mice, who presents Collins's indictment of Victorian marriage; in defense of his wife's part in his Machiavellian schemes he says,

"I ask if a woman's marriage obligations in this country provide for her private opinion of her husband's principles? No! They charge her unreservedly to love, honour, and obey him." Fosco too reminds Marian that "English Society . . . is as often the accomplice as it is the enemy of crime. . . ." Even the contrast between the pathetic Laura, a typical Victorian heroine in her submissive and dutiful attitude toward her father's memory, and the "masculine" but effective Marian reveals the independence of Collins's approach to female characterization. *The Woman in White* is indeed superb suspense fiction; but, like all major Victorian novels, it embodies serious comment on contemporary society. The law, as Walter Hartright says in the opening narrative, is "the pre-engaged servant of the long purse," and the novel displays a knowing appreciation of the problems of the powerless and their lack of protection under the law. Suspense and social significance are soundly embedded in character. The haunting figure of Anne Catherick, weak and terrified after her escape from an asylum, appears to Hartright on Hampstead Heath and establishes immediately an atmosphere of secrecy and fear. The mystery of her paternity, her resemblance to Laura, and the relationship between her hypocritical, selfish mother and Sir Percival link past and present. Mrs. Catherick, whose desire for social acceptance and financial security has made her the ally of Sir Percival, shares with him and Fosco a facade of respectability which cloaks an unscrupulous nature. Deception is the key here as it is in *No Name* (1862) and *Armadale* (1866). Seemingly prosperous Blackwater Park is debt ridden, the suave and gentlemanly Count Fosco is villainous, and Laura's beloved father is an adulterer. In *The Woman in White* Collins questions definitions of reality and shows how the limitations of personality entrap and mislead; people see, he says, not what *is* but what *seems* to be or what they *wish* to see.

Disguise, deception, and legal injustice are the mainsprings of the action in *No Name* where Collins once again describes a world where reality blurs, shifts, and alters. Life itself is an amateur theatrical where characters play out assigned or chosen roles. The placid and happy Vanstone family of Combe-Raven is legally no family at all; an unfortunate early marriage precluded Mr. Vanstone's marrying the woman he loves and with whom he lives in perfect amicability for a quarter century. Because of the ability of "Mrs." Vanstone "to resolve firmly, scheme patiently,

The evil count and Lady Laura, drawing by an unknown artist of a scene from the 1871 dramatic version of The Woman in White

and act promptly," they are able to live publicly as man and wife. They are eventually able to marry, but since Mr. Vanstone is killed in a train wreck before he can change his will, and she dies in childbirth, their two daughters are disinherited, and his fortune passes to his brother. The elder daughter, Norah, becomes a governess, and she accepts her fate. Her younger sister, Magdalen, who shares with other heroines of sensation fiction a marked deviation from acceptable models of female behavior and an exceptional talent as an actress, joins forces with a swindler named Captain Wragge. She does this to earn money through a series of dramatic performances and then marries, under an assumed name, her cousin and thus regains possession of her name and her father's fortune. Her conspiracy fails when her husband discovers her identity and disinherits her; but Magdalen, who is perhaps the most spirited and attractive of all Collins's heroines, is charming even when deceitful. Wragge, a comic and successful scoundrel, his slow-witted and childishly affectionate wife, and the pusillanimous Noel Vanstone (Magdalen's miserly cousin) contribute to the success of *No Name*, which blends humor, pathos, suspense, and social commentary.

Although some reviewers felt that Magdalen did not suffer severely enough for her sinful activities, critical response to *No Name* was reasonably favorable and its popular success so great that Collins was given a £5,000 advance for his next novel, *Armadale* (of which T. S. Eliot said, "it has no merit beyond melodrama, and it has every merit melodrama can have"). It is the most intricately plotted of Collins's novels. While some contemporary critics objected to the foreshadowing dream which gives the novel its basic structure as arbitrary and unbelievable, a view shared by Eliot who called the technique one of "spurious fatality," most attacked the book's morality. The characterization of Lydia Gwilt, a beautiful, scheming, criminal heroine, bore the brunt of critical attack: H. F. Chorley asked, "What artist would choose vermin as his subjects?" The *Spectator* called her "fouler than the refuse of the streets" and accused Collins of overstepping "the limits of decency" and revolting "every human sentiment." Far too complicated to summarize with any accuracy, the plot involves two young men both named Allan Armadale, the foreshadowing dream which indicates that one will, like his father before him, be murdered, and the involved plans of Miss Gwilt to marry one and become a rich widow. Modern readers, who tend to share Victorian critics' feelings that the novel is overplotted, find Lydia Gwilt fascinating; as twentieth-century critic Julian Symons puts it, she may be " 'wild and strange' . . . yet she is drawn with a conviction and assurance that compel belief."

In 1868 the second of Collins's great novels, *The Moonstone*, appeared. No novel considered a detective story has received such praise or held its public over such a period of time. Again using multiple narrators, Collins limited the focus of this novel to one event, the disappearance of the fabulous Indian diamond of the title. Through skillful revelation of detail, varied and consistently interesting characterization, and a highly original denouement, he constructed a perfectly plotted fiction, which is (as modern criticism has demonstrated) also a study of the unconscious mind and the limitations of individual perception. From the opening scene in India where the diamond is stolen from a Hindu temple to the discovery of the villain murdered in a squalid East End rooming house, every clue has been fairly given, but each clue is so enmeshed in the personal peculiarities of its narrator that the reader is apt to misinterpret its importance. Collins subverts the old maxim that seeing is believing and shows that truth is more complex and reality less easily discernible than the reader may have thought.

The characters of *The Moonstone* are individuals. The heroine, Rachel Verinder, is a vivacious and independent-minded young woman who is described by family steward Gabriel Betteredge as her own worst enemy and her own best friend because of her "secrecy" and "self-will." The hero is Franklin Blake, whose dogged pursuit of evidence that will clear him of suspicion of theft impresses the reader. Betteredge's devotion to *Robinson Crusoe*, his jaundiced view of matrimony, and his understanding that "Gentlefolks have a very awkward rock ahead in life–the rock of their own idleness" distinguish him from the usual family retainer. Collins's sympathy for the lower classes is evident in all his portrayals of servants but appears nowhere more compellingly than in Rosanna Spearman, the lame former thief whose hopeless love for Blake is both dignified and pathetic and whose suicide in the Shivering Sand is one of the most memorable moments in the story. Religious fanatic Drusilla Clack is a

*"The Master of Sensation," caricature of Collins by Adriano Cecioni (*Vanity Fair, *February 1872)*

paradigm of her species, a frustrated spinster who sees sin everywhere and whose excessive admiration for philanthropist Godfrey Ablewhite first warns the reader of Ablewhite's true nature. Collins's satirical view of organized charity is presented with humor, but his critical attitude toward it is nonetheless clear. Miss Clack says of the Select Committee of the Mothers' Small-Clothes-Conversion Society, "The object of this excellent Charity is . . . to rescue unredeemed fathers' trousers from the pawnbroker, and to prevent their resumption on the part of the irreclaimable parent, by abridging them immediately to suit the proportions of the innocent son." Ablewhite, though not as original a villain as Fosco, is a smooth-tongued hypocrite and ideally suited to his part; like most of Collins's villains, he presents a respectable facade to conceal his criminal activities. Few novels present such an abundance of memorable characters, but perhaps in terms of subsequent influence Sergeant Cuff, the detective, is most important. Astute, experienced, and devoted to the culture of roses, Sergeant Cuff is, as T. S. Eliot says, "the ancestor of the healthy generation of amiable, efficient, professional but fallible inspectors of fiction among whom we live today." Cuff's failure to solve the crime is oddly appealing. Ezra Jennings, the doctor's assistant who is an opium addict and whose experiences parallel Collins's own, discovers the series of clues which reveal the identity of the criminal through a process closely approximating Freudian word association techniques. Contemporary critics, obtuse as usual, repeated their praise of Collins's ingenuity and puzzle-making ability without understanding either the originality of his narrative method or his psychological perceptiveness.

Integrating suspense and social criticism proved a difficult and often impossible feat for Collins in his later years. He had made a reading tour of the United States and Canada in 1873-1874 in order to take advantage of his considerable popularity there. The tour was only moderately successful–Collins did not possess Dickens's histrionic talent nor his ability to hold an audience–and a continued decline in his health, constant pain relieved only by laudanum, and the effects of long-term addiction resulted in increasing reclusiveness in the late 1870s and 1880s. His association with Charles Reade, who replaced Dickens as a close friend and important influence after Dickens's death in 1870, is at least partially responsible for the inferior quality of his later work. The impact of Reade's melodramatic didacticism can be seen in the increasingly propagandistic tone of Collins's novels, as well as in their treatment of specific social grievances. It is also possible that critics' failure to appreciate the seriousness of his work and their dismissal of him as a mere entertainer encouraged the erroneous belief that attention to social problems might strengthen his reputation. The results were unfortunate. Swinburne's famous couplet, while unfair, sums up what many critics, contemporary and modern, have seen as the central flaw in the novels that followed *The Moonstone*:

What brought good Wilkie's genius nigh perdition?
Some demon whispered–Wilkie! have a mission.

Margaret Oliphant, one of the more intelligent Victorian commentators on Collins, expressed a similar view: his "strength, which lies in plot and complication, does not lend itself to polemics."

In *Man and Wife* (1870), Collins's novel after *The Moonstone*–and one showing the weakening of his talent–he addresses himself to three actual public grievances: the inconsistency and ambiguity of the Irish and Scottish marriage laws; the En-

glish property laws which gave a husband control of his wife's earnings and possessions; and the cult of athleticism. The most powerful portion of the novel concerns Hester Dethridge, a working-class woman who, after years of abuse, murders her husband in order to keep control of her wages. The weakest portion of the novel concerns Geoffrey Delamayne, a famous athlete who seduces Anne Sylvester, and when their Scottish marriage by intent is proved valid, plots to murder her in order to marry a woman with an income of £10 thousand a year. Collins offers no explanation for Delamayne's decline from public hero to would-be murderer except his devotion to sports. In his condemnation of athleticism Collins badly overstates his case: "The manhood and muscle of England resemble the wool and mutton of England in this respect; that there is almost as much variety in a flock of athletes as in a flock of sheep." His discussion of marriage laws, treated in the relationship between Delamayne and Anne Sylvester, is preceded by analysis of the situation of Anne's mother. Her husband, desirous of finding a wife who could aid his aspirations to a parliamentary career, found a loophole in the Irish statutes under which they were wed and disowned her and their child. The involvement of both mother and daughter in similar predicaments strains credibility, but Collins's characterization of women, as usual, is good, and the portrayal of Hester Dethridge's long struggle to survive the brutal treatment of a drunken husband is moving, even though the method which she uses to murder him detracts from the intensity of her sufferings.

In subsequent novels Collins wove plots around such topical subjects as the fallen woman, divorce, antivivisection, the relationship between heredity and environment, and a woman's place in the business world. *Poor Miss Finch* (1872), written to demonstrate that physical handicaps could be a source of happiness, has what is perhaps the most implausible plot in English fiction: Lucilla Finch, blind since early childhood, when she developed a morbid horror of dark colors, falls in love with Oscar Dubourg. She recovers her sight shortly after a series of medical treatments have turned him dark blue. Fortunately, Lucilla's blindness returns, Oscar's twin brother's plot to win her hand is foiled, and she finds happiness since she cannot see her lover. The novel was popular with the public, as Collins's novels continued to be. His outstanding failure was *The Fallen Leaves* (1879), which features a hero called Amelius

Goldenheart and his love for a redeemed prostitute named Simple Sally; Swinburne found it "ludicrously loathsome." *The New Magdalen* (1873) employs the deception theme; Mercy Merrick, a former prostitute, assumes the identity of Lady Janet Roy and, despite exposure, wins the affection of her employer and the hand in marriage of Julian Gray, a renowned preacher. The novel is weakened by too sharp a contrast between the fallen woman and her respectable foil, Grace Rosenberry, whose only virtue is chastity. Collins's rejection of conventional morality is clear, but he sacrifices sound characterization to promulgate his message. Similar criticism can be made of *Heart and Science* (1883), where an oversimplified attack on vivisection yields an implicit though unintentional condemnation of scientific inquiry, and *The Legacy of Cain* (1888), where Collins's misunderstanding of Darwinian theory creates an untenable hypothesis–that the daughter of a murderess will inherit her criminal tendencies–and a forced contrast between the evil daughter of a minister and the good daughter of the murderess.

Among the most interesting of the later novels is *Jezebel's Daughter* (1880) which, although marred by a melodramatic conclusion in the Frankfurt deadhouse, offers a striking portrait of a frustrated woman whose natural abilities have no outlet. Unhappily married to a physician who has devoted himself to chemical research in a provincial German town, Madame Fontaine finds her social ambitions thwarted and chafes at the restricted boundaries of her life. She writes to a friend: "Gossip and scandal, with an eternal accompaniment of knitting, are not to my taste, and while I strictly attend to my domestic duties, I do not consider them as constituting, in connection with tea-drinking, the one great interest of a woman's life." She sublimates her frustrations first in purchasing expensive goods and then in becoming a poisoner. When Madame Fontaine first administers poison she says, "The Power that I have dreamed of is mine at last!" By contrasting her unfulfilled life with that of Mrs. Wagner, who becomes on her husband's death "sole successor" and senior partner in his import-export firm, Collins gives explicit form to his long-held aversion to the social and economic restrictions placed on women. His sympathetic presentation of a socially ostracized divorced woman in *The Evil Genius* (1886) expresses his continuing concern with the destructive effects of an uncharitable moral code. Collins's discussion of the problems of women and his portrayals of independent, capable women who defy the Victorian stereotype irritated many of his contemporaries who found his unconventional approach immoral, but these things have been singled out as two of his major achievements by modern critics tired of the pallid, insipid heroines so common in Victorian fiction.

Of special interest to readers of mystery fiction are two late novels. *The Law and the Lady* (1875), is the first English detective story with a female protagonist. Valeria Woodville, with the help of a family lawyer, successfully undertakes the investigation of the death of her husband's first wife. *My Lady's Money and Percy the Prophet* (1877), although weakly plotted, reveals the influence of Émile Gaboriau in its detective, Old Sharon, modeled upon Père Tabaret, the elderly detective of his *The Widow Lerouge* (1873), and it is unique in that the vital clue is discovered by a dog. Of the later novelettes "Mr. Policeman and the Cook" deserves mention. Written in confessional form, the story follows a young policeman through the investigation of his first murder case. His admirable determination to solve the murder after his superiors have given up produces an ironic result: the criminal is his own fiancée.

Despite the inferior quality of Collins's later works, he continued to be popular with the public and was widely reviewed in influential periodicals and newspapers. His last years, marred by deteriorating eyesight and the constant pain of rheumatic gout, were not happy, but he continued working until his death, 23 September 1889, from a stroke. He was buried at Kensal Green Cemetery. The inscription on his tombstone reads, by his own direction, his full name, the dates of his birth and death, and the words "Author of the Woman in White and Other Works of Fiction."

The obituaries which followed Collins's death emphasized his skill as a storyteller and expressed gratitude for the delight which he had given audiences for forty years. Swinburne called him a "genuine artist" of the second rank, comparable in merit to Anthony Trollope and Charles Reade. Although his reputation, like that of many other Victorian writers, was in eclipse during the early twentieth century, it began to revive in the 1920s when T. S. Eliot turned critical attention to his work. Today his reputation is secure with both academic critics and the mystery-story reading public.

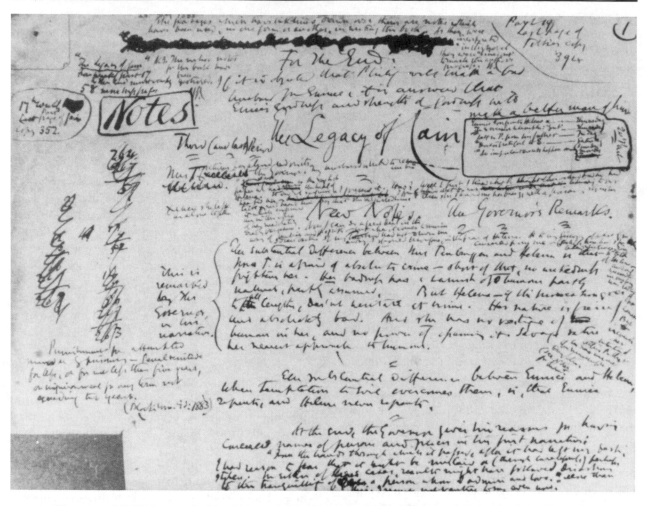

First page of Collins's notes for his 1888 novel, The Legacy of Cain *(courtesy of Durham University Library)*

The significance of Collins's work, aside from its intrinsic merit, lies in its fusion of the romantic and the realistic and its creation of suspense and terror in ordinary, middle-class settings. In *The Moonstone* Gabriel Betteredge questions the intrusion of crime into "our quiet English house": "Whosoever heard of it–in the nineteenth century, mind, in an age of progress, and in a country which rejoices in the blessings of the British constitution?" The most cursory familiarity with mystery and detective fiction, from Conan Doyle through Agatha Christie and Sayers to the present, reveals the crucial importance of Collins's domestication of criminal activities and the great debt which subsequent authors owe to his emphasis upon the actual. By integrating accurate depiction of contemporary manners and customs with the secrecy and romance of crime, he established a pattern which modern writers of mystery fiction still follow.

Bibliography:

Kirk H. Beetz, *Wilkie Collins: An Annotated Bibliography* (Metuchen, N.J. & London: Scarecrow, 1978).

References:

R. V. Andrew, "A Wilkie Collins Check-List," *English Studies in Africa*, 3 (March 1960): 79-98;

Robert Ashley, *Wilkie Collins* (New York: Roy, 1952);

Ashley, "Wilkie Collins and the Detective Story," *Nineteenth-Century Fiction*, 6 (June 1951): 47-60;

Ashley, "Wilkie Collins," in *Victorian Fiction: A Second Guide to Research*, edited by George H. Ford (New York: Modern Language Association, 1978);

Bradford A. Booth, "Wilkie Collins and the Art of Fiction," *Nineteenth-Century Fiction*, 6 (September 1951): 131-143;

Robert Louis Brannan, ed., *Under the Management of Mr. Charles Dickens: His Production of "The Frozen Deep"* (Ithaca, N.Y.: Cornell University Press, 1966);

Nuel Pharr Davis, *The Life of Wilkie Collins* (Urbana: University of Illinois Press, 1956);

T. S. Eliot, "Wilkie Collins and Dickens," in *Selected Essays* (New York: Harcourt, Brace & World, 1964);

S. M. Ellis, *Wilkie Collins, LeFanu, and Others* (London: Constable, 1931);

Winifred Hughes, "Wilkie Collins: The Triumph of the Detective," in her *The Maniac in the Cellar: Sensation Novels of the 1860s* (Princeton: Princeton University Press, 1980), pp. 137-165;

Albert D. Hutter, "Dreams, Transformations, and Literature: The Implications of Detective Fiction," *Victorian Studies*, 8 (1975): 181-209;

Clyde K. Hyder, "Wilkie Collins and The Woman in White," *PMLA*, 54 (March 1939): 297-303;

Walter M. Kendrick, "The Sensationalism of *The Woman in White*," *Nineteenth-Century Fiction*, 32 (1977): 18-35;

U. C. Knoepflmacher, "The Counterworld of Victorian Fiction and *The Woman in White*," in *The Worlds of Victorian Fiction*, edited by Jerome H. Buckley (Cambridge: Harvard University Press, 1975), pp. 351-369;

Gavin Lambert, *The Dangerous Edge* (London: Barrie & Jenkins, 1975);

Lewis Lawson, "Wilkie Collins and *The Moonstone*," *American Imago*, 20 (Spring 1963): 61-79;

Sue Lonoff, "Charles Dickens and Wilkie Collins," *Nineteenth-Century Fiction*, 35 (1980): 150-170;

Dougald B. MacEachen, "Wilkie Collins and British Law," *Nineteenth-Century Fiction*, 5 (1950): 121-139;

MacEachen, "Wilkie Collins' *Heart and Science* and the Vivisection Controversy," *Victorian Newsletter*, no. 29 (Spring 1966): 22-25;

William Marshall, *Wilkie Collins* (New York: Twayne, 1970);

C. H. Muller, "Incident and Characterization in *The Woman in White*," *Unisa English Studies*, 11, no. 2 (1973): 33-50;

Muller, "Victorian Sensationalism: The Short Stories of Wilkie Collins," *Unisa English Studies*, 11, no. 1 (1973): 12-24;

Ian Ousby, "Wilkie Collins and Other Sensation Novelists," in his *Bloodhounds of Heaven: The Detective in English Fiction from Godwin to Doyle* (Cambridge: Harvard University Press, 1976), pp. 111-136;

Norman Page, ed., *Wilkie Collins: The Critical Heritage* (London: Routledge & Kegan Paul, 1974);

Walter C. Philips, *Dickens, Reade, and Collins: Sensation Novelists* (New York: Columbia University Press, 1919);

John R. Reed, "English Imperialism and the Unacknowledged Crime of *The Moonstone*," *Clio*, 2 (June 1973): 281-290;

Kenneth Robinson, *Wilkie Collins, A Biography* (London: The Bodley Head, 1951);

Charles Rycroft, "A Detective Story: Psychoanalytic Observations," *Psychoanalytic Quarterly*, 26 (1957): 229-245;

Dorothy Sayers, *Wilkie Collins: A Critical and Biographical Study*, edited by E. H. Gregory (Toledo, Ohio: The Friends of the University of Toledo Libraries, 1977).

Papers:

Princeton University Library holds letters, manuscripts, and other papers of Wilkie Collins. Columbia University Library holds the correspondence of Collins and Henry Rider Haggard in a collection of Haggard papers.

Charles Dickens

(7 February 1812-9 June 1870)

Albert Borowitz

See also the Dickens entries in *DLB 21, Victorian Novelists Before 1885*, and *DLB 55, Victorian Prose Writers Before 1867*.

BOOKS: *Sketches by Boz, Illustrative of Every-Day Life and Every-Day People* (first series, 2 volumes, London: Macrone, 1836; second series, London: Macrone, 1837); republished as *Watkins Tottle and Other Sketches Illustrative of Every-Day Life and Every-Day People*, 2 volumes (Philadelphia: Carey, Lea & Blanchard, 1837), and *The Tuggs's at Ramsgate and Other Sketches Illustrative of Every Day People* (Philadelphia: Carey, Lea & Blanchard, 1837);

The Village Coquettes: A Comic Opera in Two Acts, as "Boz" with music by John Hullah (London: Bentley, 1836);

The Posthumous Papers of the Pickwick Club, Edited by "Boz" (20 monthly parts, London: Chapman & Hall, 1836-1837; 26 monthly parts, New York: Turney, 1836-1838);

The Strange Gentlemen: A Comic Burletta, in Two Acts, as "Boz" (London: Chapman & Hall, 1837);

The Life and Adventures of Nicholas Nickleby (20 monthly parts, London: Chapman & Hall, 1837-1839; 20 monthly parts, Philadelphia: Lea & Blanchard, 1839);

Sketches of Young Gentlemen, Dedicated to the Young Ladies (London: Chapman & Hall, 1838);

Memoirs of Joseph Grimaldi, Edited by "Boz," 2 volumes (London: Bentley, 1838; Philadelphia: Carey, Lea & Blanchard, 1838);

Oliver Twist; or, The Parish Boy's Progress, by "Boz" (3 volumes, London: Bentley, 1838; 26 monthly parts, New York: Turney, 1838);

Sketches of Young Couples, with an urgent Remonstrance to the Gentlemen of England (Being Bachelors or Widowers), on the Present Alarming Crisis (London: Chapman & Hall, 1840);

The Old Curiosity Shop (2 volumes, London: Chapman & Hall, 1841); republished in part as *Master Humphrey's Clock* (Philadelphia: Lea & Blanchard, 1840); republished in full as *Mas-*

Charles Dickens, 1843

ter Humphrey's Clock (Philadelphia: Lea & Blanchard, 1841);

Barnaby Rudge: A Tale of the Riots of 'Eighty (London: Chapman & Hall, 1841; Philadelphia: Lea & Blanchard, 1841);

American Notes for General Circulation (2 volumes, London: Chapman & Hall, 1842; 1 volume, New York: Harper, 1842);

The Life and Adventures of Martin Chuzzlewit (20 monthly parts, London: Chapman & Hall, 1842-1844; 1 volume, New York: Harper, 1844);

A Christmas Carol, in Prose: Being a Ghost Story of Christmas (London: Chapman & Hall, 1843; Philadelphia: Carey & Hart, 1844);

The Chimes: A Goblin Story of Some Bells That Rang an Old Year Out and a New Year In (London: Chapman & Hall, 1845; New York: Harper, 1845);

Pictures from Italy (London: Bradbury & Evans, 1846); republished as *Travelling Letters: Written on the Road* (New York: Wiley & Putnam, 1846);

The Cricket on the Hearth: A Fairy Tale of Home (London: Bradbury & Evans 1846; New York: Harper, 1846);

The Battle of Life: A Love Story (London: Bradbury & Evans, 1846; New York: Wiley & Putnam, 1847);

Dealings with the Firm of Dombey and Son, Wholesale, Retail, and for Exportation (20 monthly parts, London: Bradbury & Evans, 1846-1848); 20 monthly parts in 19 (parts 1-17, New York: Wiley & Putnam, 1846-1847; parts 18-19, New York: Wiley, 1848);

The Haunted Man and the Ghost's Bargain: A Fancy for Christmas-time (London: Bradbury & Evans, 1848; Philadelphia: Althemus, 1848);

The Personal History of David Copperfield (20 monthly parts, London: Bradbury & Evans, 1849-1850; Philadelphia: Lea & Blanchard, 1851);

A Child's History of England (3 volumes, London: Bradbury & Evans, 1852-1854; 2 volumes, New York: Harper, 1853-1854);

Bleak House (20 monthly parts, London: Bradbury & Evans, 1852-1853; 1 volume, New York: Harper, 1853);

Hard Times: For These Times (London: Bradbury & Evans, 1854; New York: McElrath, 1854);

The Holly-Tree Inn, by Dickens and Wilkie Collins, *Household Words* (Christmas 1855); (New York: Dix & Edwards, 1855);

Little Dorrit (20 monthly parts, London: Bradbury & Evans, 1855-1857; 1 volume, Philadelphia: Peterson, 1857);

After Dark, by Collins, includes material by Dickens, 2 volumes (London: Smith, Elder, 1856; New York: Dick & Fitzgerald, 1856);

The Wreck of the Golden Mary, by Dickens and Collins (London: Bradbury & Evans, 1856);

The Two Apprentices. With a History of Their Lazy Tour, by Dickens and Collins (Philadelphia: Peterson, 1857); republished in *The Lazy Tour of Two Idle Apprentices. No Thoroughfare. The Perils of Certain English Prisoners* (London: Chapman & Hall, 1890);

A Tale of Two Cities (London: Chapman & Hall, 1859; Philadelphia: Peterson, 1859);

Great Expectations (3 volumes, London: Chapman & Hall, 1861; 1 volume, Philadelphia: Peterson, 1861);

The Uncommercial Traveller (London: Chapman & Hall, 1861; New York: Sheldon, 1865);

Our Mutual Friend (20 monthly parts, London: Chapman & Hall, 1864-1865; 1 volume, New York: Harper, 1865);

Reprinted Pieces (New York: Hearst's International Library, 1867);

Hunted Down: A Story, with Some Account of Thomas Griffiths Wainewright, The Poisoner (London: Hotten, 1870; Philadelphia: Peterson, 1870);

The Mystery of Edwin Drood (6 monthly parts, London: Chapman & Hall, 1870; 1 volume, Boston: Fields, Osgood, 1870);

A Child's Dream of a Star (Boston: Fields, Osgood, 1871);

Is She His Wife?, or, Something Singular: A Comic Burletta in One Act (Boston: Osgood, 1877);

No Thoroughfare. A Drama in Five Acts, by Collins, Charles Fechter, and Dickens (New York: DeWitt, n.d.); republished in *The Lazy Tour of Two Idle Apprentices. No Thoroughfare. The Perils of Certain English Prisoners* (London: Chapman & Hall, 1890);

The Life of Our Lord (New York: Simon & Schuster, 1934);

The Speeches of Charles Dickens, edited by K. J. Fielding (Oxford: Clarendon Press, 1960);

Under the Management of Mr. Charles Dickens: His Production of "The Frozen Deep," by Dickens and Collins, edited by Robert Louis Brannan (Ithaca: Cornell University Press, 1966);

Uncollected Writings from Household Words, 1850-1859, 2 volumes (Bloomington: Indiana University Press, 1968; London: Allen Lane, 1969);

Charles Dickens' Book of Memoranda: A Photographic and Typographic Facsimile of the Notebook Begun in January 1855, transcribed and annotated by Fred Kaplan (New York: New York Public Library; Astor, Lenox and Tilden Foundations, 1981).

Collections: *Cheap Edition of the Works of Mr. Charles Dickens* (12 volumes, London: Chapman & Hall, 1847-1852; 3 volumes, London: Bradbury & Evans, 1858);

The Charles Dickens Edition, 21 volumes (London: Chapman & Hall, 1867-1875);

The Works of Charles Dickens, 21 volumes (London: Macmillan, 1892-1925);

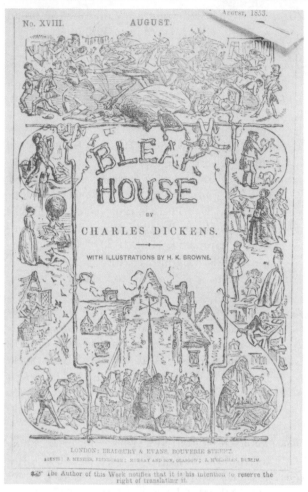

Cover for one of the monthly parts for the novel in which Dickens drew upon his observations of the Bermondsey murderess, Maria Manning, at her trial in 1849, for his characterization of Mademoiselle Hortense, the murderess of Tulkinghorn (courtesy of Otto Penzler)

Watercolor by Kyd (Clayton Clark) of the inspector whom Dickens based on his friend Inspector Field, one of the investigators in the case against Maria Manning (Tage la Cour and Harald Mogensen, The Murder Book, *1971)*

The Works of Charles Dickens, Gadshill Edition, 36
    volumes (London: Chapman & Hall/New
    York: Scribners, 1897-1908);
The Nonesuch Edition, edited by Arthur Waugh
    and others, 23 volumes (London: Nonesuch
    Press, 1937-1938);
The New Oxford Illustrated Dickens, 21 volumes (Ox-
    ford: Oxford University Press, 1947-1958);
The Clarendon Dickens, edited by Kathleen Tillot-
    son and others, 6 volumes, ongoing (Ox-
    ford: Clarendon Press, 1966-   ).

PLAY PRODUCTIONS: *The Strange Gentleman*,
    London, St. James's Theatre, 29 September
    1836;
The Village Coquettes, London, St. James's Theatre,
    6 December 1836;
Is She His Wife?, or, Something Singular, London,
    St. James's Theatre, 6 March 1837;
The Lighthouse, by Wilkie Collins and Dickens, Lon-
    don, Tavistock House, 16 June 1855; Lon-
    don, Olympic Theatre, 10 August 1857;
The Frozen Deep, by Collins and Dickens, London,
    Tavistock House, 6 January 1857; London,
    Olympic Theatre, 27 October 1866;
No Thoroughfare, by Collins, Charles Fechter, and
    Dickens, London, Adelphi Theatre, 26 De-
    cember 1867;
The Battle of Life, London, Gaiety Theatre, 26 De-
    cember 1873;
The Old Curiosity Shop, London, Opera Comique,
    12 January 1884.

Drawing his narrative themes from the sensation novel and the popular stage, Charles Dickens heavily freighted most of his plots with
mystery, crime, and suspense. His chief legacies
to crime literature, as it is narrowly understood, include his vibrant portrait of the London underworld in *Oliver Twist* (1838); the introduction of
the first police detective in English fiction, Inspector Bucket of *Bleak House* (1852-1853); and one
of the most intriguing literary puzzles of all time,
the unfinished *The Mystery of Edwin Drood* (1870).
    Dickens's mystery and crime fiction is not
generally remarkable for plot construction, ingenious detection, or formal innovation. His major
contributions to the genre are his imaginative understanding of criminal psychology and of the
destructive and self-destructive impulses that outwardly normal people share with the outlaw; his
relation of fictional crime and punishment to social concerns; and his loving portrayal of early
police detectives. With these strengths and inter-

Charles Dickens, 1861

ests, Dickens's work has much in common with
twentieth-century crime and police-procedural
novels.
    Charles John Huffam Dickens was born
near Portsmouth on 7 February 1812 to John and
Elizabeth Barrow Dickens. His expansive and im-
provident father (to be immortalized in the characters of Mr. Micawber and Mr. Dorrit) served in
the navy pay office. The family moved to London, and then to Chatham, which melted into
the neighboring cathedral town of Rochester (the
model for Cloisterham, the site of *The Mystery of
Edwin Drood*). After their return to London, John
Dickens's financial situation became desperate,
and a double disaster struck the young Charles:
at age twelve he was removed from school and
sent to work at a boot-blacking warehouse, and
shortly thereafter his father was committed to
Marshalsea debtors' prison. Although both these
misfortunes lasted only a few months, they made
permanent imprints on Dickens's personality and
art. They left him with a deeply concealed sense
of suffering and a determination to succeed.
They are probably responsible for his ineradica-

ble sympathy for children, the poor, and the oppressed.

After his wretched days at the blacking warehouse, Dickens returned briefly to school (but owed most of his education to avid reading at the British Museum). In 1827 he took a job as office boy in a firm of solicitors. He then worked as a shorthand reporter of court proceedings and parliamentary debates, having first gained admission to the gallery of the House of Commons in the tumultuous days that led to passage of the Reform Bill of 1832. In time Dickens developed into a versatile journalist, covering political meetings in the country when Parliament was not in session and contributing sketches of London life to the *Morning Chronicle* and various periodicals. Dickens married Catherine Hogarth on 2 April 1836; they had ten children, one of whom died in infancy. The same year he married, a collection of his London pieces in book form, *Sketches By Boz*, was published. It was warmly received and launched him on his literary career, but Dickens never abandoned journalism; he briefly served as founding editor of the *Daily News* (1846) and later controlled and edited two weekly miscellanies, *Household Words* (1850-1859) and *All The Year Round* (1859-1870).

From early childhood Dickens, like most good Victorians, was fascinated with crime. His nursemaid Mary Weller regaled him with bedtime tales of dreadful murderers, which he parodied in "Nurses' Stories" in *The Uncommercial Traveller* (1861). His familiarity with contemporary criminal cases is reflected in the large number of fictional characters he based on real-life criminals. Fagin of *Oliver Twist*, for example, was recognizable to readers as a portrait of the celebrated thief and fence, Ikey Solomon; the murder of Montague Tigg in *The Life and Adventures of Martin Chuzzlewit* (1842-1844) recalled the Thurtell-Hunt case of 1823; Mademoiselle Hortense in *Bleak House* (1852-1853) was closely modeled on the Bermondsey murderess, Maria Manning; and Jonas Slinkton, the murderer run to earth in the story "Hunted Down" (written in 1859) was based on the mass poisoner, Thomas Griffiths Wainewright. In addition to being strongly attracted by the drama of criminal cases, Dickens throughout his career took an active interest in social issues of crime and punishment. His views were conflictive and changeable, reflecting as they did not only shifts in public moods but also ambivalent tendencies of his own personality: an abhorrence of murder and violence com-

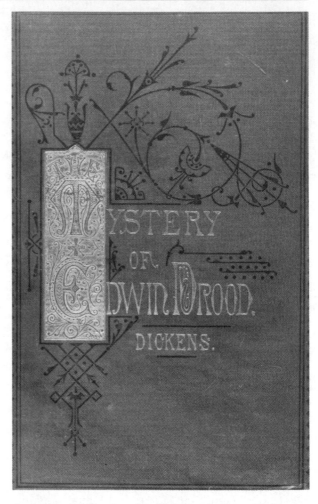

Cover for the first American edition of the novel that was only half finished at Dickens's death. Dickens told John Forster that he planned to have the novel end with "the review of the murderer's career by himself . . . , when its temptations were to be dwelt upon as if, not he the culprit, but some other man, were the tempted" (courtesy of Otto Penzler).

bined with an imaginative insight into criminal psychology, and a streak of rebelliousness, sometimes at war with his belief in law and order.

Dickens's lifelong interest in prisons and the death penalty announced itself in his first book, *Sketches By Boz*, which includes a restrained but profoundly moving account of his visit to Newgate Prison and its cells of the condemned, "A Visit to Newgate." In the mid 1840s Dickens urged the absolute abolition of capital punishment but soon shifted to the more moderate position of advocating the end of public hanging. In *American Notes for General Circulation* (1842) he attacked as inhumane the regime of solitary confinement (the "separate system") used in Philadelphia's Cherry Hill Prison, but some of his later writings ranged him among the foes of prison reforms that were seen as creating living standards superior to those enjoyed by honest workers. Although skeptical about the possibility of rehabilitating hardened criminals, he felt better disposed toward "fallen women," who were received in a charitable home that he ably helped his friend Angela Burdett Coutts organize and administer. A warm admirer of the police and particularly of the detectives of Scotland Yard, Dickens praised London's detective force in three lively *Household Words* articles that were collected in *Reprinted Pieces* (1867); however, in his last years, he came to lament the lack of energy with which the police administration was dealing with crime in London's streets.

Dickens's first crime novel, *Oliver Twist*, reflects—in its blend of lurid sensation and urban realism—a combination of literary and social impulses. In no small measure the work capitalized on the early Victorian taste for the "Newgate novel," which romanticized crime and lowlife and often featured underworld heroes drawn from criminal annals such as the Newgate Calendar. At the same time, however, Dickens shaped the narrative of Oliver's fall (from a workhouse orphanage into a den of thieves) to serve his reformist purposes of attacking England's harsh poor laws and illustrating the thesis that city slums could breed crime even in the innocent. Across Oliver's path come two of Dickens's most renowned criminals—the unspeakably brutal thief and housebreaker, Bill Sikes, with his intimidating ruffian's scowl, stocky build, and much-abused dog, Bull's-Eye; and Fagin, the rascally thief trainer and receiver of stolen goods. Although Dickens in his nonfiction wasted no love on vicious criminals, his deeply cleft artistic psyche summoned up sympathy for both the villains of *Oliver Twist* when they were brought to feel the full weight of society's wrath. Sikes cruelly murders his mistress, the prostitute Nancy (in an episode which became Dickens's favorite piece in his later recital tours), but arouses compassion when a misguided and vengeful mob hounds him to a public hanging. Despite Dickens's reference to Fagin in a letter as an "out-and-outer" (an utter scoundrel), the old man also becomes an object of pity as he awaits his last morning in a condemned cell. Moreover, Fagin, despite repulsive traits, seems to watch over Oliver and his other young "apprentices" as a kind of surrogate father, a role that the critic Steven Marcus has ingeniously traced to the befriending of young Dickens by an older boy named Bob Fagin at the dismal blacking warehouse.

Mystery and murder are major ingredients in the plot of *Bleak House*. The villain of the piece is Mademoiselle Hortense, Lady Dedlock's French maid. Hortense's broken English, volubility, impatient gestures, and tasteful dress were close imitations of the speech and manners of the Bermondsey murderess, Maria Manning, whose trial and execution, with her husband Frederick, for the murder of her lover Patrick O'Connor were attended by Dickens and his friends in 1849. The common criticism that Hortense's actions lack adequate motivation misses the mark, for she represents one of Dickens's many studies of inexplicable criminal malice, a phenomenon that he undoubtedly thought he observed in the enigmatic Mrs. Manning as she stood resolutely in the dock of Old Bailey. With great economy Dickens evoked Hortense's camouflaged evil: "Through all the good taste of her dress and little adornments . . . she seems to go about like a very neat She-Wolf imperfectly tamed."

Discharged from the service of Lady Dedlock, a reigning society beauty married to Sir Leicester Dedlock, Hortense nurses a double grudge against Lady Dedlock and also against Sir Leicester's solicitor, Tulkinghorn; the lawyer had enlisted Hortense's help in spying into Lady Dedlock's scandalous past and had resisted her demands for more money. The murderous maid shoots Tulkinghorn through the heart and throws the pistol into a country pond. She then sends letters to Sir Leicester which charge his wife with the crime.

Pitted against Hortense is Inspector Bucket, who has been hailed by A. E. Murch as the "first police detective-hero in English fiction." The lavishly detailed description of Bucket, including his habit of employing his "fat forefinger" for emphasis, proclaimed his original to be Dickens's friend Inspector Field, one of the real-life pursuers of Maria Manning. The fictional detective is genial, friendly, charismatic, talkative, even confidential, but he is all those things only to the extent he wants to be, and he never forgets his mission. Though he is capable of using bribery and threats to bar the gates of the community to a poor sick boy who knows too much of Lady Dedlock's secret, there are occasions when he shows genuine sympathy for victims of poverty, humiliation, or grief. Above all, Dickens emphasizes the professionalism of Bucket that typified the methodical competence of the newly organ-

John Jasper in the opium den, a scene from The Mystery of Edwin Drood *sketched by Charles Collins, Dickens's son-in-law
(Tage la Cour and Harald Mogensen,* The Murder Book, *1971)*

*In January 1914 a group of well-known writers and attorneys held a mock trial for John Jasper in London, with G. K. Chesterton
as judge and Bernard Shaw as foreman of the jury. When the jury found Jasper guilty, Chesterton fined them for contempt of
court and pronounced the case unsolvable (Tage la Cour and Harald Mogensen,* The Murder Book, *1971).*

ized Scotland Yard. Self-controlled, unobtrusive, and a master of disguise, Bucket observes quietly and comes and goes as if invisible. He recognizes every criminal and policeman he meets on the street. But beyond sheer competence Bucket has one essential virtue that makes him invincible: he is dogged and unrelenting to an unusual degree. Dickens wrote of him: "Time and place cannot bind Mr. Bucket. Like man in the abstract, he is here to-day and gone to-morrow–but very unlike man indeed, he is here again the next day."

Despite his professional prowess, Bucket owed the capture of Hortense primarily to coincidence and to his wife, Mrs. Bucket. The maid happens to become the Buckets' lodger around the time she begins stalking her victim. Mrs. Bucket watches Hortense post her accusing letters and is the first to suspect the hiding place of the murder weapon.

In several other novels Dickens portrays deep-dyed murderers. The crimes of the steward Rudge were perpetrated twenty years before the action of *Barnaby Rudge* (1841) begins, and until he is ultimately caught and hanged he spends his long fugitive years terrorizing his poor wife and hiding in the dark, a prey to an unremitting sting of conscience that Edgar Allan Poe found to be "inconsistent with his brutality." The murders committed by the unrelievedly evil Rigaud in *Little Dorrit* (1855-1857) are also in the distant past, but unlike Rudge, he feels no remorse; compared constantly to the Devil, he is moved, like the French murderer Lacenaire, by "utter disregard of other people," "brute selfishness," and by a determination to "subdue the society" which he believes has "grievously wronged" him. A more highly individualized portrayal of a murderer's soul is to be seen in Dickens's characterization of Jonas Chuzzlewit in *The Life and Adventures of Martin Chuzzlewit*. Jonas's crimes are inspired by an extreme strain of the malady of selfishness which is the dominant theme of the book; the rendering of his hallucinatory fears not only "*for* himself but *of* himself" induced by memories of the murder of Montague Tigg is a high point of Dickens's crime fiction. A rare Dickensian example of an endearing adult criminal is the escaped convict, Abel Magwitch, who is the secret benefactor of Pip in *Great Expectations* (1861). But Magwitch is not a murderer, and his favorable treatment may have been inspired by the fate of Dickens's own maternal grandfather, who was an embezzler.

In the last two novels of Dickens, the exploration of criminal behavior takes on added complexity: now the murderers, anticipating Robert Louis Stevenson's *The Strange Case of Dr. Jekyll and Mr. Hyde* (1896), are respectable members of society who suffer from split personalities. In *Our Mutual Friend* (1864-1865) Bradley Headstone is by day a conscientious schoolmaster. Suffering from low self-esteem partly because of his humble birth, he is driven to desperate violence by jealousy of the contemptuous gentleman Eugene Wrayburn, who wins the love of Lizzie Hexam on whom Headstone has hopelessly set his heart. When he is unable, in a graveyard confrontation, to frighten Lizzie into accepting his addresses, Headstone erupts in fury, smashing his fist on the stone coping of the burial ground wall. He later attempts (unsuccessfully) to murder Wrayburn and finally meets a suitably violent end in a death struggle with his villainous confederate, Rogue Riderhood.

A similar theme of the dual capacity of man for good and evil appears to dominate Dickens's last work, *The Mystery of Edwin Drood*, his only pure mystery novel. Left half-finished at his death on 9 June 1870 with no indication in his notes as to how the story was to end, *Edwin Drood* has itself become an eternal puzzle which has spawned an enormous number of critical commentaries and attempted solutions and completions (including one claimed to have been derived by a medium from the ghost pen of Dickens, and an American musical comedy in which the solution is left to the audience). At the beginning of *Edwin Drood* the readers are plunged into an opium dream of John Jasper, lay precentor and choirmaster of Cloisterham Cathedral, and a secret drug addict. The choirmaster's nephew, Edwin Drood, was in infancy betrothed by his parents to Rosa Bud; the two are fond of each other but not in love. Jasper, who teaches Rosa music, is, on the other hand, passionately enamored of her and apparently seeks to subject her to his powers of mesmerism (of which Dickens was himself a practitioner). The choirmaster appears to plot against Edwin, stirring up bad blood between him and Neville Landless, who (with his sister Helena) has arrived from Ceylon. As the narrative proceeds, Jasper begins to behave even more strangely: one of his most unaccountable actions is a nocturnal expedition with the tombstone mason, Durdles, through the tower and crypt of Cloisterham Cathedral. Shortly afterward, Edwin disappears without a trace (except for a watch

Dickens on his deathbed, drawing by Sir John Everett Millais (courtesy of the Trustees of the Dickens House)

and a tie pin found in a weir). The work breaks off with the arrival in Cloisterham of Datchery, who is apparently a detective in disguise.

The principal puzzle of *Edwin Drood* is whether or not Jasper murdered or attempted to murder Edwin and, if so, how and where. Although some commentators have suggested surprise endings and revelations more inventive than any Dickens ever composed, the consensus holds that Jasper would ultimately have been unmasked as Edwin's attacker, and that he would accordingly stand revealed as a double personality in the same mold as Bradley Headstone. This conclusion would accord with the plan Dickens reportedly confided in his biographer Forster: that "the originality [of the work] was to consist in the review of the murderer's career by himself at the close, when its temptations were to be dwelt upon as if, not he the culprit, but some other man, were the tempted."

Letters:

The Letters of Charles Dickens, Pilgrim Edition, edited by Nina Burgis, Kenneth J. Fielding, Madeline House, Graham Storey, and Kath-

leen Tillotson, 5 volumes (Oxford: Clarendon Press, 1965-1981).

Biographies:

John Forster, *The Life of Dickens*, 2 volumes (New York: Scribners, 1905);

Edgar Johnson, *Charles Dickens: His Tragedy and Triumph* (2 volumes, New York: Simon & Schuster, 1952; 1 volume, revised and abridged, New York: Viking, 1977; London: Lane, 1977);

Norman MacKenzie and Jeanne MacKenzie, *Dickens: A Life* (New York: Oxford University Press, 1979).

References:

Richard M. Baker, *The Drood Murder Case* (Berkeley: University of California Press, 1951);

Albert Borowitz, "The Mystery of Edwin Drood," in his *Innocence and Arsenic: Studies in Crime and Literature* (New York: Harper & Row, 1977); pp. 53-62;

Borowitz, *The Woman Who Murdered Black Satin: The Bermondsey Horror* (Columbus: Ohio State University Press, 1981);

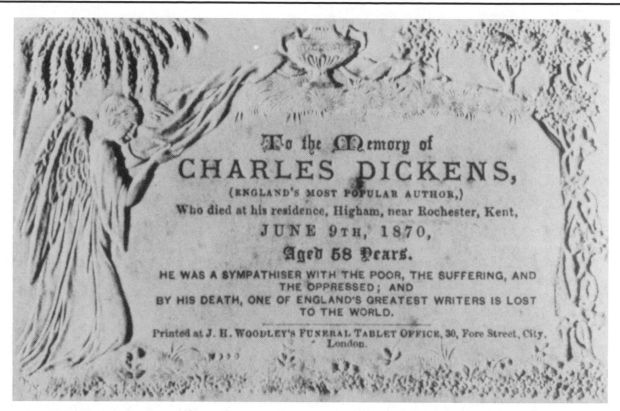

Memorial card reproducing the inscription on Dickens's gravestone in Poets' Corner, Westminster Abbey

Philip Collins, *Dickens and Crime* (London: Macmillan/New York: St. Martin's, 1962);

Charles Forsyte, *The Decoding of Edwin Drood* (London: Gollancz, 1980);

Leon Garfield, *The Mystery of Edwin Drood* (London: Andre Deutsch, 1980);

Andrew Lang, *The Puzzle of Dickens's Last Plot* (London: Chapman & Hall, 1905);

Steven Marcus, *Dickens From Pickwick to Dombey* (New York: Basic Books, 1965);

A. E. Murch, *The Development of the Detective Novel* (London: Owen, 1958; New York: Philosophical Library, 1958);

W. Robertson Nicoll, *The Problem of "Edwin Drood"* (London: Hodder & Stoughton, 1912);

Ian Ousby, *Bloodhounds of Heaven: The Detective in English Fiction from Godwin to Doyle* (Cambridge: Harvard University Press, 1976), pp. 80-110;

Richard A. Proctor, *Watched by the Dead: A Loving Study of Dickens' Half-Told Tale* (London: Allen, 1887);

Edmund Wilson, "Dickens: The Two Scrooges," in his *The Wound and the Bow* (Cambridge: Houghton, Mifflin, 1941), pp. 1-104.

Papers:

Major collections of the surviving manuscripts of Dickens's sketches and essays are at the Beinecke Rare Book and Manuscript Library, Yale University; the Huntington Library, San Marino, California; and the Free Library of Philadelphia, which also has a substantial collection of Dickens's letters. The most extensive collection of letters is housed at the Pierpont Morgan Library in New York. Other important repositories for correspondence are the Dickens House in London and the Berg Collection at the New York Public Library. The Berg Collection also includes several manuscripts and one of Dickens's notebooks.

Sir Arthur Conan Doyle

(22 May 1859-7 July 1930)

J. Randolph Cox
St. Olaf College

See also the Doyle entry in *DLB 18, Victorian Novelists After 1885.*

BOOKS: *A Study in Scarlet* (London: Ward, Lock, 1888; Philadelphia: Lippincott, 1890);

The Mystery of Cloomber (London: Ward & Downey, 1889; New York: Fenno, 1896);

Micah Clarke (London: Longmans, Green, 1889; New York: Harper, 1889);

Mysteries and Adventures (London: Scott, 1890); republished as *My Friend the Murderer and Other Mysteries and Adventures* (New York: Lovell, Coryell, 1893);

The Captain of the Polestar and Other Tales (London & New York: Longmans, Green, 1890);

The Firm of Girdlestone (London: Chatto & Windus, 1890; New York: Lovell, 1890);

The Sign of Four (London: Blackett, 1890; New York: Collier, 1891); republished as *The Sign of the Four* (Philadelphia: Lippincott, 1890);

The White Company (3 volumes, London: Smith, Elder, 1891; 1 volume, New York: Lovell, 1891);

The Doings of Raffles Haw (New York: Lovell, 1891; London: Cassell, 1892);

The Adventures of Sherlock Holmes (London: Newnes, 1892; New York: Harper, 1892);

The Great Shadow (Bristol: Arrowsmith, 1892; New York: Harper, 1893);

The Refugees (3 volumes, London: Longmans, Green, 1893; 1 volume, New York: Harper, 1893);

Jane Annie; or, The Good Conduct Prize: A New and Original English Comic Opera, by Conan Doyle and James M. Barrie (London: Chappell, 1893);

The Great Shadow and Beyond the City (Bristol: Arrowsmith, 1893);

The Memoirs of Sherlock Holmes (London: Newnes, 1894; New York: Harper, 1894);

An Actor's Duel and The Winning Shot (London: Dicks, 1894);

Round the Red Lamp: Being Facts and Fancies of Medical Life (London: Methuen, 1894; New York: Appleton, 1894);

The Parasite (London: Constable, 1894; New York: Harper, 1895);

The Stark Munro Letters (London: Longmans, Green, 1895; New York: Appleton, 1895);

The Exploits of Brigadier Gerard (London: Newnes, 1896; New York: Appleton, 1896);

Rodney Stone (London: Smith, Elder, 1896; New York: Appleton, 1896);

Uncle Bernac: A Memory of the Empire (London: Smith, Elder, 1897; New York: Appleton, 1897);

The Tragedy of the Korosko (London: Smith, Elder, 1898); republished as *A Desert Drama* (Philadelphia: Lippincott, 1898);

Songs of Action (London: Smith, Elder, 1898; New York: Doubleday & McClure, 1898);

A Duet with an Occasional Chorus (London: Richards, 1899; New York: Appleton, 1899);

Hilda Wade: A Woman with Tenacity of Purpose, by Doyle and Grant Allen (London: Richards, 1900; New York & London: Putnam's, 1900);

The Green Flag and Other Stories of War and Sport (London: Smith, Elder, 1900; New York: McClure, Phillips, 1900);

The Great Boer War (London: Smith, Elder, 1900; New York: McClure, Phillips, 1900);

The Immortal Memory (Edinburgh: Mitchell, 1901);

The Hound of the Baskervilles (London: Newnes, 1902; New York: McClure, Phillips, 1902);

The War in South Africa: Its Cause and Conduct (London: Smith, Elder, 1902; New York: McClure, Phillips, 1902);

Adventures of Gerard (London: Newnes, 1903; New York: McClure, Phillips, 1903);

A Duet (A Duologue) (London: French, 1903);

The Return of Sherlock Holmes (London: Newnes, 1905; New York: McClure, Phillips, 1905);

The Fiscal Question: Treated in a Series of Three Speeches (Hawick: Henderson, 1905);

Arthur Conan Doyle, 1894, in his study at the house in South Norwood that he bought in 1891

An Incursion into Diplomacy (London: Smith, Elder, 1906);

Sir Nigel (London: Smith, Elder, 1906; New York: McClure, Phillips, 1906);

The Story of Mr. George Edalji (London: Roberts, 1907); republished as *The Case of Mr. George Edalji* (Putney: Blake, 1907);

Through the Magic Door (London: Smith, Elder, 1907; New York: Doubleday, Page, 1908);

The Croxley Master: A Great Tale of the Prize Ring (New York: McClure, Phillips, 1907);

Waterloo (London & New York: French, 1907);

Round the Fire Stories (London: Smith, Elder, 1908; New York: McClure, Phillips, 1908);

The Crime of the Congo (London: Hutchinson, 1909; New York: Doubleday, Page, 1909);

Divorce Law Reform: An Essay (London: Divorce Law Reform Union, 1909);

Why He Is Now in Favour of Home Rule (London: Liberal Publication, 1911);

Songs of the Road (London: Smith, Elder, 1911; Garden City: Doubleday, Page, 1911);

The Last Galley: Impressions and Tales (London: Smith, Elder, 1911; Garden City: Doubleday, Page, 1911);

The Speckled Band: An Adventure of Sherlock Holmes (New York & London: French, 1912);

The Case of Oscar Slater (London: Hodder & Stoughton, 1912; New York: Doran, 1913);

The Lost World (London: Hodder & Stoughton, 1912; New York: Doran, 1912);

The Poison Belt (London: Hodder & Stoughton, 1913; New York: Doran, 1913);

Great Britain and the Next War (Boston: Small, Maynard, 1914);

To Arms! (London: Hodder & Stoughton, 1914);

The German War (London: Hodder & Stoughton, 1914);

The Valley of Fear (London: Smith, Elder, 1915; New York: Doran, 1915);

A Visit to Three Fronts (London: Hodder & Stoughton, 1916; New York: Doran, 1916);

The British Campaign in France and Flanders, 6 volumes (London: Hodder & Stoughton, 1916-1919; New York: Doran, 1916-1920);

His Last Bow: Some Reminiscences of Sherlock Holmes (London: Murray, 1917); republished as *His Last Bow: A Reminiscence of Sherlock Holmes* (New York: Doran, 1917);

The New Revelation (London: Hodder & Stoughton, 1918; New York: Doran, 1918);

Danger! and Other Stories (London: Murray, 1918; New York: Doran, 1919);

The Vital Message (London: Hodder & Stoughton, 1919; New York: Doran, 1919);

Spiritualism and Rationalism (London: Hodder & Stoughton, 1920);

The Wanderings of a Spiritualist (London: Hodder & Stoughton, 1921; New York: Doran, 1921);

The Coming of the Fairies (London: Hodder & Stoughton, 1922; New York: Doran, 1922);

The Poems of Sir Arthur Conan Doyle: Collected Edition (London: Murray, 1922);

The Case for Spirit Photography (London: Hutchinson, 1922; New York: Doran, 1923);

Our American Adventure (London: Hodder & Stoughton, 1923; New York: Doran, 1923);

Three of Them: A Reminiscence (London: Murray, 1923);

Our Second American Adventure (London: Hodder & Stoughton, 1924; Boston: Little, Brown, 1924);

Memories and Adventures (London: Hodder & Stoughton, 1924; Boston: Little, Brown, 1924; revised, London: Hodder & Stoughton, 1930);

Psychic Experiences (London & New York: Putnam's, 1925);

The Land of Mist (London: Hutchinson, 1926; New York: Doran, 1926);

The History of Spiritualism, 2 volumes (London: Cassell, 1926; New York: Doran, 1926);

Pheneas Speaks (London: The Psychic Press and Bookshop, 1927; New York: Doran, 1927);

The Case-Book of Sherlock Holmes (London: Murray, 1927; New York: Doran, 1927);

The Maracot Deep and Other Stories (London: Murray, 1929; Garden City: Doubleday, Doran, 1929);

Our African Winter (London: Murray, 1929);

The Edge of the Unknown (London: Murray, 1930; New York: Putnam's, 1930);

The Field Bazaar (London: Athenaeum, 1934; Summit, N.J.: Pamphlet House, 1947);

The Professor Challenger Stories (London: Murray, 1952);

The Crown Diamond: An Evening with Sherlock Holmes, a Play in One Act (New York: Privately printed, 1958);

Strange Studies from Life: Containing Three Hitherto Uncollected Tales (New York & Copenhagen: Candlelight Press, 1963);

The Unknown Conan Doyle: Uncollected Stories, edited by John Michael Gibson and Richard Lancelyn Green (London: Secker & Warburg, 1982; Garden City: Doubleday, 1984);

The Unknown Conan Doyle: Essays on Photography, edited by Gibson and Green (London: Secker & Warburg, 1982; North Pomfret, Vt.: David & Charles, 1983).

PLAY PRODUCTIONS: *Jane Annie*, by Doyle and J. M. Barrie, London, Savoy Theatre, 13 May 1893;

Foreign Policy, London, Terry's Theatre, 3 June 1893;

A Story of Waterloo, Bristol, Princess's Theatre, 21 September 1894; London, Lyceum Theatre, 4 May 1895;

Halves, Aberdeen, Scotland, Haymarket Theatre, 10 April 1899; London, Garrick Theatre, 10 June 1899;

Brigadier Gerard, London, Imperial Theatre, 3 March 1906;

The Fires of Fate, London, Lyric Theatre, 15 June 1909;

The House of Temperley, London, Adelphi Theatre, 27 December 1909;

A Pot of Caviare, London, Adelphi Theatre, 19 April 1910;

The Speckled Band, London, Adelphi Theatre, 4 June 1910;

The Crown Diamond, London, London Coliseum, 16 May 1921.

It is difficult to imagine the shape which detective fiction might have taken had it not been for the creation by Arthur Conan Doyle of Sherlock Holmes. Conan Doyle took a form of fiction which had become popular through the works of his predecessors, Edgar Allan Poe and Emile Gaboriau, and reshaped it, adding elements which made his own contributions among the most popular fiction of all time. The stories themselves have been considered in several contexts, both serious and facetious.

The period within which the stories were set and against which they can be examined was one of social, economic, and political change. They came at a time when the growing degree of literacy was combined with an expanding amount of leisure time. Thus, the era was right for the particular type of story which they represent. The periodical was a significant channel of communication; fiction had a growing influence; and a new concept, the best-seller, was developing. There

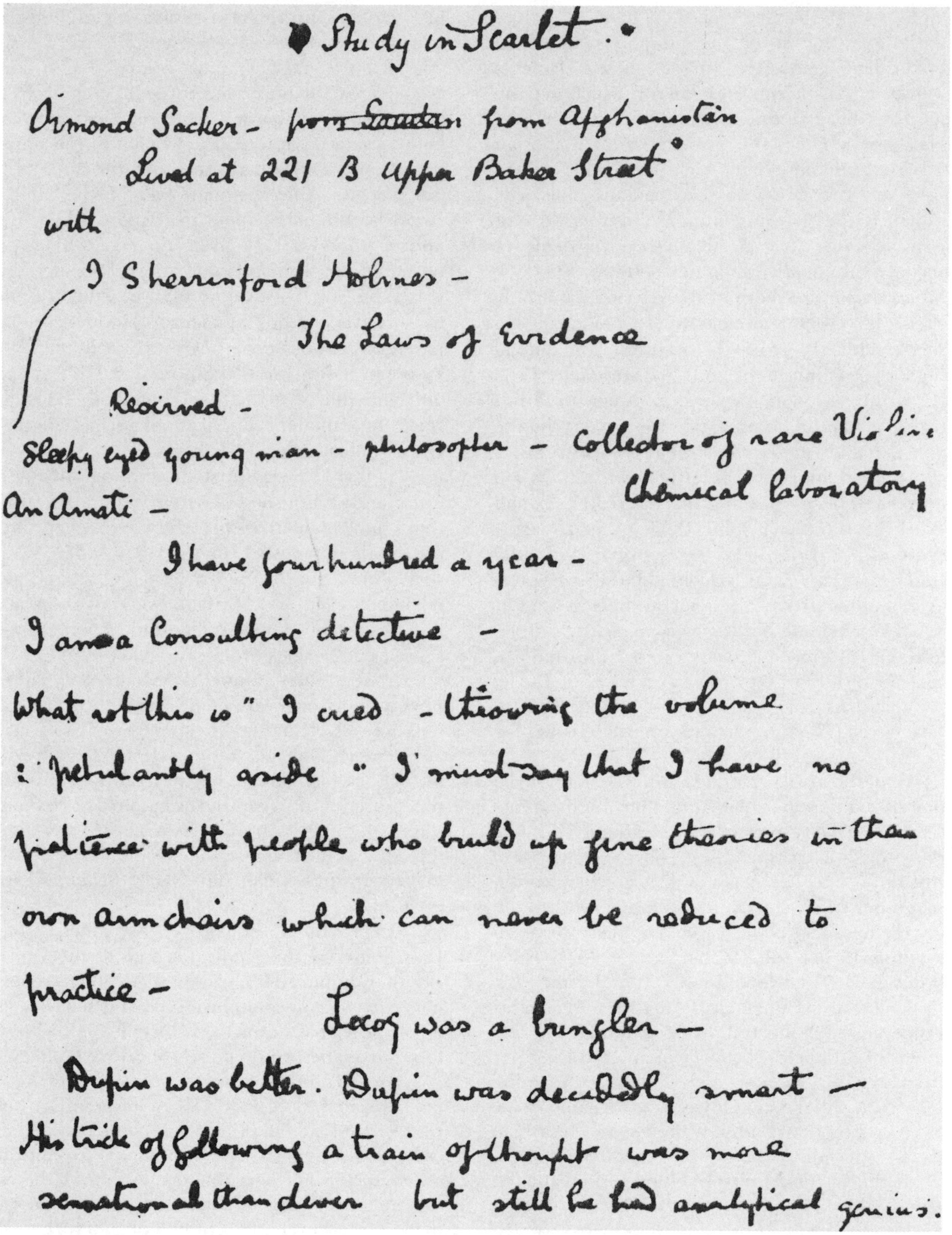

Study in Scarlet.

Ormond Sacker - from ~~Sudan~~ from Afghanistan
        Lived at 221 B Upper Baker Street
with
    I Sherrinford Holmes -
                The Laws of Evidence

    Reserved -
Sleepy eyed young man - philosopher - Collector of rare Violins
An Amati -   Chemical laboratory

        I have four hundred a year -

I am a Consulting detective -

What rot this is" I cried - throwing the volume
: petulantly aside " I must say that I have no
patience with people who build up fine theories in their
own armchairs which can never be reduced to
practice -
                Lecoq was a bungler -
    Dupin was better. Dupin was decidedly smart -
His trick of following a train of thought was more
sensational than clever   but still he had analytical genius.

Notes for Conan Doyle's first novel demonstrating how his initial conceptions of Sherlock Holmes and John Watson were modified
(Stanley Mackenzie Collection)

was a literature not for the elite, but for the people.

The Gothic novel, the Newgate novel, even the so-called Penny Dreadful, contained elements of mystery, suspense, and horror which set the stage for what Poe called the tale of ratiocination. A few years later, the French writer Gaboriau used some of these same elements in his novels, collectively referred to as his "romans policiers," but which the growing number of followers of the form came to call the mystery or detective story. In *A Study in Scarlet* (1888) Sherlock Holmes disparages both of these writers, but only because his creator wished to add personality to his character. In reality, the author was among the greatest admirers of both Poe and Gaboriau.

Arthur Conan Doyle was born in Edinburgh, Scotland, on 22 May 1859. "Art in the blood is liable to take the strangest forms," Sherlock Holmes once said about his own family. He might have been speaking of his creator. Conan Doyle's grandfather, John Doyle, was an artist and political cartoonist of the Georgian and early Victorian era. Conan Doyle's father, Charles Doyle, made a precarious living at the Scottish Office of Works, but he was also an artist, supplementing his income with book illustrations. Charles's older brother, Richard (Dickie) Doyle, drew pictures for *Punch* and designed the famous cover which appeared on each issue for 100 years.

Conan Doyle's mother, Mary Foley Doyle, was well read and a great storyteller, both characteristics clearly responsible for leading his interests toward literature. Less obvious, but also significant, was her passion for genealogy. On her mother's side she could trace her roots to the Plantagenets, and she projected a fierce pride in his family to her son. To her family, Mary Foley Doyle was always referred to as "the Ma'am."

For Arthur Conan Doyle, art would mean literature and not illustration or painting. He was named for an uncle, Michael Conan, and King Arthur. Later he came to prefer Conan Doyle (unhyphenated), rather than Doyle, as a surname.

As a boy he read Sir Walter Scott's historical novels, especially *Ivanhoe*. This book by the father of the historical novel helped to implant the spirit of chivalry in young Arthur's character. It also led him to emulate Scott in writing his own historical novels. In Conan Doyle's personality, as well as in his writing, there are the same traits of courage, nobility, fairness, courtesy, respect for women, protection of the poor, and all the rest

of the attributes of knighthood. And though Sherlock Holmes professes a dislike for and distrust of women and says in *The Sign of Four*: "I assure you that the most winning woman I ever knew was hanged for poisoning three little children for their insurance money," he remains courteous and considerate toward the women in the stories.

Conan Doyle had other favorite authors besides Scott. Among them was Mayne Reid, a writer of popular adventure fiction, whose best-known work was *The Scalp-Hunters* (1851), a tale of marauding Indians in northern Mexico.

The Conan Doyle family was Roman Catholic, so young Arthur was sent to Hodder, the preparatory school for Stonyhurst, a Jesuit public school in Lancashire. At Stonyhurst life was Spartan, and one was toughened in both body and spirit by frequent applications of a length of India rubber called a "Tolley."

It was at Stonyhurst that young Arthur became a distinguished amateur at sports, something he remained all his life. He excelled in the use of the singlestick (a sort of wooden swordstick with a guard, used in fencing) as well as in boxing, cricket, and football. Some of these abilities (especially singlestick and boxing) were shared by Sherlock Holmes.

At the same time that his intellectual and physical horizons were being broadened, his spiritual life was changing. He spent a year in Austria at Feldkirch College, another Jesuit school, when he was sixteen, but he began to draw away from the church and organized religion. He never became an atheist, however. Atheism was something he found incomprehensible. This attitude may help to explain his later belief in spiritualism.

In 1876, at the age of seventeen, Conan Doyle entered the medical school at the University of Edinburgh. It was here that he seems to have first become interested in spiritualism, and it was here that he met Dr. Joseph Bell, who was to serve as the prototype for Sherlock Holmes.

In his autobiography, *Memories and Adventures* (1924), he recalls his experience in Dr. Bell's classes. Bell was a skillful surgeon, but his specialty was diagnosis, not only of disease but also of character and occupation. Although he was sometimes incorrect, usually the results were dramatic and accurate. He could look at a former soldier, not long discharged, and tell him what regiment he had served in and where he had been stationed. Conan Doyle was able to use the method of medical diagnosis in explaining the

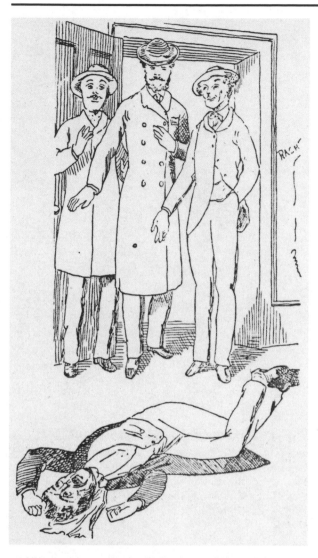

Illustration by Charles Doyle, the author's father, for the first edition of A Study in Scarlet

working of Holmes's method of "scientific deduction." When Holmes says to Dr. Watson, "You know my methods," he is speaking the literal truth. The methods Holmes applies are also those of Dr. Watson, but in a different context.

While in medical school, Conan Doyle had begun to write fiction and sold his first short story, "The Mystery of Sasassa Valley," to *Chambers's Journal* in 1879. This story of the search for diamonds in Africa gives little evidence that its author would ever make his living from anything except medicine. Even medicine was anything but a certain path. Newcomers to the profession found little work and less money.

While still a student he signed to go as a surgeon aboard the steam whaler *Hope*, bound for the Arctic. After this adventure he was gradu-

ated in 1881 with the degrees of Bachelor of Medicine and Master of Surgery and returned to the sea on a passenger liner to West Africa.

Conan Doyle returned from Africa in 1882 to take up a partnership with a former fellow student, Dr. George Budd. An account of the partnership may be found in the semi-autobiographical novel *The Stark Munro Letters* (1895). A flamboyant character, half genius and half quack, Dr. Budd was distrusted by Conan Doyle's mother, who did not hesitate to speak her mind in her letters to her son. Dr. Budd and his wife contrived to extract these letters from Conan Doyle's pocket when he hung up his coat. Told that his services in the partnership would no longer be needed, Dr. Conan Doyle removed his brass nameplate from the door and moved his office to No. 1, Bush Villas, Elm Grove, Southsea, a suburb of Portsmouth.

Patients were few and far between and so were the number of stories he wrote which were accepted for publication. In 1883 he sold "Habakuk Jephson's Statement," a story about the mystery ship, the *Mary Celeste*, to James Payn's *Cornhill*, one of the most respected of the journals. (It was in that same journal that Dr. Watson would read Sherlock Holmes's article, "The Book of Life," in *A Study in Scarlet* [1888].)

In 1885 Conan Doyle received his M.D. from Edinburgh and did what many an impoverished young man had done before: he added to his living expenses by getting married. His bride, Louise Hawkins, was the sister of one of his patients. His writing continued, and he added a novel, "Girdlestone & Co.," to the manuscripts which went the rounds of the publishers and were returned. It would take him years to find a publisher for it under its new title of *The Firm of Girdlestone* (1890). A novel of business life, it is scarcely read today.

In 1886 he began to jot down ideas, names, and bits of dialogue and description for a story he intended to call "A Tangled Skein." All that appears to remain of the manuscript of what became the first Sherlock Holmes story are those fragmentary notes. He apparently planned to have the story narrated by a man named Ormond Sacker, who had once lived in Afghanistan and now had rooms at 221B Upper Baker Street. Sacker's friend's name was I. Sherrinford Holmes. (In Conan Doyle's handwritten notes there is no period after the letter "I" in "I Sherrinford Holmes." Did he forget to include it or did he intend the letter to stand for the personal pronoun? The question remains unanswered and his intention ambiguous.) As Conan Doyle was to remark later in reconstructing his creation, he was preparing the way for a new kind of detective, one who would be an improvement on Poe's Dupin and Gaboriau's Lecoq: where those detectives achieved their results largely by chance, Holmes was to achieve his by scientific reasoning.

Today, a writer of detective literature can turn to many textbooks on police methods to keep the stories reasonably accurate. In 1886 there was no such textbook. Hans Gross's pioneering work, *Criminal Investigation*, was not published until 1891. Conan Doyle had to rely primarily on his imagination, his encyclopedic knowledge, his eye and memory for detail, his faculty for relating facts to causes, his ability to reconstruct the past from the present, plus some knowledge of human nature–in short, some of the methods of Sherlock Holmes himself. The anecdotes which support the suggestion that the stories had some influence on real-life crime detection are probably apocryphal. Neither the claim that the French police, the Sureté, once named its crime laboratories at Lyons after the detective nor the story that the Egyptian police used the stories themselves as a textbook in crime detection are supported by concrete evidence. Conan Doyle soon abandoned the names Ormond Sacker and Sherrinford Holmes for the ones by which the characters are known today. Those discarded names were replaced by John H. Watson (a name borrowed, perhaps, from a friend at Southsea, Dr. *James* Watson) and Sherlock Holmes (*Holmes*, perhaps, after the American author Oliver Wendell Holmes, and *Sherlock* for a cricketer against whom Conan Doyle once bowled). "A Tangled Skein" became *A Study in Scarlet* from the comments Holmes makes at the end of the fourth chapter: that there is a scarlet thread of murder running through this skein of life and that it is his and Watson's duty to unravel and expose it.

Conan Doyle began writing the story in March 1886 and completed it the following month. It was not until December 1887 that it finally appeared, after having been rejected by several other publishers, in the pages of *Beeton's Christmas Annual*. The publishers Ward, Lock offered the author twenty-five pounds for the complete rights, and Conan Doyle, not being in a position to argue, accepted.

While awaiting the publication of his first novel, the author began the research into

A 1904 "portrait" of Sherlock Holmes by Sidney Paget, illustrator of the first editions of The Adventures of Sherlock Holmes, The Memoirs of Sherlock Holmes, The Hound of the Baskervilles, *and* The Return of Sherlock Holmes *(Holding Together, or The Ink of the Octopus [Pine Cove, Cal.: A. & J. Hime, 1983])*

seventeenth-century history which resulted in the first of his historical novels, *Micah Clarke*. When the novel was published in 1889 it was an immediate success, both critically and commercially.

There has been some difference of opinion regarding the reception of *A Study in Scarlet*. Some histories of the genre have indicated that it was an immediate success, but the truth is somewhat different. While not generating wild enthusiasm, sales were sufficient for Ward, Lock to publish it as a hardcover book in 1888. By 1892 it had gone through six printings, but three of those appeared after the success of the first series of short stories about Sherlock Holmes in the *Strand Magazine*.

A Study in Scarlet is historically important for more reasons than that it was its author's first novel and that it was the story which introduced Holmes and Watson. It follows the pattern of Gaboriau's novels in that there are really two stories: in the first the reader follows the investigation of a murder by the detective; in the second there is a detailed explanation of the entire family history and situation which lead up to the murder. Gaboriau had presented this structure in the form of two separate volumes; Conan Doyle dealt with the same situation in a single volume divided into two parts. (The final chapter is a return to the style and content of part one.) *A Study in Scarlet* can, therefore, be viewed as a transitional work in the genre; it is a transition to the detective novel in which the murderer's motivation is integrated into the main plot.

While Gaboriau had used the third-person point of view in his novels, Poe had employed a first-person narrator in the Dupin short stories. Conan Doyle applied the latter method but replaced Poe's nameless friend of the detective with John Watson, a fully developed character in his own right. In so doing he added a dimension to the detective story which had been lacking in the works of his predecessors: the human element. But like most strokes of genius, this one was not fully grasped by the author at the time. Doyle abandoned Sherlock Holmes for other endeavors. In 1889 he wrote and published a novel which is decidedly among his minor works and deservedly obscure. Only those interested in tracing his development as a writer are likely to derive much pleasure from *The Mystery of Cloomber*, a somewhat confusing and unconvincing story of the retribution visited upon Maj. Gen. J. B. Heatherstone forty years after his murder of a holy man in India. The novel does gain some significance in its author's biography from its early evidence of his interest in spiritualism, as well as for some of the elements in it which he used with greater success the following year in *The Sign of Four*. The mysterious Indians; Cpl. Rufus Smith, an ague-ridden old India hand with a lame foot; the pursuit by dog across the countryside; the love story; and the fateful Hole of Cree, which swallows up the object of the antagonists' quest, all have their parallels in the second Sherlock Holmes novel: Jonathan Small and his wooden leg; the pursuit by dog across London; Dr. Watson's love for Mary Morstan; and the Thames, which swallows up the Great Agra Treasure.

"The Sign of the Four"—the original magazine story title and the phrase used in the text itself—was first published in *Lippincott's Magazine* for February 1890. It was retitled *The Sign of Four* when published in book form in London that year, but the American edition, also published in 1890, restores the second *the*.

The year 1890 also saw the first official collection of Conan Doyle's short fiction (there had been an earlier, unauthorized collection), *The Captain of the Polestar and Other Tales*. In April Chatto and Windus published *The Firm of Girdlestone*, with its subtitle *A Romance of the Unromantic*. Few of Conan Doyle's biographers pay much attention to this novel; one of them dismisses it as being of interest only for its portrait of medical life, while another claims that it contains all of its author's merits and faults. The book is padded with descriptions of extraneous things, and the reader may wonder whether it is intended to be a guidebook to the University of Edinburgh or a thriller. The work is primarily important for what it reveals of its author's development as a writer.

It was also in 1890 that Conan Doyle completed one of his best historical novels, *The White Company*. Having steeped himself in the seventeenth century for *Micah Clarke*, which is set against a background of Monmouth's Rebellion, he now turned to the world of chivalry. The earlier novel had been compared to R. D. Blackmore's *Lorna Doone* (1869); but where Blackmore's novel used the historical setting as a pretext for its romantic plot, *Micah Clarke* consists of episodes strung together on the thread of its historic narrative. The same is true of *The White Company*.

The result of months of study of books on the Middle Ages in England, *The White Company* became a celebration of chivalry and a personal code for Conan Doyle's life and career. It is also a good adventure story. When he completed the manuscript in July 1890, he was so elated that he threw his pen across the room, splashing the wall with ink, as he shouted, "That's done it!" The novel was serialized in the *Cornhill Magazine* in 1891 and published as a book the same year.

While Conan Doyle could write that he was as fond of Hordle John, Samkin Aylward, and Sir Nigel Loring—all characters in *The White Company*—as though he knew them in the flesh, he could have had no idea that another publication of 1891 would place him in the realm of the immortals. The first Sherlock Holmes short story, "A Scandal in Bohemia," appeared that year in the *Strand Magazine*.

Today it is difficult to imagine the impact that a general-interest magazine could have on the reading public in 1891. The passing of the Ed-

Robert Barr; Conan Doyle's sister Lottie; Conan Doyle; Louise Conan Doyle; and Robert McClure, circa 1894

ucation Act of 1870 had made it possible for more people to learn to read and thus made it almost necessary that there be something for them to read. The mass reading public demanded something lighter in tone than the periodicals available at the time, and thus the popular magazine came into being. From today's perspective the formula that developed seems simple: a price of sixpence or less an issue, plenty of light fiction and amusing nonfiction, and a multitude of illustrations. But such a formula would not have worked had there not been editors who could judge the demands of the great mass of new readers. H. Greenhough Smith, who launched the monthly *Strand* in January 1891, was such an editor.

In his autobiography Conan Doyle explained how the idea of writing a series of short stories about Sherlock Holmes came to him. The current periodicals had disconnected short stories; a series with a single character running through it should serve to attract the reader of those stories to a particular magazine. Furthermore, using a series of short stories rather than a serialized novel would remove the risk of a reader missing one number of the magazine and losing interest. As far as anyone has been able to determine, Conan Doyle was the first person to hit upon this idea, and the *Strand* was the first magazine to put it into practice.

According to the author's diary, the first half-dozen of the Sherlock Holmes stories were written in a remarkably short period of time. He mailed in "A Scandal in Bohemia," received the encouragement of the editor to submit more, and followed with five more within two months. Only the flu prevented him from mailing "The Five Orange Pips," the fifth story, until the middle of May. He was paid more for each story than he had received for the entire rights to the first Sherlock Holmes novel, but in spite of this handsome remuneration, he returned to the historical genre for his next novel, *The Refugees* (1893), set in Canada in the seventeenth century.

Conan Doyle had no intention of writing more than those first six Holmes stories. He had to plan each as carefully as though it were a novel and he felt that he might just as well be writing a novel. But when the first story appeared in the July 1891 *Strand*, the publishers knew they had something new, unique, and successful.

To illustrate the stories (one of the reasons the *Strand* was itself so popular was its lavish use of illustrations) a young artist named Sidney Paget was commissioned; the editor thought he had hired Paget's older and better-known brother Walter and had confused the names. Sidney used his brother as a model for the detective, and his illustrations became for many the definitive visual image of Sherlock Holmes. It was in the fourth story, "The Boscombe Valley Mystery," that Holmes was seen for the first time in what has become in the popular mind his standard uniform: the deerstalker cap and Inverness Coat. Paget drew this outfit based on what Dr. Watson described as a "long grey travelling-cloak and close-fitting cloth cap."

As public acceptance of Sherlock Holmes grew, the supply of stories which remained to be published dwindled, and Smith asked Conan Doyle for more. Impatient to get on with *The Refugees*, Conan Doyle said he would write more Holmes stories only if he received more money for them; he named what he considered an outrageous figure of fifty pounds per story. To his surprise, the editor agreed; so he set aside *The Refugees* in order to write six more stories, beginning with "The Adventure of the Blue Carbuncle." Once he had supplied those six, he was asked to write even more. He raised his price drastically and asked for one thousand pounds for the next dozen stories. Again the editor accepted. Conan Doyle set to work, although he warned Smith that he could not be expected to deliver these twelve stories as quickly as he had the previous ones.

By November 1891 he had the idea that in order to be quit of this assignment he would have to kill off his detective. He would have preferred to do so in "The Adventure of the Copper Beeches," but when he reported his intention to his mother she was horrified. "You won't!" she said. "You can't! You *mustn't*!" Holmes's life was spared for the time being.

The new cycle of Sherlock Holmes stories began in the December 1892 issue of the *Strand* and continued until December 1893. The twelve stories actually appeared in thirteen issues, for "The Adventure of the Naval Treaty" was sufficiently long to be divided into two parts for publication in October and November. Before that December 1893 issue, the author had written three minor novels, *The Doings of Raffles Haw* (1891), *The Great Shadow* (1892), and "Beyond the City" (1893). *The Doings of Raffles Haw* concerns a

chemist who learns to transmute base metals into gold, upsetting the economy and society. *The Great Shadow* is the first in a series of historical works set in Napoleonic times; it was to be overshadowed by the Brigadier Gerard stories. "Beyond the City" is one of several stories set in the London suburb of South Norwood, where the author and his family made their home.

The success of the Sherlock Holmes short stories has been the subject of much speculation. Certainly the unique factor of having a single character running through the series explains part of their appeal. What Conan Doyle did with the character and his vision for the series also account for much of it. In addition, there are many touches from the pen of a gifted storyteller and so many felicitous turns of phrase that the stories continue to please even on repeated readings.

The first of the series, "A Scandal in Bohemia" has often been held up as a model for the rest. It is the prototypical Holmes tale. In *The Private Life of Sherlock Holmes* (1933), Vincent Starrett says that it contains nearly all of the elements which made the stories so enjoyable. There is the prologue set in Baker Street with an example of Holmes's use of his science of deduction, the reference to an earlier adventure which has not yet been recorded, the discussion of the problem at hand (or about to be presented), and the entrance of the client (in this instance the illustrious hereditary king of Bohemia) with an additional elaboration of the problem. These preliminaries are followed by the adventure itself and the solution and explanation of the mystery. This structure was based on the conventional pattern of tragic drama: the introduction or exposition, rising action, climax or crisis, falling action, and catastrophe or denouement. The Sherlock Holmes stories are well plotted and well told without material extraneous to the point of the story. The author once claimed that Dr. Watson was without humor as a narrator, but the opportunities for humor in the stories were not avoided, and there are examples which belie that claim. The series is overflowing in humorous concepts: a league of redheaded men, a romantic meeting at the gasfitters' ball, Holmes's remark (in "The Man with the Twisted Lip") that Watson's gift of silence makes him an invaluable companion, and the entire quest for the Blue Carbuncle lost in the crop of a goose.

Equally indicative of the author's intended humor are the references to the many other cases which Dr. Watson has yet to chronicle. The

Tennyson Road.
Nov 11 /91.

Dearest mam -

I have done five of the Sherlock Holmes stories of the new Series. They are 1. The Adventure of the Blue Carbuncle 2. The Adventure of the Speckled Band 3. The Adventure of the Noble Bachelor 4 The Adventure of the Engineer's Thumb 5. The Adventure of the Beryl Coronet. I think that they are up to the standard of the first series, & the twelve ought to make a rather good book of the sort. I think of slaying Holmes in the sixth & winding him up for good & all. He takes my mind from better things. I think your golden haired idea has the making of a tale in it, but I think it would be better not as a detective tale, but as a separate one.

Letter in which Conan Doyle told his mother that he was thinking of "slaying" his famous detective at the end of his second series of Sherlock Holmes stories, so that he could go on to writing "better things" (John Dickson Carr, The Life of Sir Arthur Conan Doyle, *1949)*

case of Wilson, the notorious canary trainer; the Giant Rat of Sumatra ("for which the world is not yet prepared"); the affair of the aluminum crutch; and the story of the politician, the lighthouse, and the trained cormorant are dropped teasingly into the texts of the stories. They are tantalizing in their puckish humor and effective in the way they suggest a greater dimension to the career of the detective; there is a world beyond the confines of the present case.

The author's debt to Poe is apparent in that first short story. It may be read as a tribute to the best and most "Sherlockian" of the Dupin trilogy, "The Purloined Letter," not only in the involvement in both cases of royalty but in the basic premise of concealing an object where it is most likely to be overlooked due to the obviousness of its hiding place. In both stories the place of concealment is revealed after a smoke bomb is thrown by a confederate of the detective.

The short stories include many of the basic devices and traditional concepts upon which the literature of detection is founded. The seemingly guilty party is invariably innocent ("The Boscombe Valley Mystery"); the character who is too good to be true is the one to watch ("The Adventure of the Beryl Coronet"); a clue is found on a scrap of paper clutched in a dead man's hand ("The Reigate Squire"–published in the collected edition as "The Reigate Squires" and in the United States as "The Reigate Puzzle"). Conan Doyle enlivened his stories with appropriately and imaginatively named characters: Dr. Grimesby Roylott, Charles Augustus Milverton, Hosmer Angel, Bartholomew Sholto, Prof. James Moriarty, Col. Sebastian Moran. The name is often indicative of how the reader is intended to respond to the character; the most villainous frequently bear names of ornate splendor.

The examples of deductive reasoning for which Sherlock Holmes has become famous are used by the author both to advance the story and for humorous effect. Holmes's arrogant certainty is occasionally deflated when he makes the wrong diagnosis, but when he is correct the scene crackles with drama. His quick eye surveys Jabez Wilson in "The Red-Headed League," and his observation is almost offhand when he says that he can deduce nothing beyond the fact that the man has done manual labor, takes snuff, is a Freemason, has been to China, and has done a lot of writing lately. Mr. Wilson may be excused for seeming incredulous.

In 1892 the first twelve stories were collected as *The Adventures of Sherlock Holmes*. By then the Conan Doyle household included a daughter, Mary Louise; Louise's mother; and Conan Doyle's sister Connie. Toward the end of the year his sister Lottie moved in with them, and his son Kingsley was born.

The historical novel which had been interrupted by his work on the second series of Sherlock Holmes short stories was completed and published in 1893. One critic considered *The Refugees* to combine the worst parts of French historical fiction with a bad imitation of Mayne Reid, but Robert Louis Stevenson enjoyed it and wrote the author what amounted to a fan letter.

In 1893 the family traveled to Switzerland; the climate there was thought to be beneficial for Louise Conan Doyle, who was ill with tuberculosis. It was there that the author first saw the Reichenbach Falls and realized how he could dispose of Sherlock Holmes. He was finding the requests for more of the detective's adventures irksome; he felt that he had more arrows in his quiver than those aimed at the market for detective fiction. And so, in the last of the new series, the world's greatest consulting detective met his "Final Problem" locked in mortal combat with his old enemy, Prof. James Moriarty. Dr. Watson closed his casebook on "him whom I shall ever regard as the best and wisest man whom I have ever known," paraphrasing Plato's description of the death of Socrates.

London and the rest of the world went into mourning when "The Final Problem" appeared in the *Strand* in 1893. Conan Doyle could not understand the public reaction. The death of his father and the illness of his wife were real-life tragedies with which the one of his imagination could not compare.

The second series of Sherlock Holmes stories was collected in 1894 under the title *The Memoirs of Sherlock Holmes*. In addition to "The Final Problem" it contained "Silver Blaze," with its famous cryptic remark about the significance of the actions of the dog in the nightmare. In keeping with the "memoirs" theme the author revealed something of the detective's earlier life in "The *Gloria Scott*" and "The Musgrave Ritual" and in "The Greek Interpreter" introduced Sherlock Holmes's older brother Mycroft. By expanding the stage on which the dramas were enacted, Conan Doyle added to the verisimilitude of the stories. The great detective did have a life beyond what had been preserved in book form to date.

In the meantime, the author had much to occupy his time and mind. As his wife's health improved, he found new interests to fill the hours when he was not writing. The snow-covered mountains of Switzerland were a perfect place to try out an activity he had discovered on a visit to Norway–skiing. He sent for a pair of skis and astonished the Swiss, to whom the sport was something new. He predicted that someday visitors would come to Switzerland as much for the skiing as for health reasons.

He continued his writing, creating new characters who would appear in a series of stories designed to bind readers to the *Strand*. One was the Brig. Etienne Gerard, whose adventures partially filled the gap left by the death of Sherlock Holmes. He also published *Round the Red Lamp* (1894), a collection of stories about doctors.

His growing interest in spiritualism led him to write a novel about it. *The Parasite* (1894), however, is a strange novel in many ways. He later disowned it and hoped it would be forgotten. It concerns a doctor who is converted to belief in spiritualism by an unattractive female mesmerist who turns on him when she learns what he really thinks of her. Under her spell he commits acts he considers to be criminal, and she makes him speak nonsense at his lectures. When he refuses to retract his statements about her, she forces him to break into a bank and to attempt to disfigure his girlfriend with acid. The novel is out of character for the creator of Sherlock Holmes, the master of logic.

In 1895 he published *The Stark Munro Letters*, the story of his experience with Dr. Budd of the previous decade. The requests for more Sherlock Holmes stories continued. But readers had to be content with the two novels and the two collections of short stories which remained in print. There seemed to be no diminution in the popularity of the four books.

The first eight Brigadier Gerard stories were collected as *The Exploits of Brigadier Gerard* (1896). Its success was matched by Conan Doyle's Regency novel of prizefighting, *Rodney Stone* (1896), which was serialized in the *Strand* with illustrations by Sidney Paget. In 1897 another Napoleonic novel, *Uncle Bernac*, appeared. An uneven work, it has its moments of interest but seems to lose momentum when its hero joins the army of the emperor. Included in its cast of characters is a young officer named Etienne Gerard. Other minor works followed: *The Tragedy of the Korosko* (1898), about the reconquest of the Sudan and its restoration to Anglo-Egyptian control; a collection of verse, *Songs of Action* (1898); and a new collection of short fiction, *The Green Flag and Other Stories of War and Sport* (1900).

When the Boer War began, Conan Doyle attempted to enlist in the Middlesex Yeomanry but was rejected due to his age, for he was nearly forty. He joined a hospital unit and went to South Africa in 1900. The Boers had captured the water supply at Bloemfontein, and before long the hospital was filled with men dying of enteric fever; one quarter of the forty-eight members of the hospital staff, including Conan Doyle, were stricken. At one point during the epidemic, a London journalist asked Conan Doyle which of the Sherlock Holmes stories was his favorite. The answer given by the weary senior physician has not been recorded for posterity.

His experiences in the war resulted in *The Great Boer War* (1900), which was known for years as the standard history of that segment of the story of British imperialism. His description of the people against whom the British fought between 1899 and 1902 was both objective and compassionate. Napoleon and his veterans had never treated the British as roughly as those fierce farmers of Dutch extraction.

In 1901, inspired by conversations with the journalist Fletcher Robinson (1871-1907), Conan Doyle dreamed up a ghost story with a rational explanation. *The Hound of the Baskervilles* (1902) was not originally intended as a Sherlock Holmes story; but, needing a hero, Conan Doyle used Holmes, who fit the part admirably. He made it clear, however, that this was an adventure from before May 1891–that is, before the events at the Reichenbach Falls described in "The Final Problem." Holmes had not been revived except in a historical sense.

The Hound of the Baskervilles, serialized in the *Strand* between August 1901 and April 1902, was an instant success. It is considered by many to be the finest of the entire canon and certainly the finest of the four novels. As a ghost story it belongs more to the literature of skepticism than to the literature of belief, as the ghostly hound is integrated into a story of scientific materialism. It is interesting to contrast it with another terror tale of two decades earlier, Stevenson's *Strange Case of Dr. Jekyll and Mr. Hyde* (1886), in which reality is redefined.

Crayon sketch by G. K. Chesterton of Holmes and Moriarty struggling at the top of Reichenbach Falls (courtesy of the Lilly Library, Indiana University)

Readers have often complained that for a Sherlock Holmes story, the detective spends far too much time offstage, leaving Dr. Watson to carry on the bulk of the investigation. A close reading of the novel reveals this to be a necessity and even a strength of the story. The opening chapters are devoted to setting up the tale of the spectral hound and then demolishing the legend. There are repeated references to the men of science who have to deal with this supernatural situation, men whose logic refuses to believe in the hound or the curse visited upon the Baskervilles. The phrase "man of science" is used repeatedly to refer to Sherlock Holmes, to Dr. James Mortimer, to men of precise minds. The theme of the novel clearly is that of science versus superstition.

The legend of the Baskerville family is presented in the classic manner which is traditional in ghost stories: an ancient document is produced by Dr. Mortimer and read aloud. Its authenticity is attested to in the first of a series of reassurances that we are dealing with fact and not fancy. The passage in which Hugo Baskerville swears to sell his soul to the devil also belongs to the tradition.

When Dr. Mortimer has finished reading the document from the past, he turns to one from the present—the 1880s, when the events of the novel are supposed to occur. A newspaper account of the facts surrounding the death of Sir Charles Baskerville emphasizes the cause of death as having been natural, in spite of the circumstances which were suspiciously unusual. As Dr. Mortimer says, putting away the folded newspaper clipping, these are the *public* facts. He then goes into the *private* facts, based on his own observations, and ends his account with one of the most memorably chilling lines in all of literature, ranking with Robinson Crusoe's discovery of a footprint on an otherwise uninhabited island. He had seen traces around the body of Sir Charles, traces that no one else had observed: "Mr. Holmes, they were the footprints of a gigantic hound."

Having taken pains to establish the scientific background and training of the characters in his novel, Conan Doyle continues to emphasize these qualities when he describes Dr. Mortimer's observant nature. He is not one to jump to conclusions or make hasty judgments. Readers are as certain that he has seen the footprints as if they had been there and seen them.

All of the mysterious occurrences in these opening chapters—the message made up of words clipped from a newspaper, the man who seems to be following Dr. Mortimer and Sir Henry Baskerville on the street—can be explained by rational means. The case against this being a true tale of the supernatural has been set up so concretely that the ghost seems to have been exorcised. The only way for the author to restore the superstition theme is to arrange for Sherlock Holmes to be absent from most of the rest of the story, and so Dr. Watson is sent to accompany Sir Henry to Baskerville Hall.

Once Dr. Watson is on center stage, the tone of the novel changes. On the journey to Baskerville Hall, the author is able to use his powers of description to restore the eerie quality to the story. It is autumn, when things are dying. Baskerville Hall is described in terms that emphasize its ancient Gothic architecture. The only hint of science to dispel the gloom is Sir Henry's desire to install electric lights in front of the main entrance.

Every event from that point up to the reappearance of Sherlock Holmes is there for the purpose of emphasizing the supernatural and the power of superstition. Mystery is added to mystery until Holmes returns as a deus ex machina to set things right, and the powers of light and science triumph. The denouement is handled with fitting dramatic effect. The explanation of the spectral hound is made back at Baker Street when the tension of the final chase over the moor has been relieved and there is a period for objective analysis.

From this temporary return of Sherlock Holmes the author turned to some of his other concerns. He published a sixty-thousand-word pamphlet, *The War in South Africa: Its Cause and Conduct* (1902), in which he defended the British soldier's role in the war and refuted the charges of barbarism, rape, and murder which were appearing in newspapers both abroad and at home. Shortly thereafter he received a knighthood from King Edward VII for his services to his country.

The new Sir Arthur, like the former Dr. Conan Doyle, was besieged by requests for more Holmes stories. Finally, offered $5,000 per story by the editors of *Collier's Weekly*, an American popular periodical, and about half that sum per story for the English rights by the editor of the *Strand*, Conan Doyle agreed. And so, in the fall of 1903, readers on both continents learned that Holmes had really survived the battle with Professor Moriarty: it was Moriarty alone who went over the cliff and into the dreadful abyss at the

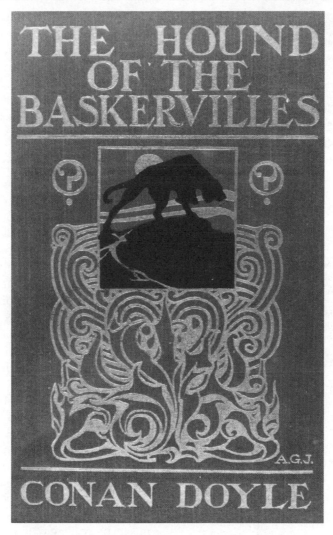

Cover for Conan Doyle's 1902 Sherlock Holmes novel, written after "The Final Problem," the 1893 short story in which he attempted to "kill" his fictional detective, but set before Holmes's plunge over Reichenbach Falls (courtesy of Otto Penzler)

Reichenbach Falls. As luck would have it, Conan Doyle had written "The Final Problem" in such a way that he had never really described Holmes's death. He was able to come up with an exotic explanation for what had happened to account for the detective's being absent from London for three years. During the period, which has become known to students of the detective's career as the Great Hiatus, he had been traveling incognito through the Middle East and Europe as a Norwegian explorer named Sigerson.

People lined up for blocks to buy the magazines containing the new story, "The Empty House." The stories appeared on a monthly schedule for the next year before being collected into book form as *The Return of Sherlock Holmes* in 1905.

There are those who maintain that the sto-

ries which appeared after Holmes's return are not as good as the earlier ones. Certainly there is not quite the same level of imagination and inspired genius, or the same touches of humor in the later years. Many of the later stories repeat ideas and situations found in the early ones, but there are many which are the equal of anything in *The Adventures of Sherlock Holmes* or *The Memoirs of Sherlock Holmes*, just as there are weak efforts among the early gems.

The novelty of those early years of the 1890s had worn off, and the host of imitators and detractors in the fictional detectives who followed Holmes through the pages of the popular magazines tended to take some of the glory away from the original. By the time that *The Return of Sherlock Holmes* had been published the leading

Jean Leckie shortly before her marriage to Conan Doyle on 18 September 1907

character and his creator were household names. Some of this fame was due to the appearance of the detective on the stage in a play written by and starred in by the American actor William Gillette, which premiered in New York in November 1899. The stories in *Collier's* were illustrated by the American artist Frederic Dorr Steele, who based his image of Holmes on the rugged-looking Gillette. It was this licensing of his character for use in other media which helped to preserve the persona of Sherlock Holmes and make of him a sort of folk hero. Conan Doyle himself had written a play about Sherlock Holmes, the text of which has been lost; Gillette received permission to rewrite this play, and what survives is more Gillette than Conan Doyle. Conan Doyle did have some success with the Sherlock Holmes drama *The Speckled Band* (1912), which premiered in 1910.

The return of Sherlock Holmes and his perpetuation on the stage having added to his financial security, Conan Doyle continued gathering material for more historical novels. He also purchased two motor cars and a motorcycle for use at his country home, Undershaw, at Hindhead in Surrey. In his *Life of Sir Arthur Conan Doyle* (1949), John Dickson Carr tells the story of the time the author was driving his mother in one of the cars, a Wolseley, and collided with two farm wagons loaded with turnips. The horses bolted, overturning the wagons and covering the old lady with the vegetables. Her son sprang out of the car, rushed to see if his mother was injured, and found that she was not even disturbed. She took out her knitting and worked away while the celebrated author and the farmer debated their driving abilities in voices that could be heard for miles around. News of the acquisition of a motorcycle by the author having reached the ears of a reporter for a magazine, Conan Doyle was asked whether Sherlock Holmes would soon begin pursuing villains, accompanied by the faithful Watson, both riding the latest model of that vehicle. Conan Doyle replied in all seriousness that the detective had retired from active duty and that the motorcycle was something he would not care to utilize.

The historical novel *Sir Nigel* (1906) was planned as a companion volume to *The White Company*. Like that work it is set in medieval England, but at an earlier day, and tells the story of the boyhood and early manhood of the knight Nigel Loring. (Rather than a sequel to *The White Company*, it is what is now termed a "prequel.") The author hoped that it would be considered his masterpiece, a bit of living history which reproduced the Middle Ages in all their Gothic splendor, but the critics only pronounced it a rousing adventure yarn.

The only time Conan Doyle addressed himself directly to a discussion of literature was in 1906, in a series of twelve articles for *Cassell's Magazine* collected in 1907 as *Through the Magic Door*. The essays take the form of appreciations or "book chats" that were popular at the time. In the articles he discusses his favorite authors from earlier days: Scott, Boswell, Gibbon, Samuel Pepys, George Borrow, Poe, and Stevenson. He considers Poe the supreme writer of short fiction; all subsequent writers of short stories, and especially detective stories, owe a monumental debt to Poe. His two masterpieces, which could not have been bettered, are "The Gold Bug" and "The Murders in the Rue Morgue"; the proportion and perspective lacking in his other works are definitely present in those two. The horror and weirdness are intensified by the coolness of the protagonists, Le Grand in the first story and Dupin in the second.

In the year in which these articles appeared in *Cassell's* and *Sir Nigel* saw publication as a book, Conan Doyle's wife Louise died. On 18 September of the following year he married Jean Leckie, a friend of several years standing. He had been in love with Jean for nearly as long as he had known her, but he had refused to treat their relationship as anything but platonic until after his wife's death. Just before the marriage he had bought a modest country house, Windlesham, in Sussex. Enlarged and improved by the time they moved in, it remained his home for the rest of his life.

It was there, in his study on the second floor, that he wrote the rest of the Sherlock Holmes stories, consisting of a final novel and twenty short stories. He also wrote letters and articles pleading the cause of justice for individuals who had been unjustly imprisoned, playing Sherlock Holmes himself on behalf of George Edalji and Oscar Slater. His articles to the press were instrumental in reopening the cases of the accused sufficiently for them to receive their freedom if not a just recompense.

While not remembered for his contributions to the dramatic art, he did compose a number of plays based on his own stories, including one about his favorite creation, Brigadier Gerard.

In 1912 he wrote the first of several stories about Prof. George Edward Challenger, *The Lost World*. The story of a lost race of dinosaurs existing in the twentieth century on a plateau in South America, it has served as inspiration for a number of writers of science fiction and producers of films and has itself been filmed several times.

He was so excited about his creation of the brusque and memorable scientist with the great black beard that he sold the *Strand* on the idea of illustrating the serial with photos of himself made up as Challenger. The editor acquiesced but was afraid that readers would think that the magazine was trying to perpetrate a hoax to convince them that the story was factual. Conan Doyle was so proud of his disguise that he drove thirty miles to try it out on E. W. Hornung, who was the husband of his sister Connie and the creator of the "gentleman burglar" Raffles. Calling at Hornung's house, he kept in character as Challenger, and it was several minutes before Hornung realized he was the butt of a joke. Conan Doyle's brother-in-law swore that he

would never forgive him. This taste for dressing up and mimicry backfired on another occasion when he dressed up as a sort of Jabberwocky figure, frightening his children so severely that they took a long time to be comforted. He followed up *The Lost World* with another Challenger novel, *The Poison Belt* (1913), which deals with the supposed destruction of the entire planet when a belt of deadly gas drifts across the earth.

World War I gave Conan Doyle an opportunity to contribute to the growing number of writings and commentaries on the conflict, along with propaganda articles and pamphlets. In a prophetic vein he wrote about the possibility of digging a tunnel under the English Channel and the advisability of using steel helmets and tanks. His belief that he had actually heard from his wife's brother after the latter's death in the war was the final incident which made him a convert to spiritualism in 1916. For the remainder of his life he lectured, wrote, and lived this philosophy of communication with the dead. The deaths of his son Kingsley, a victim of influenza in 1918 after he was wounded in the war, and his brother Brig. Gen. Innes Doyle in 1919 only strengthened his convictions.

There had been no hint of his impending change in philosophy in 1914 when he wrote *The Valley of Fear* (1915). This fourth and final novel about Sherlock Holmes is a return to the structure established by Gaboriau. Like *A Study in Scarlet* it was constructed in two parts and an epilogue, the first describing the aftermath of the murder of John Douglas and the solution to the mystery provided by Sherlock Holmes, the second telling what led up to the murder. As in the earlier novel, the solution lies in the American background of the murdered man.

Although the author had disposed of Holmes's archenemy, Professor Moriarty, more than twenty years earlier in "The Final Problem," there are suggestions here that he may have regretted such hasty action. The professor, though offstage, is very much alive in *The Valley of Fear*, giving rise to the inference that this story, like *The Hound of the Baskervilles*, predates the events at the Reichenbach Falls. In the two decades since "The Final Problem" was written, the author had evidently forgotten that Dr. Watson had never heard of Professor Moriarty before the flight to Switzerland. Since Conan Doyle's death, this type of inconsistency has fueled much debate among those aficionados of the stories–called "Sherlockians" in the United States and "Holmesians"

Sir Arthur Conan Doyle, 1921

in Great Britain–who study the tales as though they represented factual accounts.

The problem in *The Valley of Fear* concerns not only the identity of the murderer but also that of the victim. The physical and psychological clues are distributed fairly enough so that the reader should have some idea of the significance of the events surrounding the murder; thus, there is an even chance that the reader can predict the ending before arriving at it. While not as dramatic as those in *The Hound of the Baskervilles*, the deductions made by the detective are as interesting as any in the canon and the puckish humor of the author is in evidence. In addition, the passing years seem to have made Holmes less arrogant and more quietly self-confident.

So much of the mystery has been dispelled by the final chapter of the first section that only an epilogue should have been required to complete the tale. Instead, the author has one of the characters hand a bundle of papers to Dr. Watson ("You are the historian of this bunch"), who dutifully inserts it in the text. There is a seven-chapter flashback to events two decades earlier involving Jack McMurdo and the Scowrers, a secret society in the Vermissa Valley in the Pennsylvania coalfields, before the narrative returns to Baker Street for the real epilogue.

The double-plot structure of *The Valley of Fear* demonstrates the weakness of most Sherlock Holmes novels and suggests the real strength of the short stories. When Holmes is not present with a startling display of his science of deduction there is a diminution of the tension and a resulting lack of interest on the part of the reader. While the story of the Scowrers has its moments, most readers are in the habit of skimming quickly the second half of the novel in order to get back to basics and the "wonderful happenings" (in Dr. Watson's words) of the rooms at Baker Street.

The events of World War I seem to have increased Conan Doyle's sense of social consciousness. Like many of his contemporaries in popular letters (John Buchan, William Le Queux, and Edgar Wallace among them) he wrote a multivolume history of some aspects of the war while it was still being waged, *The British Campaign in France and Flanders* (1916-1919). He also wrote a prophetic story, "Danger!" (1918), in which he warned of the threat from submarine torpedoes before they were ever in wide use.

He continued to write Sherlock Holmes stories, but no longer at the rate of one every month. The eight stories in the penultimate collection, *His Last Bow* (1917), represent a span of nearly a decade in their original periodical publications, the earliest having appeared in 1908. One story, "The Adventure of the Cardboard Box," actually dates from 1893, when it was omitted from all collections but the first American edition of *The Memoirs* because its story of an illicit love affair was thought to be too scandalous for a Victorian audience. The title story of the collection serves both as an account of the war service of the great detective and as an epilogue to his career. "His Last Bow," with its third-person narration to preserve the secret until the end, depicts an older Holmes come out of retirement to serve his country.

The majority of his publications for the next decade concerned spiritualism or were accounts of his travels. His mother died in 1921, still unconvinced by those matters he found so convincing. He debated the subject of spiritualism with the American magician Harry Houdini, an avowed skeptic who gained an incredible amount of publicity from his regular challenges to mediums.

In 1925 Conan Doyle resurrected Professor Challenger for a novel published the following year, *The Land of Mist*. The semi-autobiographical book presents its author's years as a spiritualist in narrative form and provides an accurate picture of the spiritualist movement in the 1920s. The third novel in the Challenger series presents a considerable change in that character: Prof. George Edward Challenger, man of science, is a convert to spiritualism following the death of his wife, "that little bird of a woman (who) had made her nest in the big man's heart." The novel was not the most successful in the series, either artistically or commercially, and has survived only in an omnibus edition with its companions, *The Professor Challenger Stories* (1952).

While Conan Doyle had intended "His Last Bow" to be the final Sherlock Holmes story, he was persuaded to continue writing them by the success of a series of filmed versions starring Eille Norwood. He wrote a one-act play, *The Crown Diamond*, with Holmes in it, and then turned it into a short story, "The Adventure of the Mazarin Stone," which was published in the *Strand* in September 1921. After the editor of the magazine supplied him with the idea for the plot, he wrote "The Problem of Thor Bridge," which appeared early in 1922. The remaining ten stories were completed, by all accounts, by 1925. The last of them, "Shoscombe Old Place," was published early in 1927, and all twelve were collected in *The Case-Book of Sherlock Holmes* that same year.

The author's final years were spent in the cause of spiritualism, although he published a short science-fiction collection *The Maracot Deep and Other Stories* (1929), which included two short stories about Professor Challenger, "The Disintegration Machine" and "When the World Screamed." The last two stories indicate that their author's puckish humor was still intact. Stricken with angina pectoris in the fall of 1929, he maintained his working schedule to the best of his ability. He died on the morning of 7 July 1930 and was buried on his estate at Windlesham. The inscription on his headstone reads "Steel True, Blade Straight."

Arthur Conan Doyle is an author whose major creation has long outlived him. Sherlock Holmes has taken on a life beyond anything his creator intended or could have predicted. Unlike many writers of detective stories who use a recurring character, Conan Doyle had a vision for his series which did not allow him to write an infinite number of stories about an ageless figure. While it is not described in detail, Sherlock Holmes has a chronological life, with a period of young manhood, ancestors referred to briefly, a year when he definitely retired, and a brief emergence from that retirement. It is easy to believe in him as a real person.

Before Doyle wrote his historical novels he steeped himself in the periods treated in them. He was justifiably proud of his work in that field and hoped to be remembered for it. Ironically, he is remembered chiefly for his stories of Sherlock Holmes–which, after *The Hound of the Baskervilles*, were just as much historical fiction as *Micah Clarke* or *The White Company*. By keeping them set in Victorian or early Edwardian times he was writing of the recent past, his own past.

A few years after Conan Doyle's death, his creation took on an immortality which has been granted to few literary figures. The American writer Christopher Morley proposed in his column, "The Bowling Green," in the *Saturday Review of Literature*, an organization of followers of Sherlock Holmes to be called the Baker Street Irregulars. The purpose of the society was the study of what came to be called the Sacred Writings, the sixty stories about Sherlock Holmes. In emulation of other learned societies and in a spirit of fun, the members began to exchange notes and write "scholarly" papers concerning the minutiae of the stories. Eventually these "scholarly" activities came to form a sort of satire on the world of academic research.

At about the same time, in 1933, the Chicago critic, novelist, and short-story writer, Vincent Starrett, published a loving tribute to Conan Doyle and his work called *The Private Life of Sherlock Holmes*. Apart from a reading of the stories themselves, it may be the best explanation of their continued appeal. It fueled the growing interest in having fun with the character of the great detective.

The movement might have foundered as a sort of elaborate joke of its day but for the arrival on the scene in 1938 of a General Motors executive, Edgar W. Smith, who collected the better of the Sherlockian studies in *Profile by Gaslight* (1944). More important, he founded and edited a quarterly journal devoted to the study of Holmes and his times called the *Baker Street Journal*. First published in 1946, it continues publication, having had five editors since Smith. In 1975 the publication and subscription offices were transferred to Fordham University Press in the Bronx.

Since 1934 there has been an annual dinner in New York City, on or near 6 January, which Morley had established as the birthday of the Master, as Holmes has come to be called. Since a handful of scholarly papers are presented at this function it serves as the parallel to the annual conference of scholars in any discipline. The major Sherlockian periodicals as of 1988 are the *Baker Street Journal* and the *Baker Street Miscellanea* in the United States and the *Sherlock Holmes Journal* in Great Britain. A European periodical with a strong claim to be included for its longevity alone is *Sherlockiana,* the publication of the Danish Baker Street Irregulars.

In the half century since Conan Doyle's death, most critical attention paid to his work has been about Sherlock Holmes. With rare exceptions, such as Alvin E. Rodin and Jack D. Key's *The Medical Casebook of Dr. Arthur Conan Doyle* (1984), only the biographies touch on his other writings at all. And of the multitude of publications about Sherlock Holmes, the emphasis until recently has been on the internal world of the stories, examinations of those inconsistencies of which the author was well aware, but which did not matter because of the story he wanted to tell.

In 1912, when Ronald Knox wrote his satire on the higher criticism as applied to the Bible, "Studies in the Literature of Sherlock Holmes," he had to invent titles and authors for the "learned publications" which he cited. Today, so many of the same topics have been the subject of real publications that no writer need invent sources to cite. The vast literature of Sherlock Holmes has achieved its own bibliographical control in two publications by Ronald De Waal (1974, 1980).

Arthur Conan Doyle is a minor but significant figure in English literature. Since 1980, biographies do not merely repeat the platitudes of the past but examine his relationship to his times and the people with whom he came in contact. Even the publications of the various Sherlockian societies acknowledge him as more than the "literary agent" for John H. Watson. His position in the history of the literature of detection remains secure. No other figure, with the possible exception of G. K. Chesterton, represents the detective story of the early twentieth century so well as Conan Doyle. His accomplishment was in creating two characters who are recognizable even to those who have never read the stories. For the

real readers the recognition is much the same. Long after the details of their adventures have receded from memory, the readers remember those two good comrades.

How did he do it? The answer is a complex formula: take two well-drawn central characters. Surround them with a story which is not so remarkable for its incidents as for the manner in which it is told. Use a setting which seems familiar but is not mundane. Filter it through a mesh made from the strings of your own inner being, finely tuned to that of a majority of your readers. The result may well be a kind of immortality.

Letters:

Letters to the Press, edited by John Michael Gibson and Richard Lancelyn Green (London: Secker & Warburg, 1986; Iowa City: University of Iowa Press, 1986).

Interviews:

R. Blathwayt, "Talk with Dr. Conan Doyle," *Bookman* (London), 2 (May 1892): 50-51;

Harry How, "A Day with Dr. Conan Doyle," *Strand Magazine,* 4 (August 1892): 182-188;

Robert Barr, "A Chat with Conan Doyle," *Idler,* 6 (October 1894): 340-349; republished in *McClure's Magazine,* 3 (November 1894): 503-513.

Bibliographies:

Harold Locke, *A Bibliographical Catalogue of the Writings of Sir Arthur Conan Doyle, M.D., LL.D., 1879-1928* (Tunbridge Wells: Webster, 1928);

Edgar W. Smith, *Baker Street Inventory: A Sherlockian Bibliography* (Summit, N.J., 1945);

Jay Finley Christ, *The Fiction of Sir Arthur Conan Doyle* (N.p.: Privately printed, 1959);

Ronald Burt De Waal, *The World Bibliography of Sherlock Holmes and Dr. Watson* (Boston: New York Graphic Society, 1974);

De Waal, *The International Sherlock Holmes: A Companion Volume to the World Bibliography of Sherlock Holmes and Dr. Watson* (Hamden, Conn.: Archon, 1980; London: Mansell, 1980);

Richard Lancelyn Green and John Michael Gibson, *A Bibliography of A. Conan Doyle* (Oxford: Clarendon Press, 1983).

Biographies:

John Lamond, *Arthur Conan Doyle: a Memoir* (London: Murray, 1931; Port Washington, N.Y.: Kennikat Press, 1972);

Hesketh Pearson, *Conan Doyle: His Life and Art* (London: Methuen, 1943; New York: Walker, 1961);

Adrian Conan Doyle, *The True Conan Doyle* (London: Murray, 1945; New York: Coward McCann, 1946);

John Dickson Carr, *The Life of Sir Arthur Conan Doyle* (London: Murray, 1949; New York: Harper, 1949);

Sir Arthur Conan Doyle Centenary, 1859-1959 (London: Murray, 1959; Garden City: Doubleday, 1959);

Michael and Mollie Hardwick, *The Man Who Was Sherlock Holmes* (London: Murray, 1964; Garden City: Doubleday, 1964);

Pierre Nordon, *Sir Arthur Conan Doyle: L'Homme et L'Oeuvre* (Paris: Didier, 1964); translated as *Conan Doyle: A Biography* (London: Murray, 1966; New York: Holt, Rinehart & Winston, 1967);

Ivor Brown, *Conan Doyle, a Biography of the Creator of Sherlock Holmes* (London: Hamish Hamilton, 1972);

Charles Higham, *The Adventures of Conan Doyle: The Life of the Creator of Sherlock Holmes* (New York: Norton, 1976; London: Hamish Hamilton, 1976);

Ronald Pearsall, *Conan Doyle: a Biographical Solution* (London: Weidenfeld & Nicolson, 1977; New York: St. Martin's Press, 1977);

Julian Symons, *Portrait of an Artist–Conan Doyle* (London: Whizzard Press, 1979; New York: Mysterious Press, 1987);

Owen Dudley Edwards, *The Quest for Sherlock Holmes: A Biographical Study of Arthur Conan Doyle* (Edinburgh: Mainstream, 1983);

Jon L. Lellenberg, ed., *The Quest for Sir Arthur Conan Doyle: Thirteen Biographies in Search of a Life* (Carbondale: Southern Illinois University Press, 1987).

References:

William S. Baring-Gould, *Sherlock Holmes of Baker Street: A Life of the World's First Consulting Detective* (New York: Potter, 1962; London: Hart-Davis, 1962);

Baring-Gould, ed., *The Annotated Sherlock Holmes*, 2 volumes (New York: Clarkson N. Potter, 1967);

H. W. Bell, *Sherlock Holmes and Dr. Watson: A Chronology of Their Adventures* (London: Consta-

ble, 1932; Morristown, N.J.: Baker Street Irregulars, 1953);

Bell, ed., *Baker Street Studies* (London: Constable, 1934; Morristown, N.J.: Baker Street Irregulars, 1955);

T. S. Blakeney, *Sherlock Holmes: Fact or Fiction?* (London: Murray, 1932; Morristown, N.J.: Baker Street Irregulars, 1954);

Gavin Brend, *My Dear Holmes: A Study in Sherlock* (London: Allen & Unwin, 1951);

Bryce L. Crawford, Jr., and Joseph B. Connors, eds., *Cultivating Sherlock Holmes* (LaCrosse, Wis.: Sumac Press, 1978);

Michael and Mollie Hardwick, *The Sherlock Holmes Companion* (London: John Murray, 1962; Garden City: Doubleday, 1963);

Michael Harrison, *In the Footsteps of Sherlock Holmes* (London: Cassell, 1958; New York: Fell, 1960);

Harrison, *The London of Sherlock Holmes* (Newton Abbot: David & Charles, 1972; New York: Drake, 1976);

Harrison, *A Study in Surmise: The Making of Sherlock Holmes* (Bloomington, Ind.: Gaslight Publications, 1984);

Harrison, ed., *Beyond Baker Street: A Sherlockian Anthology* (Indianapolis & New York: Bobbs-Merrill, 1976);

Irving Kamil, "In the Beginning," *Baker Street Journal* (new series), 33 (December 1983): 217-224;

H. R. F. Keating, *Sherlock Holmes: The Man and His World* (New York: Scribners, 1979);

Walter Klinefelter, *Sherlock Holmes in Portrait and Profile* (Syracuse, N.Y.: Syracuse University Press, 1963);

Ronald A. Knox, "Studies in the Literature of Sherlock Holmes," *Blue Book* (Oxford), 1 (July 1912): 111-132;

Ely M. Liebow, *Dr. Joe Bell: Model for Sherlock Holmes* (Bowling Green, Ohio: Bowling Green University Popular Press, 1982);

E. W. McDiarmid and Theodore C. Blegen, eds., *Sherlock Holmes: Master Detective* (LaCrosse, Wis.: Sumac Press, 1952);

Janice McNabb, *The Curious Incident of the Hound on Dartmoor: A Reconsideration of the Origins of the Hound of the Baskervilles* (Toronto: Bootmakers, 1984);

Sam Moskowitz, "Arthur Conan Doyle: A Study in Science Fiction," in his *Explorers of the Infinite* (Cleveland: World, 1963), pp. 157-171;

Ian Ousby, *The Bloodhounds of Heaven* (Cambridge: Harvard University Press, 1976), pp. 140-175;

Michael Pointer, *The Public Life of Sherlock Holmes* (Newton Abbot: David & Charles, 1975; New York: Drake, 1975);

Donald A. Redmond, *Sherlock Holmes: A Study in Sources* (Downsview, Ontario: McGill-Queen's University Press, 1982);

S. C. Roberts, *Holmes and Watson: A Miscellany* (London: Oxford University Press, 1953);

Alvin E. Rodin and Jack D. Key, *The Medical Casebook of Dr. Arthur Conan Doyle: from Practitioner to Sherlock Holmes and Beyond* (Malabar, Fla.: Krieger, 1984);

Samuel Rosenberg, *Naked is the Best Disguise: The Death and Resurrection of Sherlock Holmes* (Indianapolis & New York: Bobbs-Merrill, 1974);

Dorothy L. Sayers, *Unpopular Opinions* (London: Gollancz, 1946);

Philip A. Shreffler, ed., *The Baker Street Reader: Cornerstone Writings about Sherlock Holmes* (Westport, Conn. & London: Greenwood Press, 1984);

Edgar W. Smith, ed., *The Incunabular Sherlock Holmes* (Morristown, N.J.: The Baker Street Irregulars, 1958);

Smith, ed., *Profile by Gaslight: An Irregular Reader about the Private Life of Sherlock Holmes* (New York: Simon & Schuster, 1944);

Vincent Starrett, *The Private Life of Sherlock Holmes* (New York: Macmillan, 1933; London: Nicholson & Watson, 1934; revised edition, Chicago: University of Chicago Press, 1960; revised and expanded edition, New York: Pinnacle, 1975);

Starrett, ed., *221B: Studies in Sherlock Holmes* (New York: Macmillan, 1940);

Chris Steinbunner and Norman Michaels, *The Films of Sherlock Holmes* (Secaucus, N.J.: Citadel Press, 1978);

Jack Tracy, *The Encyclopaedia Sherlockiana* (Garden City: Doubleday, 1977);

Tracy, ed., *Sherlock Holmes: The Published Apocrypha* (Boston: Houghton Mifflin, 1980);

Guy Warrack, *Sherlock Holmes and Music* (London: Faber & Faber, 1947).

Papers:

Manuscript material by Conan Doyle is housed in the Berg Collection, New York Public Library; the Lilly Library, Indiana University, Bloomington; and the Humanities Research Center, University of Texas, Austin. The largest collection of Conan Doyle material, including correspondence, is in the Arthur Conan Doyle Collection, Metropolitan Toronto Library, Toronto, Ontario; the largest collection of Sherlockiana in a public institution is the Philip S. and Mary Kahler Hench Collection, O. Meredith Wilson Library, University of Minnesota, Minneapolis; the largest private collection of Sherlockiana belongs to John Bennett Shaw, Santa Fe, New Mexico, and is designated for deposit at the University of Minnesota.

J. S. Fletcher

(7 February 1863-30 January 1935)

Gerald H. Strauss
Bloomsburg University

BOOKS: *The Bride of Venice* (London: Poole/ Dartford, 1879);

The Juvenile Poems of Joseph S. Fletcher (Dartford: Snowden, 1879);

Songs After Sunset (London: Poole/Dartford, 1881);

Early Poems (London: Poole, 1882);

Anima Christi (London: Washbourne, 1887);

Deus Homo (London: Washbourne, 1887);

Jesus Calls Thee! (London: Washbourne, 1887);

Our Lady's Month (London: Washbourne, 1887);

Frank Carisbroke's Stratagem (London: Jarrold, 1888);

Andrewlina (London: Kegan Paul, 1889);

Mr. Spivey's Clerk (London: Ward & Downey, 1890);

A Short Life of Cardinal Newman (London: Ward & Downey, 1890);

The Winding Way (London: Kegan Paul, 1890);

Adventures of Richard Fletcher of York (London: Chambers, 1892);

Old Lattimer's Legacy (London: Jarrolds, 1892; New York: Clode, 1929);

Through Storm and Stress, Being a History of the Remarkable Adventures of Richard Fletcher of York (London: Chambers, 1892);

When Charles the First Was King (3 volumes, London: Bentley, 1892; 1 volume, London: Gay & Bird/Chicago: McClurg, 1895);

Poems, Chiefly Against Pessimism (London: Ward & Downey, 1893);

The Quarry Farm (London: Ward & Downey, 1893);

The Remarkable Adventure of Walter Trelawney (London & Edinburgh: Chambers, 1894);

Where Shall We Go for a Holiday? (York: Waddington, 1894);

The Wonderful City (London & New York: Nelson, 1894);

Where Highways Cross (London: Dent, 1895; New York & London: Macmillan, 1895);

The Wonderful Wapentake (London: Lane, 1895);

At the Gate of the Fold (New York & London: Macmillan, 1896);

J. S. Fletcher

In the Days of Drake (London: Blackie, 1896; Chicago & New York: Rand McNally, 1897);

Life in Arcadia (London: John Lane/New York: Macmillan, 1896);

Mistress Spitfire (London: Dent, 1896);

Ballads of Revolt (London & New York: John Lane, 1897);

The Builders (London: Methuen, 1897; New York: Mansfield, 1898); republished as *The Furnace of Youth* (London: Pearson, 1914);

God's Failures (London & New York: John Lane, 1897);

At the Blue Bell Inn (Chicago & New York: Rand McNally, 1898);

The Making of Matthias (London & New York: John Lane, 1898);

Pasquinado (London & New York: Ward, Lock, 1898);

The Death that Lurks Unseen (London: Ward, Lock, 1899);

From the Broad Acres (London: Richards, 1899);

The Paths of the Prudent (London: Methuen, 1899);

A Picturesque History of Yorkshire, 3 volumes (London: Dent, 1899-1901);

Baden-Powell of Mafeking (London: Methuen, 1900);

The Harvesters (London: Long, 1900);

Morrison's Machine (London: Hutchinson, 1900);

Roberts of Pretoria (London: Methuen, 1900);

The Golden Spur (London: Long, 1901; New York: Dial, 1928);

The Three Days' Terror (London: Long, 1901; New York: Clode, 1927);

The Arcadians (London: Long, 1902);

Bonds of Steel (London: Digby, Long, 1902);

The History of the St. Leger Stakes, 1776-1901 (London: Hutchinson, 1902); revised as *The History of the St. Leger Stakes, 1776-1926* (London: Hutchinson, 1927);

The Investigators (London: Long, 1902; New York: Clode, 1930);

The Air-Ship (London: Digby, Long, 1903);

Anthony Everton (London & Edinburgh: Chambers, 1903);

The Fear of the Night: A Cluster of Stories (London: Routledge, 1903);

Lucian the Dreamer (London: Methuen, 1903);

Owd Poskitt (London & New York: Harper, 1903);

The Secret Way (London: Digby, Long, 1903; Boston: Small, Maynard, 1925);

David March (London: Methuen, 1904);

The Diamonds (London: Digby, Long, 1904); republished as *Green Ink, and Other Stories* (London: Jenkins, 1926; Boston: Small, Maynard, 1926); republished again as *The Diamond Murders* (New York: Doubleday, Doran, 1929);

For Those Were Stirring Times! And Other Stories (London: Everett, 1904);

The Pigeon's Cave (London: Partridge, 1904);

Grand Relations (London: Unwin, 1905);

The Threshing-Floor (London: Unwin, 1905);

Highcroft Farm (London: Cassell, 1906);

A Maid and Her Money (London: Digby, Long, 1906; Garden City: Doubleday, Doran, 1929);

Daniel Quayne, a Morality (London: Murray, 1907; New York: Doran, 1926);

Grand Relations (London: T. Fisher Unwin, 1907);

The Harringtons of Highcroft Farm (New York: Dodge, 1907);

The Ivory God, and Other Stories (London: Murray, 1907);

Mr. Poskitt (London: Nash, 1907); republished as *Mr. Poskitt's Nightcaps* (London: Nash, 1910);

The Queen of a Day (London: Unwin, 1907; Garden City: Doubleday, Doran, 1929);

A Book About Yorkshire (London: Methuen, 1908; New York: McClure/London: Methuen, 1908);

The Enchanting North (London: Nash, 1908);

The Harvest Moon (London: Nash, 1908; New York: McBride, 1909);

Mothers in Israel (London: Murray, 1908; New York: Moffat, Yard, 1908);

Paradise Court (London: Unwin, 1908; Garden City: Doubleday, Doran, 1929);

The Adventures of Archer Dawe (Sleuth-Hound) (London: Digby, Long, 1909); republished as *The Contents of the Coffin* (London: London Book, 1928);

The Mantle of Ishmael (London: Nash, 1909);

Marchester Royal (London: Everett, 1909; New York: Doran, 1926);

The Wheatstack and Other Stories (London: Nash, 1909);

Hardican's Hollow (London: Everett, 1910; New York: Doran, 1927);

Recollections of a Yorkshire Village (London: Digby, Long, 1910);

Nooks & Corners of Yorkshire (London: Nash, 1911);

The Pinfold (London: Everett, 1911; Garden City: Doubleday, Doran, 1928);

The Adventures of Turco Bullworthy (London: Washbourne, 1912);

The Fine Air of Morning (London: Nash, 1912; Boston: Estes, 1913);

The Golden Venture (London: Nash, 1912);

Memories of a Spectator (London: Nash, 1912);

The Town of Crooked Ways (Boston: Estes, 1912; London: Nash, 1912);

The Bartenstein Case (London: Long, 1913); republished as *The Bartenstein Mystery* (New York: Dial, 1927);

I'd Venture All for Thee! (London: Nash, 1913; Garden City: Doubleday, Doran, 1928);

Perris of the Cherry-Trees (London: Nash, 1913; Garden City: Doubleday, Doran, 1930);

The Secret Cargo (London: Ward, Lock, 1913);

Both of this Parish (London: Nash, 1914);

The Marriage Lines (London: Nash, 1914);

The Ransom for London (London: Long, 1914; New York: Dial, 1929);

The Shadow of Ravenscliffe (London: Digby, Long, 1914; New York: Clode, 1928);

The Wolves and the Lamb (London: Ward, Lock, 1914; New York: Knopf, 1925);

Cover for one of Fletcher's 1909 novels

The King Versus Wargrave (London: Ward, Lock, 1915; New York: Knopf, 1924);

Leet Livvy (London: Simpkin, Marshall, 1915);

The Annexation Society (London: Ward, Lock, 1916; New York: Knopf, 1925);

Families Repaired (London: Allen & Unwin, 1916);

Lynne Court Spinney (London: Ward, Lock, 1916); republished as *The Mystery of Lynne Court* (Baltimore: Norman, Remington, 1923);

Malvery Hold (London: Ward, Lock, 1917); republished as *The Mystery of the Hushing Pool* (New York: Hillman-Curl, 1938);

Memorials of a Yorkshire Parish (London & New York: John Lane, 1917);

The Perilous Crossways (London: Ward, Lock, 1917; New York: Hillman-Curl, 1917);

The Rayner-Slade Amalgamation (London: Allen & Unwin, 1917; New York: Knopf, 1922);

The Amaranth Club (London: Ward, Lock, 1918; New York: Knopf, 1926);

The Chestermark Instinct (London: Allen & Unwin, 1918; New York: Knopf, 1921);

Heronshawe Main (London: Ward, Lock, 1918);

The Making of Modern Yorkshire, 1750-1914 (London: Allen & Unwin, 1918);

Paul Campenhaye, Specialist in Criminology (London: Ward, Lock, 1918); republished as *The Clue of the Artificial Eye* (New York: Hillman-Curl, 1939);

The Borough Treasurer (London: Ward, Lock, 1919; New York: Knopf, 1921);

The Cistercians in Yorkshire (London: Society for Promoting Christian Knowledge/New York: Macmillan, 1919);

Droonin' Watter: A Story of Berwick and the Scottish Coast (London: Allen & Unwin, 1919); republished as *Dead Men's Money* (New York: Knopf, 1920);

Leeds (London: Society for Promoting Christian Knowledge/New York: Macmillan, 1919);

The Middle Temple Murder (London: Ward, Lock, 1919; New York: Knopf, 1919);

The Seven Days' Secret (London: Jarrolds, 1919; New York: Clode, 1930);

Sheffield (London: Society for Promoting Christian Knowledge/New York: Macmillan, 1919);

The Talleyrand Maxim (London: Ward, Lock, 1919; New York: Knopf, 1920);

The Valley of Headstrong Men (London: Hodder & Stoughton, 1919; New York: Doran, 1924);

Exterior to the Evidence (London: Hodder & Stoughton, 1920; New York: Knopf, 1923);

Harrogate and Knaresborough (London: Society for Promoting Christian Knowledge/New York: Macmillan, 1920);

The Herapath Property (London: Ward, Lock, 1920; New York: Knopf, 1921);

The Lost Mr. Linthwaite (London: Hodder & Stoughton, 1920; New York: Knopf, 1923);

The Orange-Yellow Diamond (London: Newnes, 1920; New York: Knopf, 1921);

The Paradise Mystery (New York: Knopf, 1920); republished as *Wrychester Paradise* (London & Melbourne: Ward, Lock, 1921);

Pontefract (London: Society for Promoting Christian Knowledge/New York: Macmillan, 1920);

Scarhaven Keep (London: Ward, Lock, 1920; Knopf, 1922);

The Root of all Evil (London: Hodder & Stoughton, 1921; New York: Doran, 1924);

Yorkshiremen of the Restoration (London: Allen & Unwin, 1921);

The Heaven-kissed Hill (London: Hodder & Stoughton, 1922; New York: Doran, 1924);

In the Mayor's Parlour (London: John Lane, 1922); republished as *Behind the Panel* (London & Glasgow: Collins, 1931);

The Markenmore Mystery (London: Jenkins, 1922; New York: Knopf, 1923);

The Middle of Things (London & Melbourne: Ward, Lock, 1922; New York: Knopf, 1922);

Ravensdene Court (London & Melbourne: Ward, Lock, 1922; New York: Knopf, 1922);

The Ambitious Lady (London & Melbourne: Ward, Lock, 1923);

The Charing Cross Mystery (London: Jenkins, 1923; New York & London: Putnam's, 1923);

The Copper Box (London & New York: Hodder & Stoughton, 1923; New York: Doran, 1923);

Halifax (London: Sheldon/New York & Toronto: Macmillan, 1923);

Many Engagements (London: Long, 1923);

The Mazaroff Murder (London: Jenkins, 1923); republished as *The Mazaroff Mystery* (New York: Knopf, 1924);

The Million-Dollar Diamond (London: Jenkins, 1923); republished as *The Black House in Harley Street* (Garden City: Doubleday, Doran, 1928);

The Cartwright Gardens Murder (London: Collins, 1924; New York: Knopf, 1926);

False Scent (London: Jenkins, 1924; New York: Knopf, 1925);

The Kang-He Vase (London: Collins, 1924; New York: Knopf, 1926);

Rippling Ruby (New York & London: Putnam's, 1923); republished as *The Mysterious Chinaman* (London: Jenkins, 1924);

The Safety Pin (London: Jenkins, 1924; New York & London: Putnam's, 1924);

The Secret of the Barbican, and Other Stories (London: Hodder & Stoughton, 1924; New York: Doran, 1925);

The Time-Worn Town (New York: Knopf, 1924; London: Collins, 1929);

The Bedford Row Mystery (London: Hodder & Stoughton, 1925); republished as *The Strange Case of Mr. Henry Marchmont* (New York: Knopf, 1927);

The Great Brighton Mystery (London: Hodder & Stoughton, 1925; New York: Knopf, 1926);

The Life and Work of St. Wilfrid of Ripon, Apostle of Sussex (Chichester: Thompson, 1925);

The Mill of Many Windows (London: Collins, 1925; New York: Doran, 1925);

The Reformation in Northern England (London: Allen & Unwin, 1925);

Sea Fog (London: Jenkins, 1925; New York: Knopf, 1926);

The Massingham Butterfly, and Other Stories (London: Jenkins, 1926; Boston: Small, Maynard, 1926);

The Mortover Grange Mystery (London: Jenkins, 1926); republished as *The Mortover Grange Affair* (New York: Knopf, 1927);

Safe Number Sixty-Nine, and Other Stories (Boston: International Pocket Library, 1926);

The Stolen Budget (London: Hodder & Stoughton, 1926); republished as *The Missing Chancellor* (New York: Knopf, 1927);

The Green Rope (London: Jenkins, 1927; New York: Knopf, 1927);

The Murder in the Pallant (London: Jenkins, 1927; New York: Knopf, 1928);

The Passenger to Folkstone (London: Jenkins, 1927; New York: Knopf, 1927);

Behind the Monocle, and Other Stories (London: Jarrolds, 1928; Garden City: Doubleday, Doran, 1930);

Cobweb Castle (London: Jenkins, 1928; New York: Knopf, 1928);

The Double Chance (London: Nash & Grayson, 1928; New York: Dodd, Mead, 1928);

The Wild Oat (London: Jarrolds, 1928; Garden City: Doubleday, Doran, 1929);

The Wrist Mark (New York: Knopf, 1928; London: Jenkins, 1929);

The Box Hill Murder (New York: Knopf, 1929; London: Jenkins, 1931);

The House in Tuesday Market (New York: Knopf, 1929; London: Jenkins, 1930);

The Ravenswood Mystery, and Other Stories (London: Collins, 1929); republished as *The Canterbury Mystery* (Glasgow: Collins, 1933);

The Secret of Secrets (New York: Clode, 1929);

The Matheson Formula (New York: Knopf, 1929; London: Jenkins, 1930);

Historic York (London: Photochrom, 192?);

The Borgia Cabinet (New York: Knopf, 1930; London: Jenkins, 1932);

The Dressing-Room Murder (London: Jenkins, 1930; New York: Knopf, 1931);

The Malachite Jar, and Other Stories (London: Collins, 1930); republished as *The Flamstock Mystery* (London: Collins, 1932); republished again and abridged as *The Manor House Mystery* (London: Collins, 1933);

The Marrendon Mystery, and Other Stories of Crime and Detection (London: Collins, 1930);

The South Foreland Murder (London: Jenkins, 1930; New York: Knopf, 1930);

Illustration by Paul Durden for "The Magician of Cannon Street," one of the stories in Fletcher's Paul Campenhaye, Specialist in Criminology *(1918)*

The Yorkshire Moorland Mystery (London: Jenkins, 1930); republished as *The Yorkshire Moorland Murder* (New York: Knopf, 1930);

Collected Verse, 1881-1931 (London: Harrap, 1931);

The Guarded Room (New York: Clode, 1931);

The Man in No. 3 and Other Stories of Crime, Love, and Mystery (London: Collins, 1931);

Murder at Wrides Park; Being Entry Number One in the Case-book of Ronald Camberwell (London: Harrap, 1931; New York: Knopf, 1931);

Murder in Four Degrees; Being Entry Number Two in the Case-book of Ronald Camberwell (London: Harrap, 1931; New York: Knopf, 1931);

The Burma Ruby (London: Benn, 1932; New York: Dial, 1933);

The Man in the Fur Coat and Other Stories (London: Collins, 1932);

Murder in the Squire's Pew; Being Entry Number Three in the Case-book of Ronald Camberwell

(London: Harrap, 1932; New York: Knopf, 1932);

Murder of the Ninth Baronet; Being Entry Number Four in the Case-book of Ronald Camberwell (London: Harrap, 1932; New York: Knopf, 1932);

The Solution of a Mystery: Documents Relative to the Murder of Roger Maidment at Ullathwaite in the County of Yorkshire in October 1899 (London: Harrap, 1932; Garden City: Doubleday, Doran, 1932);

The Grocer's Wife (London: Hutchinson, 1933);

The Murder in Medora Mansions (London: Collins, 1933);

Who Killed Alfred Snowe? Being Entry Number Five in the Case-book of Ronald Camberwell (London: Harrap, 1933); republished as *Murder of the Lawyer's Clerk* (New York: Knopf, 1933);

Murder of the Only Witness; Being Entry Number Six in the Case-book of Ronald Camberwell (London: Harrap, 1933; New York: Knopf, 1933);

Mystery of the London Banker; Being Entry Number Seven in the Case-book of Ronald Camberwell (London: Harrap, 1933); republished as *Murder of a Banker* (New York: Knopf, 1933);

The Ebony Box; Being the First of the Further Adventures of Ronald Camberwell (London: Butterworth, 1934; New York: Knopf, 1934);

Murder of the Secret Agent; Being Entry Number Eight in the Case-book of Ronald Camberwell (London: Harrap, 1934; New York: Knopf, 1934);

The Carrismore Ruby and Other Stories (London: Jarrolds, 1935);

The Eleventh Hour; Being the Second of the Further Adventures of Ronald Camberwell (London: Butterworth, 1935; New York: Knopf, 1935);

Todmanhawe Grange, by Fletcher and Edward Powys Mathers (as Torquemada) (London: Butterworth, 1937); republished as *The Mill House Murder; Being the Last of the Adventures of Ronald Camberwell* (New York: Knopf, 1937);

And Sudden Death (New York: Hillman-Curl, 1938).

A journalist and historian who wrote extensively about his native Yorkshire, J. S. Fletcher also published detective fiction during almost half a century of prolific output. In a five-year period between 1920 and 1925, for example, he turned out seventeen whodunits, about which a reviewer for the *New York Times* commented, "Each one is an ingenious, cleverly constructed tale, distinctive in plot and incidents and written with as much zest and freshness as if it were his first. The type of mental equipment that can produce each year three or more complicated plots, each dressed out with multitudinous thrilling incidents, will always be a marvel to those who do not possess it." Early in his career he attracted a large audience for his detective fiction in Great Britain, and by the 1920s he rivaled in popularity the equally prolific Edgar Wallace; but in the United States Fletcher was relatively unknown until Woodrow Wilson praised *The Middle Temple Murder* (1919). The president's acclaim led to all of Fletcher's later whodunits being published in the United States as well as in England, but popular as they were in his lifetime, his books have been generally forgotten on both sides of the Atlantic. Most critics since the 1940s either have ignored or denigrated him. Julian Symons in 1972, for instance, in a review of the golden age of detective fiction, includes Fletcher in "the Humdrum school, most of whose members came late to writing fiction, and few [of whom] had much talent for it. They had some skill in constructing puzzles, nothing more. . . ." H. R. F. Keating, however, said in 1982 that Fletcher's "two best books, at least, deserve to be dragged from limbo." According to him, these are *The Middle Temple Murder* and *The Charing Cross Mystery* (1923).

Joseph Smith Fletcher was born in 1863 in Halifax, Yorkshire, the son of a Nonconformist clergyman. Orphaned early, he was raised by his grandmother and educated by private tutors and at Silcoates School. At eighteen, having published two books of verse, he went south to London. He became a journalist and wrote about rural subjects under the pseudonym "A Son of the Soil" for newspapers and periodicals. He wrote editorials for the *Leeds Mercury* and in 1892 produced his first historical study, *When Charles the First Was King*. Within the next few years he wrote *The Wonderful Wapentake* (1895), *Mistress Spitfire* (1896), and other romances. By 1898 he had quit journalism in order to write books full time. The following year his three-volume *A Picturesque History of Yorkshire* began to come out; it and such later books as *The Cistercians in Yorkshire* (1919) and *Yorkshiremen of the Restoration* (1921) led to his being made a Fellow of the Royal Historical Society. He also was a historian of racing–*The History of the St. Leger Stakes, 1776-1901* (1902; revised

1927)–and continued to write poetry throughout his life.

Fletcher was married to the former Rosamund Langbridge, author of *The White Moth* (1932), whose father also was a canon. They had one son. The Fletchers lived at Dorking in Surrey in his later years, and he died there on 30 January 1935.

Though his obituaries in the London *Times* and the *New York Times* did not mention *The Middle Temple Murder*, it is his major achievement and the one that has endured. Its significance extends beyond the fact that it is a carefully plotted narrative, for its popularity in the United States came at a time when the American whodunit scene needed the stimulation of a writer who developed complex puzzles in a fluent style. The urban realism that pervades the book provided a welcome change from the works of such popular writers as Isabel Ostrander and Mary Roberts Rinehart, and it offered a full-length whodunit to admirers of Melville Davison Post, whose output was restricted to short stories. The novel symbolized to many American readers a step forward for the whodunit, which is ironic because *The Middle Temple Murder* and many of Fletcher's subsequent books are set in a Holmesian England. The book is historically important for another reason: Frank Spargo, the novel's sleuth, is an early journalist-detective (preceded by Gaston Leroux's Joseph Rouletabille) of the type that was to become popular on both sides of the Atlantic.

The Middle Temple Murder opens with the discovery of the bludgeoned body of an elderly man in Middle Temple Lane. Newspaperman Frank Spargo, on his way home, happens upon the scene and, curious, becomes involved in the case. At first he and a Scotland Yard detective work as partners, but soon Spargo is off on his own, using his newspaper to draw forth witnesses. The murdered man initially is identified as John Marbury, recently returned to England from Australia; but then he is identified as John Maitland, convicted decades earlier of bank embezzlement and sentenced to prison, and who disappeared after his release. Maitland's son, it turns out, is Ronald Breton, a young barrister friend of Spargo's. Breton, who thought he was an orphan, was raised by a barrister who became his guardian at the behest of his maternal aunt. Stephen Aylmore, a member of Parliament and father of Breton's fiancée, is originally charged with the murder of Marbury-Maitland (it is learned that Aylmore, under a different name,

Dust jacket for the first American edition of one of Fletcher's 1924 novels, in which a safety pin is the clue that leads to the murderer of a wealthy man

had been in prison years earlier with Marbury-Maitland). But through Spargo's efforts (which take him all the way to the Yorkshire moors) Marbury-Maitland is posthumously cleared of the embezzlement (as he claimed at his trial, he indeed had been duped by another), and his murderer is shown to be Breton's aunt, who hated him. Aylmore is freed, and young Breton looks forward to marrying Evelyn Aylmore. Spargo, meanwhile, seems to be well on his way to making a match with her sister Jessie.

A string of coincidences, to be sure, provides vital support to the unfolding plot, but the complications nevertheless mesh neatly, and Fletcher maintains a high degree of suspense throughout. Further, though the puzzle is his primary concern, Fletcher does develop Spargo as an engaging, likable character who not only is lucky but who also is diligent and perceptive.

The only other Fletcher novel that is of continuing interest is *The Charing Cross Mystery*, originally published as a magazine serial entitled

"Black Money." It is similar to *The Middle Temple Murder* in many ways. Again, the sleuth is a young man, this time a barrister named Hetherwick who is wealthy enough to indulge his private interests rather than tend to his profession. Like Spargo, he happens accidentally upon a crime (the first of several coincidences in the book) and assiduously pursues his investigations increasingly independent of the police. Conveniently, a barrister friend of his is from the same town as the first victim and also knows the murdered man's granddaughter, Rhona, who is his only heir. Hetherwick and Rhona fall in love, and at the end of the novel are on the verge of marrying. The most significant similarity between the books is the pervasive influence of the past upon the present. The death by poisoning of retired police superintendent Hannaford of Sellithwaite, which begins the novel, has its roots in events over a decade old, and Hetherwick travels to Sellithwaite–as Spargo goes to Market Mulcaster and the Yorkshire moors–to learn about the past in order to understand present events. Yet another similarity is that a key character (Mrs. Whittingham) disappears under questionable circumstances, reemerges years later with a different identity (as Madame Listorelle), vindicates herself of the suspected wrongdoing, and is victimized by the men who killed Hannaford, her pursuer. Her reappearance not only reopens old wounds but also spawns new crimes, as in *The Middle Temple Murder*.

The Charing Cross Mystery does not measure up to the earlier novel, in part because the resolution, which also involves a chase, is predictable but also because the villains Ambrose and Baseverie are unrealistic. Another character, peripheral though omnipresent, is a grotesque, stereotypical Jew of the sort often seen in Victorian and Edwardian whodunits. Further, too many scenes lack verisimilitude, though there are some dramatically realistic London sequences.

For most of his long and prolific career Fletcher created different sleuths for his full-length mysteries, but in his later years he made Ronald Camberwell the hero of a series of books, including *Murder of the Ninth Baronet* (1932), *The Ebony Box* (1934), and *The Eleventh Hour* (1935). Among his many collections of short stories are early volumes which feature sleuths Archer Dawe and Paul Campenhaye. The best of these is *Paul Campenhaye, Specialist in Criminology* (1918). The ten stories in the book are narrated by a private investigator who states precisely what he is: "I am a

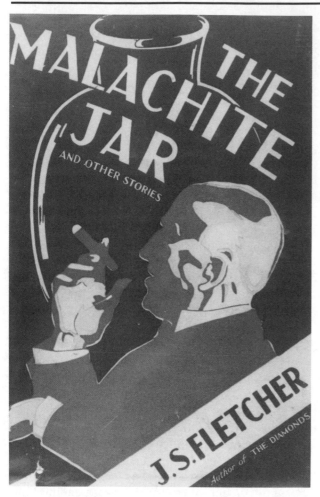

Dust jacket for one of two collections of Fletcher's short stories published in 1930 (courtesy of Otto Penzler)

specialist in criminology. . . . I am not a detective; I have nothing to do with the police." Indeed, Campenhaye works completely independently of the authorities, and some of his cases do not lead to police or legal action. His only helpmates are his clerk, Killingley, and a mysterious man about London, Tregarthan, both of whom figure prominently in the last two stories, "The Settling Day" and "The Magician of Cannon Street." The two pieces are complementary, and Campenhaye does not apprehend the Moriarty-like Mendoba (who is his nemesis) until the conclusion of the second adventure.

Campenhaye's investigations are varied, with several (such as in "The French Maid" and "The Champagne Bottle") involving affairs of the heart that reveal him to be sympathetic to women in distress, even those who have committed indiscretions and crimes. He is a man of action as much as he is ratiocinative, and his assignments take him as far afield as Fletcher's native Yorkshire, but most of the stories are set in London, about which Campenhaye is as knowledgeable as Holmes. A master of disguise (though in "The Magician of Cannon Street" Mendoba recognizes him and hypnotizes him), Campenhaye also is a keen observer of people, places, and things. Some of his successes are not attributable to these skills, however, but rather to chance. In "The Champagne Bottle," for instance, the accidental discovery of a handkerchief leads him to the murderer, and in "The Yorkshire Manufacturer" Campenhaye is searching a murder scene on a desolate moor when, he says, "I suddenly espied at a little distance some object which was shining brightly in the glancing sunlight. . . . I had no other thought in my mind as I walked towards it than that it was a piece of quartz. . . . But what I found was a small case of leather, oval in shape, the sort of thing in which jewellers place rings between pads of satin; what I had seen shining in the sun's rays was certain gilt lettering on the lid—'Armstead, Optician, Hallaton.' " His lucky discovery of a man's spare glass eye, in its case with the optician's name and location, is all he needs to identify James Harthwaite's killer. Despite such occasional weaknesses in some of the stories in the volume, the agreeable personality of Campenhaye, other sensitive characterizations, and the skillfully developed milieus combine to sustain interest.

Though a number of Fletcher's many works in the genre still offer a modicum of pleasure, *The Middle Temple Murder* is the one upon which whodunit historians focus and from which readers can expect a compelling narrative and challenging puzzle. Howard Haycraft and Ellery Queen properly included the novel in their 1951 compilation, "Definitive Library of Detective-Crime-Mystery Fiction," for the passage of time has not dimmed its luster.

Reference:

John T. Hardy, "The Romance of Crime," in his *Books on the Shelf* (London: Allan, 1934), pp. 219-235.

R. Austin Freeman
(11 April 1862-28 September 1943)

John McAleer
Boston College

BOOKS: *Travels and Life in Ashanti and Jaman* (London: Constable, 1898; New York: Stokes, 1898);

The Adventures of Romney Pringle, by Freeman and John James Pitcairn, as Clifford Ashdown (London: Ward, Lock, 1902; Philadelphia: Train, 1968);

The Golden Pool: A Story of a Forgotten Mine (London & New York: Cassell, 1905);

The Red Thumb Mark (London: Collingwood, 1907; New York: Newton, 1911);

John Thorndyke's Cases (London: Chatto & Windus, 1909); republished as *Dr. Thorndyke's Cases* (New York: Dodd, Mead, 1931);

The Eye of Osiris: A Detective Romance (London: Hodder & Stoughton, 1911); republished as *The Vanishing Man* (New York: Dodd, Mead, 1911);

The Mystery of 31 New Inn (London: Hodder & Stoughton, 1912; Philadelphia: Winston, 1913);

The Singing Bone (London & New York: Hodder & Stoughton, 1912; New York: Dodd, Mead, 1923); republished as *The Adventures of Dr. Thorndyke* (New York: Popular Library, 1946);

The Unwilling Adventurer (London & New York: Hodder & Stoughton, 1913);

The Uttermost Farthing: A Savant's Vendetta (Philadelphia: Winston, 1914); republished as *A Savant's Vendetta* (London: Pearson, 1920);

A Silent Witness (London: Hodder & Stoughton, 1914; Philadelphia: Winston, 1915);

The Exploits of Danby Croker, Being Extracts from a Somewhat Disreputable Autobiography (London: Duckworth, 1916);

The Great Portrait Mystery (London: Hodder & Stoughton, 1918);

Social Decay and Regeneration (London: Constable, 1921; Boston & New York: Houghton Mifflin, 1921);

Helen Vardon's Confession (London: Hodder & Stoughton, 1922);

R. Austin Freeman, circa 1898

The Cat's Eye (London: Hodder & Stoughton, 1923; New York: Dodd, Mead, 1927);

Dr. Thorndyke Intervenes (London: Hodder & Stoughton, 1923; New York: Dodd, Mead, 1933);

Dr. Thorndyke's Case-Book (London: Hodder & Stoughton, 1923); republished as *The Blue Scarab* (New York: Dodd, Mead, 1924);

The Mystery of Angelina Frood (London: Hodder & Stoughton, 1924; New York: Dodd, Mead, 1925);

The Puzzle Lock (London: Hodder & Stoughton, 1925; New York: Dodd, Mead, 1926);

The Shadow of the Wolf (London: Hodder & Stoughton, 1925; New York: Dodd, Mead, 1925);

The D'Arblay Mystery (London: Hodder & Stoughton, 1926; New York: Dodd, Mead, 1926);

A Certain Dr. Thorndyke (London: Hodder & Stoughton, 1927; New York: Dodd, Mead, 1928);

The Magic Casket (London: Hodder & Stoughton, 1927; New York: Dodd, Mead, 1927);

The Surprising Adventures of Mr. Shuttlebury Cobb (London: Hodder & Stoughton, 1927);

As a Thief in the Night (London: Hodder & Stoughton, 1928; New York: Dodd, Mead, 1928);

Flighty Phyllis (London: Hodder & Stoughton, 1928);

Mr. Pottermack's Oversight (London: Hodder & Stoughton, 1930; New York: Dodd, Mead, 1930);

Pontifex, Son and Thorndyke (London: Hodder & Stoughton, 1931; New York: Dodd, Mead, 1931);

When Rogues Fall Out (London: Hodder & Stoughton, 1932); republished as *Dr. Thorndyke's Discovery* (New York: Dodd, Mead, 1932);

For the Defence: Dr. Thorndyke (London: Hodder & Stoughton, 1934; New York: Dodd, Mead, 1934);

The Penrose Mystery (London: Hodder & Stoughton, 1936; New York: Dodd, Mead, 1936);

Felo De Se? (London: Hodder & Stoughton, 1937); republished as *Death at the Inn* (New York: Dodd, Mead, 1937);

The Stoneware Monkey (London: Hodder & Stoughton, 1938; New York: Dodd, Mead, 1939);

Mr. Polton Explains (London: Hodder & Stoughton, 1940; New York: Dodd, Mead, 1940);

The Jacob Street Mystery (London: Hodder & Stoughton, 1942); republished as *The Unconscious Witness* (New York: Dodd, Mead, 1942);

The Further Adventures of Romney Pringle, by Freeman and Pitcairn, as Clifford Ashdown (Philadelphia: Train, 1969);

The Best Dr. Thorndyke Detective Stories, edited by E. F. Bleiler (New York: Dover, 1973);

The Queen's Treasure, by Freeman and Pitcairn, as Clifford Ashdown (Philadelphia: Train, 1975);

From a Surgeon's Diary, by Freeman and Pitcairn, as Clifford Ashdown (London: Ferret Fantasy, 1975; Philadelphia: Train, 1977).

PERIODICAL PUBLICATIONS:
FICTION
"The Resurrection of Matthew Jephson," *Cassell's Magazine* (October 1898): 534-542;

"Caveat Emptor: The Story of a Pram," *Cassell's Magazine* (August 1900): 247-252;

"Victims of Circumstance," *Cassell's Magazine* (March 1901): 360-365;

"The Costume Model," *Cassell's Magazine* (January 1902): 233-237;

"The Great Tobacco 'Plant,' " *Cassell's Magazine* (March 1902): 417-420;

"Beyond the Dreams of Avarice," *Cassell's Magazine* (May 1902): 685-691;

"The Ebb Tide," *Cassell's Magazine* (February 1903): 352-356;

"Ye Olde Spotted Dogge," *Cassell's Magazine* (April 1904): 591-598;

"Bird of Passage," *Cassell's Magazine* (June 1904): 212-217;

"A Suburban Autolycus," *Cassell's Magazine* (November 1904): 652-657;

"The Great Slump," *Red Magazine* (November 1912);

"The Mutiny on the *Speedwell*," *People's* (October 1914): 815-828;

"A Question of Salvage," *Cassell's Magazine* (September 1916): 33-38.

NONFICTION
"The Coastwise Lights of England," *Cassell's Magazine* (December 1902): 624-631;

"The Royal Yacht," *Cassell's Magazine* (April 1903): 499-507;

"A Thames Sailing Barge Match," *Cassell's Magazine* (September 1903): 411-416;

"Down the River," *Cassell's Magazine* (June 1906): 50-57;

"The Art of the Detective Story," *Nineteenth Century and After* (May 1924): 713-721.

R. Austin Freeman, the son of Richard Freeman and Ann Maria Dunn, was born in Soho on 11 April 1862. His father was a journeyman tailor. Freeman, the youngest of four sons, had been named for his father, but (apparently in his teens) he assumed Austin as his given name in compliance with the wishes of the tailor who employed his father and eventually left him the business. In later years Freeman would put off interviewers who wanted to know something of his private life with the observation, "I have no desire for personal publicity." The fact is, he wished his progenitors were people of greater distinction. Thus, at fifty-three, he wrote to Constance Freeman, his brother Robert's daughter,

*Freeman visiting the Limamu (or Imam), head of the Moslems in Bontuku, Gold Coast (now Ghana), in 1889 (from the frontis-
piece for Freeman's* Travels and Life in Ashanti and Jaman)

whom his son Lawrence was about to visit: "Do not be expansive . . . on the subject of our rather complicated family history . . . very little has been said to him by me . . . the less he knows about these matters the better. Young people very often fail to realize how much mischief they may do to their own prospects & other people's by making injudicious confidences." That his father had been an alcoholic may have been a further source of discomfiture to Freeman.

Freeman's early schooling at "a boarding school in North London" is another matter about which he said little. Certainly, the instruction must have been adequate, for he was an excellent Latin scholar. He apprenticed as an apothecary, and in 1880, at eighteen, he entered Middlesex Hospital, London, embarking on a pro-

gram that led to his being admitted a licentiate of the Society of Apothecaries in June 1886. In the following year, as house physician at Middlesex, he became head surgeon in the throat and ear department. He also passed the qualifying examinations for membership in the Royal College of Surgeons and the Royal College of Physicians.

In those years Freeman was simultaneously preparing for the writing career which, as the creator of Dr. John Evelyn Thorndyke, would bring him fame. The thorough knowledge of London which Freeman gained as a result of living in the West End was one of his major resources. Of the sixty-five novels and short stories he wrote, thirty take place in or near London. He describes London's streets and byways, buildings and landmarks, restaurants and railways with intimate

Illustration by Fred Pegram from the 1902 publication in Cassell's Magazine of Fiction *of one of the six stories co-authored by Freeman and John James Pitcairn under the pseudonym Clifford Ashdown. These stories were collected as* The Adventures of Romney Pringle, *which is very rare in its first edition.*

and meticulous care. Freeman's topography, no matter what region he was describing, was invariably excellent. He professed to have talents in geography which circumstances of ill health prevented him from exercising.

The atmosphere in which he studied influenced his fiction. The high spirits of the young medical students who come together to discuss, under Dr. Thorndyke's instruction, the things they have experienced and the problems they have come up against convey a sense of the interest and eagerness which Freeman himself must have experienced in his student years. Freeman declared that, in those years, "I gave rather special attention to the legal aspects of medicine and the medical aspects of law." At that time he began to see that medical jurisprudence offered

the fiction writer a wealth of materials. The Rugeley and Madeline Smith poisoning cases engrossed him, as did the Tichbourne case, which involved the disputed identity of a corpse—a topic which is a repeated concern in his fiction.

Alfred Swaine Taylor's classic work *Principles and Practice of Medical Jurisprudence* (1865) was a major influence on Freeman. A criminologist and pathologist, Taylor (1806-1880) was unrivaled in his time. He had retired before Freeman came into the field of medicine, and Freeman knew him only through his books and reputation. Physically Taylor did not resemble Dr. Thorndyke, but otherwise he stood as a model for him. Freeman said, "In a professional sense, he [Thorndyke] may have been suggested to me by Dr. Alfred Swaine Taylor (the father of medical jurisprudence), whose great work on that subject I studied closely when I was a student."

In Thorndyke Freeman created an exemplary scientist and criminologist. E. A. Seaborne has called Freeman's creation "the greatest of fictional scientific detectives." To Howard Haycraft he is "the shining exception for all time." Albert Sherman Osborn's *The Problem of Proof* (1922), a textbook on the laws of evidence, lists the Thorndyke books as works of reference. Some of the Thorndyke stories have even been published in Palmer shorthand, presumably for the pleasure and edification of court reporters.

On 15 April 1887, just before he was registered as a medical practitioner, Freeman married his childhood sweetheart, Annie Elizabeth Edwards—a Roman Catholic—at her parish church in London. At this time in his life Freeman was drawn to Catholicism and may have been received into that faith. If so his conversion did not hold up. Much taken with eugenics, he seems to have been attracted to evolution, a process which he believed could be given impetus by the segregation of the fittest, and counted himself an agnostic. Passages from scripture found scattered through his works probably offer evidence of his exposure to it in his younger years.

Soon after his marriage Freeman went to the Gold Coast (now Ghana) as an assistant colonial surgeon. The region was malaria-ridden; the death toll annually among Europeans was forty percent. With perspicacity, though science in general would not accept that conclusion officially until 1898, Freeman conjectured that malaria was mosquito-borne. Eighteen months after reaching Accra he was sent inland to Ashanti and Jaman as part of an expedition to take over the kingdom of Jaman as a British protectorate. His task was to describe the flora, fauna, and natural features of the regions he was passing through and to fix geographical positions through astronomical observations. In *The Mystery of 31 New Inn* (1912) Thorndyke locates a house in London by constructing a track chart based upon time, compass bearings, and horse hoofbeats per minute, "a modification," Freeman said, of one devised by him many years ago when he was crossing Ashanti to the city of Bontuku. He was appointed a member of the Anglo-German Boundary Commission for Togoland next and asked to fix the boundary by astronomical data. Just as it appeared that a career of some consequence awaited him in the colonial service, he came down with malaria in its most lethal manifesta-

tion, blackwater fever. Smitten terribly, he had to be hoisted aboard ship in a basket.

In England, his health shattered, Freeman was invalided out of the service two months short of qualifying for a pension. Seven years later Freeman would receive critical acclaim for *Travels and Life in Ashanti and Jaman* (1898), but the book was not a money-maker for him. Indeed, in those years, none of his ventures prospered. He sought to set up practice as an eye, ear, nose, and throat specialist, but continuing poor health did not allow this. For a brief period he held a post at the Westminster Ophthalmic Hospital. While there, as he relates in "The Art of the Detective Story" (1924), he came to realize that a pair of eyeglasses could constitute "an infallible record of personal identity," a seemingly trivial fact but one which he was convinced "finally determined the character of my detective stories and incidentally the character of John Thorndyke."

Two sons were born to the Freemans—Clifford John Austin (Jack), in 1893, and Lawrence (Polly Wolly), in 1897. In 1900 Freeman served as acting assistant medical officer at London's Holloway Prison (the highly tentative title suggests he had no official standing). He probably entered into some private arrangement with John James Pitcairn, Holloway's chief medical officer, with whom Freeman and his family were then living. Holloway gave Freeman a dislike for prisons, death houses, and executions. He was reluctant to follow his fictional villains to the gallows: two die accidentally; two die while resisting arrest; seven kill themselves; only four are executed.

Late in 1902 and during 1903 *Cassell's Magazine* published, as the work of Clifford Ashdown, a dozen short stories recounting the activities of Romney Pringle, an amiable rogue and trickster who victimizes people who exploit others. In 1902 the first six of these stories were published in book form as *The Adventures of Romney Pringle* in an edition which survives now in fewer than a dozen copies. While it was soon known that Freeman was one-half of the duo of writers who produced these stories, the identity of his collaborator, evidently in accordance with the latter's wishes, was not disclosed. P. M. Stone has been able to establish that the coauthor was Pitcairn. Freeman, who had lived for a time at Clifford's Inn and had named his firstborn son Clifford, had contributed the given name. Ashdown had been Pitcairn's mother's maiden name.

A 1905 photograph of John James Pitcairn, Freeman's collaborator on the stories collected in The Adventures of Romney Pringle

The Pringle stories did not capture the market of E. W. Hornung's popular miscreant, Raffles (then at the height of his fame), and the second half-dozen stories did not achieve publication in book form, as *The Further Adventures of Romney Pringle*, until 1969.

A third Freeman-Pitcairn collaboration was published in 1975 as *From a Surgeon's Diary*. The protagonist, Dr. Wilkinson, is a nomadic practitioner who relieves others. He encounters and solves six mysteries in as many locales. In Wilkinson can be discerned Freeman's first tentative gropings toward the characterization that would emerge, in *The Red Thumb Mark* (1907), as Dr. Thorndyke–although Freeman may have first sketched out the character of Thorndyke as early as 1901 in the first draft of *The Mystery of 31 New Inn*. Freeman said: "the construction of that story determined . . . not only the general character of my future work but of the hero around whom the plot would be woven."

That Freeman, like Arthur Conan Doyle, hankered for a reputation more serious than as a writer of crime fiction is attested to by his publica-

tion in 1905 of *The Golden Pool*, a novel which draws heavily on his African experiences. While it was a critical success and, in fact, required reading for members of the colonial service until the African colonies won independence, the little that it added to Freeman's income left him with a clear mandate to follow the avenue of greatest promise. In that year Conan Doyle, with *The Return of Sherlock Holmes*, had shown that detective stories, properly managed, could produce riches.

Freeman claimed that he seldom read detective stories because he did not want to be influenced, even unconsciously, by the work of others. Even so, he does show himself susceptible on occasion to outside influences. Certainly his narrative style owes something to Robert Louis Stevenson. One contemporary critic described his early work as "anemic W. W. Jacobs." Freeman had other favorites–Izaak Walton, Samuel Pepys, Daniel Defoe, Samuel Johnson, Charles Dickens, Lewis Carroll, and John Evelyn, the seventeenth-century diarist (who may have furnished Thorndyke his given names). He also read Edgar Allan Poe, G. K. Chesterton, Henry Christopher Bailey, Dorothy Sayers, Freeman Willis Crofts, and S. S. Van Dine.

Influences aside, when he created Thorndyke, Freeman must have known that readers would measure him against Conan Doyle's Holmes. He would have been conscious of the parallels–an omniscient sleuth; a doting, slow-witted friend; cozy, familiar premises for their domicile. Both Thorndyke and Holmes have boundless energy. "My practice is my recreation," Thorndyke says. Holmes might well have made the same statement. The conspicuous difference separating the two men is that Thorndyke is a medico-legal expert and Holmes is not; and out of this difference Thorndyke's other traits derive. Thorndyke is "quiet, reserved, self-contained." Though not sentimental, "he has a kindly nature." He is "addicted to occasional touches of humor." Not surprisingly he has tolerance for romance in the lives of other men and has little of Holmes's angular aloofness. His logic is superior to that of Holmes–he is, says E. M. Wrong, "less cock-sure"–and generally goes deeper. His method, Freeman says, "consists in the interrogation of things rather than persons." The theatricality of Holmes is absent in Thorndyke; while the absence of this quality makes him seem, at times, overdeliberate and deficient in passion, his competence ultimately causes the reader to accept him as a dominant living character. A fondness for Trichinopoly cheroots able to pollute an entire stadium saves Thorndyke from being a complete monster of rectitude, but since he seldom indulges, it cannot be counted a major vice.

In 1903 Freeman moved his family from London to Gravesend, Kent, a town on the Thames estuary. He stayed there for the remaining forty years of his life and settled into a pattern of existence that suited his full-time commitment to writing. He was an able landscaper, marine painter, wax and clay modeler, plaster molder, worker in wood and metal; and he could bind books in leather and engrave finishing tools. There was a laboratory on the top floor of his house.

When Freeman published *The Red Thumb Mark*, the first Thorndyke novel in print, he was already forty-five and settling into the odd ways that probably were necessary to his peace of mind and to his work. His study was off limits to his wife and sons, and it suited him well when Annie and the boys left him free from all distractions. He would never allow either a telephone or a radio in his home–Thorndyke never uses a

Front cover for the book in which Freeman introduced Dr. John Evelyn Thorndyke

phone or rushes about "in motor cars, aeroplanes, or motor boats." Freeman's sons, who dubbed him the emperor, were always dependent on him for financial support even as emotionally they disowned him. Neither would ever marry. Lawrence died a suicide (his death came after his father's though his attempts to end his life began earlier). Jack bummed out his last years on a houseboat, his war service constituting the high point of his life. Freeman thus seems to have paid a steep price for the conditions he needed to write, but, pursued by chronic ill health, his options were limited.

In the mornings he took long walks alone, planning his books. "A sharp walk sets the mind working," he said. His writing day began at 4:00 P.M. and ran into the early morning hours. Five hundred words, done in longhand, was an average day's output. He did not try to stimulate his productivity with alcohol–"He that drinks beer thinks beer," was his observation.

Dust jacket for a reprint of the 1912 novel in which Dr. Thorndyke locates a house in London by calculating horse hoofbeats per minute and devising a track chart from compass bearings

The Red Thumb Mark, perhaps the first scientific detective novel, introduces Thorndyke and his aides, Dr. Christopher Jervis and Nathaniel Polton. There is every reason to believe that Freeman, who made gelatin stamps of his own fingerprints and meticulously tested out his theories, established in this book that fingerprints can be counterfeited. Howard Haycraft says *The Red Thumb Mark* is "one of the undisputed milestones of the genre," but Freeman had to hire a job printer to put it through the press.

John Evelyn Thorndyke is a medical jurist, a barrister-at-law of the Inner Temple, and, ultimately, professor of medical jurisprudence at St. Margaret's Hospital Medical School, his alma mater. He is tall, 5 feet 11 inches, well proportioned, 182 pounds, and has a Grecian nose and a classical face to go with it. He is in his prime—in his late thirties in *The Red Thumb Print*, about fifty when, thirty-eight years later, he makes his final appearance; "I need not saddle him with the infirmities of age, and I can (in his case) put

the brakes on the passing years," Freeman said. In a typical Thorndyke story an inquest leads to a verdict which, either through lack or error, is deficient. Thorndyke goes after the facts and comes up with the true answer. He has, says Freeman, "the capacity to perceive the essential nature of a problem before the detailed evidence comes into sight." Thorndyke's methods have been criticized on these grounds—he is too painstaking; his solutions come from facts so unusual that, until he explains their significance they are unrecognized by the reader. As Dorothy Sayers put it: "Thorndyke can cheerfully show you all his finds. You will be none the wiser, unless you happen to have an intimate acquaintance with the fauna of the local ponds; the effect of belladonna on rabbits; the physical and chemical properties of blood; optics; tropical diseases; metallurgy; hieroglyphics, and a few other trifles." In his own defense Freeman said, the "failure of the reader to perceive the evidential value of facts is the foundation on which detective fiction is built." Thorndyke's solutions always stand up in a court of law.

Although the task of reporting Thorndyke's cases is distributed among several narrators, Dr. Jervis is the first among them. In some novels he plays a minor role or no role at all, but he is present in thirty-six out of the forty Thorndyke short stories. He calls himself "second violin in the Thorndyke orchestra." Freeman sums up his role in these terms: "to observe and record all the facts, and to fail completely to perceive their significance. Thereby he gives the reader all the necessary information, and he affords Thorndyke the opportunity to expound its bearing on the case." "Duckweed is just duckweed, and there's an end of it," Jervis says once in a phrase that catches perfectly his limitations and justifies his reputation as misunderstander. Jervis is a lesser character than his parallel, Holmes's Watson, but better rounded. Thorndyke's presence intimidates him, but on his own he can be quite sharp.

Nathaniel Polton, Thorndyke's confidential servant and laboratory assistant, has been described by Stone as "one of the most fascinating, finely portrayed, convincing characters in the entire gallery of detective fiction." He is younger than Thorndyke, yet because of a hard life he seems older. Thorndyke sees in him "a shining example of the social virtues; industry—loyalty—integrity, and contentment; moreover, as an artificer, he is a positive genius." Diminutive, crinkled, with rather the look of "a rural dean or a chancery judge," he is a resource to both Thorn-

Dust jacket for the 1923 collection of seven stories published in the United States as The Blue Scarab

dyke and Jervis. As an artificer he consistently provides Thorndyke material aid at crucial moments–retro-spectacles in *The Cat's Eye* (1923); a periscope cane in *Mr. Pottermack's Oversight* (1930); a keyhole camera in *When Rogues Fall Out* (1932). For Freeman craftsmanship was synonymous with integrity. For this character he drew on two men: Pollard, a lab assistant in the Middlesex Hospital museum who gave Freeman, when he was a student, many valuable tips on matters of technique; and "Uncle Parsons," a watchmaker near the Royal Exchange, "a man of vast ingenuity and technical resources." Polton is in more than half the Thorndyke short stories and in all the novels except *For the Defence: Dr. Thorndyke* (1934).

Thorndyke's chambers are at 5A King's Bench Walk, in London's Inner Temple. They combine a workshop, laboratory, office, and museum. Freeman captures this environment best in the lab-workshop scene in *A Silent Witness* (1914). Because of Polton's competence, Thorndyke is ahead of the police in analyzing blood, hair, and dust and preserving footprints. *The Eye of Osiris* (1911) is a case solved by the use of X rays, a resource newly come into use. His green canvas research tote-kit, one foot square and four inches deep, is in itself a portable laboratory. While Freeman modestly deprecated the assertions of those who said the police had to go to Thorndyke to learn their business, he was amused when he learned that the French Sûreté had adopted his kit idea and set up laboratories patterned on Thorndyke's.

The Singing Bone (1912), a collection of Thorndyke short stories, introduces the inverted method into mystery fiction. This is plotting which centers not on whether the criminal will be caught but how. The first of the four inverted method stories appearing in *The Singing Bone*, "The Case of Oscar Brodski," which Freeman wrote for *Pearson's Magazine*, was based on an 1867 case, that of R. V. Watson and his wife, in which Alfred Swaine Taylor figured. (Although *Dr. Thorndyke Intervenes*, 1923, was based on the 1907 Druce-Portland case, Freeman used few actual cases.)

A Silent Witness was Freeman's next Thorndyke novel. It is narrated by Dr. Jardine, whose life is threatened by the villain. Opinion regarding this book is divided. Oliver Mayo finds the characterization crude and the action melodramatic. Norman Donaldson commends the lab scene, the "remarkable yet utterly convincing analysis of ash and bone fragments" and the "superb summing-up." This book contains an excellent instance of a criminal at bay making others pay a high cost for his defeat.

From 1915 to 1919 Freeman served in the Royal Army Medical Corps. His health made unfeasible his wish to serve in France, where his son Jack was severely wounded in 1917. *The Exploits of Danby Croker* (1916), a book about a rogue much like Romney Pringle, was his only publication in the war years. At war's end he brought out *The Great Portrait Mystery* (1918), a collection of short stories, two of them featuring Thorndyke.

After the war Freeman set to work on a book which he hoped would be recognized as a major contribution to human understanding, *Social Decay and Regeneration* (1921), for which Havelock Ellis wrote an introduction. In *A Silent Witness* Freeman had aligned himself with Gregor

R. Austin Freeman (photograph by William T. Munns)

Mendel, one of whose early champions he was. He saw the industrial revolution with its separation of skill from labor and of producer from consumer as a major cause of man's miseries. Rejecting both capitalism and collectivism, Freeman's social theory, akin to Eric Gill's distributism, was to be bolstered by a program of positive eugenics (founded on voluntary segregation of the fittest). His dreams of a better world carried over into the next Thorndyke novel, *Helen Vardon's Confession* (1922), in which Polton's sister Margaret is affiliated with a commune for women artists.

The Mystery of Angelina Frood (1924) is a lighthearted handling of Dickens's unfinished *Mystery of Edwin Drood* which debunks the fallacious belief that quicklime corrodes dead bodies. After it and the collection *The Puzzle Lock* (1925) Freeman published his next Dr. Thorndyke story, *The Shadow of the Wolf* (1925). It is an expanded version of "The Dead Hand," a two-part inverted story Freeman first published in 1912. When he expanded "31 New Inn" he added to it page by page. Here he spliced a large swatch of new material into the middle of the story. Thorndyke's pow-

ers of deduction operate at their finest, a standard Freeman maintained in his next Thorndyke book, *The D'Arblay Mystery* (1926), a novel in which Polton plays an important role.

The next four years would bring a new collection of Thorndyke short stories (*The Magic Casket*, 1927) and four novels: *A Certain Dr. Thorndyke* (1927); *As a Thief in the Night* (1928); *Flighty Phyllis* (1928); and *Mr. Pottermack's Oversight*. In *The Magic Casket*, a Thorndyke book, Freeman drew on his African experiences. Thorndyke makes a memorable microscopic examination of dust from a worm-eaten sparrow-hawk block. *As a Thief in the Night* is an authentic achievement. Somber, dramatic, and scientifically compelling, it enlists sympathies for both victim and murderer. The latter, who uses arsenic ingeniously, proves to be one of the main characters, an uncommon circumstance in a Thorndyke tale. Matters are carried a step further in *Mr. Pottermack's Oversight*, by some considered Freeman's masterpiece. Pottermack, a gentleman-scientist who studies mollusks, is being blackmailed. Thorndyke not only sympathizes with the murderer (who is discovered through use of a telephoto camera) but allows him to go free in a humane confrontation scene.

Freeman produced four books of interest in the decade before the war. *When Rogues Fall Out* (1932) was published when Freeman was seventy; yet it shows no marked diminution of his powers. In *For the Defence: Dr. Thorndyke* (1934) Thorndyke helps extricate a man from complications, including a murder charge, that arise out of his assumption of another's identity. In *The Penrose Mystery* (1936) Thorndyke investigates the disappearance of Daniel Penrose, an eccentric archaeologist. He rightly suspects that the murderer has ingeniously hidden the body in an ancient barrow, or burial mound, in Kent. With difficulty he achieves permission from the Ministry of Works to excavate. Ronald Jessup, intrigued by the book, got permission from the owner of the actual barrow and excavated it. *Felo De Se?* (1937) creates dramatic interest in the process of gathering and assessing minute evidence and using it for discovery and proof. Some elements of characterization are weak in *The Stoneware Monkey* (1938), but its villain is well done and the plotting is skillful. It is notable for humor, a rarity in Freeman's work.

Freeman's last two books, *Mr. Polton Explains* (1940) and *The Jacob Street Mystery* (1942), were written while Britain was under siege and

Freeman in failing health. He worked on them in his garden, in a bomb shelter he had personally designed. Polton is the central character in both books, perhaps an unconscious admission that the world had arrived at an impasse from which not logic but only cunning mechanisms could extricate it. Polton's autobiography takes up the first, and best, half of *Mr. Polton Explains*, the better of the two books. He solves the murder of a man named Moxon in the second half. Freeman died on 28 September 1943 and was buried in the old Gravesend and Milton Cemetery at Gravesend. A fund drive was launched through *The Thorndyke File* (a Freeman journal founded in 1976 by Philip Asdell and, since 1981, continued by John McAleer) to procure a granite marker for the grave, and it was put in place in September 1979.

"When in doubt stick to Dr. Thorndyke," said Christopher Morley. "He has no equal in his genre and he is also a much better writer than you might think," said Raymond Chandler of Thorndyke's creator. Freeman gathered that he found his readership in men of the intellectual class. Of the titles in *Queen's Quorum*, three are Freeman's—*John Thorndyke's Cases; The Singing Bone;* and *The Adventures of Romney Pringle*. The Haycraft-Queen Cornerstone List adds *The Red Thumb Mark* and *The Eye of Osiris*.

Freeman's detractors say he was an old-fashioned writer, that he had little talent for creating either villains or suspense. They say he ran to formula in his conception of life and character, that he rarely made more than one of his characters sound genuine, and that they voiced only those opinions that Freeman himself held. The truth is, most of his books are out-of-print and difficult to obtain so that those who deprecate his achievement often base their judgment on a knowledge of his work that is haphazard and scanty.

Biographies:

Norman Donaldson, *In Search of Dr. Thorndyke* (Bowling Green, Ohio: Popular Press, 1971);

Oliver Mayo, *R. Austin Freeman: The Anthropologist at Large* (Hawthornedene, South Australia: Investigator Press, 1980).

References:

P. M. Stone, Introduction and "5A King's Bench Walk," in Freeman's *Dr. Thorndyke's Crime File*, edited by Stone (New York: Dodd, Mead, 1941), pp. ix-xv, 1-18;

Thorndyke File (Ashton, Md.), 21 issues to date (Spring 1976-).

Papers:

The manuscripts of many of Freeman's novels are held at Occidental College, Los Angeles, California.

H. Rider Haggard
(22 June 1856-14 May 1925)

Richard C. Carpenter
Bowling Green State University

BOOKS: *Cetywayo and His White Neighbours; or, Remarks on Recent Events in Zululand, Natal, and the Transvaal* (London: Trübner, 1882; enlarged, 1888);

Dawn, 3 volumes (London: Hurst & Blackett, 1884; New York: Harper, 1887);

The Witch's Head (3 volumes, London: Hurst & Blackett, 1885; 1 volume, New York: Appleton, 1885);

King Solomon's Mines (London, Paris, New York & Melbourne: Cassell, 1885; New York: Harper, 1886);

She: A History of Adventure (New York: Harper, 1886; London: Longmans, Green, 1887);

Jess (London: Smith, Elder, 1887; New York: Munro, 1887);

Allan Quatermain, Being an Account of his Further Adventures and Discoveries in Company with Sir Henry Curtis, Bart., Commander John Good, R. N., and One Umslopogaas (London: Longmans, Green, 1887; New York: Harper, 1887);

A Tale of Three Lions (New York: Lovell, 1887);

Mr. Meeson's Will (London, 1888 [as the summer number of the *Illustrated London News*]; New York: Harper, 1888);

Maiwa's Revenge; or, The War of the Little Hand (London & New York: Longmans, Green, 1888; New York: Harper, 1888);

My Fellow Laborer [and *The Wreck of the "Copeland"*] (New York: Munro, 1888);

Colonel Quaritch, V. C.: A Tale of Country Life (3 volumes, London: Longmans, Green, 1888; 1 volume, New York: Lovell, 1888);

Cleopatra, Being an Account of the Fall and Vengeance of Harmachis, the Royal Egyptian, as Set Forth by His Own Hand (New York: Munro, 1889; London: Longmans, Green, 1889);

Allan's Wife and Other Tales (London: Blackett, 1889; New York: Lovell, 1889);

Beatrice: A Novel (London: Longmans, Green, 1890; New York: Munro, 1890);

The World's Desire, by Haggard and Andrew Lang

H. Rider Haggard, circa 1902 (courtesy of Commander M. E. Cheyne, DSC, RN, DL)

(London: Longmans, Green, 1890; New York: Harper, 1890);

Eric Brighteyes (London: Longmans, Green, 1891; New York: Lovell, 1891);

Nada the Lily (New York: Longmans, Green, 1892; London & New York: Longmans, Green, 1892);

An Heroic Effort (Frome & London: Butler & Tanner, 1893);

Montezuma's Daughter (London & New York: Longmans, Green, 1893; New York: Longmans, Green, 1894);

The People of the Mist (London & New York: Longmans, Green, 1894; New York: Longmans, Green, 1894);

Church and State, An Appeal to the Laity (London, 1895);

Heart of the World (New York: Longmans, Green, 1895; London, New York & Bombay: Longmans, Green, 1896);

Joan Haste (London & New York: Longmans, Green, 1895; New York: Longmans, Green, 1895);

The Wizard (Bristol: Arrowsmith/London: Simpkin, Marshall, Hamilton, Kent, 1896 [as a volume of *Arrowsmith's Christmas Annual*]; New York, London & Bombay: Longmans, Green, 1896);

Doctor Therne (London, New York & Bombay: Longmans, Green, 1898; New York, London & Bombay: Longmans, Green, 1898);

Swallow: A Tale of the Great Trek (New York, London & Bombay: Longmans, Green, 1899; London, New York & Bombay: Longmans, Green, 1899);

A Farmer's Year, being his Commonplace Book for 1898 (London, New York & Bombay: Longmans, Green, 1899);

The Last Boer War (London: Kegan Paul, Trench, Trübner, 1899); republished as *A History of the Transvaal* (New York: New Amsterdam Book Company/London: Kegan Paul, Trench, Trübner, 1899);

Black Heart and White Heart and Other Stories (London, New York & Bombay: Longmans, Green, 1900); republished in part as *Elissa: The Doom of Zimbabwe; Black Heart and White Heart: A Zulu Idyll* (New York, London & Bombay: Longmans, Green, 1900);

Lysbeth: A Tale of the Dutch (New York, London & Bombay: Longmans, Green, 1901; London, New York & Bombay: Longmans, Green, 1901);

A Winter Pilgrimage, Being an Account of Travels through Palestine, Italy, and the Island of Cyprus, accomplished in the Year 1900 (London, New York & Bombay: Longmans, Green, 1901);

Rural England, Being an Account of Agricultural and Social Researches Carried Out in the Years 1901 & 1902, 2 volumes (London, New York & Bombay: Longmans, Green, 1902);

Pearl-Maiden: A Tale of the Fall of Jerusalem (London, New York & Bombay: Longmans, Green, 1903; New York, London & Bombay: Longmans, Green, 1903);

Stella Fregelius: A Tale of Three Destinies (New York, London & Bombay: Longmans, Green, 1903; London, New York & Bombay: Longmans, Green, 1904);

The Brethren (London, Paris, New York & Melbourne: Cassell, 1904; New York: McClure, Phillips, 1904);

A Gardener's Year (London, New York & Bombay: Longmans, Green, 1905);

Report on the Salvation Army Colonies in the United States and at Hadleigh, England, with Scheme of National Land Settlement (London: Printed for His Majesty's Stationery Office, 1905); enlarged as *The Poor and the Land, Being a Report on the Salvation Army Colonies in the United States and at Hadleigh, England, with a Scheme of National Settlement and an Introduction* (London, New York & Bombay: Longmans, Green, 1905);

Ayesha: The Return of She (London: Ward, Lock, 1905; New York: Doubleday, Page, 1905);

The Way of the Spirit (London: Hutchinson, 1906);

Benita: An African Romance (London, Paris, New York & Melbourne: Cassell, 1906); republished as *The Spirit of Bambatse: A Romance* (New York: Longmans, Green, 1906);

Fair Margaret (London: Hutchinson, 1907); republished as *Margaret* (New York: Longmans, Green, 1907);

Reports of the Royal Commission on Coast Erosion, 3 volumes (N.p., 1907-1911);

The Real Wealth of England (London, 1908);

The Ghost Kings (London, Paris, New York, Toronto & Melbourne: Cassell, 1908); republished as *The Lady of the Heavens* (New York: Lovell, 1909);

The Yellow God: An Idol of Africa (New York: Cupples & Leon, 1908);

The Lady of Blossholme (London: Hodder & Stoughton, 1909);

Morning Star (London, New York, Toronto & Melbourne: Cassell, 1910; New York, London, Bombay & Calcutta: Longmans, Green, 1910);

Queen Sheba's Ring (London: Nash, 1910; New York: Doubleday, Page, 1910);

Regeneration, Being an Account of the Social Work of The Salvation Army in Great Britain (London:

Pages from the first draft of She (*J. E. Scott,* A Bibliography of the Works of Sir Henry Rider Haggard, 1856-1925, *1947*)

indeed expected ft an engaged woman – circumstances have altered it

now & I am not engaged any more'

Then I broke out. I raved I upbraided her. I appealed to her pity
& to my own deep devotion. Yes I told her what she was a
vile thing, a thing to be bought for money – and all the while
her lovely face grew harder & colder & a strange angry light grew
in the great eyes –

'Stop' she said at last. 'Take the candle & come here' she led the
way to a great mirror that ran down from the ceiling to the floor
'Now' she continued look at me in the glass. Am I not beautiful?
I looked – she was indeed royally beautiful

'Yes' I answered –

'Ah. Now look at yourself'.

Again I looked & again my own broad dwarfish form in
its stooping shoulders, the vast breadth of chest, its pale face
& deep set glowing eyes shining out beneath a dense growth
of black overhanging hair –

'If I am Beauty' what are you' she said in a little silvery laugh –
I made no answer. The sense of my own uncouthness crushed
me so that I could not speak.

'Do y think Horace, that any woman could love y if yourself? I
do not love y I never did – I have always been hateful to me.
I was forced to engage myself too – & I rejoice ah I rejoice that
this opportunity has come to avenge myself upon y. Now go on
y knees again & implore me not to free y self. I like to see y so'
Then I turned & cursed her in such frightful energy that she fell
back upon a chair & covered her face in her hands –

'y are not a man – y are a devil' she cried – 'go away before I
say any more – I feel as though y were driving the life out of me'
and I went – nor have I seen or heard of her ft that day to this

& three months after this my life was one long nightmare of
debauchery & drink – I did not return to college & to this day I have
never taken my degree – As it happened there was a sum of £1000
in cash which my father had lodged in my name in the day of prosperity
This I drew & spent to the last farthing. It was only when the money
was all gone & I paused in my career of shameless vice. Had there been a
little more I should never have paused till I was dead, & as it was nothing
but my own extraordinary strength of body & constitution saved me

Longmans, Green, 1910; New York & London: Longmans, Green, 1910);

Rural Denmark and Its Lessons (London, New York, Bombay & Calcutta: Longmans, Green, 1911);

Red Eve (London, New York & Toronto: Hodder & Stoughton, 1911; Garden City: Doubleday, Page, 1911);

The Mahatma and The Hare: A Dream Story (London, New York, Bombay & Calcutta: Longmans, Green, 1911; New York: Holt, 1911);

Reports of the Dominions Royal Commission, 24 volumes (N.p., 1912-1917);

Marie (London, New York, Toronto & Melbourne: Cassell, 1912; New York: Longmans, Green, 1913);

Child of Storm (London, New York, Toronto & Melbourne: Cassell, 1913; New York: Longmans, Green, 1913);

The Wanderer's Necklace (London, New York, Toronto & Melbourne: Cassell, 1914; New York: Longmans, Green, 1914);

A Call to Arms To the Men of East Anglia (London & Bungay: Privately printed, 1914);

The Holy Flower (London, Melbourne & Toronto: Ward, Lock, 1915); republished as *Allan and the Holy Flower* (New York: Longmans, Green, 1915);

The Ivory Child (London, New York, Toronto & Melbourne: Cassell, 1916; New York: Longmans, Green, 1916);

The After-War Settlement & Employment of Ex-Service Men in the Overseas Dominions: Report to Royal Colonial Institute (London: Published for the Royal Colonial Institute by the Saint Catherine Press, 1916);

Finished (London, Melbourne & Toronto: Ward, Lock, 1917; New York: Longmans, Green, 1917);

Love Eternal (London, New York, Toronto & Melbourne: Cassell, 1918; New York: Longmans, Green, 1918);

Moon of Israel: A Tale of the Exodus (London: Murray, 1918; New York: Longmans, Green, 1918);

When the World Shook, Being an Account of the Great Adventure of Bastin, Bickley and Arbuthnot (London, New York, Toronto & Melbourne: Cassell, 1919; New York: Longmans, Green, 1919);

The Ancient Allan (London, New York, Toronto & Melbourne: Cassell, 1920; New York: Longmans, Green, 1920);

Smith and the Pharaohs and Other Tales (London: Simpkin, Marshall, Hamilton, Kent, 1920; New York: Longmans, Green, 1921);

She and Allan (New York: Longmans, Green, 1921; London: Hutchinson, 1921);

The Virgin of the Sun (London, New York, Toronto & Melbourne: Cassell, 1922; Garden City & Toronto: Doubleday, Page, 1922);

Wisdom's Daughter: The Life and Love Story of She-Who-Must-Be-Obeyed (London: Hutchinson, 1923; Garden City: Doubleday, Page, 1923);

Heu-Heu, or The Monster (London: Hutchinson, 1924; Garden City: Doubleday, Page, 1924);

Queen of the Dawn: A Love Tale of Old Egypt (Garden City: Doubleday, Page, 1925; London: Hutchinson, 1925);

Treasure of the Lake (Garden City: Doubleday, 1926; London: Hutchinson, 1926);

The Days of My Life: An Autobiography, edited by C. J. Longman, 2 volumes (London, New York, Toronto, Bombay, Calcutta & Madras: Longmans, Green, 1926);

Allan and the Ice-Gods: A Tale of Beginnings (London: Hutchinson, 1927; Garden City: Doubleday, Page, 1927);

Mary of Marion Isle (London: Hutchinson, 1929); republished as *Marion Isle* (Garden City: Doubleday, Doran, 1929);

Belshazzar (London: Stanley Paul, 1930; Garden City: Doubleday, Doran, 1930);

The Private Diaries of Sir H. Rider Haggard, edited by D. S. Higgins (New York: Stein & Day, 1980).

Henry Rider Haggard, K.B.E., wrote tales of romantic adventure which may be termed "mysteries" only in a nonconventional sense of the term. The reader encounters no Poirots, no Lord Peter Wimseys, no clues; and while there are murders aplenty, they are never mysterious nor unsolved. Instead Haggard presents his readers with bizarre situations and events in exotic settings: a demigoddess 2,000 years old, the most beautiful woman ever seen; a treasure greater than any other in the world, hidden since Solomon's time; a white civilization, ruled over by two queens, in the heart of Africa. In some ways these tales are fantastic–librarians usually catalog them under the rubric of "fantasy"–but they are also mysteries in the root sense of the word: "Something that has not been, or cannot be explained; hence something beyond human comprehension. A profound secret; an enigma." From this perspective H. Rider Haggard wrote some of the classic mysteries of all time.

Only a relative few of his fifty-eight works of fiction can be categorized in this way, however. Ranging far and wide in both time and space, he wrote novels of pure adventure and conflict; tales of the Zulus and their tortured history; imitations of sagas; anti-Boer stories; and a kind of Neanderthal tale about the distant ancestor of one of his most memorable characters, Allan Quatermain. His mysteries are *King Solomon's Mines* (1885), *She* (1886), *Allan Quatermain* (1887), *Mr. Meeson's Will* (1888), *Ayesha: The Return of She* (1905), and *She and Allan* (1921). Ultimately Haggard's reputation rests on *King Solomon's Mines* and *She*, the works that have been most read through the years, have never been out of print, and still maintain their perennial attraction.

Most of Haggard's romances, including his mysteries, belong to the high-romantic tradition, wherein certain exceptional people encounter extraordinary experiences of apparently profound significance. Their basic fictional mode is that of the quest: the journey through innumerable perils and crises toward a goal of great consequence, the mode of romantic adventure from Odysseus to Indiana Jones. In Haggard's time this type of writing had not been highly regarded; and his work in the genre, along with that of contemporaries such as Robert Louis Stevenson, Sir Arthur Conan Doyle, Sir Arthur Quiller-Couch, and Rudyard Kipling, signified a revival of interest in romantic fiction. In fact, one of Haggard's major accomplishments was his aid in bringing this revival about through his adventure tales. His great talent lay not only in the ability to imagine exotic situations but also to create one adventure after another, so that the reader is swept breathlessly along on a current of suspense. His plots carry extraordinary vividness and conviction, partly through the empathy he creates by the sheer peril of the situations but also—and this quality sets him apart from most other writers of romance—through the wealth of circumstantial detail that embeds his exotic locales and events in a matrix of reality. Haggard was the kind of writer who makes one believe that King Solomon's mines *must* be somewhere in Africa.

Unfortunately for his reputation as a literary artist, he was a hasty and careless writer who looked on his romantic novels, with a few exceptions, as ephemera, which is actually the case. His employment of different plots and settings does not disguise the fact that most of his later books are repetitions in one way or another of his earlier ones. He created one great character, Allan Quatermain, and two great imaginary locales, the mines of Solomon in Kukuanaland and the Caves of Kor, where Ayesha has sojourned for 2,000 years. Occasionally in other books he strikes sparks (because he was always a writer of vivid imagination) but on the whole he would have done better to have written eight rather than fifty-eight works of fiction.

Much of the blame—and also much of the credit, positive and negative, for the qualities of his fiction—undoubtedly lies in Haggard's upbringing and early life. Born into an old and respected Norfolk family, the son of Ella and William Haggard, he was an imaginative child noticeably different from his nine siblings. He reputedly named a sinister-looking rag doll kept in a dark cupboard in his home "She-Who-Must-Be-Obeyed," the same cognomen he gave to the white African demigoddess in his most celebrated book, *She*, many years later. However, his surroundings were far from literary and his education helter-skelter, from one school to another, with none of them the kind of institution—public school and university—attended by his six brothers. Of principal importance to his formative years was the arbitrary and capricious way in which his father dictated his career, until he was finally dispatched to South Africa in July 1875, at the age of nineteen, to serve on the staff of Sir Henry Bulwer, lieutenant-governor of Natal. Perhaps because of his upbringing, Haggard was always a restless, energetic, and dissatisfied man. On the other hand, perhaps influenced by his mother, he was also a good worker, able to assume heavy responsibilities and carry out demanding tasks successfully.

Except for eighteen months in England in 1879-1880—during which Haggard married Mariana Louisa (Louie) Margitson on 11 August 1880—he lived in South Africa until the end of August 1881, holding different positions in government and legal service of an unusually responsible nature for one so young. He traveled widely on various missions, met important Zulu leaders, hobnobbed with the social elite of Natal, shot big game, learned much about the customs of the natives and the complex and critical political situation of the times, and finally found himself living on the fringe of savage conflicts between the English, the Zulus, and the Boers. It was an exciting life for Haggard, who absorbed these experiences enthusiastically, particularly

Ayesha entering the Pillar of Fire, illustration by E. K. Johnson for the first edition of She

the dramatic landscape and peoples of this land so different from anything he had previously known. He began to write of his experiences and to analyze the political problems of the region, thus entering on what was to become his lifelong vocation.

After his return to England in 1881 and, in 1883, an abortive venture at farming in Natal, he wrote his first novel, *Dawn* (1884), a farrago of plots and characters that was unsuccessful yet demonstrated his ability to write suspenseful narrative. He had already produced a book, *Cetywayo and His White Neighbours* (1882), and articles about Africa. He would continue such journalistic endeavors along with romance writing throughout his lifetime. In 1884 he wrote a second novel, *The Witch's Head* (1885), more autobiographical than *Dawn* and with certain scenes, the best in the book, laid in Africa. Haggard was slowly feeling his way toward his metier.

In 1883-1885 Haggard studied law, having decided that his writing was not financially profitable; but this decision was soon reversed because in September 1885 *King Solomon's Mines* was pub-

lished. He was launched on a writing career that would make him perhaps the most popular writer in England during the latter part of the nineteenth and the early twentieth centuries. The book has all the ingredients of high-romantic adventure, with intrepid English heroes, sinister African villains–and a splendid African hero as well–a witch of incredible power and unimaginable age, and an epic exploration for fabulous treasure.

The story begins with the meeting of Allan Quatermain, famous elephant hunter, and Sir Henry Curtis and his friend, Capt. John Good, a retired naval officer. Curtis is in Africa trying to find his younger brother, who had disappeared while searching for the mines of King Solomon. Quatermain happens to have a map, inscribed by one José Silvestra, who had been lost in 1590 while seeking the mines. With this evidence in hand the three companions set out on the quest, taking with them various servants, including Umbopa, a superb Zulu warrior who later turns out to be a king, escaped and wandering far from his native land, where his evil brother has

Illustrations by A. Forestier (left) and G. Montbard (right) for the first edition of Mr. Meeson's Will

usurped his throne. They cross a fearsome desert, are almost frozen while climbing the lofty Sheba's Breasts mountains, and find the frozen body of José Silvestra in a cave on the mountain's slope. They are captured by natives, who do not put them to death because they are overawed by Good's false teeth, his "beautiful" bare legs, and his half-shaven face. (He had been scrupulously shaving when the natives came.) Through the remainder of the story he must maintain this appearance in order to keep the tribesmen convinced that the companions are, as they say, gods from another star.

They are taken to meet the evil Twala (Umbopa's brother), subjected to perilous trials of their nerve, and witness the barbaric ceremony of the "smelling out," in which the witch Gagool, a horrible hag of great age, presides in singling out Twala's enemies and having them murdered on the spot. When she tries to subject Umbopa to this fate he reveals himself as the usurped king. Quatermain, Curtis, and Good threaten to shoot Twala and Gagool if they try further to imperil Umbopa. With the aid of the companions he begins a revolution to reclaim his inheritance. A great battle ensues in which Curtis, a huge and immensely powerful fighter, slays Twala in single combat.

The companions force Gagool to lead them to the treasure; on the way they come to an eerie sight: a huge cave in which the dead kings of Kukuanaland sit at a table presided over by a figure of Death, all of them, including Twala, having been turned into stalagmites. They reach the treasure room, revealed when Gagool, who knows the secret combination, raises a huge slab of rock. While they are admiring the riches she sneaks out and lowers the slab to trap them with the treasure, but she is caught as it descends and is crushed. The friends think escape impossible until Quatermain, always alert, discovers a trapdoor, which leads them to passages through which they make their escape. He also has had the foresight to stuff his pockets with diamonds because, as a poor hunter, he has to think about practical matters. Although the bulk of the treasure remains forever immured, enough has been saved through his practical common sense to make them all wealthy. Curtis finds his brother, and they all return to England.

This amazing tale was an immediate and resounding success, selling in large numbers for those days—thirty-one thousand copies in the first twelve months—and eliciting a veritable storm of public interest. It has continued to be read ever since, and several motion-picture versions have been made, including an excellent 1950 production with Stewart Granger and Deborah Kerr and another in 1984 starring Richard Chamberlain. Still widely available, the book will no doubt continue enthralling readers for years to come. Critical esteem also was not wanting in its own time. Stevenson, Walter de la Mare, and Gerard Manley Hopkins found it immensely appealing, while many reviewers had good things to say about its vividness and excitement.

In 1885 Haggard wrote two novels that were first serialized in magazines before their publication as books in 1887. *Allan Quatermain* is an adventure in which Quartermain, Curtis, and Good discover a lost civilization of white people in an impenetrable valley in the heart of Africa and find themselves involved in a power struggle, with Curtis eventually marrying a queen and becoming King-Consort; *Jess* is a "novel," rather than a romance, about Boers in Africa. *Allan Quatermain*, it may be observed, is a quest merely in search of adventure per se because the three friends find life in England boring and dull. The next novel Haggard wrote, however, is one of the most imaginative quest romances ever produced and the work for which he will be most remembered.

As in *King Solomon's Mines*, *She* begins with the preparation for the quest, but here Haggard shows greater ingenuity and skill in providing a sense of verisimilitude for a bizarre situation. Ludwig Horace Holly, scholar of Cambridge University, had, some twenty years before the novel opens, promised a friend, Leo Vincey, that he would bring up Leo's son and namesake, giving him his inheritance, an iron box, when he turned twenty-five. When young Leo opens the box an incredible tale emerges from the inscription on a broken potsherd he finds there: Leo is the sole descendant of an ancient Egyptian priest of Isis, Kallikrates, who had broken his vows and loved a princess, Amenartas, by whom he had conceived a son before he was slain by the jealous goddess-queen of a savage people, a beautiful white woman. The inscription also begs that some courageous descendant may avenge the death of Kallikrates.

Holly, a more educated Quatermain with great physical strength instead of the hunter's skills; Leo, a veritably godlike young Englishman of great physical beauty and keen mind; and Job, their sensible servant, set out on this dangerous

Haggard at Abydos Temple during his 1924 visit to Egypt (courtesy of Commander M. E. Cheyne, DSC, RN, DL)

mission. After great perils and vicissitudes they finally come to the land of the queen, named Ayesha but called She-Who-Must-Be-Obeyed by her subject race of savages. Leo has been seriously wounded in a fracas with the savages before they arrived at her City of Kor, so she does not see him at first but gives Holly an audience, unveiling her incredible beauty to him as she never does to her subjects. He at once falls under the seductive spell of this 2,000-year-old woman, whose beauty has increased for all that period of time along with her knowledge and power. They converse and he learns her story, as well as the curious anachronism of her thinking, immured as she has been in her cave-city for two millennia. Holly falls more deeply in love with her but is distracted by what appears to be Leo's imminent death. Finally Ayesha agrees to try to save him with her medical skills. Of course, as soon as she sees him she realizes that he is "her Kallikrates," reincarnated, as she believes, and returned to her. She saves his life; he rapidly mends and also falls in love with her, this love reciprocated by Ayesha. When Ustane, who loves Leo and has nursed him faithfully, will not give him up to Ayesha, She-Who-Must-Be-Obeyed strikes the native girl dead with a blast of magic power. Leo, still under the queen's spell, continues to love her despite his realizing her capacity for evil.

Ayesha then wants Leo to bathe in the Pillar of Fire, which is responsible for her apparent imperviousness to time, and leads the companions on a hazardous journey into the depths of a mountain where the Pillar of Fire is to be found. They cross a fathomless abyss on a plank which falls into the depths after they have passed over it and come to the great cave where the Pillar of Fire whirls round and round eternally. They feel a wonderful sense of vitality and youth as it goes by because, as Haggard implies, it is the very essence of Being, what Henri Bergson termed the élan vital. Leo is afraid to step into it, so Ayesha sets the example. Taking off her robes and clothed only in her long black hair, she steps into the flames. At first she seems to revel in their caress, but then, to the horror of the watchers, she slowly shrivels into a bundle of skin and bones, then into dust, then nothing. The Pillar of Fire giveth and the Pillar of Fire taketh away; Ayesha is no longer. Job dies from the shock of the experience; Holly and Leo make a desperate escape from the cave, leaping the gap across the abyss, and finally, aided by an old retainer of Ayesha, get to the coast and back to England.

She was as fabulously successful as the story was fabulous. It sold in very large numbers and achieved an enthusiastic reception from all kinds of readers. Nearly all the reviews were strong in praising the tale's imaginative power and its vivid creation of scene and event. As time went on a good deal of critical attention was paid to the work, especially because of its mythic qualities and the spectacular way in which it transcended the usual categories of fiction. *She* has also held the imagination of the reading public over time and space. It is still available in several editions and has been translated into many languages. One of those extraordinary books, like *Moby-Dick* (1851), *Wuthering Heights* (1847), or *The Lord of the Rings* trilogy (1954-1956), it appeals to a wide variety of readers because of its astonishing originality. It is Haggard's masterpiece; he did not write another work to match it in the long career that followed.

Mr. Meeson's Will is as close as H. Rider Haggard ever came to writing a conventional crime novel; even so, this novel fits uncomfortably into the tradition of courtroom drama. An elaborate satire of both the publishing business and the judicial system, both of which Haggard knew by firsthand experience, *Mr. Meeson's Will* is the story of an unscrupulous publisher who supervises a very large company with the ultimate goal of cheating authors. One of his novelists is a lovely lady who comes by chance to be shipwrecked with Mr. Meeson and his party. When it seems they will perish, the publisher, in a change of heart, decides to recant his disinheritance of his nephew—who happens to be the lover of the lady novelist—by tattooing a nine-word last will on her back. Only she and a child survive, setting up the amusing conclusion in which the will is filed, contested, and examined scrupulously in court. The novel was considered to be sexually daring in its day, but now it is interesting primarily for its satiric elements.

In the late 1880s Haggard settled into a steady routine of romance writing and overseeing the country estate, Ditchingham, which his wife had inherited and which the money from his writing kept going. He became much concerned over the plight of the English farmer, writing two excellent books of nonfiction on the subject—*A Farmer's Year* (1899) and *Rural England* (1902). In the second he advocated agricultural reforms which might well have alleviated the farmers' desperate economic situation. These works attest both to Haggard's serious social interests and to his capacity for hard work. He continued this type of selfless labor throughout the rest of his life, establishing for himself another reputation besides that of romance writer—that of the public servant and social reformer. From 1906 to 1911 he was a member of a royal commission on coast erosion and afforestation, and from 1912 to 1914 he served on a distinguished commission to survey the dominions. In both of these capacities he worked long and hard, traveling many thousands of miles and interviewing scores of people. For his services to the country he was awarded a knighthood in 1912.

The romances he wrote during this long later part of his career are less admirable than his public service and show that his heart was not really in them, despite the efforts he made to find new plots and milieus. Some of them are nonetheless worth reading—especially *Cleopatra* (1889), an imaginative re-creation of political intrigue in the days of that great queen; *Eric Brighteyes* (1891), a fairly successful attempt to reproduce the feeling and tone of the sagas; and the sequels to *King Solomon's Mines* and *She: Ayesha: The Return of She* (1905), in which Ayesha has been reincarnated, this time in the depths of Central Asia, and is sought out by Leo, who finally marries her but then dies; and *She and Allan* (1921), in which he brings his two most important characters ingeniously together. Each of these novels–and a few others–has rewards for the enthusiastic reader of Haggard although other readers may find them too derivative.

Haggard's best works are those in which his vivid imagination is most apparent, those in which his solidly realized milieus, with all their circumstantial detail, serve to lodge that imagination in a world of credible reality. His two greatest characters–Quatermain and Ayesha–are genuine creations, Allan for his reliability, common sense, cleverness, modesty, and courage–Natty Bumppo and Odysseus combined; Ayesha as a compelling vision of the Eternal Feminine brought to life. She is Mystery personified; in fashioning her Haggard demonstrated the power of romance to plumb the depths of psychic experience.

Bibliography:

J. E. Scott, *A Bibliography of the Works of Sir Henry Rider Haggard, 1856-1925* (Takeley: Elkin Mathews, 1947).

Biographies:

Morton Cohen, *Rider Haggard: His Life and Works* (London: Hutchinson, 1960);

Peter Berresford Ellis, *H. Rider Haggard: A Voice from the Infinite* (London & Henley: Routledge & Kegan Paul, 1978);

D. S. Higgins, *Rider Haggard: The Great Storyteller* (London: Cassell, 1981).

Reference:

Norman Etherington, *Rider Haggard* (Boston: Twayne, 1984).

Papers:

Haggard materials are located in the Columbia University library; the Huntington Library, San Marino, California; the Lockwood Memorial Library, State University of New York, Buffalo, New York; and the Norfolk Record Office.

William Hope Hodgson

(15 November 1877-19 April 1918)

Albert Borowitz

BOOKS: *The Boats of the "Glen Carrig"* (London: Chapman & Hall, 1907);

The House on the Borderland (London: Chapman & Hall, 1908);

The Ghost Pirates (London: Paul, 1909);

The Night Land (London: Nash, 1912);

"Poems" and "The Dream of X" (London: Watt, 1912; New York: Paget, 1912);

Carnacki, The Ghost-finder (London: Nash, 1913; enlarged edition, Sauk City, Wis.: Mycroft & Moran, 1947);

Men of the Deep Waters (London: Nash, 1914);

Cargunka, and Poems and Anecdotes (New York: Paget/London: Watt, 1914);

The Luck of the Strong (London: Nash, 1916);

Captain Gault, Being the Exceedingly Private Log of a Sea-Captain (London: Nash, 1917; New York: McBride, 1918);

The Calling of the Sea (London: Selwyn & Blount, 1920);

The Voice of the Ocean (London: Selwyn & Blount, 1921);

Deep Waters (Sauk City, Wis.: Arkham House, 1967);

Out of the Storm: Uncollected Fantasies, edited, with a critical biography, by Sam Moskowitz (West Kingston, R.I.: Grant, 1975).

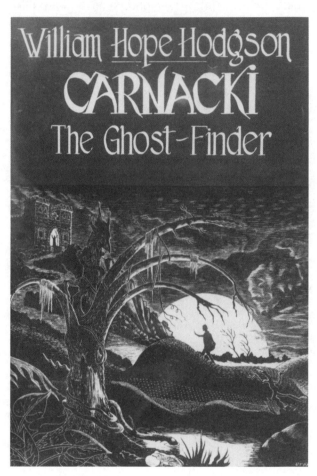

Dust jacket for the 1947 enlarged edition of Hodgson's stories about the occult detective. Carnacki observes, "when you are meddling with this sort of thing you've got to take notice of queer fancies and risk being laughed at" (courtesy of Otto Penzler).

William Hope Hodgson, an acknowledged master of horror, science fiction, and the supernatural, is also the author of a classic work of occult detection, *Carnacki, The Ghost-finder* (1913). The fundamental theory expounded by Hodgson on the writing of ghost stories is adhered to in the Carnacki series as firmly as in his purely supernatural fiction: "A ghost story that is worth anything . . . must cling to reality by some sort of explanation, however fantastic the story be, to be truly effective."

Hodgson was born in Essex, England, 15 November 1877, the son of Samuel Hodgson, an Anglican clergyman, and Lissie Sarah Brown Hodgson. His father's lively opinions, eloquently expressed, caused him to be shifted from parish to parish and kept the family on the brink of pov-

erty. At the age of thirteen William ran away from boarding school, hoping to go to sea, and in 1891 he won his father's permission to undertake a four-year apprenticeship as a cabin boy. After his apprenticeship expired Hodgson obtained his mate's certificate and served as a seaman until 1899. While on board ship Hodgson diverted himself with judo exercises and became an expert photographer, taking magnificent pictures of storms at sea. Although awarded a Royal

Humane Society Medal in 1898 for his heroism in rescuing a first mate from shark-infested waters off New Zealand, Hodgson conceived an uncompromising bitterness against the brutal treatment of sailors and apprentices and came to hate the seafaring life and the sea itself. Returning to a life ashore in 1899, William, now twenty-two, opened in Blackburn W. H. Hodgson's School of Physical Culture. Though the enterprise ultimately failed, Hodgson's knowledge of muscular activity won him brief notoriety in 1902 at the Blackburn Palace Theatre. On the theater's stage he severely tested Harry Houdini's escape artistry with six specially designed pairs of handcuffs, and other restraining devices, that caused painful injuries to the magician before he came free after two hours.

Shutting down his physical culture establishment in 1901, Hodgson turned to his true vocation as a writer, beginning with articles that combined his interests in bodybuilding and photography. In 1905 Hodgson capitalized on his loathing for the sea by publishing a story of a dreadful sea serpent, "A Tropical Horror." From this beginning Hodgson soon grew to become one of the most celebrated twentieth-century writers of supernatural fiction. His famous novels in this genre include *The House on the Borderland* (1908) and *The Night Land* (1912). Hodgson's short stories often evoke the horrors of the deep, particularly the legendary Sargasso Sea, which first appeared in Hodgson's fiction as the setting of a 1906 story, "From the Tideless Sea."

Beginning in January 1910 Hodgson began to publish in the *Idler* a series of stories about Carnacki, an occult detective often compared with Algernon Blackwood's psychic sleuth, *John Silence* (1908). In 1913 a set of the Carnacki stories appeared in book form under the name *Carnacki, The Ghost-finder* (an expanded collection including several stories unpublished during Hodgson's lifetime was issued by Mycroft and Moran in 1947). The Carnacki stories are rigidly formulaic in narrative pattern. The ghost-finder periodically invites a quartet of friends (including the author's stand-in named Dodgson) to his home in Cheyne Walk, Chelsea, and regales them after dinner with an account of a recent exploit. He also tantalizes the reader with cryptic allusions to other unwritten cases with thrilling names, such as the "Black Veil," the "Grunting Man," and the "Nodding Door." At the end of each story his guests take their leave and go out into the night and the "quiet of the Embankment." Unlike Sherlock Holmes, one of his obvious prototypes, Carnacki is not delineated strongly either in physical appearance or personality, and his circle of admirers are mere ciphers. The detective's literary fame is probably due to his unique investigative technique, which combines a pseudoscholarship in occult doctrine, a variety of devices for protection against the "Outer Monstrosities," and the use of Hodgson's beloved photography and other practical means of recording intrusion into reputedly haunted houses. The principal basis of Carnacki's understanding of the supernatural is the fourteenth-century "Sigsand MS," which describes the powerful "Saaamaaa Ritual" often invoked by the detective to ward off malign forces (including the semi-materializing "Aeiirii" and the "Saiitii" that acquire control over material substance). From Professor Gardner's "Experiments With a Medium" Carnacki has learned the modern technological defense provided by the Electric Pentacle (a five-pointed glowing star composed of intertwining vacuum tubes operated by a battery), which he employs in combination with more primitive devices such as bunches of garlic, water and chalk circles, and drawn pentagrams.

In some of the Carnacki stories a seemingly occult phenomenon is demonstrated by the detective to have a natural explanation. For example, in "The Thing Invisible" an apparently self-propelled dagger that stabs intruders in an old chapel is shown by Carnacki's photography to have been released by a lever in a chancel gatepost, an ancient trap that the (senile) present owner continues to operate. In an eerie tale, "The Searcher of the End House," supernatural and natural explanations of strange events are combined: the vision of a frightened, naked child is identified by Carnacki with "the primal Ego or Child's soul" fleeing before "the Mother Spirit," but a noisome smell that accompanies the apparitions is eventually traced to a rotting mutton bone gnawed on by a former tenant who is lurking in a well in the cellar. In other stories the mystery relates to the origin of a supernatural event; often evil powers intrude through the agency of an ancient crime associated with the haunted house. In "The Horse of the Invisible" Hodgson shows the genesis of a ghost out of a present act of violence: Parsket, a disappointed lover who injures and terrorizes an engaged couple by impersonating a ghostly horse associated by legend with the girl's family, is frightened to death by a genuine Horse Monster whose haunting of Parsket is produced as "a kind of induced simulation of his mental conceptions due to his desperate thoughts and broodings."

Through all this varied interplay of the real and unreal Carnacki remains an "unprejudiced sceptic"; he recognizes that "when you are meddling with this sort of thing you've got to take notice of queer fancies and risk being laughed at." By contrast with other famous sleuths, he never loses his sense of fear and foreboding, for he knows that none of his defenses against the extraterrestrial are absolute.

Hodgson's second entry in the field of crime fiction is *Captain Gault, Being the Exceedingly Private Log of a Sea-Captain* (1917), an amusing collection of ten short stories that first appeared in the *London Magazine* in 1914 and 1915. Captain G. Gault secures commands on transoceanic passenger ships, windjammers, and tramp steamers although he is a notoriously successful smuggler. He is under constant surveillance by customs officers and their shipboard spies. Despite the perseverance of his adversaries, Gault is never caught in possession of his contraband, which ranges from the traditional diamonds and pearls to cigars, saccharine, military plans, and a visitant from Hodgson's world of horror—an amber carving of a nameless deity of Blood Lust. There is sometimes a profit-making motive in Gault's smuggling, for the sea captain lives high and has a passion for fine paintings. But often he is moved by humorous spite against his customs service antagonists or even by altruism or gallantry. As he remarks at the beginning of "My Lady's Jewels," "Women have a great trick of asking me to help them through the Customs with their jewellery."

A master of legerdemain and an adept manipulator of decoys and red herrings, Gault relies more often on distracting the attention of customs agents than on exotic hiding places. An example of his methods is provided by one of the best stories in the collection, "The Red Herring." Here Gault bribes two U.S. customs searchers to receive from him in a port restaurant bag number one filled with shore clothes and to substitute it in the customs hall for an identical bag number two containing smuggled pearls. The inspectors take his money and bag number one but one of them betrays him: he subjects bag number two to a rigorous search when it comes off the ship but finds nothing dutiable. Gault, counterfeiting anger, storms off with both bags. Ultimately the smuggler reveals to the duplicitous searcher that the pearls were in fact packed in bag number one and that he had intentionally paid the agents bribes too low to dissuade them from pouncing in earnest on the wrong bag in their hopes of making a great professional coup.

In 1915 Hodgson obtained a commission as a lieutenant in the Royal Field Artillery. After a mandatory discharge from the service as a result of severe injuries suffered when he was thrown by a horse in 1916, he made a remarkable recovery and reenlisted. He was killed by a shell at Ypres on 19 April 1918. Despite his lamentably brief career, Hodgson has left us in the Carnacki stories a long-lived literary curiosity: an idiosyncratic blending of the supernatural with scientific detection.

References:

H. C. Koenig, Introduction to Hodgson's *The House on the Borderland and Other Novels* (Sauk City, Wis.: Arkham House, 1946);

Sam Moskowitz, Introduction to Hodgson's *Out of the Storm* (West Kingston, R.I.: Grant, 1975);

A. Langley Searles, "Bibliography of the Published Books of William Hope Hodgson," in Hodgson's *The House on the Borderland and Other Novels* (Sauk City, Wis.: Arkham House, 1946).

E. W. Hornung

(7 June 1866-22 March 1921)

Alison Janice McNabb Cox

BOOKS: *A Bride from the Bush* (London: Smith & Elder, 1890; New York: United States Book Company, 1890);

Under Two Skies (London: Black, 1892);

Tiny Luttrell (2 volumes, London: Cassell, 1893; 1 volume, New York: Cassell, 1893);

The Boss of Taroomba (London: Bliss, Sands & Foster, 1894; New York: Scribners, 1900);

The Unbidden Guest (London & New York: Longmans, Green, 1894; New York: Longmans, Green, 1894);

Irralie's Bushranger (London: Beeman, 1896; New York: Scribners, 1896);

The Rogue's March (London: Cassell, 1896; New York: Scribners, 1896);

My Lord Duke (London: Cassell, 1897; New York: Scribners, 1897);

Some Persons Unknown (London: Cassell, 1898; New York: Scribners, 1898);

Young Blood (London: Cassell, 1898; New York: Scribners, 1898);

The Amateur Cracksman (London: Methuen, 1899; New York: Scribners, 1899);

Dead Men Tell No Tales (London: Methuen, 1899; New York: Scribners, 1899);

Belle of Toorak (London: Richards, 1900); republished as *The Shadow of a Man* (New York: Scribners, 1901);

Peccavi (London: Richards, 1900; New York: Scribners, 1900);

The Black Mask (London: Richards, 1901); republished as *Raffles: Further Adventures of the Amateur Cracksman* (New York: Scribners, 1901);

At Large (New York: Scribners, 1902);

The Shadow of the Rope (London: Chatto & Windus, 1902; New York: Scribners, 1902);

Denis Dent (London: Isbister, 1903; New York: Stokes, 1903);

No Hero (London: Smith, Elder, 1903; New York: Scribners, 1903);

Stingaree (London: Chatto & Windus, 1905; New York: Scribners, 1905);

A Thief in the Night: The Last Chronicle of Raffles (London: Chatto & Windus, 1905); republished as *A Thief in the Night: Further Adven-tures of A. J. Raffles, Cricketer and Cracksman* (New York: Scribners, 1905);

Raffles: The Amateur Cracksman (London: Nash, 1906)–collects stories in *The Amateur Cracksman* (1899) and *The Black Mask* (1901);

Mr. Justice Raffles (London: Smith, Elder, 1909; New York: Scribners, 1909);

The Camera Fiend (London: Unwin, 1911; New York: Scribners, 1911);

Fathers of Men (London: Smith, Elder, 1912; New York: Scribners, 1912);

The Thousandth Woman (London: Nash, 1913; Indianapolis: Bobbs-Merrill, 1913);

Witching Hill (London: Hodder & Stoughton, 1913; New York: Scribners, 1913);

The Crime Doctor (London: Nash, 1914; Indianapolis: Bobbs-Merrill, 1914);

Trusty and Well Beloved: The Little Record of Arthur Oscar Hornung (Colchester, Essex: Privately printed, 1915);

The Ballad of Ensign Joy (New York: Dutton, 1917);

Wooden Crosses (London: Nisbet, 1918);

Notes of a Camp-Follower on the Western Front (London: Constable, 1919; New York: Dutton, 1919);

The Young Guard (London: Constable, 1919);

Old Offenders and a Few Old Scores (London: Murray, 1923);

E. W. Hornung and His Young Guard, 1914, edited by Shane R. Chichester (Crowthorne, Berkshire: Wellington College Press, 1941).

PLAY PRODUCTIONS: *Raffles, The Amateur Cracksman*, by Hornung and Eugene W. Presbrey, New York, Princess Theatre, 27 October 1903; London, Comedy Theatre, 12 May 1906;

Stingaree, the Bushranger, London, Queen's Theatre, 1 February 1908;

A Visit from Raffles, by Hornung and Charles Sansom, Brixton, Empress Theatre, 1 November 1909.

PERIODICAL PUBLICATIONS: "Stroke of Five; a story," *Belgravia*, 64 (1887): 70;

George Gissing, E. W. Hornung, Arthur Conan Doyle, and H. G. Wells in Rome, 1905

"Spoilt Negative; a story," *Belgravia*, 65 (1887): 76;

"Nettleship's Score," *Cornhill Magazine*, 61 (January 1890): 1-25;

"A Bride From The Bush," *Cornhill Magazine*, 62 (July 1890): 89-112; (August 1890): 201-224; (September 1890): 315-336; (October 1890): 429-448; (November 1890): 543-560;

"Thunderbolt's Mate; a story," *Chambers's Journal*, fifth series 9 (5 March 1892): 154-157; (12 March 1892): 169-171; (19 March 1892): 183-186; (22 March 1892): 200-201;

"Kenyon's Innings; a story," *Longman's Magazine*, 19 (April 1892): 614-637;

"The Burrawurra Brand; a story," *Idler*, 4 (November 1893): 349-365;

"The Boss of Taroomba," *Detroit Free Press* (1894);

"The Unbidden Guest," *Longman's Magazine*, 24 (May 1894): 76-102; (June 1894): 191-210; (July 1894): 296-321; (August 1894): 412-432; (September 1894): 522-543; (October 1894): 628-654;

"The Governess at Greenbush," *Chambers's Journal*, fifth series 12 (2 February 1895): 74-77; (9 February 1895): 89-91; (16 February 1895): 104-107; (23 February 1895): 119-122;

"After the Fact," *Chambers's Journal*, fifth series 13 (4 January 1896): 6-9; (11 January 1896): 23-26; (18 January 1896): 41-44; (25 January 1896): 55-58;

"A Villa in a Vineyard," *Cornhill Magazine*, 79 (May 1899): 662-665;

"No Sinecure: More Adventures of the Amateur Cracksman," *Scribner's Magazine*, 29 (January 1901): 30-43;

"A Jubilee Present: More Adventures of the Amateur Cracksman," *Scribner's Magazine*, 29 (February 1901): 220-231;

"The Fate of Faustina: More Adventures of the Amateur Cracksman," *Scribner's Magazine*, 29 (March 1901): 277-291;

"The Last Laugh: More Adventures of the Amateur Cracksman," *Scribner's Magazine*, 29 (April 1901): 483-494;

"To Catch a Thief: More Adventures of the Amateur Cracksman," *Scribner's Magazine*, 29 (May 1901): 591-600;

"An Old Flame: More Adventures of the Amateur Cracksman," *Scribner's Magazine*, 29 (June 1901): 707-720;

"The Wrong House: More Adventures of the Amateur Cracksman," *Scribner's Magazine*, 30 (September 1901): 343-350;

"Chrystal's Century," *Atlantic Monthly*, 91 (June 1903): 738-748;

"Charles Reade," *London Mercury*, 4 (June 1921): 150-163.

E. W. Hornung owes his place in the history of crime and mystery fiction to his popular scoundrel, the gentleman-burglar A. J. Raffles. Although the twenty-five Raffles stories and one novel constitute a very small portion of Hornung's canon, the Raffles character endures as one of the most successful fictional creations of British crime fiction.

Apart from his popular stories about sports, the bulk of Hornung's work explores the clash between legality and justice in both the frontier culture of Australia and within the more sophisticated European society of the time. Over the course of his career, Hornung's work showed steady maturation; initially, he wrote simple, entertaining adventure stories for magazines. By the end of his writing life, he was grappling with complex moral issues and exploring the psychology of guilt and the role of science in the study of evil. He frequently chose to write from the perspective of the criminal who devises, rather than the outsider who must solve, the puzzle of the crime, and usually the focus of interest in Hornung's works is the consequences of an act on the lives of his characters.

Hornung was a highly regarded writer in his day, not only for his ingenious plots and colorful local settings but also for his wit. (He commented, for example, about Sherlock Holmes, "Though he might be more humble, there is no police like Holmes.") He was considered one of the finest writers in the England of the British Empire about cricket in popular literature: the role of this game as a metaphor for life can hardly be overemphasized, and Hornung's descriptions of play far overreach the game itself. He was acknowledged as the writer of boys' books for men; his recreation of the boys' school environment and his sensitive portrayals of friendship between masters and boys ensured the popularity of his work among a nation of public-school graduates. He was also greatly esteemed as a true sentimentalist, favorably compared to the renowned James M. Barrie. His readers appreciated the strongly moral base from which he wrote his best stories. They could depend on him to lead them through the titillation of evil and injustice to a resolution they could endorse with satisfaction.

Ernest William Hornung was born in Middlesbrough, Yorkshire, on 7 June 1866, the youngest son of a solicitor, John Peter Hornung. He was educated at the Anglican boys' school, Uppingham, and, in spite of an asthmatic condition and poor eyesight, his lifelong interest in cricket was encouraged. He never achieved robust health, and when he graduated from school at the age of eighteen, he immigrated to Australia to take advantage of the milder climate of New South Wales.

He arrived in the Riverina district as a tutor to the children of Charles Joseph Parsons at Mossgiel Station. Much of the material he later used in his writings was drawn from this two-year experience, and the Australian influence is seen in fully two-thirds of his life's work. While still tutoring he began work on what was to become his first novel and contributed material to the Sydney *Bulletin*. When he returned to London in 1886 at the age of twenty, it was with some journalistic credentials and a partially completed manuscript.

During the late 1880s Hornung was a member of the London circle of journalists and magazine writers, and his short stories began to appear in the quality journals. Until that time he had made a precarious living writing, usually anonymously, for various newspapers. His lifelong interest in crime and social conditions date from this period; certainly it was at this time that

RAFFLES.

THE AMATEUR CRACKSMAN

BY

E. W. HORNUNG

ILLUSTRATED BY
F. C. YOHN

CHARLES SCRIBNER'S SONS

NEW YORK ::::::::::::::: 1908

Frontispiece and title page for an American edition of the first collection of stories about Hornung's most enduring character, Raffles, the gentleman thief (courtesy of Otto Penzler)

he developed an admiration for George Gissing, who shared these interests.

Hornung became a member of both the Idler's Club (in 1891) and (apparently) its amiable rival, the Strand Club. Both groups were primarily social, dinner and conversation groups, organized by the contributors and editors of the two most popular fiction magazines of the day.

On 27 September 1893, Hornung and Constance (Connie) Doyle, sister of Arthur Conan Doyle, were married at Conan Doyle's home in South Norwood. Before the marriage, Conan Doyle himself paid generous tribute to Hornung's literary ability and personality, praising his sweet nature and delicacy of mind.

Contemporary references to Hornung are few. Photographs show him to have been almost of a height with Conan Doyle, who stood over six feet, but he was altogether a slighter figure of a

man than the burly Conan Doyle. He seems to have been noted for rather precise habits of speech and manner; fussy, dapper, and strutting are all terms that have been used to describe his person, while Conan Doyle himself remarked that his neat and witty turn of phrase showed "a finer wit" than Dr. Johnson. Conan Doyle also complained that at times of disagreement Hornung's tone resembled that of an attorney dissecting a case. Hornung was a highly principled man, whose work reflected his beliefs.

Set in Australia, Hornung's first novel, *A Bride from the Bush* (1890), established him firmly in the role of a colonial romancer. Australian critics praised his accuracy and detail while they deplored the sensationalism which sold the books. He was an adept craftsman and commonly used popular plot devices. Disinherited young girls, mistaken identities, missing heirs, masquerades, im-

Illustration by Albert Levering from Mrs. Raffles, *the 1905 parody by John Kendrick Bangs in which Bunny Manders narrates the adventures of Raffles's widow. Hornung's Raffles died without having married.*

personations, and misplaced loyalties–all these themes enliven the four more Australian novels that Freeman produced from 1890 to 1896: *Tiny Luttrell* (1893), *The Boss of Taroomba* (1894), *The Unbidden Guest* (1894), and *Irralie's Bushranger* (1896).

In 1896 Hornung published *The Rogue's March,* a carefully researched novel about the Australian convict transportation system. Reviews of *The Rogue's March* were unenthusiastic as critics felt that the burden of facts and material quite overpowered the story he told. Nonetheless, the book is important because it shows his growing fascination with the motivation behind criminal behavior and a deliberate sympathy for the criminal hero as a victim of events.

In the Raffles tales–collected in *The Amateur Cracksman* (1899), *The Black Mask* (1901), *A Thief in the Night: The Last Chronicle of Raffles* (1905)–the reader vicariously participates in the planning and execution of crimes, rather than their deduction and solution.

The Raffles series, set in late Victorian London for the most part, shows a striking similarity in narrative form to Arthur Conan Doyle's Sherlock Holmes stories. Indeed, *The Amateur Cracksman* was dedicated "To A.C.D. THIS FORM OF FLATTERY." The role of the bumbling narrator-assistant is played by Bunny Manders; A. J. Raffles is the schemer, a cricket master who uses Bunny as an accomplice in his thefts. Former schoolmates, Bunny and Raffles are always-strapped-for-cash gentlemen-on-the-make. Raffles manages to live elegantly at the Albany; Bunny lives less lavishly nearby. As gentlemen, they are bound by certain standards of propriety; nonetheless, they survive by stealing from members of their own class. In "Ides of March," the initial story in the first Raffles collection, *The Amateur Cracksman*, Bunny asks Raffles how he came to be a burglar. Raffles replies: "Ah! that's a long story.... It was in the Colonies, when I was out there playing cricket. It's too long a story to tell you now, but I was in much the same fix that you were in tonight, and it was my only way out. I never meant it for anything more; but I'd tasted blood, and it was all over with me. Why should I work when I could steal? Why settle down to some humdrum uncongenial billet, when excitement, romance, danger and a decent living were all going begging together? Of course it's very wrong, but we can't all be moralists, and the distribution of wealth is very wrong to begin with." In fact, thievery is much like a game of cricket to Raffles and is played according to the same rules of deportment and the same standards of engagement.

The most notable display of Raffles's gentlemanly gamesmanship comes in "The Knees of the Gods," the last story in the second Raffles collection, *The Black Mask*. At the start of the Boer War Raffles is compelled by the patriotism appropriate to his class to enlist in the service of his country, and Bunny follows him. At the battlefront the two discover a spy and identify him, even though it means exposing themselves as thieves.

Permitted to fight on by a general who admires their principles, Raffles and Bunny are allowed one more glorious day in combat–his best day ever, Raffles says–during which Raffles is killed and Bunny is wounded as the result of an engagement with the Boers that is described in terms of a cricket match. Thus, the volume concludes with apparent finality.

Nonetheless, four years later a third collection of Raffles stories, *A Thief in the Night*, appeared with an explanatory narrator's note: "If I must tell more tales of Raffles, I can but go back to our earliest days together, and fill in the blanks left by discretion in existing annals. In so doing I may indeed fill some small part of an infinitely greater blank, across which you may conceive me to have stretched my canvas for a first frank portrait of my friend. The whole truth cannot harm him now. I shall paint in every wart. Raffles was a villain, when all is written; it is no service to his memory to gloze the fact; yet I have done so myself before to-day. I have omitted whole heinous episodes. I have dwelt unduly on the redeeming side. And this I may do again, blinded even as I write by the gallant glamour that made my villain more to me than any hero. But at least there shall be no more reservations, and as an earnest I shall make no further secret of the greatest wrong that even Raffles ever did me."

Even so, the nine stories in *A Thief in the Night* do not conclude the accounts of Raffles adventures. The success of the stories prompted Hornung to attempt a Raffles novel, *Mr. Justice Raffles*, in 1909, a book that most critics feel was ill-advised. The failure of the novel convinced Hornung to abandon his most successful character for good.

Raffles was adapted for the stage and later for the screen, initially by Hornung, and later by several other writers. Barry Perowne revived Raffles in *The Return of Raffles* (1933), *She Married Raffles* (1936), and *Raffles and the Key Man* (1940).

In any consideration of Raffles, it is useful to examine Hornung's *Stingaree*, the title of both a collection of ten stories (1905) and a stage play (*Stingaree, the Bushranger*, 1908). Hornung gave many of Raffles's qualities to the well-bred New South Wales bushranger (or highwayman) who calls himself Stingaree, but the eight third-person stories collected in this novel lack the dark charm of the early Raffles stories.

Many of Hornung's novels are studies on the theme of guilt. In *Peccavi* (1900) a British cler-

Illustration by Frederic Dorr Steele from Hornung's 1914 novel, The Crime Doctor

gyman lives a life of penance in exoneration of an early crime against his community. *The Shadow of the Rope* (1902) is a powerful portrayal of a troubled woman unjustly tried for her husband's murder. *No Hero* (1903) describes the restricted life of a divorced woman, as well as broader questions of loyalty, deception, and virtue. *Fathers of Men* (1912) treats the conflicts and loyalties of the students and faculty of a boys' school, and *The Thousandth Woman* (1913) describes a woman's act of faith when a tangle of circumstantial evidence implicates her lover in a murder. She trusts blindly to her conviction, and he is vindicated. These novels all show a deep interest in

the ramifications of guilt. While they are not properly mysteries, the plots often begin with a crime. As the Hornung-like character Langholm in *The Shadow of the Rope* explains, his interest is not in the murder the heroine is accused of having committed but in "her after life, the psychology of the woman and her subsequent adventures." Novels such as *The Shadow of the Rope, No Hero,* and *The Thousandth Woman* also demonstrate Hornung's concern with the inequities women faced in his society, a concern that extended from his earliest works.

Hornung was fascinated with developments in scientific and medical research and incorpo-

Ronald Colman with Kay Francis in the 1930 United Artists film, Raffles

rated into his plots the new techniques of psychiatry and medicine, as well as inventions such as the camera. *The Camera Fiend* (1911) and *The Crime Doctor* (1914) both depend on modern technology for their solutions to criminal activities, and *Witching Hill* (1913) is a series of short stories in which two modern young men resolve a series of unpleasant incidents that had been provoked by malign psychic influences.

The advent of World War I in 1914 put an effective end to Hornung's work as a writer of fiction. His only child, a son, enlisted in the early days of the war and was among the first who died at Ypres. Hornung himself then volunteered, in spite of his increasingly poor health, and served as an ambulance driver, rest-station attendant, and officer in the YMCA services. An account of these activities was published in 1919 under the title *Notes of a Camp-Follower on the Western Front*. It has been considered one of the best records of the war as experienced on the front lines. He published three short volumes of war poetry, *The Ballad of Ensign Joy* (1917), *Wooden Crosses* (1918), and *The Young Guard* (1919), which received considerable attention both during and after the war years, and a privately published memoir of his son's life, *Trusty and Well Beloved* (1915).

In broken health after the war, Hornung retired with his wife to the south of France and died on 22 March 1921. His brother-in-law, Arthur Conan Doyle, returning from a spiritualist tour of Australia, reached France just in time to attend Hornung's funeral and wrote later of Hornung's gravesite, adjacent to that of George Gissing in St.-Jean-de-Luz Cemetery. Obituaries appeared in both the London *Times* and the *New York Times*, noting Hornung's twin identities as the brother-in-law of Conan Doyle and the creator of Raffles. The *New York Times* even went so far as to suggest that this virtually made Raffles and Sherlock Holmes brothers-in-law.

References:

William Vivyan Butler, *The Durable Desperadoes* (London: Macmillan, 1973);

John Dickson Carr, *The Life of Sir Arthur Conan Doyle* (London: Murray, 1949);

Frank Wordleigh Chandler, *The Literature of Roguery*, 2 volumes (Boston: Houghton, Mifflin, 1907);

Arthur Conan Doyle, *Memories and Adventures* (London: Murray, 1924);

Conan Doyle, Preface to *Old Offenders and a Few Old Scores* (London: Murray, 1923);

Owen Dudley Edwards, *The Quest for Sherlock Holmes* (Edinburgh: Mainstream, 1983);

H. M. Green, *A History of Australian Literature*, volume 2 (London: Angus & Robertson, 1971), pp. 675-676;

Peter Haining, Foreword to *The Complete Short Stories of Raffles–The Amateur Cracksman* (New York: St. Martin's, 1984);

Michael Harrison, *Hornung's Revenge . . . Raffles; Greatest Sherlockian Spoof of All* (New York: Magico Magazine, 1984);

Jerome K. Jerome, *My Life and Times* (London: Hodder & Stoughton, 1926), pp. 98, 130, 176;

Jeremy Lewis, Introduction to *Classic Thrillers: The Collected Raffles*, edited by Lewis (London: Dent, 1985), pp. vii-xviii;

E. H. Mullin, "The Rambler," *The Book Buyer; a Review and Record of Current Literature*, 22 (March 1901): 90-105;

George Orwell, "Raffles and Miss Blandish," *Horizon*, 10 (October 1944): 232-244;

Hesketh Pearson, *Conan Doyle; His Life and Art* (London: Methuen, 1943), pp. 108-109, 177;

Otto Penzler, Introduction to Barry Perowne's *Raffles Revisited: New Adventures of a Famous Gentleman Crook* (New York: Harper & Row, 1974);

A. M. Robertson, " 'Ally Pally Mosis!' Wigmore Street Post-Bag," *Sherlock Holmes Journal*, 5 (Winter 1960): 27;

Colin Watson, *Snobbery with Violence* (London: Eyre & Spottiswoode, 1971), pp. 44-52, 242;

Evan M. Wilson, "Sherlock Holmes and A. J. Raffles," *Baker Street Journal*, 34 (September 1984): 155-158.

Fergus Hume

(8 July 1859-13 July 1932)

Dorothy Goldman
University of Kent, Canterbury

BOOKS: *The Mystery of a Hansom Cab* (Melbourne: Privately printed, 1886; London: Hansom Cab Publishing Company, 1887; New York: Munro, 1888);

Professor Brankel's Secret (Melbourne: Privately printed, 1886);

Madame Midas (London: Hansom Cab Publishing Company, 1888; New York: Munro, 1888);

The Girl from Malta (London: Hansom Cab Publishing Company, 1889; New York: Lovell, 1889);

The Piccadilly Puzzle (London: F. V. White, 1889; enlarged edition, New York: Lovell, 1889);

The Gentleman Who Vanished (London: F. V. White, 1890); republished as *The Man Who Vanished* (New York: Liberty Book Company, 1892);

The Man with a Secret, 3 volumes (London: F. V. White, 1890);

Miss Mephistopheles (London: F. V. White, 1890; New York: Lovell, 1890);

Whom God Hath Joined, 3 volumes (London: F. V. White, 1891);

The Year of Miracle: A Tale of the Year One Thousand Nine Hundred (London: Routledge, 1891; New York: Lovell, 1891);

A Creature of the Night (London: Low, 1891; New York: Lovell, 1891);

The Fever of Life (1 volume, New York: Lovell, 1891; 2 volumes, London: Low, 1892);

Monsieur Judas (London: Blackett, 1891; New York: Waverly, 1891);

The Black Carnation (London: Gale & Polden, 1892; New York & Chicago: United States Book Company, 1892);

Aladdin in London (London: A. & C. Black, 1892; Boston & New York: Houghton, Mifflin, 1892);

The Chronicles of Faeryland (London: Griffith, Farran, 1892?; Philadelphia: Lippincott, 1893);

The Island of Fantasy (3 volumes, London: Griffith, Farran, 1892; 1 volume, New York: Lovell, Coryell, 1892);

Cover for the 1887 London edition of Hume's first and best-known book (courtesy of Otto Penzler). All 5,000 copies of the first edition, which Hume had privately printed in Melbourne in 1886, were sold within three weeks of publication.

When I Lived in Bohemia (Bristol: Arrowsmith, 1892; New York: Tait, 1892);

A Speck of Motley (London: Innes, 1893);

The Harlequin Opal (3 volumes, London: W. H. Allen, 1893; 1 volume, Chicago & New York: Rand, McNally, 1893);

The Chinese Jar (London: Low, 1893);

The Best of Her Sex, 2 volumes (London: W. H. Allen, 1894);

The Gates of Dawn (London: Low, Marston, 1894; Chicago & New York: Neeley, 1894);

The Lone Inn (London: Jarrold, 1894; New York: Cassell, 1895);

A Midnight Mystery (London: Gale & Polden, 1894);

The Mystery of Landy Court (London: Jarrold, 1894);

The Nameless City (London: Osgood, McIlvaine, 1894);

The Crime of the "Liza Jane" (London: Ward, Lock & Bowden, 1895);

The Masquerade Mystery (London: Digby, Long, 1895);

The Third Volume (New York: Cassell, 1895);

The White Prior (London: Warne, 1895);

The Expedition of Captain Flick (London: Jarrold, 1895; New York: New Amsterdam Book Company, 1899);

The Carbuncle Clue (London & New York: Warne, 1896);

The Dwarf's Chamber and Other Stories (London: Ward, Lock & Bowden, 1896; New York, 1900);

A Marriage Mystery (London: Digby, Long, 1896);

Tracked by Tattoo (London: Warne, 1896);

Claude Duval of the Ninety-five (London: Digby, Long, 1897; New York: Dillingham, 1897);

For the Defense (Chicago & New York: Rand, McNally, 1897);

The Tombstone Treasure (London: Jarrold, 1897);

The Clock Struck One (London & New York: Warne, 1898);

The Devil-Stick (London: Downey, 1898);

Lady Jezebel (London: Pearson, 1898; New York: Mansfield, 1898);

The Rainbow Feather (London: Digby, Long, 1898; New York: Dillingham, 1898);

Hagar of the Pawn-Shop (London: Skeffington, 1898; New York: Buckles, 1899);

The Indian Bangle (London: Low, Marston, 1899);

The Red-Headed Man (London: Digby, Long, 1899);

The Silent House in Pimlico (London: John Long, 1899); republished as *The Silent House* (New York: Doscher, 1907; London: John Long, 1912);

The Bishop's Secret (London: Long, 1900); republished as *Bishop Pendle; or, The Bishop's Secret* (Chicago & New York: Rand, McNally, 1900);

The Crimson Cryptogram (London: Long, 1900; New York: New Amsterdam Book Company, 1902);

Shylock of the River (London: Digby, Long, 1900);

A Traitor in London (London: John Long, 1900; New York: Buckles, 1900);

The Lady from Nowhere (London: Chatto & Windus, 1900; New York: Brentano's, 1900);

The Vanishing of Tera (London: F. V. White, 1900);

A Woman's Burden (London: Jarrold, 1900);

The Crime of the Crystal (London: Digby, Long, 1901);

The Mother of Emeralds (London: Hurst & Blackett, 1901);

The Millionaire Mystery (London: Chatto & Windus, 1901; New York: Buckles, 1901);

The Pagan's Cup (London: Digby, Long, 1902; New York: Dillingham, 1902);

The Turnpike House (London: John Long, 1902);

Woman: The Sphinx (London: John Long, 1902);

The Jade Eye (London: Long, 1903);

The Miser's Will (London: Traherne, 1903);

The Silver Bullet (London: John Long, 1903);

The Guilty House (London: F. V. White, 1903);

The Yellow Holly (London: Digby, Long, 1903; New York: Dillingham, 1903);

A Coin of Edward VII (London: Digby, Long, 1903; New York: Dillingham, 1903);

The Mandarin's Fan (London: Digby, Long, 1904; New York: Dillingham, 1904);

The Lonely Church (London: John Long, 1904);

The Red Window (London: Digby, Long, 1904; New York: Dillingham, 1904);

The Wheeling Light (London: Chatto & Windus, 1904);

The White Room (London: F. V. White, 1904);

The Wooden Hand (London: F. V. White, 1905);

The Fatal Song (London: F. V. White, 1905);

Lady Jim of Curzon Street (London: Laurie, 1905; New York: Dillingham, 1906);

The Opal Serpent (London: John Long, 1905; New York: Dillingham, 1905);

The Scarlet Bat (London: F. V. White, 1905);

The Secret Passage (London: John Long, 1905; New York: Dillingham, 1905);

The Black Patch (London: Long, 1906);

The Dancer in Red and Other Stories (London: Digby, Long, 1906);

Jonah's Luck (London: F. V. White, 1906);

The Mystery of the Shadow (London: Cassell, 1906; New York: Dodge, 1906);

The Purple Fern (London: Everett, 1907);

The Sealed Message (New York: Dillingham, 1907; London: Digby, Long, 1908);

The Yellow Hunchback (London: F. V. White, 1907);

The Amethyst Cross (London: Cassell, 1908);

The Crowned Skull (London: Laurie, 1908); republished as *The Red Skull* (New York: Dodge, 1908);

Flies in the Web (London: F. V. White, 1908);

The Green Mummy (London: Long, 1908; New York: Dillingham, 1908);

The Mystery of a Motor Cab (London: Everett, 1908);

The Sacred Herb (London: John Long, 1908; New York: Dillingham, 1908);

The Devil's Ace (London: Everett, 1909);

The Disappearing Eye (London: Digby, Long, 1909; New York: Dillingham, 1909);

The Top Dog (London: F. V. White, 1909);

The Solitary Farm (London: Ward, Lock, 1909; New York: Dillingham, 1909);

The Lonely Subaltern (London: C. H. White, 1910);

The Mikado Jewel (London: Everett, 1910);

The Peacock of Jewels (London: Digby, Long, 1910; New York: Dillingham, 1910);

The Spider (London: Ward, Lock, 1910);

High-Water Mark (London: F. V. White, 1911);

The Jew's House (London: Ward, Lock, 1911);

The Pink Shop (London: F. V. White, 1911);

The Rectory Governess (London: C. H. White, 1911);

Red Money (New York: Dillingham, 1911; London: Ward, Lock, 1912);

The Steel Crown (London: Digby, Long, 1911; New York: Dillingham, 1911);

Across the Footlights (London: F. V. White, 1912);

The Blue Talisman (London: Laurie, 1912; New York: Clode, 1925);

Mother Mandarin (London: F. V. White, 1912);

The Mystery Queen (London: Ward, Lock, 1912; New York: Dillingham, 1912);

A Son of Perdition (London: Rider, 1912);

The Curse (London: Laurie, 1913?);

In Queer Street (London: F. V. White, 1913);

The Thirteenth Guest (London: Ward, Lock, 1913);

Seen in the Shadow (London: F. V. White, 1913);

The 4 P.M. Express (London: F. V. White, 1914);

Not Wanted (London: F. V. White, 1914);

The Lost Parchment (London: Ward, Lock, 1914; New York: Dillingham, 1914);

Answered: A Spy Story (London: F. V. White, 1915);

The Caretaker (London: Ward, Lock, 1915);

The Red Bicycle (London: Ward, Lock, 1916);

The Silent Signal (London: Ward, Lock, 1917);

The Grey Doctor (London: Ward, Lock, 1917);

Heart of Ice (London: Hurst & Blackett, 1918);

The Black Image (London: Ward, Lock, 1918);

Next Door (London: Ward, Lock, 1918);

Crazy-Quilt (London: Ward, Lock, 1919);

The Master-Mind (London: Hurst & Blackett, 1919);

The Dark Avenue (London: Ward, Lock, 1920);

The Other Person (London: F. V. White, 1920);

The Singing Head (London: Hurst & Blackett, 1920);

The Woman Who Held On (London: Ward, Lock, 1920);

Three (London & Melbourne: Ward, Lock, 1921);

The Unexpected (London: Odhams, 1921);

A Trick of Time (London: Hurst & Blackett, 1922);

The Moth-Woman (London: Hurst & Blackett, 1923);

The Whispering Lane (London: Hurst & Blackett, 1924; Boston: Small, Maynard, 1925);

The Caravan Mystery (London: Hurst & Blackett, 1926);

The Last Straw (London: Hutchinson, 1932);

The Hurton Treasure Mystery (London: Mellifont, 1937).

PLAY PRODUCTIONS: *The Mystery of a Hansom Cab*, by Hume and Arthur Law, London, Princess's Theatre, 23 February 1888;

Indiscretion, Folkestone, Kent, Exhibition Palace, 13 November 1888;

Madame Midas, The Gold Queen, by Hume and P. Beck, Exeter, Victoria Theatre, 5 December 1888;

The Fool of the Family, London, Duke of York's Theatre, 30 January 1896;

Teddy's Wives, Eastbourne, Sussex, 4 April 1896; London, Strand Theatre, 24 September 1896;

Honours Divided, Margate, Kent, Grand Theatre, 1 September 1902;

A Scotch Marriage, London, Criterion Theatre, 26 December 1907;

The Mystery of the Red Web, by Hume and Newman Harding, Liverpool, Olympia Theatre, 13 March 1908; London, Canterbury music hall, 18 April 1908.

Fergus Hume is remembered now only as the writer of best-selling detective fiction in the nineteenth century, the first to sell more than

Cover for Hume's 1888 novel, which employs the same Melbourne setting as The Mystery of a Hansom Cab

half a million copies of one novel, *The Mystery of a Hansom Cab* (1886). The customary judgment—reflected in Howard Haycraft's calling it "this shoddy pot-boiler"—is hardly a fair assessment of the book. Hume's abilities in incorporating rigorous social analysis within the detective genre deserve greater recognition.

Fergusson Wright Hume was born in England, the son of a New Zealand doctor, James Hume, who was also a founder of Dunedin College in New Zealand. His family subsequently returned to their native country, where he was educated at the Boys' High School and read law at Otago University. After a period in the New Zealand Attorney General's Office he was admitted to the bar in 1885 and later moved to Australia. By 1886 he was working in Melbourne as a barrister's clerk and completing his first book, *The Mystery of a Hansom Cab*. When it was re-

jected by the important Australian publisher George Robertson on the grounds that "no Colonial could write anything worth reading," Hume published it at his own expense, selling the entire first edition of 5,000 copies in three weeks, at one shilling each. The novel was dedicated to the novelist James Payn (1830-1898), whose latest work, *The Luck of the Darrells* (1885), Hume had read and admired. Copies of the first edition are among the rarest of the detective genre, with only two known copies extant.

Hume subsequently sold the copyright for fifty pounds to a group of London speculators, who, calling themselves the Hansom Cab Publishing Company, reaped enormous profits from the sales of the novel. Sales of various British and American editions passed the half-million mark, and its unrivaled success was marked by a contemporary full-length parody. Hume had always wanted to write for the stage, and *The Mystery of a Hansom Cab* was deliberately planned to catch the eye of theater managers; a dramatic version, by Hume and Arthur Law, was eventually produced on the London stage in 1888.

In the preface to the 1896 edition Hume described his first novel's origins: "I enquired of a leading Melbourne bookseller what style of book he sold most of. He replied that the detective stories of Gaboriau had a large sale, and as I had never even heard of this author I bought all his works—eleven or thereabouts—and read them carefully. The style of these attracted me, and I determined to write a book of the same class, containing a mystery, a murder and a description of low life in Melbourne." While it is more than a mere imitation of Emile Gaboriau, the book obviously owes a great deal to him, and Hume further acknowledged his debt to the Frenchman within the novel itself: "Indeed, from the nature of the crime itself, the place where it was committed, and the fact that the assassin had escaped without leaving a trace behind him, it would seem as though the case itself had been taken bodily out of one of Gaboriau's novels, and that his famous detective Lecoq only would be able to unravel it." Actually Hume's detectives are much more insignificant than Lecoq. Stephen Knight calls them "more like a pair of modern anti-heroes, plump, erring Gorby and soft-footed malignant Kilsip." Hume uses both amateur and professional detectives in his story of a murder that is not only a personal tragedy for the family of Frettlby the wool baron but a social evil which cannot be ignored. This dual approach is as old as the first detective story; equally part of a still-developing tradition was Hume's later decision to reemploy both his original detectives in *Madame Midas* (1888), even setting the second murder in that novel in the house where Frettlby lived and died.

Predictably for a book in the Gaboriau tradition, *The Mystery of a Hansom Cab* contains scenes of low life; indeed they are essential to the explanation of the hidden story of illegitimacy and bigamy which culminates in murder and blackmail. At the very center of the book lies the noxious and criminal section of Melbourne around Little Bourke Street (an area where Hume confessed he had spent many nights in research). On either side are what Knight describes as the "shabby-genteel, landlady-ridden suburbs" and the world of recently obtained wealth, only slowly consolidating its position. Members of society–represented by Frettlby and the young men-about-town, liberally sprinkled with newcomers from England–live a good life: indeed the entire plot rests on the drunken incapacity of three young playboys and the uniform appearance of evening dress in Melbourne society. The novel deals with the tensions and disturbances in this city where wealth and high living were still inextricably intertwined with suburban respectability and low-life dives. Despite increasing stratification, social hierarchies were not firmly established; Melbourne was shown to be a society where the position of any member might be challenged, where wealth and respectability were newly achieved, and where the servant might be the rightful heiress and the daughter of the house an unwitting imposter. Significantly the subtitle to the London edition is "a startling and realistic story of Melbourne social life."

While Melbourne's dockland slums were a new setting for detective fiction, they provided more than background, more than local color. Appearing at a time when wealthy Australian settlers were much in the news in England, the exciting portrayal of this exotic and racy society may provide a partial explanation for the novel's success outside Australia. Hume's descriptions are dramatically adept, essential to the plot, and an accurate depiction of a city whose social instability can be gauged by its doubling in size during the 1880s from a quarter to half a million inhabitants. Indeed Hume's social descriptions may have been too explicit; for Jarrold's 1896 edition he agreed to clean up the language and cut out some of the more sordid and more obscure Australian references.

Cover for Hume's 1900 book, a novel of the Boer War

The startling setting for the murder may also have something to do with the book's success: the victim is found lying dead in a cab at the station door, a chloroform-soaked silk handkerchief knotted tightly around his mouth. Hume contrasts this shocking image with an appeal to documentary evidence, a device which was to become typical of many later crime writers: "The following report appeared in the *Argus* newspaper of Saturday, the 28th July, 18--." He continues this reliance on reported evidence throughout the book, with "quotations" from newspapers, the inquest, and the trial, culminating in a written explanation.

Hume decided to become a professional writer after the 1886 publication in Australia of his second book, *Professor Brankel's Secret*, and in 1888 he sailed for England to pursue his career. He settled there and went on to write eight plays and more than 140 other novels–the majority were mysteries and the rest mainly romances. None of them was as successful as *The Mystery of a Hansom Cab,* but they earned him a comfortable enough living. Only one other of his detective novels, *Madame Midas,* is currently in print. While written and set in Australia, it was published in London in 1888 by the Hansom Cab Publishing Company. A later edition claims it had sold 100,000 copies.

Madame Midas is a fine companion piece to *The Mystery of a Hansom Cab.* Taking its portrait of the rapid translation of wealth into respectability one step further back by including a vivid picture of the actual acquisition of raw wealth at the Pactolus mine, the novel shows the vulnerability which this change creates and the close relation of the disreputable underworld of Melbourne to its beau monde. While Hume's first novel portrays the rough, vigorous, dissolute world of men, *Madame Midas* shows the effects that world had on women. Both the major women characters, Madame Midas (the reader never learns her first name, and even Midas is a nickname) and Kitty Marchurst, are destroyed by the world in which they live. Though neither is murdered nor murderer by the end of the book Madame Midas is "one who went forth into the world brokenhearted and friendless, with no belief in anyone and no pleasure in life" and Kitty, "with white face and staring eyes . . . covered her face with her hand and fled rapidly away into the shadowy night." Both can only flee a world which they have discovered to be too harsh and cruel for them. The two murders are finally solved—the

original one in rather a perfunctory manner—but they are more interesting for their symbolic representation of the world's evil, which society cannot control, than for any ingenious or innovative method of committal or discovery.

Three other detective novels by Hume established new conventions in the genre of mystery writing. The hero of *The Chinese Jar* (1893) is Octavius Fanks of Scotland Yard, a forerunner of the professional detective who is also a gentleman. As R. F. Stewart explains, he "was a man of good family, and followed the profession of detective, as one for which he was particularly adapted by nature. . . . In Scotland Yard he was known solely as Octavius Fanks; but in clubland he assumed the role of Octavius Rixton, idler and man-about-town." In *Hagar of the Pawn-Shop* (1898) Hume develops the role of the woman detective with his exotic and beautiful gypsy Hagar Stanley, and in *A Traitor in London* (1900), a mystery set against a background of the Boer War, the mystery is solved by a deathbed confession.

References:

Howard Haycraft, *Murder for Pleasure: The Life and Times of the Detective Story* (London: Davies, 1942), pp. 62-68;

Stephen Knight, Introduction to Hume's *The Mystery of a Hansom Cab* (London: Hogarth Press, 1985);

A. E. Murch, *The Development of the Detective Novel* (London: Owen, 1958);

R. F. Stewart, *. . . and Always a Detective* (Newton Abbot & North Pomfret, Vt.: David & Charles, 1980), pp. 259-260.

Sheridan Le Fanu

(28 August 1814-7 February 1873)

Judith J. Kollmann
University of Michigan-Flint

See also the Le Fanu entry in *DLB 21, Victorian Novelists Before 1885.*

BOOKS: *The Cock and Anchor being A Chronicle of Old Dublin City*, anonymous (3 volumes, Dublin: William Curry/London: Longmans/Edinburgh: Fraser, 1845; 1 volume, New York: Colyer, 1848); revised as *Morley Court* (London: Chapman & Hall, 1873); republished as *The Cock and the Anchor* (London: Downey, 1895);

The Fortunes of Colonel Torlogh O'Brien; A Tale of the Wars of King James, anonymous (Dublin: James McGlashan/London: William S. Orr, 1847; New York: Colyer, 1847);

Ghost Stories and Tales of Mystery, anonymous (Dublin: James McGlashan/London: William S. Orr, 1851);

The House by the Churchyard (3 volumes, London: Tinsley, 1863; 1 volume, New York: Carleton, 1866);

Wylder's Hand (3 volumes, London: Bentley, 1864; 1 volume, New York: Carleton, 1865);

Uncle Silas: A Tale of Bartram-Haugh (3 volumes, London: Bentley, 1864; 1 volume, New York: Munro, 1878);

The Prelude, Being a Contribution towards a History of the Election for the University, as John Figwood, Esq., Barrister at Law (Dublin: G. Herbert, 1865);

Guy Deverell (3 volumes, London: Bentley, 1865; 1 volume, New York: Harper, 1866);

All in the Dark (2 volumes, London: Bentley, 1866; 1 volume, New York: Harper, 1866);

The Tenants of Malory: A Novel (3 volumes, London: Tinsley, 1867; 1 volume, New York: Harper, 1867);

A Lost Name, 3 volumes (London: Bentley, 1868);

Haunted Lives, 3 volumes (London: Tinsley, 1868);

The Wyvern Mystery, 3 volumes (London: Tinsley, 1869);

Checkmate (3 volumes, London: Hurst & Blackett,

Sheridan Le Fanu, circa 1843; portrait by an unknown artist (courtesy of Mrs. Susan Digby-Firth)

1871; 1 volume, Philadelphia: Evans, Stoddart, 1871);

The Rose and the Key, 3 volumes (London: Chapman & Hall, 1871);

The Chronicles of Golden Friars, 3 volumes (London: Bentley, 1871);

In a Glass Darkly, 3 volumes (London: Bentley, 1872);

Willing to Die, 3 volumes (London: Hurst & Blackett, 1873);

The Purcell Papers, 3 volumes (London: Bentley, 1880);

The Poems of Joseph Sheridan Le Fanu, edited by Alfred Perceval Graves (London: Downey, 1896).

Collections: *Madame Crowl's Ghost and Other Tales of Mystery*, edited and collected by M. R. James (London: Bell, 1923);

The Collected Works of Joseph Sheridan Le Fanu, 52 volumes (New York: Arno, 1977).

The son of Thomas Philip and Emma Dobbin Le Fanu, Joseph Thomas Sheridan Le Fanu was born in Dublin on 28 August 1814. His family belonged to the professional and upper classes and were related to several of the leading families in Dublin, including the Sheridans (Le Fanu's paternal grandmother was a sister of Richard Brinsley Sheridan). Le Fanu's father, a Church of Ireland clergyman, was appointed chaplain for the Royal Hibernian Military School in 1815, so Joseph, along with his older sister, Catherine Frances, and his younger brother, William, spent his early childhood in Phoenix Park, a large public park just northwest of Dublin, which contained the school and the residences of British administrators. In 1815 the park, which still looks much the same today, was the site of duels, military pageantry, and upper-class life. On its edges were several villages, including Chapelizod, the setting for *The House by the Church-yard* (1863). The family stayed in residence at the school for eleven years.

In 1823 the Reverend Le Fanu became rector of Abingdon in County Limerick, a post he held in absentia until 1826, when he received the deanery of Emly and brought his family to Abingdon to take up residence in the glebe house. The family now found itself in rural Ireland, in a tiny village in the heart of Irish poverty and political ferment. The Reverend Le Fanu had alienated the resident Catholic priest by his three-year absenteeism, and the priest turned the countryside against him. As a result the move, which was promising at first, became financially disastrous. Tithe income dropped to half what it should have been in the first year, and, when in 1831 the Tithe Wars began, the situation became even worse. Catholics refused to pay the required tithes to the established Protestant Church of Ireland, and the family went deeply into debt.

The political situation was, at times, dangerous. As a young man, Le Fanu's younger brother, William, was nearly killed at least once, and Joseph absorbed what his biographer W. J. McCor-

Susanna Bennett Le Fanu, whom the novelist married in 1843

mack calls the "atmosphere of automatic, casual, and yet strangely intimate violence [that] pervaded rural Ireland" along with the acceptance of the supernatural, which was also widespread among Irish peasantry.

In 1832 Le Fanu entered Trinity College, University of Dublin, then the only college at the only university in Ireland. After studying classics he graduated with honors in 1837 and began legal training in the Dublin Inns of Court. The publication of his short story "The Ghost and the Bonesetter" in the January 1838 issue of the *Dublin University Magazine* began his lifelong interest in the *D.U.M.* He purchased the periodical in 1861 and edited it until he sold it in 1869. Most of his fiction appeared first in this magazine. He was called to the Irish Bar in 1839 but never practiced law. Instead he was attracted by politics and journalism. His attempts at politics did not succeed, but he was able to make a living of sorts with his writing. By 1840 he had bought interest in two Dublin newspapers, the *Statesman* and the *Warder*. The *Statesman* folded in 1846, but he continued his association with the *Warder* until 1870.

By 1861 he had also become part owner and coeditor of the *Dublin Evening Mail*. In spite of being an industrious and prolific writer, he could not seem to achieve financial stability.

He married Susanna Bennett on 18 December 1843, and they had four children. Both husband and wife suffered from ill health, and Susanna, who was somewhat unstable emotionally, died on 28 April 1858.

After her death Le Fanu gradually became more and more reclusive, earning over the years the title "The Invisible Prince" of letters in Dublin. From 1863 to his death in 1873 he wrote prolifically, mainly novels. The last year of his life was extremely solitary; he refused to see even old friends. He died of a heart condition on 7 February 1873. His imposing home in Dublin, in which he lived for twenty years, was leased from his wife's kinsman John Bennett, to whom he was deeply in debt. At Le Fanu's death his children were forced to leave.

The elements of Le Fanu's life play significant roles in his fiction. In his early work Irish life and history are major themes. The violence and often the treachery that he saw around him in his adolescence are reflected in many of his characters and plots; and his own financial difficulties gave him sympathy with all those characters in his stories who are in debt. His legal experience taught him not only what constituted evidence but also about lawyers and legal procedures. His experience with his neurotic wife undoubtedly contributed to his understanding of, and interest in, abnormal psychology.

Le Fanu was born in the late-romantic period, and its interest in the dark and macabre, which found expression in the Gothic novel, was the main stimulus to his literary imagination. Like many writers of the era, he was also influenced by Sir Walter Scott, Charles Dickens, and Wilkie Collins. All Le Fanu's novels depend on mystery, often murder. Only one of his novels does not contain a crime: *All in the Dark* (1866) is a romance in which the hero appears to be haunted by his aunt's ghost, but the reader finally discovers that he has been sleepwalking and playing the ghost himself.

Le Fanu wrote to make money, first by serializing his work in the *D.U.M.* and then by having it published in England. To appeal to the British market, he set all his novels written after 1863 in England. Even the poorest novels have enough suspense to keep the reader interested, and they occasionally have outstanding emotional

or descriptive passages. However, critics such as Elizabeth Bowen, Julian Symons, and W. J. McCormack agree that *Uncle Silas: A Tale of Bartram-Haugh* (1864) is Le Fanu's finest novel. In his introduction to *Uncle Silas* Frederick B. Shroyer has called it "one of the most effective, gripping novels of terror ... ever written." In addition, *The House by the Churchyard* and *Wylder's Hand* (1864) have also received acclaim. In *Checkmate* (1871), which is underrated, Le Fanu drew heavily on the plot of his first novel, *The Cock and Anchor being A Chronicle of Old Dublin City* (1845), but shifted the setting from eighteenth-century Dublin to nineteenth-century London.

The House by the Churchyard, Le Fanu's first mature novel, is a murder mystery. While a grave is being dug in the churchyard of Chapelizod, a skull is found, battered and obviously a murder victim's. With a large cast of characters and no main character, multiple plots, and considerable humor, the novel is an Irish comedy of manners. Eventually the various stories converge upon the solution to the mystery: first the reader discovers the identity of the victim; then, in the solution to yet another murder, the murderer. In this complex novel—of a sort he never attempted again—Le Fanu developed not only the mystery but also the macabre, the sentimental, and the comic. Le Fanu layered his comedy of manners elaborately around horrible and tragic events.

Writing comedy of manners was something Le Fanu obviously enjoyed, although he simplified its use in subsequent work. As a rule, he found his criminals in high places, drawing upon the lower classes for comedy or for the sinister (in the character of Mr. Larkin the comic and the sinister are combined) and upon foreigners (especially the French) for the truly villainous.

Wylder's Hand, more economic in plot and characters, centers upon the mystery of a missing man. Mark Wylder, an aggressive and somewhat vulgar gentleman, has inherited a vast fortune and is about to marry Dorcas Brandon, his cousin, in order to consolidate their financial position still further. However, Wylder is in love with Rachel Lake, and Dorcas with Rachel's brother Stanley. Wylder suddenly disappears, and people begin to receive letters from him that indicate he is taking a trip on the Continent. At the end of the novel Wylder (whose family motto is *resurgam*, "I shall return") reappears when the rain washes away some of the soil in a ditch near his home, and his hand, wearing a ring bearing the

Two of Le Fanu's four children: Emma Lucretia (born 1846) and Thomas Philip (born 1847) (courtesy of Mrs. Susan Digby-Firth)

motto, is uncovered. Stanley Lake's horse, smelling the corpse, rears, falls backward, and mortally injures its rider, who, before he dies, confesses to having killed Wylder.

Uncle Silas, Le Fanu's best-known novel, is, as McCormack describes it, "a self-conscious artefact, a verbal order" in which all elements are in perfect symmetrical balance. It contains few characters and a single plot that is divided into two parts, and everything is focused on one central issue: the character of Silas Ruthyn. Many years ago at his mansion, Bartram-Haugh, dead from a cut throat, was found in a room with a locked door, and the key was still in the lock on the inside. Because there were no trapdoors to the room, the jury brought in the verdict of suicide, but society, convinced that Silas is the murderer, has ostracized him. He has become moody and withdrawn. The shame to his family affects his brother, Austin, whose will names Silas as the guardian of Austin's only daughter and heir, Maud, the novel's narrator. Should she die before coming of age, Silas will inherit the estate. Thus, although it will in law prove nothing, Austin believes that Maud's survival at Bartram-Haugh will demonstrate Silas's innocence.

But Silas is the murderer, and when Maud refuses to marry his son, he plots to kill her. Making it appear that she has gone to France, he incarcerates her in the murder room. On the night she is to be murdered, her alcoholic maid-jailor, Mme de la Rougierre, drinks Maud's drugged wine and falls into Maud's bed. Maud, convinced that something is about to happen, cannot sleep and sees the murderer (in this case, Silas's son) enter the room by climbing down a rope and coming through the window. In the dark he slaughters de la Rougierre, and when Silas enters the room, Maud, who has been hiding behind the door, slips out and escapes.

The suspense is impeccably maintained: first the reader, like Maud, is curious about Silas's character and whether he is a murderer. When these questions are answered, the reader still does not know how the murder was done, and finally, when that question is answered, the reader is left wondering how Maud will escape.

In *Uncle Silas* much that is characteristic of Le Fanu's work is evident: the complex antagonist; great houses which are external manifesta-

WYLDER'S HAND:

A NOVEL.

BY

JOSEPH SHERIDAN LE FANU,

AUTHOR OF
'THE HOUSE BY THE CHURCHYARD.'

IN THREE VOLUMES.

VOL. I.

LONDON:

RICHARD BENTLEY, NEW BURLINGTON STREET.

1864.

Title page for the three-decker novel in which the murder victim, Mark Wylder, wears a ring with the family motto, resurgam

tions of the psyches of their owners; the use of nature, especially landscape, to emphasize human emotions or states of mind; the presence of paintings, especially those by Flemish masters, as ominous symbols of the past; and, in general, the haunting of the present by the past. One could say that the fates of Le Fanu's characters lie in their genes; they are often what they are because of their ancestry or because of self-imposed expectations due to their awareness of family and status.

Critics have often felt that Le Fanu's true forte was writing shorter narrative fiction, in which he could concentrate on the plot. Perhaps the two most notable mysteries to be found in his shorter fiction are "The Evil Guest," an early version of *A Lost Name* (1868), collected in *Ghost Stories and Tales of Mystery* (1851), and "The Room at the Dragon Volant" (collected in *In a Glass Darkly*,

1872), which deals with a trio of con artists who have murdered several people and who nearly do away with the narrator. This tale uses forensic medicine to identify a skeleton by means of a healed fracture, a handmade glass eye, and, above all, dentures for which the original plates are found by the dentist.

Le Fanu came close to writing what is now known as the classical English murder mystery. Many of its characteristics are present in his work: the drive for the rational explanation, a clear understanding of evidence, the existence (though rarely) of "red herrings," and motive. But two vital elements are missing: the detective and the "whodunit." There are a few detectives in Le Fanu's work, but they are amateur and occasional; and they are never main characters. Le Fanu's main character is the criminal, who is destroyed by his own subconscious self and the operation of fate.

Le Fanu's purpose was different from Wilkie Collins's or Arthur Conan Doyle's. As Michael H. Begnal explains, both of these men wished to maintain "a distance . . . between the reader and the event," and "we view crime and sin in a detached, deductive way as a puzzle which Sherlock Holmes may solve as an intellectual exercise but not as something which affects him or us very much. It is this very detachment which Le Fanu is trying to avoid in his work." Le Fanu wanted his readers involved with his morally and psychologically ambivalent Byronic antagonists, who are studies of the individual who commits one crime and then has to live with the consequences. Such characters include Sir Jekyl Marlowe of *Guy Deverell* (1865), Mr. Dingwell of *The Tenants of Malory* (1867), and Walter Longcluse of *Checkmate*, all of whom are psychologically haunted. The operation of fate, through the confluence of coincidences that are completely rational except for their timing, is probably the greatest affirmation of the supernatural in Le Fanu's work—ironically enough for a man better known for his tales of the supernatural than for his mysteries. In a Le Fanu mystery the operation of an invisible providence forces the criminal into a position or place in which he betrays himself. Thus, Wylder's hand reappears at the precise time when Lake rides by; Silas leaves the door open when he should have shut it. In his interest in the criminal's psyche and in the awareness of a providence that insists "murder will out," Le Fanu has more in common with Dostoyevski than with Conan Doyle.

Le Fanu has not been forgotten, and today he enjoys a modest popularity among afficionados of both mystery and fantastic fiction. Collections of his stories and *Uncle Silas*, at least, are usually in print, and in 1977 Arno Press reprinted all his works as *The Collected Works of Joseph Sheridan Le Fanu*. He has influenced Irish writers, especially James Joyce, and writers of the mystery genre, particularly Dorothy Sayers.

Biography:

W. J. McCormack, *Sheridan Le Fanu and Victorian England* (Oxford: Clarendon Press, 1980).

References:

Michael H. Begnal, *Joseph Sheridan Le Fanu* (Lewisburg: Bucknell University Press, 1971);

Begnal, "A Source for 'Distant Music,'" *James Joyce Quarterly*, 17 (1980): 303;

Elizabeth Bowen, Introduction to Le Fanu's *The House by the Churchyard* (London: Blond, 1968);

Bowen, "Uncle Silas," in *Collected Impressions* (New York: Knopf, 1950), pp. 3-17;

Julia Briggs, *Night Visitors: the Rise and Fall of the English Ghost Story* (London: Faber & Faber, 1977);

Joseph Browne, "Ghosts and Ghouls and Le Fanu," *Canadian Journal of Irish Studies*, 8 (1982): 5-15;

Nelson Browne, *Sheridan Le Fanu* (London: Morrison & Gibb, 1951);

David Brownell, "Wicked Dreams: The World of Sheridan Le Fanu," *Armchair Detective*, 9 (1976): 191-197;

Patrick F. Byrne, "Joseph Sheridan Le Fanu: a Centenary Memoir," *Dublin Historical Record*, 26 (June 1973): 80-92;

Austin Clarke, "Yeats and Le Fanu," *London Times Literary Supplement*, 12 (1968): 1409;

Patrick Diskin, "Poe, Le Fanu and the Sealed Room Mystery," *Notes and Queries*, new series 13 (September 1966): 337-339;

Walter C. Edens, "A Minor Victorian Novelist and his Publisher," Ph.D. dissertation, University of Illinois, 1963;

S. M. Ellis, "Bibliography of Sheridan Le Fanu," *Irish Book Lover*, 8 (October-November 1916): 30-33;

Ellis, *Mainly Victorian* (London: Hutchinson, 1925);

Ellis, *Wilkie Collins, Le Fanu and Others* (London: Constable, 1931), pp. 140-191;

Thomas Flanagan, *The Irish Novelists, 1800-1850* (New York: Columbia University Press, 1959);

David Gates, "An Addition to the Le Fanu Bibliography," *Notes and Queries*, new series 31 (1984): 491;

Gates, " 'A Dish of Village Chat': Narrative Technique in Sheridan Le Fanu's *The House by the Churchyard*," *Canadian Journal of Irish Studies*, 10 (1984): 63-69;

John P. Harrington, "Swift through Le Fanu and Joyce," *Mosaic*, 12 (1979): 49-58;

Edna Kenton, "A Forgotten Creator of Ghosts: Joseph Sheridan Le Fanu. Possible Inspirer of the Brontes," *Bookman*, 69 (July 1929): 528-534;

Thomas Phillip Le Fanu, *Memoir of the Le Fanu Family* (Manchester: Sherrat & Hughes, 1924);

William Richard Le Fanu, *Seventy Years of Irish Life* (London: Macmillan, 1893);

Christine Longford, Introduction to Le Fanu's *Uncle Silas* (Harmondsworth: Penguin, 1940);

Longford, "Joseph Sheridan Le Fanu," *Bell*, 4 (September 1942): 434-438;

W. E. Lougheed, "An Addition to the Le Fanu Bibliography," *Notes and Queries*, new series 11 (June 1964): 224;

Jean Lozes, "Joseph Sheridan Le Fanu: The Prince of the Invisible," in *The Irish Short Story*, edited by Patrick Rafroidi and Terence Brown (Lille: University of Lille, 1979), pp. 91-101;

M. J. MacManus, "Some Points in the Bibliography of Joseph Sheridan Le Fanu," *Dublin Magazine*, second series 9 (July/September 1934): 55-57;

J. C. Maxwell, "J. S. Le Fanu's *The Cock and Anchor*: Notes for *O.E.D.*," *Notes and Queries*, new series 6 (July/August 1959): 284-285;

W. J. McCormack, "J. Sheridan Le Fanu's *Richard Marston* (1848): the History of an Anglo-Irish Text," in *1848: the Sociology of Literature*, edited by Francis Barker and others (Colchester: University of Essex, 1978), pp. 107-125;

McCormack, "Sheridan Le Fanu's *Uncle Silas*: an Anglo-Irish Provenance," *Long Room*, no. 4 (Autumn/Winter 1971): 23-29;

Ivan Melada, *Sheridan Le Fanu* (Boston: Twayne, 1987);

Alma E. Murch, *The Development of the Detective Novel* (London: Owen, 1968);

Jolanta Nalęcz-Wojtozak, "*Uncle Silas*: A Link Between the Gothic Romance and the Detective Novel in England," *Studia Anglica Posnaniensia: An International Review of English Studies*, 12 (1980): 157-167;

Arthur H. Nethercot, "Coleridge's 'Christobel' and Le Fanu's 'Carmilla,' " *Modern Philology*, 147 (August 1949): 32-38;

Harold Orel, " 'Rigid Adherence to Facts': Le Fanu's *In a Glass Darkly*," *Ireland: A Journal of Irish Studies*, 20, no. 4 (1985): 65-88;

Audrey Petersen, *Victorian Masters of Mystery: From Wilkie Collins to Conan Doyle* (New York: Ungar, 1984);

Kel Roop, "Making Light in the Shadow Box: The Artistry of Le Fanu," *Papers on Language and Literature*, 21 (1985): 359-369;

Ken Scott, "Le Fanu's 'The Room in the Dragon Volant,' " *Lock Haven Review*, no. 10 (1968): 25-32;

Frederick B. Shroyer, Introduction to Le Fanu's *Uncle Silas* (New York: Dover, 1966);

Wilbur J. Smith, "Le Fanu's Ghost Stories Dublin 1851," *Book Collector*, 17 (1968): 78;

Kevin Sullivan, "The House by the Churchyard: James Joyce and Sheridan Le Fanu," in *Modern Irish Literature: Essays in Honour of William York Tyndall*, edited by R. J. Porter and J. D. Brophy (New York: Iona College Press/ Twayne, 1972), pp. 315-334;

Julian Symons, *Bloody Murder: from the Detective Story to the Crime Novel: a History* (London: Faber & Faber, 1972);

Devendra Varma, "Musings on the Life and Works of Joseph Sheridan Le Fanu: a Forgotten Creator of Ghosts," introduction to *The Collected Works of Joseph Sheridan Le Fanu* (New York: Arno, 1977);

Robert Lee Wolff, *Strange Stories and Other Explorations in Victorian Fiction* (Boston: Gambit, 1971), pp. 31-37.

Papers:
A large collection of Le Fanu family papers is available in microfilm through the National Library of Ireland (N. 2973-88; P. 2594-609). The diaries (1846-1894) of William Richard Le Fanu, the novelist's brother, are in the library of Trinity College, Dublin. The Bennett family papers (George Bennett was the novelist's father-in-law) are in the Brotherton Library, University of Leeds. The Dufferin and Ava papers (which include letters from Le Fanu to Helen, Lady Dufferin) are in the Public Record Office of Northern Ireland. The papers of the publishing firm of Bentley (the novelist's publishers) are in the library of the University of Illinois (see Walter C. Edens's dissertation, listed above).

William Le Queux
(2 July 1864-13 October 1927)

Kevin Radaker
Pennsylvania State University

BOOKS: *Guilty Bonds* (London: Routledge, 1891; New York: Fenno, 1895);

Strange Tales of a Nihilist (London: Ward, Lock, 1892; New York: Cassell, 1892); republished with altered contents as *A Secret Service, Being Strange Tales of a Nihilist* (London: Ward, Lock & Bowden, 1896);

The Great War in England in 1897 (London: Tower, 1894);

The Temptress (London: Tower, 1895; New York & London: Stokes, 1895);

Zoraida: A Romance of the Harem and the Great Sahara (London: Tower, 1895; New York: Stokes, 1895);

Stolen Souls (London: Tower, 1895; New York: Stokes, 1895);

Devil's Dice (London: White, 1896; Chicago & New York: Rand, McNally, 1897);

The Great White Queen (London: White, 1896);

Whoso Findeth a Wife (London: White, 1897; Chicago & New York: Rand, McNally, 1898);

A Madonna of the Music Halls (London: White, 1897); republished as *A Secret Sin; Or, A Madonna of the Music Halls* (London: Gardner, 1913);

The Eye of Istar (London: White, 1897; New York: Stokes, 1897);

If Sinners Entice Thee (London: White, 1898; New York: Dillingham, 1899);

Scribes and Pharisees: A Story of Literary London (London: White, 1898; New York: Dodd, Mead, 1898);

The Veiled Man (London: White, 1899);

The Bond of Black (London: White, 1899; New York: Dillingham, 1899);

The Day of Temptation (London: White, 1899; New York: Dillingham, 1899);

England's Peril (London: White, 1899);

Secrets of Monte Carlo (London: White, 1899; New York: Dillingham, 1900);

Wiles of the Wicked (London: White, 1900);

An Eye for an Eye (London: White, 1900);

In White Raiment (London: White, 1900);

William Le Queux

Of Royal Blood: A Story of the Secret Service (London: Hutchinson, 1900);

The Gamblers (London: Hutchinson, 1901);

The Sign of the Seven Sins (Philadelphia: Lippincott, 1901);

Her Majesty's Minister (London: Hodder & Stoughton, 1901; New York: Dodd, Mead, 1901);

The Court of Honor (London: White, 1901);

The Under-Secretary (London: Hutchinson, 1902);

The Unnamed: A Romance of Modern Italy (London: Hodder & Stoughton, 1902);

The Tickencote Treasure: Being the Story of a Silent Man, a Sealed Script and a Singular Secret (London: Newnes, 1903);

The Three Glass Eyes: A Story of To-Day (London: Traherne, 1903);

The Seven Secrets (London: Hutchinson, 1903);

Secrets of the Foreign Office (London: Hutchinson, 1903);

The Idol of the Town (London: White, 1904);

As We Forgive Them: Being the Story of a Man's Secret (London: White, 1904);

The Closed Book (London: Methuen, 1904; New York & London: Smart Set, 1904);

The Hunchback of Westminster (London: Methuen, 1904);

The Man from Downing Street (London: Hurst & Blackett, 1904);

The Red Hat (London: Daily Mail, 1904);

The Sign of the Stranger (London: White, 1904);

The Valley of the Shadow (London: Methuen, 1905);

The Spider's Eye (London: Cassell, 1905);

Who Giveth This Woman? (London: Hodder & Stoughton, 1905);

Sins of the City: A Story of Craft, Crime and Capital (London: White, 1905);

The Mask (London: Long, 1905);

Behind the Throne (London: Methuen, 1905);

The Czar's Spy (London: Hodder & Stoughton, 1905; New York: Smart Set, 1905);

Confessions of a Lady's Man (London: Hutchinson, 1905);

The House of the Wicked (London: Hurst & Blackett, 1906);

The Mysterious Mr. Miller (London: Hodder & Stoughton, 1906);

The Mystery of a Motor-Car: Being the Secret of a Woman's Life (London: Hodder & Stoughton, 1906);

Whatsoever a Man Soweth (London: White, 1906);

The Woman at Kensington (London & New York: Cassell, 1906);

The Invasion of 1910 (London: Nash, 1906);

The Great Court Scandal (London: White, 1907);

The Count's Chauffeur (London: Nash, 1907);

The Secret of the Square (London: White, 1907);

The Great Plot (London: Hodder & Stoughton, 1907);

Whosoever Loveth: Being the Secret of a Lady's Maid (London: Hutchinson, 1907);

An Observer in the Near East, anonymous (London: Nash, 1907); republished as *The Near East: The Present Situation in Montenegro, Bosnia, Servia, Bulgaria, Roumania, Turkey and Macedo-*

Cover for the 1896 collection of short stories about a Russian Nihilist that, according to Le Queux's preface, was banned in the Russian Empire by "a special order issued from the Press Bureau at St. Petersburg"

nia (New York: Doubleday, Page, 1907); republished as *The Balkan Trouble: Or, An Observer in the Near East* (London: Nash, 1912);

The Lady in the Car (London: Nash, 1908; Philadelphia: Lippincott, 1908);

The Crooked Way (London: Methuen, 1908);

The Looker-On: A Romance of Journalistic London (London: White, 1908);

The Pauper of Park Lane: A Mystery of East and West (London: Cassell, 1908; New York: Cupples & Leon, 1908);

Stolen Sweets (London: Nash, 1908);

The Woman in the Way (London: Nash, 1908);

Spies of the Kaiser. Plotting the Downfall of England (London: Hurst & Blackett, 1909);

The Red Room (London: Cassell, 1909; Boston: Little, Brown, 1911);

The House of Whispers (London: Nash, 1909; New York: Brentano's, 1910);

Fatal Thirteen (London: Stanley Paul, 1909);

Treasure of Israel (London: Nash, 1910);

The Great God Gold. (Boston: Badger, 1910);

Lying Lips (London: Stanley Paul, 1910);

The Unknown To-Morrow (London: White, 1910);

Hushed Up! A Mystery of London (London: Nash, 1911);

The Monkey-Spider: A Mystery of the Arctic (London & New York: Cassell, 1911; Boston: Badger, 1911);

Revelations of the Secret Service (London: White, 1911);

The Indiscretions of a Lady's Maid (London: Nash, 1911);

The Death-Doctor (London: Hurst & Blackett, 1912);

Fatal Fingers (London: Cassell, 1912);

The Mystery of Nine (London: Nash, 1912);

Without Trace (London: Nash, 1912);

The Price of Power, Being Chapters from the Secret History of the Imperial Court of Russia (London: Hurst & Blackett, 1913);

The Room of Secrets (London: Ward, Lock, 1913);

The Lost Million (London: Nash, 1913);

Mysteries (London: Ward, Lock, 1913);

The White Lie (London: Ward, Lock, 1914);

Sons of Satan (London: White, 1914);

The German Spy: A Present-Day Story (London: Newnes, 1914);

The War of Nations, volume 1 (London: Newnes, 1914);

German Atrocities: A Record of Shameless Deeds (London: Newnes, 1914);

The Hand of Allah (London & New York: Cassell, 1914); republished as *The Riddle of the Ring* (London: Federation Press, 1927);

The Royal Highness (London & New York: Hodder & Stoughton, 1914);

The Maker of Secrets (London: Ward, Lock, 1914);

The Four Faces (London: Stanley Paul, 1914; New York: Brentano's, 1914);

The Double Shadow (London: Hodder & Stoughton, 1915);

At the Sign of the Sword: A Story of Love and War in Belgium (London: T. C. & E. C. Jack, 1915; New York: Sully & Kleinteich, 1915);

The Mysterious Three (London: Ward, Lock, 1915);

The Mystery of the Green Ray (London: Hodder & Stoughton, 1915); republished as *The Green Ray* (London & Dublin: Mellifont, 1934);

The Sign of Silence (London: Ward, Lock, 1915);

The White Glove (London: Nash, 1915);

German Spies in England: An Exposure (London: Stanley Paul, 1915);

The German Spy System from Within (London: Hodder & Stoughton, 1915);

Britain's Deadly Peril. Are We Told the Truth? (London: Stanley Paul, 1915);

The Devil's Spawn: How Italy Will Defeat Them (London: Stanley Paul, 1915);

The Zeppelin Destroyer: Being Some Chapters of Secret History (London: Hodder & Stoughton, 1916);

Number 70, Berlin: A Story of Britain's Peril (London: Hodder & Stoughton, 1916);

The Place of Dragons (London: Ward, Lock, 1916);

The Spy Hunter (London: Pearson, 1916);

The Man About Town (London: Long, 1916);

Annette of the Argonne: A Story of the French Front (London: Hurst & Blackett, 1916);

The Broken Thread (London: Ward, Lock, 1916);

"Cinders" of Harley Street (London: Ward, Lock, 1916);

The Way to Win (London: Simpkin, Marshall, 1916);

Hushed Up at German Headquarters (London: London Mail, 1917);

Behind the German Lines (London: London Mail, 1917);

The Breath of Suspicion (London: Long, 1917);

The Devil's Carnival (London: Hurst & Blackett, 1917);

No Greater Love (London: Ward, Lock, 1917);

Two in a Tangle (London: Hodder & Stoughton, 1917);

Rasputin, The Rascal Monk (London: Hurst & Blackett, 1917);

The Bomb-Makers (London: Jarrolds, 1917);

Beryl of the Biplane (London: Pearson, 1917);

The Rainbow Mystery: Chronicles of a Colour-Criminologist (London: Hodder & Stoughton, 1917);

The Secrets of Potsdam (London: London Mail, 1917);

More Secrets of Potsdam (London: London Mail, 1917);

Further Secrets of Potsdam (London: London Mail, 1917);

Donovan of Whitehall (London: Pearson, 1917);

The Scandal-Monger (London: Ward, Lock, 1917);

The Yellow Ribbon (London: Hodder & Stoughton, 1918);

The Secret Life of the Ex-Tsaritza (London: Oldhams, 1918);

The Sister Disciple (London: Hurst & Blackett, 1918);

The Stolen Statesman (London: Skeffington, 1918);

The Little Blue Goddess (London: Ward, Lock, 1918);

The Minister of Evil (London: Cassell, 1918);

Bolo, The Super-Spy (London: Oldhams, 1918);

The Catspaw (London: Lloyds, 1918);

Sant of the Secret Service (London: Oldhams, 1918);

Love Intrigues of the Kaiser's Sons (London: Long, 1918; New York: John Lane, 1918);

Cipher Six (London: Hodder & Stoughton, 1919);

The Doctor of Pimlico (London & New York: Cassell, 1919; New York: Macaulay, 1920);

The Forbidden Word (London: Oldhams, 1919);

The King's Incognito (London: Oldhams, 1919);

The Lure of Love (London: Ward, Lock, 1919);

Rasputinism in London (London: Cassell, 1919);

Secrets of the White Tsar (London: Oldhams, 1919);

The Hotel X (London: Ward, Lock, 1919);

Mysteries of a Great City (London: Hodder & Stoughton, 1919); republished in 2 volumes as *Mysteries of a Great City* and *More Mysteries of a Great City* (London & Dublin: Mellifont, 1934);

The Heart of a Princess: A Romance of To-Day (London: Ward, Lock, 1920);

The Intriguers (London: Hodder & Stoughton, 1920; New York: Macaulay, 1921);

No. 7, Saville Square (London & Melbourne: Ward, Lock, 1920);

The Red Widow; Or, The Death-Dealers of London (London: Cassell, 1920);

The Terror of the Air (London: Lloyd's, 1920);

Whither Thou Goest (London: Lloyd's, 1920);

The Secret Telephone (New York: McCann, 1920; London: Jarrolds, 1921);

Society Intrigues I Have Known (London: Oldhams, 1920);

In Secret (London: Oldhams, 1921);

The House to Let (London: Hodder & Stoughton, 1921);

The Lady-in-Waiting: A Royal Romance (London & Melbourne: Ward, Lock, 1921);

The Open Verdict (London: Hodder & Stoughton, 1921);

The Power of the Borgias: The Story of a Great Film (London: Oldhams, 1921);

Mademoiselle of Monte Carlo: A Mystery of To-Day (London & New York: Cassell, 1921; New York: Macaulay, 1921);

The Fifth Finger (London: Stanley Paul, 1921; New York: Moffat, Yard, 1921);

The Luck of the Secret Service (London: Pearson, 1921);

Cover for one of Le Queux's six books published in 1906, a mystery-adventure novel

The Elusive Four (London: Cassell, 1921);

The Golden Face (London & New York: Cassell, 1922; New York: Macaulay, 1922);

The Stretton Street Affair (New York: Macaulay, 1922; London: Cassell, 1924);

Three Knots (London & Melbourne: Ward, Lock, 1922);

The Voice from the Void (London & New York: Cassell, 1922; New York: Macaulay, 1923);

The Young Archduchess (London & Melbourne: Ward, Lock, 1922; New York: Moffat, Yard, 1922);

Tracked by Wireless (London: Stanley Paul, 1922; New York: Moffat, Yard, 1922);

The Gay Triangle: The Romance of the First Air Adventurers (London: Jarrolds, 1922);

Landru: His Secret Love Affairs (London: Stanley Paul, 1922);

Where the Desert Ends (London & New York: Cassell, 1923);

The Bronze Face (London & Melbourne: Ward, Lock, 1923); republished as *Behind the Bronze Door* (New York: Macaulay, 1923);

Things I Know About Kings, Celebrities and Crooks (London: Nash & Grayson, 1923; New York: Stokes, 1924);

Bleke, The Butler (London: Jarrolds, 1924);

The Crystal Claw (London: Hodder & Stoughton, 1924; New York: Macaulay, 1924);

Fine Feathers (London: Stanley Paul, 1924);

A Woman's Debt (London & Melbourne: Ward, Lock, 1924);

The Valrose Mystery (London & Melbourne: Ward, Lock, 1925);

The Marked Man (London: Ward, Lock, 1925);

The Blue Bungalow (London: Hurst & Blackett, 1925);

The Broadcast Mystery (London: Holden, 1925);

Hidden Hands (London: Hodder & Stoughton, 1926); republished as *The Dangerous Game* (New York: Macaulay, 1926);

The Fatal Face (London: Hurst & Blackett, 1926);

The Letter E (London: Cassell, 1926); republished as *The Tattoo Mystery* (New York: Macaulay, 1927);

The Mystery of Mademoiselle (London: Hodder & Stoughton, 1926);

The Scarlet Sign (London & Melbourne: Ward, Lock, 1926);

The Black Owl (London & Melbourne: Ward, Lock, 1926);

The Office Secret (London & Melbourne: Ward, Lock, 1927);

The House of Evil (London & Melbourne: Ward, Lock, 1927);

The Lawless Hand (London: Hurst & Blackett, 1927; New York: Macaulay, 1928);

Blackmailed (London: Nash & Grayson, 1927);

The Chameleon (London: Hodder & Stoughton, 1927); republished as *Poison Shadows* (New York: Macaulay, 1927);

Double Nought (London: Hodder & Stoughton, 1927); republished as *The Crime Code* (New York: Macaulay, 1928);

The Crimes Club (London: Nash & Grayson, 1927);

Engelberg: The Crown Jewel of the Alps (London: Swiss Observer, 1927);

Concerning this Woman (London: Newnes, 1928);

The Rat Trap (London & Melbourne: Ward, Lock, 1928; New York: Macaulay, 1930);

The Secret Formula (London & Melbourne: Ward, Lock, 1928);

The Sting (London: Hodder & Stoughton, 1928; New York: Macaulay, 1928);

Twice Tried (London: Hurst & Blackett, 1928);

The Peril of Helen Marklove and Other Stories (London: Jarrolds, 1928);

The Amazing Count (London & Melbourne: Ward, Lock, 1929);

The Crinkled Crown (London & Melbourne: Ward, Lock, 1929; New York: Macaulay, 1929);

The Golden Three (London & Melbourne: Ward, Lock, 1930; New York: Fiction League, 1931);

The Factotum and Other Stories (London & Melbourne: Ward, Lock, 1931).

PLAY PRODUCTIONS: *The Proof*, Birmingham, Grand Theatre, 21 April 1924; produced again as *Vendetta*, London, Victoria Palace, 23 June 1924.

OTHER: Luigi, Duke of the Abruzzi, *On the "Polar Star" in the Arctic Sea, by His Royal Highness Luigi Amadeo of Savoy, Duke of Abruzzi*, translated by Le Queux (London: Hutchinson, 1903).

A prolific author of novels and short stories of mystery, crime, and international intrigue, William Le Queux is best remembered as the writer who set the guidelines for all subsequent British spy fiction until the advent of Eric Ambler. Though Le Queux's stories may be faulted for their often heavy padding, particularly in their treatment of love affairs, they are notable for what they reveal about his impressive knowledge of military and political affairs and his fascination with the intricacies of criminal activity.

Born to a French father and a British mother, William Tufnell Le Queux was educated privately in London and at Pegli, near Genoa, Italy. After studying art in Paris under Spiridon and touring France and Germany on foot, he returned to England, where he drifted into journalism. At first Le Queux reported police-court cases for the *Eastbourne Gazette*, after which he joined the staff of the *Middlesex Chronicle*, where he served as editor for five years. He then received an appointment to the parliamentary staff of the London *Globe* as a reporter in the gallery of the House of Commons. In 1891, after three years with the *Globe*, Le Queux was named foreign editor, a post that he thoroughly enjoyed. He resigned in 1893 to devote his time to writing fiction, but he returned to journalism in 1912 to

Cover for Le Queux's 1911 "Mystery of London"

spend two years as Balkan correspondent for the London *Daily Mail* during the Balkan War.

Throughout his life Le Queux loved to travel, and during the final decade of the nineteenth century he visited various parts of Europe and the Middle East. Following the advice of Émile Zola, who once encouraged him to become personally acquainted with the scenes and characters of European life, Le Queux wandered through Spain, Russia, Egypt, Norway, Sweden, Poland, and Italy. In these and other countries Le Queux came to know firsthand the settings for his fiction. He also visited fashionable European resorts such as Trouville, Etretat, San Sebastián, Carlsbad, Wiesbaden, Ems, Aix-les-Bains, Vichy, and Monte Carlo, and he would display his knowledge of them again and again in his novels of Continental life.

The bulk of Le Queux's fiction consists of mysteries involving crime, and most of these stories take place in exotic or fashionable settings where exorbitant wealth and power add allure to the tale. As an ardent criminologist, Le Queux was fascinated with all sorts of criminal types. Nevertheless, he was careful never to glorify the criminal. In fact many of his stories–including *Secrets of Monte Carlo* (1899), the best known of his early crime novels–contain moralistic passages that dwell on the vice and greed of criminal activities. The narrator of *Secrets of Monte Carlo* is

Being another curious leaf from the Diary of Villiers Beethom-Saunders, Doctor of Medicine, of Harley Street, London— known to his intimates as "Cinders"—revealed by his friend and executor, Charles Barrington Mayne, Esquire, Barrister-at-Law, of Fig Tree Court, Temple, and edited by William Le Queux.

An illustration from the 1916 Premier Magazine *serialization of* "Cinders" *of Harley Street*

Antoine Martin, the general director of the surveillance department for the casinos, who recounts various criminal cases that could have been witnessed only by such an official. But in the midst of Martin's accurate descriptions and his convincingly logical explanations, Le Queux inserted passages such as: "Over-ambition and greedy avarice, which are universal traits in human nature, are the bank's greatest safeguards. The man who wins today is almost certain, if he returns, to lose tomorrow. . . . In our close, stifling rooms, where the light of day is subdued and the fresh air excluded, avarice is, as elsewhere, the cause of the ruin of thousands." In Le Queux's fictional world, morality is simple: the desire for money is the genesis of all crime.

According to Le Queux's biographer, Norman St. Barbe Sladen, Le Queux was a British Secret Service agent before and during World War I. Le Queux himself claimed to have intimate knowledge of the secret services of other countries and to have been consulted on such matters by the British government. Whatever role he played, it is clear that he was well versed in matters of espionage. Nearly one-quarter of his fiction consists of spy stories, most of which were written between 1890 and 1910. Until the end of the nineteenth century Le Queux saw France as the primary threat to British security, a view that was common in military thinking at the time. *England's Peril* (1899) opens with the murder of Lord Casterton, a member of Parliament who has been protesting England's inadequate mili-

tary preparations. By the end of the novel the reader learns that Casterton has been the victim of an explosive cigar given him by his wife, who is in love with Gaston la Touche, the chief of the French secret service. In *The Great War in England in 1897* (1894) the Russians join the French in invading England, a fear often expressed at that time, particularly by military historians.

In the twentieth century Le Queux turned his attention to the threat posed by Germany. *The Invasion of 1910* (1906) and *Spies of the Kaiser* (1909) are especially noteworthy predictions of World War I. In the preface to *Spies of the Kaiser* Le Queux warned his readers that England was "in grave danger of invasion by Germany at a date not far distant" and suggested that five thousand German agents were active in Great Britain. For *The Invasion of 1910* Le Queux consulted military strategists and traveled more than ten thousand miles by car throughout England to determine its most vulnerable points. Le Queux produced a book of 550 pages, complete with maps and plans outlining the course of a possible invasion by Germany. As Le Queux wrote in the preface, the object of his forecast was to "bring home to the British public vividly and forcibly what really would occur were an enemy suddenly to appear in our midst." The serial publication of *The Invasion of 1910* in the *Daily Mail* was generally well received, and after Eveleigh Nash published it in book form, it went through several editions by 1917. The widespread attention accorded the book was partly due to the fact that Le Queux had received help from three of the best military minds of the day: Col. Cyril Field, Major Matson, and H. W. Wilson, who wrote the naval chapters of the novel. *The Invasion of 1910* has been translated into at least twenty-seven languages, including Arabic, Urdu, Syrian, Japanese, and Chinese. The total sales of various editions have amounted to nearly one million copies.

During the later years of his life, Le Queux concentrated primarily on producing crime fiction, including several collections of related short stories about individual criminals. The stories in *The Lady in the Car* (1908) are about "Prince Albert of Hesse-Holstein," who masquerades as the Kaiser's nephew; those in *"Cinders" of Harley Street* (1916) are presented as leaves from the diary of Dr. Villiers Beethom-Saunders, whose exploits are revealed by his friend and executor, barrister Charles Barrington-Mayne. *The Crimes Club* (1927) is a collection of stories about the detective work of ten members of that real organization. The club included among its forty members Le Queux, Melville Macnaghten of New Scotland Yard, Eveleigh Nash, and Sir Arthur Conan Doyle. The most intriguing stories in the collection are "A Secret of the Underworld," which involves hidden jewelry and secret passageways in a Spanish castle, and "The Purple Death," which reflects Le Queux's lifelong fascination with poisons and their effectiveness.

Perhaps Le Queux's best collection of short stories is *Mysteries of a Great City* (1919), which contains twelve stories told from the point of view of Monsieur Becq, former chief of the detective bureau of Paris. Not only does this volume contain some of Le Queux's best descriptive passages and tightest plots but Monsieur Becq is one of the most interesting and logical characters that Le Queux ever created. At times Becq's reasoning is reminiscent of Sherlock Holmes's. As Becq comments in "The Mysterious Mademoiselle," a story of a double poisoning executed by a jealous and ambitious doctor: "I am naturally a very close student of human nature. . . . Given a crime, my first objective has ever been to discern the motive. No crime is ever committed without some direct motive, be it ever so well concealed."

Like Becq, Le Queux was an ardent student of human nature, a student who studied and wrote about some of the most fascinating and infamous criminals of his day. Although Le Queux is no longer highly regarded as an author of crime fiction, he continues to be recognized as a seminal figure in the development of the spy novel.

Biography:
Norman St. Barbe Sladen, *The Real Le Queux* (London: Nicholson & Watson, 1938).

Marie Belloc Lowndes

(1868-14 November 1947)

Mary Jean DeMarr
Indiana State University

BOOKS: *H. R. H. the Prince of Wales*, anonymous (London: Richards, 1898; New York: Appleton, 1898); revised as *His Most Gracious Majesty King Edward VII*, published under Lowndes's name (London: Richards, 1901);

The Philosophy of the Marquise (London: Richards, 1899);

T. R. H. the Prince and Princess of Wales (London: Newnes, 1902);

The Heart of Penelope (London: Heinemann, 1904; New York: Dutton, 1915);

Barbara Rebell (London: Heinemann, 1905; New York: Dodge, 1907);

The Pulse of Life (London: Heinemann, 1908; New York: Dodd, Mead, 1909);

The Uttermost Farthing (London: Heinemann, 1908; New York: Kennerley, 1909);

Studies in Wives (London: Heinemann, 1909; New York: Kennerley, 1910);

When No Man Pursueth (London: Heinemann, 1910; New York: Kennerley, 1911);

Jane Oglander (London: Heinemann, 1911; New York: Scribners, 1911);

The Chink in the Armor (London: Methuen, 1912; New York: Scribners, 1912); republished as *The House of Peril* (London: Readers Library, 1935);

Mary Pechell (London: Methuen, 1912; New York: Scribners, 1912);

The Lodger (London: Methuen, 1913; New York: Scribners, 1913);

Studies in Love and Terror (London: Methuen, 1913; New York: Scribners, 1913);

The End of Her Honeymoon (New York: Scribners, 1913; London: Methuen, 1914);

Noted Murder Mysteries, as Philip Curtin (London: Simpkin, Marshall, Hamilton, Kent, 1914);

Told in Gallant Deeds: A Child's History of the War (London: Nisbet, 1914);

Good Old Anna (London: Hutchinson, 1915; New York: Doran, 1916);

The Price of Admiralty (London: Newnes, 1915);

The Red Cross Barge (London: Smith, Elder, 1916; New York: Doran, 1918);

Marie Belloc Lowndes

Lilla: A Part of Her Life (London: Hutchinson, 1916; New York: Doran, 1918);

Love and Hatred (London: Chapman & Hall, 1917; New York: Doran, 1917);

Out of the War? (London: Chapman & Hall, 1918); republished as *The Gentleman Anonymous* (London: Allan, 1934);

From the Vasty Deep (London: Hutchinson, 1920); republished as *From Out the Vasty Deep* (New York: Doran, 1921);

The Lonely House (London: Hutchinson, 1920; New York: Doran, 1920);

What Timmy Did (London: Hutchinson, 1921;
New York: Doran, 1922);

Why They Married (London: Heinemann, 1923);

The Terriford Mystery (London: Hutchinson, 1924;
Garden City: Doubleday, Page, 1924);

Bread of Deceit (London: Hutchinson, 1925); republished as *Afterwards* (Garden City: Doubleday, Page, 1925);

Some Men and Women (London: Hutchinson, 1925; Garden City: Doubleday, Doran, 1928);

What Really Happened (London: Hutchinson, 1926; Garden City: Doubleday, Page, 1926);

The Story of Ivy (London: Heinemann, 1927; Garden City: Doubleday, Doran, 1928);

"Thou Shalt Not Kill" (London: Hutchinson, 1927);

Cressida: No Mystery (London: Heinemann, 1928; New York: Knopf, 1930);

Duchess Laura: Certain Days of Her Life (London & Melbourne: Ward, Lock, 1929); republished as *The Duchess Intervenes* (New York: Putnam's, 1933);

Love's Revenge (London: Readers Library, 1929);

One of Those Ways (London: Heinemann, 1929; New York: Knopf, 1929);

The Key: A Love Drama in Three Acts (London: Benn, 1930);

With All John's Love (London: Benn, 1930);

Letty Lynton (London: Heinemann, 1931; New York: Cape & Smith, 1931);

Vanderlyn's Adventure (New York: Cape & Smith, 1931); republished as *The House by the Sea* (London: Heinemann, 1937);

Why Be Lonely?, by Lowndes and F. S. A. Lowndes (London: Benn, 1931);

Jenny Newstead (London: Heinemann, 1932; New York: Putnam's, 1932);

Love Is a Flame (London: Benn, 1932);

The Reason Why (London: Benn, 1932);

What Really Happened [play] (London: Benn, 1932);

Duchess Laura: Further Days of Her Life (New York & Toronto: Longmans, Green, 1933);

Another Man's Wife (London: Heinemann, 1934; New York & Toronto: Longmans, Green, 1934);

The Chianti Flask (New York & Toronto: Longmans, Green, 1934; London & Toronto: Heinemann, 1935);

Who Rides on a Tiger (New York & Toronto: Longmans, Green, 1935; London & Toronto: Heinemann, 1936);

Marie Belloc, age twenty

And Call It Accident (New York & Toronto: Longmans, Green, 1936; London: Hutchinson, 1939);

The Second Key (New York & Toronto: Longmans, Green, 1936); republished as *The Injured Lover* (London: Hutchinson, 1939);

The Marriage-Broker (London: Heinemann, 1937); republished as *The Fortune of Bridget Malone* (New York & Toronto: Longmans, Green, 1937);

Motive (London: Hutchinson, 1938); republished as *Why It Happened* (New York & Toronto: Longmans, Green, 1938);

The Empress Eugenie: A Three Act Play (New York & Toronto: Longmans, Green, 1938);

Lizzie Borden: A Study in Conjecture (New York & Toronto: Longmans, Green, 1939; London: Hutchinson, 1940);

Reckless Angel (New York & Toronto: Longmans, Green, 1939);

The Christine Diamond (London & Melbourne: Hutchinson, 1940; New York & Toronto: Longmans, Green, 1940);

Before the Storm (New York & Toronto: Longmans, Green, 1941);

"I, Too, Have Lived in Arcadia" [autobiography]
(London: Macmillan, 1941; New York: Dodd,
Mead, 1942);

A Labour of Hercules (London: Todd, 1943);

What of the Night? (New York: Dodd,Mead,
1943);

Where Love and Friendship Dwelt [autobiography]
(London: Macmillan, 1943; New York:
Dodd, Mead, 1943);

The Merry Wives of Westminster [autobiography]
(London: Macmillan, 1946);

A Passing World [autobiography] (London: Macmillan, 1948);

She Dwelt with Beauty (London: Macmillan, 1949);

The Young Hilaire Belloc (London: Kennedy, 1956);

*Diaries and Letters of Marie Belloc Lowndes
1911-1947*, edited by Susan Lowndes (London: Chatto & Windus, 1971).

OTHER: *Edmund and Jules de Goncourt, with Letters and Leaves from Their Journals*, 2 volumes, edited and translated by Lowndes and M. Shedlock (London: Heinemann, 1895; New York: Dodd, Mead, 1895).

Marie Belloc Lowndes excelled in creating terrifying psychological studies. Her interest was in character, and she effectively centered her carefully constructed plots around the ethical dilemmas faced by very ordinary people. She followed crimes of the day, sometimes attending trials, and she found in real events the materials for some of her best fiction. The subtitle of a late novel, *Lizzie Borden: A Study in Conjecture* (1939), suggests her method. Her approaches to crime fact vary from the loose adaptation of situation to relatively accurate approximation of actual facts, although even here names, dates, and settings may be changed.

Marie Adelaide Belloc was born in London in the summer of 1868. Her brother, Hilaire, who would become a poet and novelist, was born in 1870. Their parents, Louis Belloc, a Frenchman with an Irish grandfather, and Bessie Rayner Parkes Belloc, an Englishwoman who was a direct descendant of Joseph Priestley, were an unconventional couple in that their father was an invalid and a recluse and their mother was nearly forty when they married in 1867. The Bellocs divided their time between La Celle St. Cloud, a village about twelve miles from Paris and the home of Louis's mother, and the London residence of Mrs. Parkes on Wimpole Street.

In April 1872 Louis Belloc died, and Bessie, who had little interest in her children, left the care of Marie and Hilaire to a nurse, Sarah Mew, whom Marie disliked. The family still maintained residences in both England and France, providing the children with exposure to British culture as well as the less formal life-style of Continental Europe described by Marie Belloc Lowndes in the autobiographical *"I, Too, Have Lived in Arcadia"* (1941). Their dual existence ended when their maternal grandmother, Mrs. Parkes, died in 1877, leaving to their mother the property on Wimpole Street, complete with the lodgers Mrs. Parkes had taken in to keep her company while the Bellocs were in France. In 1878 Bessie Belloc unwisely entrusted her finances to one of the lodgers, a young stockbroker, who lost her modest fortune, ruining her financially.

In January 1896 Marie Belloc married Frederic Sawrey Lowndes, the youngest son of an English country parson. Some members of the Lowndes family, supporters of the Anglican Church, were distressed by Frederic's choice of a Catholic bride, for Marie, who rarely discussed her religion, was a devout Catholic who numbered among her happiest childhood years those spent at a convent school operated by the nuns of the Order of the Holy Child. The couple had two daughters and a son. At the time of their marriage Frederic Lowndes was employed by the London *Times* as a journalist, a position which he retained until 1938 when he retired. His work at the *Times* gave him access to "an alarming knowledge of what may be called the secret history of the day." Some of the information that he shared with his wife found its way into her detective novels.

Lowndes's most famous and widely read novel (its continuing interest is shown by its long publication history and by the fact that it has been filmed at least three times, in 1932, 1944, and 1953) is *The Lodger* (1913). An early work, it yet reveals many of the features that were to characterize much of her best work: her ability to depict a variety of sorts of people with sympathy, her skillful building of plots that create terror, her placing her characters in believable and wrenching situations, and her use of actual fact to undergird her fiction.

The Lodger is based on the series of murders committed by the legendary Jack the Ripper, but its central device was given to Lowndes by a chance remark: as she set it down in her diary, with the heading of 9 March 1923, the original

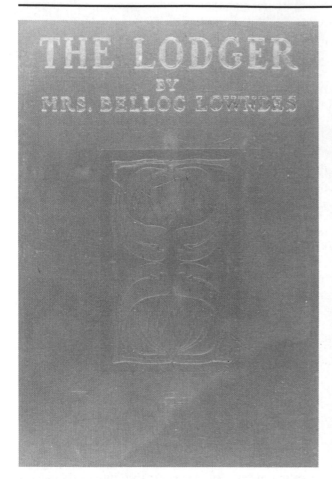 

Front covers for the first edition and later paperback publication of Lowndes's most enduring novel, based on the Jack the Ripper murders (courtesy of Otto Penzler)

short story, of which the novel was an expansion, was written after she "heard a man telling a woman at a dinner party that his mother had had a butler and a cook who married and kept lodgers. They were convinced that Jack the Ripper had spend a night under their roof." Lowndes's novel does not solve the murder–that is, it does not reveal the identity of the Ripper nor does it analyze the various identifications that have been propounded over the years. Lowndes accepted the theory that he must have been a gentleman, but he is only a secondary character in her novel. The central character is a woman, a former servant now trying to support herself and her husband by taking in lodgers. Mr. Sleuth, the ironically named gentleman who rents the upper part of her house, is seldom seen and remains a shadowy figure–even as Mrs. Bunting's fears and suspicions are gradually aroused. Willful self-deception seems her means of coping with her need for the pitiful little security he has brought them, and yet revulsion against him and

herself as well as fear of what he might do torment this inarticulate woman. The crimes are not directly shown; their effect, however, is dramatically portrayed through the terror they inflict on the citizenry, especially the Buntings, and through the hysteria whipped up by the news accounts. Although Lowndes was interested in sexuality and its impact on people's behavior, the victims are here transposed from prostitutes to drunken women so that the obsession of the criminal has been changed. The novel's end does explain the mysterious cessation of crimes, but it makes no pretensions to solving any of the other unanswered questions surrounding the Ripper's criminal career.

Exemplifying Lowndes's other approach to crime fact–the fictionalized reconstruction of a famous crime–is *What Really Happened* (1926), written near the middle of her literary career. The Bravo murder of 1876 in Balham was of continuing interest to her, as revealed by a diary entry dated 29 November 1912, in which she mentions having discussed the Bravo case with Prime Minister Asquith (she specifically indicates her belief in the innocence of the victim's widow, a chief suspect). The victim, Charles Bravo, died of poison, and suspicion was divided among his widow, her housekeeper, and her lover, a famous osteopathic surgeon. Two inquests occurred, but no one was ever brought to trial, and this unsolved mystery has attracted a number of writers, some searching for historical truth and others fictionalizing the events. Lowndes changed the time (her events occur in the early twentieth century) and the place, but neither time nor place is particularly significant in her treatment. She also renamed all the characters, changing the middle-aged doctor to a dashing young hero. She retains the shallow and careless character of the widow and the helpless dependency and unpopularity of the housekeeper. The novel follows the fictional trial of the young widow for murder (though in reality the case was never tried), using many of the facts and depicting the relationships that were revealed at the actual inquests. The title promises an inside look at the facts, and indeed the novel does suggest a solution that is in keeping with these facts. The novel is, like most of Lowndes's fiction, a psychological study rather than a historical reconstruction.

Lowndes excelled in the creation of atmosphere, and she occasionally made setting an integral part of her presentation. Her knowledge of France appears to good effect in *The End of Her Honeymoon* (1913). This study in the psychology of a suddenly deserted young woman and the man who becomes obsessed with helping her takes readers into the French investigative system and effectively portrays a family of Paris hotelkeepers. Nancy and Jack Dampier, a young English couple, conclude their blissful honeymoon by coming to a Paris hotel. Because the hotel is overcrowded they are forced to sleep in separate rooms–and Jack Dampier is never seen again. An American senator and his family take Mrs. Dampier under their care, and through their investigations the reader is taken into the prefecture and to the morgue as well as to artists' studios; Paris during an exhibition year is vividly portrayed. In some respects typical of the plot reversals at which Lowndes excelled, this novel's conclusion, unfortunately, is based upon an awkward coincidence. Jack's disappearance remains a mystery until two years after its occurrence. Nancy and her American friends are seen in an epilogue set in England. By merest chance a visitor at a din-

ner party tells an odd tale, with no names mentioned, of an Englishman who developed plague during the night while in Paris with his bride. Concealing his illness, he sought a doctor but died within a few hours. Briefly the storyteller describes the cover-up, motivated by the French horror of the disease and the necessity of maintaining calm during the Exhibition, which frustrated all attempts of his bride and her friends to learn the truth. This sudden reversal has actually been foreshadowed: Jack's incipient illness in the opening chapter becomes significant, and there are hints that not all the French officials were as forthcoming and honest as they seemed to be.

The combination of mystery and romance, as in *The End of Her Honeymoon*, was a favored form for Lowndes. *The Chianti Flask* (1934) begins with a courtroom scene of the sort she excelled in creating. Laura Dousland, on trial for the murder of her elderly husband, is acquitted. Suspicion continues to hover about her, for a missing clue, the chianti flask of the title, cannot be found. Much of the novel is seen from the point of view of the distraught young widow. The reader learns that Laura's one friend, who had testified on her behalf, had almost forced Laura into her unsuitable marriage, and the misery which Laura had endured is made plain. A young doctor falls in love with her, and, despite her scruples and fears that no marriage she contracts can be successful, he persuades her to marry him. Thus after an opening clearly in the mystery genre, the middle of the novels falls essentially into the category of romance. The end of the novel returns to the mystery as the doctor discovers the missing flask and, in one of Lowndes's more effective plot reversals, realizes that Laura is actually guilty. The romance element predominates in the ending, however, as after her full confession to him he declares that they will "expiate together . . . what has to be expiated."

Lowndes balanced her writing career with extensive travel and an active social life. She continued to spend time in both France and England and frequently visited America, which she considered her second home. She enjoyed the friendship of many leading political and literary figures, among them Robert Browning, Henry James, Arnold Bennett, Oscar Wilde, and Émile Zola. She maintained an interest in world events through both World War I and World War II, recording her impressions in her numerous memoirs.

F. S. A. Lowndes, whom Marie Belloc married in 1896

In addition to crime fiction, Lowndes also wrote romances, biography, and autobiography. Elements of suspense and tight plotting, as well as careful psychological examination, are evident in these other forms. Her long career as a writer, stretching from the first decade of the twentieth century, concluded only with several publications after her death in Eversly Cross, Hampshire, 14 November 1947. Although she is more or less forgotten now except as the author of *The Lodger* and as the sister of Hilaire Belloc, her crime fic-

tion is still readable, even absorbing. She was concerned with ordinary people facing extraordinary pressures and fears and was skilled in depicting complex human relationships. Her female characters are often assertive and competent. She built suspense and terror to gripping climaxes and was able to re-create a variety of social milieus and characters. All these factors give her best work a continuing claim on the attention of readers.

A. E. W. Mason

(7 May 1865-22 November 1948)

J. Randolph Cox
St. Olaf College

BOOKS: *Blanche de Malétroit* (London: Capper & Newton, 1894);

A Romance of Wastdale (London: Mathews/New York: Stokes, 1895);

The Courtship of Morrice Buckler (London: Macmillan, 1896; London & New York: Macmillan, 1903);

The Philanderers (London & New York: Macmillan, 1897);

Lawrence Clavering (London: Innes, 1897; New York: Dodd, Mead, 1897);

Miranda of the Balcony (London & New York: Macmillan, 1899);

The Watchers (Bristol: Arrowsmith, 1899; New York: Stokes, 1899);

Parson Kelly, by Mason and Andrew Lang (New York & London: Longmans, Green, 1900; New York: Longmans, 1909);

Ensign Knightley and Other Stories (London: Constable, 1901; New York: Stokes, 1901);

Clementina (London: Methuen, 1901; New York: Stokes, 1901);

The Four Feathers (London: Smith, Elder, 1902; New York & London: Macmillan, 1902);

The Truants (London: Smith, Elder, 1904; New York & London: Harper, 1904);

Running Water (London: Hodder & Stoughton, 1907; New York: Century, 1907);

The Broken Road (London: Smith, Elder, 1907; New York: Scribners, 1907);

Green Stockings: A Comedy in Three Acts (New York: French, 1909);

At the Villa Rose (London: Hodder & Stoughton, 1910; New York: Scribners, 1910);

Making Good (New York: Paget, 1910);

The Turnstile (London & New York: Hodder & Stoughton, 1912; New York: Scribners, 1912);

The Witness for the Defence (London: Hodder & Stoughton, 1913; New York: Scribners, 1914);

The Affair at the Semiramis Hotel (New York: Scribners, 1917);

A. E. W. Mason

The Four Corners of the World (London: Hodder & Stoughton, 1917; New York: Scribners, 1917);

The Royal Exchange (London: Royal Exchange, 1920);

The Summons (London & New York: Hodder & Stoughton, 1920; New York: Doran, 1920);

The Winding Stair (London: Hodder & Stoughton, 1923; New York: Doran, 1923);

The House of the Arrow (London: Hodder & Stoughton, 1924; New York: Doran, 1924);

No Other Tiger (London: Hodder & Stoughton, 1927; New York: Doran, 1927);

At the Villa Rose: A Play in Four Acts (London: Hodder & Stoughton, 1928);

The Prisoner in the Opal (London: Hodder & Stoughton, 1928; Garden City: Doubleday, Doran, 1928);

The Dean's Elbow (London: Hodder & Stoughton, 1930; Garden City: Doubleday, Doran, 1931);

The Three Gentlemen (London: Hodder & Stoughton, 1932; Garden City: Doubleday, Doran, 1932);

The Sapphire (London: Hodder & Stoughton, 1933; Garden City: Doubleday, Doran, 1933);

A Present from Margate, by Mason and Ian Hay (London & New York: French, 1934);

Dilemmas (London: Hodder & Stoughton, 1934; Garden City: Doubleday, Doran, 1935);

They Wouldn't Be Chessmen (London: Hodder & Stoughton, 1935; Garden City: Doubleday, Doran, 1935);

Sir George Alexander & the St. James' Theatre (London: Macmillan, 1935);

Fire Over England (London: Hodder & Stoughton, 1936; Garden City: Doubleday, Doran, 1936; abridged edition, London: University of London Press, 1949);

The Drum (London: Hodder & Stoughton, 1937; Garden City: Doubleday, Doran, 1937);

Königsmark (London: Hodder & Stoughton, 1938; New York: Doubleday, Doran, 1939);

The Life of Francis Drake (London: Hodder & Stoughton, 1941; Garden City: Doubleday, Doran, 1942);

Musk and Amber (London: Hodder & Stoughton, 1942; Garden City: Doubleday, Doran, 1942);

The House in Lordship Lane (London: Hodder & Stoughton, 1946; New York: Dodd, Mead, 1946).

PLAY PRODUCTIONS: *Blanche de Malètroit*, London, Ladbroke Hall, 30 June 1894;

The Courtship of Morrice Buckler, by Mason and Isabel Bateman, London, Grand Theatre, 6 December 1897;

Marjorie Strode, London, Playhouse, 19 March 1908;

Colonel Smith, London, St. James's Theatre, 23 April 1909;

The Princess Clementina, by Mason and George Pleydell Bancroft, as George Pleydell, London, Queen's Theatre, 14 December 1910;

The Witness for the Defence, London, St. James's Theatre, 1 February 1911;

At the Villa Rose, London, Strand Theatre, 10 July 1920;

Running Water, London, Wyndham's Theatre, 5 April 1922;

The House of the Arrow, London, Vaudeville Theatre, 11 May 1928;

No Other Tiger, London, St. James's Theatre, 26 December 1928;

A Present from Margate, by Mason and Ian Hay, London, Shaftesbury Theatre, 14 December 1933.

PERIODICAL PUBLICATION: "Detective Novels," *Nation and Athenaeum*, 36 (7 February 1925): 645-646.

A. E. W. Mason was one of the best and most popular storytellers in the first half of the twentieth century. He was remembered by his contemporaries for his genial and companionable nature and his hearty laugh and also for his enthusiasm for travel and mountaineering. His enthusiasms gave experiences and settings to his writings. His masterpiece, *The Four Feathers* (1902), combines adventure and careful character analysis so successfully that when he applied the same methods to the detective novel his contribution to the genre was considered by many to be as significant as the creation of Sherlock Holmes in the previous century. Mason's blending of characterization and psychology with high adventure is his lasting contribution to fiction. The genre was still in its infancy and did not always follow the patterns for mainstream literature, but Mason saw no reason to treat entertainment any less seriously than he would a novel of manners.

Alfred Edward Woodley Mason was born on 7 May 1865 in Camberwell, London, to a chartered accountant, William Woodley Mason, and Elizabeth Hobill Gaines Mason. The pressures from a stuffy and conventional family drove him to seek escape in books and (while at Dulwich College) to an interest in the theater. He took a second-class honors degree in classics at Trinity College, Oxford, but the friendships he made there (especially with Anthony Hope Hawkins and Arthur Quiller-Couch) influenced the direction his life would take. His choice of the stage before making the switch to writing freed him from family domination, enlarged his circle of acquaintances, and gave him that practice with dramatic construction which served him well in his second career. To the chagrin of his family he joined Edward Compton's Comedy Company and, on 6

217

boyhood.

filled the boyhood of that traveller's son with bitterness. Robin had expected a figure of arrogance, a flamboyant monarch. All he saw was a little sober glass door which might be the entrance to a hermit's cell — and indeed that door led to a tiny alcove and a small bed room which were little better. No curtains draped it. No guard stood beside it. What manner of man hid behind it?

In a little while the door slowly opened inwards and Philip of Spain stood in the doorway. No majestic conqueror, but a plain man of middle age dressed simply in black velvet with an unmistaken and sickly face. The heavy out thrust under lip gave to him a look of melancholy a brooding melancholy look. If he was master of half the world it was clear that he got no joy of his mastership, and looking at him Robin understood the complaints which Santa Cruz in his bad moods hurled at him. A conscientious plodder, a narrow computator of minutes, and overseeing brain and sail away over the proper work of underlings.

As he stood in the doorway, a little withdrawn so that he could see the high altar and hardly be seen himself, he peered — the word was Robin's, for there was no dignity in Philip's movements — round the side of the door at the altar choir filled with the chanting monks. There was an old story current that Philip had been sitting as was his custom, in the last row of stalls at the corner of that quire choir, when a messenger still booted and spurred, had pushed through a panelled door at his side and brought him the news of the victory of Lepanto and the overthrow of the Turks. The story had reached Robin's ears and he wondered now whether the memory of that afternoon was in Philip's thought and whether he was brooding over another victory which should establish his faith in the Channel as surely as Lepanto had in the Mediterranean. For more than a moment his dark eyes lingered on that corner in the high choir, and then clumsily for he was crippled of a leg, he sank upon his knees.

And with that a change came over Robin. The fire of his hatred burned

Page from the manuscript for Fire Over England, *Mason's 1936 novel of an Elizabethan secret agent (Roger Lancelyn Green, A. E. W. Mason, 1952)*

Front page of the last issue of the Mexican newspaper edited by Mason during World War I, when he served as a major in the British Secret Service. El Progreso was used to disseminate false information to the Germans. This last issue announced the peace before the Armistice.

August 1888, made his first stage appearance performing the role of a servant in William Muskberry's *Davy Garrick*. He was in the first production of George Bernard Shaw's *Arms and the Man*. His first publication, a play entitled *Blanche de Malétroit* and based on Robert Louis Stevenson's "The Sire de Maletroit's Door," appeared in 1894. Among his friends, Oscar Wilde and Quiller-Couch encouraged him to finish his first novel.

It is only for the descriptions of Lakeland scenery that *A Romance of Wastdale* (1895) can be appreciated today. His second novel, *The Courtship of Morrice Buckler* (1896), contains more of the elements which characterize Mason at his best. The hero's deeds in support of his friend Julian Harnwood against Count Lukstein are told in a lively manner which the antiquated style peculiar to the historical novel is unable to stifle. As may also be said of many of Mason's later novels, the characters are solid, credible, and interesting. Mason's method of writing a novel was simple: he began with a group of people, worked out their characters and interactions, and then looked for an appropriate setting. In his short story "The Coward" he reversed the traditional theme of the hero who is a coward until faced with a challenge by having him only believe himself to be a coward.

A visit to the Sudan in 1901 made such an impression on him that it became the setting for *The Four Feathers*. The story of Harry Feversham, a boy who believed himself a coward and lost both honor and fiancée, fired the imagination of readers. Emotions are underplayed and so gain a vivid reality.

In 1903 Mason, encouraged by the members of the Coventry Liberal Association, entered politics as a candidate for Liberal M.P. for Coventry. He was elected to the House of Commons in 1906 and served conscientiously until the end of his term in 1910. That year he wrote his first Gabriel Hanaud novel, *At the Villa Rose*. In a 1925 article Mason claimed that the personality of the detective was the heart of the appeal of a great detective novel. He might have been speaking of his own work since much of the appeal of his detective novels depends on the character of Hanaud of the Paris Sûreté. Mason seems to have wanted to create a professional detective who was unlike Sherlock Holmes, a man who was genial and friendly and willing to trust his intuition. Hanaud is all of these but is never described ex-

Front cover for the 1960 Murray paperback edition of Mason's most highly regarded work, the 1902 novel (not a mystery) about a man who believes himself to be a coward

plicitly. He is revealed by his actions, as an actor in a play is revealed.

Hanaud has been called a descendant of Emile Gaboriau's Lecoq, and the comparison is apt. Unlike Gaboriau, however, Mason does not employ sensational effects, and there is no description of the bloody murder scene as the curtain rises. Instead the reader is introduced to the characters in action and treated to a reference to the murder. Then, as if on stage, Hanaud enters the scene. Because the identity of Madame Dauvray's murderer is revealed early enough in the plot to deprive armchair detectives of the opportunity to solve the mystery, it may be more appropriate to classify *At the Villa Rose* as a novel about a detective rather than a mystery story in the traditional sense. Mason's emphasis upon characterization shifts the reader's interest from the crime itself to its effects on the individuals involved in the murder and the subsequent investigation. The novel is told from the point of view of Julius Ricardo, a wealthy widower with an appreciation for fine wines. There is rich humor in the tension between the bluff, intuitive Hanaud (who is made to resemble a professional French comedian) and the precise Ricardo.

Mason did not rush to compose a sequel. *The Witness for the Defence*, originally written as a play, was turned into a mystery novel in 1913. Again the focus of interest in the story is on character reaction to specific incidents in a specific context, not on who killed Ballantyne.

During World War I Mason was called to Wellington House, which had become a center of government propaganda turned out by some of Britain's leading authors. He visited America on behalf of the cause, but he was exposed by the American press. When he was fifty years old he returned to England where he lied about his age and joined the Royal Marine Light Infantry. Eventually he began work for the newly formed Secret Service, where his duties seem to have been supplying information from Spain and Gibraltar. He spent the last years of the war in Mexico producing a daily newspaper (*El Progreso*) which often contained false news to mislead the Germans. Near the end of the war Mason returned to writing and published a collection of his short fiction (*The Four Corners of the World*, 1917) which included a new story about Hanaud and Ricardo, "The Affair at the Semiramis Hotel." The only record he left of his wartime work may be found in some autobiographical notes and three short stories ("One of Them," "Peiffer," and "The Silver Ship").

The next novel about Hanaud is the justly praised *The House of the Arrow* (1924). Jeanne-Marie Harlowe, the widow of a wealthy art connoisseur, is found murdered in the town of Dijon, France. Suspicion falls on her niece, Betty Harlowe, and Hanaud is called in not only to solve that mystery but to learn who has been sending a series of poison-pen letters to the citizens of Dijon for the past year. The characterization in *The House of the Arrow* is more convincing; Hanaud has become a solid, three-dimensional figure. Livelier and more expansive, he seems to thrive in relation with Jim Frobisher (in the role played previously by Ricardo). Even though Ricardo is absent from *The House of the Arrow* he is present in *No Other Tiger* (1927), but without Hanaud. The following year Mason adapted *The*

Front cover for a 1979 American paperback edition of Mason's 1910 novel At the Villa Rose, *which introduced Inspector Gabriel Hanaud*

House of the Arrow for the stage, but the play was not as successful as the book.

The Prisoner in the Opal (1928) reunites Ricardo and Hanaud. The title refers to Ricardo, who sees the world as an opal with himself imprisoned within. Reminiscent of the psychic touches in *At the Villa Rose* are the warnings of danger to Diana Tasborough brought by the visions of Joyce Whipple. When Hanaud arrives it is to herald the murder—a woman's body found with the right hand hacked off. The theme of black magic and the occult is well handled but appears somewhat unorthodox in a Mason story. Ricardo is more central to the story than previously, and there are some delightful examples of Hanaud's practical jokes, but neither factor makes this a good novel.

Hanaud and Ricardo appear briefly in *The Sapphire* (1933)–in chapter 17, "The Man from Limoges," almost a separate short story–but their next appearance in a full-length novel comes two years later in *They Wouldn't Be Chessmen* (1935). Major Scott Carruthers is plotting to steal the ancestral pearls of an Indian prince. How he fails is explained by the novel's title, for the characters who serve as pawns in his perfectly plotted crime do not behave according to plan; they do not act as chessmen but as human beings. Ricardo does not arrive on the scene in this novel until the fifth chapter, and Hanaud does not arrive until midway through the story. Some readers prefer this novel to the more famous early titles, for it is the most human of the series, and the death of Oliver Ransom, one of the major characters, is as moving as *The Four Feathers*.

It would be a decade before Mason returned to the detective story in any significant way. In the meantime he composed a volume of theatrical history, *Sir George Alexander & the St. James' Theatre* (1935). Another short story about Hanaud, "The Ginger King," was published in *Strand Magazine* in 1940, but Mason devoted much of the last part of his life to writing books outside the mystery genre. In 1936 he wrote *Fire Over England*, a historical romance set in late-sixteenth-century England. Robert Aubrey, a student at Eton, has an abiding hatred of Spain because his father died in that country. He is instrumental in preserving England from the Spanish Armada. In 1937 the novel was made into a successful patriotic film. In 1942 Mason published *Musk and Amber*, considered the best of his later mainstream novels. At the age of eighty-one Mason published *The House in Lordship Lane* (1946), the fifth Hanaud novel and his last book (he died 22 November 1948).

Roger Lancelyn Green has suggested that if Mason cannot be classified as a great novelist it may be due largely to the fact that he wrote from observation and not from experience. Even the experiences he used were from the observer's viewpoint. He was adept at finding the right phrase, and his experience on the stage trained him to use the dramatic incident to its fullest effect. In an age when the detective was fast becoming a caricature he gave the world Hanaud, a well-rounded fictional character with a believable personality.

Biography:

Roger Lancelyn Green, *A. E. W. Mason* (London: Parrish, 1952).

References:

Barrie Hayne, "A. E. W. Mason," in *Twelve Englishmen of Mystery*, edited by Earl F. Bargainnier (Bowling Green, Ohio: Bowling Green University Popular Press, 1984), pp. 34-63;

Cecil Madden, Introduction to *Meet the Detective* (London: Allen & Unwin, 1935; New York: Telegraph Press, 1935), pp. 20-35.

Arthur Morrison
(1 November 1863-4 December 1945)

Richard Benvenuto
Michigan State University

BOOKS: *The Shadows around Us* (London: Simpkin & Marshall, 1891);

Tales of Mean Streets (London: Methuen, 1894; Boston: Little, Brown, 1895);

Martin Hewitt, Investigator (London: Ward, Lock & Bowden, 1894; New York: Harper, 1894);

Zig-Zags at the Zoo (London: Newnes, 1895);

Chronicles of Martin Hewitt (London & New York: Ward, Lock & Bowden, 1895; New York: Appleton, 1896);

Adventures of Martin Hewitt (London & New York: Ward, Lock, 1896);

A Child of the Jago (London: Methuen, 1896; Chicago: Stone, 1896);

The Dorrington Deed-Box (London: Ward, Lock, 1897);

To London Town (London: Methuen, 1899; Chicago & New York: Stone, 1899);

Cunning Murrell (London: Methuen, 1900; New York: Doubleday, Page, 1900);

The Hole in the Wall (London: Methuen, 1902; New York: McClure, Phillips, 1902);

The Red Triangle: Being Some Further Chronicles of Martin Hewitt, Investigator (London: Nash, 1903; Boston: Page, 1903);

The Green Eye of Goona (London: Nash, 1904); republished as *The Green Diamond* (Boston: Page, 1904);

Divers Vanities (London: Methuen, 1905);

That Brute Simmons, by Morrison and Herbert C. Sargent (New York & London: French, 1906);

Green Ginger (London: Hutchinson, 1909; New York: Stokes, 1909);

Exhibition of Japanese Screens Painted by the Old Masters (London: Yamanaka, 1910);

The Painters of Japan, 2 volumes (London & Edinburgh: T. C. & E. C. Jack, 1911; New York: Stokes, 1911);

Guide to an Exhibition of Japanese and Chinese Paintings (London: British Museum, 1914);

Fiddle O'Dreams (London: Hutchinson, 1933).

Arthur Morrison

Weary of the Sherlock Holmes stories and anxious to get on with what he considered his more important writing, Arthur Conan Doyle killed his famous Baker Street detective in December 1893. Readers protested and publicly mourned; thousands canceled their subscriptions to the *Strand Magazine*, the publisher of the Holmes stories, and a decade later Holmes returned, not dead after all. In the interim, however, in what can be seen as formative years in the history of detective literature, Holmes's successors and imitators appeared. One of the most important and successful of these was Martin Hewitt, the creation of Arthur Morrison—journalist, chronicler of London's slums, and, in the years following Holmes's "death," a popular writer of detective fiction.

Morrison was a reticent man whose life is as obscure as his work is unjustly neglected. So little is known about him that P. J. Keating, the most informative writer about Morrison, contends that a full, detailed biography of him will probably never appear. He was born to working-class parents in the East End of London, a background that Morrison himself may have tried to suppress. Practically nothing is known about his early years or his education. His writings suggest that he had a strong interest in cycling, boxing, and other sports. In 1886 he was working as a clerk for the People's Palace, a charitable institution founded by the novelist and critic Walter Besant, from whom Morrison learned basic techniques of fiction. In 1889 he was made subeditor of the *Palace Journal*, a post which he held for about a year, and then he worked briefly on the editorial staff of the *Globe*; but he preferred to be a free-lance writer. Morrison married Elizabeth Thatcher in August 1892; they had one child, Guy, who died in 1921 from malaria, which he had contracted in World War I.

In 1891 his first important article, "A Street," a sketch of the East End, appeared in *Macmillan's Magazine*, where it was read by William Ernest Henley, editor of the *National Observer*. Henley encouraged Morrison to pursue his plan of writing frank, realistic stories about the East End and made Morrison a member of his circle of young men, a group that included Rudyard Kipling and J. M. Barrie. Most of Morrison's stories appeared in the *National Observer* in 1893; in 1894 they were published together as *Tales of Mean Streets*, Morrison's first important book and a testimony to his intimate knowledge of London's poor and working classes.

Tales of Mean Streets brought Morrison to the notice of a slum priest, the Reverend A. Osborne Jay, who introduced Morrison to his own parish in one of the worst of the London slums, which Morrison named the Jago and faithfully re-created in his best novel, *A Child of the Jago* (1896). Powerfully written, with compelling scenes, *A Child of the Jago* made Morrison a major literary figure of his times, a center in the debate then being waged over realism. Other novels dealing with the East End followed: *To London Town* (1899) and *The Hole in the Wall* (1902), which has been called a minor classic. *Cunning Murrell* (1900) reveals a different Morrison, a local color-

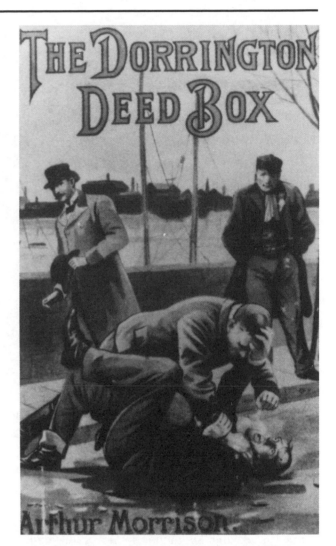

Dust jacket for Morrison's 1897 collection of stories about a thief and con man who works part-time as a "private inquiry agent"

ist who drew upon legends of witchcraft and smuggling to portray a remote Essex village in the mid-nineteenth century.

At the same time he was writing these books Morrison was helping detective fiction survive the loss of Holmes. The first Martin Hewitt story, "The Lenton Croft Robberies," appeared in the March 1894 issue of the *Strand Magazine*, with drawings by Sidney Paget, the illustrator of the Holmes stories. Recording Hewitt's adventures, Morrison's "Watson" is a journalist named Brett, who lives in the building where Hewitt has his offices. Some fifteen or twenty years earlier, while working for a firm of solicitors, Hewitt found the evidence his employers needed to clinch a difficult case and decided to work on his own. He is like Holmes in his reserve, efficiency, and powers of observation and logic, but differ-

Illustration by Stanley L. Wood in Windsor Magazine *for "The Affair of the 'Avalance Bicycle and Tyre Co. Ltd.,'" a story about the criminal-detective Dorrington*

ent from him in his appearance and habits–being a stout man of medium height, with a cheerful, round face. Virtually nothing is revealed about his private life and habits, his background or family, and aside from Brett and several policemen, he appears to have no friends. While Holmes is noted for playing his violin, spending the night in a state of profound abstraction, or filling his rooms with pipe smoke, Hewitt is the detective who is virtually indistinguishable from the average, well-dressed man of the streets.

Nineteen Martin Hewitt stories, well-written and inventive, were first published in the *Strand Magazine* and the *Windsor Magazine* and then collected into three volumes: *Martin Hewitt, Investigator* (1894), *Chronicles of Martin Hewitt* (1895), and *Adventures of Martin Hewitt* (1896). Such standard devices of detective fiction as cryptograms and crimes committed in locked or inaccessible rooms appear frequently, but Morrison also drew upon various fields of expertise for plot innovations. In "The Nicobar Bullion Case" Hewitt dons a diving suit to conduct his investigation underwater; in "The Case of the Lost Foreigner" he thwarts an anarchist plot to distribute bombs concealed in loaves of bread by interpreting the doodling of a victim of aphasia and agraphia; in "The Case of the Missing Hand," one of the most inter-

esting and complex of the stories, Hewitt speaks Romany (the language of the Gypsies) in the course of proving a supposed murder to have been a suicide.

Hewitt works methodically and objectively, seldom displaying any sense of personal involvement with the victims or the perpetrators of crime. In "The Case of Mr. Foggatt" a murderer who has been identified by Hewitt escapes but then sends Hewitt a letter which explains that years ago his victim had caused the disgrace and death of his father. Clearly not a criminal, but a young lawyer who, without premeditation, avenged a long-standing injury, he wants Hewitt, the only other person who knows what he has done, to be able to judge his actions fairly–and the letter is clearly designed to evoke sympathy from the reader. Hewitt, though he admires the man's character, includes the letter with the other evidence to be given to the police. Justice takes precedence over any question of sentiment, but Hewitt is not without feeling. When he discovers that the thief of a supposedly valuable cameo is the dealer who sold it and who has since discovered that it was a fake, he does not turn the man in, even though it will appear that he has failed to solve the crime, because exposure of that kind would destroy the dealer's reputation.

Frontispiece by Sidney Paget for Martin Hewitt, Investigator *(1894)*

Though they conform to the pattern popularized by Conan Doyle and sometimes borrow details from the Holmes stories (Morrison's use of a deceptive carriage ride in "The Loss of Sammy Crockett" was clearly inspired by "The Engineer's Thumb"), the Hewitt stories have a vitality of their own and show considerable variety of material and tone. Morrison's powers show no signs of weakening in *The Red Triangle* (1903), the last of the Hewitt books, though when it is mentioned at all by the critics it is usually called inferior to the earlier works. A collection of six connected stories, *The Red Triangle* pits Hewitt against a deadly criminal, Mayes, whose identity unfolds in a series of brutal crimes (including three deaths in the first four stories). Mayes is able to hypnotize others into becoming his accomplices and committing crime. If they disobey or become expendable, he murders them (his trade-

mark is strangulation by a tourniquet and a red triangle stamped on the victim's forehead). Except for the hypnotism—which Morrison had used effectively in "The Holford Will Case," from the *Chronicles of Martin Hewitt*, but which here strains credulity—*The Red Triangle* is fast paced and suspenseful and contains Morrison's most ingenious cryptogram: a block of numbers for which letters are substituted and then decoded by following the movements of the knight on a chessboard. Hewitt reads the cryptogram but faces more difficulties and perplexities than he has had in the earlier stories, where the solutions of crimes were seldom a problem for him. Ultimately a genuine duel develops between Hewitt and Mayes, leading to the inevitable, tense showdown in the final episode—which, like the book as a whole, shows Morrison's willingness to play fair with the reader and his considerable ability to pace the action and make it vivid.

Besides the Martin Hewitt stories, Morrison's detective fiction includes *The Green Eye of Goona* (1904) and *The Dorrington Deed-Box* (1897). *The Green Eye of Goona* (published in America as *The Green Diamond*) is a mystery-adventure about the hunt for a stolen diamond that has been hidden in one of twelve bottles of wine which have been inadvertently sold and must be traced. The protagonist (ironically named Harvey Crook), though not a detective or criminal expert but a trader in foreign goods, resourcefully traces the bottles of wine in a series of adventures and interprets a letter sent to a rich American ally by two sinister Indians. The diamond was originally stolen from an Indian Rajah, and Morrison's debt in this novel to Wilkie Collins's *The Moonstone* (1868) is evident. Though it has effective dramatic scenes (as when a murderer, posing as the man he has murdered, entertains Crook) and elements of comedy, *The Green Eye of Goona* shows no noteworthy elements of style or characterization. It ends with the diamond still unrecovered and Crook engaged to the daughter of the rich American (the only time in any of Morrison's major mysteries that the protagonist has a romantic involvement).

The Dorrington Deed-Box is a much more important work, with its opening story, "The Narrative of Mr. James Rigby," ranking among Morrison's very best. Horace Dorrington is a "private inquiry agent" whom Rigby meets on a ship taking them from Australia (Rigby's home) to England. As Rigby tells Dorrington, Rigby's father was killed years earlier by an Italian secret society, the Camorra. After a week together in Scotland, Rigby discovers he is being followed and even sees a man's face at his window. Convinced that the Camorra is now bent on complete vengeance against his family, Rigby gives his legal papers to Dorrington so that the detective, posing as Rigby, can deal with the Camorra while Rigby lodges with Dorrington's friend. The reader's suspicions, gradually aroused, are startlingly confirmed when Rigby awakens in a closed cistern that is filling with water. Managing to escape, Rigby realizes that he has been duped—drugged by Dorrington's friend; followed, not by members of the Camorra, but by Dorrington's agents—and that Dorrington's object was to obtain his papers, which included deeds to Rigby's valuable Australian possessions. With no means of establishing Rigby's identity (his body would have been dumped in the Thames to appear as that of an ordinary drowning victim), it would have been the perfect crime. Rigby rushes to Dorrington's office and finds accounts of Dorrington's earlier cases, which form the basis of the five stories to follow. None of the others matches the authentic realism, suspense, or brilliant denouement of "The Narrative of Mr. James Rigby," but the collection as a whole is equal to Morrison's best work in detective fiction.

Unlike Hewitt, Dorrington is a criminal as well as a detective, shrewd and unscrupulous, slipping from one side of the law to the other without any moral conflict. Some of his victims are innocents, like Rigby; others are criminals themselves, like the crooked bookie in "The Case of Janissary," the originator of the cistern water trap, whom Dorrington forcibly makes an accomplice. Moral distinctions do not matter to Dorrington, who admits he is only a more clever rascal than those he outwits. He wants money, of course, but also power, the feeling of mastery over others, and he represents a world in which neither justice nor moral good prevails but intelligence and single-minded cunning, and in which detection becomes predatory. Tough, ruthless, amoral, Dorrington is an important and so far unacknowledged forebear of the hard-boiled detective. There is an added interest in the stories because the reader cannot be sure how Dorrington will act; for sometimes crime, sometimes honesty, serve his purpose. As a work which blurs the distinction between criminal and detective—which makes the detective a mask or shield for the criminal and shows the methods of the detective being used to commit crime as effectively as to solve it— *The Dorrington Deed-Box* is a work of considerable psychological and moral interest.

Morrison's major work remains his studies of the East End: *Tales of Mean Streets*, *A Child of the Jago*, and *The Hole in the Wall*. Their depiction of crime and criminals is more compelling and authentic than in his detective work, where the world of Martin Hewitt and even Dorrington seems far removed from the raw brutality of desperation that governs the Jago. But Morrison's detective stories are still worth reading. Hewitt has been called the second-best detective in the age of Holmes, and Howard Haycraft has credited Morrison with helping the detective story to survive. There is little internal evidence to suggest that Morrison did not take detective writing seriously, but by the turn of the century another interest, his collection of Japanese and Oriental art, became increasingly important to him. By 1910 he had virtually ended his career in fiction and

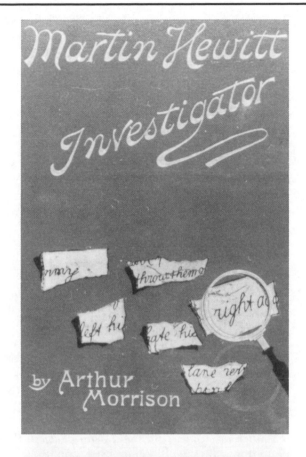

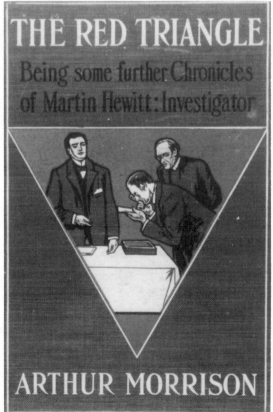

Front covers for three of the four collections of Martin Hewitt stories, which were first published in the Strand Magazine *and* Windsor Magazine. *Hewitt is frequently compared to Sherlock Holmes, whose adventures were also published in the* Strand Magazine *(courtesy of Otto Penzler).*

in 1911 published his two-volume *The Painters of Japan*, a major reference work for some time. Though he was elected to the Royal Society of Literature, later serving on its council, and was an honorary member of the Japanese Art Association, his later years are even more obscure than his earlier life. When he died on 4 December 1945 in Chalfont St. Peter, Buckinghamshire, this writer who had once attracted wide attention and stirred debate was practically unknown.

Bibliography:

Robert Calder, "Arthur Morrison: A Commentary with an Annotated Bibliography of Writings About Him," *English Literature in Transition*, 28 (1985): 276-297.

Biography:

P. J. Keating, "Biographical Study," in Morrison's *A Child of the Jago* (London: MacGibbon & Kee, 1969), pp. 11-36.

References:

"Arthur Morrison," *Scholastic*, 24 (26 March 1934): 5;

Jocelyn Bell, "A Study of Arthur Morrison," in *Essays and Studies for the English Association* (London: John Murray, 1952), pp. 77-88;

E. F. Bleiler, Introduction to Morrison's *Best Martin Hewitt Detective Stories* (New York: Dover, 1976), pp. vii-xiv;

Vincent Brome, "Arthur Morrison," in his *Four Realist Novelists* (London: Longmans, Green, 1965), pp. 7-20;

William C. Frierson, *The English Novel in Transition, 1885-1940* (Norman: University of Oklahoma Press, 1942), pp. 88-93;

Hugh Greene, Introduction to *The Rivals of Sherlock Holmes*, edited by Greene (New York: Pantheon, 1970), pp. 11-13;

Howard Haycraft, *Murder for Pleasure* (New York: Biblo & Tannen, 1968), pp. 64-65, 303;

P. J. Keating, *The Working Classes in English Fiction* (London: Routledge & Kegan Paul, 1971), pp. 167ff;

Michael Krzak, Preface to Morrison's *Tales of Mean Streets* (Woodbridge, U.K.: Boydell, 1983), pp. 7-17;

"Mr. Arthur Morrison," *Bookman* (London), 7 (January 1895): 107;

V. S. Pritchett, "An East End Novelist," in his *The Living Novel and Later Appreciations* (New York: Random House, 1964), pp. 206-212;

H. D. Traill, "The New Fiction," in his *The New Fiction and Other Essays on Literary Subjects* (London: Hurst & Blackett, 1897), pp. 8-26.

E. Phillips Oppenheim

(22 October 1866-3 February 1946)

Will Murray

BOOKS: *Expiation* (London: J. & R. Maxwell, 1887);

The Peer and the Woman (New York: Taylor, 1892; London: Ward, Lock & Bowden, 1895);

A Monk of Cruta (London: *Beeton's Christmas Annual*, 1894; London: Ward, Lock, 1894; New York: Neely, 1894); republished as *The Tragedy of Andrea* (New York: Ogilvie, 1906);

A Daughter of Marionis (London: Ward & Downey, 1895); republished as *To Win the Love He Sought* (New York: Doscher, 1910);

False Evidence (London: Ward, Lock, 1896; New York: Ward, Lock, 1897);

The Mystery of Mr. Bernard Brown (London: Bentley, 1896; Boston: Little, Brown, 1910); republished as *The New Tenant* (New York: Collier, 1912); republished as *His Father's Crime* (New York: Street & Smith, 1929);

The World's Great Snare (London: Ward & Downey, 1896; Philadelphia: Lippincott, 1896);

The Modern Prometheus (London: Unwin, 1896; London & New York: Neely, 1897);

The Wooing of Fortune (London: Ward & Downey, 1896);

The Postmaster of Market Deignton (London: Routledge, 1897);

The Amazing Judgment (London: Downey, 1897);

Mysterious Mr. Sabin (London & New York: Ward, Lock, 1898; Boston: Little, Brown, 1905);

A Daughter of Astrea (Bristol: Arrowsmith, 1898; New York: Doscher, 1909);

As a Man Lives (London: Ward, Lock, 1898; Boston: Little, Brown, 1908); republished as *The Yellow House* (New York: Doscher, 1908);

Mr. Marx's Secret (London: Simpkin, Marshall, Hamilton, Kent, 1899; New York: Street & Smith, 1899);

The Man and His Kingdom (London & New York: Ward, Lock, 1899; Philadelphia: Lippincott, 1900);

A Millionaire of Yesterday (London: Ward, Lock, 1900; Philadelphia: Lippincott, 1900);

E. Phillips Oppenheim, 1903 (Culver Pictures)

Master of Men (London: Methuen, 1901); republished as *Enoch Strone* (New York: Dillingham, 1902);

The Survivor (London: Ward, Lock, 1901; New York: Brentano's, 1901);

The Great Awakening (London: Ward, Lock, 1902); republished as *A Sleeping Memory* (New York: Dillingham, 1902);

The Traitors (London & New York: Ward, Lock, 1902; New York: Dodd, Mead, 1903);

219

The Yellow Crayon (London: Ward, Lock, 1903; New York: Dodd, Mead, 1903);

A Prince of Sinners (London & New York: Ward, Lock, 1903; Boston: Little, Brown, 1903);

The Master Mummer (Boston: Little, Brown, 1904; London: Ward, Lock, 1905);

The Betrayal (London: Ward, Lock, 1904; New York: Dodd, Mead, 1904);

Anna the Adventuress (London: Ward, Lock, 1904; Boston: Little, Brown, 1904);

A Maker of History (London: Ward, Lock, 1905; Boston: Little, Brown, 1905);

Mr. Wingrave, Millionaire (London: Ward, Lock, 1906); republished as *The Malefactor* (Boston: Little, Brown, 1906);

A Lost Leader (London: Ward, Lock, 1906; Boston: Little, Brown, 1906);

Bernice (Boston: Little, Brown, 1907; London: Ward, Lock, 1910);

The Vindicator (Boston: Little, Brown, 1907);

The Missioner (Boston: Little, Brown, 1907; London: Ward, Lock, 1908);

The Secret (London: Ward, Lock, 1907); republished as *The Great Secret* (Boston: Little, Brown, 1907);

Illustration by F. H. Townsend from the first British edition (1905) of The Master Mummer

Conspirators (London: Ward, Lock, 1907); republished as *The Avenger* (Boston: Little, Brown, 1908);

The Long Arm of Mannister (Boston: Little, Brown, 1908); republished as *The Long Arm* (London: Ward, Lock, 1909);

The Ghosts of Society, as Anthony Partridge (London: Hodder & Stoughton, 1908); republished as *The Distributors* (New York: McClure, 1908);

Jeanne of the Marshes (Boston: Little, Brown, 1908; London: Ward, Lock, 1909);

The Governors (London: Ward, Lock, 1908; Boston: Little, Brown, 1909);

The Kingdom of Earth, as Partridge (London: Mills & Boon, 1909; Boston: Little, Brown, 1909); republished as *The Black Watcher*, as Oppenheim (London: Hodder & Stoughton, 1912);

Passers-By, as Partridge (Boston: Little, Brown, 1910; London: Ward, Lock, 1911);

The Golden Web, as Partridge (Boston: Little, Brown, 1910); republished as *The Plunderers*, as Oppenheim (London: Hodder & Stoughton, 1912);

The Illustrious Prince (London: Hodder & Stoughton, 1910; Boston: Little, Brown, 1910);

The Missing Delora (London: Methuen, 1910); republished as *The Lost Ambassador* (Boston: Little, Brown, 1910);

The Moving Finger (Boston: Little, Brown, 1910); republished as *The Falling Star* (London: Hodder & Stoughton, 1911);

The Tempting of Tavernake (Boston: Little, Brown, 1911); republished as *The Temptation of Tavernake* (London & New York: Hodder & Stoughton, 1913);

Havoc (Boston: Little, Brown, 1911; London: Hodder & Stoughton, 1912);

The Double Four (London, New York, Toronto & Melbourne: Cassell, 1911); republished as *Peter Ruff and the Double Four* (Boston: Little, Brown, 1912);

Peter Ruff (London: Hodder & Stoughton, 1912);

The Court of St. Simon, as Partridge (Boston: Little, Brown, 1912); republished as *Seeing Life*, as Oppenheim (London: Lloyds, 1919);

Those Other Days (London: Ward, Lock, 1912; Boston: Little, Brown, 1913);

The Mischief-Maker (Boston: Little, Brown, 1912; London: Hodder & Stoughton, 1913);

For the Queen (London: Ward, Lock, 1912; Boston: Little, Brown, 1913);

A 1907 advertisement for Oppenheim's books (Culver Pictures)

The Lighted Way (London: Hodder & Stoughton, 1912; Boston: Little, Brown, 1912);

The Way of These Women (Boston: Little, Brown, 1913; London: Methuen, 1914);

The Double Life of Mr. Alfred Burton (Boston: Little, Brown, 1913; London: Methuen, 1914);

Mr. Laxworthy's Adventures (London & New York: Cassell, 1913);

The King's Cup: A Play in Four Acts, by Oppenheim and H. D. Bradley (London & New York: French, 1913);

A People's Man (Boston: Little, Brown, 1914; London: Methuen, 1915);

The Vanished Messenger (Boston: Little, Brown, 1914; London: Methuen, 1916);

The Amazing Partnership (London & New York: Cassell, 1914);

The Black Box (New York: Grosset & Dunlap, 1915; London: Hodder & Stoughton, 1918);

The Double Traitor (Boston: Little, Brown, 1915; London: Hodder & Stoughton, 1918);

The Game of Liberty (London: Cassell, 1915); republished as *An Amiable Charlatan* (Boston: Little, Brown, 1916);

Mr. Grex of Monte Carlo (London: Methuen, 1915; Boston: Little, Brown, 1915);

The Kingdom of the Blind (Boston: Little, Brown, 1916; London: Hodder & Stoughton, 1917);

Mysteries of the Riviera (London: Cassell, 1916);

The Hillman (London: Methuen, 1917; Boston: Little, Brown, 1917);

The Cinema Murder (Boston: Little, Brown, 1917); republished as *The Other Romilly* (London: Hodder & Stoughton, 1918);

The Zeppelin's Passenger (Boston: Little, Brown, 1918); republished as *Mr. Lessingham Goes Home* (London: Hodder & Stoughton, 1919);

The Pawns Count (London: Hodder & Stoughton, 1918; Boston: Little, Brown, 1918);

The Curious Quest (Boston: Little, Brown, 1919); republished as *The Amazing Quest of Mr. Ernest Bliss* (London: Hodder & Stoughton, 1922);

Frontispiece by F. H. Townsend for the first edition of The Missing Delora

The Strange Case of Mr. Jocelyn Thew (London: Hodder & Stoughton, 1919); republished as *The Box with the Broken Seals* (Boston: Little, Brown, 1919);

The Wicked Marquis (London: Hodder & Stoughton, 1919; Boston: Little, Brown, 1919);

The Devil's Paw (Boston: Little, Brown, 1920; London: Hodder & Stoughton, 1921);

Ambrose Lavendale, Diplomat (London: Hodder & Stoughton, 1920);

Aaron Rodd, Diviner (London: Hodder & Stoughton, 1920; Boston: Little, Brown, 1927);

The Honorable Algernon Knox, Detective (London: Hodder & Stoughton, 1920);

The Great Impersonation (London: Hodder & Stoughton, 1920; Boston: Little, Brown, 1920);

Jacob's Ladder (London: Hodder & Stoughton, 1921; Boston: Little, Brown, 1921);

Nobody's Man (Boston: Little, Brown, 1921; London: Hodder & Stoughton, 1922);

The Profiteers (Boston: Little, Brown, 1921; London: Hodder & Stoughton, 1922);

My Books and Myself (Boston: Little, Brown, 1922);

The Evil Shepherd (Boston: Little, Brown, 1922; London: Hodder & Stoughton, 1923);

The Great Prince Shan (London: Hodder & Stoughton, 1922; Boston: Little, Brown, 1922);

Michael's Evil Deeds (Boston: Little, Brown, 1923; London: Hodder & Stoughton, 1924);

The Seven Conundrums (Boston: Little, Brown, 1923; London: Hodder & Stoughton, 1924);

The Mystery Road (Boston: Little, Brown, 1923; London: Hodder & Stoughton, 1924);

The Inevitable Millionaires (London: Hodder & Stoughton, 1923; Boston: Little, Brown, 1925);

The Passionate Quest (London: Hodder & Stoughton, 1924; Boston: Little, Brown, 1924);

The Terrible Hobby of Sir Joseph Londe, Bt. (London: Hodder & Stoughton, 1924; Boston: Little, Brown, 1927);

The Wrath to Come (London: Hodder & Stoughton, 1924; Boston: Little, Brown, 1925);

The Adventures of Mr. Joseph P. Cray (London: Hodder & Stoughton, 1925; Boston: Little, Brown, 1927);

Edmund Lowe (left) as Baron von Ragastein in the 1935 film version of The Great Impersonation *(Universal)*

Gabriel Samara (London: Hodder & Stoughton, 1925); republished as *Gabriel Samara, Peacemaker* (Boston: Little, Brown, 1925);

Stolen Idols (London: Hodder & Stoughton, 1925; Boston: Little, Brown, 1925);

The Interloper (Boston: Little, Brown, 1926); republished as *The Ex-Duke* (London: Hodder & Stoughton, 1927);

The Golden Beast (London: Hodder & Stoughton, 1926; Boston: Little, Brown, 1926);

The Little Gentleman from Okehampstead (London: Hodder & Stoughton, 1926);

Harvey Garrard's Crime (Boston: Little, Brown, 1926; London: Hodder & Stoughton, 1927);

Prodigals of Monte Carlo (London: Hodder & Stoughton, 1926; Boston: Little, Brown, 1926);

The Quest for Winter Sunshine (London: Methuen, 1926; Boston: Little, Brown, 1927);

The Channay Syndicate (London: Hodder & Stoughton, 1927; Boston: Little, Brown, 1927);

Mr. Billingham, The Marquis and Medelon (London: Hodder & Stoughton, 1927; Boston: Little, Brown, 1929);

Madame (London: Hodder & Stoughton, 1927); republished as *Madame and Her Twelve Virgins* (Boston: Little, Brown, 1927);

Miss Brown of X.Y.O. (London: Hodder & Stoughton, 1927; Boston: Little, Brown, 1927);

Nicholas Goade, Detective (London: Hodder & Stoughton, 1927; Boston: Little, Brown, 1929);

The Fortunate Wayfarer (London: Hodder & Stoughton, 1928; Boston: Little, Brown, 1928);

Matorni's Vineyard (Boston: Little, Brown, 1928; London: Hodder & Stoughton, 1929);

The Light Beyond (London: Hodder & Stoughton, 1928; Boston: Little, Brown, 1928);

Chronicles of Melhampton (London: Hodder & Stoughton, 1928);

The Exploits of Pudgy Pete & Co. (London: Hodder & Stoughton, 1928);

Blackman's Wood, by Oppenheim, and *The Under Dog*, by Agatha Christie (London: Reader's Library, 1929);

The Glenlitten Murder (London: Hodder & Stoughton, 1929; Boston: Little, Brown, 1929);

The Treasure House of Martin Hews (London: Hodder & Stoughton, 1929; Boston: Little, Brown, 1929);

By the Prince of Story-tellers

THE LION AND THE LAMB

E. PHILLIPS OPPENHEIM

H&S

Dust jacket for Oppenheim's novel about a young man's search for revenge against Tottie Green, whose rooms at The Lion and the Lamb, an inn in Bermondsey, are the headquarters for London gangsters

What Happened to Forester (London: Hodder & Stoughton, 1929; Boston: Little, Brown, 1930);

Jennerton & Co. (London: Hodder & Stoughton, 1929);

The Human Chase (London: Hodder & Stoughton, 1929);

The Lion and the Lamb (London: Hodder & Stoughton, 1930; Boston: Little, Brown, 1930);

The Million Pound Deposit (London: Hodder & Stoughton, 1930; Boston: Little, Brown, 1930);

Slane's Long Shots (London: Hodder & Stoughton, 1930; Boston: Little, Brown, 1930);

Up the Ladder of Gold (London: Hodder & Stoughton, 1931; Boston: Little, Brown, 1931);

Simple Peter Cradd (London: Hodder & Stoughton, 1931; Boston: Little, Brown, 1931);

Sinners Beware (London: Hodder & Stoughton, 1931; Boston: Little, Brown, 1932);

Inspector Dickins Retires (London: Hodder & Stoughton, 1931; republished as *Gangster's Glory* (Boston: Little, Brown, 1931);

Moran Chambers Smiled (London: Hodder & Stoughton, 1932); republished as *The Man from Sing Sing* (Boston: Little, Brown, 1932);

The Ostrekoff Jewels (London: Hodder & Stoughton, 1932; Boston: Little, Brown, 1932);

Crooks in the Sunshine (London: Hodder & Stoughton, 1932; Boston: Little, Brown, 1933);

Jeremiah and the Princess (London: Hodder & Stoughton, 1933; Boston: Little, Brown, 1933);

Murder at Monte Carlo (London: Hodder & Stoughton, 1933; Boston: Little, Brown, 1933);

The Ex-Detective (London: Hodder & Stoughton, 1933; Boston: Little, Brown, 1933);

The Strange Boarders of Palace Crescent (Boston: Little, Brown, 1934; London: Hodder & Stoughton, 1935);

The Bank Manager (London: Hodder & Stoughton, 1934); republished as *The Man without Nerves* (Boston: Little, Brown, 1934);

The Gallows of Chance (London: Hodder & Stoughton, 1934; Boston: Little, Brown, 1934);

The Battle of Basinghall Street (London: Hodder & Stoughton, 1935; Boston: Little, Brown, 1935);

The Spy Paramount (London: Hodder & Stoughton, 1935; Boston: Little, Brown, 1935);

General Besserley's Puzzle Box (London: Hodder & Stoughton, 1935; Boston: Little, Brown, 1935);

Advice Limited (London: Hodder & Stoughton, 1935; Boston: Little, Brown, 1936);

The Bird of Paradise (London: Hodder & Stoughton, 1936); republished as *Floating Peril* (Boston: Little, Brown, 1936);

Judy of Bunter's Buildings (London: Hodder & Stoughton, 1936); republished as *The Magnificent Hoax* (Boston: Little, Brown, 1936);

Ask Miss Mott (London: Hodder & Stoughton, 1936; Boston: Little, Brown, 1937);

The Dumb Gods Speak (London: Hodder & Stoughton, 1937; Boston: Little, Brown, 1937);

Envoy Extraordinary (London: Hodder & Stoughton, 1937; Boston: Little, Brown, 1937);

The Mayor on Horseback (Boston: Little, Brown, 1937);

Curious Happenings to the Rookie Legatees (London: Hodder & Stoughton, 1937; Boston: Little, Brown, 1938);

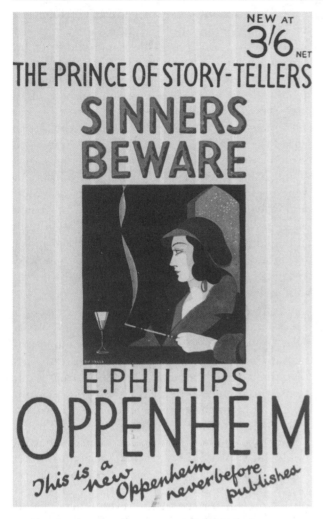

THE PRINCE OF STORY-TELLERS
NEW AT 3/6 NET
SINNERS BEWARE
E. PHILLIPS OPPENHEIM
This is a new Oppenheim never before published

Dust jacket for the 1931 novel in which gentleman-detective Peter Hames resolves "the mystery of the great robbery, . . . one of the most dramatic shocks the Principality of Monaco had experienced for many years"

The Colossus of Arcadia (London: Hodder & Stoughton, 1938; Boston: Little, Brown, 1938);

The Spymaster (London: Hodder & Stoughton, 1938; Boston: Little, Brown, 1938);

A Pulpit in the Grill Room (London: Hodder & Stoughton, 1938; Boston: Little, Brown, 1939);

And I Still Cheat the Gallows: A Series of Stories (London: Hodder & Stoughton, 1939);

Exit a Dictator (London: Hodder & Stoughton, 1939; Boston: Little, Brown, 1939);

Sir Adam Disappeared (London: Hodder & Stoughton, 1939; Boston: Little, Brown, 1939);

The Stranger's Gate (Boston: Little, Brown, 1939; London: Hodder & Stoughton, 1940);

General Besserley's Second Puzzle Box (London: Hodder & Stoughton, 1939; Boston: Little, Brown, 1940);

The Grassleyes Mystery (London: Hodder & Stoughton, 1940; Boston: Little, Brown, 1940);

Last Train Out (Boston: Little, Brown, 1940; London: Hodder & Stoughton, 1941);

The Milan Grill Room (London: Hodder & Stoughton, 1940; Boston: Little, Brown, 1941);

The Shy Plutocrat (London: Hodder & Stoughton, 1941; Boston: Little, Brown, 1941);

The Pool of Memories: Memoirs (London: Hodder & Stoughton, 1941; Boston: Little, Brown, 1942);

The Man who Changed his Plea (London: Hodder & Stoughton, 1942; Boston: Little, Brown, 1942);

Mr. Mirakel (London: Hodder & Stoughton, 1943; Boston: Little, Brown, 1943);

The Great Bear (London: Todd, 1943);

The Man who Thought He Was a Pauper (London: Todd, 1943);

The Hour of Reckoning, and The Mayor of Ballydaghan (London: Todd, 1944).

PLAY PRODUCTIONS: *The Money-Spider*, London, Collins' Music-hall, 20 July 1908;

The King's Cup, by Oppenheim and H. D. Bradley, London: Adelphi Theatre, 13 December 1909;

The Gilded Key, Blackpool Hippodrome Theatre, 26 September 1910;

The Eclipse, by Oppenheim and Fred Thompson, London, Garrick Theatre, 12 November 1919.

OTHER: *Many Mysteries*, edited by Oppenheim (London: Rich & Cowan, 1933).

While William LeQueux was the father of the espionage novel, E. Phillips Oppenheim made the genre his own. Like LeQueux, Edgar Wallace, and many other mystery novelists of his generation, E. Phillips Oppenheim was a prolific writer. The author of more than 150 books, Oppenheim produced only one truly classic mystery novel, *The Great Impersonation* (1920) over the course of a career that spanned fifty-eight productive years.

The so-called Prince of Storytellers, Edward Phillips Oppenheim was born in London on 22 October 1866, to Edward John and Henrietta Susannah Budd Oppenheim. Oppenheim's father, a leather merchant, later took his family to live in Leicester, where the future novelist attended Wyggeston Grammar School, leaving in

Dust jacket for the first American edition of Oppenheim's 1935 novel about an international spy who responds to a major threat to the great powers of the world

December 1882 to go to work for his father. Although he continued his connection with the leather business until he was forty, he began writing early, in his spare time. His first novel *Expiation* (1887), with its publication partly subsidized by his parents, sufficiently impressed the editors of the Sheffield *Weekly Telegraph* that he was given a contract to write six stories for serialization in that newspaper. Having begun his long career as a published writer, Oppenheim married Elsie Clara Hopkins in 1891; they had one daughter, and, when Oppenheim left the leather business, they went to live in Norfolk. After serving in the British Ministry of Information during World War I, Oppenheim established a winter home in 1922 on the French Riviera, where royalties from his books enabled him to live the life of an aristocrat. The outbreak of World War II forced him to leave France in 1940. Later, when the Germans invaded the Channel Islands, they made his house on Guernsey the local Luftwaffe headquarters. In October 1945 Oppenheim was able to return to Guernsey, where he died on 3 February 1946.

Oppenheim's earliest works include romances, mysteries, and political novels, many of which were popular with his contemporaries but have no lasting distinction. His forte was the spy novel; his mystery novels are almost invariably suspenseful and often deal with some aspect of secret service. Many of his best novels deal with European intrigues, and in later years, when he realized the immense market the United States presented for his work, he wrote fiction with a strong American focus. Oppenheim's sensibilities were distinctly nineteenth century. He was a monarchist whose fictional characters sneer at democracy, socialism, and communism. This attitude imbues his work from his early historical novels to his later espionage fantasies, many of which advocate the establishment of benevolent European monarchies.

Oppenheim's reputation as a writer of popular spy novels began with the publication of *Mysterious Mr. Sabin* in 1898. The novel's nominal protagonist steals secret British defense documents, planning to sell them to a hostile Germany and to use the money to finance a new French revolution. To obtain these documents, Sabin resorts to blackmail, extortion, and other crimes. Then a mysterious character, who announces that he holds high office in a secret society to which Sabin also belongs, orders Sabin to burn the documents and cease his mischief. Despite all his previous efforts in service of his revolutionary ideals, Sabin agrees, and the rest of the novel—a substantial portion of the book—focuses on Sabin's efforts to rehabilitate his reputation among the book's many other characters.

Oppenheim's most successful novel, *The Great Impersonation*, written immediately after World War I, chronicles the efforts of a German nobleman, Baron von Ragastein, to impersonate his physical double and Eton schoolmate, dissolute English aristocrat Everard Dominey, in British society of East Africa. Von Ragastein's purpose is to influence British public opinion and keep England out of World War I. Oppenheim ignores the improbability of such a plot: since Dominey is married, his wife will have to accept the impersonation. Resolving his story with a classic twist of plot and counterplot, he holds his readers' interest while mollifying their incredulity.

Oppenheim's most convincing works are a handful of novels anticipating the expansionist aims of Germany, the Soviet Union, and Japan and predicting the ultimate impotency of such in-

Dust jacket for Oppenheim's 1942 novel about a Scotland Yard inspector's unraveling of a murder case in which an innocent man pleads guilty in order to shield a woman whom he mistakenly believes to be the murderer

ternational bodies as the League of Nations and the United Nations. Novels such as *The Great Prince Shan* (1922), set in 1934; *The Wrath to Come* (1924), set in 1950; and *The Dumb Gods Speak* (1937), set in 1947 are fascinating extrapolations of the political dangers that faced Europe and America in the first half of the twentieth century.

The Dumb Gods Speak, perhaps the most intriguing of Oppenheim's predictive novels, concerns the international struggle resulting from the discovery and implementation of an ultimate weapon in the year 1947. While this much of the plot is remarkably prescient, Oppenheim's vision of the ultimate weapon and the result of its employment are not: it is an electrical neutralizing ray capable of stopping entire fleets of warships dead in the water without causing casualties. After one American warship uses the weapon to defeat the entire Japanese naval fleet, which is attacking the Philippines, aggressive nations of the

world are so horrified by this weapon that, by the novel's end, war has been universally banned. Many of Oppenheim's espionage novels turn upon similarly preposterous plot devices. For example in *The Wrath to Come*, a joint German-Japanese attack on America is foiled after the discovery of a deathbed document. While modern readers tend to be critical of such implausibility, Oppenheim's contemporaries seemed to expect and enjoy such surprising twists of plot.

Late in life, Oppenheim came to believe in the moral superiority of the rich, and his later novels could be termed fantasies of aristocracy. *Up the Ladder of Gold* (1931) illustrates Oppenheim's naive but unshakable belief in the power of the wealthy when their aims are politically pure. Millionaire American Warren Rand tries to insure world peace by cornering the gold market and bribing the world's most powerful nations not to go to war for forty years. As in many of his spy novels, Oppenheim attempts to contrast the high ideals of a protagonist who commits espionage and other crimes on behalf of a greater good against the sordidness of those who work for evil regimes or, for what is in Oppenheim's eyes the ultimate sin, mere money. To modern readers of spy novels, accustomed to more pragmatic protagonists, these distinctions may seem ludicrous.

Oppenheim's final novel, *Mr. Mirakel* (1943), is clearly his response to World War II and to the consequences of his predictions becoming reality. Disgusted by the global conflict he cannot quell, the wealthy Mr. Mirakel creates a remote paradise where he and his followers begin a new civilization dedicated to peace. Oppenheim believed that international discord was not a natural condition but the result of improper leadership—specifically the absence of a single authoritative ruler.

Throughout his long career, Oppenheim seems to have been influenced by Baroness Orczy. Many of Oppenheim's early heroes are outwardly innocuous even as they set great events in motion, much in the manner of Orczy's Scarlet Pimpernel. In Oppenheim's late short-story collections, *A Pulpit in the Grill Room* (1938) and *The Milan Grill Room* (1940), the character of Louis, a crippled veteran of World War I and maitre d' of the Milan Hotel, who solves crimes from his table in the grill room of the hotel, owes much to Orczy's seminal armchair detective, the Old Man in the Corner.

At his best, Oppenheim was the consummate entertainer. His characters are artificial but

E. Phillips Oppenheim (photograph by George Grantham Bain; Culver Pictures)

amusing, most often members of the European upper-class social set to which Oppenheim himself belonged. Although his fiction was enormously popular during his lifetime, Oppenheim has suffered the fate of many early, prolific genre novelists. Since his death in 1946, all but a few of his books have slipped out of print, and even the best of his fiction is now read only by a shrinking circle of specialists.

Biography:

Robert Standish, *The Prince of Story-Tellers: The Life of E. Phillips Oppenheim* (London: Davies, 1957).

References:

Reg Gadney, "Switch off the Wireless—It's on Oppenheim," *London Magazine*, new series 10 (June 1970): 19-27;

Grant Overton, "A Great Impersonation by E. Phillips Oppenheim," in his *Cargoes for Crusoes* (New York: Appleton/Boston: Little, Brown, 1925), pp. 126-142;

Leroy L. Panek, "E. Phillips Oppenheim," in his *The Special Branch: The British Spy Novel, 1890-1980* (Bowling Green, Ohio: Popular Press, 1981), pp. 17-31;

Ellen Wellman and Wray D. Brown, "Collecting E. Phillips Oppenheim (1866-1946)," *Private Library, Quarterly Journal of the Private Libraries Association*, third series 6 (Summer 1983): 83-89.

Emma, Baroness Orczy

(23 September 1865-12 November 1947)

Katherine Staples
Austin Community College, Texas

BOOKS: *The Emperor's Candlesticks* (London: Pearson, 1899; New York: Doscher, 1908);

By the Gods Beloved (London: Greening, 1905); republished as *The Beloved of the Gods* (New York: Knickerbocker Press, 1905); republished as *The Gates of Kamt* (New York: Dodd, Mead, 1907);

The Case of Miss Elliott (London: Unwin, 1905);

The Scarlet Pimpernel (London: Greening, 1905; New York & London: Putnam's, 1905);

I Will Repay (London: Greening, 1906; Philadelphia: Lippincott, 1906);

A Son of the People (London: Greening, 1906; New York & London: Putnam's, 1906);

In Mary's Reign (New York: Cupples & Leon, 1907);

The Tangled Skein (London: Greening, 1907);

Beau Brocade (Philadelphia: Lippincott, 1907; London: Greening, 1908);

The Elusive Pimpernel (London: Hutchinson, 1908; New York: Dodd, Mead, 1908);

The Old Man in the Corner (London: Hodder & Stoughton, 1908); republished as *The Man in the Corner* (New York: Dodd, Mead, 1909);

The Nest of the Sparrowhawk (London: Greening, 1909; New York: Stokes, 1909);

Lady Molly of Scotland Yard (London & New York: Cassell, 1910);

Petticoat Government (London: Hutchinson, 1910); republished as *Petticoat Rule* (New York: Hodder & Stoughton, 1910);

A True Woman (London: Hutchinson, 1911); republished as *The Heart of a Woman* (New York: Hodder & Stoughton/Doran, 1911);

Fire in the Stubble (London: Methuen, 1912); republished as *The Noble Rogue* (New York: Hodder & Stoughton/Doran, 1912);

Meadowsweet (London: Hutchinson, 1912; New York: Hodder & Stoughton/Doran, 1912);

The Traitor (New York: Paget, 1912);

Two Good Patriots (New York: Paget, 1912);

Eldorado (London: Hodder & Stoughton, 1913; New York: Hodder & Stoughton/Doran, 1913);

Emma, Baroness Orczy

The Laughing Cavalier (London: Hodder & Stoughton, 1914; New York: Doran, 1914);

Front covers for the first British and American editions of Orczy's 1908 collection of purely ratiocinative tales. There were seven Old Man in the Corner collections, of which this was the first (courtesy of Otto Penzler).

Unto Caesar (London: Hodder & Stoughton, 1914; New York: Doran, 1914);

A Bride of the Plains (London: Hutchinson, 1915; New York: Doran, 1915);

The Bronze Eagle (London: Hodder & Stoughton, 1915; New York: Doran, 1915);

Leatherface: A Tale of Old Flanders (London: Hodder & Stoughton, 1916; New York: Doran, 1916);

The Old Scarecrow (New York: Paget, 1916);

Lord Tony's Wife: An Adventure of the Scarlet Pimpernel (London: Hodder & Stoughton, 1917; New York: Doran, 1917);

A Sheaf of Bluebells (London: Hutchinson, 1917; New York: Doran, 1917);

Flower o' the Lily (London & New York: Hodder & Stoughton, 1918; New York: Doran, 1919);

The Man in Grey, Being Episodes of the Chouan Conspiracies in Normandy During the First Empire (London & New York: Cassell, 1918; New York: Doran, 1918);

Silver-Leg (New York: Doran, 1918);

The League of the Scarlet Pimpernel (London: Cassell, 1919; New York: Doran, 1919);

His Majesty's Well-Beloved (London & New York: Hodder & Stoughton, 1919; New York: Doran, 1919);

The First Sir Percy: An Adventure of the Laughing Cavalier (London: Hodder & Stoughton, 1920; New York: Doran, 1921);

Castles in the Air (London & New York: Cassell, 1921; New York: Doran, 1922);

Nicolette (London: Hodder & Stoughton, 1922; New York: Doran, 1922);

The Triumph of the Scarlet Pimpernel (London: Hodder & Stoughton, 1922; New York: Doran, 1922);

The Old Man in the Corner Unravels the Mystery of the Khaki Tunic (New York: Doran, 1923);

Dust jacket for the first American edition of Orczy's 1928 collection of stories about the crude Irish lawyer Patrick Mulligan (courtesy of Otto Penzler)

Les Beaux et les Dandys des Grands Siècles en Angleterre (Monaco: Société des Conferences, 1924);

The Honorable Jim (London: Hodder & Stoughton, 1924; New York: Doran, 1924);

The Old Man in the Corner Unravels the Mystery of the Pearl Necklace and the Tragedy in Bishop's Road (New York: Doran, 1924);

The Old Man in the Corner Unravels the Mystery of Brundell Court and the Tytherton Case (New York: Doran, 1924);

The Old Man in the Corner Unravels the Mystery of the Russian Prince and of Dog's Tooth Cliff (New York: Doran, 1924);

Pimpernel and Rosemary (London & New York: Cassell, 1924; New York: Doran, 1925);

The Old Man in the Corner Unravels the Mystery of the Fulton Gardens Mystery, and the Moorland Tragedy (New York: Doran, 1925);

The Old Man in the Corner Unravels the Mystery of the White Carnation and the Montmartre Hat (New York: Doran, 1925);

The Miser of Maida Vale (New York: Doran, 1925);

A Question of Temptation (New York: Doran, 1925);

Unravelled Knots (London: Hutchinson, 1925; New York: Doran, 1926);

The Celestial City (London: Hodder & Stoughton, 1926; New York: Doran, 1926);

Sir Percy Hits Back: An Adventure of the Scarlet Pimpernel (London: Hodder & Stoughton, 1927; New York: Doran, 1927);

Blue Eyes and Grey (London: Hodder & Stoughton, 1928; Garden City: Doubleday, Doran, 1929);

Skin o' My Tooth (London: Hodder & Stoughton, 1928; Garden City: Doubleday, Doran, 1928);

Adventures of the Scarlet Pimpernel (London: Hutchinson, 1929; Garden City: Doubleday, Doran, 1929);

Marivosa (London: Cassell, 1930; New York: Doubleday, Doran, 1932);

In the Rue Morgue (Garden City: Doubleday, Doran, 1931);

A Child of the Revolution (London: Cassell, 1932; Garden City: Doubleday, Doran, 1932);

A Joyous Adventure (London: Hodder & Stoughton, 1932; Garden City: Doubleday, Doran, 1932);

The Scarlet Pimpernel Looks at the World (London: John Heritage, 1933);

The Way of the Scarlet Pimpernel (London: Hodder & Stoughton, 1933; New York: Putnam's, 1934);

A Spy of Napoleon (London: Hodder & Stoughton, 1934; New York: Putnam's, 1934);

The Turbulent Duchess: H.R.H. Madame la Duchesse de Berri (London: Hodder & Stoughton, 1935; New York: Putnam's, 1936);

The Uncrowned King (London: Hodder & Stoughton, 1935; New York: Putnam's, 1935);

Sir Percy Leads the Band (London: Hodder & Stoughton, 1936);

The Divine Folly (London: Hodder & Stoughton, 1937);

No Greater Love (London: Hodder & Stoughton, 1938);

Mam'zelle Guillotine: An Adventure of the Scarlet Pimpernel (London: Hodder & Stoughton, 1940);

Pride of Race (London: Hodder & Stoughton, 1942);

Links in the Chain of Life (London & New York: Hutchinson, 1947);

Will-o'-the-Wisp (London: Hutchinson, 1947).

PLAY PRODUCTIONS: *The Scarlet Pimpernel,* by Orczy and Montagu Barstow, Nottingham, Theatre Royal, 15 October 1903; London, New Theatre, 5 January 1905;

The Sin of William Jackson, by Orczy and Barstow, London, Lyric Theatre, 28 August 1906;

Beau Brocade, by Orczy and Barstow, Eastbourne, Sussex, Devonshire Park Theatre, 4 May 1908; London, Cornet Theatre, 1 June 1908;

The Duke's Wager, Manchester, Prince's Theatre, 8 November 1911;

The Legion of Honour, Bradford, Theatre Royal, 27 May 1918; London, Aldwych Theatre, 24 August 1921;

Leatherface, by Orczy and Caryl Fiennes, Portsmith, Theatre Royal, 25 September 1922.

OTHER: *Old Hungarian Fairy Tales,* edited, illustrated, and translated by Orczy and Montagu Barstow (London: Dean/Philadelphia: Wolf, 1895);

The Enchanted Cat, edited and translated by Orczy (London: Dean, 1895);

Fairyland's Beauty (The Suitors of Princess Fire-Fly), edited and translated by Orczy (London: Dean, 1895);

Uletka and the White Lizard, edited and translated by Orczy (London: Dean, 1895).

Successful as an author of popular adventure and romance fiction, Baroness Orczy also wrote elaborately plotted detective tales. Orczy's Old Man in the Corner stories develop a brilliant, eccentric, and unlikely armchair detective, a disagreeable raconteur who helps a young woman journalist unravel obscure crimes. Orczy's Lady Molly of Scotland Yard tales feature one of the first fictional woman detectives.

Emma Madgalena Rosalia Maria Josefa Barbara Orczy was born into the Hungarian landed aristocracy in Tarna-Örs, Hungary, on 23 September 1865. She was named Emma (or Emmuska) after her mother, Countess Wass. Her father, Baron Felix Orczy, a gifted amateur composer who was friends with Liszt, Wagner, Gounod, and Massenet, was forced to leave Hungary because of an 1868 peasant uprising against his agricultural innovations. The family moved to Budapest, to Brussels, to Paris, and finally to London.

Frontispiece by Cyrus Cuneo for Lady Molly of Scotland Yard *(1910), one of the earliest collections of stories about a female detective. The stories are narrated by Lady Molly's loyal maid (courtesy of Otto Penzler).*

Orczy was educated at schools in Brussels and Paris, where she unsuccessfully studied music. In London she studied painting at the West London School of Art and at Heatherley's. While at school she exhibited her work at the Royal Academy. During her studies at Heatherley's she met Montagu Barstow, an illustrator, whom she married in 1894. Their only child, John Montagu Orczy Barstow, was born in 1899.

During the early years of their marriage the Barstows were very active in the aristocratic London social circles to which Orczy's family had introduced her. However, they were poor. To supplement the family income Orczy began to translate and illustrate fairy tales. She also wrote romance and adventure tales for the popular press. Her first novel, *The Emperor's Candlesticks* (1899), was a failure. Orczy's widespread popularity came only in 1905 with the enormous London

Dust jacket for Orczy's ninth novel about Sir Percy Blakeney, an Englishman who risks his life to save victims of the French Revolution (courtesy of Otto Penzler)

stage success of *The Scarlet Pimpernel*, which ran for years in many different productions. The play called attention to the novel of the same title. It had been written in 1902 but failed to find a publisher until 1905. The Scarlet Pimpernel, Sir Percy Blakeney, is an English rescuer of French aristocrats during the Reign of Terror. His rescues depend on a double identity: at home in England he is known as a foppish, effete socialite, but, as the daring Scarlet Pimpernel, he risks his life to save those unjustly accused in France. Orczy wrote many sequels to her most famous book.

All of Orczy's works sold profitably, and the Barstows lived very comfortably. After World War I they purchased a small estate in Monte Carlo, where, apart from trips, they lived until the last years of Orczy's life, which were spent in a secluded country home at Henley-on-Thames. Orczy died in London on 12 November 1947.

The first Old Man in the Corner stories date from the days before the stage success of *The Scarlet Pimpernel*. The thirty-eight tales make a special contribution to the armchair detective genre because they begin with the denouement, devoting the narrative to the gradual development of the plot by flashback. The first collection (there were seven in all) was published in 1908. Bill Owen, the disagreeable Old Man in the Corner, compulsively knots and unravels a bit of string as he reveals the solutions to unsolved crimes publicized in newspaper accounts and spectacular trials. The Old Man's cases include the whole range of sensational and complex detective puzzles: grisly murder ("The Tremarn Case"), fiendish blackmail ("The Murder of Miss Pebmarsh"), perfect alibis ("The Case of Miss Elliott"), masked motive and identity ("The Regent's Park Murder"), and brilliantly planned thefts ("The Affair at the Novelty Theatre").

Despite his vanity about his own ratiocinative talents, Bill Owen is an unlikely detective. A balding, watery-eyed, mild-mannered little man in violently checked tweed, he haunts a corner of the ABC Teashop. His listener and protégé is the attractive young journalist Polly Burton. Polly is fascinated by the unlikely unravelings she hears, but despite her sarcasm and pride in her own investigative talents she remains the learner, impressed in spite of herself.

Typical of the Old Man in the Corner tales is "The Fenchurch Street Mystery." William Kershaw reveals to his wife and an unsavory friend that he has evidence to blackmail Francis Smethurst, a millionaire who has made his fortune in speculations in Russia (where he has lived for many years). Smethurst's letters to Kershaw reveal the millionaire's willingness to meet on his return to England. After the meeting Kershaw vanishes. A decomposed body found later is identified as Kershaw's by its clothes and property. When Smethurst is brought to trial he proves that he did not write the letters to Kershaw and produces witnesses who saw Kershaw after the time of his supposed death. Bill Owen shows that the murdered man was Smethurst, not Kershaw. Kershaw had murdered Smethurst and has impersonated his victim so completely that he conceals his identity, even from his wife who sees him testify as Smethurst. Those who could uncover the deception by identifying Smethurst are in Russia. Bill Owen's unravelings are completely convincing.

Although Orczy's Old Man is not the first armchair detective who solves crimes from second-hand evidence (an honor belonging to Edgar Allan Poe's C. Auguste Dupin in "The Mystery of Marie Roget"), he is the first truly Socratic problem solver, forcing his listener (and the reader) to question seemingly logical conclusions about a crime to reach a more difficult, but more valid, solution.

Orczy's other contributions to the detective genre include *Lady Molly of Scotland Yard* (1910), among the first stories featuring a woman detective, and *Skin o' My Tooth* (1928). The twelve tales narrated by Lady Molly's loyal maid praise her daring, intelligence, and savoir faire, but they do not develop a truly independent woman-detective character. Lady Molly's cases all involve women and show her social insight into their sexually and socially motivated behavior. Lady Molly depends as much on her sensitivity and intuition as her brilliance and bravery. Her motivation as a crime solver lies in her wish to clear her falsely accused beloved. This task accomplished, she leaves detection forever. *Skin o' My Tooth* features twelve stories about a particularly sharp Irish lawyer, Patrick Mulligan. Like the Lady Molly series, these tales are elaborately plotted and narrated by an admiring assistant.

Some of Orczy's adventure tales include mystery elements. Most memorable are the M. Hector Ratichon stories of *Castles in the Air* (1921). These are narrated by Ratichon himself, a vain, unscrupulous trickster and shopworn investigator. Ratichon solves crime puzzles in the Paris of the corrupt early republic–always to his own advantage and often at the expense of his equally shady valet, Theodore.

Orczy's contribution to detective fiction lies chiefly in popularizing the armchair detective, the Socratic Old Man in the Corner, and her introduction of one of the first woman detective characters. At times she transcends the stock conventions of popular fiction to develop fast-moving, cleverly plotted, ratiocinative tales.

References:

Earl F. Bargainnier, "Lady Molly of Scotland Yard," *Mystery FANcier*, 7 (July-August 1983): 15-19;

Bargainnier, "The Old Man in the Corner," *Mystery FANcier*, 7 (November-December 1983): 21-23;

E. F. Bleiler, Introduction to Orczy's *The Old Man in the Corner* (New York: Dover, 1980), pp. v-ix;

Fred Dueren, "Was the Old Man in the Corner an Armchair Detective?," *Armchair Detective*, 14 (1981): 232-233.

Sir Max Pemberton
(19 June 1863-22 February 1950)

Julia Hardie
Pennsylvania State University

BOOKS: *The Diary of a Scoundrel* (London: Ward & Downey, 1891);

The Iron Pirate (London: Cassell, 1893; Chicago: Rand, McNally, 1897);

Jewel Mysteries I Have Known (London: Ward, Lock & Bowden, 1894); republished as *Jewel Mysteries from a Dealer's Notebook* (New York: Fenno, 1904);

The Sea Wolves (London: Cassell, 1894; New York: Harper, 1894);

Lights Out: A Farce in One Act (London: French, 1894);

The Impregnable City (London: Cassell, 1895; New York: Dodd, Mead, 1895);

The Little Huguenot (London: Cassell, 1895; New York: Dodd, Mead, 1895);

A Gentleman's Gentleman (London: Innes, 1896; New York: Harper, 1896);

A Puritan's Wife (London: Cassell, 1896; New York: Dodd, Mead, 1896);

Christine of the Hills (London: Innes, 1897; New York: Dodd, Mead, 1897);

Queen of the Jesters (London: Pearson, 1897; New York: Dodd, Mead, 1897);

Kronstadt (London: Cassell, 1898; New York: Appleton, 1898); republished as *A Woman of Kronstadt* (Leipzig: Tauchintz, 1898);

The Phantom Army (London: Pearson, 1898; New York: Appleton, 1898);

The Garden of Swords (London: Cassell, 1899; New York: Dodd, Mead, 1899);

Signors of the Night (London: Pearson, 1899; New York: Dodd, Mead, 1899);

Féo (London: Hodder & Stoughton, 1900; New York: Dodd, Mead, 1900);

Love the Harvester (New York: Dodd, Mead, 1900; London: Methuen, 1908);

The Footsteps of a Throne (London: Methuen, 1900; New York: Dodd, Mead, 1900);

The Giant's Gate (London: Cassell, 1901; New York: Stokes, 1901);

Pro Patria (London: Ward, Lock, 1901; New York: Dodd, Mead, 1901);

I Crown Thee King (London: Methuen, 1902);

Max Pemberton (Culver Pictures)

The House Under the Sea (London: Newness, 1902; New York: Appleton, 1902);

Doctor Xavier (London: Hodder & Stoughton, 1903; New York: Appleton, 1903);

The Gold Wolf (London: Ward & Lock, 1903; New York: Dodd, Mead, 1903);

Red Morn (London: Cassell, 1904); republished as *A Daughter of the States* (New York: Dodd, Mead, 1904);

Beatrice of Venice (London: Hodder & Stoughton, 1904; New York: Dodd, Mead, 1904);

The Hundred Days (London: Cassell, 1905; New York: Appleton, 1905);

235

Mid the Thick Arrows (London: Hodder & Stoughton, 1905);

The Lady Evelyn (London: Hodder & Stoughton, 1906; New York: Authors and Newspapers Association, 1906);

The Prima Donna: A Farce in One Act (London: French, 1906);

My Sword for Lafayette (London: Hodder & Stoughton, 1906; New York: Dodd, Mead, 1906);

The Lodestar (London: Ward, Lock, 1907; New York: Authors and Newspapers Association, 1907); republished as *Aladdin of London: or, Lodestar* (New York: Empire Book Company, 1907);

The Amateur Motorist (London: Hutchinson, 1907; Chicago: McClurg, 1907);

The Diamond Ship (London: Cassell, 1907; New York: Appleton, 1907);

The Shadow on the Sea (Cleveland: Westbrook, 1907);

The House of the Nightingales (London: French, 1907);

Sir Richard Escombe (London: Cassell, 1908; New York: Harper, 1908);

Wheels of Anarchy (London: Cassell, 1908);

The Show Girl (London: Cassell, 1909; Philadelphia: Winston, 1909);

The Adventures of Captain Jack (London: Mills & Boon, 1909);

The Fortunate Prisoner (London: Hodder & Stoughton, 1909; New York: Dillingham, 1909);

The Man Who Drove the Car (London: Nash, 1910);

The Mystery of the Green Heart (London: Methuen, 1910; New York: Dodd, Mead, 1910);

White Walls (London: Ward, Lock, 1910);

The Girl With the Red Hair (London: Cassell, 1910);

The Summer Book (London: Mills & Boon, 1911);

Captain Black (London: Cassell, 1911; New York: Hodder & Stoughton/Doran, 1911);

White Motley (New York: Sturgis & Walton, 1911; London: Cassell, 1913);

War and the Woman (London: Cassell, 1912); republished as *Swords Reluctant* (New York: Dillingham, 1912);

The House of Fortune (London: Nash, 1912);

The Virgin Fortress (London: Cassell, 1912);

Millionaire's Island (London: Cassell, 1913);

Leila and Her Lover (London: Ward, Lock, 1913);

Two Women (London: Methuen, 1914);

The Great White Army (London: Cassell, 1915);

Behind the Curtain (London: Nash, 1916);

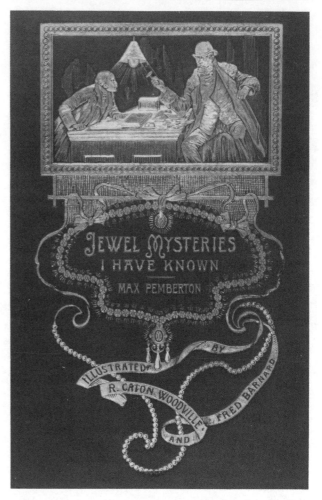

Cover for Pemberton's 1894 collection of ten stories narrated by jewel dealer Bernard Sutton (courtesy of Otto Penzler)

The Man of Silver Mount (London: Cassell, 1918);

Her Wedding Night: A Story from the German Lines and Others (London: Jenkins, 1918);

A Bagman in Jewels (London: Skeffington, 1919);

Prince of the Palais Royal (London: Cassell, 1921);

A Woman Who Knew (London: Hutchinson, 1921);

Paulina (London: Cassell, 1922);

Lord Northcliffe: A Memoir (London: Hodder & Stoughton, 1922; New York: Doran, 1922);

John Dighton, Mystery Millionaire (London: Cassell, 1923);

Lucienne, with Isabelle, and Horizon of God (London: Mills & Boon, 1925);

The Mad King Dies (London: Cassell, 1928);

Night Lights and Others (London: Mills & Boon, 1929);

Hyde Park and the House of Grosvenors: A History Thereof (London: Grosvenor House, 1930);

Dolores and Some Others (London: Mills & Boon, 1931);

The Life of Sir Henry Royce (London: Selwyn & Blount, 1934);

Sixty Years and After: Reminiscences (London: Hutchinson, 1936).

PLAY PRODUCTIONS: *A Private Detective*, by Pemberton and S. Leigh, London, St. James's Theatre, 1 April 1886;

The Dancing Master, by Pemberton and M. Wellings, London, Opera Comique, 2 October 1899;

The Huguenot Lover, by Pemberton and James McArthur, London, Globe Theatre, 24 April 1901;

The Finishing School, London, Wyndham's Theatre, 16 June 1904;

A Woman of Kronstadt, by Pemberton and George Fleming, London, Garrick Theatre, 8 February 1908;

The Lady of the Pageant, by Pemberton and C. W. Hogg, Eastbourne, 20 July 1908;

The Grey Room, by Pemberton and Eille Norwood, York, 23 November 1911;

Diane's Diamonds, London, Collins' Music-hall, 12 August 1912;

Garrick, London, Collins' Music-hall, 14 July 1914;

The Bells of St. Valoir, London, Collins' Music-hall, 30 November 1914;

The Haunted Husband, London, Collins' Music-hall, 5 April 1915;

Oh! Don't, Dolly!, by Pemberton and Eustace Ponsonby, music by G. Dorlay, Folkestone, Kent, Pleasure Garden, 16 January 1919; London, Criterion Theatre, 3 March 1919.

OTHER: *The Dickens Souvenir of 1912*, edited by Pemberton and Dion Clayton Calthorp (London: Chapman & Hall, 1912);

Pelman Pie, edited by Pemberton (London: Pelman Institute, 1919);

Famous Crime Mysteries and Romances, 2 volumes, edited by Pemberton (London: Newnes, 1924);

Tit-bits Jubilee Book, edited by Pemberton (London: Newnes, 1931).

Max Pemberton wrote more than sixty books in his eighty-seven years, enjoying wide popularity. Today his work is almost completely forgotten, and his mystery novels have been no more timeless. What interest they have comes from his accurate depiction of the new products of the modern age: automobiles, airplanes, and ships. Such elements, however, seem distinctly out of place with both the Victorian sentiment and style of Pemberton's work. His failure to reconcile his nineteenth-century values with the world he saw changing has contributed to his current obscurity.

Born in Birmingham, Warwickshire, on 19 June 1863, the son of a prosperous merchant in the Rice Market, Pemberton was early drawn to the idea of a writing career. He recalls in *Lord Northcliffe* (1922), his memoir of Alfred Harmsworth, how he and his friend planned to write a mystery novel to be called "The Black Hand." The book was inspired by Harmsworth's imagining that "a man going home late at night sees a white hand sticking out of the black waters of a silent pool." Only a first chapter was ever written, but both men submitted articles to the *Globe* newspapers; Harmsworth sold a few, but Pemberton's were returned at first. Harmsworth and Pemberton were more than literary friends. Both were avid bicyclists, having met for the first time when out cycling. Pemberton's first published article grew out of this hobby. The *Bicycling News* accepted his account of a cycling tour made when he was fifteen.

Pemberton was formally educated at Merchant Taylors' School in London and at Caius College, Cambridge, which he attended in the early 1880s. There he studied law and, after receiving his M.A., tried unsuccessfully for a position as a schoolmaster. "These disappointments greatly pleased me," he recalled in his autobiography *Sixty Years and After: Reminiscences* (1936), because they enabled him to become, without great success for a time, a Fleet Street free-lancer.

In the summer of 1885 he met Harmsworth coming out of the reading room of the British Museum, and the two renewed both their friendship and their literary ties. Pemberton and Harmsworth directed their attention toward *Vanity Fair* and *Young Folks*, the periodical where Robert Louis Stevenson's *Treasure Island* (1883) was first published (under the title *The Sea Cook*). None of the papers in which Pemberton and Harmsworth published paid well, and they were in a precarious financial position until they met Sir George Newnes, publisher of *Tit-bits*, who gave them higher fees for the articles he accepted. Both learned enough from Newnes's methods to become involved eventually with the founding of other papers.

In 1892 Pemberton was offered a position by Thomas Wemyss Reid, general manager of the Cassell publishing company, to start a newspa-

Illustration by P. Caton Woodville for the 1893 English Illustrated Magazine *serialization of* Jewel Mysteries
I Have Known

per for boys. *Chums,* which Pemberton edited, was from its outset a modest success. Reid suggested that to boost circulation Pemberton should write a serial for *Chums* readers, and he responded with *The Iron Pirate* (1893). This well-received novel is the story of a modern-day pirate, Captain Black, and the attempts of the narrator, Mark Strong, to stop Captain Black and his crew from their greedy and murderous rampages. *The Iron Pirate* introduces several elements that recur in Pemberton's later novels. The ship descriptions show Pemberton's fascination with

machinery, for "The Nameless Ship" is made of phosphor bronze and runs on gas. The brooding and almost tragic captain of this ultramodern, fast ship demonstrates Pemberton's attraction to the romantic. Captain Black, though falling into rages and unrepentant over the lives lost when he and his men make ships disappear from the ocean, has the gentlemanly taste to appreciate fine spirits, the best furnishings, and beautiful jewels—objects that appear often in Pemberton's novels. *The Iron Pirate* ends with the sinking of "The Nameless Ship" after a battle with British ships. Adrift with him on a raft for several days, Mark learns what has driven Captain Black to a life of piracy: After a crooked partner had caused the death of his wife and child, Black turned against civilization and vowed revenge upon the world. Mark also finds out why Black has repeatedly protected him from his men: Mark resembles Black's dead son. Finally, Mark is rescued; Black is presumed dead.

In 1911 Pemberton published a sequel, *Captain Black*, set only a few months after *The Iron Pirate*. This novel, in which Mark attempts to recover the booty from Black's raids, begins with Mark setting out on his yacht with friends to explore Ice Haven, Black's Greenland hideout. Like *The Iron Pirate*, *Captain Black* is filled with exotic locales. The mysteriously still-alive Black is now captain of the *Zero*, a submarine that can outrun any other vessel. Its speed in diving makes the *Zero* vulnerable only when the batteries that power it must be recharged. As in the earlier novel, Black's vessel is destroyed, but once again his own fate is uncertain.

Pemberton resigned from his editorial position with *Chums* in 1893, and in 1894 he became editor at *Cassell's Magazine* (resigning in 1906 after the death of Reid). He also joined Harmsworth at his *Daily Mail* in 1900. Pemberton kept to a busy writing schedule while working for *Cassell's* and the *Daily Mail*, publishing almost yearly his novels of romance, history, and crime and detection. *Jewel Mysteries I Have Known* (1894), narrated by Bernard Sutton, jewel dealer, consists of amusing accounts of escapades described with wit, a quality lacking in some of Pemberton's more fantastic adventure stories. Set in some of the exotic locales which Pemberton enjoyed visiting, the book contains ten stories about mysteries such as the disappearance of a jeweled scimitar in Algiers and the secret workings of a jewel-theft ring operating in the best circles of British society. *A Gentleman's Gentleman* (1896) features more rogues in society, this time Sir Nicolas Steele and his valet, Hildebrande Bigg. Pemberton's two later collections of mystery stories, *Queen of the Jesters* (1897) and *The Man Who Drove the Car* (1910), also feature a central character around whom events revolve. Corinne de Montesson immerses herself in a rescue mission for criminals, giving up her wealth to save both those willing to repent and their victims. For those who refuse to repent, she acts as nemesis. *The Man Who Drove the Car*, a collection of six sto-

ries, centers around events witnessed by a chauffeur.

In the only critical assessment to date of Pemberton's work, Affroditi Panaghis asserts that Pemberton departs from the conventions of the romance by using elements taken from real life. "His novels are not improbable, nor are they the total product of the author's imagination, for he never avoids an opportunity to depict real life." *The Phantom Army* (1898) demonstrates the mingling of real world events with romantic elements. The unstable political climate of Europe in the late nineteenth century is the backdrop against which Neal Falconer joins a political cause he later abandons after discovering the evil nature of those who are plotting the revolution. *The Giant's Gate* (1901) deals with modern scientific advances that man can use for either good or evil.

This mixing of styles that permeates Pemberton's novels is not always completely successful. *The Mystery of the Green Heart* (1910) is too sentimental. The novel opens with the discovery of a body in a boat. The victim, Lady Anna Maclain, has been a houseguest of Prince Maurevale of Dara, who performs mysterious tests in his laboratory for the good of mankind. When Lady Anna is killed, the prince has been working on a new type of torpedo which he hopes will keep England (his adopted home) safe from war. She has been poisoned, not by one of the prince's enemies but by a disgruntled employee of a French pharmaceutical company who had put poison in headache powders. He has been hanged for his crimes by the time of Anna's death. Captain Ferman, a British agent accused of her murder, is willing to hang rather than reveal that Anna had borne an illegitimate child by Tahir Pasha, an Egyptian soldier who tricked Anna into believing that he had married her. The prince unravels the mystery, discovering in the process his love for his ward, Stella.

White Motley (1911) is confused, too, with the mingling of murder and adventure. The novel opens with the once honorable Sir Luton Delayne, disgraced by shady business dealings and the subsequent, mysterious disappearance of his wife. She has gone to Switzerland where she is posing as a widow and being courted by Benjamin Benson, an early aviation enthusiast. Delayne comes to Switzerland, discovers her, and commits murder when he pushes a zealous creditor over a cliff. Benson forces him to go into hiding in Italy. By novel's end Delayne has come back, only to die in a snowstorm; conveniently he both takes

THE BOOKLOVERS MAGAZINE

Mr. Max Pemberton.

Drawn by David Wilson   *The Tatler*

MAX PEMBERTON

A 1904 caricature of Pemberton by David Wilson (Culver Pictures)

his punishment and leaves Benjamin free to marry Lily Delayne. *White Motley* is convincing in its descriptions of the trials Benjamin faces as he attempts to fly over Mount Blanc and back. Pemberton conveys the difficulties and excitement of early aviation.

The Gold Wolf (1903), with its questions of both the possibility of murder and the identity of the murderer, is a more fully realized mystery than *White Motley*. Dudley falls asleep in the library after an argument with his wife, Hermione. When he wakes he finds his wife dead on her bedroom floor. Though the doctor pronounces the cause of death as heart failure, Dudley feels at least partially responsible. His sense of guilt leads him to fall in love with Daphne, a

woman who looks a great deal like Hermione. Confiding in Daphne the events of the night, Dudley realizes that when he found his wife's body she was no longer wearing the diamond necklace she had on before their quarrel. Eventually he deduces that the butler has taken it.

Pemberton is typically most comfortable with writing novels that mix private relations with public, often political, spheres. *Wheels of Anarchy* (1908) is the story of a Canadian railway magnate, Jehan Cavanaugh, who hunts down anarchists after his father has been killed by fanatics at Baku. These hunts are narrated by Bruce Ingersoll, Cavanaugh's secretary. The *Times Literary Supplement* found that "save that Ingersoll pro-

Max Pemberton (photograph by Russell, Culver Pictures)

ent story. Dighton, head of a large firm, disappears. His son Gilbert leads a global search for him. Dighton's partner searches Mexico; another searcher goes to Canada. All are engaged in strange adventures, but they never find Dighton since he never really went away, a fact clear to the reader much earlier than to the searchers. In this novel, as is typical in Pemberton's work, the final resolution of the mystery itself may not be totally convincing, but the scenery, the scientific inventions, and the backgrounds are well worked out.

Pemberton devoted himself to many activities besides novel writing. In 1920 he and Lord Northcliffe founded the London School of Journalism. He wrote a number of plays, tried writing adaptations of some of his novels for the stage, and remained socially active. Along with George R. Sims (the journalist), Churton Collins (a professor of literature), and Sir Arthur Conan Doyle, Pemberton was a member of Our Society, a dining club devoted to discussing both fictional and actual crimes. He was knighted in 1928 and died in London in 1950.

Pemberton's work is unlikely to come into favor again, and he remains interesting more as a portrait of the gentleman author than as a lasting literary figure. Perhaps he sensed the shift in public taste, for in *Sixty Years and After* he offers this assessment: "Novelists of this age have, I believe, even less chance of survival than the men and women of the 'nineties and the early days of the new century. The immortal of last year is the 'What's his name' of this . . . we are here today and but 'remainders' tomorrow. Let us then cry 'Kismet' and, lifting our glasses to dead memories, see that the vintage is good and that the wine is red."

claims a little too loudly his determination to keep the reader excited, it is a keen and lively tale told with effect." *Two Women* (1914) also received favorable notice from the *Times:* "Mr. Max Pemberton, with his keen eye for actuality, preys upon recent history—the imprisonment of Reggie Ainsworth, an Englishman, on a charge of espionage in a German fortress. This . . . [is] pictured with zest and bravura which the author always has at his disposal."

John Dighton, Mystery Millionaire (1923), Pemberton's last mystery novel, is marred by a wealth of story lines that never becomes one coher-

Reference:

Affroditi Panaghis, "An Edition and Study of Max Pemberton's Short Stories," Ph.D. dissertation, Pennsylvania State University, 1978.

Eden Phillpotts

(4 November 1862-29 December 1960)

Gerald H. Strauss
Bloomsburg University

See also the Phillpotts entry in *DLB 10, Modern British Dramatists, 1900-1945*.

BOOKS: *My Adventure in the Flying Scotsman: A Romance of London and North-Western Railway Shares* (London: Hogg, 1888);

The End of a Life (Bristol: Arrowsmith/London: Simpkin, Marshall, Hamilton, Kent, 1891);

Folly and Fresh Air (London: Trischler, 1891; New York: Harper, 1892; revised edition, London: Hurst & Blackett, 1899);

A Tiger's Cub (Bristol: Arrowsmith/London: Simpkin, Marshall, Hamilton, Kent, 1892);

In Sugar-Cane Land (London: McClure/Simpkin, Marshall, Hamilton, Kent, 1893);

Summer Clouds and Other Stories (London, Paris & New York: Tuck, 1893);

Some Every-Day Folks (3 volumes, London: Osgood, McIlvaine, 1894; 1 volume, New York: Harper, 1895);

A Deal with the Devil (London: Bliss, Sands & Foster, 1895; New York: Warne, 1917);

A Breezy Morning (London & New York: French, 1895);

The Prude's Progress, by Phillpotts and Jerome K. Jerome (London: Chatto & Windus, 1895);

Down Dartmoor Way (London: Osgood, McIlvaine, 1896);

My Laughing Philosopher (London: Innes, 1896);

Lying Prophets (London: Innes, 1897; New York: Stokes, 1898);

Children of the Mist (London: Innes, 1898; New York & London: Putnam's, 1899);

Loup-Garou! (London: Sands, 1899);

A Golden Wedding, by Phillpotts and Charles Groves (London & New York: French, 1899);

The Human Boy (London: Methuen, 1899; New York & London: Harper, 1900);

A Pair of Knickerbockers (New York & London: French, 1900);

Sons of the Morning (London: Methuen, 1900; New York & London: Putnam's, 1900);

The Good Red Earth (Bristol: Arrowsmith/London: Simpkin, Marshall, Hamilton, Kent, 1901; New York: Doubleday, Page, 1901); republished as *Johnny Fortnight* (Bristol: Arrowsmith, 1904; revised, 1920);

The Striking Hours (London: Methuen, 1901; New York: Stokes, 1901);

Fancy Free (London: Methuen, 1901);

The River (London: Methuen, 1902; New York: Stokes, 1902);

242

The Transit of the Red Dragon and Other Tales (Bristol: Arrowsmith/London: Simpkin, Marshall, Hamilton, Kent, 1903);

The Golden Fetich (London: Harper, 1903; New York: Dodd, Mead, 1903);

My Devon Year (London: Methuen, 1903; New York: Macmillan, 1903);

The American Prisoner (London: Methuen, 1904; New York & London: Macmillan, 1904);

The Farm of the Dagger (London: Newnes, 1904; New York: Dodd, Mead, 1904);

The Secret Woman (London: Methuen, 1905; New York & London: Macmillan, 1905);

Knock at a Venture (London: Methuen, 1905; New York & London: Macmillan, 1905);

The Portreeve (London: Methuen, 1906; New York: Macmillan, 1906);

The Unlucky Number (London: Newnes, 1906);

My Garden (London: Newnes/New York: Scribners, 1906);

The Poacher's Wife (London: Methuen, 1906); republished as *Daniel Sweetland* (New York & London: Authors & Newspapers Association, 1906);

Doubloons, by Phillpotts and Arnold Bennett (New York: McClure, Phillips, 1906); republished as *The Sinews of War* (London: Laurie, 1906);

The Whirlwind (London: Chapman & Hall, 1907; New York: McClure, Phillips, 1907);

The Folk Afield (London: Methuen, 1907; New York & London: Putnam's, 1907);

The Mother (London: Ward, Lock, 1908); republished as *The Mother of the Man* (New York: Dodd, Mead, 1908);

The Statue, by Phillpotts and Bennett (London, Paris, New York, Toronto & Melbourne: Cassell, 1908; New York: Moffat, Yard, 1908);

The Human Boy Again (London: Chapman & Hall, 1908);

The Virgin in Judgment (London, Paris, New York, Toronto & Melbourne: Cassell, 1908; New York: Moffat, Yard, 1908);

The Three Brothers (London: Hutchinson, 1909; New York: Macmillan, 1909);

The Fun of the Fair (London: Murray, 1909);

The Haven (London: Murray, 1909; New York: John Lane, 1909);

The Thief of Virtue (London: Murray, 1910; New York: John Lane, 1910);

Tales of the Tenements (London: Murray, 1910; New York: John Lane, 1910);

The Flint Heart: A Fairy Story (London: Smith, Elder, 1910; New York: Dutton, 1910; revised edition, London: Chapman & Dodd, 1922);

A Fight to a Finish (London: Cassell, 1911);

Wild Fruit (London & New York: John Lane, 1911);

Demeter's Daughter (London: Methuen, 1911; New York: John Lane, 1911);

The Beacon (London: Unwin, 1911; New York: John Lane, 1911);

Dance of the Months (London & Glasgow: Gowans & Gray, 1911);

The Secret Woman: A Play in Five Acts (London: Duckworth, 1912; New York: Brentano's, 1914; revised, London: Duckworth, 1935);

The Forest on the Hill (London: Murray, 1912; New York: John Lane, 1912; revised edition, London: Newnes, 1914); republished as *The Forest* (London: Macmillan, 1927);

The Iscariot (London: Murray, 1912; New York: John Lane, 1912);

The Three Knaves (London: Macmillan, 1912);

From the Angle of Seventeen (London: Murray, 1912; Boston: Little, Brown, 1914);

The Lovers: A Romance (London, Melbourne & Toronto: Ward, Lock, 1912; Chicago & New York: Rand, McNally, 1912);

Curtain Raisers (London: Duckworth, 1912; New York: Brentano's, 1914);

Widecombe Fair (London: Murray, 1913; Boston: Little, Brown, 1913);

The Old Time Before Them (London: Murray, 1913); revised as *Told at "The Plume"* (London: Hurst & Blackett, 1921);

The Joy of Youth: A Comedy (London: Chapman & Hall, 1913; Boston: Little, Brown, 1913);

The Shadow (London: Duckworth, 1913; New York: Brentano's, 1914);

The Mother: A Play in Four Acts (London: Duckworth, 1913; New York: Brentano's, 1914);

The Master of Merripit (London, Melbourne & Toronto: Ward, Lock, 1914);

The Judge's Chair (London: Murray, 1914);

Faith Tresilion (New York: Macmillan, 1914; London, Melbourne & Toronto: Ward, Lock, 1916);

Brunel's Tower (London: Heinemann, 1915; New York: Macmillan, 1915);

My Shrubs (London & New York: John Lane, 1915);

The Angel in the House, by Phillpotts and Basil Macdonald Hastings (London & New York: French, 1915);

Old Delabole (London: Heinemann, 1915; New York: Macmillan, 1915);

The Human Boy and the War (London: Methuen, 1916; New York: Macmillan, 1916);

MY ADVENTURE

IN

THE FLYING SCOTSMAN:

A ROMANCE OF

London and North-Western Railway Shares.

BY

EDEN PHILLPOTTS.

LONDON:
JAMES HOGG AND SONS,
7 LOVELL'S COURT, PATERNOSTER ROW.
1888.

Title page for Phillpotts's first book, a story of stolen railroad stocks that may have been written as an advertisement for the London and North-Western Railway

The Green Alleys (London: Heinemann, 1916; New York: Macmillan, 1916);

"Delight" (London: Palmer & Hayward, 1916);

The Girl and the Faun (London: Palmer & Hayward, 1916; Philadelphia: Lippincott/London: Palmer & Hayward, 1917);

The Farmer's Wife: A Play in Three Acts (London: Duckworth/New York: Brentano's, 1916);

The Nursery (Banks of Colne) (London: Heinemann, 1917); republished as *The Banks of Colne* (New York: Macmillan, 1917);

Plain Song 1914-1916 (London: Heinemann, 1917; New York: Macmillan, 1917);

The Chronicles of St. Tid (London: Skeffington, 1917; New York: Macmillan, 1918);

The Spinners (London: Heinemann, 1918; New York: Macmillan, 1918);

A Shadow Passes (London: Palmer & Hayward, 1918; New York: Macmillan, 1919);

Storm in a Teacup (London: Heinemann, 1919; New York: Macmillan, 1919);

St. George and the Dragons: A Comedy in Three Acts (London: Duckworth, 1919);

Evander (London: Richards, 1919; New York: Macmillan, 1919);

Miser's Money (London: Heinemann, 1920; New York: Macmillan, 1920);

As the Wind Blows (London: Elkin Mathews/New York: Macmillan, 1920);

A West Country Pilgrimage (London: Parsons, 1920; New York: Macmillan, 1920);

Orphan Dinah (London: Heinemann, 1920; New York: Macmillan, 1921);

The Bronze Venus (London: Richards, 1921);

Eudocia: A Comedy Royal (London: Heinemann, 1921; New York: Macmillan, 1921);

A Dish of Apples (London & New York: Hodder & Stoughton, 1921);

The Grey Room (New York: Macmillan, 1921; London: Hurst & Blackett, 1922);

Pan and the Twins (London: Richards, 1922; New York: Macmillan, 1922);

Pixies' Plot (London: Richards, 1922);

Number 87, as Harrington Hext (London: Butterworth, 1922; New York: Macmillan, 1922);

The Red Redmaynes (New York: Macmillan, 1922; London: Hutchinson, 1923);

Black, White, and Brindled (London: Richards, 1923; New York: Macmillan, 1923);

Children of Men (London: Heinemann, 1923; New York: Macmillan, 1923);

The Market-Money: A Play in One Act (London & Glasgow: Gowans & Gray/Boston: Phillips, 1923); republished in *Three Short Plays* (London: Duckworth, 1928);

The Lavender Dragon (London: Richards, 1923; New York: Macmillan, 1923);

Cherry-Stones (London: Richards, 1923; New York: Macmillan, 1924);

The Thing at Their Heels, as Harrington Hext (London: Butterworth, 1923; New York: Macmillan, 1923);

"Cheat-the-Boys" (London: Heinemann, 1924; New York: Macmillan, 1924);

A Human Boy's Diary (London: Heinemann, 1924; New York: Macmillan, 1924);

Thoughts in Prose and Verse (London: Watts, 1924);

Bed Rock: A Comedy in Three Acts, by Phillpotts and Hastings (London: "The Stage," 1924);

Redcliff (London: Hutchinson, 1924; New York: Macmillan, 1924);

The Treasures of Typhon (London: Richards, 1924; New York: Macmillan, 1925);

A Harvesting (London: Richards, 1924);

Who Killed Diana?, as Harrington Hext (London: Butterworth, 1924); republished as *Who Killed Cock Robin?* (New York: Macmillan, 1924);

A Comedy Royal (London: Laurie, 1925; revised edition, London: Duckworth, 1932);

Devonshire Cream: A Comedy in Three Acts (London: Duckworth, 1925; New York: Macmillan, 1925);

A Voice from the Dark (London: Hutchinson, 1925; New York: Macmillan, 1925);

Up Hill, Down Dale (London: Hutchinson, 1925; New York: Macmillan, 1925);

George Westover (London: Hutchinson, 1925; New York: Macmillan, 1925);

The Monster, as Harrington Hext (New York: Macmillan, 1925);

Circé's Island and The Girl and the Faun (London: Richards, 1926; New York: Macmillan, 1926);

The Marylebone Miser (London: Hutchinson, 1926); republished as *Jig-Saw* (New York: Macmillan, 1926);

Peacock House and Other Mysteries (London: Hutchinson, 1926; New York: Macmillan, 1927);

The Augustan Books of Modern Poetry: Eden Phillpotts, edited by Edward Thompson (London: Benn, 1926);

The Miniature (London: Watts, 1926; New York: Macmillan, 1927);

A Cornish Droll (London: Hutchinson, 1926; New York: Macmillan, 1928);

Yellow Sands: A Comedy in Three Acts, by Phillpotts and Adelaide Eden Phillpotts (London: Duckworth, 1926; New York: French, 1927);

Brother Man (London: Richards, 1926);

The Blue Comet: A Comedy in Three Acts (London: Duckworth, 1927);

The Jury (London: Hutchinson, 1927; New York: Macmillan, 1927);

It Happened Like That (London: Hutchinson, 1927; New York: Macmillan, 1928);

Arachne (London: Faber & Gwyer, 1927; New York: Macmillan, 1928);

The Ring Fence (London: Hutchinson, 1928; New York: Macmillan, 1928);

Brother Beast (London: Secker, 1928);

Three Short Plays (London: Duckworth, 1928);

Goodwill (London: Watts, 1928);

The Runaways: A Comedy in Three Acts (London: Duckworth, 1928);

Tryphena (London: Hutchinson, 1929; New York: Macmillan, 1929);

The Torch (London: Hutchinson, 1929; New York: Macmillan, 1929);

A Hundred Sonnets (London: Benn, 1929);

Buy a Broom: A Comedy in Three Acts (London: Duckworth, 1929);

The Apes (London: Faber & Faber, 1929; New York: Macmillan, 1929);

The Three Maidens (London: Hutchinson, 1930; New York: Smith, 1930);

A Hundred Lyrics (London: Benn, 1930; New York: Smith, 1930);

Alcyone (A Fairy Story) (London: Benn, 1930);

Cherry Gambol (London: Hutchinson, 1930);

Jane's Legacy: A Folk Play in Three Acts (London: Duckworth, 1931; London & New York: French, 1932);

"Found Drowned" (London: Hutchinson, 1931; New York: Macmillan, 1931);

Essays in Little (London: Hutchinson, 1931);

Stormbury (London: Hutchinson, 1931; New York: Macmillan, 1932);

The Broom Squires (London: Benn, 1932; New York: Macmillan, 1932);

Becoming (London: Benn, 1932);

A Clue from the Stars (London: Hutchinson, 1932; New York: Macmillan, 1932);

Bred in the Bone (London: Hutchinson, 1932; New York: Macmillan, 1932);

The Good Old Days: A Comedy in Three Acts, by Phillpotts and Adelaide Eden Phillpotts (London: Duckworth, 1932; New York: French, 1932);

They Could Do No Other (London: Hutchinson, 1932; New York: Macmillan, 1933);

The Captain's Curio (London: Hutchinson, 1933; New York: Macmillan, 1933);

Mr. Digweed and Mr. Lumb (London: Hutchinson, 1933; New York: Macmillan, 1934);

Witch's Cauldron (London: Hutchinson, 1933; New York: Macmillan, 1933);

A Shadow Passes [novel] (London: Hutchinson, 1933; New York: Macmillan, 1934);

A Cup of Happiness: A Comedy in Three Acts (London: Duckworth, 1933);

Nancy Owlett (London, Paris & New York: Tuck, 1933; New York: Macmillan, 1933);

Song of a Sailor Man: Narrative Poem (London: Benn, 1933; New York: Macmillan, 1934);

A Year with Bisshe-Bantam (London & Glasgow: Blackie, 1934);

Minions of the Moon (London: Hutchinson, 1934; New York: Macmillan, 1935);

The Oldest Inhabitant: A Comedy (London: Hutchinson, 1934; New York: Macmillan, 1934);

Portrait of a Gentleman (London: Hutchinson, 1934);

Ned of the Caribees (London: Hutchinson, 1935);

Sonnets from Nature (London: Watts, 1935);

The Wife of Elias (London: Hutchinson, 1935; New York: Dutton, 1937);

Physician, Heal Thyself (London: Hutchinson, 1935); republished as *The Anniversary Murder* (New York: Dutton, 1936);

Once Upon A Time (London: Hutchinson, 1935);

A Close Call (London: Hutchinson, 1936; New York: Macmillan, 1936);

The Owl of Athene (London: Hutchinson, 1936);

The White Camel (London: Country Life, 1936; New York: Dutton, 1938);

Wood-Nymph (London: Hutchinson, 1936; New York: Dutton, 1937);

Farce in Three Acts (London: Hutchinson, 1937);

A Dartmoor Village (London: Watts, 1937);

Lycanthrope: The Mystery of Sir William Wolf (London: Butterworth, 1937; New York: Macmillan, 1938); republished as *The Mystery of Sir William Wolf* (London: Butterworth, 1938);

Portrait of a Scoundrel (London: Murray, 1938; New York: Macmillan, 1938);

Dark Horses (London: Murray, 1938);

Golden Island (London: Joseph, 1938);

Saurus (London: Murray, 1938);

Monkshood (London: Methuen, 1939; New York: Macmillan, 1939);

Tabletop (New York: Macmillan, 1939);

Thorn in Her Flesh (London: Murray, 1939);

Awake Deborah! (London: Methuen, 1940; New York: Macmillan, 1941);

Chorus of Clowns (London: Methuen, 1940);

A Mixed Grill (London: Watts, 1940);

Goldcross (London: Methuen, 1940);

A Deed Without a Name (London & Melbourne: Hutchinson, 1941; New York: Macmillan, 1942);

Ghostwater (London: Methuen, 1941; New York: Macmillan, 1941);

Pilgrims of the Night (London: Hutchinson, 1942);

Miniatures (London: Watts, 1942);

Flower of the Gods (London & New York: Hutchinson, 1942; New York: Macmillan, 1943);

A Museum Piece (London & New York: Hutchinson, 1943);

At the 'Bus-Stop: A Duologue for Two Women (London: French, 1943);

They Were Seven (London & New York: Hutchinson, 1944; New York: Macmillan, 1945);

The Changeling (London & New York: Hutchinson, 1944);

The Drums of Dombali (London & New York: Hutchinson, 1945);

Quartet (London & New York: Hutchinson, 1946);

There Was an Old Woman (London & New York: Hutchinson, 1947);

Fall of the House of Heron (London & New York: Hutchinson, 1948);

The Enchanted Wood (London: Watts, 1948);

Address Unknown (London & New York: Hutchinson, 1949);

Dilemma (London: Hutchinson, 1949);

The Waters of Walla (London & New York: Hutchinson, 1950);

The Orange Orchard, by Phillpotts and Nancy Price (London: French, 1951);

Through a Glass Darkly (London & New York: Hutchinson, 1951);

From the Angle of 88 [autobiography] (London & New York: Hutchinson, 1951);

George and Georgina (London & New York: Hutchinson, 1952);

The Hidden Hand (London: Hutchinson, 1952);

His Brother's Keeper (London: Hutchinson, 1953);

One Thing and Another (London: Hutchinson, 1954);

The Widow Garland (London: Hutchinson, 1955);

Connie Woodland (London: Hutchinson, 1956);

Giglet Market (London: Methuen, 1957);

There Was an Old Man (London: Hutchinson, 1959).

PLAY PRODUCTIONS: *The Policeman*, by Phillpotts and Walter Helmore, Ealing, Lyric Hall, 12 January 1887;

A Platonic Attachment, Ealing, Lyric Hall, 20 February 1889;

A Breezy Morning, Leeds, Grand Theatre, 27 April 1889;

The Councillor's Wife, New York, Empire Theatre, 6 November 1892; revised as *The Prude's Progress*, by Phillpotts and Jerome K. Jerome, Cambridge, Theatre Royal, 16 May 1895;

Allendale, by Phillpotts and G. B. Burgin, London, Strand Theatre, 14 February 1893;

The MacHaggis, by Phillpotts and Jerome, Peterborough, Theatre Royal, 22 February 1897;

For Love of Prim, London, Court Theatre, 24 January 1899;

A Pair of Knickerbockers, London, St. George's Hall, 26 December 1899;

A Golden Wedding, by Phillpotts and Charles Graves, London, Playhouse Theatre, 22 February 1908;

The Carrier Pigeon, Glasgow, Royal Theatre, 7 April 1913;

Hiatus, Manchester, Gaiety Theatre, 22 September 1913;

The Shadow, Manchester, Gaiety Theatre, 6 October 1913;

The Mother, Liverpool, Playhouse, 22 October 1913;

The Point of View, London, St. George's Hall, 18 November 1913;

The Angel in the House, by Phillpotts and Basil MacDonald Hastings, London, Savoy Theatre, 3 June 1915;

Bedrock, Manchester, Gaiety Theatre, 16 October 1916;

The Farmer's Wife, by Phillpotts and Adelaide Eden Phillpotts, Birmingham, Repertory Theatre, 11 November 1916;

St. George and the Dragons, Birmingham, Repertory Theatre, 30 March 1918;

The Secret Woman, Birmingham, Repertory Theatre, 14 October 1922;

Devonshire Cream, by Phillpotts and Adelaide Eden Phillpotts, Birmingham, Repertory Theatre, 6 December 1924;

Jane's Legacy, Birmingham, Repertory Theatre, 24 October 1925;

The Blue Comet, Birmingham, Repertory Theatre, 11 September 1926;

Yellow Sands, by Phillpotts and Adelaide Eden Phillpotts, London, Haymarket Theatre, 3 November 1926;

The Purple Bedroom, London, Colosseum, 27 December 1926;

Something to Talk About, London, Colosseum, 17 January 1927;

My Lady's Mill, by Phillpotts and Adelaide Eden Phillpotts, London, Lyric Theatre, 2 July 1928;

The Runaways, Birmingham, Repertory Theatre, 1 September 1928;

The Market-Money, Liverpool, Playhouse, 5 June 1929;

The Good Old Days, by Phillpotts and Adelaide Eden Phillpotts, Birmingham, Repertory Theatre, December 1931;

A Cup of Happiness, London, Royalty Theatre, 24 December 1932;

The Orange Orchard, by Phillpotts and Nancy Price, London, New Lindsay Theatre, 12 April 1950.

During a prolific literary career that spanned the reigns of five monarchs, Eden Phillpotts wrote novels, stage and radio plays, memoirs, essays, poetry, short stories, fables, and mystery fiction. He published his first book, *My Adventure in the Flying Scotsman: A Romance of London and North-Western Railway Shares*, in 1888, possibly as an advertisement of the railway. The evil half brother of the narrator steals his valuable railway shares. There is a fight on the train, but the hero is finally triumphant in the yards at Carlisle.

Phillpotts was still writing novels and radio plays in the 1950s, by which time his output totaled more than 250 books. He was successful from the beginning of his career. His first significant novel was *Lying Prophets* (1897), a work commended by James Payn, an influential editor and essayist. *Children of the Mist* (1898) sold in even greater numbers. It was praised by R. D. Blackmore, author of *Lorna Doone* (1869). By the first decade of the twentieth century, Phillpotts was widely recognized as a leading regionalist, notable for his ability to evoke his native Devon and Cornwall. His series of Dartmoor novels were compared to Hardy's novels of Wessex. Though his earliest books have elements of detective fiction, *The Three Knaves* (1912) is his first full-fledged whodunit. He did not turn in earnest to the form until the 1920s, and just a small number of his total output is in the genre; but beginning with *The Grey Room* (1921) and continuing into the 1950s, Phillpotts produced whodunits regularly.

Julian Symons in 1972 dismissed Phillpotts's crime fiction as "among the most ridiculous of the time"; Phillpotts's contemporaries, however, reacted more favorably. For instance, Willard Huntington Wright (in 1927) wrote that "Eden Phillpotts has written some of the best detective stories in England," and in 1929 Dorothy Sayers also praised his work in the genre.

Critical judgment notwithstanding, Phillpotts should be conceded a place in the whodunit pantheon if only because he encouraged a young Torquay, Devonshire, neighbor, Agatha Miller, to pursue a literary career. In his memoir *From the Angle of 88* (1951), he recalls Agatha Miller Christie as "a little girl of tender years, the daughter of acquaintance who dwelt not far from me just then. . . . I lent her books, many of which it is possible she may have read, but they were

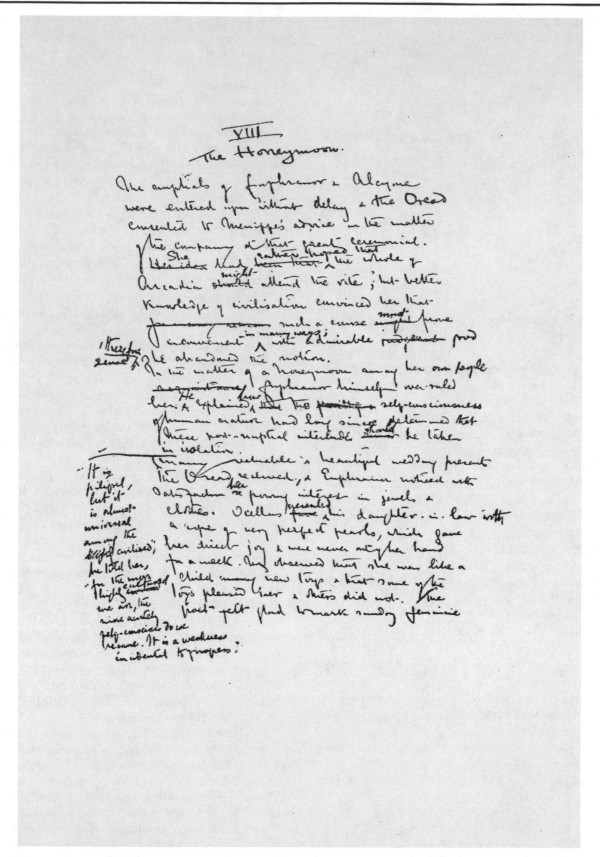

Page from the manuscript for Alcyone (A Fairy Story) *(Percival Hinton,* Eden Phillpotts: A Bibliography of First Editions, *1931)*

not of a kind to quicken her own secret promise, for, when she grew up, it was to find herself a popular novelist with unique qualities of invention."

Eden Phillpotts was born at Mount Aboo, Rajputana, India, on 4 November 1862, to Henry and Adelaide Waters Phillpotts. His father was an officer in the Indian Army and a British political agent in Harrowtec and Rajputana; when he died, his widow returned with her three young boys to England. Eden, the eldest, went to Mannamead School in Plymouth and at seventeen came to London to work in the Trafalgar Square office of Sun Fire, an insurance company. During his ten years as a clerk, he took acting lessons and began writing. When he left the insurance office after a decade, he became assistant editor of a weekly, *Black and White,* a part-time position he soon relinquished in order to become a full-time writer. He married Emily Topham in 1892. The couple had a daughter and a son. His first wife died in 1928, and he married Lucy Robina Webb the following year.

Phillpotts was a regular contributor to the *Idler.* Early in his career he also began writing plays, one an 1895 collaboration with Jerome K. Jerome (*The Prude's Progress*). His greatest theatrical success was *The Farmer's Wife,* which he coauthored with his daughter Adelaide Eden Phillpotts. It was produced by Barry Jackson in 1916 at the Birmingham Repertory Theatre after a dozen others had rejected it. Though the critics were not enthusiastic, this broad comedy of a Devonshire farmer's search for a wife opened at the Court Theatre in London in 1924 and ran for 1,329 performances over three years (at the time, the third longest run in British stage history for a straight play). By this time Phillpotts also was gaining popular recognition as a writer of detective fiction.

A noteworthy early example of his work is *The Grey Room,* published first in the United States in 1921, then the following year in England. Set in a Devonshire nobleman's Tudor mansion, it opens during a house party at which old Sir Walter Lennox, the host, tells the story of the Grey Room, an upstairs bedroom that has been closed since a nurse inexplicably died in it twelve years earlier. Before retiring for the night, Sir Walter shows the room to the curious guests, who marvel at its rich antique furnishings. Later in the evening, Henry Lennox, Sir Walter's nephew and heir to the baronetcy, and Thomas May, new husband of Mary Lennox, Sir Walter's daughter, resume talking about the room, and on a dare May

Front cover for Phillpotts's 1931 novel in which a murder by poison is solved by a country investigator (courtesy of Otto Penzler)

spends the night in it. The next morning he is dead. Peter Hardcastle, a star detective of New Scotland Yard, is brought in, but while alone in the room, he too dies. (Hardcastle is the first of Phillpotts's vulnerable and unsuccessful detectives, a character type he favored.) The next victim of the mysterious force is the Reverend Septimus May (the father of Thomas). He is a religious fanatic who wrongly believes that he can exorcise the malignant spirit of the room through fervent prayer.

The mystery finally is solved, not by a Scotland Yard or private detective, but by an Italian visitor who recognizes the antique furnishings of the Grey Room as having been built for the Borgias of Renaissance Florence. Signor Mannetti passes a night in the room accompanied by an old dog who is slated to be put to sleep later in the week. Unlike most previous occupants of the room, the Italian survives; but the dog dies while sleeping on the bed. Mannetti explains: "The moment the heat of his ancient body penetrated the mattress under him, it released its awful venom." London experts elaborate: "A thin supple wire was found to run between the harmless flock of the mattress and the satin casing.... Experiments showed that ... the wire, of which fifty miles wound over the upper and lower surfaces of the mattress under its satin upholstery, proved infinitely sensitive to heat, and gave off, or ejected at tremendous speed, an invisible, highly poisonous matter even when subjected to a lower temperature than that of a normal human being."

Unconventional though the resolution may be—having the Borgias prove to be the villains because of a centuries-old mattress—the novel has many of the typical trappings of English detective fiction of its day: a country estate, a highly regarded New Scotland Yard detective, a house party, and a potential conflict of interest between the heir and someone who marries into the family. Motive, suspects, and opportunities abound. But Phillpotts introduces a novel twist when the detective becomes a victim, and the various characters' claims of psychical causes for the deaths thus seem for a while to be possible.

There are obvious similarities between *The Grey Room* and *The Red Redmaynes*, which was published in the United States in 1922 (though not until 1923 in England). The serial deaths in both novels appear to be exterminating a family, and there is the suggestion that a supernatural force is responsible for the deaths. The English police detective in the novel also fails to solve the case: Mark Brendon early on loses his objectivity by falling in love with Jenny Pendean, a woman who turns out to be one of the murderers. Solving the case is Peter Ganns, a member of the New York City police force. Once the American arrives on the scene (halfway through the novel), Brendon in effect becomes his Watson. Ganns perceptively judges character, adeptly orchestrates events to serve his needs, and determinedly avoids being swayed by personal considerations. He succeeds in solving the case, but his victory is a Pyrrhic one, for the friend at whose request he joined the hunt is the last victim.

The book begins with the apparent murder of Michael Pendean, Jenny's husband (though his body is not found) by Robert Redmayne, one of her three uncles (they are, with her, the last of the Redmaynes). Robert had not approved of the

marriage. By it, Jenny lost her share of the family inheritance. The mystery is heightened both by confessional correspondence from the fugitive Robert after he disappears and also by his frequent fleeting reappearances; further, though on the run for more than a year, he always re-emerges in exactly the same clothes.

Brendon's initial inquiries are fruitless, and when months later he goes to the Devon coast home of Jenny's uncle Bendigo, she and Doria (Bendigo's new Italian boatman) report that they chanced upon the fugitive and have arranged for Bendigo to meet his brother alone. The outcome of this intrigue is the apparent death of the Bendigo; again, however, there is no body, though the presumed killer is the missing Robert Redmayne. As her remaining uncle, Albert, says to Jenny when he arrives from Italy, "It is your poor husband's case over again—blood, alas, but nought else!" When he leaves for home, he promises to write to a friend, New York police detective Peter Ganns, "without doubt, the most accomplished of men in the dreadful science of detecting crime.... [whose] brain has a quality which one can only describe as a mental X-ray, which probes and penetrates in a fashion denied to ordinary thinking apparatus."

During the period prior to Ganns's arrival, Jenny marries Doria; they move to Italy, and the problems of the past seem to have been forgotten. Then one day, when the fugitive Robert briefly appears near Albert Redmayne's home like "some apparition limned in the air," Albert asks Brendon and Ganns to go to Italy as soon as possible.

Phillpotts introduces Ganns as "white-haired, somewhat corpulent ... clean shaved, with a heavy face modelled to suggest a rhinoceros. The features were large; the nose swollen and a little veinal with purple, the eyes hidden behind owl-like spectacles with tortoise-shell rims, and the brow very broad, but not high." Based on what he has been told about the case by Albert and Brendon, Ganns calls Brendon's "cast-iron facts" just "elaborate and deliberate fictions." He is able to discover that the appearances of the previous Robert Redmayne were Doria's ploys. As Ganns nears the conclusion of the case, he tries to protect the last of the Redmayne brothers, but Albert is killed anyway. Soon after, however, Ganns and the police apprehend Michael Pendean, alias Doria, for murdering the three Redmaynes. When he attempts to

A VOICE FROM THE DARK

EDEN PHILLPOTTS

Dust jacket for Phillpotts's 1925 novel about a recently re-
tired CID agent who becomes involved in international in-
trigue while vacationing on the Dorset downs (courtesy of
Otto Penzler)

escape, a bullet meant for him kills his wife and accomplice, Jenny, instead.

In a lengthy written confession, Pendean provides support for Ganns's deductions about his
scheme, and though warders constantly watch
him in the days prior to his execution, he manages to poison himself with cyanide of potassium
and thus cheats the gallows. He wills to Ganns an
artificial eye he has worn since an accident in his
youth, and Brendon reports: "Behind an eye of
glass . . . had lain concealed, until he required it,
the capsule of poison found crushed within his
mouth after death."

Phillpotts's immediate popular success as a
writer of crime fiction can be attributed in part
to the fact that he already was a well-known novelist; but he used a pseudonym that was also successful. Under the name Harrington Hext he wrote
Number 87 (1922), *The Thing at Their Heels* (1923),
Who Killed Diana? (1924, published in the United

States as *Who Killed Cock Robin?*, 1924), and *The
Monster* (1925). The Hext books were more popular in the United States than in the United Kingdom, but the pseudonym did not fool many
readers in either country.

The Thing at Their Heels is Phillpotts's Hext
masterpiece. It, like *The Red Redmaynes*, deals with
the destruction of a family, in this case that of Sir
Augustine Templer (a devout Anglo-Catholic and
scion of an ancient house whose ancestral seat is
Kingscresset, an Inigo Jones mansion in southern
England). Though his family is small, seventy-five-
year-old Sir Augustine has every reason to feel secure about the continuation of the Templer line,
but within a short time, several male members
are struck down. First, Captain Matthew
Templer, Sir Augustine's remaining son, is shot
and killed; then Thomas Templer, Matthew's
fifteen-year-old son, is drowned. Two nephews
remain as potential heirs: Major Montague
Templer, who also is shot and killed, and Father
Felix Templer, an Anglo-Catholic priest so devout that he joins "the Great Mother Church"
and becomes a member of a Roman Catholic
order in London. Soon after, he reports being attacked one night while going to a bed-ridden pa-
rishioner but survives and says that his assailant
was the same "stout, black-bearded man with
dark glasses—the familiar figure" who had been reported at the scenes of the prior attacks.

The attack on Father Templer is curious. As
he himself speculates: "To me the most extraordinary feature of the affair is that the murderer always appears as the same man. That points to
the fact, surely, that he does not trouble to disguise himself. At Kingscresset, in Derbyshire, in
Devon—always the black beard and big spectacles,
so that everybody connected with this horrible ex-
termination knows and expects one thing. Why
did he dress himself up in this conspicuous way
to challenge and destroy me? If it were a disguise, surely it has more than served its turn?
Had a strange man passed me in the alley, or suddenly emerged from one of those doors, he
might have come to my side, said 'Good evening,'
and blown my brains out, as he killed poor Montague. Instead, the one sinister figure in the world—
the one human being I have most to dread and
avoid—suddenly starts up in front of me—with the
result that he defeats his own object. I take instant fright and leap forward as he fires. I also
faint from shock, and fall in such a way that he believes he has done what he attempted."

Sir Augustine, whose twin passions are his Anglo-Catholicism and his family line, makes a final futile attempt to dissuade Felix Templer from becoming a Roman Catholic and to persuade him to marry his cousin Petronell in order to beget an heir and avoid "the death-knell of the family–the end of the race." Soon after Felix Templer returns to London for his conversion, Sir Augustine dies, the victim of poisoning. The murderer is undiscoverable. Father Templer, new master of Kingscresset, reveals his plans for the legacy: "I have determined to turn Kingscresset into a great asylum for boys–the unwanted, the waifs and strays. The institution will be endowed, and the revenues and accommodations of this huge place are such that we shall always be able to support and educate a thousand lads."

On his deathbed, Father Templer reveals he has murdered his family. In a written statement, he says, "I had long considered with uneasiness the Kingscresset millions and the sorry uses to which, through generation after generation, they were applied . . . and I perceived that it must be my great and terrible task to set aside those who stood between me and the Templer fortune and turn it to a rightful purpose . . . I alone am responsible for the destruction of my family. . . . By their sacrifice, thousands and thousands of lads will pass into the world equipped for noble actions, sustained by highest teaching and precept, healthy of body and soul, endowed to let their light so shine that others may be uplifted and advanced thereby."

In the course of the novel Phillpotts effectively develops suspense, which increases with the serial deaths of family members and thus eliminates potential suspects. In addition, the reader is prepared for the concluding revelations about motivation by the focus throughout on social issues and religion. As in much of his other detective fiction, these philosophical and sociological digressions occasionally distract and become tedious. Familiarity with others of his novels also prepares the reader for the failure of the detective Inspector Midwinter to solve the case to which he has devoted so much time. As in *The Red Redmaynes*, the detective fails because he has "a

warm heart." Father Felix is one of Midwinter's "enthusiasms"; he "admired the young priest . . . and he was proud of the real friendship that existed between them." The closeness of the relationship blurs his insight.

Eden Phillpotts died at his home at Broad Clyst, Exeter, 29 December 1960. He brought to his detective fiction the skills of an experienced storyteller, for his narratives have complex plots and are peopled by characters who are sometimes fully three-dimensional. His milieus also are more fully developed than is the norm, whether the locale be England or Italy. Further, his practice of having the source and resolution of crime found in past generations, even centuries earlier, also provides depth to his work. His likable, yet vulnerable, detectives similarly are an imaginative departure from the typical type of the omniscient superman. But Phillpotts must be faulted for his discursiveness, particularly the tendency to have his characters preach. The writer of detection who envelopes his puzzles in such peripheral concerns always risks alienating his readers. Finally, surprising though his resolutions frequently are, Phillpotts too often–as in *The Grey Room*–comes up with ones that are largely external to the plots. The weaknesses notwithstanding, at least some of the detective novels that Phillpotts wrote during a long, varied, and prolific career, remain compelling reading experiences, not at all dated by the passage of time.

Bibliography:

Percival Hinton, *Eden Phillpotts: A Bibliography of First Editions* (Birmingham, U.K.: Worthington, 1931).

References:

Waveney Girvan, ed., *Eden Phillpotts: An Assessment and a Tribute* (London: Hutchinson, 1953);

Adelaide Eden Phillpotts, *Yellow Sands; The Story of the Famous Play by Eden & Adelaide Eden Phillpotts* (London: Chapman & Hall, 1930).

Papers:

The manuscript of *"Cheat-the-Boys"* is at Brown University.

Angus Reach

(23 January 1821-25 November 1856)

Carol M. Dole
Cornell University

BOOKS: *The Natural History of "Bores"* (London: Bogue, 1847; New York: Leavitt, Trow, 185?);

The Natural History of Humbugs (London: Bogue, 1847);

The Natural History of Tuft-Hunters and Toadies, anonymous (London: Bogue, 1848); republished, with *The Natural History of "Bores"* and "The Bal Masqué," as *Men of the Hour* (London: Ward & Lock, 1856);

The Comic Bradshaw; or, Bubbles from the Boiler (London: Bogue, 1848);

London on the Thames; or, Life above and below Bridge (London: Office of the *Puppetshow,* 1848);

A Romance of a Mince-Pie, An Incident in the Life of John Chirrup of Forty-winks (London: Bogue, 1848);

Clement Lorimer; or, The Book with the Iron Clasps: A Romance (6 monthly parts, London: Bogue, 1848-1849; 1 volume, London: Bogue, 1849; London & New York: Routledge, 1856);

Leonard Lindsay; or, The Story of a Buccaneer, 2 volumes (London: Bogue, 1850);

Claret and Olives, from the Garonne to the Rhone (London: Bogue, 1852; New York: Putnam's, 1852);

A Story with a Vengeance; or, How Many Joints Go Into a Tale?, by Reach and Shirley Brooks (London: Printed by Robson, Levey & Franklyn, 1852; revised edition, London: Cooke, 1953);

Jenny Lind at Last (Boston: W. V. Spencer, 1856);

Christmas Cheer, in Three Courses, by Reach, James Hannay, and Albert Smith (London: Ward & Lock, 1858);

Manchester and the Textile Districts in 1849, edited by C. Aspin (Rossendale: Helmshore Local History Society, 1972).

PLAY PRODUCTIONS: *Which Mr. Smith,* London, Lyceum Theatre, 8 October 1846;

Jenny Lind at Last; or, The Swedish Nightingale, London, Lyceum Theatre, 14 April 1847;

Fleur de Lys; or, Love's Triumph, by Reach and Hamilton Herbert, London, Lyceum Theatre, 19 July 1847;

The Special, London, Olympic Theatre, 3 May 1848;

The Czarina; or, Ivan the Armourer, by Reach and Morris Barnett, London, Surrey Theatre, 21 April 1851;

The Shot Tower, London, Strand Theatre, 4 August 1851;

Dreaming and Waking, by Reach and Barnett, London, Surrey Theatre, 20 October 1851.

OTHER: *Gavarni in London: Sketches of Life and Character,* sketches by Gavarni, with essays by Reach, Albert Smith, and others (London: Bogue, 1848-1849); republished as *Sketches of London Life and Character* (London: Dean, 1858).

A prolific journalist who wrote for some of the leading periodicals of his day, Angus Reach turned his hand as well to several other genres, including the mystery novel. His romance *Clement Lorimer* (1849) is illustrative of the difficulties mystery writers faced before the rise of the detective in British fiction.

Born in Inverness, Angus Bethune Reach was educated at the Inverness Royal Academy and Edinburgh University, where he began his journalistic career by writing articles for the *Inverness Courier.* At the age of twenty-one he went to London to help his father scratch out a living for them. His father, Roderick Reach, a solicitor and onetime proprietor of the *Inverness Courier,* had encountered financial difficulties and later became the London correspondent for the newspaper he had once run, a position that the son assumed on his father's death in 1853.

With the help of Charles Mackay, a Scottish poet and an editor at the influential London *Morning Chronicle,* young Reach secured occasional free-

Illustrations by George Cruikshank for Clement Lorimer

lance employment and eventually a position on the *Morning Chronicle,* covering first the central criminal court and later the House of Commons. Hardworking and punctual, Reach made good at the *Chronicle,* eventually becoming their music and art critic. His series of articles on labor and the poor in northern England, published in the *Chronicle* during October and November 1849, was highly regarded and was published as a book in 1972. A similar investigation into labor practices in the vineyards of southern France, commissioned for serialization in the *Chronicle* in 1850, was republished as *Claret and Olives* (1852). According to Mackay, Reach "introduced a style till then unpractised" in journalism, "except in the editorial articles, by means of which he brought before the reader's mind a vivid picture, such as a novelist would paint, of every occurrence that passed under his eye–rapid, correct, graphic, and full of life and animation." This "immense advance upon the old reporting style ... immediately found imitators in other journals."

Reach was employed by the *Chronicle* throughout his working life, also writing for the *Sunday Times,* the *Illustrated London News, Bentley's Miscellany,* and many other newspapers and magazines. His "operatic bagatelle" *Jenny Lind at Last* was produced in London in 1847. The same year his social satires *The Natural History of "Bores"* and *The Natural History of Humbugs* appeared as part of David Bogue's Social Zoologies series, and in 1848 Bogue published Reach's *The Comic Bradshaw.* In 1847 Reach joined his friend Albert Smith, a writer embittered by his experiences on the staff of *Punch,* in editing the *Man in the Moon,* one of the most successful rivals of the famous humor magazine. Despite the satires on *Punch* in the *Man in the Moon,* Reach and his friend Shirley Brooks, another contributor to both the *Morning Chronicle* and the *Man in the Moon,* managed to get on the staff of *Punch* in 1849 after the *Man in the Moon* folded in mid year. Reach then found himself subject to the barbs of one of the reigning wits of *Punch,* Douglas Jerrold (an enemy of Smith's), who delighted in teasing Reach on his insistence that his name be pronounced as a disyllable. Typical of Jerrold's nettling was his question one night at a *Punch* dinner: "Mr. Re-ack, may I pass you a pe-ack?"

During these years Reach also found time to write several novels and to appear frequently at playhouses and supper rooms where literary men gathered; Edmund Yates recalled seeing the "earnest-faced long-haired young man" at French plays. To do so much Reach maintained an exhausting schedule. George Augustus Sala recorded that he and Reach frequently dined together "at half-past two in his rooms in Tavistock Street, Covent Garden, and punctually at a quarter to four he would go to the House to slave at reporting and transcribing his notes until perhaps two in the morning; but he was at his desk again on the morrow at nine, and did not rise therefrom until dinner-time." The taxing schedule Reach set himself in an effort to maintain his parents and, eventually, his wife resulted at last in a mental breakdown. In 1854 he became unable to work. Hoping for his recovery, the *Morning Chronicle* continued his salary for some months. When those payments stopped Shirley Brooks arranged to take on all his friend's work for the paper on the condition that Reach's paychecks be continued–an arrangement that lasted almost a year. Reach's wife established a stationery shop, but, in spite of the patronage of friends, the enterprise failed. When it became clear that Reach would not recover, his friends in the Fielding Club put on a burlesque for his benefit. Staged on 31 March 1855, Albert Smith's pantomime *Harlequin Guy Fawkes* helped Reach financially, but his friends could do nothing to restore his health. He died on 25 November 1856.

Reach's breakdown at the age of thirty-three seems less surprising when one considers that during the previous six years he had not only supplemented his work on the *Morning Chronicle* and *Punch* with free-lance articles but had also produced four works of fiction. Only one of these is a standard mystery novel, but the others incorporate several of the characteristic themes of mystery fiction, including crime and the supernatural.

Reach's first volume of fiction, *A Romance of a Mince-Pie,* appeared in 1848 with twenty-seven illustrations by Phiz (H. K. Browne), who also illustrated Charles Dickens's books. A crime story without a crime, this ghoulish fable alternately amuses and horrifies. It concerns the dilemma of a good-natured pastry cook, John Chirrup, whose plan to poison his nefarious neighbor's equally nefarious dog goes amiss when the pie prepared for the purpose is stolen. A series of misunderstandings and thefts brings the plot full circle, so that only the intended victim ends up dead– but meanwhile Chirrup is arrested, after an unsuccessful suicide attempt, on the strength of his vague confession to murder. Chirrup's release when his niece notices that no one has produced a victim adds to the comedy, of course, but it also reflects the emerging importance of evidence over accusation, which had been the basis of most convictions in the eighteenth and early nineteenth centuries.

Set in the town of Forty-winks and featuring characters with names such as Snitch and Fuzz, the tale is lighthearted and frankly unrealistic at the outset, but it ends as a moral exemplum. The last-minute didacticism may have been a way to make the grisly tale acceptable to the parents of the children who were the book's chief audience, or *A Romance of a Mince-Pie* may simply be the first example of Reach's perennial difficulty in maintaining his original conception throughout a sustained piece of writing.

The obituary for Reach in the *Inverness Courier* (4 December 1856) speculates that Reach's facility of composition, which allowed him to dash off "readable, even instructive, papers on almost any subject," also prevented him from achieving much success in writing of a less ephemeral order. The structural flaws of *Clement Lorimer* (published in six parts, October 1848-March 1849), Reach's only mystery for an adult audience, suggest that the *Courier* analysis is accurate.

The novel is filled with promising beginnings that lead nowhere. In the first two-thirds of the volume almost every chapter begins with a detailed description of a new setting, establishes a new plot line, and introduces new characters. Some of these characters never reappear, and some turn up again only long enough to fulfill minor functions in the plot. A detailed introduction of the entire Dumple family, for instance, serves only to establish the availability of Gill Dumple to run a couple of errands for the principal characters later in the story. Characters who do remain prominent in the plot are subject to drastic changes over the course of the novel. The loss of a horse race on which he had staked his fortune suddenly transforms the title character not just from a rich man to a poor man but from a "thoroughly dissipated, thoroughly extravagant, thoroughly selfish" man-about-town to a brave, faithful, resolute hero.

Some of the flaws of *Clement Lorimer* may be excused by the lack of models for a novel with a prominent detection theme. Gothic romances had featured characters enmeshed in mysterious situations, but those characters do not attempt to solve the mysteries. In Charlotte Brontë's 1847 novel, for example, Jane Eyre finally learns the se-

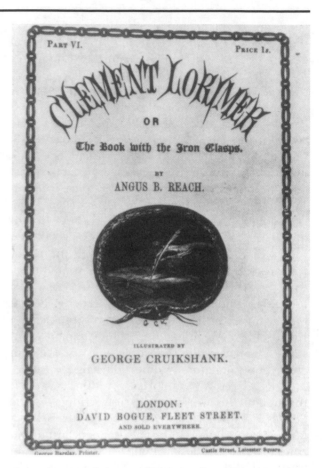

Cover for one of the monthly parts of Reach's only mystery novel for adults, in which the long-sought-after secret in "The Book with the Iron Clasps" is never revealed because the book is accidentally set afire just as it is about to be opened

cret of the madwoman in the attic not through deductive reasoning or the gathering of evidence but through a timely revelation. In contrast Lorimer determines to solve the mystery of his past—in short, to play detective—as soon as he recognizes that he is the victim of "a dark complot."

That complot is dark indeed. In the seventeenth century an old Italian named Raphael Benosa had declared a secret vendetta against Stephen Vanderstein and all his family. Benosa told his son that only when his descendants had annihilated the Vandersteins, whom they must poison in spirit as well as in flesh, might the Book with the Iron Clasps be opened to reveal the wrong that inspired the vendetta. Two centuries later the last Benosa marries the woman he believes to be the last Vanderstein but poisons her only after she has had his child. Thus his own son, renamed Clement Lorimer, is marked as his final victim. Sending his son to be raised apart from him, Benosa secretly supplies Lorimer with a fortune for the purpose of making him dependent and weak of character, so that the collapse of that fortune will destroy him. When Lorimer loses his money his determination to find out who is engineering his doom poses a problem for Reach. Professional detectives, though occasionally featured in fictionalized memoirs, were unknown in ordinary novels; indeed, they were little known in real life, since the detective department of the Metropolitan Police (Scotland Yard) had not been established until 1842. Thus Lorimer does not call for professional help, though he does once threaten Harry Trumps, Benosa's tool, with the "sleuth hounds of the law" (according to Chris Steinbrunner and Otto Penzler's *Encyclopedia of Mystery and Detection,* the first application of this phrase to detectives). Lacking a single detective figure, Reach is forced to develop various unrelated plot lines, including those involving a journalist in need of a story, a dishonest jockey and his duped son, the two wives of a bigamist, and a young woman Lorimer rescues from drowning who turns out to be the descendant of an underground branch of the Vandersteins. The detective function is divided among these characters and others, each of whom provides a different key to the mystery. The proliferating plot lines prevent Reach from establishing a point-of-view character, and the action is so fragmented that the reader would be overly confused if forced to view each facet of the mystery from the outside. So Reach lets his reader in on all the secrets, effectively eliminating the joys of deduction and discovery. Even the one secret kept from the reader, the nature of the wrong recorded in the Book with the Iron Clasps, is a disappointment. At the moment of imminent revelation the book is accidentally set afire.

In his last two works of fiction Reach abandoned the mystery genre and tried to circumvent his problems with sustaining a narrative. *A Story with a Vengeance* (1852), written in collaboration with Shirley Brooks, adopts a highly unusual form that actually demands some inconsistency from chapter to chapter. To while away their journey eight railway travelers each agree to tell a single story, each picking up the tale where the previous teller left off. As each traveler imposes his own interests on the original situation the tale becomes increasingly disjointed and bizarre. The many elements of potential mystery—disappearances, false identity, crime—get lost in the tale's comic anarchy.

For his longest novel, the two-volume *Leonard Lindsay* (1850), Reach found a form suitable to his bent for quick sketches: the picaresque adventure. By announcing in the preface that *Leonard Lindsay* was "an unpretending and plotless story of personal adventure, constructed expressly in order to throw full light upon the Buccaneers," Reach absolved himself from the necessity of providing either depth of character or a sustained plot. By setting his tale in the West Indies, he created plenty of opportunities to put his descriptive powers to work.

Among the novel's many episodes are several mysterious tales. Two of these, a story and a poem, are the English and Spanish legends about the origin of a mysterious light that periodically appears on ships. A fully developed ghost story, "The Legend of Foul-Weather Don," appears as one of the tales the buccaneers tell for their own amusement at night around the fire. In it, a sailor, cursed by the phantom of a cruel Spanish captain to be followed everywhere by sharks, escapes the curse by locating the captain's lost treasure. This chapter-long story is unified in structure and tone, but when Reach tries to maintain a tale of mystery for a longer time he is less successful. A longer episode opens with an intriguing figure, a dwarf pilot who unaccountably turns up in the middle of the sea in a canoe with an offer to guide the buccaneers' ship off a shoal. Eerie and almost demonic in the initial chapter, the dwarf is revealed later in the episode to be a rather prosaic treasure hunter.

Reach's novels were popular enough to go through several editions in his own era, but none has been reprinted since 1924. Although his mysteries seem crude in comparison with those that appeared even slightly later, notably Charles Dickens's and Wilkie Collins's novels of the 1850s and 1860s, they retain historical interest as examples of the predetective novel of detection.

References:

Charles Mackay, *Forty Years' Recollections of Life, Literature, and Public Affairs from 1830 to 1870,* 2 volumes (London: Chapman & Hall, 1877), I: 148-157;

George Augustus Sala, *The Life and Adventures of George Augustus Sala,* 2 volumes (New York: Scribners, 1895), I: 166-167;

M. H. Spielmann, *The History of "Punch"* (New York: Cassell, 1895).

Sax Rohmer
(Arthur Henry Sarsfield Ward)
(15 February 1883-1 June 1959)

Will Murray

BOOKS: *Pause!*, anonymous (London: Greening, 1910);

The Mystery of Dr. Fu-Manchu (London: Methuen, 1913); republished as *The Insidious Dr. Fu-Manchu* (New York: McBride, Nast, 1913);

The Sins of Séverac Bablon (London: Cassell, 1914);

The Romance of Sorcery (London: Methuen, 1914; New York: Dutton, 1915);

The Yellow Claw (New York: McBride, Nast, 1915; London: Methuen, 1915);

The Devil Doctor (London: Methuen, 1916); republished as *The Return of Dr. Fu-Manchu* (New York: McBride, 1916);

The Exploits of Captain O'Hagan (London: Jarrolds, 1916);

The Si-Fan Mysteries (London: Methuen, 1917); republished as *The Hand of Fu-Manchu* (New York: McBride, 1917);

Brood of the Witch-Queen (London: Pearson, 1918; Garden City: Doubleday, Page, 1924);

Tales of Secret Egypt (London: Methuen, 1918; New York: McBride, 1919);

The Orchard of Tears (London: Methuen, 1918);

The Quest of the Sacred Slipper (London: Pearson, 1919; Garden City: Doubleday, Page, 1919);

Dope: A Story of Chinatown and the Drug Traffic (London: Cassell, 1919; New York: McBride, 1919);

The Golden Scorpion (London: Methuen, 1919; New York: McBride, 1920);

The Dream Detective, Being Some Account of the Methods of Moris Klaw (London: Jarrolds, 1920; Garden City: Doubleday, Page, 1925);

The Green Eyes of Bâst (London: Cassell, 1920; New York: McBride, 1920);

The Haunting of Low Fennel (London: Pearson, 1920);

Bat-Wing (London: Cassell, 1921; Garden City & Toronto: Doubleday, Page, 1921);

Fire-Tongue (London: Cassell, 1921; Garden City & Toronto: Doubleday, Page, 1922);

Tales of Chinatown (London: Cassell, 1922; Garden City: Doubleday, Page, 1922);

Grey Face (London: Cassell, 1924; Garden City: Doubleday, Page, 1924);

Yellow Shadows (London: Cassell, 1925; Garden City: Doubleday, Page, 1926);

Moon of Madness (Garden City: Doubleday, Page, 1927; London: Cassell, 1927);

She Who Sleeps (Garden City: Doubleday, Doran, 1928; London: Cassell, 1928);

The Emperor of America (Garden City: Doubleday, Doran, for the Crime Club, 1929; London: Cassell, 1929);

The Day the World Ended (Garden City: Doubleday, Doran, for the Crime Club, 1930; London: Cassell, 1930);

Daughter of Fu Manchu (Garden City: Doubleday, Doran, 1931; London: Cassell, 1931);

Yu'an Hee See Laughs (Garden City: Doubleday, Doran, for the Crime Club, 1932; London: Cassell, 1932);

Tales of East and West (London: Cassell, 1932); republished with different contents (Garden City: Doubleday, Doran, for the Crime Club, 1933);

The Mask of Fu Manchu (Garden City: Doubleday, Doran, for the Crime Club, 1932; London: Cassell, 1933);

Fu Manchu's Bride (Garden City: Doubleday, Doran, for the Crime Club, 1933); republished as *The Bride of Fu Manchu* (London: Cassell, 1933);

The Trail of Fu Manchu (Garden City: Doubleday, Doran, for the Crime Club, 1934; London: Cassell, 1934);

The Bat Flies Low (Garden City: Doubleday, Doran, for the Crime Club, 1935; London: Cassell, 1935);

President Fu Manchu (Garden City: Doubleday, Doran, for the Crime Club, 1936; London: Cassell, 1936);

White Velvet (Garden City: Doubleday, Doran, 1936; London: Cassell, 1936);

Sax Rohmer

Salute to Bazarada and Other Stories (London: Cassell, 1939);

The Drums of Fu Manchu (Garden City: Doubleday, Doran, for the Crime Club, 1939; London: Cassell, 1939);

The Island of Fu Manchu (New York: Doubleday, Doran, for the Crime Club, 1941; London: Cassell, 1941);

Seven Sins (New York: McBride, 1943; London: Cassell, 1944);

Egyptian Nights (London: Hale, 1944); republished as *Bimbâshi Barûk of Egypt* (New York: McBride, 1944);

Shadow of Fu Manchu (Garden City: Doubleday, for the Crime Club, 1948; London: Jenkins, 1949);

Hangover House (New York: Random House, 1949; London: Jenkins, 1950);

Nude in Mink (New York: Fawcett, 1950); republished as *Sins of Sumuru* (London: Jenkins, 1950);

Wulfheim, as Michael Furey (London: Jarrolds, 1950);

Sumuru (New York: Fawcett, 1951); republished as *Slaves of Sumuru* (London: Jenkins, 1952);

The Fire Goddess (New York: Fawcett, 1952); republished as *Virgin in Flames* (London: Jenkins, 1953);

The Moon is Red (London: Jenkins, 1954);

Return of Sumuru (New York: Fawcett, 1954); republished as *Sand and Satin* (London: Jenkins, 1955);

Sinister Madonna (London: Jenkins, 1956; New York: Fawcett, 1956);

Re-Enter Fu Manchu (Greenwich, Conn.: Fawcett, 1957); republished as *Re-Enter Dr. Fu Manchu* (London: Jenkins, 1957);

Emperor Fu Manchu (London: Jenkins, 1959; Greenwich, Conn.: Fawcett, 1959);

The Secret of Holm Peel and Other Strange Stories (New York: Ace, 1970);

The Wrath of Fu Manchu and Other Stories (London: Stacey, 1973; New York: DAW, 1976).

PLAY PRODUCTIONS: *Round in Fifty,* by Rohmer and Julian and Lauri Wylie, Cardiff, Empire Theatre, 6 March 1922; London, Hippodrome, 16 March 1922;

The Eye of Siva, London, New Theatre, 8 August 1923;

Secret Egypt, London, Q Theatre, 4 August 1928;

Rohmer and his wife, Elizabeth, shortly after their secret marriage in 1909 (Cay Van Ash and Elizabeth Sax Rohmer, Master of Villainy, *1972)*

The Nightingale, by Rohmer and Michael Martin-Harvey, London, Princess Theatre, 15 July 1947.

OTHER: Harry Relph, *Little Tich: A Book of Travels and Wanderings,* ghostwritten by Rohmer (London: Greening, 1911).

Sax Rohmer, one of the most popular and influential thriller writers of the first half of the twentieth century, owes his continued renown principally to the international popularity of the character of Dr. Fu Manchu, whom he created in 1911.

Born Arthur Henry Ward in Birmingham, England, Rohmer was the son of Irish parents, William and Margaret Mary Furey Ward. The family moved to South London when Rohmer was two or three. There are no records of his formal schooling, which ended in 1901, the same year his mother, an alcoholic, died. At about this time he took the middle name Sarsfield, and, having failed a civil-service examination, he went to work briefly as a bank clerk. After leaving that job he made his first attempt at writing short sto-

ries, which were rejected by all the popular magazines, while toiling at several minor business positions. His short tenure as a cub reporter with the *Commercial Intelligence,* a weekly newspaper, was colorful but not suited to either his temperament or his interests, which included Egyptology, Islamic culture, and the Orient. Rohmer, who belonged to an occult society known as the Hermetic Order of the Golden Dawn (and possibly the Rosicrucians as well), also maintained a lifelong interest in the occult, which was prompted by personal experiences that he perceived as evidence of psychic phenomena.

In 1903, just twenty years old, Rohmer's attempts to market his fiction resulted in the acceptances of "The Mysterious Mummy" by *Pearson's Magazine* (which appears not to have published the story) and "The Leopard-Couch" by *Chambers's Journal* (which included it in the 30 January 1904 issue). Both stories were steeped in mysticism and showed evidence of Rohmer's interest in Egyptology. Over the next several years Rohmer wrote a variety of stories for British magazines under his original byline, A. Sarsfield Ward, while writing newspaper articles anony-

Illustration by W. W. Dewar for Rohmer's The Dream Detective *(1920), a collection of stories about Moris Klaw, who solves crimes by sleeping at their scenes and reconstructing them in his dreams*

mously and involving himself in the theater as an agent and a sketch and song-lyric writer. Around 1905, when one of his short stories, "The McVillin," prompted the editor of *Pearson's Magazine* to offer Rohmer a contract for a series of stories, Rohmer was stricken by a severe case of writer's block and took a voyage to Holland. Upon his return he had a new pen name, Sax Rohmer, which he did not use exclusively until 1912. As he explained in a 1947 *New Yorker* interview, "In ancient Saxon, 'sax' means 'blade'; 'rohmer' equals 'roamer.' I substituted an 'h' for the 'a' as a gesture in the direction of phonetics–pretty obscure gesture, I guess." Rohmer came to use this name even in his personal life.

On 14 January 1909 Rohmer married Rose Elizabeth Knox, but, because Rohmer's income was both modest and erratic, they kept the marriage secret and lived apart for nearly two years

until they bought a house in the Herne Hill section of London with the help of Rohmer's father, who settled there with them. Rohmer's first book, *Pause!*, a collection of sketches conceived by comedian George Robey and written by Rohmer, was published anonymously in 1910. Many of the stories Rohmer produced at this time were written to suit cover illustrations that magazines commissioned before they found authors to write stories to go with them. Rohmer was also ghostwriter for *Little Tich: A Book of Travels and Wanderings* (1911), the autobiography of another comedian, Harry Relph.

Work on Relph's autobiography interrupted a series of ten short stories he was writing for the *Story-Teller*, which ran them in the October 1912-July 1913 issues. Published as a novel, *The Mystery of Dr. Fu-Manchu*, in June 1913, the stories brought Rohmer immediate popular and financial success. (The novel was published in the United States in 1913 as *The Insidious Dr. Fu-Manchu*.) In later years Rohmer gave several quite different accounts of how he came to create his most memorable character (whose name lost its hyphen in later books). In the version reported by Cay Van Ash and Elizabeth Sax Rohmer in *Master of Villainy: A Biography of Sax Rohmer* (1972), Rohmer heard about the prototype for Dr. Fu Manchu in 1911 while researching an article he had been commissioned to write about Limehouse, London's Chinatown district. He had heard about a mysterious Chinese man called Mr. King, who was reputed to be involved in gambling and narcotics traffic and backed by a large international syndicate. After many attempts to learn more about the man, Rohmer convinced a Limehouse merchant to tell him where he could catch a glimpse of King. Rohmer waited in an alley one foggy night and finally saw a "tall, dignified Chinese, wearing a fur-collared overcoat and a fur cap," getting out of a limousine and going into a building. As he said later, he saw a man whose "face was the living embodiment of Satan," and, "in that instant my imaginary monster came to life."

Because of their magazine-serial origins the first three Fu Manchu novels are extremely episodic. (*The Mystery of Dr. Fu-Manchu* was followed by *The Devil Doctor* in 1916 and *The Si-Fan Mysteries* in 1917; both were republished in the United States with Fu-Manchu's name in their titles.) Whatever the weaknesses of construction, the novels' characters make them–and all subsequent books in the series–memorable. The books are,

Rohmer in his study at Lovelands Way, the country house that the Rohmers had built about 1930 (Cay Van Ash and Elizabeth Sax Rohmer, Master of Villainy, *1972)*

in essence, an extended narrative of two adversaries, Dr. Fu Manchu and Denis Nayland Smith. When introduced, Fu Manchu is the agent of a Chinese secret society with sinister political aims, and Nayland Smith, his nemesis and pursuer, is an agent of the British government. Over the years, as Fu Manchu becomes head of the Si-Fan and Nayland Smith is knighted, their relationship remains bitter but always mutually respectful. Nayland Smith's description of the Devil Doctor (as he is often termed) in the first novel reflects something akin to awe: "Imagine a person, tall, lean and feline, high-shouldered, with a brow like Shakespeare and a face like Satan, a close-shaven skull, and long, magnetic eyes of the true cat-green. Invest him with all the cruel cunning of an entire Eastern race, accumulated in one giant intellect, with all the resources, if you will, of a wealthy government–which, however, already has denied all knowledge of his existence. Imagine that awful being, and you have a mental picture of Dr. Fu-Manchu, the yellow peril incarnate in one man."

Although Nayland Smith is the hero of the series and Rohmer kept his villain, Fu Manchu, in the background–concentrating instead on the attempts of Nayland Smith and others to frustrate Fu Manchu's agents in their aims–Fu Manchu, who takes center stage only two or three times per novel, dominates the series. Rohmer was not the first writer to focus upon a criminal in a series, nor was he the first to capitalize on public perception of the so-called Yellow Peril by creating a sinister Chinese mastermind; but Rohmer produced unforgettable results, as witnessed by the fact that his Fu Manchu stories have remained in print. Part of their popularity may be due to the fact that they are dated, much in the manner of Arthur Conan Doyle's Sherlock Holmes stories, which they more than casually resemble. In many ways the series is a variation on the Sherlock Holmes stories, with Nayland Smith as a Holmes counterpart nearly as idiosyncratic as the great detective himself, but with Dr. Fu Manchu playing the Dr. Moriarity role so successfully that antagonist clearly overshadows protagonist–a dominance Rohmer created by characterizing Fu Manchu as a genius, a man of his word, and, his cruel methods aside, strangely sympathetic. A variety of characters play Watson to Smith's Holmes; the first, Dr. Petrie, is the narrator of the first four Fu Manchu novels.

The Devil Doctor (published in the United States as *The Return of Dr. Fu-Manchu*, 1916) and *The Si-Fan Mysteries* (published in the United States as *The Hand of Fu-Manchu*, 1917) continue to detail Fu Manchu's campaign against enemies of his new China on British soil. Nayland Smith and Petrie invariably win the skirmishes, in spite of Fu Manchu's superior resources (which include all manner of venomous creatures, human and otherwise). At the conclusion of *The Si-Fan Mysteries* Fu Manchu evidently dies after failing in his bid to take over the Si-Fan. After having been compelled by the success of *The Mystery of Dr. Fu-Manchu* to write a second novel about the Devil Doctor in 1914-1915 and a third in 1916, Rohmer hoped to rid himself of Fu Manchu, just as Conan Doyle had tried to kill off Sherlock Holmes.

A year after the publication of the first Fu Manchu novel, *The Sins of Séverac Bablon* (1914), which he had written in 1912 at the same time as the early Fu Manchu episodes, appeared in book form. Séverac Bablon is a mystery man, a descendant of Jewish royalty who, as a sort of unacknowledged leader of the Jewish people, takes it upon himself to discipline Jews whose behavior discredits their heritage. While Bablon is a fascinating figure, the novel has never been popular.

In 1913, with fifty pounds earned from the book publication of *The Mystery of Dr. Fu-Manchu*, Rohmer and his wife visited Egypt, which inspired one of his best works, *Brood of the Witch-Queen* (1918), which he wrote upon his return to England, but not until he had finished his only nonfiction book, *The Romance of Sorcery* (1914), a history of the occult and its chief practitioners. Serialized in the *Premier* magazine beginning in May 1914, *Brood of the Witch-Queen* is also deeply concerned with sorcery: Anthony Ferrara, a student of the occult, learns the secrets of ancient Egyptian wizardry and uses them for evil. Although Ferrara commands action from disembodied hands and fire elementals, among other forces, Rohmer claimed in a prefatory note to the novel that "In no case do the powers attributed to him exceed those which are claimed for a fully equipped Adept." For all its improbabilities and impossibilities, *Brood of the Witch-Queen* is a striking novel, and undoubtedly much of its power and convincingness derive from the author's own belief in the supernatural. Rohmer's Egyptian visit also resulted in his first short-story collection, *Tales of Secret Egypt* (1918). For the most part Rohmer's

short stories do not come up to the level of his novels, and *Tales of Secret Egypt* is no exception.

Life in Limehouse intrigued Rohmer, and he would popularize the Chinatowns of Britain and the United States as places of mystery and danger in many of his later books, not all of them concerning Fu Manchu. Written during the first year of World War I, Rohmer's *The Yellow Claw* (1915) concerns narcotics traffic emanating from Limehouse. The novel's villain is not named Fu Manchu but is instead named after the Devil Doctor's inspiration, Mr. King. The novel also introduces Gaston Max of the Paris police, who figures in later books by Rohmer. In 1915 Rohmer entered officers training with the Artists' Rifles. He was assigned to military intelligence, but after he was hospitalized for the recurrence of lung problems he had had as a child, he was invalided out in early 1917.

Rohmer's next book, *The Orchard of Tears* (1918), is neither a thriller nor a mystery but the story of a seeker after religious truth, Paul Mario. Because it was not typical of the public conception of a Sax Rohmer book, it did not do well, but it is of interest because it reflects many of Rohmer's personal attitudes, especially about religion. Earlier Rohmer had departed from writing melodramatic popular novels with *The Exploits of Captain O'Hagan* (1916), which proved unsuccessful and is now sought after only by collectors of Rohmer's books.

The year 1919 saw the publication of three new novels, all of which met with favorable response from his readers: *The Quest of the Sacred Slipper*, *Dope: A Story of Chinatown and the Drug Traffic* and *The Golden Scorpion*. Rohmer's popularity was growing, and late in that year he made the first of several trips to the United States, where he met with his American publishers. He made important contacts (a friendship with the magician Harry Houdini developed) and learned something of the lives and interests of his American audience.

In *The Quest of the Sacred Slipper*, which was serialized before the war in *Short Stories* magazine (November 1913-June 1914), Hassan of Aleppo comes to England to retrieve the stolen slipper of the Prophet Mohammed in spite of the efforts of an American criminal and Scotland Yard to prevent him. Completed in fall 1918, *Dope* introduces the pugnacious Chief Inspector Red Kerry of the C.I.D. Kerry, a delightfully down-to-earth investigator pitted against Chinese drug trafficking, reportedly had a real-life counterpart, an In-

Dust jacket for the first British edition of Rohmer's 1939 novel, in which Fu Manchu plots the assassinations of several European heads of state, including Rudolph Adlon, who is clearly recognizable as Adolf Hitler (courtesy of Otto Penzler)

spector Yeo, whom Rohmer had met in 1911. *The Golden Scorpion* brings back Gaston Max and pits him against a new Chinese villain, Fo-Hi, or the "Scorpion," who, after the apparent demise of Fu Manchu, has taken control of the Si-Fan. Though he is not named, Fu Manchu makes an unmistakable appearance in this novel, an indication that Rohmer had decided to revive that character.

The Dream Detective, Being Some Account of the Methods of Moris Klaw (1920) is the only one of Rohmer's short-story collections which can be favorably compared to his novels. The ten stories deal with Moris Klaw, the "dream detective" of the title, who is an eccentric character noted for his frequent spraying of his large forehead with verbena perfume. Possessing the ability to absorb psychic impressions of his surroundings, Klaw is able, by sleeping in the scene of a crime, to dream the crime as it happened, which naturally

leads to the apprehension of the perpetrator. After Rohmer's return from the United States and a trip to the south of France with his wife, he had moved with his wife and father to a house in the fashionable Mayfair district of London. Certain occurrences led them to believe the house might be haunted, and Rohmer's imagination was triggered to write *The Green Eyes of Bâst* (1920), which concerns a mysterious woman, Nahémah, whose feline characteristics have a supernatural origin. Less a thriller than a novel of the occult, it is neither Rohmer's best nor worst book.

Fire-Tongue (1921), Rohmer's next novel, also had an unusual background. Having signed a contract to write a mystery story for *Collier's Weekly*, Rohmer set up the murder of a well-known medical consultant and in his opening chapters eliminated any possible solution he thought the reader might imagine; then, however, he found that he could not solve the crime either. He notified his agent that he had abandoned the story and would send *Collier's* a different mystery story but learned that the agent had given the opening chapters to the *Collier's* editors and that they had already published the first installment. Sailing to the United States, Rohmer continued the novel, which introduces London private investigator Paul Harley and deals with the mystery surrounding an Indian cult whose head is known only as Fire-Tongue. It was the magician Houdini who, aware of Rohmer's plight, suggested the solution which enabled the novel to be successfully completed. This experience cooled Rohmer's creative fires for a time. The novel *Bat-Wing* (1921), which he had written for *Collier's* when he had decided he was unable to complete *Fire-Tongue*, is another Paul Harley story, a more traditional mystery novel than any book Rohmer had attempted until that time. Like *Fire-Tongue*, *Bat-Wing* concerns a cult, in this case voodoo worshipers whom a Cuban expatriate believes have pursued him to England.

For a period of three years Rohmer confined his activities to work on short fiction and plays. With Julian and Lauri Wylie he wrote *Round in Fifty*, a musical spoof on Jules Verne's *Around the World in Eighty Days* (1873), which starred George Robey and, opening on 16 March 1922 in London, enjoyed a run of 471 performances. In 1923 he wrote *The Eye of Siva*, a moderately successful melodrama in which Paul Harley was the protagonist. At about this time a film based on *The Yellow Claw* was completed in the

United States by the Stoll production company; Rohmer had no part in writing the scenario. During this period two more short-story collections appeared: *The Haunting of Low Fennel* (1920), which includes some of Rohmer's early magazine cover stories as well as a story in which Nayland Smith appears without Fu Manchu; and *Tales of Chinatown* (1922), containing several short stories featuring Paul Harley or Red Kerry.

Grey Face (1924) signaled Rohmer's return to the novel, which was no longer constrained by earlier serialization fashions with magazines requiring each episode of a serialized novel to be a complete story in itself. Rohmer could now write each new novel as a whole, and as a result *Grey Face* is an extraordinarily complicated account of a man who discovers the secrets of the magician Cagliostro and the terrible consequences of his experiments. Thematically similar to *Brood of the Witch-Queen*, *Grey Face* ranks as one of Rohmer's best works, and he settled into a steady routine of producing one novel per year. His next was *Yellow Shadows* (1925), the last Limehouse novel to feature Red Kerry.

Moon of Madness (1927) is atypical of Rohmer's fiction. While outwardly a novel of intrigue, it is at heart a romance about the love of an older man, Maj. Edmond O'Shea, for a teenage girl, Nanette, and the difficulties of their unorthodox relationship. Semi-autobiographical, it is based upon Rohmer's brief affair with an eighteen-year-old girl during a vacation in Funchal, Madeira. While not a great success with his popular audience, *Moon of Madness* stands as one of Rohmer's sharper narratives, proving that his talents were not limited to the occult or the melodramatic.

More typical of Rohmer's work, *She Who Sleeps* (1928) is set partly in Egypt and partly in the United States, where Rohmer had spent six months after his affair in Madeira had brought estrangement from his wife. A story about the resurrection of an Egyptian princess, Zalithea, and the twentieth-century man who falls in love with her, the novel is intriguing but ultimately unsatisfying.

Not long after Rohmer completed this novel, *Collier's* magazine offered a contract for a new novel featuring Fu Manchu, whom their editors had decided was due for a revival. Returning to America, this time with his wife, Rohmer began to write a Fu Manchu novel but stopped work on it to produce the exciting novel *The Emperor of America* (1929), his first novel set entirely in the United States. Although Rohmer considered the book hackwork, American readers responded favorably to this story of navy Comdr. Drake Roscoe's battle with the self-styled Emperor of America, whose criminal network holds the country in thrall. The Rohmers returned to England, and *Daughter of Fu Manchu* (1931) was not completed for three more years.

In 1928 Rohmer wrote another stage play, *Secret Egypt,* which proved less successful than his earlier theatrical ventures, and another Gaston Max adventure, *The Day the World Ended* (1930). Set in Germany and inspired by a visit to the Black Forest, this rather fantastic story pits Max against Anubis, a dwarfish Fu Manchu type, whose chief ambition is to destroy the world by sound waves.

Daughter of Fu Manchu brought the Devil Doctor back. His earlier Fu Manchu books continued through numerous editions; there had been two-reel silent films based on the Fu Manchu novels; and in 1929 the first of several Fu Manchu sound films was completed. These films brought Rohmer's character to a larger audience, creating an even greater demand for new Fu Manchu novels, to which Rohmer acquiesced, somewhat unwillingly. *Daughter of Fu Manchu* concerns the reactivation of the Si-Fan by Fu Manchu's Eurasian daughter Fah Lo Suee. Nayland Smith, Dr. Petrie, and narrator Shan Greville find themselves allied with their old adversary Fu Manchu (who does not appear until the novel's conclusion) in their ironic campaign to thwart Fah Lo Suee.

The proceeds from Rohmer's writing and film rights enabled the Rohmers to build a country house, Lovelands Way, outside Reigate, about an hour from London. While the house was being completed they spent three months touring the Middle East, which served as the setting for Rohmer's next two novels, *Yu'an Hee See Laughs* and *The Mask of Fu Manchu,* both published in 1932.

Hoping to convince his public to forget Fu Manchu, Rohmer created a new Chinese villain for *Yu'an Hee See Laughs.* Head of Middle Eastern slave traffic, Yu'an Hee See is more realistically portrayed than Fu Manchu. Rohmer considered *Yu'an Hee See Laughs* to be one of his best books, but Yu'an Hee See proved unpopular and Rohmer wrote no sequels.

The Mask of Fu Manchu deals with Fu Manchu's attempt to stir up the Middle East by passing himself off as El Mokanna, a long-dead

Shirley Eaton (center) as Sumuru in The Million Eyes of Su-Muru, *the 1967 American International film based on the novels about the female villain whom Rohmer had created for a BBC radio series in 1945, after the BBC rejected Rohmer's proposal for a series about Fu Manchu for fear of offending England's Chinese allies*

prophet of Islam. In fall 1932, while this novel was appearing serially in *Collier's,* the Rohmers visited the United States and Jamaica.

Rohmer's next novel, *Fu Manchu's Bride* (1933), is generally considered to be the best Fu Manchu book. Set on the French Riviera, which Rohmer visited frequently, it deals with Fu Manchu's attempt to sire an heir through selective mating with a white woman, Fleurette. One of the patterns in the Fu Manchu novels is the narrator's falling in love with Fu Manchu's female agent. This motif is most successful in *Fu Manchu's Bride,* in which narrator Alan Sterling falls in love with Fleurette, because it is the only Fu Manchu novel in which the woman in question is not indispensable to Fu Manchu's plans.

The Trail of Fu Manchu (1934) is set once again in Limehouse, where Fu Manchu has discovered a process of manufacturing gold. Having been expelled from the Si-Fan, he is in dire straits, cut off from his resources, and the elixir which has prolonged his life (Nayland Smith estimates his age at 160) has run out. Only Dr. Petrie can, and does, save his life.

Though they spent weekends at Lovelands Way, the Rohmers had kept the London flat at

Braemar House, where they had lived since the mid 1920s. In 1934 they decided to build a larger country house, near Gatton Park, as their home base and to rent a smaller flat in London. During the fifteen months that it took to build the large house that Rohmer modestly named Little Gatton, he wrote another narrative of ancient Egyptian science and sorcery loosed upon the modern world, *The Bat Flies Low* (1935). Inspired by Rohmer's third and most recent trip to Egypt, this novel involves the discovery of the fragment of the *Book of Thoth* that holds the key to a lost scientific secret, the Egyptians' method of storing sunlight. The plot is grounded in an American electric company's efforts to rediscover this formula for solar-powered lighting.

In May 1935, while their new house was being completed, the Rohmers went to New York, where Rohmer explored that city's Chinatown, the setting for his next novel, *President Fu Manchu* (1936), clearly written to please the American public. Fu Manchu's latest attempt to conquer the world involves taking control of the United States by insuring the election of his handpicked presidential candidate. Nayland Smith, now attached to the U.S. Secret Service, enlists the aid of a popular priest (based on Father Charles Coughlin) to prevent Harvey Bragg (modeled on Huey Long) from fulfilling Fu Manchu's dream. It is a compelling novel, but Rohmer professed little affection for it.

His next novel, *White Velvet* (1936), began the scenario for a Hollywood film that was to star Marlene Dietrich. Rohmer was invited to Hollywood to work on a final script, but he refused to go and the deal fell through. He then rewrote the scenario, which involved an Egyptian theatrical touring group, as both a novel and a BBC radio series.

After a break from novel writing Rohmer produced two. In *The Drums of Fu Manchu* (1939) the Devil Doctor plans the assassination of several heads of European nations, whose aims are at cross-purposes to his own, among them Rudolph Adlon, who is clearly meant to be recognized as Adolf Hitler. *The Island of Fu Manchu* (1941)—set in Haiti, where Rohmer had gone for background research in 1938—is the last of the classic Fu Manchu novels. It takes place during World War II, and voodooism, espionage, and the safety of the Panama Canal all figure prominently. This would be the final Fu Manchu novel for the duration of the war. Orientals like Fu Manchu offended England's Chinese allies, and paper rationing had reduced the number of markets for fiction. As he had during World War I, Rohmer worked for British military intelligence; the details of his activities are unknown.

Only two more Sax Rohmer books were published during World War II: *Seven Sins* (1943), a final Gaston Max adventure about Nazi agents in London; and *Egyptian Nights* (1944), a collection of short stories about the exploits of an Egyptian camel driver named Bimbâshi Barûk. Gaston Max had earlier been the main character in *Myself and Gaston Max*, a short-lived BBC radio series Rohmer adapted in 1942 from a group of uncollected stories about another character, whom Rohmer replaced with Max. In 1945 he wrote a series of eight radio plays, *Shadow of Sumuru*, for the BBC. The shows featured a new character, a seemingly Eurasian female supercriminal, Sumuru, whom Rohmer created when plans to revive Fu Manchu met with a cool reaction from the BBC. Later Rohmer adapted these scripts into the first of a series of Sumuru novels. Faced with the difficulties of maintaining a large household during wartime, the Rohmers sold Little Gatton in 1944 and went to live in their London flat. After the war ended, Rohmer wrote two

plays, "The Body's Upstairs" and "The Shadow of Fu Manchu." Neither was produced. Rohmer then collaborated with Michael Martin-Harvey on *The Nightingale*, a play based on a Hans Christian Andersen fairy tale, which failed miserably when it opened in 1947.

Shortly after writing his Fu Manchu play and adapting his Sumuru scripts as a novel, Rohmer and his wife went to live in the United States, where, finding no one willing to produce his play about the Devil Doctor, he rewrote it as a novel. In 1948 *Shadow of Fu Manchu* was serialized in *Collier's* before its publication as a book later that year. Heartened by this success, Rohmer converted "The Body's Upstairs" into *Hangover House* (1949), a murder mystery that met with what may have been the worst critical response accorded any Rohmer book. At least one critic expressed the wish that the author would return to Fu Manchu as soon as possible. *Shadow of Fu Manchu* suffers from its dramatic origins; for practical reasons the setting had been limited to a few locations in Manhattan. Its plot revolves around the discovery by an American scientist, Dr. Morris Craig, of a destructive scientific secret. In this book Fu Manchu is now the archenemy of communism, which has taken over his beloved China and dashed his hopes of a rebirth for that nation.

In 1950 Rohmer found a publisher for his novelization of the Sumuru radio series, the American paperback house Fawcett Books, which was then opening up the market for the original paperback novel. They retitled the book *Nude in Mink* (1950), much to Rohmer's displeasure. Over the next six years there would be four more Fawcett paperback editions of novels featuring Sumuru: *Sumuru* (1951), *The Fire Goddess* (1952), *Return of Sumuru* (1954), and *Sinister Madonna* (1956). A beautiful female version of Fu Manchu, Sumuru has achieved wealth and power through a series of carefully chosen but passionless marriages, each of which has ended with the untimely demise of her husband. Not as charismatic as Fu Manchu, Sumuru has similar goals. As the head of a secret society known as the Order of Our Lady, Sumuru hopes to establish a worldwide matriarchy. She despises ugliness, which she considers a male trait, and barely tolerates men themselves. The novels, which were published in Great Britain in hardcover, are more sexually explicit than Rohmer's previous work because his American editors demanded such frankness. Rohmer, who was still living in the United States, felt that he could hardly refuse, although this interference rankled him. The Sumuru novels are second-rate, in some cases thematic recyclings of earlier, better, work. Unlike the Fu Manchu books, they contain no main protagonist in the mold of Nayland Smith, although the hero of *The Emperor of America*, Drake Roscoe, is a continuing character. Broken by Sumuru, he struggles back in the final Sumuru novel, *Sinister Madonna*, which ends on an uncertain note and with the promise of a sequel which was not to be.

While writing about Sumuru's adventures, Rohmer returned to the short-story form, mostly for a newspaper supplement, *This Week*. He also revived an unproduced, mystical play that he had written some twenty-five years earlier and converted it into a novel, *Wulfheim* (1950), which was published under the pen name Michael Furey. It did not have an American edition during his lifetime, nor did his American-based mystery novel *The Moon is Red* (1954), despite its many excellences.

At the end of his life Sax Rohmer was forced by financial circumstances to return to Fu Manchu, about whom he produced two final novels and four short stories. *Re-Enter Fu Manchu* (1957) continues the Devil Doctor's war against communism. Because Nayland Smith is also anticommunist, the adversarial relationship between the two has lost much of its fire. Of the four stories–all published in *This Week* and not collected in book form until 1973, long after Rohmer's death–"The Eyes of Fu Manchu," "The Word of Fu Manchu," and "The Mind of Fu Manchu" are extremely short and minor efforts. The novelette "Wrath of Fu Manchu" is noteworthy for the final appearance of Fah Lo Suee.

Emperor Fu Manchu (1959), published after Rohmer's return to live in London and shortly before his death, was his final novel. The only book about Fu Manchu that is set in China, it is the only novel Rohmer set in a place he had never visited and is something of a nostalgic exercise in which Fu Manchu and Nayland Smith reflect upon their long association and things that might have been. The novel ends appropriately. Fu Manchu may be dead, and Nayland Smith has fallen heir to a list of every Si-Fan member in China. As Nayland Smith says of this discovery, "It will shatter his dream empire!"

Early in 1959 Rohmer contracted Asiatic flu and suffered complications which ultimately led to his death in London on 1 June 1959. Reprintings of the Fu Manchu novels continue unabated. Sax Rohmer created in Fu Manchu a compelling, *living* being, one who has not been tarnished or cheapened by the imitations of lesser authors, by his transformation from an archetype into a stereotype by the popular mind, or by the forward march of history, which has dated the attitudes and situations in even the later books. Dr. Fu Manchu is an original creation in every sense, and, like Sherlock Holmes, Dracula, Tarzan, and a very few other popular characters, he has achieved a universal acceptance and popularity which will not be forgotten.

References:

Rohmer Review, nos. 1-18 (1968-Spring/Summer 1981);

Cay Van Ash and Elizabeth Sax Rohmer, *Master of Villainy: A Biography of Sax Rohmer*, edited, with a foreword, notes, and a bibliography, by Robert E. Briney (Bowling Green, Ohio: Bowling Green University Popular Press, 1972).

Joseph Shearing
(Gabrielle Margaret Vere Campbell)

(29 October 1886-23 December 1952)

Mary Jean DeMarr
Indiana State University

BOOKS: *The Viper of Milan*, as Marjorie Bowen
(London: Alston Rivers, 1906; New York:
McClure, Phillips, 1906);

The Glen o' Weeping, as Bowen (London: Alston Rivers, 1907); republished as *The Master of Stair*
(New York: McClure, Phillips, 1907);

The Leopard and the Lily, as Bowen (New York:
McClure, Phillips, 1907; London: Methuen,
1920);

The Sword Decides!, as Bowen (London: Alston Rivers, 1908; New York: McClure, Phillips,
1908);

Black Magic: A Tale of the Rise and Fall of Antichrist,
as Bowen (London: Alston Rivers, 1909);

I Will Maintain, as Bowen (London: Methuen,
1910; New York: Dutton, 1911; revised edition, Harmondsworth & New York: Penguin, 1943);

Defender of the Faith, as Bowen (London: Methuen, 1911; New York: Dutton, 1911);

God and the King, as Bowen (London: Methuen,
1911; New York: Dutton, 1912);

Lovers' Knots, as Bowen (London: Everett, 1912);

The Quest of Glory, as Bowen (London: Methuen,
1912; New York: Dutton, 1912);

The Rake's Progress, as Bowen (London: Rider,
1912);

The Soldier from Virginia, as Bowen (New York: Appleton, 1912); republished as *Mr. Washington*
(London: Methuen, 1915);

God's Playthings, as Bowen (London: Smith, Elder,
1912; New York: Dutton, 1913);

The Governor of England, as Bowen (London: Methuen, 1913; New York: Dutton, 1914);

A Knight of Spain, as Bowen (London: Methuen,
1913);

The Two Carnations, as Bowen (London: Cassell,
1913; New York: Reynolds, 1913);

Prince and Heretic, as Bowen (London: Methuen,
1914; New York: Dutton, 1915);

Because of These Things . . ., as Bowen (London:
Methuen, 1915);

Gabrielle Margaret Vere Campbell, whose pen names included Joseph Shearing, Marjorie Bowen, and George Preedy

The Carnival of Florence, as Bowen (London: Methuen, 1915; New York: Dutton, 1915);

"William, By the Grace of God," as Bowen (London:
Methuen, 1916; New York: Dutton, 1917);

Shadows of Yesterday: Stories from an Old Catalogue,
as Bowen (London: Smith, Elder, 1916;
New York: Dutton, 1916);

The Third Estate, as Bowen (London: Methuen,
1917; New York: Dutton, 1918); revised as
Eugenie (London: Fontana, 1971);

Curious Happenings, as Bowen (London: Mills & Boon, 1917);

The Burning Glass, as Bowen (London: Collins, 1918; New York: Dutton, 1920);

Kings-at-Arms, as Bowen (London: Methuen, 1918; New York: Dutton, 1919);

Crimes of Old London, as Bowen (London: Odhams, 1919);

Mr. Misfortunate, as Bowen (London: Collins, 1919);

The Cheats, as Bowen (London: Collins, 1920);

The Haunted Vintage, as Bowen (London: Odhams, 1921);

Roccoco, as Bowen (London: Odhams, 1921);

The Pleasant Husband and Other Stories, as Bowen (London: Hurst & Blackett, 1921);

The Jest, as Bowen (London: Odhams, 1922);

Stinging Nettles, as Bowen (London & Melbourne: Ward, Lock, 1923; Boston: Small, Maynard, 1923);

Seeing Life! and Other Stories, as Bowen (London: Hurst & Blackett, 1923);

The Presence and the Power, as Bowen (London: Ward, Lock, 1924);

Five People, as Bowen (London & Melbourne: Ward, Lock, 1925);

"Luctor et Emergo," Being an Historical Essay on the State of England at the Peace of Ryswyck, 1697, as Bowen (Newcastle-upon-Tyne: Northumberland Press, 1925);

Boundless Water, as Bowen (London & Melbourne: Ward, Lock, 1926);

Nell Gwyn: A Decoration, as Bowen (London: Hodder & Stoughton, 1926); republished as *Mistress Nell Gwyn* (New York: Appleton, 1926; London: Mellifont Press, 1949);

The Seven Deadly Sins, as Bowen (London: Hurst & Blackett, 1926);

The Netherlands Display'd; or, The Delights of the Low Countries, as Bowen (London: John Lane, 1926; New York: Dodd, Mead, 1927);

"Five Winds," as Bowen (London: Hodder & Stoughton, 1927);

The Pagoda (Le Pagode de Chanteloup), as Bowen (London: Hodder & Stoughton, 1927);

Dark Ann and Other Stories, as Bowen (London: John Lane/Bodley Head, 1927);

General Crack, as George Preedy (London: John Lane, 1928; New York: Dodd, Mead, 1928);

The Countess Fanny, as Bowen (London: Hodder & Stoughton, 1928);

The Golden Roof, as Bowen (London: Hodder & Stoughton, 1928);

Holland, Being a General Survey of the Netherlands, as Bowen (London: Harrap, 1928; Garden City: Doubleday, Doran, 1929);

The Winged Trees, as Bowen (Oxford: Blackwell, 1928);

The Story of the Temple and Its Associations, as Bowen (London: Griffin, 1928);

Sundry Great Gentlemen: Some Essays in Historical Biography, as Bowen (London: John Lane/New York: Dodd, Mead, 1928);

William, Prince of Orange (Afterwards King of England), Being an Account of His Early Life, as Bowen (London: John Lane/New York: Dodd, Mead, 1928);

Dickon, as Bowen (London: Hodder & Stoughton, 1929);

The Gorgeous Lovers and Other Tales, as Bowen (London: John Lane, 1929);

Sheep's-Head and Babylon, and Other Stories of Yesterday and To-Day, as Bowen (London: John Lane, 1929);

The Lady's Prisoner, as Bowen, and *The Story of Mr. Bell,* by Geoffrey M. Boumphrey (Oxford: Blackwell, 1929);

Mademoiselle Maria Gloria, as Bowen, and *The Saving of Castle Malcolm,* by Madeleine Nightingale (Oxford: Blackwell, 1929);

The Third Mary Stuart, Being a Character Study with Memoirs and Letters of Queen Mary II of England 1662-1694, as Bowen (London: John Lane, 1929);

The English Paragon, as Bowen (London: Hodder & Stoughton, 1930);

The Devil's Jig, as Robert Paye (London: John Lane, 1930);

The Rocklitz, as Preedy (London: John Lane, 1930);

Old Patch's Medley; or, A London Miscellany, as Bowen (London: Selwyn & Blount, 1930);

Captain Banner: A Drama in Three Acts, as Preedy (London: John Lane, 1930);

A Family Comedy (1840): A Comedy in One Act, as Bowen (London & New York: French, 1930);

Exits and Farewells, Being Some Account of the Last Days of Certain Historical Characters, as Bowen (London: Selwyn & Blount, 1930);

Bagatelle and Some Other Diversions, as Preedy (London: John Lane, 1930; New York: Dodd, Mead, 1931);

Brave Employments, as Bowen (London: Collins, 1931);

Tumult in the North, as Preedy (London: John Lane, 1931; New York: Dodd, Mead, 1931);

Dust jacket for the 1939 novel that Campbell had published under the pen name Joseph Shearing (courtesy of Otto Penzler). During the same year she produced three books as Marjorie Bowen, three more as George Preedy, and an autobiography under her real name.

Grace Latouche and the Warringtons: Some Nineteenth-Century Pieces. Mostly Victorian, as Bowen (London: Selwyn & Blount, 1931);

The Question, as Bowen (London & New York: French, 1931);

Withering Fires, as Bowen (London: Collins, 1932);

The Shadow on Mockways, as Bowen (London: Collins, 1932);

Forget-Me-Not, as Joseph Shearing (London: Heinemann, 1932); republished as Lucile Cléry (New York: Harper, 1932); republished as The Strange Case of Lucile Cléry (New York: Harper, 1941);

The Devil Snar'd, as Preedy (London: Benn, 1932);

Dark Rosaleen, as Bowen (London: Collins, 1932; Boston & New York: Houghton Mifflin, 1933);

Passion Flower, as Bowen (London: Collins, 1932); republished as Beneath the Passion Flower, as Preedy (New York: McBride, 1932);

Idlers' Gate, as John Winch (London: Collins, 1932; New York: Morrow, 1932);

The Pavilion of Honour, as Preedy (London: John Lane, 1932);

Violante: Circe and Ermine, as Preedy (London: Cassell, 1932);

Fond Fancy and Other Stories, as Bowen (London: Selwyn & Blount, 1932);

The Last Bouquet: Some Twilight Tales, as Bowen (London: John Lane, 1932);

Julia Roseingrave, as Paye (London: Benn, 1933);

I Dwelt in High Places, as Bowen (London: Collins, 1933);

"Set with Green Herbs," as Bowen (London: Benn, 1933);

The Stolen Bride, as Bowen (London: Lovat Dickson, 1933);

The Veil'd Delight, as Bowen (London: Odhams, 1933);

Double Dallilay, as Preedy (London: Cassell, 1933); republished as Queen's Caprice (New York: King, 1934);

The Knot Garden: Some Old Fancies Re-Set, as Preedy (London: John Lane, 1933);

Album Leaf, as Shearing (London: Heinemann, 1933); republished as The Spider in the Cup (New York: Smith & Haas, 1934);

Dr. Chaos, and The Devil Snar'd, as Preedy (London: Cassell, 1933);

Moss Rose, as Shearing (London: Heinemann, 1934; New York: Smith & Haas, 1935);

The Triumphant Beast, as Bowen (London: John Lane, 1934);

The Autobiography of Cornelius Blake, 1773-1810, of Ditton See, Cambridgeshire, as Preedy (London: Cassell, 1934);

Mary, Queen of Scots, Daughter of Debate, as Bowen (London: John Lane, 1934; New York: Putnam's, 1935);

The Scandal of Sophie Dawes, as Bowen (London: John Lane, 1934; New York & London: Appleton-Century, 1935);

Laurell'd Captains, as Preedy (London: Hutchinson, 1935);

Patriotic Lady: A Study of Emma, Lady Hamilton, and the Neapolitan Revolution of 1799, as Bowen (London: John Lane, 1935; New York & London: Appleton-Century, 1936);

The Angel of Assassination: Marie-Charlotte de Corday d'Armont, Jean-Paul Marat, Jean-Adam Lux: Three Disciples of Rousseau, as Shearing (London & Toronto: Heinemann, 1935; New York: Smith & Haas, 1935);

Peter Porcupine: A Study of William Cobbett, 1762-1835, as Bowen (London: Longmans, Green, 1935);

The Golden Violet: The Story of a Lady Novelist, as Shearing (London & Toronto: Heinemann, 1936; New York: Smith & Durrell, 1941);

The Poisoners, as Preedy (London: Hutchinson, 1936);

Trumpets at Rome, as Bowen (London: Hutchinson, 1936);

William Hogarth: The Cockney's Mirror, as Bowen (London: Methuen, 1936; New York & London: Appleton-Century, 1936);

Crowns and Sceptres: The Romance & Pageantry of Coronations, as Bowen (London: Long, 1937);

The Lady and the Arsenic: The Life and Death of a Romantic, Marie Capelle, Madame Lafarge, as Shearing (London & Toronto: Heinemann, 1937; New York: Barnes, 1944);

This Shining Woman: Mary Wollstonecraft Godwin 1759-1797, as Preedy (London: Collins, 1937; New York & London: Appleton, 1937);

Wrestling Jacob: A Study of the Life of John Wesley and Some Members of His Family, as Bowen (London & Toronto: Heinemann, 1937);

My Tattered Loving, as Preedy (London: Jenkins, 1937); republished as *The King's Favourite,* as Bowen (London: Fontana, 1971);

Painted Angel, as Preedy (London: Jenkins, 1938);

Orange Blossoms, as Shearing (London: Heinemann, 1938);

A Giant in Chains: Prelude to Revolution (France 1775-1791), as Bowen (London: Hutchinson, 1938);

God and the Wedding Dress, as Bowen (London: Hutchinson, 1938);

World's Wonder and Other Essays, as Bowen (London: Hutchinson, 1938);

The Trumpet and the Swan: An Adventure of the Civil War, as Bowen (London: Pitman, 1938);

Blanche Fury; or, Fury's Ape, as Shearing (London & Toronto: Heinemann, 1939; New York: Harrison-Hilton, 1939);

The Fair Young Widow, as Preedy (London: Jenkins, 1939);

Mr. Tyler's Saints, as Bowen (London: Hutchinson, 1939);

The Circle in the Water, as Bowen (London: Hutchinson, 1939);

Dove in the Mulberry Tree, as Preedy (London: Jenkins, 1939);

The Debate Continues, by Margaret Campbell, Being the Autobiography of Marjorie Bowen (London: Heinemann, 1939);

Ethics in Modern Art, as Bowen (London: Watts, 1939);

Child of Chequer'd Fortune: The Life, Loves and Battles of Maurice de Saxe, Maréchal de France, as Preedy (London: Jenkins, 1939);

Exchange Royal, as Bowen (London & Melbourne: Hutchinson, 1940);

Primula, as Preedy (London: Hodder & Stoughton, 1940);

Strangers to Freedom, as Bowen (London: Dent, 1940);

The Life of John Knox, as Preedy (London: Jenkins, 1940);

The Life of Rear-Admiral John Paul Jones, 1747-1792, as Preedy (London: Jenkins, 1940);

Aunt Beardie, as Shearing (London & Melbourne: Hutchinson, 1940; New York: Harrison-Hilton, 1940);

Laura Sarelle, as Shearing (London & Melbourne: Hutchinson, 1940); republished as *The Crime of Laura Sarelle* (New York: Smith & Durrell, 1941);

Today is Mine, as Bowen (London & Melbourne: Hutchinson, 1941);

Black Man–White Maiden, as Preedy (London: Hodder & Stoughton, 1941);

Findernes' Flowers, as Preedy (London: Hodder & Stoughton, 1941);

Lindley Waters, as Preedy (London: Hodder & Stoughton, 1942);

The Courtly Charlatan: The Enigmatic Comte de St. Germain, as Preedy (London: Jenkins, 1942);

The Fetch, as Shearing (London: Hutchinson, 1942); republished as *The Spectral Bride* (New York: Smith & Durrell, 1942);

Airing in a Closed Carriage, as Shearing (London: Hutchinson, 1943; New York & London: Harper, 1943);

Lady in a Veil, as Preedy (London: Hodder & Stoughton, 1943);

The Fourth Chamber, as Preedy (London: Hodder & Stoughton, 1944);

Nightcap and Plume, as Preedy (London: Hodder & Stoughton, 1945);

The Church and Social Progress: An Exposition of Rationalism and Reaction, as Bowen (London: Watts, 1945);

The Abode of Love, as Shearing (London: Hutchinson, 1945);

For Her to See, as Shearing (London & New York: Hutchinson, 1947); republished as *So Evil My Love* (New York: Harper, 1947);

No Way Home, as Preedy (London: Hodder & Stoughton, 1947);

Mignonette, as Shearing (New York: Harper, 1948; London: Heinemann, 1949);

The Bishop of Hell and Other Stories, as Bowen (London: John Lane/Bodley Head, 1949);

The Sacked City, as Preedy (London: Hodder & Stoughton, 1949);

Within the Bubble, as Shearing (London: Heinemann, 1950); republished as *The Heiress of Frascati* (New York: Berkley, 1966);

To Bed at Noon, as Shearing (London: Heinemann, 1951);

Julia Ballantyne, as Preedy (London: Hodder & Stoughton, 1952);

In the Steps of Mary, Queen of Scots, as Bowen (London: Rich & Cowan, 1952);

The Man with the Scales, as Bowen (London: Hutchinson, 1954);

Night's Dark Secret, as Campbell (New York: Signet, 1975);

Kecksies and Other Twilight Tales, as Bowen (Sauk City, Wis.: Arkham, 1976).

PLAY PRODUCTIONS: *Captain Banner,* as George Preedy, London, Arts Theatre, 25 April 1929;

The Rocklitz, as Preedy, London, Duke of York's Theatre, 4 February 1931;

Rose Giralda, as Preedy, London, 1933;

Court Cards, as Preedy, London, Shilling Theatre, 7 November 1934;

Royal Command, as Preedy, Wimbledon, Surrey, 1952.

OTHER: *Great Tales of Horror,* edited, with an introduction, as Marjorie Bowen (London: John Lane, 1933);

More Great Tales of Horror, edited, with a foreword, as Bowen (London: John Lane, 1935);

Some Famous Love Letters, edited as Bowen (London: Jenkins, 1937).

By 1932, when she produced her first crime novel, *Withering Fires,* under the pen name Marjorie Bowen, Gabrielle Margaret Vere Campbell had been writing histories, biographies, and historical novels under that pseudonym for more than twenty-five years. She had also published novels as Robert Paye and as George Preedy, and in 1932 she employed a fourth pen name: John Winch. That same year she adopted the pseudonym under which she is best known as a crime writer: Joseph Shearing (though she sometimes published her crime fiction as Bowen or Preedy). In the course of her long career she also wrote children's stories (as Bowen) and plays (most successfully as Preedy). Campbell once explained that, when she used a new pseudonym, it helped her to assume a new personality as a writer. She also realized that critics tended to be unkind to prolific writers. Because she earned her living by writing, she devised a practical solution to this dilemma: by using pen names and keeping their identity secret from everyone except her publishers, she established a series of different reputations for herself. Though she had earlier acknowledged that she was Marjorie Bowen and George Preedy, Campbell did not admit that she was also Joseph Shearing until 1942. She is suspected to have also written under the names Evelyn Winch, Edgar Winch, E. M. Winch, and Bertha Winch.

Born on Hayling Island, Hampshire, Gabrielle Margaret Vere Campbell was a member of a penurious Moravian clerical family whose eccentric life-style gave her a permanent distaste for bohemianism. Her formal schooling–in Paris, Rome, and London–was sporadic, and she liked to say that she had been educated largely by life and herself. Campbell married Zeffrino Emilio Costanzo in 1912. She was widowed in 1916 and married Arthur L. Long in 1917; she had three sons, one by Costanzo and two by Long.

Set in the past, her crime novels fall into two general groups: fictionalized reconstructions of actual crimes and depictions of fictional crimes in historically accurate settings. The first group–which includes *Forget-Me-Not* (1932), *Airing in a Closed Carriage* (1943), and *For Her to See* (1947)–is thought to contain her best work. These novels examine famous nineteenth-century murder cases in which the suspects were women, and each is primarily concerned with the characters of these women, examination of the events leading up to the crimes, and investigation of the psychological as well as practical impact of crime on their lives.

Forget-Me-Not (also published as *Lucile Cléry* and *The Strange Case of Lucile Cléry*) is based on the Praslin case of 1847, often credited with precipitating the French rebellion of 1848. The Du-

Dust jacket for Shearing's 1947 fictional reconstruction of the Bravo murder case of 1876 (courtesy of Otto Penzler)

chesse de Praslin was brutally murdered by her husband, who made an amateurish effort to conceal his guilt. While the police questioned a young governess in the household, who was suspected of being his mistress and his accomplice, he poisoned himself and died. The governess was not held for the murder, and, after being freed, she found her way to the United States, where she married a minister. One of her brothers-in-law was Cyrus Field, the promoter of the transatlantic cable; a grandniece was Rachel Field, whose novel *All This, and Heaven Too* (1938) is a much more sympathetic portrayal of the governess, carrying her story into her American life and making an interesting contrast to Shearing's version of characters and events.

Forget-Me-Not presents the governess, called Lucile Cléry through most of the novel, unsympathetically from the beginning, when—as a young woman desperately trying to find her way in a hostile world—she elopes with a young man she does not even like much. After he reveals that he has learned of her multitudinous lies to him and that he does not feel bound to marry her, she finds herself condemned to the life of a governess for the Boccage family (based on the de Praslins). The thwarting of her marriage plans has made her cold and manipulative, and she is surprised to discover a passion for the Duc growing within her. That passion, as well as her desire to grasp the luxury of the Boccage household for herself, leads to disaster. Like Field, Shearing finds her innocent of actual complicity in the murder, but, unlike Field, Shearing considers her morally guilty. For Shearing's governess her subsequent marriage to a young American minister is only a hated expedient, giving her safety and comfort but trapping her in a relationship with a man she scorns and a society of which she is contemptuous. She is no happier than she had been at the beginning of her adventure. The meaning of the novel's original title is set up in the prologue, in which the future governess refuses to read a tale about the unhappy lives of governesses in a volume of prose and poetry titled *Forget-Me-Not*. The same words are inscribed on her thimble, one of her few pretty possessions. Yet the past she cannot forget is far from pretty.

Olivia Sacret, a widow who is a hired companion to a shallow and wealthy young wife, Susan Rue, in *For Her to See* (also published as *So Evil My Love*), is equally desperate to make her way in a hostile world. While she is less unpleasant than Lucile Cléry, the reader's response to her is more pity than liking. The novel is based on the Bravo case of 1876, in which Florence Bravo was the chief suspect in the murder of her husband, Charles Bravo, in the Balham district of London. They were known to have quarreled often, and details about her affair with a well-known osteopathic surgeon were revealed at two inquests (no trial was ever held and the case remained unsolved). No consensus of opinion was ever reached on the complicity or innocence of the wife's companion, a Mrs. Cox, upon whom Mrs. Sacret (whom Shearing casts as the murderer) was based. Shearing's novel examines the relationship between the two women, stressing the helplessness of well-bred, educated women, like Mrs. Sacret, who are forced into servitude by their lack of resources. Like Lucile Cléry, Mrs. Sacret makes a desperate effort to find physical passion if not love, and her effort, similarly, leads to disaster as she allows herself to be dominated by her lover, who forces her to blackmail Susan and to poison Martin Rue.

Airing in a Closed Carriage is based on the Maybrick murder of 1889, a case in which a young wife was accused of murdering her husband, an elderly businessman. She was believed to have taken a lover, and the poison which killed her husband had been available to her. She was tried, convicted, sent to prison, and ultimately released. In 1941 news of Florence Maybrick's death in South Kent, Connecticut, where she had been living for twenty years under an assumed name, prompted the writing of *Airing in a Closed Carriage*. Shearing follows the actual events quite closely. The presentation of May Tyler, as Florence Maybrick is called here, is somewhat sympathetic, but, like Lucile Cléry and Olivia Sacret, she is characterized as shallow and selfish. The title refers to May's sense of her entire life: she never has any freedom. Persuaded to enter a confining marriage with a cruel, much older man, living in a dreary provincial city, and having no friends, she is manipulated by her husband's resentful brother and has no chance of happiness. Innocent of both adultery and the murder, she is convicted and condemned to death, although this sentence is commuted. Her years in prison are simply an exchange of one sort of confinement for another. An epilogue describes her funeral and reveals the anonymity and desperate poverty in which she spent the final third of her life. The novel's controlling symbol is the mayfly, representing May's prettiness and her few moments of happiness as a girl. In the novel's closing passage one woman remarks that the insects live for only a day but are terrible pests; another responds, "I often wonder what it seems like to *them*–a pity they haven't the sense to tell you. . . ." This statement serves as May's epitaph. As Edward Wagenknecht said in an essay-review of *Airing in a Closed Carriage,* the novel is "from every point of view quite first-class Shearing. It tells an absorbing horror story, which is all the more terrible because no physical horror is presented in it . . ." (*New York Times Book Review,* 2 May 1943).

In some of Shearing's novels the effect of the past on the present is a central theme. Lavinia Pierrepoint, the heroine of *Album Leaf* (1933; also published as *The Spider in the Cup,* 1934), one of the historical mystery novels not based on an actual case, barely remembers her profligate father or alcoholic mother, but she knows that her father cruelly beat her mother and that her mother was a suicide. Reared by a scholarly grandfather, who has impoverished himself to pay her father's debts, she is eager to escape the provincial English town in which she lives. She agrees to marry a young officer who bores her, and, after he is sent to India for three years, she accepts a position as paid companion to two women who live as recluses in Provence. Like Lucile Cléry and Olivia Sacret, she becomes enmeshed in an obsessive passion, and the result is disastrous. After her two employers die mysteriously she flees, fearing she will be accused of complicity in their murder. Like other of Shearing's manipulative women, she has masked her true feelings until she seems only a player of roles. Her fiancé stands by her until in a desperate fury she reveals her contempt for him; her French lover refuses to take her back because of her cowardice in leaving him. She is left with nothing except the need for drink. The novel's last pages follow her as she furtively buys brandy, and the last line makes clear that she will follow her mother's example into drunken self-destruction.

Lavinia's repetition of the past, clearly foreshadowed throughout the novel, is unintentional on her part, suggesting the power of inheritance. In *Laura Sarelle* (1940; also published as *The Crime of Laura Sarelle*, 1941), a past crime inspires another in the novel's present, 1840. The Laura of the present is a petulant girl who, quite justifiably, hates gloomy Leppard Hall, where she is forced to live. Of particular distress to her are two portraits, one of her namesake and distant relative of several generations earlier and the other of an unknown young man. Her insensitive brother not only refuses to allow them to be removed, but he attempts to force Laura into a marriage she resists. Laura falls passionately in love with her brother's impecunious steward, whom she hopes to marry and thus escape her brother's domination. When she learns the truth of the portraits–that her namesake had committed murder, blaming her husband (the model for the other portrait) in hopes of freeing herself from their marriage so she could marry the man she loved–Laura sees her way to escape. She carefully plans the murder of her brother, using her predecessor's method (poison distilled from laurel leaves), and so contrives events that her hated suitor must be accused. But in the process her obsession leads to madness.

The use of symbols which both reveal character and foreshadow fate is a particularly important aspect of Shearing's craft. The laurel leaves that are alluded to in Laura Sarelle's name and become her murder weapon, the mayfly that represents May Tyler's hopelessness, and the forget-me-nots that suggest Lucile Cléry's passion are all introduced early and recur as key motifs in the novels.

Always set in an accurately depicted past, Shearing's novels have been accused of containing unbelievable reversals and obtrusive symbolism, but these gripping psychological studies, with their mood of foreboding, their compelling suspense, and their realistic portrayals of women trapped by circumstances they can alter only to their own destruction, are highly readable and worthy of respect. As Wagenknecht wrote in 1943, "the artist in Joseph Shearing is drawn to crime and mystery as Conrad or the Brontës were drawn to them, not because they can be wrapped up in neat little artificial packages but because it is in extreme situations that the real capacities of human nature are revealed, and because human life itself is a mystery. . . ."

George R. Sims

(2 September 1847-4 September 1922)

Christopher D. Murray
University of Regina

See also the Sims entry in *DLB 35, Victorian Poets After 1850*.

BOOKS: *The Social Kaleidoscope* (London: Francis, 1879);

The Dagonet Ballads (London: Francis, 1879);

The Ballads of Babylon (London: Fuller, 1880);

Zeph, and Other Stories (London: Fuller, 1880; enlarged edition, London: Chatto & Windus, 1892);

The Theatre of Life (London: Fuller, 1881);

The Social Kaleidoscope, second series (London: Francis, 1881);

Three Brass Balls (London: Fuller, 1882);

How the Poor Live (London: Chatto & Windus, 1883);

The Lifeboat, and Other Poems (London: Fuller, 1883);

Ballads and Poems (London: Fuller, 1883);

Stories in Black and White (London: Fuller, 1885);

Rogues and Vagabonds (London: Chatto & Windus, 1885; New York: Munro, 1886);

The Ring o' Bells (London: Chatto & Windus, 1886);

Mary Jane's Memoirs (London: Chatto & Windus, 1887; New York: Ivers, 1887);

Mary Jane Married: Tales of a Village Inn (London: Chatto & Windus, 1888);

The Land of Gold, and Other Poems (London: Fuller, 1888);

The Dagonet Reciter and Reader, in Prose and Verse (London: Chatto & Windus, 1888);

Tales of To-Day (London: Chatto & Windus, 1889; New York: Lovell, 1889);

How the Poor Live, and Horrible London (London: Chatto & Windus, 1889);

The Case of George Candlemas (London: Chatto & Windus, 1890);

Dramas of Life (London: Chatto & Windus, 1890; New York: United States Book Company, 1890);

A Bunch of Primroses (London & New York: Tuck, 1890);

Nellie's Prayer (London & New York: Tuck, 1890);

From a Photograph by G. & R. Lavis

Faithfully Yours
Geo R Sims

A Missing Husband and Other Tales (London: Chatto & Windus, 1890);

Tinkletop's Crime (London: Chatto & Windus, 1891; New York: Webster, 1891);

Dagonet Ditties (London: Chatto & Windus, 1891);

Memoirs of a Mother-in-Law (London: Newnes, 1892; New York: Waverly, 1892);

My Two Wives, and Other Stories (London: Chatto & Windus, 1894);

Memoirs of a Landlady (London: Chatto & Windus, 1894);

277

Dagonet on Our Islands (London: Unwin, 1894);

Scenes from the Show (London: Chatto & Windus, 1894);

Dagonet Abroad (London: Chatto & Windus, 1895);

The Ten Commandments (London: Chatto & Windus, 1896);

As It Was in the Beginning: Life Stories of To-Day (London: White, 1896);

The Coachman's Club: or, Tales Told Out of School (London: White, 1897);

Dorcas Dene, Detective: Her Adventures (London: White, 1897);

Dorcas Dene, Detective: Her Adventures, second series (London: White, 1898);

Dagonet Dramas of the Day (London: Chatto & Windus, 1898);

Once Upon a Christmastime (London: Chatto & Windus, 1898);

In London's Heart (London: Chatto & Windus, 1900; New York: Buckles/London: Chatto & Windus, 1900);

Without the Limelight: Theatrical Life as it is (London: Chatto & Windus, 1900);

The Small-Part Lady and Other Stories (London: Chatto & Windus, 1900);

A Blind Marriage, and Other Stories (London: Chatto & Windus, 1901);

Nat Harlowe, Mountebank (London: Cassell, 1902);

Biographs of Babylon: Life-Pictures of London's Moving Scenes (London: Chatto & Windus, 1902);

Young Mrs. Caudle (London: Chatto & Windus, 1904);

Among My Autographs (London: Chatto & Windus, 1904);

The Life We Live (London: Chatto & Windus, 1904);

The King's Pardons. The Martyrdom of Adolf Beck (London: Daily Mail, 1904);

Li Ting of London, and Other Stories (London: Chatto & Windus, 1905);

The Mysteries of Modern London (London: Pearson, 1906);

Two London Fairies (London: Greening, 1906);

For Life–and After (London: Chatto & Windus, 1906);

London by Night (London: Greening, 1906; revised, 1910);

His Wife's Revenge (London: Chatto & Windus, 1907);

Watches of the Night (London: Greening, 1907);

The Mystery of Mary Anne, and Other Stories (London: Chatto & Windus, 1907);

The Black Stain (London: Jarrolds, 1907);

Joyce Pleasantry, and Other Stories (London: Chatto & Windus, 1908);

The Devil in London (London: S. Paul, 1908; New York: Dodge, 1909);

The Death Gamble (London: S. Paul, 1909);

The Cabinet Minister's Wife (London: S. Paul, 1910);

Off the Track in London (London: Jarrolds, 1911);

Behind the Veil: True Stories of London Life (London: Greening, 1913);

The Bluebeard of the Bath (London: Pearson, 1915);

Anna of the Underworld (London: Chatto & Windus, 1916);

My Life: Sixty Years' Recollections of Bohemian London (London: Nash, 1917);

Glances Back (London: Jarrolds, 1917);

Prepare to Shed Them Now: The Ballads of George R. Sims, edited by Arthur Calder-Marshall (London: Hutchinson, 1968).

PLAY PRODUCTIONS: *The Lights o' London,* London, Princess's Theatre, 10 September 1881; New York, Union-Square Theatre, 5 December 1881;

The Romany Rye, London, Princess's Theatre, 10 June 1882; New York, Booth's Theatre, 18 September 1882;

In the Ranks, by Sims and Henry Pettitt, New York, Standard Theatre, 1 November 1883; London, Adelphi Theatre, 6 November 1883;

Harbour Lights, by Sims and Pettitt, London, Adelphi Theatre, 23 November 1885; New York, Wallack's Theatre, 26 January 1887;

The English Rose, by Sims and Robert Buchanan, London, Adelphi Theatre, 2 August 1890; New York, Proctor's Theatre, 9 March 1892;

The Trumpet Call, by Sims and Buchanan, London, Adelphi Theatre, 1 August 1891.

OTHER: *Balzac's Contes Drolatiques,* translated by Sims (London: Chatto & Windus, 1874);

Living London, edited by Sims, 3 volumes (London & New York: Cassell, 1901-1903).

In his day George Sims was regarded primarily as a journalist and dramatist, but little of his journalism and his drama survives in print. What was clearly a sideline for him, writing detective fiction, has become one of the chief reasons that he is remembered today. He also wrote verse; his reports of some of his forays into the worst of Lon-

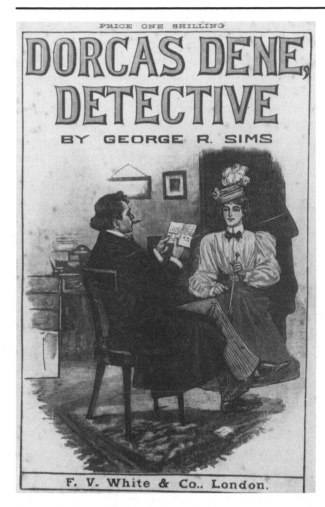
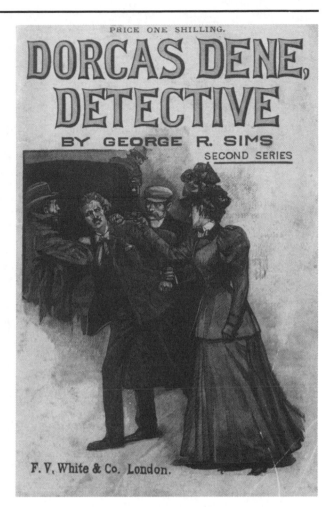

Covers for Sims's "shilling shockers" about an actress-turned-private-detective who employs her theatrical talent to solve her cases (courtesy of Otto Penzler)

don slums, commissioned by *Pictorial World*, were subsequently published as *How the Poor Live* (1883), but most of his books are collections of short stories. He wrote a few novels, but often they are series of episodes involving the same characters, and it is clear that Sims favored the short-story form. Many of his stories are sentimental romances; some are pure whimsy; but many others involve mystery or crime, and some of these are very good indeed.

George Robert Sims was born into a prosperous London family. From his father's side he inherited a sound business sense, an acute interest in everything around him, and, above all, a taste for the good life. Early he became a bon vivant, interested in good food, good entertainment, and the worlds of horse racing, boxing, showing dogs, and, particularly, the London criminal. From his mother's side, however, his grandfather having been prominent in the Chartist movement in the 1840s, he developed a keen and abiding sympa-

thy for the plight of the poor. He may have been a man of the world, but he knew well the injustices of that world, and he worked hard to correct them.

He was educated at Hanwell Military College and the university at Bonn. Other than adding German to his fluent French and getting to know the other upper-class English students there for a good time, Sims did not greatly benefit from his German education, and he was sent home after failing to obey a curfew imposed by the Bonn police. Back in London he worked in his father's furniture business in the city by day and got caught up in the bohemian life of writers and artists by night. After several years and several false starts he managed to make a living by his pen, and he quit his father's employment for good in 1874.

Sims's nocturnal habits and wide variety of interests naturally led him to become a journalist. Having a gift for comic writing, he was invited in

Cover for Sims's 1900 mystery novel about insurance fraud

esty about his many successes, his whimsical and self-effacing sense of humor, his knowledge both of Londoners and London, and, most of all, because he was seen to embody the qualities that Englishmen of his day admired. His sense of right and wrong could offend no one; yet he often championed the rights of those whom respectable English people considered beneath their notice. Though by today's standards he may seem to have been overly patriotic, he strove harder than most popular writers of his day to broaden the sympathies and outlook of his readers. While many of his villains are foreigners, many of their victims are too, and those victims are often among the East European labor of the Cheapside or Wapping slums. Though Sims rarely became indignant in his writings, he drew public attention to a variety of social abuses and by so doing helped to end them.

While Sims published a collection of short stories in 1879, the success of his melodramas and comedies in the next decade allowed him little time for fiction. His first big stage hit came with *The Lights o' London,* a melodrama, in 1881. Thereafter nearly every play he wrote enjoyed success, and at one time he had four plays running in the West End, a feat matched only once in his lifetime. When he began writing good fiction at the end of the decade it showed some of the weaknesses of melodrama, but as he discovered fiction's advantages he became remarkably proficient.

As with many of his contemporaries, Sims at first depended all too frequently on coincidence for solving plot problems, and on occasion he somewhat mechanically, and quite unnecessarily, had his characters give information about themselves in dialogue. He soon discovered the advantage of the first-person narrator, often seeming to write in his own person or telling a story that, he asserts, he has heard from a friend in the police or someone closely connected with the case. In his *Dorcas Dene, Detective* series (1897, 1898) his narrator is a successful London dramatist called Saxon, who gave Dorcas Lester parts in some of his plays before she left the stage to become Mrs. Dene and later a private detective. He is happy to help her when needed and plays a role that is parallel with Dr. Watson's. In fact Sims took up detective fiction seriously only after Arthur Conan Doyle's success with Sherlock Holmes.

As one might expect from a dramatist, Sims's dialogue is usually good. He had a fine

1874 to join the staff of *Fun,* a downmarket *Punch,* to replace Tom Hood. In 1876, employing the pseudonym Dagonet, he began to write "Mustard and Cress," a weekly column for the *Referee* that appeared without fail until the week of his death forty-six years later. The success of this column suggests a quality not often associated with the easygoing world of bohemian London: discipline. Sims was hardworking and scrupulous about honoring contracts. Also discreet and trustworthy, he gained the confidence of both the police and the criminal element of London. In order to gain safe passage through dangerous London slums he needed police protection and, more often than not, contacts in the underworld as well.

Sims put his inborn inquisitiveness and resourcefulness to good use both in his melodramas and his fiction. He soon became a celebrity, one of the most popular Englishmen of his day, mainly because of his easygoing manner, his mod-

Covers for the 1910 revised edition of Sims's exposé of white-slave traffic in London. Tatcho "hair grower" is one of several products that Sims endorsed.

ear for dialect, particularly Cockney. One of the unexpected pleasures of his work is his knowledge of London slang. Some of it does have overtones of the period, but much of it remains up-to-date.

Again, as a practicing playwright, Sims is especially good at creating character through dialogue. At worst his people are recognizable types; at best he manages to convey idiosyncrasies sufficient to individualize them. One of his happiest creations is Dorcas Dene. After her marriage to an artist, who becomes blind, and—to provide for her husband, her mother, and the family bulldog—she becomes a detective. As an actress she can become an American tourist, a housemaid, or an heiress to solve a case. She is refreshingly frank with men, not to be bullied, matter-of-fact, highly imaginative, independent, and intelligent. She may owe something to George Bernard Shaw's Vivie Warren and much

to the New Woman. Sims clearly had achieved something in his two "shilling shockers" about her, but, rather than employing this successful character again, he wrote no more about her.

Sims continued to write fiction, which was published annually for more than another ten years; during this period he married Florence Wykes in 1901. A judicious editor could establish Sims's reputation as a writer of crime fiction by taking a story or two from each volume from *Tales of To-Day* (1889) through *Behind the Veil* (1913). From *Tinkletop's Crime* (1891), a collection of mostly humorous pieces, would come "Bismarck in London." In only twenty pages Sims develops an amusing idea and heightens the effect by reference to prominent contemporary figures such as Lord Rosebery or Sir Charles Dilke. Having saved Otto von Bismarck from drowning early in his career, the narrator establishes close friendships with both Kaiser Wilhelm and Bismarck.

Years later when seeing him off at the Berlin station Bismarck tells the narrator that one day he would like to visit London incognito to understand the English better. Sometime thereafter the German ambassador visits the narrator and tells him that Bismarck will be arriving in London within the week heavily disguised as a Lutheran pastor and wanting to meet prominent politicians and leaders of society. The narrator refurbishes his apartment at great expense and proceeds to show his visitor the London he wishes to see. After each visit to a great house, however, a theft is discovered. On contacting Berlin after his guest has left, the narrator discovers that a confidence man–having overheard Bismarck expressing his wish to visit London in disguise–has impersonated him after having his brother play the role of German ambassador, thus helping set up the operation. In this story Sims's plotting is at its near best, but even here he needs the coincidence of a larcenous railway employee overhearing Bismarck's confidential remark to trigger the action.

Having turned to mystery fiction first in the late 1880s when the Sherlock Holmes craze was at its height, Sims, a decade later, signed a contract with London publisher F. V. White to produce "shilling shockers." At this time Sims, now prosperous, cut back on his stage work and wrote more mystery and romance novels. They are not very good; Sims needed the constrictions of the short story to do his best work, and by 1914 his career was just about finished.

During the first decade of the twentieth century he fought some new causes. In 1904, for the only time in his career, he attacked Scotland Yard in the press. Persuaded that Adolf Beck, a Norwegian citizen, had been unjustly convicted of fraud, Sims used the columns of the *Daily Mail* to prove him innocent. A grateful King Oscar created Sims a Knight of the Order of St. Olaf. As a direct result of Sims's work on the Beck case the Court of Criminal Appeal was instituted.

A year later Sims, working this time for the *Daily Telegraph,* vigorously defended the police from charges that they had wrongly arrested a well-known and well-connected woman for living off the avails of prostitution. He then proceeded to show the extent of a white-slavery ring flourishing in the heart of London. This writing was vintage Sims, one of the best pieces of investigative journalism of the time; the series was published in book form as *London by Night* (1906) and *Watches of the Night* (1907).

As his two memoirs, *My Life* and *Glances Back* (both published in 1917), show, Sims never lost his breezy bonhomie. He was known among his wide circle of friends as a raconteur, and what lifts his work above that of many of his contemporaries is his ability to tell a good story. He had imagination, as well as access to both the London underworld and London society, and he wrote well. Some of his stories turn on the workings of the law, many on confidence tricks or impersonations, some on mistaken identity; all celebrate human ingenuity; and helping to set the conventions of the mystery genre, while playing fair, he inevitably leads his readers in a false direction. Loss of caste, loss of money, and loss of life are the principal fears of his victims, and whether his stories are set in high society or the worlds of the racetrack, commerce, the stage, or the slums, Sims–because of his experience of those worlds and his capacity as a writer–remains an impressive practitioner of mystery fiction. His best work deserves republication for a new audience.

Bram Stoker

(8 November 1847-20 April 1912)

Brian Murray
Youngstown State University

See also the Stoker entry in *DLB 36, British Novelists, 1890-1929: Modernists.*

BOOKS: *The Duties of Clerks of Petty Sessions in Ireland* (Dublin: Privately printed, 1879);

Under the Sunset (London: Low, Marston, Searle & Rivington, 1882);

A Glimpse of America: A Lecture Given at the London Institution, 28th December, 1885 (London: Low, Marston, 1886);

The Snake's Pass (New York: Harper, 1890; London: Low, Marston, Searle & Rivington, 1891);

Crooken Sands (New York: De Vinne, 1894);

The Man from Shorrox's (New York: De Vinne, 1894);

The Watter's Mou' (London: Constable, 1895; New York: Appleton, 1895);

The Shoulder of Shasta (London: Constable, 1895);

Dracula (London: Constable, 1897; New York: Doubleday & McClure, 1899);

Miss Betty (London: Pearson, 1898);

Sir Henry Irving and Miss Ellen Terry (New York: Doubleday & McClure, 1899);

The Mystery of the Sea (New York: Doubleday, Page, 1902; London: Heinemann, 1902);

The Jewel of Seven Stars (London: Heinemann, 1903; New York & London: Harper, 1904; revised and abridged edition, London: Rider, 1912);

The Man (London: Heinemann, 1905); abridged as *The Gates of Life* (New York: Cupples & Leon, 1908);

Personal Reminiscences of Henry Irving, 2 volumes (London: Heinemann, 1906; New York: Macmillan, 1906; revised, London: Heinemann, 1907);

Lady Athlyne (London: Heinemann, 1908; New York: Lovell, 1909);

Snowbound (London: Collier, 1908);

The Lady of the Shroud (London: Heinemann, 1909);

Famous Impostors (London: Sidgwick & Jackson, 1910; New York: Sturgis & Walton, 1910);

The Lair of the White Worm (London: Rider, 1911);

Dracula's Guest, and Other Weird Stories (London: Routledge, 1914; New York: Hillman-Curl, 1937).

PERIODICAL PUBLICATION: "The Censorship of Stage Plays," *Nineteenth Century & After*, 66 (December 1909): 974-989.

Though he was shy and sickly as a child, Bram Stoker grew up to be a man with many talents and interests, and a seemingly endless supply of energy. He was simultaneously an amateur athlete, a businessman, a journalist, and an impresario; he maintained countless friendships and read widely, particularly in subjects related to spiritualism and the occult. Stoker was also the author of nine novels, most of which are ignored today—and justifiably so. But Stoker's best book, the extensively researched *Dracula* (1897), effectively combines macabre atmospherics with high suspense, and not only set the standard for subsequent novels in the horror-mystery genre but also helped establish the vampire as one of the most recognizable figures in the popular arts.

Stoker—the third of seven children—was born in Clontarf, north of Dublin Bay, on 8 November 1847. His father, Abraham Stoker, was a civil servant; his mother, Charlotte Thornley Stoker, was a social activist with a particular concern for impoverished women. Though the precise nature of his illness remains unknown, the young Stoker was so chronically weak that, until the age of seven, he rarely left his bed. He kept himself occupied with books from his father's well-stocked library and was frequently entertained by the grisly folktales involving spirits and plagues that his mother liked to tell. As a boy, Stoker wrote many poems and ghost stories and promised his family that one day he would enjoy literary fame.

In 1864 Stoker began his studies at Dublin's Trinity College, where he was named president of the Philosophical Society and the Historical Society, both of them prestigious undergraduate organizations. Now large and robust, he participated in a variety of sports and began to evince an increased enthusiasm for both the theater and Walt Whitman's verse. As a young man, Stoker sent Whitman a series of lengthy, unrestrained fan letters and continued to plan for a literary career of his own. Still, acceding to his father's wishes, Stoker, upon graduation, entered the Irish civil service and was soon promoted to inspector of petty sessions—a position that, perhaps not surprisingly, failed to develop into a consuming passion.

In 1871 Stoker began writing play reviews for the *Dublin Mail*; he also continued to work on making marketable his own plays and stories. In 1875 he sold to the *Shamrock* "The Chain of Destiny"—a lengthy, serialized tale that features, among other things, a phantom and a curse. In 1876 Stoker met the British actor Henry Irving, who was already famous for his interpretations of Shakespearean roles including—most notably—*Hamlet*. Stoker and Irving quickly became close friends, and in 1878 Stoker began to manage Irving's Lyceum Theatre in London. Stoker's association with Irving—which lasted until the actor's death in 1905—provided him with considerable stimulation. Traveling four times to the United States, Stoker met many notable figures, including Whitman and Theodore Roosevelt (then head of New York City's department of police).

On 4 December 1878 Stoker married Florence Balcombe, a stunning but apparently rather austere woman who—a year later—bore Stoker his only child, a son named Noel. Though his duties as theater manager and tour arranger for the mercurial Irving took up enormous amounts of his time, Stoker did not cease in his attempts to produce profitable fiction in the romance-adventure vein. His first published novel, *The Snake's Pass* (1890), features a dashing hero named Arthur who looks for treasure and competes for the heart of a virginal young woman in a region rich in "legends and myths" and "gloomy scenes." The wide success of *The Snake's Pass* encouraged Stoker to continue extensive research on a much more ambitious work, *Dracula*, which appeared in 1897.

Dracula is constructed principally and masterfully of journal entries and letters written by several characters, including Jonathan Harker, an English real-estate agent who, in the book's opening chapters, describes his journey through Transylvania to the castle of Count Dracula, who wants to buy property in London. Transylvania, he observes, is a rugged, mysterious realm full of the descendants of "Attila and the Huns"; it is a country without maps—a place where "every known superstition in the world is gathered." Dracula, Harker discovers when they meet, is a tall old man with pointed ears, hairy palms, "massive" eyebrows, a "heavy" moustache, and "peculiarly sharp white teeth" which "protruded over the lips." Moreover he shares his castle—which sits "on the edge of a terrific precipice"—with several alluring women endowed with "brilliant white teeth" and "voluptuous lips." They appear before Harker one bright moonlit night and—with a "deliberate voluptuousness which was both thrilling and repulsive"—hover about his neck, their "sweet" scent offset by a "bitter offensiveness, as one smells in blood." One of the women "licked her lips like an animal, till I could see in

Cover for the first American edition (1899) of Stoker's 1897 novel, the culmination of years of research on vampires that Stoker began in 1890 after Prof. Arminius Vambery, the model for Dr. Abraham Van Helsing in the novel, introduced him to some of the stories about these supernatural beings

the moonlight the moisture shining on the scarlet lips and on the red tongue as it lapped the white sharp teeth."

Later, after realizing that his host steals infants, sleeps in a coffin, scurries "lizard fashion" up and down the castle wall, and in fact sucks blood "like a filthy leech," Harker flees Dracula's castle and returns to England and to his fiancée, Mina Murray, whom he describes as "so sweet, so noble, so little an egoist"–as "one of God's women fashioned by His own hand to show us men and other women that there is a heaven where we can enter, and that its light can be here on earth." But Dracula also makes his way to London, where he attacks Mina's close friend–Lucy Westenra–before finally sinking his fangs into Mina herself. As a result of her encounter with the count, Lucy becomes emaciated and dies; she returns, however, as an eerie and erotic ghoul and must finally be stopped with a tar-tipped stake through the heart.

Mina also begins to behave weirdly but is in due course cleansed of her curse when–at the novel's well-paced, riveting conclusion–Dracula (her seducer and controller) is cornered near his Transylvanian castle and killed by a team of men that includes Harker and Dr. Abraham Van Helsing, a Dutch physician and hypnotist. Van Helsing is familiar with the habits of vampires and continually provides his fellow characters and the novel's readers with the facts necessary to anticipate and understand Dracula's actions. For example, he notes that vampires fear religious articles and must periodically return to their native soil. As several critics have pointed out, Stoker modeled Van Helsing on Professor Arminius Vambery, the Hungarian professor of Oriental languages who in 1890 first exposed Stoker to some of the arcana regarding vampires and their haunts in eastern Europe and the Balkans.

Dust jacket for the 1914 collection of short stories compiled by Stoker's widow after his death (courtesy of Otto Penzler). The title story was originally written as an early chapter in Dracula.

A fascination with vampirism was not uncommon among European intellectuals and artists of the eighteenth and nineteenth centuries. In "The Bride of Corinth" Johann Wolfgang von Goethe writes of a young woman doomed to wander eternally from the grave, hoping to "seek the Good's long-sever'd link" while drinking "the life-blood" of the lover she has lost. Samuel Taylor Coleridge alludes to vampiric activity in "Christabel," as does Sir Walter Scott in *Rokeby* (1813), Lord Byron in *The Giaour* (1813), and Robert Southey in *Thalaba the Destroyer* (1801)—a verse fantasy set in the Orient that includes a vivid portrayal of a female "fiend" with "livid cheeks, and lips of blue." The literary male vampire—typically magnetic, brooding, and pale—made his first appearance in the form of a character called Lord Ruthven in John Polidori's *The Vampyre, A Tale* (1819), a work similar to such Gothic novels as Horace Walpole's *Castle of Otranto* (1764) and Ann Radcliffe's *The*

Mysteries of Udolpho (1794). Perhaps even better known, however, was "Carmilla," an 1871 novella written by Joseph Sheridan Le Fanu, an Irishman who also studied at Trinity and who later produced numerous stories and novels with supernatural themes. Like *Dracula*, "Carmilla" includes the observations of a young male narrator who visits a "feudal residence" in an isolated region of eastern Europe; it features a female vampire who is at once a "playful, languid, beautiful girl" and a "writhing fiend" with a "horrible lust for living blood."

Stoker acknowledged a special fondness for "Carmilla," and—as surviving notes for *Dracula* clearly reveal—he had absorbed, at the British Museum and elsewhere, an extraordinary amount of information about the ways in which vampires have been portrayed in the literature and lore of various cultures. He knew then that accounts of creatures who sipped blood and stalked by night were common in ancient times; that European legends about a particularly monstrous aristocrat owed much to Voivode of Wallachia, a very real fifteenth-century Transylvanian landowner who became known as both Vlad the Impaler and "the son of the devil"—or Dracula—because of his fondness for indiscriminately torturing and murdering in a variety of horrific ways.

Still, Stoker was not a particularly deep thinker; it is unlikely that he viewed his own *Dracula* as anything more than a well-constructed and highly suspenseful story which features several memorable characters and a deft blending of the ghastly and the grotesque with a convincingly rendered normality. Indeed, the publicly prudish Stoker—who once wrote an essay calling for the censorship of works that exploit "sex impulses"— would probably be shocked to read much of the recent criticism of *Dracula*, which perceptively points to the many ways in which the novel not only plays to man's fear of disease and foreignness and his own animality but to the Victorian middle-class male's fear of women and female sexuality. *Dracula* repeatedly reveals an intense interest in a woman's capacity to extend and to receive physical pleasure but simultaneously reinforces the notion that, in the end, a man ought to settle for nothing less than an angel constrained and doting; that a woman who has attained carnal knowledge—especially illicitly—has been rendered unclean and thus much too tainted for the respectable bourgeois male. Lucy, for example, becomes diseased and monstrous after having been touched by unbridled sex, here

Edward Van Sloan as Dr. Van Helsing and Bela Lugosi as Count Dracula in the 1931 Universal Studios film version of Stoker's best-known novel

symbolized by the rather satyric count; Mina can be redeemed only when she in effect renounces her bestial seducer and presents Harker, her husband, with a child.

Dracula received more than one unfriendly review: the *Athenaeum*, for instance, described it as "a mere series of grotesquely incredible events" that was "wanting in the constructive art as well as in the higher literary sense." But the novel was also enthusiastically praised by such influential publications as the *Bookman* and the *Pall Mall Gazette*. *Dracula* sold steadily and well and can certainly be credited with reigniting in both Europe and America a craze for vampires, which probably reached its peak in the 1920s and 1930s when Irish actor Hamilton Deane adapted *Dracula* into a highly successful stage play.

After *Dracula* Stoker remained as manager of the Lyceum and continued to devote a fair portion of his free time to the writing of fiction. His fourth novel, *The Mystery of the Sea* (1902), meticulously describes a hunt for lost treasure in Cruden Bay—and runs on, often laboriously, for nearly 500 pages. Archie Hunter, the novel's hero, possesses a "big body and athletic powers" as well as a keen interest in occult matters. "The

whole earth and sea, and air," he announces in an early chapter, "all that of which human beings generally ordinarily take cognisance, is but a film or crust which hides the deeper moving powers of forces." "These forces," he decides (and the novel's plot is structured to bear him out), do not clash arbitrarily; rather, "there was somewhere a purposeful cause of universal action. An action which in its special or concrete working appeared like the sentience of nature in general, and of the myriad items of its cosmogony."

The Lady of the Shroud (1909) opens with a lengthy, deadly dull discussion of the provisions of a will but becomes—by book 3—perhaps the best paced and most readable of Stoker's later novels. Structured like *Dracula* around a series of interconnected documents, this work focuses on a brawny and very earnest fellow named Rupert St. Leger and his attempts to discover the identity of a young, shroud-clad woman who visits him nightly in his room on the Adriatic estate where he is temporarily staying. St. Leger dubs his visitor "the Lady of the Shroud," and though he fears that she might be a vampire (she is not), he soon falls in love with her and begins a chain of thought and action that suggests the sexual tension and confusion that is so abundant in *Dracula*. Rupert kisses the very cushions where his mysterious lady rests her head; he admits that she has awakened in him a passion "quick, hot and insistent." Early on, he is shocked by her proposal that the two of them spend the night together holding hands by the fire and proclaims that, in the final analysis, nothing can be more "sweet" than "to restore the lost or seemingly lost soul of the woman you love!"

The title of Stoker's final novel, *The Lair of the White Worm* (1911), is a Freudian's delight. Put simply, the story focuses on Lady Arabella, "a girl of the Caucasian type, beautiful, Saxon blonde, with a complexion of milk and roses"– who is able to transform herself into a large and deadly snake. This book illustrates the principal characteristics and weaknesses of the bulk of Stoker's book-length fiction. It features stereotypical characters involved in utterly implausible adventures in an exotic setting; it has a strong boy-gets-girl subplot, and its muzzy occultism is paralleled by a sense that large white British males are the crowning achievement of all creation and can always be counted on to save the day. Thus, much of the ridicule that Stoker perhaps intended as comic relief is aimed at Lady Arabella's black servant, Oolanga. Stoker routinely refers to this character as "the nigger" and occasionally uses his appearance in the text to introduce racist slurs.

The Lair of the White Worm sold surprisingly well, but none of Stoker's other novels came close to achieving the popular or critical success of *Dracula*. Stoker, moreover, suffered a series of disappointments and setbacks in the later years of his life, beginning with the closing of the Lyceum in 1902 and the death of his idol Irving in 1905. Stoker contracted syphilis in the 1880s, and, Daniel Farson suggests, as a result he suffered from a gradual decline in his mental health–a fact that might explain the particular awfulness of his final novel. Stoker died in 1912 of general paresis and exhaustion.

Following her husband's death, Florence Stoker released a collection of his shorter fiction entitled *Dracula's Guest, and Other Weird Stories* (1914). In the vivid, strongly paced title piece–originally conceived as an early chapter of *Dracula*–Jonathan Harker again makes his way to the count's castle. This time he encounters, among other things, a very nervous coachman, a hailstorm, and a female vampire who turns into a wolf and spends the night nestled protectively against his chest. Even more curious, however, is "The Squaw," which begins with a detailed description of a carelessly tossed rock shattering out the "little brains" of a playful kitten and concludes with a scene in which one man's eyeball is gouged out; another is crushed inside a spiked torture device; and the narrator picks up a sword and cuts in half yet another cat. This brief story is so thoroughly gory that the reader is tempted to view it as a subtle parody of the horror genre, especially when–early on–the narrator matter-of-factly observes that the infamous Iron Virgin of Nuremberg "has been handed down as an instance of the horrors of cruelty of which man is capable" and then adds that he and his wife had "long looked forward to seeing it." Stoker was not noted for his subtlety, and most evidence also suggests that he was not prone to take himself or his work lightly. "The Squaw" can be viewed only as the particularly fascinating, unsettling product of a late-Victorian gentleman writer oddly preoccupied not only with matters mysterious and frightening but with the brutal mutilation of innocent life: with impalements, gaping wounds, and great showers of blood.

Stoker's death attracted relatively little attention in the world's press. Today he remains far less famous than his best-known fictional character, who–at least in his Bela Lugosi guise–is probably as recognizable to most Americans as Mickey Mouse or Batman. Broadly and essentially, Stoker was himself the creator of prose cartoons. But *Dracula* is a marvel: its murky depths will surely keep readers and critics intrigued for many years to come.

Bibliography:
Richard Dalby, *Bram Stoker: A Bibliography of First Editions* (London: Dracula Press, 1983).

Biographies:
Harry Ludlam, *A Biography of Dracula: The Life Story of Bram Stoker* (London: Foulsham, 1962);
Daniel Farson, *The Man Who Wrote Dracula: A Biography of Bram Stoker* (London: Joseph, 1975; New York: St. Martin's, 1976).

References:
C. F. Bentley, "The Monster in the Bedroom: Sexual Symbolism in Bram Stoker's *Dracula*," *Literature and Psychology*, 22, no. 1 (1972): 27-33;
Joseph S. Bierman, "The Genesis and Dating of *Dracula* from Bram Stoker's Working

Notes," *Notes and Queries*, new series 24 (1977): 39-41;

Charles S. Blinderman, "Vampurella: Darwin and Count Dracula," *Massachusetts Review* (Summer 1980): 411-428;

M. M. Carlson, "What Stoker Saw: An Introduction to the History of the Literary Vampire," *Folklore Forum*, 10, no. 1 (1977): 26-32;

Stephanie Demetrakopoulos, "Feminism, Sex Role Exchanges, and Other Subliminal Fantasies in Bram Stoker's *Dracula*," *Frontiers*, 2, no. 3 (1977): 104-113;

Radu Florescu and Raymond T. McNally, *Dracula: A Biography of Vlad the Impaler, 1431-1476* (New York: Hawthorn, 1973);

Carrol L. Fry, "Fictional Conventions and Sexuality in *Dracula*," *Victorian Newsletter*, 42 (Fall 1972): 20-22;

Donald F. Glut, *The Dracula Book* (Metuchen, N.J.: Scarecrow Press, 1975);

Mark M. Hennelly, Jr., "*Dracula*: The Gnostic Quest and Victorian Wasteland," *English Literature in Transition*, 20, no. 1 (1977): 13-26;

Eric Irvin, "Dracula's Friends and Forerunners," *Quadrant*, 135 (October 1978): 42-44;

Elizabeth MacAndrew and Susan Gorsky, "Why Do They Faint and Die?–The Birth of the Delicate Heroine," *Journal of Popular Culture*, 8 (Spring 1975): 735-745;

Raymond T. McNally and Radu Florescu, *In Search of Dracula: A True History of Dracula and Vampire Legends* (New York: Warner, 1976);

McNally, ed., *A Clutch of Vampires: These Being Among the Best from History and Literature* (Greenwich, Conn.: New York Graphic Society, 1974);

Lowry Nelson, Jr., "Night Thoughts on The Gothic Novel," *Yale Review*, 52 (Winter 1963): 236-257;

Phyllis A. Roth, *Bram Stoker* (Boston: Twayne, 1982);

Harry A. Senn, *Were-Wolf and Vampire in Romania* (New York: Columbia University Press, 1982);

John Allen Stevenson, "A Vampire in the Mirror: The Sexuality of *Dracula*," *PMLA*, 103 (March 1988): 139-149;

Richard Wasson, "The Politics of *Dracula*," *English Literature in Transition*, 9, no. 1 (1966): 24-27;

Judith Weissman, "Women and Vampires: *Dracula* as a Victorian Novel," *Midwest Quarterly*, 18 (Summer 1977): 392-405;

Leonard Wolf, ed., *The Annotated Dracula* (New York: Ballantine, 1975);

Dudley Wright, *The Book of Vampires* (New York: Causeway Books, 1973).

Papers:

Seventy-eight pages of Bram Stoker's diagrams, notes, and outlines for *Dracula* are held by the Rosenbach Museum and Library, Philadelphia.

Edgar Wallace

(1 April 1875-10 February 1932)

J. Randolph Cox
St. Olaf College

BOOKS: *The Mission That Failed! A Tale of the Raid and Other Poems* (Cape Town: Miller, 1898);

War! and Other Poems (Cape Town: Eastern Press, 1900);

Writ in Barracks (London: Methuen, 1900);

Unofficial Dispatches (London: Hutchinson, 1901);

"Smithy" (London: Tallis, 1905); revised as *Smithy, Not to Mention Nobby Clark and Spud Murphy* (London: Newnes, 1914);

The Four Just Men (London: Tallis, 1905; revised, 1906; Boston: Small, Maynard, 1920);

Angel Esquire (Bristol: Arrowsmith, 1908; New York: Holt, 1908);

The Council of Justice (London: Ward, Lock, 1908);

The Duke in the Suburbs (London: Ward, Lock, 1909);

Smithy Abroad: Barrack Room Sketches (London: Hulton, 1909);

Captain Tatham of Tatham Island (London: Gale & Polden, 1909); revised as *The Island of Galloping Gold* (London: Newnes, 1916); republished as *Eve's Island* (London: Newnes, 1926);

The Nine Bears (London: Ward, Lock, 1910); revised as *The Other Man* (New York: Dodd, Mead, 1911); original version republished as *Silinski, Master Criminal* (Cleveland: World Syndicate, 1930); republished as *The Cheaters* (London: Brown, Watson, 1964);

Sanders of the River (London: Ward, Lock, 1911; Garden City: Doubleday, Doran, 1930);

Private Selby (London: Ward, Lock, 1912);

The People of the River (London: Ward, Lock, 1912);

Grey Timothy (London: Ward, Lock, 1913); republished as *Pallard the Punter* (London: Ward, Lock, 1914);

The River of Stars (London: Ward, Lock, 1913);

The Fourth Plague (London: Ward, Lock, 1913; Garden City: Doubleday, Doran, 1930);

Bosambo of the River (London: Ward, Lock, 1914);

The Admirable Carfew (London: Ward, Lock, 1914);

The Story of My Life, as Evelyn Thaw (London: John Long, 1914);

The Standard History of the War, 4 volumes (London: Newnes, 1914-1916);

Heroes All: Gallant Deeds of the War (London: Newnes, 1914);

Smithy's Friend Nobby (London: Town Topics, 1914); republished as *Nobby* (London: Newnes, 1916);

Field Marshall Sir John French and His Campaigns (London: Newnes, 1914);

Famous Scottish Regiments (London: Newnes, 1914);

"Bones": Being Further Adventures in Mr. Commissioner Sanders' Country (London: Ward, Lock, 1915);

"Smithy" and the Hun (London: Pearson, 1915);

The Melody of Death (Bristol: Arrowsmith, 1915; New York: Dial, 1927);

"1925": The Story of a Fatal Peace (London: Newnes, 1915);

The Man Who Bought London (London: Ward, Lock, 1915);

Kitchener's Army and the Territorial Forces: The Full Story of a Great Achievement (London: Newnes, 1915);

War of the Nations, 11 volumes (London: Newnes, 1915-1917);

A Debt Discharged (London: Ward, Lock, 1916);

The Tomb of Ts'in (London: Ward, Lock, 1916);

The Clue of the Twisted Candle (Boston: Small, Maynard, 1916; London: Newnes, 1917);

The Just Men of Cordova (London: Ward, Lock, 1917; Garden City: Doubleday, Doran, 1929);

The Secret House (London: Ward, Lock, 1917; Boston: Small, Maynard, 1919);

The Keepers of the King's Peace (London: Ward, Lock, 1917);

Kate, Plus Ten (Boston: Small, Maynard, 1917; London: Ward, Lock, 1919);

Down Under Donovan (London: Ward, Lock, 1918);

Those Folk of Bulboro (London: Ward, Lock, 1918);

Lieutenant Bones (London: Ward, Lock, 1918);

Edgar Wallace (photograph by Sasha, courtesy of BBC Hulton)

Tam of the Scouts (London: Newnes, 1918); republished as *Tam O' the Scoots* (Boston: Small, Maynard, 1919); republished and abridged as *Tam* (London: Newnes, 1928);

The Man Who Knew (Boston: Small, Maynard, 1918; London: Newnes, 1919);

The Fighting Scouts (London: Pearson, 1919);

The Adventures of Heine (London & Melbourne: Ward, Lock, 1919);

The Green Rust (London & Melbourne: Ward, Lock, 1919; Boston: Small, Maynard, 1920);

Jack o' Judgment (London & Melbourne: Ward, Lock, 1920; Boston: Small, Maynard, 1921);

The Daffodil Mystery (London & Melbourne: Ward, Lock, 1920); republished as *The Daffodil Murder* (Boston: Small, Maynard, 1921);

Bones in London (London & Melbourne: Ward, Lock, 1921);

The Book of All-Power (London & Melbourne: Ward, Lock, 1921);

The Law of the Four Just Men (London: Hodder & Stoughton, 1921); republished as *Again the Three Just Men* (Garden City: Doubleday, Doran, 1933);

The Angel of Terror (London: Hodder & Stoughton, 1922; Boston: Small, Maynard, 1922); republished as *The Destroying Angel* (London: Pan, 1959);

Sandi, the King-Maker (London & Melbourne: Ward, Lock, 1922);

The Flying Fifty-Five (London: Hutchinson, 1922);

The Crimson Circle (London: Hodder & Stoughton, 1922; Garden City: Doubleday, Doran, 1929);

Mr. Justice Maxell (London & Melbourne: Ward, Lock, 1922);

The Valley of Ghosts (London: Odhams Press, 1922; Boston: Small, Maynard, 1923);

Captains of Souls (Boston: Small, Maynard, 1922; London: Long, 1923);

Chick (London & Melbourne: Ward, Lock, 1923);

The Clue of the New Pin (London: Hodder & Stoughton, 1923; Boston: Small, Maynard, 1923);

The Books of Bart (London & Melbourne: Ward, Lock, 1923);

The Green Archer (London: Hodder & Stoughton, 1923; Boston: Small, Maynard, 1924);

The Missing Million (London: Long, 1923); republished as *The Missing Millions* (Boston: Small, Maynard, 1925);

Bones of the River (London: Newnes, 1923);

Blue Hand (Boston: Small, Maynard, 1923; London: Ward, Lock, 1925);

The Fellowship of the Frog (Boston: Small, Maynard, 1923; London: Ward, Lock, 1925);

The Dark Eyes of London (London: Ward, Lock, 1924; Garden City: Doubleday, Doran, 1929);

Educated Evans (London: Webster, 1924);

The Sinister Man (London: Hodder & Stoughton, 1924; Boston: Small, Maynard, 1925);

Room 13 (London: Long, 1924);

The Three Oak Mystery (London: Ward, Lock, 1924);

Double Dan (London: Hodder & Stoughton, 1924); republished as *Diana of Kara-Kara* (Boston: Small, Maynard, 1924);

The Face in the Night (London: Long, 1924; Garden City: Doubleday, Doran, 1929);

Flat 2 (Garden City: Garden City Publishing, 1924; London: Long, 1927);

The Black Avons, 4 volumes (London: Gill, 1925);

The Strange Countess (London: Hodder & Stoughton, 1925; Boston: Small, Maynard, 1926);

A King By Night (London: Long, 1925; Garden City: Doubleday, Page, 1926);

The Gaunt Stranger (London: Hodder & Stoughton, 1925); republished as *The Ringer* (Garden City: Doubleday, Page, 1926);

The Mind of Mr. J. G. Reeder (London: Hodder & Stoughton, 1925); republished as *The Murder Book of J. G. Reeder* (Garden City: Doubleday, Doran, 1929);

The Three Just Men (London: Hodder & Stoughton, 1925; Garden City: Doubleday, Doran, 1929);

The Man from Morocco (London: Long, 1925); republished as *The Black* (Garden City: Doubleday, Doran, 1930);

The Daughters of the Night (London: Newnes, 1925);

The Hairy Arm (Boston: Small, Maynard, 1925); republished as *The Avenger* (London: Long, 1926);

The Door with Seven Locks (London: Hodder & Stoughton, 1926; Garden City: Doubleday, Page, 1926);

Sanders (London: Hodder & Stoughton, 1926); republished as *Mr. Commissioner Sanders* (Garden City: Doubleday, Doran, 1930);

We Shall See! (London: Hodder & Stoughton, 1926); republished as *The Gaol Breaker* (Garden City: Doubleday, Doran, 1931);

The Black Abbot (London: Hodder & Stoughton, 1926; Garden City: Doubleday, Page, 1927);

The Terrible People (London: Hodder & Stoughton, 1926; Garden City: Doubleday, Page, 1926);

The Day of Uniting (London: Hodder & Stoughton, 1926; New York: Mystery League, 1930);

Penelope of the "Polyantha" (London: Hodder & Stoughton, 1926);

The Joker (London: Hodder & Stoughton, 1926); republished as *The Colossus* (Garden City: Doubleday, Doran, 1932);

The Square Emerald (London: Hodder & Stoughton, 1926); republished as *The Girl from Scotland Yard* (Garden City: Doubleday, Page, 1927);

The Yellow Snake (London: Hodder & Stoughton, 1926);

More Educated Evans (London: Webster's, 1926);

Barbara on Her Own (London: Newnes, 1926);

The Million Dollar Story (London: Newnes, 1926);

The Northing Tramp (London: Hodder & Stoughton, 1926; Garden City: Doubleday, Doran, 1929); republished as *The Tramp* (London: Pan, 1965);

People: A Short Autobiography (London: Hodder & Stoughton, 1926; Garden City: Doubleday, Doran, 1929); republished as *Edgar Wallace: A Short Autobiography* (London: Hodder & Stoughton, 1929);

The Ringer [play] (London: French, 1926);

The Hand of Power (London: Long, 1927; New York: Mystery League, 1930);

The Brigand (London: Hodder & Stoughton, 1927);

The Traitor's Gate (London: Hodder & Stoughton, 1927; Garden City: Doubleday, Page, 1927);

The Ringer [novel] (London: Hodder & Stoughton, 1927);

The Man Who Was Nobody (London: Ward, Lock, 1927);

The Feathered Serpent (London: Hodder & Stoughton, 1927; Garden City: Doubleday, Doran, 1928);

Terror Keep (London: Hodder & Stoughton, 1927; Garden City: Doubleday, Page, 1927);

Big Foot (London: Long, 1927);

Number Six (London: Newnes, 1927);

This England (London: Hodder & Stoughton, 1927);

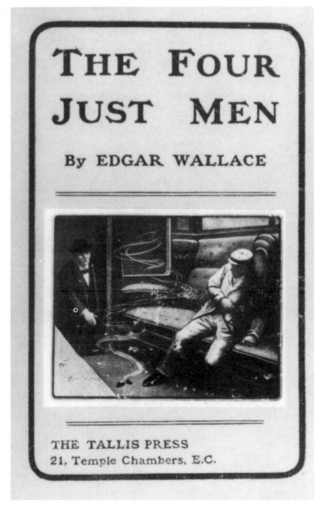

Front covers for the first and second issues of Wallace's 1905 novel, which he published himself under the imprint Tallis. In the first issue, the final chapter of the novel is omitted and the last pages announce a contest, with monetary rewards for the most accurate solutions to the book's murder mystery. In the second issue, these pages are cancelled and replaced with the last chapter, an explanatory letter from the murderer. When Wallace, who had spent freely for advertising, found himself unable to cover the expenses of his contest or to deal with the thousands of entries (many of which solved the mystery), he sought assistance from his employer at the Daily Mail *and was granted a £1000 salary advance.*

APPENDIX

WHO KILLED SIR PHILIP RAMON, AND HOW WAS HE KILLED?

£500 (FIVE HUNDRED POUNDS) PRIZE OFFER

IN the foregoing pages Mr. Edgar Wallace has told in a style which, we submit, at once places him in the forefront of living impressionist writers, a story of enthralling interest. He has in the course of the story shown how apparently inexplicable occurrences have had the simplest explanation, and has differed from most writers of mystery fiction in this respect, that he has explained as he went along the minor secrets of the Four Just Men. At the conclusion of the book only two mysteries remain unsolved :

1. How did the Four Just Men encompass the death of Sir Philip Ramon ?
2. Who killed Thery, and what was the explanation of the stained hands ?

So far the answer to these two questions is only known to the author and publisher, but there are

sufficient clues scattered through the book to enable the astute reader to unravel the mystery to his or her satisfaction. To the readers who give the correct solution, the Tallis Press will award

PRIZES AMOUNTING TO

FIVE HUNDRED POUNDS STERLING

DIVIDED AS FOLLOWS :

For the best and most accurate solution, gathered from the clues, £250 in one prize.
For the next best, £100 in one prize.
For the next most feasible solution, £50 in one prize.
For the two next most accurate, two prizes of £25 each.
And fifty consolation prizes of £1.

(*The solution will be published in the form of a diagram in the " Daily Mail."*)

INSTRUCTIONS.

1. Readers may send in as many solutions as they wish, but each explanation must either be written on or accompanied by the numbered and perforated page overleaf. All solutions unaccompanied by the perforated leaf will be disqualified without further notice.
2. Explanations should be written in detail, which should not, however, exceed 300 words. Absence of detail will not disqualify, but

---

224 APPENDIX

should, for instance, " A " write " Ramon was shot by Thery " and " B " write " Ramon was shot from the window by Thery ; the gun exploded and Thery had his hands destroyed," and if such were in substance the correct solution, the superior prize would go to " B."

3. The 1st, 2nd, 3rd, 4th and 5th prizes will NOT BE DIVIDED.
4. Mr. Edgar Wallace will adjudicate on the prize award, and HIS DECISION WILL BE FINAL.
5. The reader will compete expressly under the conditions laid down in these rules, and agrees to bind himself by these rules.
6. SOLUTIONS should be sent by REGISTERED LETTER POST, addressed to

THE TALLIS PRESS
(Competition Department),
21, Temple Chambers, E.C., London.

Readers enclosing a stamped addressed POST-CARD will receive a receipt for their letters.

Butler & Tanner, The Selwood Printing Works, Frome, and London.

№ 13062

"THE FOUR JUST MEN."

£500 SOLUTION COMPETITION.

(Note.—This sheet is numbered to prevent fraud. Readers before despatching this coupon should take careful note of the number.)

To the Publisher of
" The Four Just Men."

Sir,—

Having read the rules, to the terms of which I bind myself, I send hereunder (or attached)* my explanation of the killing of Sir Philip Ramon.

Name in full_____

Profession_____

Address_____

_____

* Cross out one of these.

Contest rules and entry blank for Wallace's The Four Just Men *"Solution Competition"*

The Squeaker [novel] (London: Hodder & Stoughton, 1927); republished as *The Squealer* (Garden City: Doubleday, Doran, 1928);

The Mixer (London: Long, 1927);

The Forger (London: Hodder & Stoughton, 1927); republished as *The Clever One* (Garden City: Doubleday, Doran, 1928);

Good Evans! (London: Webster's, 1927); republished as *The Educated Man (Good Evans!)* (London: Collins, 1929);

The Double (London: Hodder & Stoughton, 1928; Garden City: Doubleday, Doran, 1928);

The Twister (London: Long, 1928; Garden City: Doubleday, Doran, 1929);

The Flying Squad [novel] (London: Hodder & Stoughton, 1928; Garden City: Doubleday, Doran, 1929);

The Gunner (London: Long, 1928); republished as *Gunman's Bluff* (Garden City: Doubleday, Doran, 1929);

Again Sanders (London: Hodder & Stoughton, 1928; Garden City: Doubleday, Doran, 1929);

The Orator (London: Hutchinson, 1928);

The Thief in the Night (London: Readers Library, 1928);

Elegant Edward (London: Readers Library, 1928);

Again the Three Just Men (London: Hodder & Stoughton, 1928); republished as *The Law of the Three Just Men* (Garden City: Doubleday, Doran, 1931); republished as *Again the Three* (London: Pan, 1968);

Four Square Jane (London: Readers Library, 1929);

Forty-Eight Short Stories (London: Newnes, 1929); abridged as *The Cat Burglar* (London: Newnes, 1929); abridged again as *Circumstantial Evidence* (London: Newnes, 1929); abridged again as *The Prison-Breakers* (London: Newnes, 1929); abridged again as *The Governor of Chi-Foo* (London: Newnes, 1929); abridged again as *The Stretelli Case and Other Mysteries* (Cleveland: World Syndicate, 1930); abridged again as *Nig-Nog and Other Humorous Stories* (Cleveland: World Syndicate, 1934);

The India-Rubber Men (London: Hodder & Stoughton, 1929; Garden City: Doubleday, Doran, 1930);

Planetoid 127 and the Sweizer Pump (London: Readers Library, 1929);

The Flying Squad [play] (London: Hodder & Stoughton, 1929);

Again the Ringer (London: Hodder & Stoughton, 1929); republished as *The Ringer Returns* (Garden City: Doubleday, Doran, 1931);

Fighting Snub Reilly (London: Newnes, 1929);

The Ghost of Down Hill and The Queen of Sheba's Belt (London: Readers Library, 1929);

The Squeaker [play] (London: Hodder & Stoughton, 1929);

The Little Green Man (London: Newnes, 1929);

Red Aces (London: Hodder & Stoughton, 1929; Garden City: Doubleday, Doran, 1930);

The Terror (London: Collins, 1929; expanded edition, London: Brown, Watson, 1962);

The Lone House Mystery (London: Collins, 1929);

The Black (London: Readers Library, 1929; expanded edition, London: Brown, Watson, 1962);

For Information Received (London: Newnes, 1929);

The Lady of Little Hell (London: Newnes, 1929);

The Reporter (London: Readers Library, 1929);

The Big Four (London: Readers Library, 1929);

The Golden Hades (London: Collins, 1929);

The Iron Grip (London: Readers Library, 1929);

The Green Ribbon (London: Hutchinson, 1929; Garden City: Doubleday, Doran, 1930);

The Man Who Changed His Name [play] (London: Hodder & Stoughton, 1929);

Killer Kay (London: Newnes, 1930);

The Lady Called Nita (London: Newnes, 1930);

Mrs. William Jones and Bill (London: Newnes, 1930);

White Face (London: Hodder & Stoughton, 1930; Garden City: Doubleday, Doran, 1931);

The Calendar [novel] (London: Collins, 1930; Garden City: Doubleday, Doran, 1931);

The Clue of the Silver Key (London: Hodder & Stoughton, 1930); republished as *The Silver Key* (Garden City: Doubleday, Doran, 1930);

The Lady of Ascot (London: Hutchinson, 1930);

The Devil Man (London: Collins, 1931; Garden City: Doubleday, Doran, 1931);

On the Spot (London: Long, 1931; Garden City: Doubleday, Doran, 1931);

The Man at the Carlton (London: Hodder & Stoughton, 1931; Garden City: Doubleday, Doran, 1932);

The Coat of Arms (London: Hutchinson, 1931); republished as *The Arranways Mystery* (Garden City: Doubleday, Doran, 1932);

The Guv'nor, and Other Stories (London: Collins, 1932); republished as *Mr. Reeder Returns* (Garden City: Doubleday, Doran, 1932); republished as *The Guv'nor* (London: Col-

Dust jacket for the 1908 sequel to The Four Just Men

lins, 1933); republished again as *Mr. J. G. Reeder Returns* (London: Collins, 1934);

When the Gangs Came to London (London: Long, 1932; Garden City: Doubleday, Doran, 1932);

My Hollywood Diary (London: Hutchinson, 1932);

The Case of the Frightened Lady (London: French/ New York: French, 1932);

Sergeant Sir Peter (London: Chapman & Hall, 1932); republished as *Sergeant Dunn, C.I.D.* (London: Brown, Watson, 1962);

The Steward (London: Collins, 1932);

The Calendar [play] (London & New York: French, 1932);

The Frightened Lady (London: Hodder & Stoughton, 1932; Garden City: Doubleday, Doran, 1933);

The Governor of Chi-Foo and Other Stories (Cleveland: World Syndicate, 1933);

Fighting Snub Reilley and Other Stories (Cleveland: World Syndicate, 1934);

The Last Adventure (London: Hutchinson, 1934);

The Woman from the East, and Other Stories (London: Hutchinson, 1934);

The Undisclosed Client (London: Brown, Watson, 1962);

An African Millionaire (London: Davis-Poynter, 1972);

The Man Who Married His Cook and Other Stories (London: White Lion, 1976);

Two Stories and the Seventh Man (Oxford: Penelope Wallace, 1981);

"The Sooper" and Others, edited by Jack Adrian (London: Dent, 1984);

The Death Room, edited by Adrian (London: Kimber, 1986).

PLAY PRODUCTIONS: *An African Millionaire*, Cape Town, South Africa, Cape Town Opera House, 1904;

Dolly Cutting Herself, London, Hippodrome Theatre, 2 January 1911;

The Forest of Happy Dreams, London, Queen's Theatre, 15 April 1911;

Hello, Exchange!, London, Pavilion Theatre, 7 April 1913;

The Manager's Dream, Chelsea, Palladium Theatre, 14 April 1913;

The Soldier Boy, by Wallace and Rida Johnson Young, London, Apollo Theatre, 26 June 1918;

M'Lady, London, Playhouse Theatre, 18 July 1921;

The Ringer, London, Wyndham's Theatre, 1 May 1926;

The Mystery of Room 45, Chelsea, Theatrical Garden Party, 22 June 1926;

The Terror, New Brighton, Winter Garden Theatre, 4 April 1927;

A Perfect Gentleman, London, New Theatre, 26 April 1927;

Double Dan, London, Savoy Theatre, 7 May 1927;

The Yellow Mask, London, Carlton Theatre, 8 February 1928;

The Man Who Changed His Name, London, Apollo Theatre, 14 March 1928;

The Squeaker, London, Apollo Theatre, 29 May 1928;

The Flying Squad, London, Lyceum Theatre, 7 June 1928;

The Lad, London, Shaftsbury Theatre, 24 December 1928;

Persons Unknown, London, Shaftsbury Theatre, 8 May 1929;

The Calendar, London, Wyndham's Theatre, 18 September 1929;

On the Spot, London, Wyndham's Theatre, 2
    April 1930;
Smoky Cell, London, Wyndham's Theatre, 1930;
The Case of the Frightened Lady, London, Wynd-
    ham's Theatre, 1931;
The Green Pack, London, Wyndham's Theatre,
    1932.

MOTION PICTURES: *Should a Doctor Tell?*, dia-
    logue by Wallace, British Lion, 1930;
King Kong, screenplay by Wallace and Merian C.
    Cooper, RKO, 1933.

The name Edgar Wallace too often suggests
the sensational thriller, with dark deeds on
darker nights, which is easily parodied or dismissed. What is overlooked is the fact that this prodigious writer was one of the most popular
writers of this century. Measured by the standard
of number of publications over a specific period
of time, Edgar Wallace was one of the most prolific writers of the first third of the twentieth century. In number of titles, he may not have been
the equal of the mystery writers John Creasey
(1908-1973) or Georges Simenon (1903-   ) but to
produce 173 novels, 24 plays, 61 sketches, over
200 short stories, and countless articles and adaptations in a period of about twenty-five years is
still a prodigious feat. Unfortunately, a recitation
of statistics like these has been substituted for
any substantive discussion of those works.

Richard Horatio Edgar Wallace was born in
Greenwich, 1 April 1875, the illegitimate son of
Richard Horatio Edgar, a sometime actor, and
Mary Jane (Polly) Richards, an actress. He was
brought up as the adopted child of George Freeman, a Billingsgate fish porter. Wallace held a variety of jobs as a boy, storing up experiences he
later used as a writer. His lifelong association
with journalism began when he sold newspapers
at Ludgate Circus a few yards from where the
bronze plaque which now commemorates him is located. When he was twelve years old he began
work as a printer's boy. At eighteen he enlisted
in the Royal West Kent Regiment, later transfer-
ring to the Medical Staff Corps. His first attempts at writing were lyrics for Arthur Roberts,
a popular singer of the day. When he took unofficial leave to hear them sung, he was given thirty-
six hours of hard labor in the military prison.

In 1896, at the age of twenty-one, he was
transferred to Simonstown, South Africa, where
he continued his writing. He commemorated a
visit to South Africa by Rudyard Kipling in the

Dust jacket for the 1929 American edition of The Mind of
J. G. Reeder, *the first collection of stories about Wallace's med-
itative crime solver introduced in the 1924 novel* Room 13
(courtesy of Otto Penzler)

poem, "Good Morning, Mr. Kipling." The reception of this work encouraged him to continue writing. Within two years his first book, a collection
of verse titled *The Mission That Failed!* (1898), was
published.

In addition to composing poetry, Wallace
began writing political articles for South African
newspapers which were not well received by his superior officers. He bought himself out of the
army and took a position as a correspondent for
Reuters. His typist sent his articles impartially to
Reuters, the *Daily News*, and the *Daily Mail*,
thereby giving him wider recognition through a
sort of improvised syndication. In 1900 Wallace returned to England for the publication of his
third collection of verse, *Writ in Barracks*. He
came back to South Africa in a new position as
war correspondent for the *Daily Mail*. His collected articles were published the following year

as *Unofficial Dispatches* (1901). Wallace's outspokenness was responsible for his many conflicts with the military. The ingenuity he used in getting the story of the signing of the peace treaty with the Boers resulted in his being banned as a war reporter by Lord Kitchener, a restriction which lasted into World War I.

Wallace married Ivy Maud Caldecott in April 1901. By the next year he was the father of a daughter (who died in childbirth of meningitis) and the first editor of a Johannesburg newspaper, the *Rand Daily Mail*. With the flair which would make him famous in years to come, he spent the paper's money on sensational material and a staff of foreign correspondents. He rented a large house, engaged a staff of native servants, and entertained lavishly. He was fired by the paper's owner. Wallace and his wife went to England, arriving with only a few shillings and a half-finished play about Cecil Rhodes.

He took a reporter's job at the *Daily Mail* which sent him to Canada, Spain, the Belgian Congo, and Morocco. His wife gave birth to a son, Bryan, at about the time his play, *An African Millionaire* (1904), closed in Cape Town after a run of only six nights.

Wallace's next venture was one which he hoped would make him rich. It did not, but this first novel, *The Four Just Men* (1905), encouraged him to write thrillers for a living. Unable to find a publisher for his manuscript, Wallace decided to publish it himself under the imprint of the Tallis Press. He spent lavishly for advertising and offered £500 to the reader who could solve the mystery. Although the book sold well, the profits could not cover his expenses. Moreover, thousands of solutions, many of them correct, were sent to the office of the Tallis Press. To deflect the adverse publicity which might come to his paper as a result of the unforeseen outcome of Wallace's publicity stunt, Alfred Harmsworth, publisher of the *Daily Mail*, rescued Wallace from possible scandal and certain bankruptcy by advancing him £1,000 against his salary.

The Four Just Men set a pattern which Wallace followed with greater success in later books. The highly improbable story of a plot against the English foreign secretary is told in a plain style with precise, realistic details which lend credibility to a series of events which would not have been believable if written in a more flamboyant style. The main characters punish evildoers whom the law cannot touch. The book was popular enough to make sequels possible and profit-

Dust jacket for the American edition of Wallace's 1926 science-fiction novel in which a comet threatens to destroy Earth

able. *The Council of Justice* (1908), *The Just Men of Cordova* (1917), *The Law of the Four Just Men* (1921), *The Three Just Men* (1925), and *Again the Three Just Men* (1928) complete the canon.

Wallace did not remain in Harmsworth's good graces for long. When he allowed himself to become careless in reporting on the atrocities in the Congo in 1907, the possibility of a libel suit made it necessary for the newspaper owner to let him go. No other newspaper would hire him. His wife was expecting another child, and the bill collectors began to hound him. He forced himself to write for periodicals, and some money was forthcoming–although it often left him at the racetrack along with the horses he backed. Commissioned to write some racing articles for George Beech of Shurey's Publications, he met their fiction editor, Mrs. Isabel Thorne. Her advice on that occasion and a subsequent meeting, regarding the technique of short-story writing and the use of source material, resulted in the creation of Mr. Commissioner Sanders.

Edgar Wallace and his daughter Penelope, circa 1928

The stories about Sanders may represent Wallace's strongest contributions to English literature. Wallace developed a format for the short story which he would use for the rest of his career. He described a series of events to a specific point, and suddenly he broke off to begin an apparently independent story. This sequence continued for some time until the several threads met to merge into one story, a knot tied up into a comic or dramatic ending. Set in an unspecified territory in West Africa, the stories center around Sanders, a commissioner who speaks the Bomongo tongue to perfection and is little short of a king in the river territories. Wallace based these stories on his own experiences and knowledge gained in Africa, fortified by research and his own fertile imagination. The characters of Sanders, Bosambo, and the rest were popular

with the readers of the *Weekly Tale-Teller*, where they appeared prior to being collected into books—beginning with *Sanders of the River* (1911).

The success of his West African stories inspired Wallace to create a character named Bones who was featured in books beginning with *"Bones": Being Further Adventures in Mr. Commissioner Sanders' Country* (1915). His new reputation led to fresh assignments from other publishers. Soon he had returned to Fleet Street as a reporter for the *Standard*.

When World War I began, Wallace was thirty-nine, too old to be a soldier, and prohibited by Kitchener from resuming his post as a war correspondent. Amid changes in his personal life brought on by the war, he wrote a daily column analyzing the war news for the Birmingham *Daily Post*. His capacity for presenting the popular attitude was a significant factor in his later success as a writer. Wallace lost his secretary Robert Curtis, who enlisted for the duration of the war, and he hired Ethel Violet King to replace him. Wallace and Ivy, who had two sons and a daughter, were divorced in 1918. Wallace married King, whom he nicknamed Jim, in 1921. The couple had one daughter.

Until the early 1920s Wallace had been content to write serials, short stories, and articles, selling them outright for whatever price he could get. His new wife was a practical woman. She ordered his affairs, and he acquired a literary agent, A. S. Watt. Watt introduced him to Sir Ernest Hodder-Williams, head of the publishing firm of Hodder and Stoughton. Hodder-Williams had been aware of Wallace and thought he had potential as a writer of thrillers. In short order Wallace signed a contract for six novels with a £250 payment on receipt of each manuscript and a sliding scale of royalties dependent on sales.

The basis for this contract and the future ones Wallace was to sign was Hodder-Williams's belief in the quantity of work needed. The reading public was to be saturated with novels by Edgar Wallace. In banking his investment on Wallace's ability as a journalist to write clearly, superficially, and quickly, he found a sure thing. In the next decade, before Wallace's death in 1932, Hodder and Stoughton published no less than forty-six of his books. Wallace aspired to reach millions of readers; anything less meant failure. Like all great storytellers, he sought to entertain. He also wanted to make a fortune.

Edgar Wallace

It is not true that each Edgar Wallace novel is just like every other, but the great quantity must be divided into categories and discussed on the grounds of their similar elements before the author's achievement can be properly appreciated. The typical Edgar Wallace book is a straightforward crime novel or thriller in which the plot is the most significant point. *The Crimson Circle* (1922), *The Green Archer* (1923), *The Dark Eyes of London* (1924), *A King by Night* (1925), *The Man from Morocco* (1925), and *Terror Keep* (1927) can be placed in this category. His plot construction for the thriller novels was a variation of the scheme he had devised for his African stories. Instead of a series of seemingly unrelated threads being brought together at the end, there was a main mystery introduced at the beginning and not solved until the end. In addition, Wallace used several minor mysteries introduced at various points in the story which were solved shortly after the introduction of a subsequent minor mystery.

Many Wallace novels have strong central characters who recur. This created strong reader identification with the personality of the hero. The Just Men series, the J. G. Reeder books (*The Mind of Mr. J. G. Reeder* [1925], *Terror Keep, Red Aces* [1929], and *The Guv'nor, and Other Stories* [1932] form this group), and the stories of Evans, the little cockney tipster–*Educated Evans* (1924), *More Educated Evans* (1926), and *Good Evans!* (1927)–all feature such characters. *The Ringer* (1927) features a criminal protagonist as does its sequel, *Again the Ringer* (1929). Many of Wallace's books have a racing background and protagonists associated with it. The Educated Evans series and works like *Grey Timothy* (1913), *Down Under Donovan* (1918), and *The Flying Fifty-Five* (1922) are in this category.

Wallace did not always create truly three-dimensional characters, but many of his characters are vivid and memorable nonetheless. His heroes are intelligent and able reporters or detectives, often employed by Scotland Yard or some other agency (the River Police or the Public Prosecutor's Office). His heroines are beautiful, partly responsible for solving the mystery, and they are usually the object of the villain's machinations. The identity of some of the villains might be obvious from the first page, but Wallace always saved the identity of the chief villain for the final chapter. There is comic relief supplied by petty thieves, criminals, and philosophical asides of the author. A similarity in characterization and plot structure between Wallace's thrillers and motion picture thrillers of the 1930s and 1940s (both features and serials) is due to the recognition by scriptwriters of the entertainment value of his work.

Wallace wrote a number of books which are not easily categorized. In *The Day of Uniting* (1926) he wrote one of his rare science-fiction stories about the predicted end of the world in a collision with a comet. *The Devil Man* (1931) is a fictionalized account of the life of criminal Charles Peace, and *Barbara on Her Own* (1926) is a comic novel in the vein of P. G. Wodehouse.

On occasion Wallace was able to command a kind of inspiration that belied his seemingly mechanical approach to writing. One example is *On the Spot* (1931) which was written first as a play, then as a novel (following the author's visit to Chicago in 1929). Al Capone seemed to Wallace to be the personification of all of the master criminals he had ever imagined for his fiction. In consequence, the character of Tony Perelli, based on

Endsheets, with scenes from the movie, for the first American edition of King Kong. *Based on an idea proposed by Wallace when he worked at RKO in 1930, the movie was released in 1933, the year after he died, and the book, by Delos W. Lovelace, was based on the movie (courtesy of Otto Penzler).*

Capone, is one of the most convincing criminals Wallace ever created.

Edgar Wallace began his working day around five or six o'clock in the morning after no more than five or six hours of sleep. His ability to sleep soundly, as well as to take a nap of five or ten minutes at a time during the day, explains much of this. By the time his wife arrived at the breakfast table, Wallace would have put in two or three hours of work. He smoked cigarettes constantly in a characteristic holder, slaking the thirst created by his smoking with weak tea, heavily sweetened and diluted with milk. This routine was varied by the occasional round-the-clock sessions when a serial, play, or series of articles had been promised for the following Monday. He dictated much of his work for his secretary Robert Curtis to put into presentable manuscript form. His wife protected him from external disturbances.

Wallace wrote twenty-four plays, producing many of them himself. His first real success was

The Ringer in 1926, which starred Leslie Banks, featured Nigel Bruce, and was produced by Gerald Du Maurier. He turned some of his plays into novels.

He also wrote screenplays for British Lion. In 1930 RKO Studios offered him a two-month contract at £600 a week if he would come to Hollywood. He left England in November 1931. He missed his family but settled to work in a rented house, savoring the warm climate which he hoped would prove beneficial to his health. He looked forward to a visit from his wife and the production of one of his movie ideas. The visit never took place, and the film that came from his idea, *King Kong,* was not produced until after his death.

Early in 1932 Wallace fell into a coma. E. C. Fishbaugh, a physician called in by Wallace's secretary, diagnosed diabetes brought on by years of drinking abnormal quantities of heavily sweetened tea. Double pneumonia set in, and he died on 10 February. His widow, already on her way to America by ship, disembarked at Cherbourg to await her husband's remains. The coffin carrying Wallace's body, draped with a Union Jack and covered with flowers, was put ashore at Southampton, where the flags of the city were at half-mast.

The legend of Edgar Wallace persists more than half a century after his death. His extravagances, his love of horse racing, his generosity, and his petty annoyances, have all been discussed. A rumor that his works were ghostwritten was never completely dispelled in spite of no one coming forward to accept his offer of £5,000 for proof that every word was not his own. He was not a great writer, for all of his flashes of genius and inspiration. He never claimed to be, and he did not need to be. He was a great storyteller who appealed mainly to his own generation.

Bibliographies:

W. O. G. Lofts and Derek Adley, *The British Bibliography of Edgar Wallace* (London: Howard Baker, 1969);

Charles Kiddle, *A Guide to the First Editions of Edgar Wallace* (Motcombe, Dorset: Ivory Head Press, 1981).

Biographies:

Robert Curtis, *Edgar Wallace–Each Way* (London: Lane, 1932);

Ethel V. Wallace, *Edgar Wallace by his Wife* (London: Hutchinson, 1932);

Margaret Lane, *Edgar Wallace: The Biography of a Phenomenon* (London: Heinemann, 1938; Garden City: Doubleday, Doran, 1939); revised edition (London: Hamilton, 1964).

References:

J. Randolph Cox, "So You Think You Know the Story? Ringing the Changes on The Ringer," *Edgar Wallace Society Newsletter*, nos. 20-21 (November 1973-February 1974): 2-3, 4-5;

Cox, "So You Think You Know the Story? Some Variant Readings of the Works of Edgar Wallace," *Edgar Wallace Society Newsletter*, nos. 18-19 (May-August 1973): 2-3, 3-4;

Edgar Wallace Society Newsletter (1969-1985); continued as *Crimson Circle Magazine* (1985-   );

John A. Hogan, "Exhumation of *The Tomb of Ts'in*," *Armchair Detective*, 6 (April 1973): 167-171;

Hogan, "Stranger Than Fiction," *Armchair Detective*, 9 (February 1976): 119-121;

Nigel Morland, "The Edgar Wallace I Knew," *Armchair Detective*, 1 (April 1968); 68-70;

Jack Edmund Nolan, "Edgar Wallace," *Films in Review*, 18 (February 1967): 71-85;

Penelope Wallace, "Edgar Wallace–Master of Mystery," *Pontine Dossier*, new series 1 (1970): 19-23.

H. G. Wells

(21 September 1866-13 August 1946)

Brian Murray
Youngstown State University

See also the Wells entry in *DLB 34, British Novelists, 1890-1929: Traditionalists.*

BOOKS: *Text-Book Of Biology*, 2 volumes (London: Clive, 1893; volume 1 revised, 1894);

Honours Physiography, by Wells and R. A. Gregory (London: Hughes, 1893);

Select Conversations With An Uncle (now extinct) and two other reminiscences (London: John Lane/ New York: Merriam, 1895);

The Time Machine: An Invention (London: Heinemann, 1895; New York: Holt, 1895);

The Wonderful Visit (London: Dent/New York: Macmillan, 1895);

The Stolen Bacillus, And Other Incidents (London: Methuen, 1895);

The Island of Doctor Moreau (London: Heinemann, 1896; New York: Stone & Kimball, 1896);

The Wheels of Chance (London: Dent/New York: Macmillan, 1896);

The Plattner Story And Others (London: Methuen, 1897);

The Invisible Man: A Grotesque Romance (London: Pearson, 1897; enlarged edition, New York: Arnold, 1897; London: Pearson, 1900);

Certain Personal Matters: A Collection of Material, Mainly Autobiographical (London: Lawrence & Bullen, 1897);

Thirty Strange Stories (New York: Arnold, 1897);

The War of The Worlds (London: Heinemann, 1898; New York & London: Harper, 1898);

When the Sleeper Wakes (London & New York: Harper, 1899); revised as *The Sleeper Awakes* (London: Nelson, 1910);

Tales of Space and Time (London & New York: Harper, 1899; New York: Doubleday, McClure, 1899);

Love and Mr. Lewisham (London & New York: Harper, 1900);

The First Men in the Moon (London: Newnes, 1901; Indianapolis: Bowen-Merrill, 1901);

Anticipations Of The Reaction Of Mechanical And Scientific Progress Upon Human Life And Thought (London: Chapman & Hall, 1901; New York & London: Harper, 1902);

The Discovery Of The Future: A Discourse Delivered To The Royal Institution On January 24, 1902 (London: Unwin, 1902; New York: Heubsch, 1913);

The Sea Lady (London: Methuen, 1902; New York: Appleton, 1902);

Mankind in the Making (London: Chapman & Hall, 1903; New York: Scribners, 1904);

Twelve Stories and a Dream (London & New York: Macmillan, 1903; New York: Scribners, 1905);

The Food of the Gods And How It Came To Earth (London: Macmillan, 1904; New York: Scribners, 1904);

A Modern Utopia (London: Chapman & Hall, 1905; New York: Scribners, 1905);

Kipps: The Story Of A Simple Soul (London: Macmillan, 1905; New York: Scribners, 1905);

In The Days Of The Comet (London: Macmillan, 1906; New York: Century, 1906);

The Future in America: A Search After Realities (London: Chapman & Hall, 1906; New York & London: Harper, 1906);

Faults of the Fabian (London: Fabian Society, 1906);

Socialism and the Family (London: Fifield, 1906; Boston: Ball, 1906);

This Misery of Boots (London: Fabian Society, 1907; Boston: Ball, 1908);

Will Socialism Destroy the Home (London: Independent Labour Party, 1907);

New Worlds for Old (London: Constable, 1908; New York: Macmillan, 1908);

The War In The Air And Particularly How Mr Bert Smallways Fared While It Lasted (London: Bell, 1908; New York: Macmillan, 1908);

First & Last Things: A Confession of Faith and Rule of Life (London: Constable, 1908; New York & London: Putnam's, 1908; revised and enlarged edition, London, New York, Melbourne & Toronto: Cassell, 1917);

H. G. Wells, 1915

Tono-Bungay (New York: Duffield, 1908; London: Macmillan, 1909);

Ann Veronica: A Modern Love Story (London: Unwin, 1909; New York & London: Harper, 1909);

The History Of Mr. Polly (London, Edinburgh, Dublin, New York, Leipzig & Paris: Nelson, 1910; New York: Duffield, 1910);

The New Machiavelli (New York: Duffield, 1910; London: John Lane/Bodley Head, 1911);

The Country Of The Blind And Other Stories (London, Edinburgh, Dublin, Leeds, New York, Leipzig & Paris: Nelson, 1911);

Floor Games (London: Palmer, 1911; Boston: Small, Maynard, 1912);

The Door in the Wall And Other Stories (New York & London: Kennerley, 1911; London: Richards, 1915);

The Labour Unrest (London: Daily Mail, 1912);

Marriage (London: Macmillan, 1912; New York: Duffield, 1912);

War and Common Sense (London: Daily Mail, 1913);

Little Wars: A Game for Boys from Twelve Years of Age to One Hundred and Fifty and for That More Intelligent Sort of Girls Who Like Boys' Games (London: Palmer, 1913; Boston: Small, Maynard, 1913; revised edition, London & Toronto: Dent, 1931);

The Passionate Friends (London: Macmillan, 1913; New York & London: Harper, 1913);

An Englishman Looks at the World (London, New York, Toronto & Melbourne: Cassell, 1914); republished as *Social Forces in England and America* (New York & London: Harper, 1914);

The World Set Free: A Story of Mankind (London: Macmillan, 1914; New York: Dutton, 1914);

The Wife of Sir Isaac Harman (London: Macmillan, 1914; New York: Macmillan, 1914);

The War That Will End War (London: Palmer, 1914; New York: Duffield, 1914);

The Peace Of The World (London: Daily Chronicle, 1915);

Boon, The Mind of the Race, The Wild Asses of The Devil, and The Last Trump, Being a First Selection from the Literary Remains of George Boon, Appropriate to the Times. Prepared for Publication by Reginald Bliss . . . With An Ambiguous Introduction by H. G. Wells (London: Unwin, 1915; New York: Doran, 1915);

Bealby: A Holiday (London: Methuen, 1915; New York: Macmillan, 1915);

The Research Magnificent (London: Macmillan, 1915; New York: Macmillan, 1915);

What Is Coming? A Forecast of Things after the War (London, New York, Toronto & Melbourne: Cassell, 1916); republished as *What Is Com-*

H. G. Wells, circa 1890 (courtesy of the University of Illinois Library, Urbana-Champaign)

ing? A European Forecast (New York: Macmillan, 1916);

Mr. Britling Sees It Through (London, New York, Toronto & Melbourne: Cassell, 1916; New York: Macmillan, 1916);

The Elements of Reconstruction (London: Nisbet, 1916);

War and the Future: Italy, France, and Britain at War (London, New York, Toronto & Melbourne: Cassell, 1917); republished as *Italy, France, and Britain at War* (New York: Macmillan, 1917);

God, The Invisible King (London, New York, Toronto & Melbourne: Cassell, 1917; New York: Macmillan, 1917);

The Soul of a Bishop: A Novel (with Just a Little Love in It) about Conscience and Religion and The Real Troubles of Life (London, New York, Toronto & Melbourne: Cassell, 1917; New York: Macmillan, 1917);

In the Fourth Year: Anticipations of a World Peace (London: Chatto & Windus, 1918; New York: Macmillan, 1918);

Joan And Peter: The Story of an Education (London, New York, Toronto & Melbourne: Cassell, 1918; New York: Macmillan, 1918);

British Nationalism and the League of Nations (London: League of Nations Union, 1918);

The Undying Fire (London, New York, Toronto & Melbourne: Cassell, 1919; New York: Macmillan, 1919);

History Is One (New York: Ginn, 1919);

The Idea of a League of Nations, by Wells, Viscount Grey, Gilbert Murray, J. A. Spender, A. E. Zimmern, H. Wickham Steed, Lionel Curtis, William Archer, and Viscount Bryce (London: Oxford University Press, 1919; Boston: Atlantic Monthly Press, 1919);

The Way to the League of Nations, by Wells, Grey, Murray, Spender, Zimmern, Steed, Curtis, Archer, Ernest Barker, G. Lowes Dickinson, John Hilton, and L. S. Woolf (London: Oxford University Press, 1919);

The Outline of History, Being a Plain History of Life and Mankind (24 parts, London: Newnes, 1919-1920; 1 volume, London: Newnes, 1920; 2 volumes, New York: Macmillan, 1921);

Frank Swinnerton, Personal Sketches: Together With Notes and Comments on the Novels of Frank Swinnerton, by Wells, Arnold Bennett, and G. M. Overton (New York: Doran, 1920);

Russia in the Shadows (London: Hodder & Stoughton, 1920; New York: Doran, 1921);

The Salvaging Of Civilisation (London, New York, Toronto & Melbourne: Cassell, 1921; New York: Macmillan, 1921);

The New Teaching Of History, With a Reply to some Recent Criticisms of The Outline of History (London, New York, Toronto & Melbourne: Cassell, 1921);

Washington And The Hope of Peace (London, Glasgow, Melbourne & Aukland: Collins, 1922); republished as *Washington and the Riddle of Peace* (New York: Macmillan, 1922);

The Secret Places of the Heart (London, New York, Toronto & Melbourne: Cassell, 1922; New York: Macmillan, 1922);

A Short History of The World (London, New York, Toronto & Melbourne: Cassell, 1922; New York: Macmillan, 1922);

The World, Its Debts And The Rich Men: A Speech (London: Finer, 1922);

Men Like Gods (London, New York, Toronto & Melbourne: Cassell, 1923; New York: Macmillan, 1923);

The Story Of A Great Schoolmaster, Being A Plain Account Of The Life And Ideas Of Sanderson Of Oundle (London: Chatto & Windus, 1924; New York: Macmillan, 1924);

The Dream: A Novel (London: Cape, 1924; New York: Macmillan, 1924);

A Year of Prophesying (London: Unwin, 1924; New York: Macmillan, 1925);

The Atlantic Edition of the Works of H. G. Wells, 28 volumes, revised by Wells (London: Unwin, 1924; New York: Macmillan, 1924);

Christina Alberta's Father (London: Cape, 1925; New York: Macmillan, 1925);

A Forecast of the World's Affairs (New York & London: Encyclopaedia Britannica, 1925);

The World of William Clissold: A Novel at a New Angle (3 volumes, London: Benn, 1926; 2 volumes, New York: Doran, 1926);

Mr. Belloc Objects to the Outline of History (London: Watts, 1926; New York: Doran, 1926);

Democracy Under Revision: A Lecture Delivered at the Sorbonne, March 15th, 1927 (London: Leonard & Virginia Woolf, 1927; New York: Doran, 1927);

Meanwhile: The Picture of a Lady (London: Benn, 1927; New York: Doran, 1927);

Experiments on Animals: Views For and Against, by Wells and George Bernard Shaw (London: British Union for the Abolition of Vivisection, 1927);

The Short Stories of H. G. Wells (London: Benn, 1927; Garden City: Doubleday, Doran, 1929);

The Way the World Is Going: Guesses and Forecasts of the Years Ahead (London: Benn, 1928; Garden City: Doubleday, Doran, 1929);

The Open Conspiracy: Blue Prints for a World Revolution (London: Gollancz, 1928; Garden City: Doubleday, Doran, 1928; revised edition, London: Leonard & Virginia Woolf, 1930); revised again as *What Are We To Do With Our Lives?* (London: Heinemann, 1931; Garden City: Doubleday, Doran, 1931);

Mr. Blettsworthy on Rampole Island (London: Benn, 1928; Garden City: Doubleday, Doran, 1928);

The King Who Was a King: The Book of a Film (London: Benn, 1929); republished as *The King Who Was a King: An Unconventional Novel* (Garden City: Doubleday, Doran, 1929);

The Common Sense of World Peace: An Address Delivered to the Reichstag at Berlin, on Monday, April 15th, 1929 (London: Leonard & Virginia Woolf, 1929);

The Adventures of Tommy (London: Harrap, 1929; New York: Stokes, 1929);

Imperialism and the Open Conspiracy (London: Faber & Faber, 1929);

The Science of Life: A Summary of Contemporary Knowledge about Life and Its Possibilities, by H. G. Wells, Julian Huxley, and G. P. Wells (31 parts, London: Amalgamated Press, 1929-1930; 3 volumes, London: Amalgamated Press, 1930; 4 volumes, Garden City: Doubleday, Doran, 1931);

The Autocracy of Mr. Parham: His Remarkable Adventures in this Changing World (London: Heinemann, 1930; Garden City: Doubleday, Doran, 1930);

The Way to World Peace (London: Benn, 1930);

The Problem of the Troublesome Collaborator: An Account of Certain Difficulties in an Attempt to Produce a Work in Collaboration and of the Intervention of the Society of Authors Therein (Woking, U.K.: Privately printed, 1930);

Settlement of the Trouble between Mr. Thrung and Mr. Wells: A Footnote to The Problem of the Troublesome Collaborators (Woking, U.K.: Privately printed, 1930);

The Work, Wealth and Happiness of Mankind (2 volumes, Garden City: Doubleday, Doran, 1931; 1 volume, London: Heinemann, 1932);

After Democracy: Addresses and Papers on the Present World Situation (London: Watts, 1932);

What Should Be Done—Now: A Memorandum on the World Situation (New York: John Day, 1932);

The Bulpington of Blup (London: Hutchinson, 1932; New York: Macmillan, 1933);

The Shape of Things to Come: The Ultimate Revolution (London: Hutchinson, 1933; New York: Macmillan, 1933);

Experiment in Autobiography: Discoveries and Conclusions of a Very Ordinary Brain (Since 1866), 2 volumes (London: Gollancz & Cresset, 1934; New York: Macmillan, 1934);

Stalin-Wells Talk: The Verbatim Record, and a Discussion by G. Bernard Shaw, H. G. Wells, J. M. Keynes, Ernst Toller and Others (London: New Statesman and Nation, 1934);

The New America: The New World (London: Cresset, 1935; New York: Macmillan, 1935);

Things to Come: A Film Story Based on the Material Contained in His History of the Future 'The

H. G. and Jane Wells, 1890s (courtesy of the University of Illinois Library, Urbana-Champaign)

Shape of Things to Come' (London: Cresset, 1935; New York: Macmillan, 1935);

The Anatomy of Frustration: A Modern Synthesis (London: Cresset, 1936; London: Macmillan, 1936);

The Croquet Player: A Story (London: Chatto & Windus, 1936; New York: Viking, 1937);

The Idea of a World Encyclopaedia: A Lecture Delivered at the Royal Institution, November 20th, 1936 (London: Leonard & Virginia Woolf, 1936);

Man Who Could Work Miracles: A Film Story Based on the Material Contained in His Short Story (London: Cresset, 1936; New York: Macmillan, 1936);

Star Begotten: A Biological Fantasia (London: Chatto & Windus, 1937; New York: Viking, 1937);

Brynhild (London: Methuen, 1937; New York: Scribners, 1937);

The Camford Visitation (London: Methuen, 1937);

The Brothers: A Story (London: Chatto & Windus, 1938; New York: Viking, 1938);

World Brain (London: Methuen, 1938; Garden City: Doubleday, Doran, 1938);

Apropos of Delores (London: Cape, 1938; New York: Scribners, 1938);

The Holy Terror (London: Joseph, 1939; New York: Simon & Schuster, 1939);

Travels of a Republican in Search of Hot Water (Harmondsworth: Penguin, 1939);

The Fate of Homo Sapiens (London: Secker & Warburg, 1939); republished as *The Fate of Man* (New York: Alliance/Longmans, Green, 1939);

The New World Order, Whether It Is Obtainable, How It Can Be Attained, and What Sort of World a World at Peace Will Have to Be (London: Secker & Warburg, 1940; New York: Knopf, 1940);

The Rights of Man, Or What Are We Fighting For? (Harmondsworth & New York: Penguin, 1940);

Babes in the Darkling Wood (London: Secker & Warburg, 1940; New York: Alliance, 1940);

The Common Sense of War and Peace: World Revolution or War Unending? (Harmondsworth & New York: Penguin, 1940);

All Aboard for Ararat (London: Secker & Warburg, 1940; New York: Alliance, 1941);

Two Hemispheres or One World? (N.p., 1940);

Guide to the New World: A Handbook of Constructive World Revolution (London: Gollancz, 1941);

You Can't Be Too Careful. A Sample of Life 1901-1951 (London: Secker & Warburg, 1941; New York: Putnam's, 1942);

The Outlook for Homo Sapiens, "amalgamation and modernization" of *The Fate of Homo Sapiens* and *The New World Order* (London: Secker & Warburg, 1942);

Modern Russia and English Revolutionaries: A Frank Exchange of Ideas between Commander Lev Uspensky, Soviet Writer, and H. G. Wells (London: Privately printed, 1942);

Science and the World-Mind (London: New Europe Publishing, 1942);

Phoenix: A Summary of the Inescapable Conditions of World Organization (London: Secker & Warburg, 1942; Girard, Kans.: Haldeman-Julius, 1942);

A Thesis on the Quality of Illusion in the Continuity of Individual Life of the Higher Metazoa, with Particular Reference to the Species Homo Sapiens (London: Privately printed, 1942);

The Conquest of Time, by H. G. Wells: Written to Replace His First and Last Things (London: Watts, 1942);

The New Rights of Man (Girard, Kans.: Haldeman-Julius, 1942);

Crux Ansata. An Indictment of the Roman Catholic Church (Harmondsworth & New York: Penguin, 1943; New York: Agora, 1944);

'42 to '44: A Contemporary Memoir upon Human Behaviour during the Crisis of the World Revolution (London: Secker & Warburg, 1944);

The Happy Turning: A Dream of Life (London & Toronto: Heinemann, 1945);

Mind at the End of its Tether (London: Heinemann, 1945);

Mind at the End of Its Tether and The Happy Turning, A Dream of Life (New York: Didier, 1946);

The Desert Daisy, edited by Gordon N. Ray (Urbana, Ill.: Beta Phi Mu, 1957);

Hoopdriver's Holiday, edited by Michael Timko (West Lafayette, Ind.: Purdue University Press, 1964);

The Wealth of Mr. Waddy: A Novel, edited by Harris Wilson (Carbondale: Southern Illinois University Press/London: Feffer & Simons, 1969);

H. G. Wells: Early Writings in Science and Science Fiction, edited by Robert M. Philmus and David Y. Hughes (Berkeley & London: University of California Press, 1975);

H. G. Wells's Literary Criticism, edited by Patrick Parrinder and Philmus (Brighton, U.K.: Harvester, 1980; Totowa, N.J.: Barnes & Noble, 1980);

H. G. Wells in Love, edited by G. P. Wells (London & Boston: Faber & Faber, 1984);

The Man with a Nose and Other Uncollected Short Stories of H. G. Wells, edited by J. R. Hammond (London: Athlone, 1984).

OTHER: "The Past and the Great State," in *The Great State: Essays in Construction*, edited by Wells and others (London & New York: Harper, 1912); republished as *Socialism and the Great State* (New York: Harper, 1914), pp. 1-46;

Amy Catherine Wells, *The Book of Catherine Wells*, edited, with an introduction, by Wells (London: Chatto & Windus, 1928; Garden City: Doubleday, Doran, 1928);

The New Russia: Eight Talks Broadcast, includes a contribution by Wells (London: Faber & Faber, 1931);

Reshaping Man's Heritage: Biology in the Service of Man, includes an essay by Wells (London: Allen & Unwin, 1944).

H. G. Wells at about the time he was contributing stories such as "The Hammerpond Park Burglary" and "The Red Room" to popular magazines

Over a career that spanned five decades, H. G. Wells produced nearly a hundred full-length books, a large portion of them novels and collections of short fiction. In his 1934 autobiography Wells accurately admitted that "much of my work has been slovenly, haggard, and irritated, much of it hurried and inadequately revised." But Wells possessed exceptional literary gifts, and several of his novels–including *Kipps* (1905), *Tono-Bungay* (1908), and *The History of Mr. Polly* (1910)–deserve to be ranked among the best of their time. Wells is widely regarded as the father of modern science fiction; *The Time Machine* (1895) and *The War of the Worlds* (1898) employ strong elements of carefully paced suspense and amply illustrate Wells's remarkable ability to render convincingly the most bizarre and improbable characters and events. Indeed, many of Wells's earlier works reveal him working within a tradition of narrative fiction shaped in large part by, among others, Nathaniel Hawthorne, Edgar Allan Poe, and Robert Louis Stevenson. Like them, Wells makes frequent use of the mysterious and the horrific as he develops serious artistic themes.

Herbert George Wells was born into a rather grim lower-middle-class environment in Bromley, Kent. His father, Joseph Wells, was a celebrated cricket player turned failed shopkeeper; his rather domineering mother, Sarah Neal Wells, was a housekeeper and lady's maid whose fondest dream was that young "Bertie" and his two older brothers should become respectable tradesmen in service to the upper classes. When he was nearly seventeen, Wells finally convinced his mother that apprentice positions with a dispenser of medicines and with various drapers had left him desperately unhappy. She allowed him to enroll as a pupil-tutor at the Midhurst Grammar School, and—two years later—to accept a scholarship at the Normal School of Science in South Kensington (which later became Imperial College, London University). Here, preparing for a teaching career, Wells studied biology, geology, and astronomical physics; he was particularly influenced by the views of one of his instructors, Thomas Huxley, already famous or—some would say—infamous as Charles Darwin's most blunt and articulate defender.

Like Huxley, Wells embraced fully Darwin's theory of organic evolution and with it the implication that human beings share a common ancestor with other primates and must struggle to survive in a world of nature that is indifferent and often cruel. Wells did not then hold the common Victorian belief that human progress was divinely ordained, supervised, and thus guaranteed: he agreed with Huxley that men and women must work continuously to assure not only their material well-being but their ethical evolution. Thus in his novels and stories Wells often sets out to expose the animalistic streak that runs through humankind, that is ultimately responsible for the fear, irrationality, and violence that could lead to its decline—and extinction.

In 1889, after completing his training at Kensington, Wells taught for a year at a wretched boy's school in Wales. A year later he was back in London, conducting adult-education classes at the University Correspondence College and supplementing his income by selling brief articles on scientific subjects to newspapers and magazines seeking large circulations among members of Britain's growing middle class. On 31 October 1891 Wells married his first cousin Isabel Mary Wells but soon realized that he had committed a serious mistake. Wells and his young wife were of

diverse temperaments and shared few interests; they had married—Wells's writings came to suggest—because of an intense and mutual physical attraction and because in late Victorian England young men and women who desired respectability as well as sexual activity had no other choice.

Despite his marital discontent and the many distractions of teaching, Wells continued to write. In the more serious of his early publications Wells wrote about dreams, angels, and flying machines, among other diverse subjects; he began to point out that a continuing knowledge explosion coupled with advances in communication and transportation were rapidly bringing about the world's radical transformation. Wells wanted to help set a constructive course for the century to come, calling for bold and massive social planning; for more opportunities for women and all members of the lower classes; for better, more democratic systems of education that would be based largely in the study of science and history, and that—given time—would free all people of crippling superstitions and fears. Wells's *Anticipations Of The Reaction Of Mechanical And Scientific Progress Upon Human Life And Thought* (1901), *Mankind in the Making* (1903), and *A Modern Utopia* (1905), were widely read and discussed and contributed enormously to the character of Britain's socialist movement as it grew and developed during the twentieth century's first decades.

Wells first attracted notice as a writer of fiction when—in 1893—he began to publish short stories in such popular magazines as the *Pall Mall Budget* and the *Pall Mall Gazette*. Many of these pieces, which employ strange settings and sustained suspense, reveal particularly well Wells's early debt to such writers as Stevenson and Poe and illustrate some of the concerns that turn up in Wells's later fiction. For example, "Pollock and the Porroh Man" (*New Budget*, 23 May 1895) and "The Red Room" (*Idler*, March 1896)—both collected in *The Plattner Story And Others* (1897)—center on characters who are the terrified victims of their own irrationality. In "Pollock and the Porroh Man," set principally in Sierra Leone, an English trader named Pollock grows convinced that he is being haunted by a man whose murder he had arranged—a witch doctor or "porroh man" from a tribe given to vengeful curses. Pollock becomes obsessed with the image of the porroh man's severed head; it turns up in his daydreams and his sleep. Once, acting on his doctor's advice, Pollock takes up football for exercise and diversion, but–in a bit of black humor that is not uncommon in Wells's early fiction–he finds himself "kicking a furious inverted head about a field." Worse, the head "was no longer a thing of the eye merely; it gibbered at him, spoke to him." Alone, Pollock would "curse the thing, defy it, entreat it; once or twice, in spite of his grim self-control, he addressed it in the presence of others." Finally Pollock kills himself, admitting that he has been beaten by fear–by his failure to control the hallucination that haunts him to the end.

In "The Red Room" the narrator, a young man visiting eerie Lorraine Castle, insists on spending the night in a large room that his hosts assert is full of ghosts. Initially, despite the room's many shadowy recesses and alcoves, the intrepid guest manages to remain "matter-of-fact," but he grows uneasy as the night becomes darker and the winds begin to howl. Frantic for light, he fills the room with candles that give off "reassuring" flames. When the candles begin to flicker and fade, the narrator panics: screaming, he bounces around in the darkness until he finally crashes into a piece of furniture and blacks out. And yet, in the morning, when he regains his bearings, the narrator reasserts his belief that "there is neither ghost of earl nor ghost of countess in that room, there is no ghost at all." Instead "there is the worst of all things that haunt mortal man, . . . and that is, in all its nakedness–*Fear*! Fear that will not have light nor sound, that will not bear with reason, that deafens and darkens and overwhelms."

Wells also depicts characters encountering what they believe might be ghosts in other fictional works, including "The Presence by the Fire" (*Penny Illustrated Paper*, 14 August 1897; collected in *The Man with a Nose and Other Uncollected Short Stories of H. G. Wells*, 1984) and "The Story of the Inexperienced Ghost" (*Strand Magazine*, March 1902; collected in *Twelve Stories and a Dream*, 1903)–a piece that, as the novelist and critic Susan Hill notes, "makes us laugh," though "increasingly hollowly and falteringly." But as Catherine Rainwater suggests, "The Red Room" illustrates particularly well Wells's early "affinities" with Poe who, in such stories as "The Fall of the House of Usher" and "The Tell-Tale Heart," similarly portrays characters who are the victims of "paranoid delusions." "Except for a few subtle stylistic differences (amid a number of striking similarities), 'The Red Room,' " Rainwater points out, "might have been written by Poe himself."

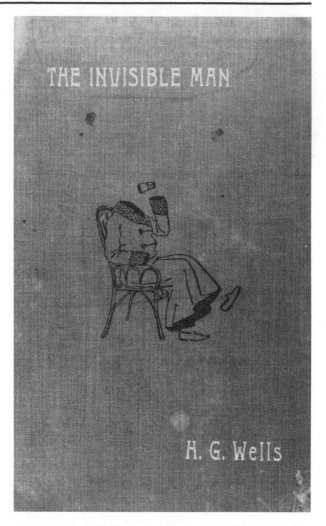

Cover for Wells's 1897 novel, in which an albino scientist's discoveries in his research on cell structure and light refraction enable him to become invisible (courtesy of Otto Penzler)

In several of his early stories Wells portrays characters who solve mysteries and crimes by piecing together available clues. In "The Thing in Number 7" (*Pall Mall Budget*, 25 October 1894; collected in *The Man with a Nose and Other Uncollected Short Stories of H. G. Wells*), two young men looking for a friend in a thunderstorm also discover the badly disfigured corpse of a man who, they conclude, was struck by lightning while trying to pilfer plumbing fixtures from an unoccupied house. In "The Thumbmark" (*Pall Mall Budget*, 28 June 1894; collected in *The Man with a Nose and Other Uncollected Short Stories of H. G. Wells*), a professor studies a thumbprint as he seeks to uncover the identity of a bomb-making anarchist. In this early story, one of several that display something of the ambience of the Normal School of Science, Wells's principal character refers to the researches of Francis Galton, whose "impressions from inked thumbs at the Anthropometric laboratory at South Kensington" had recently revealed that "in no two human beings are these impressions alike." This is one of the first references to the technique of fingerprinting in British or American fiction.

Another early story, "The Hammerpond Park Burglary" (*Pall Mall Budget*, 1894; collected in *The Stolen Bacillus, And Other Incidents*, 1895), combines a dose of social satire with what is clearly intended to be a fairly realistic portrayal of criminal activity in Victorian England. Teddy Watkins, an accomplished thief, gathers up "two virgin canvases, a brand-new easel," and "a paintbox" and poses as an artist in order to gain access to grounds near Hammerpond House, where–according to the newspapers–the wealthy Lord Aveling and his new bride are about to commence their honeymoon. As Watkins attempts to enter Aveling's house under the cover of darkness, he is interrupted by a couple of bumbling amateur burglars who attract unwanted attention and are captured after a chaotic scuffle with Watkins, and "a vast multitude of people," including Aveling, who–like everyone else–is convinced that the inarticulate Watkins is a great artist and a hero whose efforts helped prevent the removal of expensive wedding gifts and the family jewels. The new groom then invites Watkins to spend the night as his guest; Watkins, accordingly, walks off with the goods while the young lord snores. By portraying Aveling as both obtuse and naive, Wells displays a decidedly irreverent attitude toward the upper classes–a trait which appears in several of his later works, including *In The Days Of The Comet* (1906) and the more masterful *Tono-Bungay*.

In much of his early fiction Wells creates tension and impact by suddenly juxtaposing the cozily familiar with the sometimes terrifyingly strange. He delighted in describing menacing and often man-eating creatures, generally as a way of underscoring his sense of man's vulnerable place in the eat-or-be-eaten world of nature. In "The Flowering of the Strange Orchid" (*Pall Mall Budget*, 2 August 1894; collected in *The Stolen Bacillus, And Other Incidents*), for example, Wells portrays a mild-mannered flower breeder who purchases an exotic flower that gradually turns into a large, sweet-smelling, tentacular thing that one day seizes him and sucks his blood. In "The Sea Raiders" (*Weekly Sun Literary Supplement*, 6 December 1896; collected in *The Plattner Story And Others*), a group of octopuslike

creatures the size of "fair-sized swine" devour several citizens of an English coastal town. Similarly, in a somewhat later piece of fictional reportage, "The Empire of the Ants" (*Strand Magazine*, December 1905; collected in *The Country Of The Blind And Other Stories*, 1911), an Englishman accustomed to a world where nature is "hedged, ditched, and drained into a perfection of submission," travels to the tropics where he finds a land of "inhuman immensity" and huge, poisonous ants who have begun to kill humans in what appears to be a drive for global domination. In "The Star" (*Graphic*, Christmas number 1897; collected in *Tales of Space and Time*, 1899) Wells brilliantly builds suspense as he describes the approach of another symbol of nature's indifference–a comet, a "vast mass of matter"–that nearly collides with the earth as it rushes "without warning out of the black mystery of the sky." As the early critic W. T. Stead pointed out, Wells revealed in "The Star" and elsewhere in his early fiction that he had "caught the trick of describing events which only exist in his imagination with the technical precision of a newspaper reporter." According to Stead, Wells was "a seer of gruesome visions," a "past master in the art of producing creepy sensations" (*Review of Reviews*, April 1898).

In 1894 Wells left his wife and began living with Amy Catherine Robbins, one of his former students. In 1895 Wells and Isabel Wells were divorced, freeing him to marry Robbins, whom he would come to call Jane, on 27 October 1895. Meanwhile, he kept turning out great quantities of publishable prose, including his first novel, *The Time Machine*, which further enhanced Wells's reputation as a writer of adventure and suspense fiction much in the manner of Stevenson and H. Rider Haggard. In this short novel–surely one of the most imaginative and innovative in the English language–Wells created a Victorian scientist who discovers a means of traveling forward through the centuries and finds himself on earth in the year 802701 A.D. Though it appears to be beautiful and calm, the part of the world in which he finds himself is dominated by odious, cannibalistic creatures called Morlocks, who clearly represent–among other things–man's animalistic tendencies given free reign. After fleeing the Morlocks, the time traveler again speeds far ahead, to a time when he finds earth on the verge of extinction and sees on a long beach, beneath an "inky black sky," little that is alive except for some lichenlike plants, huge white

H. G. Wells arriving in New York, 1934

butterflies emitting "dismal cries," and crablike creatures with mouths "alive with appetite," eyeballs "wriggling on their stalks," backs "corrugated and ornamented with ungainly bosses," and claws "smeared with an algal slime."

The suspense in Wells's second novel, *The Island of Doctor Moreau* (1896), begins when its narrator, a shipwrecked Englishman named Edward Prendick, seeks shelter on a small, faraway island that is largely populated by oddly shaped, "amazingly ugly" creatures who function as human beings but bear unsettling similarities to a variety of beasts. Indeed, as Prendick learns, the island's ruler, the secretive Moreau, is–like Mary Shelley's Victor Frankenstein–a dangerously obsessed scientist whose sadistic experiments have produced grotesque results. Employing tissue transplants and chemical alterations, he has transformed dogs and apes and other creatures into "humanised animals"–a practice Wells describes in a brief author's note as "within the possibilities of vivisection." Eventually, Moreau is murdered by a puma he has tortured, and his unfortunate "Beast Folk"–free of tyrannical supervision– revert increasingly to more thoroughly animal

ways. Prendick escapes the island, but when he returns to "civilization" he finds that he cannot leave behind the horrors he has witnessed. He continues to see bestial qualities in the men and women he passes daily and must eventually retreat "from the confusion of cities and multitudes" to a place where he is surrounded by books, those "bright windows in this life of ours lit by the shining souls of men."

Missing its more subtle concerns, early critics of *The Island of Doctor Moreau* tended to view the work as little more than a particularly brutal exercise in fictional horror–so brutal, in fact, that Stead called it a book "which ought never to have been written" (*Review of Reviews*, April 1898). But as later critics have pointed out, the work is a powerful indictment of science without ethics, and it remains particularly relevant at a time when research into the creation and alteration of simple and complex life-forms has become increasingly more sophisticated. *The Island of Doctor Moreau* remains provocative, moreover, because it plainly attempts to establish parallels between the Judeo-Christian conception of God and the cruel and capricious Moreau, and between Christian churchgoers and the Beast Folk, who worship Moreau out of what Wells makes clear is a combination of ignorance and fear. As John Batchelor notes, *The Island of Doctor Moreau* aims to make its readers confront "the humiliating implications of the Darwinian revolution: that man is no more than a talking animal, that all moral systems are arbitrary and man-made, that the sanctions traditionally endorsing the social order are illusions." Still, as Batchelor suggests, the book is not only "austere" but "exhilarating," largely because of the way Wells–with "unflagging energy and relish"–describes, among other things, "the fire which destroys Moreau's 'house of pain' " and the way in which Pendick has to develop "the defensive skills of an animal" in order to leave the island alive.

As V. S. Pritchett has aptly put it, Wells's third novel, *The Invisible Man* (1897), is "a good thriller . . . held up by horseplay and comedy." In this–yet another of Wells's frequently imitated works–an albino scientist named Griffin manages to make himself transparent as a result of long experimentation with cell structure and light refraction. As a result he is able to harass and befuddle several residents of the towns through which he passes; one of them, a tramp called Thomas Marvel, emerges as one of Wells's most memorable minor figures. The obsessed, irascible Griffin is not interested in using his invisibility for jokes and tricks; he turns to crime and–before he is finally tracked down and killed–begins planning to establish "the Epoch of the Invisible Man," a reign of terror maintained by his ability to murder and extort at will. As Frank McConnell has observed, *The Invisible Man* appeared at a time when people in Europe and America were particularly aware of "the threat presented by the figure of the anarchist, that outwardly normal, rational man who might, unsuspected, be harboring thoughts and plans of the most unthinkable violence and hatred." Calling Wells's novel "an early, very resonant expression of this fear," McConnell suggests that Joseph Conrad's *The Secret Agent* (1907) and G. K. Chesterton's *The Man Who Was Thursday* (1908) "would both treat the theme of anarchy in ways perhaps suggested by *The Invisible Man*"–as a social plague that has "the terrible quality of being unrecognizable until it is too late." As Brian Ash has noted, Griffin's sinister acts take place largely in the deceptively calm and sunny lanes of Sussex–"a striking departure from the damp cellars of the Gothic genre and an inspired touch which makes his invisibility all the more strange."

The War of the Worlds is perhaps Wells's best-written and most-gripping romance. Its plot centers on the invasion of present-day England by scores of hideous Martians who employ "Heat-Rays" to level large parts of the country before they succumb to bacteria against which they have no defense. Particularly brilliant are the narrator's descriptions of the destruction of Weybridge and Shepperton and the exodus from London, as well as his tense and detailed account of being trapped in a corner of a demolished house, watching a curious Martian's long grey tentacle "waving towards me and touching and examining the wall, coals, wood, and ceiling." Because of its convincing, brilliantly paced depiction of an unprecedentedly major and theoretically possible news event, *The War of the Worlds* has often been adapted for film and radio, most notably in 1938 by Orson Welles and the Mercury Players. That version, broadcast in the United States as a mock-news event on the CBS radio network, resulted in considerable hysteria; similar, somewhat later radio versions produced in South America proved even more provocative. In Ecuador, for example, fifteen people were killed in panics brought on by a 1949 broadcast of *The War of the Worlds*.

The War of the Worlds is full of messages–none of them subtle. Early in the work, Wells's unnamed narrator points out that, prior to the invasion, few people realized "the immensity of vacancy in which the dust of the material world swims"; most, "blinded by vanity," had simply assumed that throughout the universe no intelligence could possibly transcend "its earthly level." They had assumed too that their little towns and villages were "safe and tranquil," forgetting that life is, after all, "an incessant struggle for existence"; that for centuries homo sapiens wrought "ruthless and utter destruction" not only upon less-intelligent animals but upon other women and men. He thus hopes the Martian's massive destruction of soldiers and civilians–eerily prefiguring the indiscriminate slaughterings of both world wars–will finally teach humans "pity–pity for those witless souls that suffer our dominion" and will, as well, "promote the conception of the commonweal of mankind."

By 1900 Wells's reputation was secure. On the strength of his growing income, he built in Sandgate, near Folkestone, a large house, Spade House, where Jane Wells continued to combine her work as Wells's typist and the organizer of his time with the rearing of their two small sons, George Philip and Frank Richard. At Spade House Wells remained as productive as ever, turning out, among other things, *The Food of the Gods And How It Came To Earth* (1904), a romance in which yet another scientific experiment goes awry. In this case a supernourishing substance dubbed "Boomfood" is carelessly consumed by animals and humans alike and creates gigantic chickens, wasps, rats, and men and women tall enough to tower above the highest structures. Inevitably these giants conflict with those they call "the little folks," but ultimately–embodying the traits of foresight and courage that Wells prized–they undertake the construction of a new and improved world order that will finally provide all people with the means of moving "out of these shadows and darknesses, into greatness and light!" *The Food of the Gods* contains several well-constructed and highly dramatic episodes, including those that depict giant rats being tracked down and "bagged." But as more than one of its reviewers noted, *The Food of the Gods* is a rather muddled and too baldly didactic work that is itself too large by several chapters. As Pritchett adds, the novel's descriptions of love scenes between the giants are "the most embarrassing in English fiction."

H. G. Wells, circa 1936 (courtesy of the University of Illinois Library, Urbana-Champaign)

By 1905 Wells had grown tired of wearing the label of "the English Jules Verne" and began focusing his creative energies on producing book-length fiction in a more realistic vein. In the classic *Kipps*–the source for the popular 1966 film *Half-a-Sixpence*–Wells presents the simple, likable Arthur Kipps and shows how he escapes from a repressive lower-class environment. After experiencing life among men and women obsessed with money and eager for social respectability, he winds up running a small bookshop and finally securing peace of mind. The equally fine *Tono-Bungay* is narrated by George Ponderevo, a housekeeper's son whose up-and-down life, like Wells's, included a stint as a druggist's apprentice and the study of science at a new university in South Kensington. He is indeed–as J. R. Hammond has noted–"the epitome of Wells in his restlessness, his sceptical attitude towards orthodox religion, his dislike of convention and his almost mystical belief in the veracity of science." Wells's central figure in *The History of Mr. Polly* is another sympathetically drawn figure from the lower class, who–despite a series of hardships

and blunders–maintains a sense of delight and wonder about life and musters the courage to escape from a domestic realm he finds thoroughly deadening. *The History of Mr. Polly* is in fact a blunt illustration of one of Wells's most basic themes. "If the world does not please you," its narrator observes, *"you can change it.* You may change it to something sinister and angry, to something appalling, but it may be you will change it to something much more interesting. There is only one sort of man who is absolutely to blame for his own misery, and that is the man who finds life dull and dreary."

Despite his prolific output of articles and books, Wells managed to lead a rich and varied life away from his desk. He ran for Parliament as a member of the Labour party; he traveled widely, visiting the Soviet Union and the United States. He interviewed both Lenin and Theodore Roosevelt and came to know many of the twentieth century's leading literary and political figures. George Gissing, Stephen Crane, George Bernard Shaw, and Henry James were among Wells's literary acquaintances; writers Rebecca West and Dorothy Richardson were among the notable women with whom he had what would become well-publicized affairs. West bore Wells a son, Anthony, who became a talented essayist and novelist, producing, among other things, several insightful writings on the subject of his father's work.

At least one of Wells's later–and better–novels, *The Croquet Player* (1936), makes use of some of the conventions common to the mystery genre. Its narrator, a youngish man named George Frobisher, announces at the outset that since his boyhood discovery of Poe he has maintained "a taste for the weird and the eerie," and that he is about to unfold "a ghost story" of his own. This tale, he adds, is "not an ordinary ghost story"; it is not "a story of a haunted churchyard or anything so limited." Instead, it is the story of the haunting of "a whole countryside" and of a fear that grew in power and intensity until it became "a continual overshadowing dread."

Frobisher is a self-described member of the upper crust, "the floating cream of humanity"–a rather idle and shallow fellow who spends his time perfecting his skills at croquet. While on holiday at "the Source Hotel at Perona above Les Noupets," he meets an English physician called Finchatton, whose otherwise handsome face reveals "the jaded look of a man who doesn't sleep well." Finchatton regales Frobisher with a story of malign forces and "evil" events, claiming that his hometown–Crainmarsh–is haunted by the spirits of brutal cavemen, "grisly ghosts" who are capable of causing ordinary citizens to become paranoid and commit violent acts. Later, Frobisher meets Dr. Norbert, Finchatton's psychiatrist, who asserts that although the doctor is "mad" and given to flights of fantasy, he is not inaccurate in his diagnosis that a contagion of fear and brutality afflicts the world. After all, Norbert notes, science is now confirming the fact that man "unmasked and disillusioned, is the same fearing, snarling beast he was a hundred thousand years ago." Indeed, "civilization, progress, *all* that, we are discovering, was a delusion. Nothing was secured. Nothing."

Wells's earliest writings reveal that–regarding the quality of humanity's future–he shifted often between qualified hope and frank despair. Such later works as *Mr. Blettsworthy on Rampole Island* (1928), *The Croquet Player*, and the notoriously bleak *Mind at the End of its Tether* (1945) suggest that, in the main, Wells's pessimistic impulses won. He spent his life campaigning for the triumph of reason and order in a messy world. In the wake of World War I, he called increasingly for the construction of a world state in which social and economic opportunities would be widened and weapons of mass destruction strictly controlled; but of course during the 1930s the world careened once more toward war. Like Dr. Norbert, who winds up warning of "The Wrath to Come," Wells energetically exhorted and prophesied, and the men and women he sought to sway–symbolized by the easily distracted, self-absorbed Frobisher–paid him no heed. "I'm all for peace, order, social justice, service, and all that," Frobisher asserts at the novel's conclusion. "But if I'm to think! If I'm to find out what to do with myself ! That's too much."

In his lifetime Wells was frequently criticized not only by those who disagreed with his socialist and agnostic tendencies but by those–such as Virginia Woolf and Henry James–who looked past the extraordinary range and vitality evident in even the least of Wells's fiction and focused instead on its occasional lack of polish and its tendency to drift into propaganda. In some academic quarters–perhaps particularly in America–Wells, in many ways so much the antithesis of the widely admired Woolf and James, continues to be regarded with condescension. In his review of David Smith's 1986 biography of Wells, Stanley Weintraub, for example, asserts that Wells "was

not a great artist, nor was he a major prophet. He was an undersized boy from the working class who, after a Dickensian childhood, heightened the imaginations of readers all over the world and in the process became rich, famous, self-indulgent, and sloppier as a writer."

Those who admired Wells in his lifetime included Anatole France, who described Wells as "the greatest force in the English speaking world." Though he deplored the propagandistic streak in Wells's later novels, H. L. Mencken greatly admired the strength and vigor of Wells's mind, calling it "one of the most extraordinary that England has produced in our time." In 1941–five years before Wells's death–Sinclair Lewis suggested that "there is no greater novelist living than Mr. H. G. Wells." More recent biographies and critical studies by Smith, Patrick Parrinder, John R. Reed, and John Batchelor reveal that a sympathetic interest in Wells and his work continues to grow. "Wells," Batchelor suggests, "is a great artist, and those of us who enjoy his work need not feel ashamed of the pleasure we take in reading him."

Certainly, Wells was highly skilled at evoking mystery and maintaining suspense. He was among the first novelists and short-story writers to employ humor in the telling of a macabre tale and to realize that elements of horror and episodes of terror can be rendered more horrible and terrifying–and memorable–when placed within the context of a carefully detailed, seemingly secure middle-class world. Not surprisingly, his best works, including *The Time Machine*, *The Island of Doctor Moreau*, and *The War of The Worlds*, continue to sell steadily nearly a century after their publication.

Letters:

Henry James and H. G. Wells, edited by Leon Edel and Gordon N. Ray (Urbana: University of Illinois Press, 1958; London: Hart-Davis, 1958);

Arnold Bennett and H. G. Wells, edited by Harris Wilson (Urbana: University of Illinois Press, 1960; London: Hart-Davis, 1960);

George Gissing and H. G. Wells, edited by Royal A. Gettmann (Urbana: University of Illinois Press, 1961; London: Hart-Davis, 1961).

Bibliographies:

Geoffrey H. Wells, *The Works of H. G. Wells, 1887-1925: a Bibliography, Dictionary and Subject-Index* (London: Routledge, 1926);

H. G. Wells Society, *H. G. Wells: A Comprehensive Bibliography* (London: H. G. Wells Society, 1972);

J. R. Hammond, *H. G. Wells: An Annotated Bibliography* (New York & London: Garland, 1977).

Biographies:

Geoffrey West, *H. G. Wells: A Sketch for a Portrait* (London: Howe, 1930);

Vincent Brome, *H. G. Wells: A Biography* (London & New York: Longmans, Green, 1951);

Lovat Dickson, *H. G. Wells: His Turbulent Life and Times* (London: Macmillan, 1969; New York: Atheneum, 1969);

Norman and Jeanne MacKenzie, *The Time Traveller* (London: Weidenfeld & Nicolson, 1973; New York: Simon & Schuster, 1973);

Gordon N. Ray, *H. G. Wells & Rebecca West* (New Haven: Yale University Press, 1974);

Frank Wells, *H. G. Wells: A Pictorial Biography* (London: Jupiter, 1977);

J. R. Hammond, *H. G. Wells: Interviews and Recollections* (London: Macmillan, 1980);

Anthony West, *H. G. Wells: Aspects of a Life* (London: Hutchinson, 1984; New York: Random House, 1984);

David C. Smith, *H. G. Wells: Desperately Mortal* (New Haven: Yale University Press, 1986).

References:

Brian Ash, *Who's Who in H. G. Wells* (London: Hamilton, 1979);

John Batchelor, *H. G. Wells* (Cambridge: Cambridge University Press, 1985);

Bernard Bergonzi, *The Early H. G. Wells* (Manchester: Manchester University Press, 1961; Toronto: Toronto University Press, 1961);

Bergonzi, ed., *H. G. Wells: A Collection of Critical Essays* (Englewood Cliffs, N.J.: Prentice-Hall, 1976);

Richard Haur Costa, *H. G. Wells*, revised edition (Boston: Twayne, 1985);

J. R. Hammond, *An H. G. Wells Companion* (London: Macmillan, 1980);

Roslynn D. Haynes, *H. G. Wells: Discoverer of the Future* (New York: New York University Press, 1980);

Mark R. Hillegas, *The Future as Nightmare: H. G. Wells and the Anti-Utopians* (New York: Oxford University Press, 1967);

Peter Kemp, *H. G. Wells and the Culminating Ape* (London: Macmillan, 1982; New York: St. Martin's Press, 1982);

Frank McConnell, *The Science Fiction of H. G. Wells* (New York: Oxford University Press, 1981);

H. L. Mencken, "H. G. Wells *Redivivus,*" in *H. L. Mencken's Smart Set Criticism,* edited by William H. Nolte (Ithaca: Cornell University Press, 1968);

Patrick Parrinder, *H. G. Wells* (Edinburgh: Oliver & Boyd, 1970; New York: Putnam's, 1977);

Parrinder, ed., *H. G. Wells: The Critical Heritage* (London & Boston: Routledge & Kegan Paul, 1972);

Catherine Rainwater, "Encounters with the 'White Sphinx': Poe's Influence on Some Early Works of H. G. Wells," *English Literature in Transition,* 26 (1983): 35-51;

Ingvald Raknem, *H. G. Wells and His Critics* (London: Allen & Unwin, 1962);

John R. Reed, *The Natural History of H. G. Wells* (Athens: Ohio University Press, 1982);

Alan Wykes, *H. G. Wells in the Cinema* (London: Jupiter, 1977).

Papers:

Wells's books, letters, and papers are preserved at the University of Illinois Library, Urbana-Champaign. The most extensive collection of Wells material in Great Britain is at the Bromley Central Library in London.

Victor L. Whitechurch
(12 March 1868-25 May 1933)

Nancy Ellen Talburt
University of Arkansas

BOOKS: *The Course of Justice* (London: Isbister, 1903);

The Canon in Residence (London: Unwin, 1904; New York: Baker & Taylor, 1911);

The Locum Tenens (London: Unwin, 1906);

Concerning Himself: The Story of An Ordinary Man (London: Unwin, 1909; New York: Baker & Taylor, 1911);

The Canon's Dilemma and Other Stories (London: Unwin, 1909);

Off the Main Road (London: Long, 1911; New York: Baker & Taylor, 1911);

Thrilling Stories of the Railway (London: Pearson, 1912); republished as *Stories of the Railway* (London: Routledge & Kegan Paul, 1977);

A Downland Corner (London: Unwin, 1912; New York: Holt, 1913);

Left in Charge (London: Long, 1912; Garden City: Doubleday, Page, 1912);

Three Summers: A Romance (London: Long, 1915);

Parochial Processions (London: S.P.C.K., 1917);

If Riches Increase (London: Long, 1923);

A Bishop Out of Residence (London: Unwin, 1924; New York: Duffield, 1924);

The Templeton Case (London: Long, 1924; New York: Clode, 1924);

Downland Echoes (London: Unwin, 1924; New York: Duffield, 1925);

The Adventures of Captain Ivan Koravitch (Edinburgh & London: Blackwood, 1925);

Concerning Right and Wrong (London: Faith Press, 1925);

The Dean and Jecinora (London: Unwin, 1926; New York: Duffield, 1926);

The Truth in Christ Jesus (London: Faith Press, 1927);

The Crime at Diana's Pool (London: Unwin, 1927; New York: Duffield, 1927);

Shot on the Downs (London: Unwin, 1927; New York: Duffield, 1928);

Mixed Relations (London: Benn, 1928);

First and Last (London: Collins, 1929; New York: Duffield, 1930);

Canon Victor L. Whitechurch

The Robbery at Rudwick House (New York: Duffield, 1929);

Murder at the Pageant (London: Collins, 1930; New York: Duffield, 1931);

Murder at the College (London: Collins, 1932); republished as *Murder at Exbridge* (New York: Dodd, Mead, 1932);

Mute Witnesses (London: Benn, 1933).

OTHER: *The Floating Admiral,* includes contributions by Whitechurch, G. K. Chesterton, Dorothy L. Sayers, and others (London: Hod-

317

der & Stoughton, 1931; New York: Doubleday, 1932).

Unlike Arthur Conan Doyle, whose mysteries resulted at least in part from a dearth of patients to support his intended medical career, Canon Victor L. Whitechurch wrote fiction while filling increasingly responsible positions in the Church of England. He was ordained in 1891, just as Conan Doyle was enjoying the first successes of the Sherlock Holmes stories. Whitechurch's mysteries, "merely detective yarns," as he called them, are few but include the very rare collection *Thrilling Stories of the Railway* (1912). Published just one year after the appearance of G. K. Chesterton's *The Innocence of Father Brown* (1911), these stories show a decided kinship with the Holmes adventures while simultaneously defining a world of their own. Whitechurch wrote a relatively small body of work in which the contemporary conventions of the mystery story are expanded with skill and sympathy. He was one of the first writers to submit manuscripts to Scotland Yard for verification of police procedure. In Thorpe Hazell, British fiction's only railroad detective, he created the first specialty detective.

One measure of Whitechurch's acceptance by his fellow writers is his authorship of the first chapter, depicting the crime and laying the foundation for the mystery, of *The Floating Admiral* (1931), a novel jointly written by Dorothy L. Sayers, G. K. Chesterton, Agatha Christie, and other members of the Detection Club. The prefatory statement to his *The Crime at Diana's Pool* (1927), in which he describes his unusual method of composition, may explain why he was chosen to write the opening chapter: "To begin with, I had no plot. When I had written the first chapter I did not know why the crime had been committed, who had done it, or how it was done. Then, with an open mind, I picked up the clues which seemed to show themselves, and found, as I went on, their bearing on the problem. In many respects the story appeared to work itself out to that inevitable conclusion about which, to begin with, I was in entire ignorance."

Whitechurch was honorary canon of Christ Church, Oxford, but his career in the Church of England bears little direct relation to the mysteries which were to him only a second avocation, the writing of so-called clerical romances being the first. Nevertheless his experiences as a cleric and in a cathedral community provide matter for his craft, and his fictional clerics are persuasively cast in the roles of detective, lover, and police confidant, among others.

Victor Lorenzo Whitechurch was born 12 March 1868, the son of the Reverend W. F. Whitechurch and his half-Spanish wife, Matilda Cornwall Whitechurch. He was educated at Chichester Grammar School, Sussex; Chichester Theological College; and Durham University. After his ordination at the age of twenty-three, he held curacies at Aston Clinton, Buckinghamshire, from 1891 to 1894, and at All Souls, Harlesden, London, from 1894 to 1896. He served as senior curate at St. Luke's, Maidenhead, Berkshire, from 1896 to 1904. He was vicar at Blewbury, Berkshire, from 1904 to 1913. In that year he was appointed diocesan chaplain to the Bishop of Oxford and organizing secretary in the diocese for the Church of England Men's Society. After a year he went to Aylesbury as vicar and chaplain of the Royal Buckinghamshire Hospital. In 1923 he moved from Aylesbury to Hartwell-with-Stone, Buckinghamshire, where he was rector until 1931. Other offices he held included that of rural dean of Aylesbury (from 1919 to 1931), proctor in the Convocation of Canterbury for the diocese of Oxford, and member of the Church Assembly from 1922 to 1925. He married Florence Partridge, daughter of Mr. E. T. Partridge, in October 1896 and had one daughter, Bertha. Whitechurch died at the age of sixty-five on 25 May 1933.

Seven works by Whitechurch are clearly mysteries. Other works often identified as mysteries, such as *The Canon in Residence* (1904), *A Bishop Out of Residence* (1924), and *The Canon's Dilemma* (1909), only include incidental crimes. *The Adventures of Captain Ivan Koravitch* (1925) contains three railway mysteries and some spy stories.

Thrilling Stories of the Railway, perhaps by virtue of its rarity, has a measure of fame among mystery works and is Whitechurch's best-known work. In the years from the death of Queen Victoria (1901) to the beginning of World War I British railways were at the height of their development, a fact reflected in *Thrilling Stories of the Railway*. The fifteen railway stories in the collection fall into two sections: the first nine feature the detective Thorpe Hazell; the second six feature a different protagonist for each story. A comic figure, Hazell is among those detective characters whose identifying idiosyncrasies cross the line into the peculiar. Well described in each story because they first appeared serially, Hazell

Illustration by Alfred Paget for the 1899 Strand Magazine *publication of "A Station Master's Story"*

is a "strong faddist on food and 'physical culture,'" carrying vegetarianism to an extreme. He periodically practices various strange exercises. When deeply absorbed he chain-smokes cigarettes. He drinks lemonade for breakfast and carries his own provisions of plasmon biscuits or chocolate, sometimes a banana, and a flask of milk on journeys. If he has forgotten to take his special foods, he may beg bread and milk at a farm. On one occasion he asks a farm wife for a couple of onions and a broomstick and solemnly eats the onions and twirls the broomstick (a digestive exercise) before her startled gaze. Less bizarre, and more typical of early detectives, are his enthusiasm for railway arcana and his knowledge of book editions and bindings. Thorpe has independent means and functions as an amateur detective.

Whitechurch's indebtedness to Conan Doyle is unmistakable. Hazell's diction is similar to Holmes's diction: upon discovering a smuggler's scheme, he cries, "There's a pretty little dodge for you." As Holmes would, he tells a policeman who has failed to solve a murder that it is only an ordinary case. In several stories he has a typically Holmesian disregard for the law, and the unnamed narrator observes that Hazell "always declared that the chief interest to his mind was the unique method by which a very daring plan was carried out." Hazell refers to his authorship in words that recall Holmes's description of his monograph on tobacco types: "I rather aspire to be a book-collector; you may have read my little monogram [*sic*] on 'Jacobean Bindings?'"

There are five Thorpe Hazell stories in which he detects in the classical sense: he halts a smuggling operation, solves a murder and lets the murderer go, solves a kidnapping and rescues the victim, and finds a stolen picture and a necklace. In four adventures he prevents a threatened disaster: he saves a British bank from the plot of a villainous foreign financier, prevents delivery of a stolen secret document by diplomatic spies, helps a bishop keep an appointment after a train derailment, and saves many lives by halting a train engine set into motion by spies. The six remaining stories in the collection mix prevention and detection, and the assorted protagonists whose special wits or talents enable them to solve a crime or prevent disaster include a professional railway detective, a railway signalman, a maid who has learned Morse code, a French spy and railway enthusiast (much like Hazell), a boy railway expert, a one-legged railwayman, and a British secret agent. The stories are as varied as their central characters.

A consistent feature of all fifteen stories is the use by the detective figure of specialized knowledge of the railway to solve or prevent crime, or to make possible a solution that challenges his ingenuity. The diagrams, the explanations of the operation of signaling devices, the jargon of the railway workers, and even the timetable minutiae relating operations of the competing railway companies combine to create a railway environment. The detective controls and shapes the way things turn out through his mastery of "railway details." On occasion, Whitechurch is able to give the reader the feeling of being a part of a select group of professionals. He comes close to creating his own countryside-and-railway version of the fog-dimmed streets of London through which Sherlock Holmes and Watson tracked their quarries, but he lacks Conan Doyle's skill in characterization.

In addition to the railway detective stories, Whitechurch wrote theological works, an autobiography, romances, and six mystery novels. Beginning with *The Templeton Case* (1924) the novels share certain characteristics. Whitechurch makes intelligent use of physical clues, and he involves the reader by revealing them fairly. These novels feature different detectives and combine police and amateur detection. All of them have clerical characters of some prominence. They are flawed by conventional and repeated incidents and contain mostly stock characters.

Opinion is divided as to whether *The Crime at Diana's Pool* or *Shot on the Downs* (1927) is Whitechurch's best mystery novel. In both he

Dust jacket for Whitechurch's 1912 short-story collection, which includes nine stories about Thorpe Hazell, vegetarian amateur detective (courtesy of Otto Penzler)

uses the same ingenious, if hardly credible, method of composition. The protagonist of *The Crime at Diana's Pool* is the vicar of Coppleswick, Francis Westerman. He discovers the body, solves the crime, lets the police take the credit, startles the villain into an admission of guilt with a stunningly symbolic reenactment of the crime, and wins the lady, Diana. Westerman is one of Whitechurch's best characters. Recollecting his exposure of the villain, he is ashamed. "Just then, parson or no parson, he was tasting that terrible excitement born of a man hunt, the latent savage, call it that if you like, that lurks beneath the veneer of polished civilisation."

Shot on the Downs is notable for its painstaking police work and the motive and method of the young woman who commits the crime. The victim is the man who seduced and ran away with her mother, something which brought her father to an early decline. Whitechurch engages reader attention by revealing in the first scene that the chief suspect, the ne'er-do-well nephew of the housekeeper, discovers and robs (but does not kill) the victim; the police do not make this discovery until late in the novel. Colonel Chadlington, typical of the author's elegant and wise chief constables, is the central intelligence for piecing together the facts his police force gathers.

The Robbery at Rudwick House (1929), essentially a lighthearted comedy, contrasts markedly with its immediate predecessor. The focus is not on the theft of valuable snuff boxes, whose perpetrator is known to the reader from the beginning, but on the archdeacon of Frattenbury, Cyril Osborne Lakenham. He must come to terms with two American relatives, Alexander Washington Lakenham and his mother, Selina. Through an error by Scotland Yard detectives (which suggests that all Americans look alike to them) the pair are shadowed. Alexander is eventually charged with the crime and spends a night in jail, to the great chagrin of his uncle. Police work improves, and the conclusion features a neat twist as the professional thieves–husband, wife, and brother–are apprehended in a family scene which suggests that, apart from their unfortunate choice of occupation, they are just ordinary people. The American characters are done in very broad strokes which suggest a limited acquaintance on the author's part with original models.

Murder at the Pageant (1930) and *Murder at the College* (1932) are well plotted and meticulously detailed in the use of clues and detecting. An unusual feature is that the murder victim in each novel is a detective. In both novels the deaths result from the detective's unauthorized intrusion into a crime or series of crimes. A former

member of the secret service, Maj. Roger Bristow, lends the police a welcome hand in *Murder at the Pageant*. Professional thieves commit a robbery, but because of the involvement of his runaway wife a retired detective dies in an attempt to prevent it. Favorite Whitechurch devices such as misappropriated clothing and incriminating personal effects mislead the police at first, but they solve the crime with careful work and Bristow's advice.

Whitechurch's last detective novel, *Murder at the College*, contains no love interest and little humor. In it police detectives do most of the work. Caught in the act of opening a secret cache of stolen items, Francis Hatton pays for his ingenuity with his life when he refuses to allow the thief, a friend and Oxford don, a head start to flee from the police. The details of the crime are confirmed in a letter in which the criminal asks for the prayers of the chief constable, a former friend. His clerical disguise effectively prevents anyone from seeing him or remembering him.

Victor L. Whitechurch occupies a small niche in the history of mystery fiction. His works appeal primarily to the reader with a taste for the carefully plotted tale firmly set in the Britain of empire days and in the sort of countryside that (doubtless) surrounded Holmes's London. His special contribution is the combination of railway lore with clever plots in the Thorpe Hazell stories, but his longer mysteries still repay the reader with the special pleasure provided by a classic detective tale.

Reference:
Bryan Morgan, Foreword to *Stories of the Railway* (London: Routledge & Kegan Paul, 1977), pp. 1-9.

Books for Further Reading

Adey, R. C. S. *Locked Room Murders and Other Impossible Crimes.* London: Ferret, 1979.

Aisenberg, Nadja. *A Common Spring: Crime Novel and Classic.* Bowling Green, Ohio: Bowling Green University Popular Press, 1979.

Albert, Walter. *Detective and Mystery Fiction: An International Bibliography of Secondary Sources.* Madison, Ind.: Brownstone Books, 1985.

Altick, Richard D. *Victorian Studies in Scarlet.* New York: Norton, 1970.

Ball, John, ed. *The Mystery Story.* San Diego & Del Mar: University of California, 1976.

Bargainnier, Earl F., and George N. Dove, eds. *Cops and Constraints: Amerian and British Fictional Policemen.* Bowling Green, Ohio: Bowling Green University Popular Press, 1986.

Barnes, Melvyn. *Best Detective Fiction: A Guide from Godwin to the Present.* London: Bingley/Hamden, Conn.: Linnet, 1975.

Barzun, Jacques, and Wendell Hertig Taylor. *A Book of Prefaces to Fifty Classics of Crime Fiction, 1900-1950.* New York: Garland, 1976.

Barzun and Taylor. *A Catalogue of Crime,* second impression, corrected. New York, Evanston, San Francisco & London: Harper & Row, 1974.

Benvenuti, Stephano, and Gianni Rizzoni. *The Whodunit: An Informal History of Detective Fiction.* Translated by Anthony Eyre. New York: Macmillan, 1980.

Borowitz, Albert. *Innocence and Arsenic: Studies in Crime and Literature.* New York: Harper & Row, 1977.

Breen, Jon L. *What About Murder? A Guide to Books about Mystery and Detective Fiction.* Metuchen, N.J. & London: Scarecrow, 1981.

Cassidy, Bruce, ed. *Roots of Detection.* New York: Ungar, 1983.

Cawelti, John G. *Adventure, Mystery, and Romance: Formula Stories as Art and Popular Culture.* Chicago: University of Chicago Press, 1976.

Champigny, Robert. *What Will Happen: A Philosophical and Technical Essay on Mystery Stories.* Bloomington: Indiana University, 1977.

Charney, Hannah. *The Detective Novel of Manners: Hedonism, Morality and the Life of Reason.* Rutherford, N.J.: Fairleigh Dickinson University Press, 1981.

Cook, Michael L. *Mystery, Detective, and Espionage Magazines.* Westport, Conn.: Greenwood Press, 1983.

De Vries, P. H. *Poe and After: The Detective Story Investigated.* Amsterdam: Bakker, 1956.

Eco, Umberto, and Thomas A. Sebeok, eds. *Dupin, Holmes, and Pierce: The Sign of Three*. Bloomington: Indiana University Press, 1983.

Edwards, P. D. *Some Mid-Victorian Thrillers: The Sensation Novel, Its Friends and Its Foes*. St. Lucia, Queensland: University of Queensland Press, 1971.

Gribbin, Lenore S. *Who's Whodunit: A List of 3218 Detective Story Writers and Their 1100 Pseudonyms*. University of North Carolina Library Studies, no. 5. Chapel Hill: University of North Carolina, 1968.

Haining, Peter. *Mystery! An Illustrated History of Crime and Detective Fiction*. London: Souvenir Press, 1977.

Harper, Ralph. *The World of the Thriller*. Cleveland: Press of Case Western Reserve University, 1969.

Haycraft, Howard. *Murder for Pleasure: The Life and Times of the Detective Story*, enlarged edition. New York: Biblio & Tannen, 1968.

Haycraft, ed. *The Art of the Mystery Story: A Collection of Critical Essays*. New York: Simon & Schuster, 1946.

Hubin, Allen J. *Crime Fiction, 1749-1980: A Comprehensive Bibliography*. New York & London: Garland, 1984.

Hughes, Winifred. *The Maniac in the Cellar: Sensation Novels of the 1860s*. Princeton: Princeton University Press, 1980.

Johnson, Timothy W., and Julia Johnson, eds.; Robert Mitchell, Glenna Dunning, and Susan J. Mackall, assoc. eds. *Crime Fiction Criticism: An Annotated Bibliography*. New York & London: Garland, 1981.

Kalikoff, Beth. *Murder and Moral Decay in Victorian Popular Literature*. Ann Arbor: UMI Research Press, 1986.

Keating, H. R. F. *Crime and Mystery: The 100 Best Books*. New York: Carroll & Graf, 1987.

Keating. *Murder Must Appetize*. London: Lemon Tree Press, 1975.

Keating. *Whodunit? A Guide to Crime, Suspense & Crime Fiction*. New York: Van Nostrand Reinhold, 1982.

Keating, ed. *Crime Writers*. London: BBC, 1978.

La Cour, Tage, and Harald Morgensen. *The Murder Book: An Illustrated History of the Detective Story*. Translated by Roy Duffell. London: Allen & Unwin, 1971.

Lambert, Gavin. *The Dangerous Edge*. London: Barrie & Jenkins, 1975.

The Lilly Library, Indiana University. *The First Hundred Years of Detective Fiction, 1841-1941, By One Hundred Authors. On the Hundred Thirtieth Anniversary of The First Publication in Book Form of Edgar Allan Poe's "The Murders in the Rue Morgue," Philadelphia, 1843*, introduction by David A. Randall. Bloomington: Lilly Library, 1973.

Mandel, Ernest. *Delightful Murder: A Social History of the Crime Story*. London: Pluto, 1984.

Mann, Jessica. *Deadlier than the Male: Why Are Respectable English Women So Good At Murder?* New York: Macmillan, 1981.

McCleary, G. F. *On Detective Fiction and Other Things*. London: Hollis & Carter, 1960.

McSherry, Frank D., Jr. *Studies in Scarlet: Essays on Murder and Detective Fiction*. San Bernardino, Cal.: Borgo, 1985.

Meet the Detective. London: Allen & Unwin, 1935.

Menendez, Albert J. *The Subject Is Murder; A Selective Subject Guide to Mystery Fiction*. New York: Garland, 1986.

Merry, Bruce. *Anatomy of the Spy Thriller*. Dublin: Gill & Macmillan, 1977.

Modern Fiction Studies, special "Detective & Suspense" issue, 29 (Autumn 1983).

Most, Glen W., and William W. Stowe, eds. *The Poetics of Murder: Detective Fiction & Literary Theory*. New York: Harcourt Brace Jovanovich, 1983.

Murch, A. E. *The Development of the Detective Novel*. London: Owen, 1958.

Nevins, Francis M., Jr., ed. *The Mystery Writer's Art*. Bowling Green, Ohio: Bowling Green University Popular Press, 1970.

Olderr, Steven. *Mystery Index: Subjects, Settings and Sleuths of 10,000 Titles*. Chicago: American Library Association, 1987.

Osborne, Eric. *Victorian Detective Fiction: A Catalogue of the Collection Made by Dorothy Glover & Graham Greene*. London, Sydney & Toronto: Bodley Head, 1966.

Ousby, Ian. *Bloodhounds of Heaven: The Detective in English Fiction from Godwin to Doyle*. Cambridge: Harvard University Press, 1976.

Palmer, Jerry. *Thrillers: Genesis and Structure of a Popular Genre*. London: Arnold, 1978.

Panek, Leroy L. *The Special Branch: The British Spy Novel, 1890-1980*. Bowling Green, Ohio: Bowling Green University Popular Press, 1981.

Panek. *Watteau's Shepherds: The Detective Novel in Britain, 1914-1940*. Bowling Green, Ohio: Bowling Green University Popular Press, 1979.

Pate, Janet. *The Book of Sleuths: From Sherlock Holmes to Kojak*. London: New English Library, 1977.

Pate. *The Book of Spies and Secret Agents*. London: Gallery Press, 1978.

Peterson, Audrey. *Victorian Masters of Mystery*. New York: Ungar, 1983.

Phillips, Walter C. *Dickens, Reade and Collins, Sensation Novelists*. New York: Columbia University Press, 1919.

Prager, Arthur. *Rascals at Large: Or, The Clue in the Old Nostalgia*. Garden City: Doubleday, 1971.

Quayle, Eric. *The Collector's Book of Detective Fiction*. London: Studio Vista, 1972.

Queen, Ellery. *The Detective Short Story: A Bibliography*. Boston: Little, Brown, 1942.

Queen. *Queen's Quorum: A History of the Detective-Crime Short Story as Revealed in the 106 Most Important Books Published in This Field Since 1845*, new edition, with supplements through 1967. New York: Biblio & Tannen, 1969.

Reilly, John M., ed. *Twentieth-Century Crime and Mystery Writers*, revised and enlarged edition. New York: St. Martin's, 1985.

Routley, Erik. *The Puritan Pleasures of the Detective Story: A Personal Monograph*. London: Gollancz, 1972.

Skene Melvin, David, and Ann Skene Melvin. *Crime, Detective, Espionage, Mystery and Thriller: Fiction and Film: A Comprehensive Bibliography of Critical Writing through 1979*. Westport, Conn.: Greenwood Press, 1980.

Smith, Myron J., Jr. *Cloak and Dagger Fiction: An Annotated Guide to Spy Thrillers*, revised and enlarged edition. Santa Barbara & Oxford: ABC-Clio, 1982.

Smyth, Frank, and Myles Ludwig. *The Detectives: Crime and Detection in Fact Fiction*. Philadelphia & New York: Lippincott, 1978.

Steinbrunner, Chris, Charles Shibuk, Otto Penzler, Marvin Lachman, and Francis M. Nevins, Jr. *Detectionary: A Biographical Dictionary of the Leading Characters in Detective and Mystery Fiction*, revised edition. Woodstock, N.Y.: Overlook Press, 1977.

Steinbrunner and Penzler, eds., with Lachman and Shibuk. *Encyclopedia of Mystery and Detection*. New York, St. Louis & San Francisco: McGraw-Hill, 1976.

Stewart, R. F. *. . . and Always a Detective: Chapters on the History of Detective Fiction*. Newton Abbot, U.K. & North Pomfret, Vt.: David & Charles, 1980.

Symons, Julian. *Bloody Murder*, revised edition. New York: Viking, 1984.

Thomson, H. Douglas. *Masters of Mystery: A Study of the Detective Story*. London: Collins, 1931. Republished, with an introduction and notes by E. F. Bleiler. New York: Dover, 1978.

Watson, Colin. *Snobbery with Violence: Crime Stories and Their Audience*. New York: St. Martin's, 1971.

Winks, Robin W. *Modus Operandi: An Excursion into Detective Fiction*. Boston: Godine, 1982.

Winks, ed. *Detective Fiction: A Collection of Critical Essays*. Englewood Cliffs, N.J.: Prentice-Hall, 1980.

Woeller, Waltraud, and Bruce Cassidy. *The Literature of Crime and Detection: An Illustrated History from Antiquity to the Present*. Translated by Ruth Michaelis-Jena and Willy Merson. New York: Ungar, 1988.

Contributors

Jeanne F. Bedell ....*Virginia Commonwealth University*
Richard Benvenuto ....*Michigan State University*
Albert Borowitz ....*Cleveland, Ohio*
Richard C. Carpenter ....*Bowling Green State University*
Alison Janice McNabb Cox ....*Northfield, Minnesota*
J. Randolph Cox ....*St. Olaf College*
Mary Jean DeMarr ....*Indiana State University*
Carol M. Dole ....*Cornell University*
Gareth W. Dunleavy ....*University of Wisconsin-Milwaukee*
Dorothy Goldman ....*University of Kent, Canterbury*
Julia Hardie ....*Pennsylvania State University*
Judith J. Kollmann ....*University of Michigan-Flint*
Thomas M. Leitch ....*University of Delaware*
John McAleer ....*Boston College*
Virginia B. Morris ....*John Jay College of Criminal Justice*
Brian Murray ....*Youngstown State University*
Christopher D. Murray ....*University of Regina*
Will Murray ....*Quincy, Massachusetts*
Kevin Radaker ....*Pennsylvania State University*
Phyllis Rozendal ....*York University*
Joan Seay ....*University of Tulsa*
Katherine Staples ....*Austin Community College, Texas*
Gerald H. Strauss ....*Bloomsburg University*
Nancy Ellen Talburt ....*University of Arkansas*